COLLEGE READING ASSOCIATION LEGACY: A CELEBRATION OF 50 YEARS OF LITERACY LEADERSHIP

Volume II

Senior Editor
Wayne M. Linek
Texas A&M University-Commerce

Associate Editors

Dixie D. Massey
University of Washington

Elizabeth G. Sturtevant
George Mason University

Louise Cochran
University of North Texas

Barbara McClanahan
Southeastern Oklahoma
State University-Idabel

Mary Beth Sampson
Texas A&M University-Commerce

Editorial Assistants
Susan Glaeser
Paula Mason
Texas A&M University-Commerce

ISBN 1-883604-36-2

Cover design by Crystal Britton, student at Texas A&M University-Commerce.

Table of Contents
Volume I

ACKNOWLEDGEMENTS AND DEDICATION xvii

INTRODUCTION: LEST WE FORGET 1
Wayne M. Linek

HISTORIES 9
The First Five Years: 1958-1963 11
J. Estill Alexander and Susan L. Strode

1963-1968 19
J. Estill Alexander and Susan L. Strode

1968-1973 25
J. Estill Alexander and Susan L. Strode

1973-1978 33
J. Estill Alexander and Susan L. Strode

1978-1983 39
J. Estill Alexander and Susan L. Strode

1983-1988 47
J. Estill Alexander and Susan L. Strode

1988-1993 55
J. Estill Alexander and Susan L. Strode

1993-1998 63
J. Estill Alexander and Susan L. Strode

1998-2003 71
Dixie D. Massey and Wayne M. Linek

2003-2008 79
Dixie D. Massey and Wayne M. Linek

EARLY LEADERS 87
Introduction to Early Leaders 89
Elizabeth G. Sturtevant

J. Estill Alexander 93
A Brief Biography
Arvinder Johri and Elizabeth G. Sturtevant

Reflection on J. Estill Alexander 95
Cathleen Doheny

Reflection on J. Estill Alexander 100
Sabiha Aydelott

Ira E. Aaron 105
A Brief Biography
Arvinder Johri and Elizabeth G. Sturtevant

My Experiences as a Literacy Educator 107
Ira E. Aaron

Reflection on Ira E. Aaron 111
Timothy V. Rasinski

Jules C. Abrams 113
A Brief Biography
Arvinder Johri and Elizabeth G. Sturtevant

A Psychologist-Educator's Journey Through the Reading World 115
Jules C. Abrams

Reflection on Jules C. Abrams 119
Patricia M. Bricklin

Robert Aukerman 121
A Brief Biography
Arvinder Johri and Elizabeth G. Sturtevant

Reflections on the Early Years of CRA and
the Focus of Reading in the 1950s and 1960s 123
Robert Aukerman

Richard Carner 131
A Brief Biography
Arvinder Johri and Elizabeth G. Sturtevant

From Metronoscopes to Megabytes 132
Richard L. Carner

Reflection on Richard Carner 137
Fritzie Chowning

Eleanor Ladd Kress 139
A Brief Biography
Arvinder Johri and Elizabeth G. Sturtevant

Perspectives from Fifty Years of Teaching: A Personal Odyssey 141
Eleanor Ladd Kress

Roy A. Kress   147
A Brief Biography
Arvinder Johri and Elizabeth G. Sturtevant

This is Reading!   148
Roy A. Kress

Martha Maxwell   155
A Brief Biography
Arvinder Johri and Elizabeth G. Sturtevant

College Reading Fifty Years Later   157
Martha Maxwell

Albert J. Mazurkiewicz   163
A Brief Biography
Arvinder Johri and Elizabeth G. Sturtevant

Reflections, Remembrances and Resonances   165
Albert J. Mazurkiewicz

Walter Pauk   171
A Brief Biography
Arvinder Johri and Elizabeth G. Sturtevant

How the SQ3R Came To Be   172
Walter Pauk

Lillian Putnam   181
A Brief Biography
Arvinder Johri and Elizabeth G. Sturtevant

Beginning Reading Methods: A Review of the Past183
Lillian Putnam

Jeannette Veatch   187
A Brief Biography
Arvinder Johri and Elizabeth G. Sturtevant

Reading From the Rear View Mirror   189
Jeannette Veatch

Reflection on Jeannette Veatch   194
Robert B. Cooter

M. Jerry Weiss   197
A Brief Biography
Arvinder Johri and Elizabeth G. Sturtevant

A Genuine Legacy 199
M. Jerry Weiss

Reflection on M. Jerry Weiss 204
Janet K. Carsetti

ORAL HISTORIES **207**
Introduction to CRA Oral Histories 209
Wayne M. Linek

Jules C. Abrams 211
Dixie D. Massey

Marino C. Alvarez 215
Christine Walsh

Lois A. Bader 223
Daniel L. Pierce

Rita M. Bean 227
Kellee Jenkins

Allen Berger 233
Ellen Jampole

William E. Blanton 243
Gary Moorman and Wayne M. Linek

Bruce W. Brigham 249
Dixie D. Massey

Karen M. Bromley 257
Maureen Boyd

Janet Carsetti 263
Dixie D. Massey and Katie Monnin

Jack Cassidy 271
Norma D. Zunker

Robert B. Cooter 277
Wayne Linek and Mary Beth Sampson

Joan B. Elliot 285
Fancine Falk-Ross

June Ewing 293
Jack Cassidy

Fred Fedorko
Mary Beth Allen 299

Thomas P. Fitzgerald
Jack Cassidy 307

Linda B. Gambrell
Ellen Jampole 313

Susan Mandell Glazer
Dixie D. Massey and Joanne L. Previts 323

Betty S. Heathington
Agnes Stryker, Wayne M. Linek and Lynn L. Rudd 327

William A. Henk
Mary W. Strong 333

Ellen Jampole
Denise H. Stuart 341

Jerry L. Johns
Dixie D. Massey 351

Patricia S. Koskinen
Terry Kindervater and Dixie D. Massey 357

Jim R. Layton
Kent Layton 367

Wayne M. Linek
Donna M. Harkins 371

George E. Mason
Dixie D. Massey 381

Jane Brady Matanzo
Beverly Bruneau Timmons 389

Martha Maxwell
Dixie D. Massey and Kristine E. Pytash 397

Albert J. Mazurkeiwicz
Dixie D. Massey and Kristine E. Pytash 401

Nancy D. Padak
Denise N. Morgan 409

Irene Payne 417
Judy S. Richardson

Uberto Price 423
Bill Blanton and Gary Moorman

Timothy V. Rasinski 431
Susan Morrison

Barbara Reinken 439
Linda K. Rogers

David Reinking 447
Louise Cochran

D. Ray Reutzel 453
Timothy G. Morrison

Judy Richardson 459
Charlene Fleener

Bob Rickelman 467
Carol Carrig

Victoria J. Risko 475
Shannon Beach

Gary Shaffer 483
Kathleen A. J. Mohr

Jon Shapiro 489
Susan Szabo

Norman A. Stahl 499
James R. King

VOLUME II **511**
Linda Thistlethwaite 513
H. Jon Jones

Richard T. Vacca 521
Maryann Mraz

Maria Valeri-Gold 527
Linda Mahoney

Barbara J. Walker 535
Susan Szabo

James E. Walker
Richard T. Vacca   543

M. Jerry Weiss
Jill Lewis   551

Robert M. Wilson
Karen Bromley   557

Presidential Addresses   **565**
Introduction to Presidential Addresses   566
Wayne M. Linek

1996   567
Those Wonderful Toys: Read-Alouds From the Classics and
Assorted Literature
Judy S. Richardson

1997   575
Adolescent Literature: Are We In Contact?
Marino C. Alvarez

1998   583
Outside of A Dog, A Book is Man's Best Friend.
Inside of A Dog, It's Too Dark to Read. (With Apologies to Groucho Marx)
Timothy V. Rasinski

1999   589
Listening to Learners
Nancy D. Padak

2000   597
Literacy 2001: What Is and What Should Be
Jack Cassidy

2001   603
What is Johnny Reading? A Research Update
Maria Valeri-Gold

2002   611
Going Beyond: The Possibilities of Thinking and Literacy
Jane Brady Matanzo

2003   621
Predicting the Whether: Lessons Learned from the Past
Robert J. Rickelman

2004   629
Mentoring Reading Colleagues in Higher Education: Paving the Path to Success
Wayne M. Linek

2005   637
Another Pothole in the Road: Asserting our Professionalism
Jon Shapiro

2006   649
The Future of Writing
Karen Bromley

2007   659
Traditions, Storying, and Crossroads
Ellen Jampole

2008   665
So What's in a Word? The Power of Words
D. Ray Reutzel

Keynote Addresses   **673**
Introduction to Keynote   675
Wayne M. Linek

1994   677
Motivation Matters
Linda B. Gambrell

1996   699
Future Controversial Issues in Literacy: The Same Old Stuff or a
Whole New Ball Game?
William A. Henk

Controversial Pathways to Literacy: The Present   711
D. Ray Reutzel

If the Horse is Dead, Get Off   719
Wayne Otto

1997   733
My Life in Reading
Jeanne S. Chall

Finding Common Ground: A Review of the Expert Study   747
Rona F. Flippo

A Social-Constructivist View of Family Literacy   755
Susan B. Neuman

1998   761
Are We Trend Spotters or Tale Spinners? A Report from the Field
Donna E. Alvermann

1999   779
Teacher Decision Making in Literacy Education: Learning to Teach
Gay Su Pinnell

2001   795
Stories That Can Change the Way We Educate
Patricia Edwards

What Research Reveals About Literacy Motivation   807
Linda Gambrell

Effective Reading Instruction: What We Know, What We Need to   819
Know, and What We Still Need to Do
Timothy V. Rasinski

2003   829
Latino Children's Literature is Mainstream
Becky Chavarria-Chariez

Preparing Elementary Teachers in Reading: Will University-Based
Programs Move Foreward or be "Left Behind?"   837
James V. Hoffman

Fast Start: Successful Literacy Instruction that Connects
Schools and Homes   849
Nancy Padak and Tim Rasinski

2004   861
Writing from the Heart
Joyce Sweeney

2005   869
Content Area Literacy: The Spotlight Shifts to Teacher Educators
Donna E. Alvermann

Thinking about our Future as Researchers: New Literacies,
New Challenges, and New Opportunities   875
Jill Castek, Julie Coiro, Douglas K. Hartman, Laurie A. Henry,
Donald J. Leu, Lisa Zawilinski

Living in the Promised Land...or Can Old and New Literacies
Live Happily Ever After in the Classroom?   895
Linda D. Labbo

2006   907
A Few Words About Sentences
Allen Berger

Advancing Children's Literacy Requires Starting with the
Right Questions in the Debate over Literacy   913
Gerald Coles

Pedagogies of the Oppressors: Critical Literacies   933
as Counter Narratives
Patrick Shannon

2007   947
Teacher Knowledge and Teaching Reading
Mia Callahan, Vicki B. Griffo, and P. David Pearson

Getting the Facts Right in Books for Young Readers:
Researching *Mailing May*   *971*
Michael Tunnel

Teachers of English Learners: Issues of Preparation and   983
Professional Development
MaryEllen Vogt

2008   997
Helping Students Appreciate the Value of Reading
Linda B. Gambrell

Speaking the Lower Frequencies 2.0: Digital Ghoststories   1007
Walter R. Jacobs

The Future of the College Reading Association   **1015**
Karen Bromley

Conclusion: Evolving From CRA to ALER   **1025**
Wayne M. Linek

Appendix A   **1029**
Thesis and Dissertation Award Winners

Appendix B   **1033**
Officers of the College Reading Association

ORAL HISTORIES

Continued from Volume I

Linda Thistlethwaite

Albert J. Mazurkiewicz CRA Special Services Award 2002

H. Jon Jones

Western Illinois University

Family Background

Linda was born in Fort Wayne, Indiana, on August 17, 1947 to Rudolph and Gerry Schulenberg. She grew up in a small rural town near Fort Wayne as an only child in a middle class family. Her father was also an only child and her mother's only brother had no children, so Linda had no close cousins growing up. While she thought that her mother had a strong influence on her, Linda said,

"[I have] a lot of my father in me." Linda's father managed an office for the Norfolk and Western Railroad and exhibited a strong work ethic. Her mother, who taught Linda her "p's and q's," worked as a beautician, a billing clerk, and sold Tupperware. Linda believes that her father's work ethic and mother's independent spirit have stood her in good stead throughout her life.

Early Influences

Church was always an important element of Linda's life. She recounted fond memories of youth group experiences and summer church camp, first as a camper, then as a counselor. She felt that these church youth group experiences were important influences in her life. Linda was also active in Girl Scouts and 4-H and said that her church, scouting, and 4-H experiences taught her self-sufficiency as well as how to be a team member.

In addition to her parents, other people played important roles in Linda's life. One such person was a family friend named Francis Brown. Francis was married, had children, and was working on a master's degree. She gave Linda sage advice that Linda followed many years later. Francis told Linda that if she chose to further her education, she should do so before she had a family. Linda was reminded of Francis three years ago when she received a letter. As she read the letter, it seemed familiar. Looking back at the letter's salutation and then at the closing, Linda realized it was a letter she had written. Puzzled, she looked further and found a note from Francis confirming this was a letter Linda had written many years ago when Francis had a serious illness. Francis went on to say that the letter had meant so much that she had saved it. Now in her 80's, Francis was returning this and other meaningful letters to their writers with notes of appreciation. She was doing this because she felt it was important to tell each person how much his or her letters meant to her while she still could. Linda explained that this gesture had a significant effect on her outlook on life. As a result, she strives to not let too many things go undone in her own life.

Schooling

Schooling was important to Linda's parents. She recalled, "I was one of the few 'country kids' to go to kindergarten at that time." That was because Linda's mother drove her eight miles one way to kindergarten each day. Teaching and learning became important to Linda early in her schooling. She credited her second grade teacher, Mrs. Jones, for this. Linda described her as an individual who was always smiling and who demonstrated her love of teaching by making every student feel that he or she was a good child. Linda said, "I always wanted to be a teacher because of Mrs. Jones."

Like all students, as Linda progressed through school she developed opinions about her most and least favorite subjects. Her favorites were reading and literature. She recounted going to the library to check out a book in the afternoon and then returning it to the library the very next morning. After a number of repetitions of this behavior the librarian said to Linda, "Don't you ever help your mother?" Linda commented, "I guess she thought that I read too much.... from that point I decided that I would only give positive reinforcement to people who read books."

Linda mentioned prejudice in her school years. She said, "With a few exceptions I lived in a fairly homogeneous town and attended a homogeneous school. Racially and ethnically, almost everyone was like me." However, she recalled that a number of her school friends were people that others seemed to avoid. Migrant workers' children and special education classmates were among those she counted as friends. Linda attributed this to the inclusiveness exemplified by her early teachers.

In junior and senior high school, Linda continued to be active in Girl Scouts and 4-H. She recalled that her mother was a very "artsy crafty" person who sewed, knitted, and quilted. Linda said, "I was a failure at all those things despite my mother's best efforts!" Linda recounted with a laugh, "I did develop an interest in photography as a hobby....[and] was involved in the Speech and Debate Society [in high school]." Linda enjoyed public speaking and competed frequently in speech contests. These competitions were extemporaneous, which meant that she and the other competitors were given a topic and allowed only two hours to prepare a speech. Linda thought this process caused her to develop skills in preparing, organizing and speaking in front of groups. "What better preparation could one have for teaching?" she remarked. Linda also recounted fond memories of family vacations through these years. Her father's position with the railroad enabled her family to travel to various parts of the country for vacations, which enriched her education.

College and Professional Years

As Linda was finishing high school, she began making plans for her future. Interestingly, her father wanted her to work for him in his railroad office as a secretary. He supervised 15 people and had a good career with the railroad. He thought that being a secretary would be a good career for Linda. Linda's mother, however, felt that college was very important. Linda said, "My mother felt strongly about this and she prevailed." It may have been the only time that Linda's mother opposed her father's wishes. Once the decision had been made for Linda to go to college, her father threw his full support behind it.

Linda obtained her BA in English with a Spanish minor at Ball State University in Muncie, Indiana. Reflecting on her years at Ball State, Linda mentioned an undergraduate professor named Harry Snyder who made a great impression on her. He quickly learned every student's name and where each person sat in his class. More important than just knowing the students' names, he emphasized the importance of getting to know each of his students. Linda was very impressed by this and it is something that she carried into her own teaching.

While an undergraduate at Ball State, Linda became friends with fellow student, Paul Thistlethwaite. They married in 1967. She smiled when she mentioned that she never even considered hyphenating her name as a number of her friends were doing. Upon completion of her BA, and mindful of the advice that Francis Brown had given her, Linda remained at Ball State as a graduate student and completed a master's degree in English.

After completing her master's program, Linda obtained her first teaching position as a high school English and Spanish teacher in Missouri. In her English classes she began to notice that many of her students were struggling with their literature assignments due to basic reading problems. After three years of teaching, she went back to school and began study for a second master's degree, this time in reading. Shortly after, Paul accepted a teaching position at Western Illinois University and they relocated there. Linda completed a master's in reading at Western and began teaching reading and study skills there.

Doctoral Program and a Family Health Crisis

When Linda was hired at Western, her permanent employment was based upon completion of her doctoral degree in a specified amount of time. Linda was accepted into the doctoral program at the University of Missouri in Columbia. However, at the same time Paul was diagnosed with cancer and Linda immediately postponed beginning her program. After two years of teaching and with the deadline looming, she began taking courses at Western that she could transfer. After Paul's surgery at the Mayo clinic and follow-up radiation therapy, his health seemed to improve and he insisted that Linda begin her doctoral program even as he continued his therapy. Given his health circumstances Paul said to Linda, "It is now even more important that you obtain your doctorate."

So, in the summer of 1979, Linda began her doctoral studies at the University of Missouri. She spent the week in Columbia, Missouri while Paul took care of their two boys, aged three and six, in Macomb, Illinois. During this time Paul continued his therapy and Linda returned home each weekend.

By the fall of that year, Paul seemed well enough for Linda to continue her studies in Missouri. Linda was granted a leave of absence from Western for a year and used that year and the preceding summer to complete coursework and fulfill her residency requirement. Even better, Paul was able to secure a fulltime lecturer's position at the University of Missouri for the upcoming year and took a leave from his position as a Marketing Professor at Western Illinois University. Linda, Paul, and their two boys moved to Columbia, Missouri for her year of doctoral residency. Linda concluded her description of this time period with the rhetorical question, "What more support could I have had?"

With coursework and residency requirements behind her, Linda went back to teaching at Western while completing research for her dissertation. She said she wondered what it would have been like to pursue her studies fulltime in residence at Missouri. "Would I have done more research and more writing? Would I have gotten to know my doctoral colleagues?" are questions she has pondered. Looking at it from another perspective, she went on to say, "But then, without the situation of limited time and a deadline, maybe I never would have finished."

When reflecting on her doctoral studies Linda noted several faculty mentors who had a significant impact.. Although she said her entire doctoral committee "was great," she lauded Dorothy Watson and Jim Leigh for giving her a broad range in her dissertation, including both experimental design and in-depth single-subject research. She also extended "vast gratitude" to Dick Robinson for helping her to move through her program in a timely manner.

CRA Involvement

Linda taught at Western Illinois University from 1977 until 2002 and it was during these years that she became involved with the College Reading Association (CRA). She was very active in the Adult Learning Division (ALD), serving as Chair, Newsletter Editor, and as a contributor and reviewer for ALD's online journal, *Exploring Adult Literacy*. She also served as CRA's Executive Secretary from 1992 to 1996 and again from 1999 to 2002.

Linda said she felt especially indebted to three CRA members who nurtured her professional growth: Judy Richardson, Nancy Padak, and Linda Gambrell.

Judy Richardson taught her the importance of coming down from the ivory tower of university teaching, exchanging places with a high school English teacher, and taking on all of that teacher's classroom and extra-curricular responsibilities for a semester. Although Linda recognized the value of university teachers working *with* classroom teachers on various research efforts and doing classroom demonstrations, she stated that actually walking in a K-12 classroom teacher's shoes for a significant period of time was very important. She said that all new literacy professionals at the university level should look for opportunities to do something similar and regretted that she did not avail herself of this opportunity.

Linda also felt indebted to Nancy Padak, not only for her expertise in adult literacy, but also for her willingness to share knowledge with Illinois adult education programs. Finally, she saw Linda Gambrell as a model of how it is possible to combine serious research with practical and informal dissemination of that research. She commented on the way that audiences enjoy both listening to, as well as learning from, Linda Gambrell. She also thanked Linda Gambrell for sharing her expertise with Illinois teachers at Western Illinois University's Issues and Trends in Reading Conference.

Retirement, Reflections, and Visions

When Linda retired from Western Illinois University in December 2002, she had taught there for "just a tad over 25 years." Work and teaching were an integral part of her life. Not surprisingly, though she left the classroom at Western, she continues to do grant and consultation work in adult literacy. While Linda had always worked as a state consultant in adult literacy, in retirement she has become a consultant on the national level through the federal STAR (Student Achievement in Reading) Project, a project focusing on training Adult Basic Education teachers in assessment and evidence-based reading instruction. In the summer Linda directs a tutoring program through a local Altrusa organization. This program serves 20 to 30 school age children each summer.

Linda and Paul have just bought a second home in Arizona and expect to spend more time in the sunny Southwest. Although Linda's father passed away 20 years ago, her mother is still active at 102 years of age and lives with Linda and Paul. She goes with them to Arizona to avoid Illinois's cold winter weather.

Without hesitation and with great enthusiasm Linda shared what she considers to be the most momentous event of her retirement. As a good teacher, she accompanied the description of this event with audiovisuals—an armful of photographs. Linda announced with great pride, "This is my first grandchild—my granddaughter Ellie. Spending time with her is the highlight of my retirement." Linda and Paul's two sons, Craig 33, and Ryan 30, both graduated from the University of Illinois. Craig, his wife, and daughter—the star of the armload of pictures—live in Chicago, while Ryan lives in the Washington D.C. area. Both are enjoying successful careers in business.

As Linda reflected on balancing her personal and professional lives, she wondered if she missed some crucial time with her two boys as they were growing up. However, son Ryan's comment in a recent conversation has somewhat ameliorated her concern. He said, "Mom, you were always there when I needed you, and also sometimes when I didn't." Linda said with a smile, "I guess their perception was that I was there for them and they seemed to have turned out all right."

Visions for the Future

Linda's professional lifetime encompassed graduate, undergraduate, and adult literacy, so she has visions in all these areas. She said that research is very important in every area of literacy, but feels that it is crucial to get research findings to the people who need them for use on a day-to-day basis—the teachers.

Linda sees two trends. The first trend applies specifically to adult literacy. Linda sees the people who teach in the various types of adult literacy as being very dedicated, but she also sees that they are facing different challenges than they did in the past. The students they teach are younger and younger. Some are young high school dropouts that think the GED route will be easier and, of course, it is not. Also, adult literacy students used to come of their own volition, now many individuals are mandated to attend by courts or social service agencies. While adult literacy teachers are rising to meet these challenges, it is important for literacy teacher educators to understand that adult literacy teachers now have different education and training needs.

The second trend is the increased accountability that all teachers and teacher educators face. Much more time is now spent assessing and writing reports that convey results of these assessments. Many teachers feel that they have less and less time to actually teach. The challenge for the immediate and long-term future, as Linda sees it, is to make the accountability a positive factor in literacy education at all levels.

Overall, Linda feels that it is paramount for teacher educators to maintain close contact with teachers in the field. It is important to periodically be out there with the teachers in a real way, whether it be as co-researchers or in other ways.

As Linda reflected on her long affiliation with CRA, she also had visions for its future. She commented that it is crucial for CRA to become involved in legislation at both state and federal levels. Linda said, "CRA will have to become more political." She sees this not just as a need at the organizational level, but as a challenge for each individual CRA member. She also envisioned the CRA Legislative Committee as assuming an active role in exploring resources, support, and advocacy for legislative issues.

Linda said CRA is one of the best organizations at nurturing its new and established members. She noted that nurturing and mentoring are two of CRA's most notable characteristics and that the association should continue in this vein.

Conclusion

Linda Thistlethwaite represents exactly the kind of teacher, scholar, literacy leader, and compassionate individual that the developers of the Albert J. Mazurkiewicz Special Services Award had in mind to honor. We would do well to pay heed to her words of wisdom regarding both the future of CRA/ALER and the broader scope of literacy on the national stage.

RICHARD VACCA

B. Herr Award 1989

Maryann Mraz
University of North Carolina at Charlotte

Starting Off

Born to Italian-American parents on February 22, 1946, Rich Vacca's early years were spent in East Harlem, New York. It was a rough-and-tumble place that Rich described as "a big melting pot of immigrants from the old world… Our building was #213," he explained, "the mob boss lived in #234." Rich's father was a painter, his mother a seamstress. Both left school hallways behind at the end of eighth grade to help support their families.

Rich's own formal education began at Public School 168. It was an arduous beginning. Having suffered ear infections as a child, the results of which likely contributed to his inability to distinguish certain sounds, Rich struggled in school. He floundered, ironically, with reading. "Reading in school did not make any sense to me," he recalled. "It was all isolated." So, as was often the case with struggling readers, he was relegated to the "buzzard" group. Through his own collection of poems, *Block Boy: Memories of Another Time and Place* (2008), he recalled the experience some five decades later:

> I'm just a buzzard stuck in school,
>   feeling like everyone's fool.
> Not a fierce eagle flying in rarified air,
>   not even a mediocre magpie heading to who knows where.
> I'm a buzzard with broken wings
>   trying hard to fly beyond the shame
> being a buzzard brings. (p. 56)

At the age of eight, when the street on which he lived was condemned and the houses were about to be torn down, Rich moved with his parents and two bothers to Long Island, which, in the 1950's, seemed to him to be "out in the country." It was there that he encountered the first teacher who became a positive and decisive influence in his life. Mrs. Fladhammer was a no-nonsense, old-school type teacher who maintained impeccable control of her class.

> Mrs. Fladhammer,
>   Plies her craft without glitz or glamour.
> But what do I know of a teacher's love
>   or passion for her work?
> I'm much too cool in "The Hammer's" class,
>   the city kid, the occasional jerk,
> the quintessential clown,
>   who has mastered the art of fooling around
> until that fateful day
>   when The Hammer turned my world upside down. (p. 70)

It was Mrs. Fladhammer who discovered that this "buzzard" could indeed *read*. While there were no books at his home, his father's passion for boxing kept *Ring* magazine around the house, and Rich recalled "picking up words" by looking over this older brother's shoulder as he was reading comic books. It was a comic book that Mrs. Fladhammer discovered him reading inside the pages of his assigned *Dick and Jane* text.

> Rather than admonish me,
> she took delight in her discovery.
>   Despite my chagrin and protestation,
> she asked me to read out loud,
>   *Aquaman and the Attack of the Giant Crustaean.* (p. 70)

The next day, Mrs. Fladhammer presented him with a gift: an adapted version of the book *The Adventures of Robinson Crusoe*, along with the invitation to read it "just for fun." That sparked Rich's interest in adventure books and marked his promotion from the buzzard reading group to the middle "magpies." He had mixed feelings, however, about being pulled away from his fellow buzzards, and lamented decades later the fate that befell some of them: One died in Vietnam; two others were lost to drugs. Sadly, not all buzzard stories had happy endings. He wondered if or how the low expectations placed on buzzards may have set some of them on an irreversible course.

A Life's Work in Teaching

Rich knew he wanted to be a teacher from the time he was in the seventh grade. "If I could teach," he explained, "then I could coach basketball." His seventh grade English teacher, Mario Shortino, served as a role model of what a teacher could be. "He was just so good at it," Rich remembered. Rich evolved into a person who could read and who liked to read. His gym teacher aspirations gave way to a desire to be an English teacher.

The start of his undergraduate work at SUNY Albany was not academically stellar. Rich described himself as "Joe Fraternity" that first year. College began as an opportunity to expand his social horizons and to play freshmen basketball. He enjoyed both that first year, but found himself flunking out of school. It was then that Rich made the decision to quit the basketball team and focused instead on his future as a teacher. During his sophomore year, he met Jo Anne, the woman who became both his wife and, as he described, "my most influential colleague." Rich and Jo Anne eloped when he was a senior and she a junior. Their collaboration as spouses and colleagues continues to this day.

As a teacher, Rich found his niche. When student-teaching, he tried to infuse a "strand of creativity" into his teaching by using non-traditional texts such as Beatles song lyrics to introduce his students to poetry. He experimented with the use of process-type questioning and strategies to engage his students. His cooperating teacher invited other teachers into the classroom to watch his lessons. He never wrote a formal lesson plan ahead of time, and, to fulfill his student-teaching requirements, recalled spending one all-nighter writing up formal plans for lessons he had already taught.

Graduating with his bachelor's degree at age 21, Rich began work as a high school English teacher. He was only a year or two older than some of his students. During his first three years of teaching, he obtained a master's degree in English Education from SUNY Albany. "I had this wife," Rich mused, "who thought I should work on my doctorate." His mentor at Albany, Frank Hodge, encouraged him to pursue that doctorate in secondary reading. Rich was reluctant at first, because he had not had a favorable experience in the secondary reading class he was required to take in his master's program.

Nevertheless, at age 23, he entered the doctoral program in reading at Syracuse. Margaret Early, past-president of NCTE and former member of the Board of Directors of IRA, whom Rich described as a great role model and the "madam of secondary reading," looked at him upon his arrival at Syracuse and flatly stated, "You're kind of young." Hal Herber was an influential mentor for Rich at Syracuse, awarding him an assistantship in the Reading Research Center and including Rich in a multitude of projects centered on content area reading.

His professors and fellow doctoral students "took me under their wing" he explained. Jo Anne gave him the confidence to persevere. Rich recalled a poster she gave him of a sea gull soaring across the sky: "They can because they think they can," it read. "Confidence and competence," he stated, "go hand in hand." At age 26, Rich completed his dissertation on the topic of the use of cooperative learning groups and text structure in eighth grade social studies.

In his first teaching appointment at Northern Illinois University, Rich recalled wonderful colleagues like Jerry Johns and Jane Davidson. Jane referred to him as her "barn burner" because he could bring the house down with his innovative presentations. Nancy Padak, who would later become his colleague at Kent State University, took her first secondary reading course from Rich. Rich started writing articles for journals such as the *Journal of Educational Research,* the *Journal of Reading,* and the *Reading Teacher.*

At the same time, Jo Anne, who had been working as an educational consultant for the State of Illinois, decided to pursue her doctorate at Boston University. As fate would have it, Judy Marr at the University of Connecticut contacted Rich about an associate professor opening, and Rich and Jo Anne were on their way to the Northeast. Upon completing her doctorate, Jo Anne accepted a position at Russell Sage College—a choice that meant a 90-mile commute for her and a 70-mile commute for Rich. After two years, two positions opened at Kent State University. Rich and Jo Anne applied separately for those positions, accepted them, and remained at Kent for over 20 years.

Reflections

When asked what he would define as his most important contributions to the field of literacy education, the texts that he and Jo Anne coauthored immediately came to mind: *Content Area Reading: Literacy and Learning Across the Curriculum,* now in its 10th edition, and *Reading and Learning to Read,* currently in its 7th edition. "Sometimes she doesn't get as much credit," he stated, "but she was instrumental in the success of both books." Rich also credited his success to having been blessed with terrific colleagues at all the universities at which he studied and worked, and to teachers from all over the country from whom he's had the opportunity to learn. He cited one of his most satisfying accomplishments as being "one of many voices pushing for an emphasis on adolescent literacy."

Rich's leadership in the field is well known, particularly in his role of President of the International Reading Association (IRA) in 1995-96. During his tenure as IRA President, Rich sought to extend the association's membership and influence beyond North America to Europe and Asia. It was, however, the College Reading Association (CRA) that marked Rich's entry into the venue of professional literacy organizations.

Jim Walker, past-president of CRA, introduced Rich to CRA during his first year at Syracuse. The annual conference that year was held in Washington and Bill Martin, Jr., was the keynote speaker. "He blew me away." Rich recalled. He remained grateful that CRA was his first conference experience. "I always looked forward to it," he said. As Rich became more active in the field, he became more active in CRA, serving on the Board of Directors and being awarded the A. B. Herr Award in 1989, an honor he never expected. "CRA continues to be a place where young literacy professionals can integrate into the field." He is pleased that CRA remains a major contributor to the field of literacy education.

Rich and Jo Anne are still connected to the field through their textbooks and some consulting work. One piece of advice he offered to other professors is to get their doctoral students involved in CRA, presenting, publishing, and networking with colleagues. He is proud to have watched some of his own former doctoral students, such as Wayne Linek, assume leadership positions in the organization.

The Second Act

"We wanted to retire while we still liked what we did." Their retirement from Kent State University marked the beginning of what Rich called, "the second act." Retiring relatively early has allowed Rich and Jo Anne to pursue new ventures from their home in Vero Beach, Florida. Jo Anne is active as a hospice volunteer. Rich devotes time to other types of writing, including poetry and a novel in-progress. Life has come full circle, in a sense, as Rich described himself as "back to being the Caddy Shack golf-bum." The game is invigorating and kid-like, analogizing his golf buddies to his fraternity brothers from years ago. Both Rich and Jo Anne enjoy traveling the world and spending time with their daughter, Courtney, who earned her PhD and is now an Assistant Professor at Kent, son-in-law Gary, and grandsons Simon, Max, and Joe.

The gift that Mrs. Fladhammer gave Rich in the first-grade changed his life. It also enriched the lives of countless students and teachers whose own contributions to the field have been influenced, in turn, by him:

Thank you Mrs. Fladhammer for the gift
that changed my life,
the gift that keeps on giving:
To be lost on an island,
and lost in a book—
A real book with a hardcover—
And hardly any pictures
except those in my head. (Vacca, 2008, p. 72)
Thank you, Mrs. Fladhammer…from all of us.

References

Vacca, R. T. (2008). *Block boy: Memories of another time and place.* Victoria B. C. Canada: Trafford Publishing.

Vacca, R.T., Vacca, J. L., & Mraz, M. (2011). *Content area reading: Literacy and learning across the curriculum,* (10th ed.). Boston: Allyn & Bacon.

Vacca, J. L., Vacca, R. T., Gove, M. K., Burkey, L. C., Lenhart, L. A., & McKeon, C. (2009). *Reading and learning to read,* (7th ed.). Boston: Allyn & Bacon.

MARIA VALERI-GOLD

CRA President 2000-2001
A. B. Herr Award 2000
Albert J. Mazurkiewicz Special Services Award 1997

Linda Mahoney

Mississippi University for Women

My correspondence with Maria Valeri-Gold began with an e-mail to introduce myself and to describe my role in this project of compiling the histories, the stories, of past CRA presidents. In the process of inquiring about how she would like to proceed, I quickly learned that Maria is a take-charge person. I asked whether she would like to share her story with me via phone or e-mail and she chose e-mail. She asked me to send her the protocol for the interview process, a style sample, and she said that she would send her responses to me. We corresponded about timelines, deadlines, and the details of meeting the editors' publication guidelines. About one month later, she sent me her life in a completed format. Through the process of our correspondence, Maria demonstrated the initiative that characterized her year as President of CRA and her successful career as an outstanding educator.

Maria Valerie-Gold's family story has close ties to the stories of immigrant families of the early and mid 1900's. Maria Valeri-Gold was born on July 10, 1948 in Clinton, Massachusetts—a small suburban town located forty-five minutes west of Boston with a population of approximately 12,000 people. Her parents were the late Frank and Adelinda (Turini) Valeri who immigrated to the United States from Pretare, Italy—a suburb located north of Rome. Both her parents came to this country by boat and landed on Ellis Island in New York. Maria's father came to the United States at 16 years of age with his three brothers to seek a better life. When he arrived in the United States, he worked as a laborer for the railroad company where he laid down tracks, and then years later, he was employed as a steel worker for over 40 years. Her mother was 2 years old when she arrived in this country. Maria's mother was a stay-at-home mom who worked for a short period of time in a doll factory. Both her parents lived and worked all of their lives in Clinton. Maria also has two older sisters, Esther Martin and Caroline Perla. She has one niece, Dr. Andrea Martin, two nephews, Joseph and James Perla, and numerous cousins who still reside in Clinton and neighboring towns throughout the state of Massachusetts.

In her Presidential Address to the College Reading Association, Maria Valerie-Gold included a quote from the writer, Janet Ruth Falon (2001), from an article titled "Life Among the Debris:" "A book, as a physical object, develops a life of its own, one other than a story written on its pages. We read books as we experience the story of our lives…." This quote described Maria's early experiences with books and reading.

Maria attended Clinton Public Schools and always wanted to be a teacher since she was a child. She enjoyed playing school in her earlier years with her cousins and other neighborhood children and always took on the role of the teacher. In her younger years, Maria developed a love for reading fairytales. Her favorites were *Little Red Riding Hood* and *Hansel and Gretel*. These books were cherished because she remembered receiving them on special occasions such as her birthdays and as Christmas gifts from her parents. These books were kept on shelves in the basement of her home along with report cards, rewards, and other school memorabilia.

Reflecting upon her parents' role and their influence upon her learning to read, Maria recollected that her parents did not read to her, and they did not stress the importance of learning to read. She remembered her mother and father reading the newspaper each day, but she never saw them read any books for pleasure. Reading was for survival purposes, for example, reading the phone bill or filling out a tax form. Finding a job and working were valued more than obtaining an education. In addition, the importance of family and helping family members who were in need always played a major role in her home and was highly valued. If any family member needed assistance with any financial or medical situation, the family was always there to support one another. Both her parents experienced the depression, and this event had a profound effect on her parents' lives.

Maria said she loved attending school. She did not attend kindergarten because it was not in existence at that time. Her elementary school, which housed grades 1-6, was located right next door to her house; so she only had to walk several hundred feet and enter the building. Her first and second grade teacher was Ms. Philbin; Ms. Gannon taught both third and fourth grades; and Mr. NcNally was her fifth and sixth grade teacher. Maria remembered that all her elementary school teachers taught every subject using the "drill and kill" approach to learning. Rote memorization was also stressed.

Maria recalled sitting at her desk that had a hole on the right hand side of it that contained an ink well and reading the *Dick and Jane* primers in first grade.

She remembered sitting in a "round robin" circle with her other classmates as each one took turns reading a page of text and answering questions about what they had just read. Maria also recollected that phonics was not taught, but the sight method of learning was used to teach reading. She remembered circling the correct answers in the workbook pages and coloring them. Her elementary school is no longer in existence because it was demolished over 30 years ago. But she has a photo of her parents sitting in the backyard with the school located in the background as a fond memory. The school now serves as a park and playground for neighborhood children.

Maria recalled that as a student she was quiet, shy, and obedient. When her teachers asked her questions, she would respond. Although Maria knew the answers, she wasn't inclined to raise her hand in class. As she gained more confidence, she started to participate more in class and respond to her teachers' questions.

After leaving elementary school, Maria recollected that she walked to junior high school (grades 7 and 8) and senior high school (grades 9-12) because there weren't any school buses. Since both schools were in close proximity to each other, walking to and from school took approximately 20 minutes each way. Her love for learning continued, and she earned good grades. Her name appeared in the local town newspaper, the *Clinton Daily Item*, where she was credited for being on the honor roll. Maria made the honor roll throughout junior and senior high school. Her inner motivation and perseverance paid off because she graduated with honors from high school. She remembered that her family was very proud of her school accomplishments.

During her high school years, she was actively involved in a variety of clubs and school organizations. Maria fondly recalled one club. She joined the Future Teachers Club of America where she had opportunities to visit and observe elementary and middle school classrooms. These classroom observations further affirmed her decision to attend college and become a classroom teacher.

Maria's during and after school experiences were characteristic of the 1950's era, the teenage years of the generation known as baby boomers, with sock hops, poodle skirts, and the Chevy convertible. During her teenage years, Maria loved dancing and purchased records that she constantly played over and over again on her record player. Maria enjoyed listening to the Motown sound. She remembered that her favorite television show was *American Bandstand* hosted by the legendary Dick Clark. When she got home from high school in the late afternoon, Maria would watch the show and try to mimic the dance steps that she learned from *American Bandstand* at the school dances. Her other favorite pastime was watching soap operas with her mother. Before *American Bandstand* started at 4 p.m., she would watch either *The Guiding Light* or *General Hospital*. Both soap operas are still on television and Maria loves watching them when she has the time. When Maria was a junior in high school, she worked full-time as a nurse's aide at Clinton Hospital to earn additional spending money. During her teenage years, Maria fondly remembered going to the beaches in Maine and New Hampshire with family and friends. She still loves eating fried clams and lobster stuffed with crabmeat!

After graduating from Clinton High School in 1966, Maria attended Anna Maria College, a small Catholic liberal arts college for women located in Paxton, Massachusetts; the college is now co-educational and offers a variety of programs. She attended this college because it was affordable, close to home, and had an excellent education program. Despite the fact that she earned good grades in high school, college was more challenging and competitive. Maria recalled sitting in classrooms with her peers who were speaking fluent French and Spanish, but she could not converse with them because of her lack of foreign language skills. She quickly realized that she would need to study more if she wanted to survive in college because she lacked the necessary study strategies to succeed. Her first two years in college were very challenging, and her grades were affected. She remembered earning B's and C's in her core courses. After completing her core requirements; however, her grades improved because she was now taking courses in her major. Maria graduated with honors from Anna Maria College with a Bachelor of Arts degree in Spanish Education in 1970. During her college years, she continued working as a nurse's aide on weekends to earn extra spending money for college expenses.

After graduating from Anna Maria College in 1970, Maria applied for teaching positions in the Massachusetts area. She recalled that there were more teachers applying for jobs than there were positions during the 1970s. Finally, Maria found employment with the Worcester Public School System—a city located 25 miles from her hometown. Her first teaching position was working in a federally funded program that taught kindergarten children how to read using phonics, called *Distar*. After two years, the funding for the program was eliminated. As she continued to search for a full-time teaching position, Maria became a substitute teacher. Her days as a substitute teacher were full of challenges and fond memories. Maria remembered serving as a month long substitute teacher for a sixth grade class in her own hometown. The majority of students in the class were at-risk learners reading below grade level, and she wanted to get them interested in reading. The students were not interested in reading their basal readers so she decided to use another strategy. She purchased comic books, placed them on a reading table, and used them as a motivational tool to get students involved in reading. When students finished their assignments, they went to the reading table and selected a comic book of their choice. Although the comic books may not have been the best choice, they served the purpose! This experience tied into the topic of her Presidential Address, the reading interests of students at different age levels. Her presentation noted that comic books continue to be of high interest to at-risk college students (Blackwood et al., 1991; Gallik, 1999; Jeffres & Atkin, 1996, Nelson, 1989).

After serving as a substitute teacher, a fifth grade teaching position was advertised in her hometown. Mr. McNally, Maria's former fifth and sixth grade teacher, decided to teach the sixth grade. As a result, a fifth grade teacher opening became available. After interviewing for the position, Maria was hired to teach the fifth grade. She taught reading and science classes. At that time, students were grouped according to their ability—homogeneous grouping.

While teaching, Maria continued her education and attended night classes at Worcester State College located in Worcester, Massachusetts. The college was located approximately thirty minutes from her home and was known for its teacher education program. Maria took additional reading and language arts courses and incorporated many of the ideas that she learned from her professors into her reading and science classes. After taking several courses in creative writing, Maria implemented the teaching ideas she learned in these courses with her fifth grade students. Regardless of their reading ability level, Maria remembers that her fifth graders were writing fairytales, folktales, and poetry. She still has a scrapbook that contains samples of her students' writings.

Maria expressed appreciation for a former professor whose advice she followed. Her reading professor and mentor at Worcester State College, Dr. Barbara Pilon, had a profound effect on her decision to pursue her doctorate in reading and language arts. She encouraged Maria to complete her Masters degree and to strongly consider getting an advanced degree. After earning her Masters degree in 1972, Maria continued teaching fifth grade and obtained her Reading Specialist certificate from Worcester State College. After she obtained her reading certificate in 1973, Maria became the reading specialist for the elementary schools in Clinton. She taught at-risk readers in grades 1 through 3.

Passion for travel

In addition to teaching and pursuing her advanced degrees, Maria traveled with colleagues during school vacation breaks. She visited England, Italy, Russia, and Aruba. She has many fond memories of her traveling experiences and a curio in her home contains artifacts from each country she visited. Maintaining a sense of balance between her career and personal life has always been, and still is, her focus and goal.

After teaching nine years in the Clinton Public School system, Maria decided that she would take the advice of her mentor, Dr. Pilon, and pursue a doctoral degree in reading and language arts. She felt that the time was right for her to leave her hometown and attend a university that had a strong reading reputation. Maria selected Florida State University located in Tallahassee, Florida where a second mentor entered Maria's life and guided her studies. She was very fortunate to find the late Dr. Edwin Smith, who took her under his wing. After taking additional reading courses and completing her dissertation titled *Trope Density in Intermediate Grade Basal Readers*, Maria graduated with a Doctorate of Philosophy degree with a concentration in reading and language arts in 1982. While pursuing her doctorate, Maria recalled that reading and language arts were considered two separate fields of study during the early 1980s.

Maria's life continues to be defined by the cultural influences of the times in which she lives. While pursuing her doctorate, Maria met her husband, Stephen Gold, in the Florida State University bookstore. She remembered that Stephen greeted her and then commented that he liked her red vinyl boots. For those of you who can remember, those were the days when Nancy Sinatra, the daughter of the legendary Frank Sinatra, had recorded a song with the phrase "These boots are made for walking, and that's just what they'll do, one of these days these boots will walk all over you!" Maria remembered that she purchased three pairs of boots in all different colors (red, white, and black) at the Tallahassee Mall. These boots proved to be a lucky charm because she married her husband a year after graduating from Florida State University in 1983.

After completing her doctorate, Maria returned to the Clinton Public Schools for one year. Then she moved to Marietta, Georgia, where her husband was employed as the southeast sales representative for a college publishing company. Maria spent some time after the move adjusting to her new life in the south and began seeking employment. She applied for part-time positions throughout the metro Atlanta area, because many full-time positions in her area of concentration were not available. Maria applied and interviewed for part-time positions at Georgia State University and Kennesaw State University. She was hired to teach reading in the developmental studies department of both universities. Maria worked as a part-time instructor for two years, and then applied for a full-time position as a developmental reading instructor at Gordon College, which is located in Barnesville, Georgia— the buggy capital of the world! Maria accepted the position at Gordon College. While teaching at Gordon College, a full-time developmental studies reading position was advertised at Georgia State University. Maria applied for this position and was hired to teach developmental reading classes to at-risk college readers. She taught developmental readers for over thirteen years until the developmental studies department was eliminated. After the department closed, Maria moved to the university's Counseling Center where she taught courses that stressed the application of study strategies. She left the Counseling Center to teach freshmen orientation courses that were offered by the university. Currently, Maria is a Professor in the Office of Undergraduate Studies where she teaches both the orientation classes and the strategic thinking and learning courses to incoming freshmen enrolled in Freshmen Learning Communities. Her research interests include retention and assessment.

Maria recalled that Dr. Charles Cope, a math colleague in the Developmental Studies Department, informed her about the College Reading Association (CRA) and gave her a packet of information concerning an upcoming conference that would be held in Baltimore, Maryland. She submitted a proposal to the *College Reading Division Idea Exchange*. This was Maria's first CRA conference, and she remembered how friendly everyone was to first time attendees. She enjoyed sharing her reading ideas with other developmental reading colleagues who had similar interests. She also recollected that CRA was always looking for members who were interested in serving in a variety of leadership positions and increasing membership. After attending her first CRA conference, Maria knew that she had chosen the right organization. Maria has been actively involved in the organization for 20 years. CRA has provided her with many leadership opportunities, and most importantly, long lasting friendships with individuals who share both personal and research interests.

Maria served as the CRA Conference Coordinator for six years. She credited Dr. Marion Patterson, the former CRA Conference Coordinator, as a wonderful mentor who taught her the necessary skills for developing a conference. As a result of serving as conference coordinator for the organization, Maria received the CRA Special Service Award in 1997. She felt honored that her CRA colleagues bestowed this honor upon her.

In addition to traveling, Maria's passion is teaching. She has always worked with at-risk learners from elementary grade levels to postsecondary levels. Working with developmental readers has always been rewarding, because Maria observed their progress as they implemented strategic thinking and learning strategies taught in their developmental classes to their core courses and major field of study. She uses literature in her classes to increase her developmental learners' motivation to read and develop an interest in reading. Maria also utilizes a variety of literary genre to reinforce the connections between reading and writing. In addition to using literature with her students, she incorporates sample chapters from content area textbooks to model study strategies. Incorporating literature and modeling study strategies have been successful teaching tools for her. Motivating her students has been a challenge at times, but Maria utilizes self-improvement books to enhance their motivation and to combat any negative feelings that they may feel toward school and reading.

Maria's professional accomplishments demonstrate her commitment to her students and professional colleagues. Maria has co-authored two textbooks for college developmental readers and writers: *Taking Charge of Your Reading: Reading and Study Strategies for College Success* with Dr. Frank Pintozzi, and *Making Connections through Reading and Writing* with Dr. Mary P. Deming. She has also published her research in many peer-reviewed journals such as *Reading Research and Instruction*, *Research and Teaching in Developmental Education*, *Journal of Developmental Education*, *Journal of Teaching Academic Survival Skills*, and the *Journal of College Literacy and Learning*. In addition, she has presented her research at numerous local, state, regional, and national conferences and conventions with colleagues who share similar interests. Currently, she serves on the Editorial Advisory Boards of the *Journal of Developmental Education* and

Reading Research and Instruction.

Maria's outgoing personality and friendly smile along with her professional qualifications have served to draw people to her. She is actively involved in service at the national level. She served as Membership Chair, Secretary, and currently, Awards Co-chair for the College Literacy and Learning Special Interest Group of the International Reading Association where she also serves on the Board of Directors. In addition, she served as Media Chair and Awards Chair for the College Reading Association.

Maria said, "It is now time to move on and venture into other venues." She and her husband want to travel abroad and visit countries that both have not had an opportunity to tour. Maria will retire after 30 years of teaching. She has many fond memories of her career, but now she is looking forward to new adventures. However, she will definitely attend the 50th CRA Anniversary in Sarasota, Florida. This event will be one that she doesn't want to miss!

References

Blackwood, C., Flowers, S. S., Rogers, J.S., & Staik, I. M. (1991, November). *Pleasure reading by college students: Fact or Fiction?* Paper presented at the annual meeting of the Mid-Southern Educational Research Association Conference, Lexington, KY.

Falon, J. R. (2001, May/June). Life among the debris. *Book: The Magazine for the Reading Life* (p. 92). New York: West Egg Communications.

Gallik, J. D. (1999). Do you read for pleasure? Recreational reading habits of college students. *Journal of Adolescent & Adult Literacy, 42,* 480-489.

Jeffries, L., W., & Atkins, D. J. (1996). Dimensions of students interest in reading newspapers. *Journalism and Mass Communication Educator, 51,* 15-23.

Nelson, R. L. (1989, October). *College students' views of reading.* Paper presented at the annual meeting of the Great Lakes Regional Reading Association, Cincinnati, OH.

Valeri-Gold, M. & Deming, M. (1994). *Making connections through reading and writing.* Florence, KY: Wadsworth Publishing Company.

Valeri-Gold, M. & Pintozzi, F. (2000). *Taking charge of your reading: Reading and study strategies for college success.* New York, NY: Addison Wesley Longman.

BARBARA J. WALKER

A. B. Herr Award 1997

Susan Szabo
Texas A&M University-Commerce

Prophetic Beginnings

Barbara Walker was the first daughter born to Francis (Frank) and Helen Shell in Hutchinson, Kansas in 1946. Frank, who was in the Army Air Corps at the time, missed the birth. When Frank came home from the service, he moved his family to Fort Hays, Kansas, so he and his wife could further their college education. Helen finished her Bachelors of Science Degree in Business Education while Frank finished a Master's Degree in Chemistry. While in Fort Hays, Barbara became a big sister, and she took her job seriously. She explained, "I became a teacher the day my younger sister was born. At the age of two-and-a-half, I

began to teach my baby sister everything I knew. That was the year I knew I would eventually become a classroom teacher."

Next, the family moved to Kentucky so that Frank could work on his PhD in chemistry. Barbara remembered two things about her life in Kentucky. First, her younger brother was born, and she states, "This is where I really honed my skills as a teacher." Second, she remembered her mother spending many hours typing and her dad dictating as they stayed up many nights working on "this magical thing called a dissertation." Thus, the seed was planted early that graduate school was where the action was to be found.

After Frank graduated, the family moved to Bartlesville, Oklahoma, where Phillips Petroleum Company had just built a large research lab. Barbara's formal schooling began when she became a first grader at the Jane Phillips Elementary School, a school full of "children of research scientists." Barbara recalled that she spent the year trying to catch up with the rest of her classmates who had attended kindergarten, while she had not. She remembered that she had to have reading both in the morning and in the afternoon, because she was a slow reader. Barbara learned to read well because her mother read her science textbook aloud and she would follow along repeating every word after her mother. And, even though the sentences were longer, Barbara found she could read better because she could use the context to help her figure out the words and their meaning. In addition, her dad took her to his lab on the weekends and demonstrated the science concepts to her that she was reading about in her science textbook. Schooling was very important in her family, and it was understood that Barbara would not only go to college, but would also get an advanced degree in education.

Throughout her school years, Barbara was a girl scout and took ballet, square dance, and ballroom dance lessons. In high school, she was an officer in Future Teachers of America and worked in a public school in the afternoon after school. She played clarinet in the band where she met her future husband, Lorrin Walker, at the young age of 15.

Mixing Higher Ed and Family Life

After high school, Barbara attended Oklahoma State University along with her high school sweetheart, Lorrin. Barbara majored in elementary education, was active on campus, and took part in the female honor society. During her senior year, she was selected to be part of the Mortar Board Honor Society. Also, during her senior year, she and Lorrin married. Barbara stated, "I was married while I was student teaching and due to the stress of these two major events, I do not recommend this to anyone." That summer after graduation in 1968, they spent their time working in the black ghetto of Gary, Indiana, but when the race rioting and looting began, they returned to Oklahoma, but had no idea what they were going to do next.

They finally decided to go right into graduate school at Oklahoma State University. Lorrin received a grant to become a rehabilitation counselor and Barbara worked as a graduate assistant in the reading clinic to help pay for her education. She majored in elementary education with a specialization in reading. "I loved it!" she said. As a graduate assistant, she taught developmental reading at the college level and worked in the reading clinic. Barbara remembered the first child she tutored in the reading clinic, "He was a very active young man and needed to go to the bathroom frequently. One day as he was charging out the room, he lowered his head and ran right through the legs of a tall lanky man. That man was my major professor, Dr. Darrel D. Ray. I was mortified. But Dr. Ray, having been a very active child, understood."

While working on her master's degree, Dr. Ray challenged Barbara to think about the reading process, learning differences, and adjusting instruction to meet each child's reading needs. At the young age of 22, she became a reading specialist and joined the International Reading Association (IRA).

However, teaching in a public school was a long way off, as Lorrin and Barbara signed up to go to Bolivia in South America to teach in a home for children who were physically handicapped. However, before they could go to Bolivia, they had to learn Spanish. They attended Ivan Illich's School in Cuernavaca, Mexico, where they learned not only Spanish, but also about Paulo Freire's work. From there, they headed to Bolivia where they worked for three years. Barbara wrote, "I learned so much about differences from being in another culture and teaching all kinds of learners." While in Cochabamba, Bolivia, Barbara gave birth to their daughter, Sharon.

When Barbara and Lorrin returned to the United States, Lorrin took a job in Vernon, Texas. Barbara found a part time job at a local junior college. First, she built a developmental reading program and taught courses to college students who needed extra help. Barbara stated, "The town was small and I missed the excitement of learning, so I started attending conferences of the International Reading Association."

It was during their first year in Vernon that she and Lorrin adopted their son, Christopher, who was 11 months old. Sharon was only 18 months old so they were like twins. To this day, they are great friends, travel well together, and talk on the phone for long periods of time. They had a wonderful time before their formal schooling began, playing in parks and the back yard. Like all parents, Barbara and Lorrin believed their children were perfect.

Doctoral Studies

After three years in Vernon, Lorrin had an opportunity to go back to graduate school at Oklahoma State University, so they packed and moved back to Stillwater. Barbara was at loose ends, as she had quit her job to make the move. That summer, she met with public school officials in Stillwater and with Dr. Ray in hopes of finding a position. Eventually, she decided that she would also go back to the university to work on her doctorate. While taking a full load of classes, she worked as a graduate assistant in the reading clinic.

Barbara remarked, "I started out fast, but slowed down when I took a public school position." She was hired as a K-3 reading specialist in an open classroom school, her first public school position. Barbara explained, "We had 100 children in the first grade suite, four teachers, and a reading specialist. This was the age of reading styles, modality preferences, and individual differences. In the schools, we gave a specialized battery of tests in kindergarten to predict learning preferences and started children in one of the four different approaches to instruction based on those preferences. The children were closely monitored and I would give them an oral passage to read while I marked miscues as they read to determine if they needed to be moved to another group. We had 90 minutes for reading instruction. The children improved at their own rate and by third grade, they were all reading successfully. By fourth grade, they were successful in the same books as their classmates."

Barbara worked as a reading specialist while taking doctoral reading classes for three years. She said this was a great combination, as she was able to put her beliefs, research, and learning into practice immediately in the classroom.

At this time, both Sharon and Chris were beginning public schooling. As the reading specialist in their school, Barbara administered the specialized battery of tests to them in kindergarten. This is when Barbara and Lorrin learned that both their children had reading problems. Sharon could not synthesize sounds, and Chris had difficulty with psychomotor tasks like drawing shapes and writing letters—even though he knew the letter names. However, because the school had a very flexible program and effective teachers, they were not evaluated as having learning disabilities. By the end of kindergarten, Chris still had difficulty paying attention and some behavioral concerns. The kindergarten teachers suggested that Chris repeat kindergarten. Barbara suggested that Chris learn to read in the morning and go to kindergarten in the afternoon. Chris learned well under this arrangement, although Chris and Sharon were no longer in the same grade. Barbara stated, "Helping both my children to learn became a welcome challenge as I tried out various reading strategies and test batteries with them."

Next, Barbara became the reading curriculum advisor in a new school where she also evaluated all the children in the school for reading performance. This job lasted one year, until Barbara took a college teaching position. However, Barbara stated, "I learned a lot about teaching during my four years in the public school system. In fact, I was a teacher-researcher. I kept notes about students, made observations about strategies students used, made adaptations for struggling readers, and collected data to analyze growth from a multitude of sources. This is one of the lenses I use to interpret and discuss reading and reading instruction."

The Synergy of Academia and Family

Barbara and Lorrin graduated from Oklahoma State University together as they had done with their master's and bachelor's degrees. In 1981, Barbara took her first job as an assistant professor at Eastern Montana College, which later became Montana State University-Billings (MSUB). Billings was a long way from Oklahoma. Lorrin developed a private practice where he helped many people deal with drug and alcohol addiction. Barbara stated that one of the perks of living in Montana was the weather and the fact that they could commune with nature and take trips to Yellowstone National Park anytime they wanted to.

Although Barbara's career was progressing, her children were struggling. "In Montana, our children had even more difficulties in school because they did not have effective, flexible teachers." Both children were eventually evaluated for learning disabilities. Sharon was evaluated in third-grade because she was having an especially hard time passing the criterion-based tests in reading. Testing determined that her performance abilities were extremely high but her verbal abilities were average to low average. In reading, her biggest problem was her inability to complete tasks involving sound blending and isolating individual phonic sounds. However, she began reading better and did not want to be pulled out of her regular classroom. She was not labeled as learning disabled and did not receive any special services until she entered college. Chris was identified in fourth grade. He was found to have a learning disability due to lack of perceptual-motor integration and visual thinking. In terms of reading, this affected his comprehension. He was placed in a special education program. In eighth grade, Chris was placed in the regular classroom as part of a pilot inclusion program. It worked wonderfully for him. Each year thereafter, the school district had to create an inclusion classroom in each subject and this continued throughout his high school career. Chris later took courses at a community college where he was consistently on the Dean's honor role. Barbara stated, "Because of my beliefs and the trouble my own two children were having with reading and learning, I became dedicated to learning differences."

During her tenure at MSUB, Barbara claimed, "I was a demanding professor." She laughed and said, "Students often plotted to break into my office to steal the test and answers." However, she has changed her assessment techniques and now uses more collaborative group projects, group problem-solving exams, case studies, and strategy demonstrations.

Scholarly Activity and the College Reading Association

Much of her published research was done in the reading clinic while she was at MSUB. Every semester, while she taught the reading clinic course at the undergraduate level, she continued to learn about how to help struggling readers and how to support novice teachers in their efforts to teach. It was at this time that Barbara joined College Reading Association because they had both a clinical division and a teacher education division. Barbara stated, "In CRA, I found many teacher educators were focusing on my same interests. Through conversations and collaborations with CRA members, I continued experimenting with multiple ways to teach preservice teachers to work with struggling readers. This led the way for much of my research in reading teacher education."

So, after two years of teaching the reading clinic course at MSUB, Barbara decided to write up the techniques she used most frequently, which led to the writing of her first book. She submitted it to Merrill Publishing during an IRA conference and received a contract that same summer. She wrote for two years trying out multiple versions before finally sending it in. She laughed and commented, "The reviewers liked the content and some of the organization, but labeled the manuscript conceptually dense. What I did the next year was to stretch out the major concepts and provide more description of them as well as a few examples. The rest is history. *Diagnostic Teaching of Reading* is now in the 6th edition."

As her interest in reading teacher education grew, so did her research. First, she focused on reflective teaching and studied her own. Next, she began changing how she taught and used more collaborative teaching methods. This led the way for much of her research in reading teacher education. Her research on reflective teaching has encouraged teachers and teacher educators to study their own methods of teaching.

Barbara published a pamphlet entitled *Remedial Reading* (1990) for the National Education Association's "What Research Says to the Teacher" series and she became a Distinguished Finalist for IRA's 1991 Albert J. Harris Award for Research in Reading Disabilities. In 1992, she published *Supporting Struggling Readers* and in 1998 she published *Interactive Handbook for Understanding Reading Diagnosis* with Kathy Roskos. Barbara states, "Kathy and I met at CRA. We began collaborating on research in our own reading clinics and sharing data. The result was the book that contained the lessons we used for our research on reading instruction and assessments."

Barbara has continued her research in reading teacher education and presented a research study every year at CRA. She reminisced, "I have made long lasting friends [at CRA]. Susan Glazer was conference chair when I made my first presentation. Two years later, we presented on *Becoming a Nation of Readers*. In fact, at CRA, I have collaborated with Susan Glazer, Jerry Johns, Linda Gambrell, Timothy Rasinski, Nancy Padak, Vicki Risko, Dee Nichols, and Mindy Smith. When Pat Koskinen was president, she asked me to create a silent book auction that would honor members. I had members bring a copy of an autographed book they had written. And the silent book auction is still held during each conference. Many CRA members taught in reading clinics and they used much of what I had written when they taught their reading clinic course. More importantly, they began doing research in their own reading clinics. Systematically studying our college teaching was in its infancy."

Barbara believes that CRA is a great professional organization that brings colleagues together to discuss research on literacy education and particularly reading teacher education. "Although I ran for president [of CRA]," Barbara remembered, "I did not win. Instead, I won the A. B. Herr Award for research and publications that influenced reading education. I have been and continue to be mentored by members in CRA. Susan Glazer, Jerry Johns, Linda Gambrell, Timothy Rasinski, Pat Koskinen, Nancy Padak, Jon Shapiro, Betty Heathington, Ray Reutzel, Karen Bromley, Vicki Risko, Marino Alvarez and many, many others." Barbara also mentioned sharing new ideas with Bill Henk, Jack Helfeldt, Kathy Roskos, Fred Ferdorko, Wayne Linek, Deb Dillon, David O'Brien, Dee Nichols, and others.

Barbara also talked about Sally and Mike Martin challenging her with their ideas and welcoming her at every conference and said, "I appreciate them greatly." She also went on to say, "I often chat with my graduate students, Nancy Hill, Mindy Smith, Stephan Sargent, and Susan Szabo. Now, I want to continue the collaboration I have had with these colleagues and meet new colleagues each year so I will continue to grow as a professional. CRA has a great future as ALER and I believe it will continue to grow uniting colleagues for a common goal."

Coming Home

After 17 years in Montana, Barbara returned to Oklahoma where she took a full professorship at Oklahoma State University. Currently, she is a full professor at Oklahoma State University-Tulsa and is teaching courses in reading dealing with struggling readers, clinical practice, and literacy coaching. Barbara stated, "This year I taught a course in literacy coaching that was very challenging and yet rewarding. I learned that so much of my career has been about coaching and supporting teachers as they change their instruction and their beliefs about instruction."

Barbara plans to teach in the reading clinic until retirement, but noted that she would continue to write professional articles and books for a long time. However, Barbara asserted, "No honor or publication is ever attained on one's own. It is the ideas that we share with colleagues that help us clarify and write about what we know. CRA is the place where I can talk and think. CRA is a family of researchers, literacy educators, and teacher educators that article by article influence reading education."

References

Walker, B. (2007). *Diagnostic teaching of reading: Techniques for instruction and assessment* (6th ed.). Upper Saddle River, NJ: Prentice Hall.

Walker, B. (1990). *Remedial reading*. Washington, DC: National Education Association.

Walker, B. (1992). *Supporting struggling readers*. Markam, Ontario: Pippin Publishing.

Roskos, K., & Walker, B. (1998). *Interactive handbook for understanding reading diagnosis*. Upper Saddle River, NJ: Prentice Hall.

JAMES E. WALKER

CRA President 1980-1981
Albert J. Mazurkiewicz Special Services Award 1984

Richard T. Vacca, Emeritus

Kent State University

Many of you will recall one of the first hit songs by the late-great Jim Croce in the early 1970's, one which is now a classic example of the folk rock era. It's the one that begins by declaring, "Uptown got its hustlers, bowery got its bums, and 42nd street got big Jim Walker, he's a pool shootin' son of a gun." I think the song always embarrassed the Jim Walker of College Reading Association (CRA) fame. Neither is our Jim "big and dumb as a man can come;" nor is he stronger than a "country hoss." Our Jim is a gentle man, a scholar, a teacher's teacher. Moreover, even when Jim was president of CRA in 1980-1981, his colleagues had little need to ever call him "boss," as was the case with Big Jim Walker in Croce's song, "You Don't Mess Around With Jim."

If you will allow me some poetic license,

IRA got it members,
NRC got its researchers,
And CRA got gentle Jim Walker,
He's a straight shootin' son of the Cloth.

For those who may not be aware, CRA's Jim is now Father Jim, a Catholic priest and Vicar General in the diocese of Gallop, New Mexico. He is still leading others, teaching others, making a difference in the lives of those around him—only the context is different. Let me tell you his story.

The Early Years as a Literacy Educator

I first met Jim when we were doctoral students at Syracuse University. The year was 1970. I was twenty-three years old and in my first year of full-time study. If memory serves me well, there were ten or more full time doctoral students in my "class." The class ahead of us had a similar number of full-time doctoral students—among them, Jim Walker. Jim adopted me as the "resident neophyte" of 508 Ostrum Avenue, home of the University's Reading and Language Arts Center. Jim took it upon himself to show me how to navigate through the sometimes challenging waters of the Reading and Language Arts Center and through higher education in general.

It was Jim who invited me to attend my first professional conference ever—CRA's 1971 conference in Bethesda, Maryland. Looking back, my reaction was quite similar to Jim's first CRA encounter the year before, one that he vividly recalled nearly 40 years later:

> I can still remember when Dr. Leonard S. Braam invited Arthur Smith and myself to get involved in the CRA. We were doctoral students at the time and our first Conference was in 1970 at the Marriott City Line Hotel in Philadelphia. Len Braam had me introduce a speaker and I was intimidated by the whole thing. Robert Wilson was the incoming President and he also brought doctoral students, including Janet Carsetti and Linda Gambrell, two future presidents of CRA, to the Conference.

As Jim remembered, CRA was a great place to get started in one's professional career, especially in higher education circles. Over the years, Jim and I have met many graduate students who began their work in CRA and went on to serve as President of the College Reading Association, the National Reading Conference, and the International Reading Association. Jim remained convinced, as do I, that CRA has always been a very welcoming group to make young professionals feel comfortable. For many of us, CRA was a true nurturing atmosphere created by mentors and professional colleagues who cared about students. It was this acceptance and a feeling of comfort that neither Jim nor I ever forgot about CRA.

How Jim Became a Literacy Educator

In 1962, Jim started teaching Latin and English in a private high school in Newark, NJ. The administration then decided to have teachers focus more on a single teaching field and, as a result, he was assigned solely to the English Department. At this time, a new effort was underway to recruit students who otherwise might not be able to attend that school because of a history of poor academic performance. A new program was introduced called Developmental Reading. It was in reality a "remedial program," and Jim was assigned to a class of struggling readers as their homeroom teacher, their first period English teacher, and their final period Developmental Reading teacher. Jim said,

> Best assignment I ever had! I got to know those freshmen students quickly because of the multiple interactions each day. I fell in love with the idea of teaching Reading. I thought: Anyone can teach a smart kid. Try teaching some who really needs you! That marked my beginning as a literacy educator.

To learn more about developmental reading and students who struggled with text, Jim began a M.A. degree in Reading at Newark State College, now Kean University of New Jersey. Lois Bader, another future president of CRA (1985-1986), was a classmate in that program. As Jim recalled, he was struck by the motto in large gold letters in the Education Building: WHO DARES TO TEACH MUST NEVER CEASE TO LEARN. Jim reflected, "I often think of that motto and try to live it to the present day. I always knew I wanted to be a teacher from the days of my own high school."

The best teacher Jim ever had was a brilliantly trained Franciscan friar named Fr. DeSales, S.A., a Graymoor Friar. According to Jim, he could teach anything; he mastered the art and craft of teaching and was a marvelous role model. Jim remembered, "Sadly, he died in a plane crash in Pennsylvania and I thought then that somehow I should try to emulate him in the profession."

Jim's Leadership in CRA

Three years after graduating from Syracuse University, Jim first joined the Board of Directors in 1976 at the invitation of Richard Carner (1975-1976) to serve as a Public Information Officer for CRA. From that year on, he continued on the Board in various roles until about 1986. Jim served as President-elect and Program Chair for the Baltimore Conference in 1979-1980 and was President in 1980-1981. That was CRA's 25th Conference Year, the year that Linda Gambrell (1981-1982) put the program together in Louisville, Kentucky. After serving as President, he automatically continued as Chair of the Awards and then the Election Committees. Jim was then invited to serve as Historian for a few years and was also head of the Adult Learning Division for a year.

Organizing the Annual Conference

The theme of the Annual Conference Jim put together was "Reading as Its Own Reward." It was from October 30-November 1, 1980 at the Baltimore Hilton at the Inner Harbor, Maryland. The Keynote speaker was Dr. Margaret J. Early, one of our mentors at Syracuse University. Her title, as you might suspect, was "Reading as Its Own Reward." Jim remembers that Margaret made quite a point of addressing the human need for story. To this day in his pastoral duties, Jim refers to Margaret's thoughts on this "need." Jim said, "It certainly applies to the homilies I give. If I do not include a story, I always find it to be flat. People connect to stories more easily than to the abstract." Margaret Early's whole point, of course, was the need and usefulness of reading for its own sake (Not a bad message in this era of teaching for the test!).

At the time of Jim's conference, there were still only three divisions in CRA: College, Clinical, and Teacher Education. The Adult Learning Division started later. As a kind of sub-theme of the Conference Jim organized, he had a featured speaker for each division. For College Reading, Milton Spann from Appalachian State University spoke on "Developmental Education: The State of the Art." For the Clinical Division, Dr. Irene Athey, then Dean of Education at Rutgers University, spoke on "Reading and the Deaf." For the Teacher Education Division, Paul Kazmierski (CRA President 1974-1975) from Rochester Institute of Technology spoke on "Cognitive Style: A Vital Vial in Reading." One of the highlights of Jim's conference was his choice of speaker at the Annual Banquet:

> An obvious change from the usual idea of an author or another featured speaker at the Annual Banquet on Friday evening was to have the deaf mute group from Washington, D.C. called Expressions give us a presentation titled "Songs in Sign." It was certainly unique and a welcome difference from the usual format for CRA Banquets.

Jim's Presidential Year

During the year that Jim served as President, a number of things stood out as a testimonial to his leadership. The biggest problem CRA faced was financial in nature. Jim's predecessor, Bill Blanton, had started to address the fiscal needs of the organization. A proposal was made to have the membership, conference registrations, publications production, and related matters handled by an outside agency. This idea was ultimately rejected because of the expense and the fact that the board members felt CRA would lose much of its character as a personable kind of organization. Yet the reality remained that CRA faced a financial crisis. Expenses were exceeding income, partly because of the annual conference, but more so from the costs of publications.

As a result, Jim appointed a special group that he termed the Carsetti Commission, chaired by past-president Janet Carsetti and consisting of former and then-current members of the Board to study the entire question of CRA's finances and to make recommendations to the Board. Dr. Carsetti and her colleagues did an outstanding job of researching all aspects of the CRA, and a series of recommendations were made to the Board. Things started to turn in a more positive direction but, as Jim noted modestly, "They are to the credit of my successor, Linda Gambrell, and subsequent presidents of CRA."

During the year of Jim's presidency, he was on sabbatical for a semester from Northern Illinois University. Thus, he had time to devote to other matters he considered "fun and special." Since that year was CRA's 25th Annual Conference, it was held at the Galt House on the Riverfront in Louisville, Kentucky. Jim arranged for a dozen CRA members to be initiated into the Honorable Order of Kentucky Colonels at the Annual Banquet. In addition, every member who attended the Conference received a copy of *Reading: A Tribute*. This was a collection of notes, jokes, and quotes about reading, literacy in general, and kids. Jim noted, "It was a lot of fun for me to put that little booklet together and people have told me several times how much they enjoyed it and used it in some way in their own teaching." Another project that Jim undertook for the special anniversary year was to have a new CRA banner made to be displayed at future conferences and to be maintained by the Executive Secretary of the organization.

Jim fondly recalled that a very special opportunity presented itself during his presidency when Lois Bader and he testified at a Hearing before the Subcommittee on Select Education of the House of Representatives' Committee on Education and Labor. Jim remembered,

> It was a very hot, humid Washington, DC day. The statement I had prepared had been circulated for replies among prominent education figures, mainly professors and researchers. Our presentations and related responses to questions from the Committee members were contained in the Congressional Record for June 18, 1981.

Finally, in the year that Jim served as President, he also reintroduced the tradition that the President would give an address as part of the annual conference. Later, for the 16th CRA Yearbook in 1994, he wrote an article titled "CRA Professionals, Programs and Progress: A Personal Twenty-five Perspective," in which he included a table of twenty traditions of the organization as he saw them. Reflecting on that article, Jim revealed,

> I intended that article as my last publication in professional education and that has been the case. I had already decided to make a major change in my life. I would retire from formal education after a thirty-three year career and begin studies for the priesthood which began in 1995.

Jim's Road to Priesthood

The Jim Walker I knew from literacy education was by no means a saint—just a good and decent man. I had known that Jim was a person of great faith, but he blew me out of the water in 1995 when he matter-of-factly shared with Jo Anne and I that he was retiring from the hallowed halls of academe to become a priest:

> From the time I was in grammar school, I thought I would be a priest. The idea never really went away. Over the years, I was always closely associated with my church, wherever I lived. I had been privileged to do so many things over my years as a teacher and professor. I saw all fifty states, traveled oversees, saw everything I wanted to see in the United States. I felt fulfilled except that there was a recurring hunger to serve peoples' needs in other ways.

That hunger led Jim to discern that he should enter a seminary and study for the priesthood. He cared for his ailing father for several years and when his father died in 1995, Jim entered Pope John National Seminary outside Boston. There, he began studies for the priesthood for service in the Diocese of Gallup in New Mexico and Arizona. That is where he is now as pastor of four parishes. As Jim said with a sense of total satisfaction, "It is the best decision I ever made. It is even more rewarding than my many years as a professional educator. This is my dream come true."

Seminary studies were challenging for Jim. He put a lot of pressure on himself to do well—after all, he was a professor of education for more than thirty years:

> When my background as a professor became more obvious to others, the Rector and staff expected me to be a mentor to other men studying. I enjoyed using my background and experiences to help them, especially in doing research for papers and the like. My 'house job' for four years was to work in the seminary library which was a natural for me.

Jim's first assignment as a priest was at the Cathedral parish in Gallup where he remained for five years. The head priest there was elected president of a national organization, a position to which Jim could relate from his CRA days. "I think I was a help to him in his position." In time, Jim moved to his present assignment and more recently was named as Vicar General of the Diocese, second-in-command to the Bishop. According to Jim,

> I find that so many areas of experience as a professional educator come into play in my everyday work as a pastor. I am constantly preparing talks, conferences, and retreats. This is so much akin to what I had done in higher education. I have no hesitation about getting up in front of groups to speak. It is second nature for me and for any teacher. Somehow, all those years teaching are simply parlayed into more refined areas of experience in my present position.

As a priest, Jim's everyday life puts him into direct contact with people who are suffering much in their lives. Most of it, of course, is highly personal. Just being present to others, and motivated to serve in whatever ways that might help them, is a source of constant energy for Jim:

> It is a gift to have found a place in the world that is so fulfilling. Even so, there are frustrations: buildings falling apart, constant financial concerns which I never had to deal with as an educator, plus the overall administrative responsibilities take a toll. I prefer the more direct contact with everyday people and their everyday concerns. It is so rewarding. I guess I just admitted that an idea of long ago that "reading is its own reward" is an idea that has continued to grow to where I now feel that my ministry is itself its own reward. At least, that is the way I see it and prefer it to be. I am a truly blessed and content person. I am grateful indeed.

That's my friend Jim—the Jim Walker that we knew and grew to respect and love in CRA. Sadly, Jim Croce died tragically in a plane crash the year that Jim and I defended our dissertations and graduated from Syracuse University. But just as he has left his legacy, our Jim is leaving his. Whenever I am with him at a baseball game, a restaurant for dinner, or even when he's leading a congregation in prayer, I can't help but hum, somewhat irreverently, the refrain from Jim Croce's memorable song that has reverberated throughout the nearly 40 years of our friendship: "You don't tug on Superman's cape, you don't spit into the wind, you don't pull the mask off the old Lone Ranger, and you don't mess around with Jim." Well, maybe just a little...

M. JERRY WEISS

CRA President 1964-1965

Jill Lewis
New Jersey City University

Early Life

What do H.G. Wells, Lucille Ball and M. Jerry Weiss have in common? You'll be surprised to learn they are among the many well-known individuals who dropped out of high school but who to the surprise of many (especially their teachers) had brilliant careers. Jerry's story is one of self-direction, perseverance, and believing in others as much as he believes in himself.

Jerry grew up in the depression era living in several cities, including Chapel Hill, North Carolina, and Scranton and Harrisburg, Pennsylvania. His father lost the family owned, small, general store while the family was living in Oxford, North Carolina and his mother worked hard to raise her only child. When Jerry reached high school, he dropped out and joined the navy, serving on LST (Landing Ship Tank) 869 in the Pacific during World War II. Jerry says, "I grew up in the service."

Following his Navy service, Jerry took advantage of the GI Bill, going to Hershey Junior College for one year, and then transferring to University of North Carolina at Chapel Hill for his BA. Although unsure of what he wanted to do, (his dad wanted him to be an accountant,) Jerry's path was becoming clear. In undergraduate school, he joined Pi Lamda Phi, and became active in the business end of his college's musical comedy club during which time he became good friends with Oscar Hammerstein's son Jim, and movie director Larry Peerce.

Teaching Career

We can see a pattern developing as we follow Jerry to his first job as an English teacher in Chase City, Virginia, a small town where his parents then lived. Having just come from a sophisticated university environment, Jerry was excited about exposing his students to more culture than what their rural community offered them, and he was also concerned about the disparities in opportunities afforded the city kids who attended his school and those of his poor rural students. Jerry took on many extracurricular responsibilities. He directed school plays and took his students to see local plays. He became yearbook advisor and in that capacity learned that students could buy votes to be queen of the senior prom or be a member of the court. Jerry felt this was especially unfair to rural seniors since they couldn't afford to buy votes. His solution was to ask famous model agent John Robert Powers to select those students whose photos qualified them for these coveted positions. Among Powers' choices were several rural students, causing an uproar among parents of city kids.

Jerry also knew he had to do something to help all students to improve their reading. With no library in town, and realizing that the textbooks the students had were quite dull, Jerry gave his students paperbacks that he soon realized the school board had not approved. This infuriated school administrators, and the superintendent decided Jerry should leave.

Graduate School

It should not be surprising that this event resulted in Jerry's having even greater determination to foster a love of reading in all children. Thus, after being fired, Jerry decided to further his education and went to Teachers College, Columbia University, where he came under the influence of some remarkable individuals. Dr. Frances Wilson, who was Director of Guidance for New York City public schools, was one of them.

Jerry's passion for theatre caught fire here. His graduate class in Group Dynamics, taught by Dr. Wilson, was given the assignment to write a play about and for adolescents that would motivate them to discuss teenage problems. Jerry wrote, "Parents are People." Dr. Wilson was so impressed that she took it to New York City's High School of Performing Arts for a trial run and ultimately Jerry's play was performed throughout the city. Dr. Wilson asked Jerry to write more, resulting in his creative dissertation of six plays. Several of these were published and Jerry led discussions throughout the city. This experience was an eye opener for Jerry who now realized that many adolescent literacy problems were really motivation problems, in that the kids were bored and didn't like school.

Another important influence on Jerry at Teachers College was Dr. Ruth Strang who advocated the use of trade books in reading programs. Jerry explains, "With all her clinical expertise she knew that bringing books and children together were important." Roma Gans and Leland Jacobs, also at Columbia, furthered Jerry's interest in children's literature and literacy education.

University Career

For a brief period, Jerry taught English and reading at Rhodes School, a private school in New York City and then at Defiance College in Defiance, Ohio, a small town near Toledo, Ohio. Despite family obligations (Jerry was married to Helen in 1950 and by 1963 they had four children), and his teaching responsibilities, Jerry had become a stellar student in college, and through rapid succession earned his MA and EdD within two years from Teachers College. Jerry actually finished his dissertation before completing his coursework! He taught briefly at Penn State University where he had the good fortune to work with George Murphy, Nell Murphy, and Jeanette Veatch. In 1961 Jerry took a position at New Jersey City University (NJCU). This new position offered Jerry the challenges and opportunities for creativity that he needed. Initially his position at NJCU was to develop a reading program, but recognizing his talents, the administration moved him often. He chaired several departments including Special Education & Reading, Communications, and English & Reading. Ultimately, Jerry became NJCU's Distinguished Service Professor, reporting directly to the Vice President for Academic Affairs and enabling him to teach in whichever department he wanted. Jerry remained at NJCU for 33 years before retiring in 1994.

Jerry's proximity to New York City while at Penn State and NJCU put him close to the publishing world. While Jerry was at Penn State, Bantam books offered him the first consultancy for their new paperback series for adolescent readers, Pathfinder and Laurel Leaf books. This gave Jerry the opportunity to meet many publishers, editors, and authors and to impress upon them the need to write for kids at all different grade and literacy levels. When he moved to NJCU, Jerry was confident he could organize a successful reading conference, and he did so throughout the 1960's and early 70's. His one-day spring conferences filled the university's entire auditorium. He was able to bring wonderful authors to campus, such as Nat Hentoff and Neil Postman. Although some thought Jerry was using the conference for political purposes, it was clear to those who knew him that Jerry's bottom line was to do all he could to introduce students and teachers to the very best adolescent literature available and to motivate everyone to read without constraint.

As Jerry met people through professional organizations such as College Reading Association (CRA), National Council of Teachers of English (NCTE), International Reading Association (IRA), and the American Library Association (ALA), he saw what could be done by bringing groups of teachers and librarians together. He knew that clinical aspects were important to increasing reading achievement, but literature could not be sacrificed. He encouraged CRA to bring authors to the conference, and he helped to make that possible. For its Philadelphia conference, Jerry brought a screening of "They Shoot Horses, Don't They?" along with its director Sidney Pollack.

Jerry and Helen live in Montclair, New Jersey where they have resided for the last 46 years. When he first retired from NJCU, it was not unusual to see Jerry on campus, visiting friends, still planning conferences. Though not there as often now, his presence is definitely felt. In his honor, the university created the M. Jerry Weiss Center for Children's and Young Adult Literature in 2006 that serves as a resource for teachers and library/media specialists looking for innovative ways to incorporate literature into urban classrooms. The Center also explores issues of censorship in children's literature; works in partnership with schools, museums, and libraries to develop programs and share innovations; and, disseminates information about literature, the creative process and censorship to parents and the community at large.

His work is also recognized by the New Jersey Reading Association, which presents an annual "M. Jerry Weiss Book Award," affectionately known as "The Jerry." The award, established in his honor in 1993, is given to a children's, juvenile, or young adult author selected by students throughout the state of New Jersey.

Future Directions

For several reasons, Jerry is concerned about teacher preparation for teaching children to read. First, he feels there is an aesthetic part of reading that must be communicated to future generations of teachers, noting that reading is a very personal and private affair in which each individual brings something to the printed page and takes something out of it that is not always measurable. Second, he feels that teachers need to have some insight as to the importance of the library and its central role in children's lives, reminding us that kids may discover Harry Potter, not as a supplementary experience, but as a meaningful life-altering event. In Jerry's view, whenever a kid picks up a book, it should be counted as reading. Another of his concerns is that teachers of elementary grades don't have experience in all the subjects they are supposed to teach. Jerry also feels that teachers need more creative approaches to teaching and to become involved in professional organizations to get ideas about what other districts and areas of the country are doing.

While he is enthusiastic about the potential of New Literacies, Jerry feels that we must make sure kids realize that most of their education will be through books, and that not everything on the computer is accurate. He also notes that many, many schools do not have the modern technology that we talk about, and not all students have computers at home. While we must teach computer skills, book learning in science, social studies, and English, language varies subject to subject and reading in content areas is as varied as subjects themselves. Thus, teachers need to help kids become comfortable with reading content areas.

Future of CRA

Jerry's vision for CRA on its 50th anniversary is drawn from his many years of working with teachers and students, as well as his long service to CRA and other professional organizations. He would like to see CRA give more recognition to the importance of visual literacy and performing arts as an integral part of literacy. Believing as others do (e.g. Christopher Fry) that imagination is our 6th sense, Jerry hopes CRA's programs and publications can become more open to visual and performing arts and creativity so that teachers will routinely ask themselves how what they are doing in their classes is stimulating our students' imaginations.

Jerry congratulates CRA on its 50th anniversary and is proud to have been its President.

ROBERT M. WILSON

CRA President 1970-1971
A. B. Herr Award 1973
Albert J. Mazurkiewicz Special Services Award 1983

Karen Bromley

Binghamton University, SUNY

My first memory of Bob Wilson is that of a tall man with a shock of white hair accenting a tanned face. It was October in Cumberland, Maryland, when Bob and several doctoral students led a series of Friday seminars for Title 1 reading teachers in Allegany County. I was one of those fortunate reading teachers. Luckily, what I learned made me think in new ways about how students learn to read and how I might be a more effective reading teacher. My good fortune also involved the fact that Bob and his students challenged my assumptions about phonics, comprehension, and teaching struggling readers. This series of monthly half-day workshops helped me pose questions about the reading process and best practices in reading. In much larger ways my good fortune in meeting Bob and receiving his guidance helped me establish my professional life and eventually led me to where I am today.

Within a year, I entered the doctoral program in reading at the University of Maryland, College Park. Like other graduate assistants in the reading center, I came to know and love Bob Wilson. From the beginning I remember his "FOS" philosophy. "Focus on Strengths" was a strategy Bob and Linda Gambrell, a former doctoral student, created at a time when diagnosis and remediation of reading problems focused on deficiencies in the reader. "FOS" targeted a reader's strengths first and used these strengths or established behaviors as avenues to develop areas of need. It resulted in their book *Focusing on the Strengths of Children* (1973). Bob didn't use the term "weaknesses" and he practiced this philosophy with approximately 80 doctoral students he mentored. Bob said, "They all went on to distinguished careers. I'd rather not pick any of them as more distinguished than others."

Mentors and Teaching Experiences

No doubt, Bob also practiced this positivist philosophy as an educator in Pennsylvania where he held several different teaching positions. With his typical directness and modesty, Bob attributed his mentors and varied teaching experiences to "...helping me do a good job as a professor later on." What follows are descriptions of some of the highlights Bob remembered as he reminisced with me, and some of my own memories.

During high school in California, Pennsylvania, Bob was on the debate team where he polished his elocution, logic, and sense of humor. He also was the lead character in a play during his senior year, but said he was not very good at it, which seems hard to believe. Bob was a leader then and served as President of his senior class.

Bob's father, a psychology professor at California State College in Pennsylvania, was an important mentor for him. "He had a strong, positive influence on my life. He was a no-nonsense guy who was always encouraging." Because of him, Bob attended California State where he also participated on the debate team. Bob graduated with a bachelor's degree in speech therapy and elementary education. His father was his professor for some of the psychology courses and Bob reflected, "My dad was my favorite teacher in those undergraduate years." Bob then taught sixth grade at West Mifflin Public Schools near Pittsburgh. A four-year stint in the Air Force, following his enlistment during the Korean War, interrupted Bob's time at Mifflin. He returned to West Mifflin after the war and taught sixth grade there for the next five years.

Bob remembered one boy in particular named William who could not seem to learn to read or do anything Bob wanted him to, and was a bit of a behavior problem. Bob said his own handwriting was not as legible as it should have been, but William had good penmanship skills. "So, I had him put everything I needed on the blackboard for me. Then he became a 'hot shot' in the classroom because he was doing important work that was useful to us, and he wasn't a behavior problem anymore." As well as teaching sixth grade, Bob taught reading to struggling secondary level students at Kiski Preparatory School for three summers.

These experiences with students who had problems with reading and learning prompted Bob to enroll in a master's program at the University of Pittsburgh. He said, "I had ambitions to be credentialed. But more important, I had no idea what to do with the kids in my class who were having trouble reading." His first master's course was with Professor Don Cleland, and Bob learned from him how little he knew about reading. During the commencement ceremony, Bob remembers seeing doctoral candidates walk across the stage to obtain their degrees. He had known some of them and the realization hit him that "If they can do it, I can do it too." Therefore, he enrolled in the doctoral program at the University of Pittsburgh with Don Cleland as his major advisor. Bob said, "Don took an interest in me and I took a shine to him." One of Bob's vivid memories from his doctoral work was that

"Don got all his students very involved in reading center activities and it wasn't long before you didn't feel like a student. You were a participant and you felt like a colleague." Bob's dissertation research involved evaluating the effectiveness of the university reading clinic at the University of Pittsburgh using case studies of children who attended there.

After obtaining his Ed.D., Bob took a position at Edinboro State College in Pennsylvania where he was a faculty member in the teacher education program for five years before joining the faculty at the University of Maryland at College Park. While at Maryland, Bob spent 28 years as a Professor and Director of the Reading Center.

Don Cleland's mentoring was one of the things that influenced the way Bob operated at the University of Maryland with his graduate assistants and other doctoral students. Bob included everyone and welcomed all to join the regular "brown bag" lunches held at the large seminar table in the Reading Center. There, professors and doctoral students alike debated everything from the difference between comprehension and learning, to nuclear war, and the most recent editorial by William Raspberry in the *Washington Post*.

One example of Bob's sense of humor with both colleagues and graduate students stands out in my mind. I remember an over-sized screwdriver that might mysteriously appear in your mailbox one day if you by chance did something embarrassing, made a faux pas, or blundered in some way. However, it always helped us laugh at ourselves. I think we even had occasion to put it in his mailbox a few times. That screwdriver helped keep the atmosphere light in the Reading Center.

Bob said he thoroughly enjoyed his work at the University of Maryland. He specifically discussed how a doctoral competency program was developed in which all doctoral students were given opportunities to demonstrate skill in such areas as professional writing, conducting research, writing proposals for grants, teaching, advising, working with children, professional speaking, etc. He said since all his doctoral students were carefully selected, it was no surprise to him that they all performed in an outstanding manner in each of these areas.

Another of Bob's major interests was teaching the struggling readers in the Reading Clinic. An experience teaching in the clinic was part of coursework requirements for all graduate students, masters and doctoral. The clinic at Maryland focused on the strengths of all readers. Results were encouraging for both the readers and their teachers.

Another of Bob's satisfactions while at the University of Maryland was the 15 off-campus graduate programs he began with Dick Jantz, a Professor and colleague in social studies education at the University of Maryland. Bob said, "It occurred to me that there were a lot of people who wanted to get a degree but lived too far away to drive to the university. So, we started an outreach program that took our masters and doctoral programs to the field." Bob, Dick, and their doctoral students drove to all corners of the state where they taught evening and summer courses that allowed many Maryland teachers and administrators the opportunity to study and extend their professional development. However, as the university shifted its focus to research and writing as criteria for promotion and tenure, it became increasingly difficult to interest new faculty in keeping these programs going. For many years, Bob and a few others provided the outreach that had a huge impact on the instruction in classrooms and schools beyond the usual scope of a university.

CRA Memories

While Bob was at Edinboro State College, he had an opportunity to attend a CRA conference held at Gannon College in nearby Erie, Pennsylvania. He recalled, "I was hooked" and remembered attending CRA conferences in Philadelphia, Bowling Green, Jersey City, and Rochester. At that time, he said CRA meetings occurred in Pennsylvania, Ohio, New Jersey, and New York, and he remembered how it was "a big deal" to some members when the conference moved one year to Nashville, Tennessee. Recently, CRA met in Salt Lake City, Utah and there are plans to meet in Omaha, Nebraska in the future. Bob is pleased to see the geographic reach of CRA continuing to expand.

I reminded Bob that he was the eleventh president of CRA and we talked some about his experiences as President. He remembered initiating the A. B. Herr Award with huge satisfaction. Bob said A. B. Herr passed away just prior to one CRA conference and his death had an emotional effect on many CRA members. Remembering A. B. Herr as an unselfish contributor to CRA, Bob said:

> He was the one to pile all the CRA materials into his car each year and drive to wherever the conference was being held. He set up registration, saw that rooms were available for presentations, and made sure all the hotel accommodations were ready for us.

The A. B. Herr award (begun in 1972) is presented annually for distinguished service in reading. It recognizes a professional educator who has made outstanding contributions to the field of reading. An Awards Committee, chaired by the Past President of CRA, determines the award recipient. The winner receives an engraved plaque and funding to attend the conference. In 1973, Bob was surprised when both he and Jerry Weiss, a Professor at Jersey City College, New Jersey and his good friend, received this award. Bob's award was most probably due to his contributions to the field through his writing for educators, presentations at conferences, and exemplary service to CRA.

Mentors and Professional Writing

Bob was and continues to be a prolific writer. A selected list of his impressive publications is included here because it shows the breadth and depth of his writing and impact on the field of reading and classroom instruction in general. Bob credited Arthur Heilman with helping him begin his professional life as a writer. He said he met Art at the 1963 International Reading Association (IRA) conference by chance when he and a colleague, Joe Nameth, hosted a cocktail party for colleagues and graduate students. They invited a few "big names" in the field because Bob wanted his doctoral students to meet some of the well-known people in reading, and Art came to the party. After IRA, Bob invited Art to speak at a conference at Edinboro State College and Art accepted. Bob remembers Art telling him that he had a choice. He could stay at Edinboro and be happy or he could move on to a larger institution and increase his outreach in the field. Art told him "You can stay here and enjoy it or you can move on. If you want to move on you have to write." Art offered to read anything Bob might send him and give Bob honest feedback.

Later, Bob sent Art a draft of something he had written and Art "tore it apart." Bob then revised the piece and this process was the start he needed. He began writing in earnest. It was at about that time that Bob had an important insight. He noticed that no one in the field was making the critical link between diagnosis and remediation. He said, "People were doing a test to determine 'X' about a student, but stopping there and failing to decide 'Y' which is what to do with that information." This notion became the premise for his well-received book *Diagnostic and Remedial Reading for Classroom and Clinic* (1972). Proof of its popularity is the fact that it went into a fifth edition in 1985. The book went into a sixth edition in 1990 when he co-authored it with Craig Cleland, another of his past doctoral students and Professor at Mansfield State University in Pennsylvania.

Besides writing books for educators included in the list at the end of this chapter, Bob published many articles in refereed journals. He also realized how important it was for his doctoral students to engage in research and begin to write and publish before they received their doctorate. He felt this would help ensure that his graduate students could obtain a position at a college or university if that was their goal. Bob helped me in this way, and I am convinced it played an important part in my being offered a position in higher education. Later, I learned the publication we had co-authored, along with my dissertation research, impressed the people who interviewed me. We had done a study together, largely conceptualized by Bob, and co-authored an article that appeared in *The Reading Teacher*. Bob really should have been first author, but knowing it would be a boost to my resume as I job-hunted, he insisted my name appear first. Bob was an unselfish and wise mentor and guide to many.

Thoughts on Retirement

Bob said he retired in 1992 when "I realized I didn't have a burning desire to work with another doctoral student. I did not want to take on another curriculum project for an off-campus degree. I felt I had done what I could do and it was time to move on." After Bob retired, he and Dick Jantz took many trips to pursue their interest in the Civil War. Together, they visited and studied almost every Civil War site east of the Mississippi. These visits sparked Bob to do more Civil War research and this work resulted in a recently co-authored book with another friend, Carl Clair, titled *They Also Served: Wives of Civil War Generals* (2006). Bob mentioned a second related book that is now in the works with Carl called *Sons and Daughters of Civil War Generals*. It is clear that retirement has not slowed Bob down. He has indeed moved on to a new chapter in life.

Advice to New Professionals and CRA

True to his penchant for directness and getting right to the point, Bob had some advice for those entering or leaving graduate work and those working in teacher education. He said, "Don't forget…if it doesn't make a difference in the classroom, we're wasting our time." Bob has certainly lived this philosophy in his teaching, writing, mentoring, and service to CRA. About the future of the profession, Bob reflected,

I have always seen the best results when teachers identify needs and develop programs to meet those needs. I call that 'bottom up.' Today most of what I hear is 'top down,' in other words the federal and state governments make rules and regulations for teachers. I doubt that such 'top down' programs will continue to be effective.

CRA was always Bob's favorite of the professional organizations. He was in favor of a name change for CRA:

I like the new name, Association of Literacy Educators and Researchers (ALER). The main reason is that it is more reflective of the membership. The name College Reading Association never really did represent us well except for the very beginning. However, as we grew, our membership broadened and we attracted not only teacher educators, but also researchers, teachers, and graduate students from colleges and universities.

Bob has a vision for the future "I hope the organization continues to be the research-based, but practical professional group, that is so badly needed in the field." He has always liked the annual conference for several reasons. He said, "The group is small enough that it is easy to get to know everyone, presentations are useful and practical while based on research and theory, and people are kind and generous with their time and ideas."

Bob helped demystify the profession for his graduate students. He nudged us to attend every CRA conference and often provided funds for those who could not afford to attend. Many graduate students had their first experience at CRA making a presentation to an audience of college and university faculty. Thanks to Bob, many of us also met some of the "big names" in the reading field at these annual events.

In Conclusion

Talking to Bob on the telephone recently to tie up loose ends for this chapter, I heard the same strong and energetic voice I knew thirty years ago when I graduated from the University of Maryland. Despite the time that has gone by, Bob remains a curious, vibrant, warm, and thoughtful person. Bob was and continues to be a wonderful role model, mentor, and friend to many. In addition, we in CRA have much to thank Bob for as one of the original creators of this vital professional organization.

References

Wilson, R. M., & Clair, C. (2006). *They also served: Wives of civil war generals.* Philadelphia: Xlibris.

Leu, D. J., Kinzer, C. K., Wilson, R. M., & Hall, M. (2005). *Phonics, phonemic awareness, and word analysis for teachers: An interactive tutorial* (8th ed.). Upper Saddle River, NJ: Prentice Hall.

Hafer, J. C., & Wilson, R. M. (1998). *Signing for reading success.* Washington, DC: Gallaudet University Press.

Wilson, R. M., & Hall, M. (1997). *Programmed word attack for teachers* (6th ed.). Des Moines, IA: Merrill Prentice Hall.

Wilson, R. M., & Hall, M. (1997). *Programmed word attack for teachers* (6th ed.). Des Moines, IA: Merrill Prentice Hall.

Hafer, J., & Wilson, R. M. (1996). *Come sign with us: Sign language activities for children* (2nd ed.). Washington, DC: Gallaudet University Press.

Wilson. R. M., & Cleland, C. (1990). *Diagnostic and remedial reading for classroom and clinic* (6th ed.). Upper Saddle River, NJ: Prentice Hall.

Wilson, R. M., & Gambrell, L. (1988). *Reading comprehension in the elementary school: A teacher's practical guide.* Boston: Allyn & Bacon.

Koskinen, P. & Wilson, R. M. (1982). *Developing a successful tutoring program.* New York: Teachers College Press.

Wilson, R. M., & Bean, R. (1981). *Effecting change in school reading programs: The resource role.* Newark, DE: International Reading Association.

Wilson, R. M., Gambrell, L., & Hall, M. (1980). *Programmed reading for teachers.* Desoto, TX: SRA/McGraw Hill.

Gambrell, L., & Wilson, R. M. (1980). *28 ways to help your child be a better reader.* Columbus, OH: Instructo/McGraw Hill

Hall, M. A., Wilson, R. M., Ribovich, J. K., & Ramig, C. J. (1979). *Reading and the elementary school child: Theory and practice for teachers* (2nd ed). New York: Van Nostrand Reinhold.

Wilson, R. M. & Barnes, M. (1975). *Using newspapers to teach reading skills.* Reston, VA: American Newspaper Publishers Association Foundation.

Wilson, R. M. & Barnes, M. (1974). *Survival Learning Materials*, York, PA: College Reading Association.

Waynant, L., & Wilson, R. M. (1974). *Learning centers: A guide for effective use.* Columbus, OH: Instructo/McGraw Hill.

Gambrell, L., & Wilson, R. M. (1973). *Focusing on the strengths of children.* Belmont, CA: Fearon Publishers.

Wilson, R. M. (1972). *Readings for diagnostic and remedial reading.* Blacklick, OH: Glencoe/McGraw Hill.

PRESIDENTIAL ADDRESSES

Introduction to Presidential Addresses

Wayne M. Linek

Texas A&M University-Commerce

Starting in 1996, with Judy Richardson's presidency, presidential Addresses were captured and published in the CRA Yearbook. Those who were present for the speeches will fondly recall instances such as: Judy Richardson giving her address wearing a pointed witches' hat, Marino Alvarez talking about paper clips, Tim Rasinski learning from his dog, Jane Matanzo waving at herself in the mirror, Jon Shapiro making us cry, and "Boss Queen of CRA" Ellen Jampole in a wig, crown, and with laryngitis. The speeches are presented in chronological order so that readers can analyze them for trends over time.

THOSE WONDERFUL TOYS: READ-ALOUDS FROM THE CLASSICS AND ASSORTED LITERATURE

Judy S. Richardson
Virginia Commonwealth University

Presidential Address
College Reading Association
1996

Since joining CRA in 1979 and as of 1996, Judy Richardson had served as Chair of the Adult Learning Division and on the Awards, Nominating, and Publications Committees. She had contributed to several studies and presentations for both the Teacher Education and Adult Learning Divisions, reviewed program proposals, and served on the Board of Reviewers for several Yearbooks and for Reading Research and Instruction.

Judy had spent more than 30 years in the teaching field, with experiences in English, reading and special education. She had taught at Virginia Commonwealth University for 17 years, both under-graduate and graduate level courses in Reading and related areas.

Judy's publications included the textbook, Reading to Learn in the Content Areas *(Wadsworth, 1990; 1994; 1997); the teacher text,* The English Teacher's Survival Guide, *articles in several* International Reading Association *and College Reading Association monographs and yearbooks; chapters in CRA's monograph* Adult Beginning Readers: To Reach Them My Hand; *articles in* Journal of Adolescent and Adult Literacy, Reading Today, Adult Literacy *and* Basic Education, Lifelong Learning, CARE, The Reading Professor, Reading News, Virginia English Bulletin, *and* Reading in Virginia. *Judy had presented at numerous national, regional, state and local conferences.*

Reprinted from *Exploring Literacy*, pp.29-36, by W. M. Linek, & E. G. Sturtevant, Eds., 1997, Commerce, TX: College Reading Association.

Judy had also contributed to the International Reading Association as Chair of the Affective Domain and of the Adult Literacy Special Interest Groups; member of the Adult Literacy Committee; conference arrangements committee member for the Third and Fourth IRA Adolescent and Adult Literacy Conference; and reviewer for Journal of Reading.

Thirty years ago I was awarded a sizable fellowship to pursue graduate studies in English literature. Personal difficulties sidetracked me to a high school where I taught ninth and twelfth graders for a year. I was hooked! Here were rapscallions who did not appreciate literature—some could not read well enough and others did not want to read—but whose appreciation for life seduced me! I wanted my students to discover the satisfaction of learning.

I abandoned my plans to become an English scholar and fell into teaching positions across the United States and on Okinawa during the Vietnam War. The more I interacted with learners of all kinds—special needs, elementary, middle, high, and adult—the more I knew my heart belonged to the teaching of reading. However, my brain has never forgotten its original plan. I retain a deep appreciation for good literature. I pursue my study of Flannery O'Connor. I take courses. I read voraciously, as I am sure you do.

And sometimes I wonder what my professional life would have been like had I taken the other road of which Robert Frost writes: . . . .

Knowing how way leads on to way,
I doubted if I should ever come back . . .

But I have found a way to travel a double path. While my heart lies with students, and my profession requires me to keep abreast, I also make time to read for pleasure. Now I explore rather than *deeply study* literature. I read many genres, from classics to light fantasies. And I think about learners always as I read.

So, when asked recently where I got all of those great ideas for my "Read It Aloud" column in the *Journal of Adolescent and Adult Literature* (JAAL), I was reminded of the Joker's line in *Batman, The Movie*. Batman has just rescued his girlfriend by employing a series of marvelous tricks. The Joker expresses his admiration for "those wonderful toys." This address is a series of stories to illustrate my parallel travels in the lands of literature and the teaching of reading, finding wonderful toys from literature to use in instruction. I have selected a slice of time, from July and August of 1996, for my stories.

My husband, son—Andrew was fifteen—and I toured Great Britain in the summer of 1996. We stayed in Stratford-Upon-Avon for several nights because we wanted to see a Royal Shakespearean play. To appease Andrew as he stoically indulged us in our enthusiasm for Shakespeare, I took him shopping for souvenirs. Andrew found a crossbow; he had to have it! The shopkeeper told me that if I purchased ten pounds more, I could avoid the tax and qualify for direct shipping to my home. So of course I looked around and found a wonderful toy. The figurine I bought is "The Intellectual Witch." She is staggering under a load of several books. I loved her immediately. And when the shopkeeper told me that she is modeled after a Terry Pratchett character, I had to read about this character.

Terry Pratchett is the popular writer of a fantasy series, The Discworld, in Great Britain. The shopkeeper could not remember in which of his books I would find The Intellectual Witch. So I was bound to read until I found her. I started with The Colour of Magic (1983). I did not find the Intellectual Witch. However, I did find the circumfence! And this passage became the topic of my March 97 column for JAAL:

". . . So why aren't we going over the edge, then?" asked Rincewind with glassy calmness.

"Because your boat hit the circumfence," said the voice behind him (in tones that made Rincewind imagine submarine chasms and lurking Things in coral reefs).

"The Circumfence?" he repeated.

"Yes, it runs along the edge of the world," said the unseen troll. Above the roar of the waterfall Rincewind thought he could make out the splash of oars. He hoped they were oars.

"Ah, you mean the circumference," said Rincewind. "The circumference makes the edge of things."

"So does the Circumfence," said the troll.

"He means this," said Twoflower, pointing down. Rincewind's eyes followed the finger, dreading what they might see .. .

Hubwards of the boat was a rope suspended a few feet above the surface of the white water. The boat was attached to it, moored yet mobile, by a complicated arrangement of pulleys and little wooden wheels. They ran along the rope as the unseen rower propelled the craft along the very lip of the Rimfall. That explained one mystery—but what supported the rope?

Rincewind peered along its length and saw a stout wooden post sticking up out of the water a few yards ahead. As he watched the boat neared it and then passed it, the little wheels clacking neatly around it in a groove obviously cut for the purpose . . .

"All things drift into the Circumfence in time," said the troll, gnomically, gently rocking in his chair. "My job is to recover the flotsam. Timber, of course, and ships. Barrels of wine. Bales of cloth. You."

Light dawned inside Rincewind's head.

"It's a net, isn't it? You've got a net right on the edge of the sea!"

"The Circumfence," nodded the troll. Ripples ran across his chest. Rincewind looked out into the phosphorescent darkness that surrounded the island, and grinned inanely.

"Of course," he said. "Amazing! You could sink piles and attach it to reefs and —good grief! The net would have to be very strong." "It is," said Tethis.[1]

Terry Prachett has written many Discworld novels. Next, I selected Witches Abroad (Pratchett, 1993), thinking it a likely title in which to find my intellectual witch. I could see her there; it must be Magrat, I reasoned, but I was not yet completely satisfied. However, here is one "toy" I found, excellent for a read-aloud whenever I am teaching about the importance of spelling or about homophones:

Local people called it the Bear Mountain. This was because it was a bare mountain, not because it had a lot of bears on it. This caused a certain amount of profitable confusion, though; people often strode into the nearest village with heavy duty crossbows, traps and nets and called haughtily for native guides to lead them to the bears. Since everyone locally was making quite a good living out of this, what with the sale of guide books, maps of bear caves, ornamental cuckoo-clocks with bears on them, bear walking-sticks and cakes baked in the shape of a bear, somehow no one had time to go and correct the spelling.*

*Bad spelling can be lethal. For example, the greedy seriph of Al-Ybi was once cursed by a badly-educated deity and for some days everything he touched turned to Glod, which happened to be the name of a small dwarf from a mountain community hundreds of miles away who found himself magically dragged to the kingdom and relentlessly duplicated. Some two thousand Glods later the spell wore off. These days, the people of Al-Ybi are renowned for being unusually short and bad-tempered.[2]

Next, I went to *Wyrd Sisters* (Pratchett, 1990), and here I found my Intellectual Witch described:

"Magrat had learned a lot of witchcraft from books" (p. 16).

But her sister witches, Nanny Ogg and Granny Weatherwax, do not necessarily take to books:

"It's all these books they read today." said Granny. "It overheats the brain. You haven't been putting ideas in her head, have you?"

(p.117)...Granny had never had much time for words. They were so insubstantial. Now she wished that she had found the time. Words were indeed insubstantial. They were soft as water, but they were also powerful as water and now they were rushing over the audience, eroding the levees of veracity, and carrying away the past" (p. 271).[3]

Also in *Wyrd Sisters*, I have found a wonderful introduction to theatre for language arts classes. In this novel, the witches "hide" the crown prince from an evil duke who has usurped the throne; they place the prince with a company of actors. Tom John becomes one of the best actors in the troupe. Ironically, his company is commissioned by the duke to stage a play in which the witches are portrayed as evil hags. Why do people enjoy plays? What happens when we watch a play? Here is Granny's impression:

> Granny subsided into unaccustomed, troubled silence, and tried to listen to the prologue. The theatre worried her. It had a magic of its own, one that didn't belong to her, one that wasn't in her control. It changed the world, and said things were otherwise than they were. And it was worse than that. It was magic that didn't belong to magical people. It was commanded by ordinary people, who didn't know the rules. They altered the world because it sounded better."[4]

After three Terry Prachett fantasies, I switched to reading another genre when Andrew began his summer reading requirements—the last three weeks before school was to start. I read along with him, to sustain him, through Flaubert's *Madame Bovary* (1857). Emma is a romantic. She is a reader. Leon is also a reader, and certainly a romantic at the start of the novel. The following passage foreshadows their relationship, as well as painting for the reader an early portrait of Emma. This passage was the subject of my May 1997 Read It Aloud column.

> "—My wife doesn't care much for it," said Charles; "she'd rather, even though she's been recommended to take exercise, stay in her room the whole time, reading."

> "—That's like me," remarked Leon; "what could be better, really, than an evening by the fire with a book, with the wind beating on the panes, the lamp burning? . . ."

> "—I do so agree," she said, fixing on him her great black eyes open wide.

> "—Your head is empty," he continued, "the hours slip away. From your chair you wander through the countries of your mind, and your thoughts, threading themselves into the fiction, play about with the details or rush along the track of the plot. You melt into the characters; it seems as if your own heart is beating under their skin."

> "—Oh, yes, that is true." she said.

> "—Has it ever happened to you," Leon went on, "in a book you come

across some vague idea you once had, some blurred image from deep down, something that just spells out your finest feelings?"

"—I have," she answered.

"—That" he said, "is why I particularly love the poets. I find verse more tender than prose, and it brings more tears to the eye."

"—Though rather exhausting after a while," Emma went on; "and at the moment, you see, I adore stories that push on inexorably, frightening stories. I detest common heroes and temperate feelings, the way they are in life."[5]

I will think of this passage when I want to talk with students about the reasons we might read, the way reading can carry us away. And I might use this passage also as a way to segue into a discussion of some of the differences between poetry and prose.

To initiate a discussion about poetry, always a challenging topic for secondary English teachers, I discovered a wonderful story by Fred Chappell. I could use the following excerpt in an English class when introducing a poetry unit: What is a poem? What does a poem look like? How do poems get made? Who is a poet? Fred Chappell (1991), noted author and master of the short story, encourages readers to explore these questions in his short story "Mankind Journeys Through the Forest of Symbols" in his collection *More Shapes Than One*. Sheriff Balsam needs to clear a major highway of a fog so dense that motorists cannot drive through it. The fog turns out to be an unwritten poem disturbing someone's unconscious so greatly that it has caused the unwitting poet to create a fog. This clouded thinking has settled on the highway. Balsam calls in the expert Dr. Litmouse to help find a way to dissolve it:

> Dusk had come to the mountains like a sewing machine crawling over an operating table, and Dr. Litmouse and Hank and Bill and Balsam were back in the sheriffs office. Balsam sat at his desk, the telephone receiver still off the hook. Bill and Hank had resumed their corner chairs. The three lawmen were listening to the scientist's explanation. "Basically, it's the same problem as a dream, so it's mostly out of our hands. Somebody within a fifty-mile radius is ripe to write a symbolist poem but hasn't gotten around to it yet. As soon as she or he does, then it will go away, just as the usual dream obstructions vanish when the dreamers wake." He took off his glasses and polished them with his handkerchief. His eyes looked as little and bare as shirt buttons and made the others feel queasy. They were glad when he replaced his spectacles.

> "It's worse than a dream, though, because we may be dealing with a subconscious poet. It may be that this person never writes poems in the normal course of his life. If this poem originated in the mind of someone who never thinks of writing, then I'm afraid your highway detour will have to be more or less permanent." (pages 160-161)

The sheriff picked up a ballpoint pen and began clicking it. "Well, let's see.... There it is, and it'll go away if somebody writes it down on paper." "Correct." (page 162)

"Well, what we got to do then is just get as many people as we can out there writing poems. Community effort. Maybe we'll luck out." "How?" asked Dr. Litmouse.

He clicked his ballpoint furiously. He got a sheet of department stationery and began printing tall uncertain letters. The other three watched in suspense, breathing unevenly. When he finished, Balsam picked up the paper and held it at arm's length to read. His lips moved slightly. Then he showed them his work. "What do you think?" he asked.

The Sheriff's Department
Of Osgood County
in cooperation with the
North Carolina State Highway Department
announces
A Poetry Contest
$50 first prize
Send entries to Sheriff Elmo Balsam
Osgood County Courthouse
Ember Forks, N. C. 26816
Symbolism Preferred!!!

"I suppose it's worth a try," Dr. Litmouse said, but he sounded dubious. (pp. 162-163)[6]

The poet, incidentally, turns out to be Sheriff Balsam's deputy, Bill. Bill sweats out his poem, which clears his head, and thus the road clears, and everyone goes back to a normal life. Adolescents are bound to have fun thinking about unwritten poems fogging up unsuspecting minds and creating all kinds of havoc in one's community. Why, anyone might write a poem, even a sheriffs deputy!

To conclude my stories, I want to take you back with me to Haworth, near the Lake Country of England. My husband and I spent three hours wandering through Haworth, in the home of the Bronte sisters. Our son sat outside and fumed in the hot sun; this was not his most exciting part of our trip! When we returned to the car, he spewed at us,

"They're just dead people! You're worshipping dead people!" And to him I respond,

"Ah, yes, my son, the Brontes are dead. But they have left us such wonderful toys."

Notes

[1]From *The Colour of Magic* (pp. 164-165), by T Pratchett, 1983, Buckinghamshire, England: Colin Smythe Ltd. Copyright 1983 by Colin Smythe Ltd. Reprinted with permission.

[2]From *Witches Abroad* (pp. 11-12), by T Pratchett, 1993, Buckinghamshire, England. Colin Smythe Ltd. Copyright 1993 by Colin Smythe Ltd. Reprinted with permission.

[3]From *Wyrd Sisters* (pp. 16, 117, 271), by T Pratchett, 1990, Buckinghamshire, England. Colin Smythe Ltd. Copyright 1990 by Colin Smythe Ltd. Reprinted with permission.

[4]From *Wyrd Sisters* (p. 265), by T. Pratchett, 1990, Buckinghamshire, England: Colin Smythe Ltd. Copyright 1990 by Colin Smythe Ltd. Reprinted with permission.

[5]From *Madame Bovary*: Provincial Lives (p. 66), by G. Flaubert (G. Wall, Trans.), 1857/1992, New York: Penguin Books. Copyright 1992 by Penguin Books.

[6]From *Mankind Journeys Through Forests of Symbols* in *More Shapes Than One* (p. 160-163), by Fred Chappell, 1991, New York: St. Martin's Press Incorporated. Copyright 1991 by Fred Chappell. Reprinted by permission of St. Martin's Press.

References

Chappell, F. (1991). *Mankind journeys through forests of symbols. more shapes than one.* New York: St. Martin's Press.

Flaubert, G. (1992). *Madame Bovary: Provincial lives.* (G. Wall, Trans.) New York: Penguin Books. (Original work published 1857).

Frost, R. The road not taken. In E. C. Lathem (Ed.), *The poetry of Robert Frost* (p. 105). NY: Holt Rinehart and Winston, Inc.

Pratchett, T. (1983). *The colour of magic.* Buckinghamshire, England: Colin Smythe Ltd.

Pratchett, T (1990). *Wyrd sisters.* Buckinghamshire, England: Colin Smythe Ltd.

Pratchett, T. (1993). *Witches abroad.* Buckinghamshire, England: Colin Smythe Ltd.

Richardson, J. S., & Gross, E. (1997). A read-aloud for mathematics. *Journal of Adolescent and Adult Literacy, 40*, 492-494.

Richardson J. S., Wimer, D. B., & Counts, J. (1997). A read-aloud for romantics and realists. *Journal of Adolescent and Adult Literacy, 40*, 658-661.

Adolescent Literacy: Are We In Contact?

Marino C. Alvarez

Tennessee State University

Presidential Address
College Reading Association
1997

In 1997 Marino Alvarez was a professor of graduate and undergraduate reading classes in the Department of Teaching and Learning in the College of Education. He was a former middle and secondary school social studies teacher. He has served on national committees, on editorial advisory boards, and as president of the Action Research Special Interest Group of the American Educational Research Association. His publications have appeared in edited chapters and in a variety of journals. Professor Alvarez was the 1995 recipient of both the Teacher-of-the-Year and Distinguished Researcher-of-the-Year Awards at TSU. He also directed the Explorers of the  *Universe, a scientific literacy project, which involves teachers and their students in various NASA earth/space projects.*

Ever wonder about the role of paper clips and staples? The only thing they have in common is that they come in a box. Staples are invariant. They don't change shape, and they serve a singular function: to keep papers in place. Paper clips, on the other hand, are flexible. They can be made of metal (like the staple) or of plastic. Plastic seems preferable because it does not leave a paper clip trace on the page like metal clips. They can be independently selected and reused again and again. Paper clips are colorful and serve multiple purposes. They can keep papers in place, they can be removed from a collection of pa-

Reprinted from *Literacy and Community*, pp. 2-10, by E. G. Sturtevant, J. R. Dugan, P. Linder, & W. M. Linek, Eds., 1998, Commerce, TX: College Reading Association.

pers and the papers can again be joined by the same paper clip. They can be manipulated into different shapes and can be used as a probe. For example, I was able to bend one into a hook and use it to retrieve a screw that fell into my garbage disposal. Paper clips can also be joined together to form a chain. Staples give one a sense of permanency. When you staple papers together you sense a final product. When you use a paper clip you get a feeling that you're not really done. These papers are in a state of transition. They either need to be revised or rearranged before they can be stapled.

Paper Clips and Staples

Students are often treated by teachers and policymakers as if they are either paper clips or staples. There are those who want students to explore, imagine, exercise critical thinking, learn from the future, and learn from mistakes. These educators and policymakers believe that students are in transition with knowledge and that learning new knowledge helps them to grasp future knowledge. However, there are others who believe in permanency and that learning involves mastering what is known. Like a staple, this knowledge is in place. All one needs to do is learn what is known to succeed in schooling. Imagination, curiosity, and exploration are fine, as long as it takes place *after* knowing what is known. For many students, thinking about learning seldom happens. For others, it takes place after formal schooling.

Although indoctrination of facts begins at an early age of one's formal schooling, no where is it more prominent than during the adolescent years. It is during this period that students either "learn how to learn," learn "how to play school" or falter by the wayside because they have never "learned how to learn," or learned "how to play school." Literacy proficiency plays a crucial role in dividing these students. Students who have the most difficulty with literacy skills are often neglected by teachers who are not aware of strategies to use to help them comprehend texts and supplementary readings. This situation is compounded by a lack of reading specialists to aid students in their understanding of narrative and expository discourse.

Limited Funding and Lack of Research

Funding for adolescent literacy programs by the federal government under Title I's compensatory education program is only 16 percent to grades 7, 8, and 9. It is even less for grades 10, 11, and 12, at 5 percent. However, 69 percent of Tide I funds are earmarked for grades 1, 2, 3, 4, 5, and 6 (U.S. Department of Education, 1994-95). These funding levels remain consistent with findings reported ten and twenty-three years ago (Davidson & Koppenhaver, 1988). Davidson and Koppenhaver (1988) further report that in 1985 only 54 out of every 100 eligible students were being served by Chapter I funds. Clearly this discrepancy in funding exemplifies the minimal priority that adolescents needing literacy support are given.

Couple this finding with a move toward licensure by the states to minimize or abolish content literacy course requirements, the lack of funding for reading specialists at the middle and secondary levels, the use of basal readers to teach reading skills by an English teacher or a teacher assigned the task, the limited number of research articles that involve middle and high school populations appearing in our literacy research journals, and you begin to understand the problem. These situations are compounded by federal and state legislators moving toward national and state curricula, common standards, and curriculum and instruction policies and procedures that hinder meaningful learning.

Fragmented Adolescent Literacy Programs

Adolescent literacy programs are fragmented into those that follow an elementary school model of structured skills instruction, those that rely on published materials and worksheets that accompany the text for literacy instruction and learning, and pull-out programs that take the student away from a subject. There are a few literacy programs that incorporate the subject discipline with conventional and electronic readings and writings from other related content areas. However, most of these programs lack a coordinated effort among the content teachers to include strategies in their lesson planning to aid students in their literacy development.

Lost in all this milieu are the voices of adolescents and those of thoughtful teachers who strive to make school a place for learning rather than endurance. These voices are out shouted by those who hold onto what was done in the past, imposing standards that they may not have attained given the same circumstances, clinging to the notion that there is a given body of knowledge that everyone needs to know. Also included are those who have difficulty with the concept that electronic literacy and the information age is upon us. The combining of narrative with expository texts that require students to select, analyze, synthesize, recombine, and think about unrealized possibilities is needed for meaningful adolescent literacy programs to flourish.

Students are already accessing, communicating, publishing papers with interactive reference linkages to other sources, and developing their own e-mail and web pages. They are using metacognitive interactive tools (e.g., concept maps and Interactive Vee Diagrams) to plan, carry-out, and finalize their assignments and research investigations. Their electronic literacy skills surpass those measured in typical pencil and paper literacy tests. It will take several years before reading tests are constructed to reflect these types of electronic reading and reasoning abilities. The obstacles that face test-makers are formidable. Many of these students are using their imagination for enhancing their learning using electronic literacy in ways that extend those of the typical teacher and extend the parameters of closure that challenge test-makers.

Electronic Literacy

A literate person living in our society is drastically different from one who lived in 14th century England. The literacy skills of yesterday are no longer practical in today's fast-pace world of information. The printing press, invented in the 1400s, changed the way people thought and accessed information; so too, is the electronic information age changing the ways we view literacy. The societal needs of the 21st century demand that literacy definitions be revised to include this new information age. This electronic literacy requires individuals to access large quantities of information, determine their accuracy and worth, communicate with others over distances, and become involved collaboratively and interactively.

Thinkers and Tinkers

Little opportunity is given for teachers and students to be thinkers and tinkers in our schools (Alvarez, 1996a; Alvarez, 1997a). Fixed curricula, required course content, and state and national policies do little to foster thinking and tinkering. Those few teachers and students that recognize the nonsense that restrictive environments impose and are willing to trust themselves and each other are succeeding in making school a place for learning and exchanging ideas.

The English teachers and librarians in the Gallatin High School Literacy Project and the astronomy and physics teachers in the Explorers of the Universe Scientific/Literacy Interdisciplinary Project (http://coe2.tsuniv.edu/ex-plorers) are part of these few (Alvarez, 1993; Alvarez, 1995; Alvarez, Binkley, Bivens, Highers, Poole, & Walker, 1991; Alvarez & Rodriguez, 1995). These teachers are willing to try something different. They are willing to trust their thinking about what is best for their students to learn. They use meaningful materials in problem-oriented contexts that invite students to "show what they can do." They also include their students in their curriculum by offering opportunities to involve them in reading both narrative and expository texts, writing reports and journals, and incorporating the curriculum with other subject disciplines. Students who have more knowledge about programming mathematical computations than their teachers are encouraged to write the programs. In situations where students wish to study a related topic for which a case has not been developed, they do so in conjunction with their teacher. The lessons that make up the emergent curriculum are more meaningful. Metacognitive tools such as concept maps and interactive Vee diagrams through the Internet are used by students to share ideas and information. The conversations that occur between teachers and their students are more inquiry than answer producing. Instead of being subjected to the "one best system," they are searching for the ways in which to tinker with the existing knowledge and to extend its meaning. These teachers "teach," and their students "student." Teachers don't speak of "covering" the material; instead, they demonstrate by example and facilitate the "teaching" of the material. Instead of focusing on compartmentalizing the subject discipline, they are looking for ways to incorporate music, art, literature, history, mathematics, industrial technology, and multimedia into their lessons and assignments—and so are their students.

Elizabeth Binkley, Judy Bivens, Patricia Highers, and Cynthia Poole (1991) are teachers who are both thinkers and tinkers at Gallatin High School. They were willing to try a case-based approach to teaching and learning with their students that revolved around the study of *To Kill A Mockingbird*. Students were given cases to explore that were thematically linked to the story. They were also given the opportunity to develop their own cases with the aid of the teacher. These students were asked to participate in a variety of literacy building activities. They read related sources, interviewed authors, lawyers, and ministers, and they videotaped related episodes that they wanted to incorporate into their cases. Students designed blueprints and built models, visited local and distant libraries seeking information, and used their critical thinking and imaginative processes to search out information. Five years later with over twenty cases written by the teacher and her students, a videodisc was developed. This videodisc was the first of its kind to be designed and developed by teachers for their students instead of by outside professionals.

Bill Rodriguez (astronomy and physics teacher) at the University School of Nashville, and Lee Ann Hennig (astronomy teacher) at Thomas Jefferson High School for Science and Technology, Alexandria Virginia are two teachers who are both thinkers and tinkers in the Explorers of the Universe Scientific/Literacy Project. They wrote a technical manual for the Explorers Project, *Finding Periods in Variable Star Data: Using Remote FORTRAN and Local Windows Software*. The manual is based on analyzing data that they are receiving from automatic photoelectric telescopes that reside at the Fairborn Observatory in Washington Camp, near Nogales, Arizona. These automatic telescopes are controlled over the Internet by astronomers at Tennessee State University in Nashville, Tennessee. These teachers field-tested this manual with their students. Students offered suggestions for revision of the materials, and a few also wrote several programs to analyze the data. The manual has been revised and is now on the web site for use by students affiliated with the project. The students who field-tested the manual and those who will do so in the future will make recommendations for change and, in all probability, develop different methods of evaluations. They will make changes and develop new methods because they will be encouraged to do so. This manual is one of many that will be developed and will remain open for revision.

This emergent curriculum is negotiated throughout the process. Students share their concept maps with each other and their teacher. They send e-mail messages to other teachers affiliated with our project and to our astronomers who in turn guide them to other sources or to specific areas of scientific papers. I have developed an Interactive Vee Diagram where students enter their research questions, describe how they plan to carry out their study, name the instruments they will use to collect the data, list the concepts that need to be defined, and state the theory they are testing (Cowin, 1981).

Electronically over the Internet they submit this information along with any problems or suggestions to our base of operations at Tennessee State University's Center of Excellence in Information Systems. I review their entries and reply with comments. Our astronomers do the same. These students can share their ideas with others at other affiliated schools and receive feedback electronically from them. These Vee diagrams are revisited several times as they carry out their case investigations with variable stars. Within their case they are encouraged to incorporate literature, music, art, history, and other subject disciplines into their case. Their papers are then published on the World Wide Web to be read and commented on by people throughout the world (Alvarez, 1996b; Alvarez, 1997b).

This process differs from conventional product-learning outcomes. Thinking of ways to achieve learning outcomes is different from focusing on ways that learning outcomes can be achieved. The former is a process, the latter an outcome. When teachers and administrators focus on students achieving prescribed outcomes, thought processes become product oriented. In contrast, when students learn in ways that involve them in thinking about problem-oriented tasks and assignments that actively engage them in mutual discussions with their teacher, peers, and others, the process becomes mufti-faceted, meaningful, and negotiable.

In both the Gallatin High School Interdisciplinary Project and the Explorers of the Universe Scientific/Literacy Projects, our efforts focus on ways that students can use a variety of processes to reach multiple resolutions. Our efforts are directed toward divergent rather than convergent learning outcomes. It is interesting to see the different types of paths that students pursue when resolving their inquiry. The emphasis is on melding society with the formal school curriculum by having students apply what they are learning to meaningful settings. Robert Frost may have had this notion in mind when he wrote *At Woodward's Garden* (Frost, 1956).

Frost's At Woodward's Garden

At Woodward's Garden is one of two poems Robert Frost wrote that has a moral similar to Aesop's Fables. The setting takes place in Woodward's Garden, which is a zoo. A boy wants to show off his knowledge to two monkeys who are caged. He has a magnifying glass which he uses to try to show the monkeys how the instrument can be used. He knows that words will not do the trick. First he uses the sun's rays and the glass to focus on one monkey's nose and then the other's. The monkeys are puzzled, and their eyes begin to blink. He then uses the glass and the sun's rays to sting the knuckles of the monkeys. Tired of this experiment, one of the monkey's reaches out from the cage and grabs the burning glass. The monkeys bite the glass. They hold it up to their ears and listen to it. They break the handle. But their lack of knowledge of the whys and wherefores of a magnifying glass leads to boredom and a lack of interest with the glass. This causes them to give up the weapon and place it under their bedding straw. Again the monkeys come to the bars of the cage no wiser than before as to the purpose, function, or use of the instrument. Frost concludes his poem with the parable, "It's knowing what to do with things that counts."

How many adolescents know what to do with things that count in their daily lessons of mathematics, science, literature, history, foreign language, art, music, health education, business education, and industrial technology? How often do they relate what they are learning in school to their society?

Conclusion

The degree of contact we have with adolescents and their literacy skills and development is codependent upon the amount of interplay between them and their teachers and their ability to exercise their imagination in an emergent curriculum. When students are given tasks and lessons under a fixed curriculum with defined outcomes, opportunities to pursue inquisitive paths of inquiry are diminished for both teachers and students. So too, are opportunities for students to "show what they can do."

Adolescents need opportunities to engage in meaningful learning experiences that include reading, writing, investigating, analyzing, synthesizing, and rethinking of facts and ideas. Teachers need these same opportunities to engage in meaningful learning experiences that include reading, writing, analyzing, synthesizing, and rethinking of facts and ideas. In an environment such as this both students and teachers become communities of thinkers. Communities where ideas are shared and valued and opportunities to engage in forums of discussion are more than just cursory exercises which direct students toward reaching that final "right" answer.

How many of our students, like the monkeys in Frost's poem, are given information of which they have little or no understanding? How many of our students are given time to think about learning what to do with this new knowledge to make it count before they are told they need to move on to a different topic? Finally, to return to the analogy from which I began: How many of our students are treated like a staple or a paper clip? For those students who master what is known about a given topic the staple is in place. However, for those students

who view knowledge in transition as they would the function of a paper clip—
the final product is elusive.

*Support for the Explorers of the Universe Project is provided, in part,
by the Tennessee State University and the Center of Excellence in Information
Systems—Astrophysics Component, and by NASA through the
Tennessee Space Grant Consortium NGT 5-40054.*

References

Alvarez, M. C. (1993). Imaginative uses of self-selected cases. *Reading Research and Instruction, 32*(2), 1-18.

Alvarez, M. C. (1995). Explorers of the universe: An action research scientific literacy project. In K. Camperell, B. L. Hayes, & R. Telfer (Eds.), *Linking literacy: Past, present, and future* (pp. 55-62). American Reading Forum, Vol. 15. Logan, UT: Utah State University.

Alvarez, M. C. (1996a). A community of thinkers: Literacy environments with interactive technology. In K. Camperell, B. L. Hayes, & R. Telfer (Eds.), Literacy: *The information highway to success* (pp. 17-29). American Reading Forum, vol. 16. Logan, UT: Utah State University.

Alvarez, M. C. (1996b). Explorers of the universe: Students using the world wide web to improve their reading and writing. In B. Neate (Ed.), *Literacy saves lives* (pp. 140-145). Winchester, England: United Kingdom Reading Association.

Alvarez, M. C. (1997a). Communities of thinkers: investigating interactive scientific literacy environments. In J. Willis, J. D. Price, S. McNeil, B. Robin, & D. A. Willis (Eds.), *Technology and Teacher Education Annual: Vol. 2* (pp. 1236-1239). Charlottesville, VA: Association for the Advancement of Computing in Education (AACE).

Alvarez, M. C. (1997b). Thinking and learning with technology: Helping students construct meaning. *NASSP Bulletin, 81*(592), 66-72.

Alvarez, M. C., Binkley, E., Bivens, J., Highers, P., Poole, C., & Walker, P. (1991). Case-based instruction and learning: An interdisciplinary project. In T. V. Rasinski, N. D. Padak, & J. Logan (Eds.), *Reading is knowledge* (pp. 53-62). Thirteenth Yearbook of the College Reading Association. Pittsburg, KS: College Reading Association.

Alvarez, M. C., Rodriguez, W. J. (1995). Explorers of the universe: A pilot study. In W. M. Linek & B. G. Sturtevant (Eds.), *Generations of literacy* (pp. 221-236). The Seventeenth Yearbook of the College Reading Association. Commerce, Texas: College Reading Association.

Davidson, J. & Koppenhaver, D. (1988). *Adolescent literacy: What works and why.* New York: Garland.

Frost, R. (1956). *Complete poems of Robert Frost.* New York: Holt, Rinehart and Winston.

Gowin, D. B. (1981). Educating. Ithaca, NY: Cornell University Press.

U.S. Department of Education. (1994-5). *Compensatory Education Programs.* Washington, DC: Author.

OUTSIDE OF A DOG, A BOOK IS MAN'S BEST FRIEND. INSIDE OF A DOG, IT'S TOO DARK TO READ. (WITH APOLOGIES TO GROUCHO MARX)

Timothy V. Rasinski

Kent State University

Presidential Address
College Reading Association
1998

In 1998 Timothy Rasinski was a Professor of Curriculum and Instruction in the College and Graduate School of Education at Kent State University. After several years of classroom and Title I teaching in Elkhorn, Nebraska, Tim earned his PhD from Ohio State. Prior to coming to Kent, Tim was a faculty member in the Department of Reading Education at the University of Georgia. Tim's professional interests include working with struggling readers, early literacy development, reading fluency, and parent involvement in reading. During the past decade he has served as co-editor of both The Reading Teacher *and the* CRA Yearbook. *Tim has also authored, co-authored, or edited several books on reading education. He and his wife Kathy have four children, Michael, Emily, Mary, and Jenny, and one dog—a beagle named Ginger.*

Reprinted from *Advancing the World of Literacy: Moving into the 21st Century*, pp. 2-6, by J. R. Dugan, P. Linder, W. M. Linek, & E. G. Sturtevant, Eds., 1999, Commerce, TX: College Reading Association.

Have you heard the one about the man who walks into a bar with his dog and bets the bartender 20 bucks that his dog can talk. The bartender takes on the bet. So the dog's owner asks the dog a series of questions. First he asks, "Where will a bad golf shot end up?" And the dog answers, "RUFF." Then the owner queries, "What's on the top of a house?" And the dog answers, "ROOF." Finally, the guy says to the dog, "Who's the best baseball player of all time?" Immediately, "RUTH" comes out of the dog's mouth. "Alright," says the bartender, "I've had enough of this baloney," and he throws the man out of the bar with the dog right behind. The dog trots over to his master, looks up with pleading eyes and asks, "Was it Dimaggio?"

Dogs and books, dogs and reading, dogs and language—What's the connection? Actually, there are plenty of connections. There are dog lovers and there are book lovers. (And judging from my chats with CRA members, those two categories have a lot of overlap.) Just as reading has become an integral part of contemporary life, dogs seem to have made themselves right at home in our world too. Just consider some of the everyday expressions we use that make reference to dogs:

Who here has ever been in the doghouse?

How many of you have ever felt like you've been treated like a dog?

How many people feel that the world is going to the dogs?

Have you ever been hounded by your boss?

And after a hard day's work, it's not unusual to feel dog-tired.

Who can remember their first puppy love?

Oh, and lets not forget that some of us believe that it's the evaluation tail that wags the reading instruction dog.

And then there is the way that literary quotes always seem more vivid and memorable when they involve dogs. Take for example:

Some days you're the dog, some days you're the hydrant. (Unknown)

Dogs feel very strongly that they should always go with you in the car, just in case the need should arise for them to bark violently at nothing right in your ear. (Dave Barry)

In dog years, I'm dead. (Unknown)

A dog teaches a child fidelity, perseverance, and to turn around three times before lying down. (Peter Benchley)

I wonder if other dogs think poodles are members of a weird religious cult? (Rita Rudner)

Cat's motto: No matter what you've done wrong, always try to make it look like the dog did it. (Unknown)

No one appreciates the very special genius of your conversation as the dog does. (Christopher Morley)

No dog should ever jump on the dining room furniture unless absolutely certain that he can hold his own in the conversation. (Fran Lebowitz)

There is no psychiatrist in the world like a puppy licking your face. (Ben Williams)

Since CRA is an association dedicated to excellence in reading, just think of all the dogs that have graced the pages of books for children, adolescents, and adults. There's that stage struck pooch Gloria in *Gloria and Officer Buckle* by Peggy Rathbone, and then there's Bandit and Slider from Beverly Cleary's *Dear Mr. Henshaw* and its sequel. *Shiloh* is now into his third book. There's *Old Yeller* and *Sounder*, and we shouldn't forget Old Dan and Little Ann from Wilson Rawls' classic *Where the Red Fern Grows*. And Jack London's *White Fang*? What about Beverly Cleary's *Henry and Ribsy* and Cynthia Rylant's *Henry and Mudge*? You also can't leave out *Clifford the Big Red Dog*, and oh yeah, *Harry the Dirty Dog*. Oh, and let's be sure to mention good old *Wishbone*, and of course, we couldn't leave out Spot. I'm sure I could add many more pooches to the list; but you get the idea.

But beyond quotations and expressions and books, there is more. The ways that dogs garner our attention and affection should be a model of the way we get our students, young and old alike, to become excited about reading.

Last year, after 22 years of marriage and 4 kids, my 2 youngest children convinced my wife to buy a dog for the family. The dog we got is a little beagle; we named her Ginger. We didn't know much about how to feed or discipline dogs. We still don't have much of a handle on training her. In fact, I think she has trained us better than we have trained her. But this little pup has woven herself into our family and in many ways enriched our lives—not only in our interactions with the dog, but in our interactions with one another.

This is an important point that seems to me to have direct and often neglected implications for reading and writing. How did Ginger enrich our lives? Mainly through the sheer vigor and playfulness and sense of wonderment she brings with her. That same sense of wonderment and passion and playfulness needs to be part of our literacy teaching. We need to have fun with reading, and we need to let our students see us have fun with reading. Indeed, we need to include them in that passion we have for the written word. How are students ever going to enjoy reading if they never see the joy we get out of it?

And yet the evidence suggests that many students do not see our own passions and playfulness for reading. In a survey study of students' reading perceptions, reported recently on the National Reading Conference Listserve, elementary students were asked toward the end of the school year if their teacher liked to read. A third said that their teacher "did not like to read," 47% responded they "didn't know," and only 20% said their teacher "liked to read." If students can't tell if their teacher has that playfulness about reading and language, how can we expect students to develop the passion and love for literacy that needs to develop concomitantly with any skills learned? Before we bring tests, skills, worksheets, and assignments to the reading classroom, we need first and foremost to bring a dog—well maybe not a real dog, but the playfulness we see in dogs has to be the same sort of playfulness we have about reading. William Steig put it nicely in his book *Caleb and Kate*, "Being a dog among dogs could be joyous sport." When we engage in that joyous sport of reading, we will inexorably draw our students into this web of meaning and wonderment and satisfaction. Reading will win its way into our students' hearts just as Ginger has won her way into my family's life. And even if she never masters any of those doggy tricks or skills or never passes any of the puppy obedience tests, or is not perfectly responsive to us in her own poochy ways, well that's okay, because we're sold on her no matter what happens. And if we can sell reading to our students in the same way, well let's just say if we win the heart over first, the rest of the reader will soon follow and they'll be in pooch paradise as they wolf down books one after another.

There's a lot we can learn from dogs. These include:

When you're happy, dance around and wag your entire body.

If what you want lies buried, dig until you find it.

Delight in the simple joy of a long walk.

Avoid biting when a simple growl will do.

Take lots of naps and always stretch before rising.

When loved ones come home, always run to greet them.

On hot days, drink lots of water, lie under a shady tree, and let yourself dream.

And now one more:

Run, romp, play, and read every day.

Children's Literature Cited.

The Adventures of Wishbone. (1999). Milwaukee, WI: Gareth Stevens Inc.

Armstrong, W. H. (1987). *Sounder*. Saint Petersburg, FL: Pages Inc.

Bridwell, N. (1985). *Clifford, the big red dog*. New York: Scholastic, Inc.

Cleary, B. (1984). *Dear Mr. Henshaw*. New York: Dell Publishing.

Cleary, B. (1954). *Henry and Ribsy*. Madison, WI: Demco Media.

Gipson. F. B. (1956). *Old Yeller*. New York: Scholastic, Inc.

Hill, E. (1999). *Spot helps out*. New York: Putnam Publishing Group.

London, J. (1935). *White Fang*. Old Tappan, NJ: MacMillan Publishing Co.

Naylor, P. R. (1991). *Shiloh*. New York: Dell Publishing.

Rathmann, P. (1995). *Gloria and Officer Buckle*. New York: Putnam Publishing Group.

Rawls, W. (1961). *Where the red fern grows: The story of two dogs and a boy*. New York: Doubleday.

Rylant, C. (1996). *Henry and Mudge under the yellow moon*. New York: Simon & Schuster Trade.

Steig, W. (1977). *Caleb and Kate*. New York: Farrar, Straus & Giroux, Inc.

Zion, G. (1956). *Harry the dirty dog*. New York: Harper Collins Children's Books.

LISTENING TO LEARNERS

Nancy Padak

Kent State University

Presidential Address
College Reading Association
1999

In 1999 Nancy Padak was a Professor in the Department of Teaching, Leadership and Curriculum Studies in the College of Education at Kent State University. She also directed the Reading and Writing Center at KSU and taught undergraduate and graduate courses in the area of literacy education. She had authored or edited books/monographs, had contributed book chapters, and written more than 70 articles on topics related to literacy development. She was a frequent presenter at meetings of learned societies and an active consultant for school districts within Ohio and in other parts of the Midwest. She had also served in a variety of leadership roles in professional organizations, including the presidency of the College Reading Association and (with others) the Editor of The Reading Teacher. *She was recently appointed by the Governor of the State of Ohio to serve on the Ohio Reads Council as the representative for higher education.*

I've been fussing with this speech for some time. There's something a little scary about preparing a "Presidential Speech"— it seems a bigger deal somehow. So I decided before beginning to write this thing to seek advice from some colleagues, who also happen to be CRA leaders. First I went to my good friend Tim Rasinski. Tim said, "You know, my dog speech went pretty well last year. Why don't you stick with the animal theme? How about fluency for ferrets or the phonemic awareness of pheasants?" I thanked Tim and went on my way.

Reprinted from *Literacy at a New Horizon*, pp. 2-8, by P. Linder, W. M. Linek, E. G. Sturtevant, & J. R. Dugan, Eds., 2000, Commerce, TX: College Reading Association.

Next I emailed our Yearbook Co-Editors, Betty Sturtevant and Wayne Linek. "What should I speak about?" I asked. "Let us think about it," they said. A couple of days later, they replied. "We've checked with the other editors. We've consulted our Editorial Advisory Board. We know what you should speak about.... Speak about 15 minutes."

OK, I thought, I guess I'm on my own here. And I began thinking about what was interesting to me (hoping that it would also be interesting to you). I settled on the importance of listening to learners, of trying to see schooling and education from the perspective of those we teach, of trying to improve students' learning by attending to what they tell us.

I've always liked to talk to learners, especially children. I find their views on things interesting—sometimes charming, sometimes sad, always thought-provoking. But I think Jerry Johns may be responsible for helping me see the scholarly value of systematically trying to understand learners' views of education. I remember learning about his "What is Reading?" studies (e.g., Johns, 1972; Johns & Ellis, 1976) during my graduate work at Northern Illinois University. I remember being stunned by kids' views and finally deciding that they were learning what we were teaching, albeit unintentionally. I now believe it's critical for us to listen to what our students have to say. I've studied learners' perceptions of things from time to time over the course of my career, and I want to share some of that work with you today. It seems to me that we should listen to learners because they can tell us both what they know and how they learn best. These are related issues, I think. Students learn when we give them an opportunity to learn. Here's what I mean:

I've been collecting children's definitions of content area concepts—those in science and social studies—to prepare for a course I'm teaching next semester. Here are a few of students' definitions from science—these may give you a new way of looking at our world:

> What is the law of gravity? The law of gravity says no fair jumping up without coming back down. Galileo dropped his balls to prove gravity.

> What is the sun? Most books say the sun is a star. But it still knows how to change back into the sun during the daytime.

> Explain genetics. Genetics explains why you look like your father. And if you don't, why you should.

Where do children get these ideas? And, perhaps, more important, how do they get these ideas? The answer lies in classrooms and the way we organize instruction, I think. Chris Leland (1999, p. 878) explained this relationship eloquently in an article called "A Lesson from the Trenches" that appeared in *The Reading Teacher*. She tells the story of how she learned to listen to learners during her fourth year of teaching fourth grade children.

Students had completed a social studies unit about maps and the globe; Chris felt good about the children's achievements. Then Stephen, tracing the equator on a globe, said, "I understand about the equator when it's over land, but how do they dig the trench when it's under water?" Although startled, Chris asked Stephen to define *equator*. He provided the textbook definition, which used the word *imaginary*, so Chris asked him to define *imaginary*, which he also did. Finally, she said, "And the equator?" Stephen replied, "There's no line where the equator is…. It's actually a trench. It's the same for latitude and longitude. They're not real lines either. But how do they get the bulldozers underwater to dig the trenches?"

Chris asked students to consider Stephen's ideas. Some agreed with him; others speculated about other imaginary lines, such as state boundaries. Chris summarized the discussion by moving her finger around the equator and asking the children if they would feel a bump—or even know—when they crossed the equator in a boat. Jane waved her hand in the air and pointed at the social studies text. "Oh, you'll know when you cross the equator!… You'll know because a big blast of hot air will hit you in the face. The book says it's the hottest place on earth." Students nodded; Jane's idea made sense to them.

Chris concluded that she had focused on mentally checking off terms that students seemed to know instead of listening and watching to find out what children actually knew. This incident taught her to listen to learners.

So listening to learners helps us understand what students know. And it also gives us some ideas about how and why they have come to know these things. At Kent we always talk to children who enroll in our summer reading program. We want to learn about what they think reading is and what they think readers should do. Sometimes their responses surprise us. For example we worked with a third grader a couple of summers ago who explained her goals for the summer like this: "I want to read a book with no pictures. And I want to be able to read one whole page. And then I want to turn the page and read some more. And I want to do all that before I have to take a breath." After I recovered my composure, I realized that she thought good readers were fast readers.

And then there was the little first grader who was talking to my friend Jane Davidson about what he did when he came to a word he didn't know. He covered up a word with his chubby index fingers and said, "WELL!! I put my fingers over the word like this. And then I pick up one finger and I peek. And then I pick up the other finger and I peek." Jane said, "And does this work?" And he replied, "Hardly ever."

On a more distressing note, our conversations with struggling readers at Kent have led us to conclude that they see reading as skills-based, not idea-based. And saddest of all, they see reading as difficult, beyond their ability, something they cannot do successfully. I have worked with developmental reading students and adult literacy students who have the same views. And these views should trouble us. We know from the rich research conducted at the National Reading Research

Center (e.g., Baumann & Duffy, 1997; Wigfield & Guthrie, 1997) that being an "engaged reader" involves will as well as skill; we know that self-efficacy, the belief in oneself as a reader, is tremendously (in fact, statistically) important to becoming an engaged reader.

OK, so kids say the darndest things—about gravity, about the equator, about reading and readers. Where do these ideas come from? They come from us. Students learn what they live. And we can listen to learners to find out more about this as well.

We have a Literacy Seminar at Kent—an informal group of faculty, former doctoral students, current doctoral students, and assorted others—who come together every now and then late on Friday afternoons to share research, talk about current literacy events, and so forth. A few years ago, we decided to launch a collaborative research study called, "Students' Perceptions of Learning to Read and Write." It's a large-scale interview study. Each of us has selected a group of learners to listen to— everyone from primary students through developmental education students, adult literacy students, and even preservice teachers. We all use the same interview protocol, which is based on Flanagan's (Patton, 1990) critical incidents technique and which involves three questions "Think of a time in school when you really learned a lot and enjoyed what you were doing. Tell me about it—what did you do? Who did you work with? How did it go? What did you learn? Why did you like it?"

And its opposite:

"Think of a time in school when you didn't learn very much and did not enjoy what you were doing. Tell me about it . . . and so on."

And a third question

"If you could change the things you do in school, what changes would you make? Why?"

I've interviewed more than 80 kids so far, primary-grade students and middle school students. I want to tell you about what 23 middle school kids had to say. These were pretty good students; some of them had been identified as gifted. Here's what they described as their "best" learning experiences: Long projects. All but two students described an experience that ranged from two weeks to an entire year—making elevation maps of the U.S., making rockets to learn about aerodynamics, studying local history and making a book about it, making bridges out of toothpicks and then testing certain shapes to see how much weight they would hold. I was first concerned that there didn't seem to be too much reading and writing in these experiences, but after more careful study, I discovered that reading and writing had and important role. In fact, there's general cycle that describes how these projects go: First students read, then they do something related to what they have read, then they present what they have learned, which often involves writing. And there's lots of doing and talking throughout.

Also, students like to work in groups. More than half of the "best learning experiences" involved collaborating with others.

Finally, students like to learn new things. They like to learn skills in the context of other learning. Here's Emily: "This year in language arts...I found out that mythology was the base of most of the English language. And every day we were told stories about each god and what they did, and what they stand for. I learned a lot. I learned how to tell what words mean just by looking at them. . . . Breaking up words isn't as boring as it used to be. It can be more fun. Words have more meaning than they seem. . . . [The] stories were not even true, but they were so fascinating. And our teacher made it fun, and we ended up having fun AND learning something."

These students were just as eloquent about their worst learning experiences. Eight students described situations where they were "taught" things they already knew. For example, one said, "Well, you learn lots of stuff when you're young, and you keep learning it, in your head. You know it. And they keep teaching you every year. And it gets boring after awhile."

Four students described teachers who do not explain, just assign, or who assign busywork: "Nobody knows how to do it, but she gets busy with something else and then you get really bored. . . . We sorta try to ask her, but the whole class is all confused. And then she gets sorta mad, you know, she just gets mad because she's trying to do stuff and she expects us to know how to do it." "A lot of us had questions, and she would explain it one way. But the way she would explain it was too confusing, so we asked again, and she just explained it the same way and didn't change anything. So we weren't really learning anything . . . we were just confused."

And students REALLY don't like situations where they "just sit"—Just sit and round-robin read out of a textbook; just sit and listen to the teacher read the textbook to them: "You sit in your chair, and you just have to sit there and listen, follow along in your book.... It's boring...it's really not interesting. I mean it doesn't make you want to learn, just to sit there and read out of a textbook, word for word...it's boring and you want to fall asleep." One student described the teacher reading a text chapter aloud: "He never elaborated on anything.... His voice, the way he read things, it was almost, he sounded like a robot. It was just carrying on and on and on and on...no emotion or anything.... I don't think that he *understood* that we couldn't understand what he was talking about. And he would just go over it again, like thinking maybe we didn't hear it. And if we heard it again, we would understand it.... But it didn't work."

Students also had some good ideas about how to change school. It probably won't surprise you to learn that they want more activity, to have fun while they are learning, to find meaning in their learning.

Fourteen of the 23 kids advised more activity in schools. Here are comments from a few of them:

"I would have more hands-on activities. Because just working out of books, it's real boring and I just feel like falling asleep . . . 'Cause in social studies we read out of the book every day . . . . We have to read it out loud. It takes a long time . . . . He picks people out of the grade book. He just looks for a name and picks one . . . [Q: Do you learn anything?] A little bit, but when you're bored the information doesn't stick."

"I'm sure that if I had more hands-on things, then I would understand it more than just reading it out of a book. . . . 'Cause I mean, yeah, when you do read you put it in your brain and you actually understand. But like I said, if you actually see it or feel it or hear it—whatever—you understand it more. It puts more perspective in for you."

And my friend Robert thinks that just "reading from the book gets boring. And I think it's a little out of date. I think now with the different computers and stuff like that ... I think even working on a computer would be more hands-on than just bookwork. I think that book work is stuff that they could do in the 50s and 60s and stuff, but I think they should update it more now . . . so I guess what I'm saying is I think hands-on is more up to date and the book work is more out of date."

Five students had advice about other teaching methods. They want us to teach concepts thoroughly

"Because some teachers . . . some of their teaching habits . . . they like go from one thing to another thing and then they just go back and forth and they don't stay on one thing very long and then they come back to it. And it's hard to keep up with them."

"Well most of the bad ones, they think we already know something, and we really don't know it that well. So they try to go ahead, or they assume we understand it and give us a test on it. The ones that are good, they make you think about what you're doing."

All right then. We can learn a lot if we listen to learners. How do students view their reading? As interesting and enjoyable, or, as Robert said, as "stuff they could do in the 50s or 60s . . . more out-of-date"? And what about learning situations? How can we best support students as learners? How can we prepare students for the unbelievable rate at which new information is growing? Consider these statistics, taken from *Healthy Times*, March/April, 1995:

- Information now doubles every 19 months.
- 75% of today's information did not exist in 1974.
- 50% of what we learn will be unusable in 10 years. And, to me, the most surprising of all:
- 90% of today's kindergartners will work at jobs that don't even exist today.

Those are some compelling reasons to listen to learners. Sometimes we'll chuckle at what they have to say. Other times we may not like what they tell us. But it's essential to listen. And to think. And, if necessary, to change.

References

Baumann, J., & Duffy, A. (1997). *Engaged reading for pleasure and learning: A report from the National Reading Research Center*. Athens, GA: National Reading Research Center.

Healthy Times. (1995, March/April).

Johns, J. (1972). Children's concepts of reading and their reading achievement. *Journal of Reading Behavior, 4*, 56-57.

Johns, J., & Ellis, D. (1976). Reading: Children tell it like it is. *Reading World, 16*, 115-128.

Leland, C. (1999). A lesson from the trenches. *The Reading Teacher, 52*, 878.

Patton, M. (1990). *Qualitative evaluation and research methods* (2nd ed.). Newbury Park, CA: Sage.

Wigfield, A., & Guthrie, J. (1997). Relations of children's motivation for reading and the amount and breadth of their reading. *Journal of Educational Psychology, 89*, 420-432.

LITERACY 2001:
WHAT IS AND WHAT SHOULD BE

Jack Cassidy

Texas A&M University-Corpus Christi

Presidential Address
College Reading Association
2000

The thought of this particular speech I have found somewhat intimidating—"PRESIDENTIAL AD-DRESS." Somehow, with that particular title, you feel some obligation to say something extremely profound and enlightening. The last time that I prepared to give a Presidential Address the venue was in the main arena at the Anaheim Convention Center. Luckily this room is not quite as overpowering.

As I thought back over the CRA Presidential Addresses that I had heard, I was amazed that I could only really remember two of them—Tim Rasinski's two years ago and Nancy Padak's last year. I'm sure part of the reason for this recollection was that those two presentations were the most immediate. However, I soon realized that my primary motivation for the vivid memories of my two predecessors was that I knew I was soon going to be in their shoes. This realization relieved some of my anxiety because I now believed that there were only two people who were going to be paying close attention to my words. They are Maria Valeri-Gold and Jane Matanzo-each of whom will be standing in this spot in the subsequent two years.

Last year, Nancy Padak recounted how she had asked two of the CRA year-book editors, "What should I talk about?" After some delay, they finally came up with an answer: "…about 15 minutes!" (Padak, 2000). I thought that was a very good idea!

Reprinted from *Celebrating the Voices of Literacy,* pp. 2-6, by W. M. Linek, E. G. Sturtevant, J. R. Dugan, & P. Linder, Eds., 2001, Commerce, TX: College Reading Association.

My wife, who used to be in public relations, tells me that you should always start a speech with a joke. Unfortunately, I can never remember punch lines of jokes. But, luckily, I remembered that Tim Rasinski had told a joke in his Presidential Address; and, luckily, I had the 1999 CRA Yearbook handy.

There was the joke-printed verbatim! Unfortunately, the joke (which was about a dog), pertained directly to Tim's Presidential Address; but, alas, it had nothing to do with mine. Thus, although I repeated the joke in my address, I'll merely refer my readers to the published version of Tim's speech (Rasinski, 1999.) Thank you Tim Rasinski, for my joke!

My remarks today are going to address the topic Literacy 2000, What Is and What Should Be! I'm going to look at some of the topics in literacy instruction that have been a focus of current and positive attention, and some that have been receiving negative or less attention. As many of you know, I do a column each year, now with my wife, but in the past with Judith Wenrich of Millersville University, entitled "What's Hot, What's Not" (Cassidy & Cassidy. 2000/2001; Cassidy & Cassidy, 1999/2000; Cassidy & Cassidy, 1998/1999; Cassidy & Wenrich, 1998; Cassidy & Wenrich, 1997). In addition more in-depth discussions of these issues have also appeared (Cassidy & Wenrich, 1998/99; Cassidy, Brozo, & Cassidy, 2000). In those columns and articles, I compiled a list of topics in literacy education that have/had been receiving attention and then surveyed literacy leaders from around the world asking them if they thought a particular topic was "hot" or "not hot."

When I thought of the idea of a "what's hot" list in early 1996, it seemed like a kind of whimsical piece. After it first appeared in *Reading Today* in early 1997, I was surprised at the reactions that I received. Reporters from several prominent newspapers called asking permission to summarize the results of my survey. During her keynote address at the Boston CRA Convention, Rona Flippo referenced it and subsequently alluded to it in her book *What Do the Experts Say* (Flippo, 1999). And, I received lots of "hate" mail with comments like: "How could you write something like this. You are contributing to the bandwagon effect-already too prevalent in literacy education."

Partially, to relieve some of the "hate" mail, I decided last year to ask my 25 experts not only what is hot, what is not, but also should this topic be hot. The dichotomy between the two sets of responses proved both interesting and disturbing. In Table One are the topics for 2001 that at least 75% of our 25 literacy experts rated as "hot" or "not hot." These are the fourteen very hottest and very coldest from the list of twenty-nine topics presented. Although all the topics were grouped alphabetically in the survey, for convenience I have grouped these fourteen topics into five categories: philosophy/approach; level; content; materials; and assessment.

Probably, there is nothing in Table 1 that is surprising to you. You knew this information without the opinions of these 25 literacy experts. Like me, you are probably disturbed by some of the topics that are receiving current and positive attention and some that are not.

Table 1.

	What's Hot	What's Not
Philosophy/ Approach	• Balanced Reading Instruction	• Whole Language
	• Research-based Practice	
	• Guided Reading	
Level	• Early Intervention	
Content	• Phonemic Awareness	• Comprehension
	• Phonics	• Vocabulary
		• Spelling
Materials	• Decodable Text	• Literature/Based Instruction
Assessment	• High Stakes Assessment	• Portfolio Assessment

Table Two confirms that the literacy leaders are also disturbed. These are their responses when they were asked "should this topic be hot." Although they were not asked why they said a topic *should be hot or not hot,* some of the experts explained their reasoning.

Sometimes, they felt that too much research attention had already been directed toward a given topic; it was now time to move on. Sometimes, however, they felt that a topic really was important and was not receiving the attention it deserved.

Table 2.

	Should Be Hot	Should Not Be Hot
Philosophy/ Approach	• Balanced Reading Instruction	• Whole Language
	Research-based Practice	
	Guided Reading	
Level	• Early Intervention	
Content	• Comprehension	• Phonemic Awareness
	Vocabulary	• Phonics
		• Spelling
		• Decodable Text
Materials	• Literature-Based Instruction	
Assessment	• Portfolio Assessment	
	• High-stakes Assessment	

The fifteen minutes suggested to Nancy Padak by the Yearbook editors does not allow me to discuss all of these topics. However, I would like to mention two: *comprehension* and *vocabulary,* the very essence of what we know as reading. They are not receiving attention in the popular media or in the research community despite the fact that virtually every literacy leader believes they are crucial to what we call **reading**. There was a time—not too long ago when I felt that these two very important topics were the "hot" topics—receiving the attention they so richly deserved. That time, from 1976 to 1991, roughly corresponded to the 15 years that the Center for the Study of Reading at the University of Illinois was receiving federal funding for its groundbreaking research on comprehension and cognition.

Yesterday, as you listened to our general session speaker, Dr. Sandra Stotsky, Deputy Commissioner of Academic Affairs for the Massachusetts Department of Education, many of you may have disagreed with some of her remarks. However, I doubt if any of you disagreed with her premise about the need to develop vocabulary knowledge in our students. There was a time, in the not too distant past, when this topic was a priority. Books and whole issues of journals were devoted to this issue. Today, discussions of word meaning/vocabulary have virtually disappeared from the professional literature.

In Summary

My fifteen minutes are just about up. Trends in literacy have existed since the dawn of recorded language and will probably continue to exist. At the advent of the last millennium, silent reading was the "hot" topic. Scribes began separating words to facilitate the silent perusal of text. Prior to that time, oral reading, primarily in church, was thought to be synonymous with reading (Manguel, 1996). In 1900, with the invention of scientific measurement instruments, "researched-based practice" became a hot issue (Smith, 1961). Luckily, it is still a focus of attention.

But, perhaps the most important finding of the 2001 survey is the discrepancy between what is not *hot,* and what should be *hot.* With the exception of *whole language* and *spelling,* all aspects of literacy on what's "not hot" list (comprehension, vocabulary, literature-based instruction, and portfolio assessment) were thought by most of those surveyed to be deserving of much greater positive attention. Similarly, several items on the hot list *(phonemic awareness, phonics, and decodable text)* were thought to be receiving too much attention. These disparities between what *is* and what *should be* suggest that literacy practices today have less to do with the informed understanding of experts than with political agendas and media hype.

As pendulums and political winds shift, I hope that in the near future, we—the literacy leaders—will be providing the momentum for those pendulums. We will be determining the literacy agenda. The *hot* topics will be those that *should be* the focus of attention and research. *What is* will be synonymous with *what should be.*

References

Cassidy, J., Brozo, W. G. & Cassidy, D. (2000). Literacy at the millennium. *Reading Online.* [online serial] Hostname reading.org director: readingonline.org/past/ past_indese. asp?HREF=../criticalkassidy/index.html

Cassidy, J., & Cassidy, D. (1998/99). What's hot, what's not for 1999. Reading Today, 16(3). pp. 1, 28.

Cassidy, J., & Cassidy, D. (1999/2000). What's hot, what's not for 2000. Reading Today, 18(3), pp. 1,18.

Cassidy, J., & Cassidy, D. (2000/2001). What's hot, what's not for 2001. Reading Today. 18(3), pp. 1,18.

Cassidy, J., & Wenrich, J. K. (1997). What's hot, what's not for 1997: A look at key topics in reading research and practice. *Reading Today, 14*(4), p. 34.

Cassidy, J., & Wenrich, J. K. (1998). What's hot, what's not for 1998. Reading Today, 15(4) p. 128.

Cassidy, J., & Wenrich, J. K. (1998/99). Literacy research and practice: What's hot, what's not and why. *The Reading Teacher 52*(4) p. 402-406.

Flippo, R. F. (1999). *What do the experts say: helping children learn to read.* Portsmouth, NH: Heinemann.

Manguel, A. (1996). A history of reading. New York: Viking.

Padak, N. (2000). Listening to learners. In P. E. Linder, W. M. Linek, E. G. Sturtevant, & J. R. Dugan (Eds.), *Literacy at a new horizon (pp.2-8).* Commerce, TX: College Reading Association.

Rasinski, T. V. (1999). Outside of a dog, a book is a man's best friend. Inside of a dog, it's too dark to read. (With apologies to Groucho Marx). In J. R. Dugan, P. E. Linder, W. M. Linek & E. G. Sturtevant. (Eds.), *Advancing the world of literacy: Moving into the 21st century. Twenty-first yearbook of the College Reading Association.* (pp. 2-6) Commerce, TX: College Reading Association.

Smith, N. B. (1961). What have we accomplished in reading? *Elementary English, 35*, 141-150.

What is Johnny Reading?
a Research Update

Maria Valeri-Gold

George State University

Presidential Address
College Reading Association
2001

I will begin my talk this morning with a quote taken from the writer, Janet Ruth Falon (2001), in her article titled "Life Among the Debris."

> *A book, as a physical object, develops a life of its own, one other than a story written on its pages. We read books as we experience the story of our lives ....*

We teach many readers who approach books as Falon has described in this quote. What draws readers to these physical objects? Why do readers choose books that appear to develop a life of their own? What books are they selecting? How do these books affect them? As a lifelong reader and as a college educator who teaches at-risk learners, I understand the importance of reading interest and its effect on reading attitude, reading behavior, intrinsic and extrinsic motivation, and reading comprehension. I have incorporated literature as a positive catalyst to motivate my reluctant college readers to read and to create that literary spark to help them develop an interest in reading.

I will present to you this morning a brief research update on the reading interests of elementary, middle, junior-high, high school, college at-risk students, and mature adults.

Reprinted from *Celebrating the Faces of Literacy*, pp.2-8, by P. E. Linder, M. B. Sampson, J. R. Dugan, & B. Brancato, Eds., 2002, Commerce, TX: College Reading Association.

The assessment of readers' reading interests has been well documented since 1889 (Weintraub, 1987), and researchers have continued to investigate the reading preferences of readers using a variety of data-gathering materials, such as open-ended questions and responses, Likert scaled survey instruments, reading logs, and journals (Monson & Sebesta, 1991).

During the past decade, numerous research studies have been conducted that examine the reading interests of elementary, middle, junior-high, and high school students (Beck, Bargiel, Koblitz, O'Connor, Pierce, & Wolf, 1998; Belden & Beckman, 1991; Cope, 1997; Diaz-Rubin, 1996; Fisher & Ayres, 1990; Fox, 1996; Fronius, 1993; Isaacs, 1992; Johns & Davis, 1990; Jordan, 1997; Laumbach, 1995; Lewis & Mayes, 1998; Richards, Thatcher, Shreeves, & Timmons, 1999; Rinehart, Gerlach, Wisell, & Welker, 1998; Simpson, 1996; Snellman, 1993; Sullivan & Donoho, 1994; Weiss, 1998; Worthy, 1996; Wray & Lewis, 1993). Yet, a limited number of research studies have been conducted to investigate the reading interests of college at-risk students (Blackwood, Flowers, Rogers, & Staik, 1991; Gallik, 1999; Jeffres & Atkin, 1996; Martinez & Nash, 1997; McCreath, 1975; Schraw, Flowerday, & Reisetter, 1998; Sheorey & Mokhtari, 1994) and mature adults (Black, 1998; Gourlie, 1996) in the last ten years.

Other research studies have examined how physical characteristics (visual appeal, size), age, grade level, reading ability, intrinsic and extrinsic motivation, reading attitude, reading habits, book choice, assigned reading, income, and gender play a significant role in determining the reading interests of students in varying grade levels (Cherland, 1994; Cope, 1997; Kincade & Kleine, 1993; Ley, 1994; Reutzel & Gali, 1998; Wigfield & Guthrie, 1997; Worthy, 1996; Worthy, Moorman, & Turner, 1999).

Additional studies have investigated the role of realistic fiction books focusing on societal issues, such as prejudice, racism, cults, child abuse, peer pressure, self-esteem, family struggles, violence, crime, rape, death, alcohol, and drugs, and their impact on reading interests (Weiss, 1998). These books discuss controversial problems that are realistic portrayals of readers' issues and their lives, and they can help students cope and solve their personal, social, and academic concerns in the real world.

Other investigations examine how self-selection, intrinsic and extrinsic motivation, peer relationships, and teacher interest influence reading interests rather than the school's media center, school collections, and libraries (Worthy et al., 1999).

After reviewing the literature, I noted that the majority of students from elementary through college grade levels enjoy listening to stories and reading books (Richards et al., 1999), and they also find pleasure in reading "light materials" such as comics and magazines (Worthy et al., 1999). Regardless of grade level; however, both females and males preferred fiction over nonfiction; females preferred fiction more strongly than males; males preferred male main characters more strongly than females; and females preferred female main characters more than the males (Segel, 1986). Simpson (1996) found that females read more, while males read less. Fox (1996) noted that students read more than they are generally believed to read, but their reading interests are not often tapped in school. Overall, the majority of students want books that they can read, relate to, think about, discuss, and write about (Harkrader & Moore, 1997).

I will present the reading interests of students by grade levels, ages, and categories. It should be noted, however, that the changes found in students' reading interests as they grow older are well documented (Wigfield & Asher, 1984). Methods of assessing readers' reading interests and the use of different populations, terminology, and data collecting methods can also affect the various reading categories. In addition, categories may represent a mixture of genre, theme, and topic and may be too broad to pinpoint students' reading interests (Monson et al., 1991).

Elementary school readers (ages-5-8) were interested in reading the following types of books: 1) picture books, 2) animals, 3) scary books /mystery/suspense/horror, 4) humor/riddles/jokes, 5) media (television/movies), and 6) adventure.

Preadolescent readers (middle and junior high school students) (ages 913) reported that they were interested in reading these types of books: 1) horror, 2) humor, 3) mystery, 4) historical fiction, 5) adventure, 6) science fiction/fantasy, 7) animals, 8) media (television/movies, 9) realistic fiction, and 10) magazines (video games, teen magazines).

Higginbotham's study (1999) conducted with middle school readers (ages 9-11) noted that females reported an interest in romance, friendship, animal stories, adventure, and historical fiction; while the males reported preferences for sports and science. The results also indicated that males had a stronger preference for non-fiction than did the females.

An earlier study conducted by Fisher and Ayres (1990) compared the reading interests of children between the ages of 8 and 11 years old in England and in the United States is noteworthy. The rank order of mean scores by country is as follows:

England	*United States*
1. Jokes	1. Jokes
2. Mystery	2. Mystery
3. Adventure	3. Crafts
4. Crafts	4. Adventure
5. Animals	5. Animals
6. Sports	6. Science
7. Fairytales	7. Sports
8. Science	8. Fairytales

9.	Poetry	9.	Poetry
10.	History	10.	History
11.	Biographies	11.	Biographies

The top 10 areas of interest for high school students (ages 14-17) are the following (Diaz-Rubin, 1996): 1) adventure, 2) horror, 3) mystery, 4) humor, 5) murder, 6) love, 7) fantasy, 8) crime, 9) sports, and 10) media (television/ movies).

The reading interests of college at-risk students (Blackwood et al., 1991; Gallik, 1999; Jeffres & Atkin, 1996; Nelson, 1989) are: 1) newspapers, 2) magazines, 3) comic books, 4) poetry, 5) letters/e-mail/chat rooms, 6) Internet, 7) novels, 8) fiction, 9) non-fiction, and 10) media (television/movies).

Black's (1998) study conducted with mature adults indicated the following interests according to genre and preferences:

Fiction Preferences for Women
1. Romance
2. Mystery
3. Historical fiction

Non-fiction Preferences for Women
1. Biography
2. History
3. Travel

Fiction Preferences for Men
1. Western fiction
2. Mystery
3. Historical fiction and Romance

Non-fiction Preferences for Men
1. Travel
2. Fine Arts
3. Biography

I would like to recommend three books written by Kathleen Odean for future reference. One book is titled *Great Books about Things Kids Love* (Odean, 2001), and two earlier guides titled *Great Books for Girls* (1997) and *Great Books for Boys* (1998). *Great Books about Things Kids Love* (Odean, 2001) describes over 750 books recommended for ages three to fourteen that are arranged by high interest subjects such as ghosts, computers, robots, insects, and disasters. *Great Books for Girls* (Odean, 1997) contains more than 600 books recommended for girls three to fourteen, and *Great Books for Boys* (1998) has more than 600 books for boys aged two to fourteen.

I will end my presentation with a quote written by the writer Charlotte Gray. This quote was found in Glaspey's (1998) book titled *A Passion for Books*:

> Books become as familiar and necessary as old friends. Each change in them, brought about by much handling and by accident only endears them more. They are an extension of oneself.

Educational Resources for Selecting Books

Recommended websites for selecting books:

Award Winning Children's Books
http://awardbooks.hypemart.net/

Bibliotherapy
http://www.indiana.edu/~eric_rec/ieo/digests/d82.html

The Bulletin of the Center for Children's Books
http://www.lis.uiuc.edu/puboff/bccb/

Horn Book Magazine
www.hbook.com

Book Links
www.ala.org/BookLinks/

Book: *The Magazine for the Reading Life*
bookmagazine.com

Children's Literature Web Guide from the University of Calgary
www.acs.calgary.ca/~dkbrown/

Fairrossa Cyber Library of Children's Literature
www.dalton.org/libraries/fairrosa/

American Library Association
www.ala.org

International Reading Association
http://www.reading.org./choices/tc2000.html
http://www.reading.org./choices/cc2000.html

HtmlResAnchor
http://www.reading.org./choices/yac2000.html

Takoma Park Maryland Library—Middle School and High School Students
Selected Resources-Books, Magazines, Websites
HtmlResAnchor http://cityoftakomapark.org/library/ya/midbook.html

Recommended websites for renting audio books:

Recorded Books
www.recordedbooks.com

Books on Tape
www.booksontape.com

Blackstone Books
HtmlResAnchor www.blackstoneaudio.com

Recommended reference books for selecting children's books that are arranged and indexed by subject.

Cavanaugh, M., Freeman, J., Jones, B., & Rivlin, H. (Eds.). (2000). *The Barnes and Noble guide to children's books*. New York: Barnes & Noble.

Gillespie, J. T., & Naden, C. J. (Eds.). (1998). *Best books for children: Preschool through grade 6* (6th ed.). New York: Bowker.

Homa, L. L. (Ed.). (2000). *Elementary school library collection* (22nd ed.). New York: Brodart.

Lima, C. W., & Lima, J. A. (1998). *A to Zoo: Subject access to children's picture books* (5th ed.). New York: Bowker.

Lipson, F. R. (Ed.). (2000). *The New York Times parent's guide to the best books for children* (3rd ed.). New York: Three Rivers Press.

Rand, D., Parker, T. T., & Foster, S. (1998). *Black books galore: Guide to great African American children's books*. New York: John Wiley.

References

Beck, C., Bargiel, S., Koblitz, D., O'Connor, A., Pierce, K. M., & Wolf, S. (1998). Books for summer reading (Talking about books). *Language Arts, 75*, 320-328.

Belden, E. A., & Beckman, J. M. (1991). Finding new harmony, then and now: Young women's rites of passage (Books for the teenage reader). *English Journal, 80*, 84-86.

Black, B. A. (1998). *Outreach services for older adults at the Wadsworth Public Library*. Unpublished master's research paper, Kent State University, Ohio.

Blackwood, C., Flowers, S. S., Rogers, J. S., & Staik, I. M. (1991, November). *Pleasure reading by college students: Fact or fiction*. Paper presented at the annual meeting of the Mid-Southern Educational Research Association Conference, Lexington, KY.

Cherland, M. (1994). Untangling gender: Children, fiction, and useful theory. *New Advocate 7*, 253-264.

Cope, J. (1997). Beyond "voices of readers": Students on school's effects on reading. *English Journal, 86*, 18-23.

Diaz-Rubin, R. C. (1996). Reading interests of high school students. *Reading Improvement, 33*, 169-175.

Falon, J. R. (2001, May/June). Life among the debris: *Book: The Magazine for the Reading Life* (p. 92). New York: West Egg Communications.

Fisher, P. J. L., & Ayres, G. (1990). A comparison of the reading interests of children in England and the United States. *Reading Improvement, 2*, 111-115.

Fox, D. L. (1996). Learning to teach through inquiry (New teachers). *English Journal, 85*, 114-117.

Fronius, S. K. (1993). *Reading interests of young adults in Medina County, Ohio*. Unpublished master's research paper, Kent State University, Ohio.

Gallik, J. D. (1999). Do you read for pleasure? Recreational reading habits of college students. *Journal of Adolescent & Adult Literacy, 42*, 480-489.

Glaspey, T. W. (1998). *A passion for books*. Eugene, OR: Harvest House.

Gourlie, S. K. (1996). Reading interests in older adult public library users. Unpublished master's thesis, Kent State University, Ohio.

Harkrader, M. A., & Moore, R. (1997). Literature preferences of fourth graders. *Reading Research and Instruction, 36*, 325-339.

Higginbotham, S. (1999). *Reading interests of middle school students and reading preferences by gender of middle school students in a southeastern state.* Unpublished master's thesis, Mercer University, Macon, Georgia.

Isaacs, K. T. (1992). "Go ask Alice": What middle schoolers choose to read. *New Advocate, 5,* 129-143.

Jeffres, L. W., & Atkin, D. J. (1996). Dimensions of student interest in reading newspapers. *Journalism and Mass Communication Educator, 51,* 15-23.

Johns, J., & Davis, S. J. (1990). Reading interests of middle school students. *Ohio Reading Teacher, 24,* 47-50.

Jordan, A. D. (1997). Space, the final frontier: Books on space and space exploration. *Teaching and Learning Literature with Children and Young Adults, 7,* 15-16.

Kincade, K. M., & Kleine, P. E. (1993). Methodological issues in the assessment of children's reading interests. *Journal of Instructional Psychology, 20,* 224-237.

Laumbach, B. (1995). Reading interests of rural bilingual children. *Rural Educator, 16,* 12-14.

Lewis, V. V., & Mayes, W. M.. (1998). *Vaki & Walter's best books for children: Lively, opinionated guide.* New York: Avon.

Ley, T. C. (1994). Longitudinal study of the reading attitudes and behaviors of middle school students. *Reading Psychology, 15,* 11-38.

Martinez, M., & Nash. M. F. (1997) Heroes and heroines. *Language Arts, 74,* 50-56.

McCreath, E. E. (1975). An investigation of reading habits, reading interests, and their relationship to reading improvement of students in an urban open door junior college. In G. McNinch & W. Miller (Eds.), *Reading: Convention and Inquiry* (pp. 100-106). Clemson, SC: National Reading Conference.

Monson, D. L, & Sebesta, S. (1991). Reading preferences. In J. Flood, J. Jensen, D. Lapp, & J. Squire (Eds.), *Handbook of Research in Teaching the Language Arts* (pp. 664-673). New York: Macmillan.

Nelson, R. L. (1989, October). *College students' views of reading.* Paper presented at the annual meeting of the Great Lakes Regional Reading Association, Cincinnati, OH.

Odean, K. (1997). *Great books for girls.* New York: Ballantine.

Odean, K. (1998). *Great books for boys.* New York: Ballantine.

Odean, K. (2001). *Great books about things kids love.* New York: Ballantine.

Reading Today. (June/July, 2001). *Reading remains popular among youths, according to polls,* p. 13.

Reutzel, D. R., & Gali, K. (1998). The art of children's book selection: A labyrinth unexplored. *Reading Psychology, 19,* 3-50.

Richards, P. O., Thatcher, D. H., Shreeves, M., & Timmons, P. (1999). Don't let a good scare frighten you: Choosing and using quality chillers to promote reading. *Reading Teacher, 52,* 830-840.

Rinehart, S. D., Gerlach, J. M., Wisell, D. L., & Welker, W. A. (1998). Would I like to read this book?: Eighth graders' use of book cover choices to help choose recreational reading. *Reading Research and Instruction, 37,* 263-279.

Schraw, G., Flowerday, T., & Reisetter, M. F. (1998). The role of choice in reader engagement. *Journal of Educational Psychology, 90,* 705-714.

Segel, E. (1986). As the twig is bent . . .: Gender and childhood reading. In E. Flynn & P. Schweickart (Eds.), *Gender and Reading: Essays on Readers, Texts, and Contexts* (pp. 165-186). Baltimore, MD: John Hopkins University Press.

Sheorey, R., & Mokhtari, K. (1994). The reading habits of college students at different levels of reading proficiency. *Reading Improvement, 31,* 351-362.

Simpson, A. (1996). Fictions and facts: An investigation of the reading practices of girls and boys. *English Education, 28*, 268-279.

Snellman, L. M. (1993). *Sixth grade reading interests: A survey.* (ERIC Document Reproduction Service No: ED 358 415).

Sullivan, E. P., & Donoho, G. E. (1994, November). *Reading interests of gifted secondary school writers.* Paper presented at the annual meeting of the Mid-South Educational Research Association, Nashville, TN.

Weintraub, S. (1987). Two significant trends in reading research. In H. A. Robinson (Ed.), *Reading and Writing Instruction in the United States: Historical Trends* (pp. 59-68). Newark, DE: International Reading Association.

Weiss, M. J. (1998). Potpourri (The Publisher's Connection). *ALAN Review, 26*, 40-41.

Wigfleld, A., & Asher, S. R. (1984). Social and motivational influences on reading. In P. D.Pearson (Ed.), *Handbook of Reading Research* (pp. 423-452). New York: Longman.

Wigfield, A., & Guthrie, J. T. (1997). Relations of children's motivation for reading to the amount and breath of their reading. *Journal of Educational Psychology, 89*, 420-432.

Worthy, J. (1996). A matter of interest: Literature that hooks reluctant readers and keeps them reading. *Reading Teacher, 50*, 204-212.

Worthy, J., Moorman, M., & Turner, M. (1999). What Johnny likes to read is hard to find in school. *Reading Research Quarterly, 34*, 12-27.

Wray, D., & Lewis, M. (1993). The reading experiences and interests of junior school children. *Children's Literature in Education, 24*, 252-263.

GOING BEYOND: THE POSSIBILITIES OF THINKING AND LITERACY

Jane Brady Matanzo

Florida Atlantic University

Presidential Address
College Reading Association
2002

In 2002 Jane Brady Matanzo had been very active in CRA for 30 years: She had served as President, President-Elect, an elected member of the CRA Board of Directors, Chair of the Public Information Committee for six years, Editor of Reading News for eight years, and a member of the Publications Committee: She had been a professor at various colleges and universities in Maryland, Washington, DC, Pennsylvania, and Ohio: She also had been an administrator in two school systems in Maryland: She was an Associate Professor at Florida Atlantic University where she had been honored as the University-wide Distinguished Teacher of the Year:

I am a collector of stories: As I travel and visit classrooms, I often leave with stories to share. My first story has its origins in India with another more familiar tale but has been retold here with different characters having a similar dilemma. As I paraphrase this story, consider which original story it reminds you of and how it might relate to the possibilities of literacy and thinking:

The title of this story is *Seven Blind Mice* (Young, 1992): It features six blind mice who are investigating a strange "something" that has landed near the pond

Reprinted from *Celebrating the Freedom of Literacy*, pp.2-11, by M. B. Sampson, P. E. Linder, J. R. Dugan, & B. Brancato, Eds., 2003, Commerce, TX: College Reading Association.

where they live. They each make guesses which none of the other mice believe. Their guesses are it's "a pillar," "a snake," "a spear," "a great cliff," "a fan," and "a rope." The mice didn't agree with each other and began to argue. When the seventh mouse appeared, she inspected ALL parts of this strange "something." She ran top to bottom, side-to-side, and end-to-end. She exclaimed that they all were right but, when it was put all together, it was an elephant. The other mice then joined her and they, too, inspected ALL parts of this thing Mouse Seven was calling an elephant until they all agreed. The moral of the tale in Young's words is "Knowing in part may make a fine tale, but wisdom comes from seeing the whole" (Young, 1992, p. 36).

In this tale, each part was important! Without those sturdy pillars, the elephant would have no foundation. Without being as supple as a snake or as stringy as a rope, it would be missing a beginning and an end! Without seeing how each of those parts would build to form a workable whole, there would be NO elephant!

I have a high respect and admiration for people—and mice—who can see and think beyond given parts and envision possibilities not yet fathomed: One such person is Mary McLeod Bethune (McKissick & McKissick, 1992). Although I read a section of the book at the conference, I will paraphrase that section here for copyright purposes.

Mary Bethune heard that living conditions for Black people were a disgrace in Daytona, Florida and that they did not even have a school. She felt she needed to go there and build a school. Upon arriving, she announced that she was going to build a school for Black girls: She got a loan and rented a cottage for eleven dollars where she and her husband lived upstairs: The three rooms on the first floor were the school. She immediately tried to get support from the Black community and winter residents such as Thomas Proctor, Henry Kaiser, and John D. Rockefeller. In 1904, Mary opened the Daytona Normal and Industrial Institute for Girls. Boxes served as desks with trashed paper and charcoal used for the school materials. Five students arrived the first day who were each charged a tuition of fifty cents. The students made and sold food to railroad workers to meet expenses. As word traveled, the students in her school soon numbered more than 100! She needed a bigger school, so she bought a trash dump.

As she was looking at her trash dump unaware of the broken bottles, furniture, and ugly trash, someone passing by asked her why she was looking at all that junk. Her reply was that she was looking at her school!

If Mary had only seen parts when she saw that trash pile, it might still be a trash heap today piled with more broken furniture, bottles, and useless junk. Without Mary's belief, it may not have developed into a workable whole: IT DID! The school became a reality and later merged with Cookman Institute to become Bethune-Cookman College as it is known today.

Mary MacLeod Bethune summed up her life and beliefs in her will:

"My worldly possessions are few. Yet, my experiences have been rich. From them I distilled principles and policies in which I firmly believe... and, finally, a responsibility to our young people." (McKissick & McKissick, 1992, p. 31).

As I considered more people of vision, I thought of our own CRA members and suddenly an idea struck me! Why not e-mail members? Hence, I combed through the CRA Directory "randomly" for this most scientific research "tongue in cheek" adventure, and selected e-mails that were, of course, representative even though a number of servers and addresses were returned or sent who knows where! My query to given members was:

I would appreciate your input for the CRA President's Address I am preparing. My title is "Going Beyond: The Possibilities of Thinking and Literacy." The description is "Examples and encouragement will be given for 'stepping outside traditional and mandated boxes' in terms of thinking and literacy practices." Please entertain some interesting ideas as to possibilities and innovations we might consider that relate to any aspect(s) of literacy, thinking, and/or CRA.

Sixty-three members responded. As the responses were examined, five predominant categories emerged:

1. Definitions of literacy and instruction,
2. Adolescent literacy,
3. Collaboration instead of "Discollaboration!,"
4. Critical thinking is critical!, and
5. Technology and media.

The five categories are not arranged in any scientific research order but sequenced according to the Matanzo Right Brain Organization Method! It would be my pleasure to share all 63 responses . . . but there are other things scheduled on the program today! I have selected several responses representative of each category and will share those with you with hopes to pique your thinking as you listen.

Definitions of literacy and instruction

Cindi Hasit, Rowan University, replied as follows:

I'm thinking of the expanded definition of literacy, which includes visualizing and viewing. Art, photography, and other media can be integrated into our literacy instruction. We should capitalize on the expertise of the specialists in our schools (or outsiders, of course) in those areas to create lessons that address these areas. I think in most schools we use the arts as an add-on or a response to a piece of literature. We should rethink to include these specialists as part of the "literacy team." Using multiple intelligences is probably not that novel, but we should think about providing students with opportunities to use areas of strength or intelligence (linguistic, logical-mathematical, spatial, musical, bodily kinesthetic, interpersonal, and intrapersonal) to enhance and demonstrate comprehension. That would include various school personnel on the "literacy team."

Jackie Peck and Steve Snyder, Kent State University, observed faculty who successfully bring innovations into their practice and faculty who resist innovative practice. They found that the innovators and the resistors used very different language when talking about teaching and learning. They concluded that uncertainty and higher-level thinking resulted with the language used by the innovators: They gave me permission to share their list with you in Table 1.

Table 1. Innovative and Status Quo Language Differences About Teaching and Learning

Innovative	Status Quo
Chaos	Order
Designing	Performing
Inquiring	Telling
Organic	Mechanistic
Social networks	Organizations
Stories	Data
Isearch	Research
Customization	One size fits all; Mandated testing
Insight	Evaluation
Risk taking	Security
Divergence	Convergence
Ambiguity	Clarity

Adolescent Literacy

Yesterday, Jack and Drew Cassidy, Texas A&M, Corpus Christi, presented their "What's Hot-2003 Survey Results." Adolescent literacy received one check on their list of "What's Hot" but responders to their survey recommended with three checks that it should be hot and, indeed, two times hotter than what is now perceived. Peggy Daisey, Eastern Michigan University, agrees with the "what should be" as she stated:

> As a secondary content area literacy professor, who teaches a required course to students from every subject area, and who come with every attitude toward the course under the sun, my life revolves around getting future teachers to

think outside the box; to not teach the way they were taught, to expand their ideas about reading and writing, and reading materials. How sad that these adults come to me in need of having their interest in reading and writing revitalized, due to chronic experiences in middle/high school and college that have beat their interest in reading and writing out of them.

Joan Elliott, Indiana University of Pennsylvania, espouses using interactive strategies with adolescents and to consider the findings of brain research. She advocates that strategies such as having Reflective Practice Groups be implemented. Wayne Linek, Texas A & M University-Commerce, also thinks the new focus on adolescent literacy is a possibility as it looks at literate behavior in all contexts and not just traditional context, such as the contextual dependence of literacy. Examples he gives are the use of cell phones, instant messaging, interactive TV, and computer games that indicate literate behavior among adolescents and their impact on what is culturally and socially accepted and expected. In other words, text that once was rigid or sequential has now become open to new avenues and interactions with much more flexibility. This should be reflected in the way we teach and motivate adolescents.

Donna Alvermann, University of Georgia, further comments on the need to focus on adolescent literacy:

> We know something needs to be done to help underachieving adolescent struggling readers but we're not sure just what, and further, we have little data on which to base our understanding of how these readers approach learning in other than formal school contexts (Hull & Schultz, 2001). Why this is the case, I'm not sure. Perhaps as researchers we feel more at home studying the pedagogies of scientific literacy in the classroom rather than in other less formal learning environments. Maybe it's a sense of having easier access to and more control over what we study when we observe in familiar and safe places Yet I would contend that it's in out-of-school contexts such as after-school clubs, community organizations, workplaces, public libraries with free Internet access, and mall video arcades where we're more likely to observe young people using their everyday literacies in ways that foster informal, but powerful and complex learning. Ways, in fact that could inform science content teaching and learning in schools.

Collaboration instead of "Discollaboration!"

Working together to encourage literacy and to solve related problems seems to be high on the list of the next three responders. Karen Bromley, SUNY at Binghamton, writes:

> How about thinking about concrete, substantive collaboration between our teacher education programs and area schools? I am co-teaching a literacy assessment course in a local middle school that has one of our most difficult populations. My co-teacher is a reading specialist in the building. We teach

our course there in the library and our graduate students tutor struggling readers for part of the class. They have the opportunity to do the assessments and instruction one-on-one as well as an in-depth case study, and we provide a needed service to the local school. We called it Partner Power last year and the district loved it.

Mary Roe, Washington State University, also encourages collaboration through partnerships. She comments:

> Instead of simply thinking outside of the "traditional and mandated boxes," I think literacy professionals also must closely consider how their thinking relates to those boxes and, especially when differences appear, ponder how their research agendas and public actions might nudge the people behind the traditional and mandated in a broader-perhaps more enlightened-direction. Especially in these highly charged times, I find it imperative to have the communicative competence to move forward in partnerships rather than embrace thinking that is too far afield or too dismissive of the "boxes" to nurture these alliances.

Linda Rogers, East Stroudsburg University, also believes that collaboration is a very significant aspect in providing students with good instruction. She tells how her university offers a block of courses that are taught by a team of five professors representing three different departments. This collaboration has made a rigorous semester exciting for her as well as for the host teachers and the faculty team. She claims the bonus is that the preservice teachers witness the collaboration of their instructors as they see the team make decisions about planning, instruction, and assessment. It also has resulted in respect for another's discipline and work. In turn, the preservice teachers collaborate with their host teacher in making decisions about how they will plan and deliver instruction in the assigned classroom. Linda, in conclusion, remarks that "No longer can we close our doors and 'do our own thing!' With 'push in' as a model, there are many people in any classroom at any given time. We truly need to think and work collaboratively so the work we do with students is the best we can provide."

Critical Thinking is Critical!

On the Cassidy's "What's Hot" list, Critical Thinking was subsumed under comprehension, which received one check for what is occurring now, but the respondents advocated two checks for the emphasis that it needs to be given: A number of our members agree. Rita Bean, University of Pittsburgh, feels that the current focus on accountability using "simple" measures reduces the focus on higher-level thinking and helping students learn to learn. She advocates that we professionals need to pursue other types of measures to assess effectiveness and that address the critical thinking skills we want students to possess. Linda

Gambrell, Clemson University, feels that not only do students in our schools need to be critical thinkers but that the "current political climate suggests that it is more important than ever that we prepare literacy teachers who are critical thinkers."

Ray Reutzel, Utah State University, goes a step further by posing critical questions that we should ask ourselves. His initial comment is that he is "not so concerned about stepping outside the box . . . : but stepping on the box! There are some among us who seem to want to step on, bum, or otherwise toss this box right out the door . . . why (has there been) such a virulent reaction from some of us in reading education against the biggest box of federal funding for reading we have ever seen?" He continues with questions for us each to consider:

> What are we "for" instead of what are we "against" in the field of reading? Will our continued "reading wars" within our scholarly community disarm us and discredit us without? Why is there a cry for scientific evidence in practice education? Why isn't there a cry for more interpretive and artistic practice in education? What is at work here? We need to have more honest conversations and fewer dogmatic pronouncements coming from the profession. We are at a crossroads in literacy and reading education. How much longer will Washington DC or state legislators have patience with a profession that can't seem to agree on whether the sun is shining today? Will we join hands at this point in time, or will we once again "circle the wagons and start shooting inward?" How can we come together, or will we as in the past, just start another organization where we can be with our own kind?

In other words, going back to our mouse parable, will the blind mouse that only "sees the something as a spear form his own spear group and the mouse that saw something as breezy as a fan form his own fan group? If so, mouse discourse and the hope of the mice listening again to each other and checking out the whole thing will no longer be one of the possibilities: It seems important that we reflect on Ray's questions and begin to discuss possibilities and inevitabilities with each other. What better forum is there than here at this CRA conference to do just that:

Technology and Media

As noted when I presented the Adolescent Literacy category, technology and media may be an important literacy vehicle for that group. Seventy two percent of the CRA members who answered my e-mail request noted technology as a category to consider in terms of its relationship to literacy instruction. Pat Koskinen, University of Maryland, feels that it is imperative that we need to help every family in the country become aware of the text in the form of captions on the highly motivating medium of television. She claims that the captions are free and plentiful as more than 1500 hours of TV programming per week are captioned. Research indicates that by just watching captioned TV at home, students' vocabulary and comprehension are enhanced. This incidental learning, however, can only occur if the captions are turned on by parents or other caregivers. She firmly believes that word needs to get out so that the potential of using captions as one way to support literacy learning can be realized.

Barbara Walker, Oklahoma State University, suggests we include multimedia and technology as tools to help us step outside the box. Creating multimedia responses to text can enhance critical thinking. Don Leu, University of Connecticut, goes a step further as he encourages one to consider the new literacies of the Internet and other Information and Communication Technologies (ICT) that are "rapidly redefining literacy in an information age and rapidly defining what students must know if we want them to succeed on life's journey." He continues to warn that "these new literacies include the new critical literacies required for evaluating and using information appropriately on the Internet. Ironically, the literacy community is the last to recognize the importance of the changes taking place around us." He also notes that it is difficult to build a consistent body of published research within traditional forums before the technology being studied develops into or is replaced by a newer technology.

Just before I left for this conference, I received a book about technology that I found impressive. It was *Technology for Literacy Teaching and Learning* (Valmont, 2003). William Valmont, University of Arizona, claims:

> Constructing meaning as you read printed words alone is quite different from constructing meaning as you interact with multimedia, from which you construct meaning not only from words but also from graphics, photographs, animations, audio, and video almost simultaneously. (p. 1).

He further suggests that new skills are needed as we expect literacy to include multi-tasking, media literacy, visual literacy, global context, and being able to be telecollaborative. As just one example of the urgency of this need is that approximately 800+ billion E-mails are now sent each day throughout the world! In the past, we have considered survivor words such as poison, exit, H for hospital, and RR for railroad crossing: Valmont states that technology words are the survivor words of tomorrow. This new vocabulary includes such terms as cybersquatters, URLs, cobweb sites, netiquette, recursive, E-materials, metasearch engines, polysymbolic, and portrait mode. On-line glossaries are a resource that must become more familiar and more frequently used by literacy learners. It is also important that professors and teachers learn to use and apply technology and media. We must consider the possibilities of the best ways to model, teach, and use technology ourselves: We must resolve to find ways to eliminate gaps between the technological haves and have nots so we don't create struggling E-literates in the same vein that struggling readers exist today.

 In the Reference section, I have included a short Webliography, another new survivor term, to offer you some additional sites that may be helpful. I highly encourage you to sign up for the CRA Listserv and to visit our newest CRA journal, *Literacy Cases Online*, and the CRA Website.

Today I have urged you to consider possibilities beyond what we are now doing in the areas of thinking and literacy. I have shared the ideas of some of our CRA members in the expressed categories of (a) definitions of literacy and instruction, (b) adolescent literacy, (c) collaboration instead of "discollaboration," (d) critical thinking is critical, and (e) technology and media. In essence, we cannot let our personal biases about what literacy is obscure or overlook where the world is going and, in many cases, has already arrived. We must encourage critical thinking so that we can evaluate and reevaluate these changes. In looking at these five areas, we have concentrated on parts. We must be like that seventh mouse and put these parts into an integrated and balanced whole. If we do not, that SOMETHING which I will name literacy will not result in a cohesive, capable, functioning, and recognizable literacy elephant...or eventually in a literate society. Think possibilities...and be aggressive in making those possibilities you envision a reality that will benefit us all.

References

Hull, G. & Schultz, K. (2001). Literacy and learning out of school: A review of theory and research. *Review of Educational Research, 71*, 575-611.

McKissack, P., & McKissack, E (1992). *Mary McLeod Bethune*. Chicago: Children's Press.

Valmont, W. J. (2003). *Technology for literacy teaching and learning*. Boston: Houghton Mifflin Company

Young, E. (1992). *Seven blind mice*. New York: Puffin Books.

Webliography

College Reading Association Sites

CRA Listserv majordomo@archon.educ.kent.edu Contact: Nancy Padak CRA Website http://explorers.tsuniv.edu/cra/Contact: Marino Alvarez

Literacy Cases on Line www.literacycasesonline.org Editors: Sandee Goetze and Barbara Walker, Oklahoma State University

Other Literacy Related Sites

Beaucoup! http://www.beaucoup.com/1metaeng.html Conducts 11 metasearches at once; links to 20 more search engines

Langenberg.com http://www.langenberg.com/ Conducts metasearches and translates web pages in English, French, German, Dutch, Danish, Spanish, Finnish, Czech, Italian, or Portuguese. Engage in projects around the world.

ProFusion http://www.profusion.com/ Tips for conducting searches with links to nine search engines

The Global Schoolhouse http://www.gsn.org/ Free worldwide collaborative projects.

PREDICTING THE WHETHER:
LESSONS LEARNED FROM THE PAST

Robert J. Rickelman

University of North Carolina-Charlotte

Presidential Address
College Reading Association
2003

Robert J. Rickelman has been an active member of CRA since attending his first conference in 1980 with John Readence, his major professor. He has served as President, President-Elect, an elected member of the Board of Directors, Co-Editor of Reading Research and Instruction *and* Reading News, *Chair of the Teacher Education Division, and Co-Chair of the Public Information Committee. In 2003 he was a Professor and Department Chair in the Reading and Elementary Education Department at the University of North Carolina-Charlotte, and had taught in middle and secondary schools in Ohio and Pennsylvania. He received his*  *BA and MEd from Ohio University and the PhD in Reading Education from the University of Georgia.*

I would like to state up front that the title of this paper is not mine. I am indebted to my good friend, Jim Cunningham, who came up with a form of this title about 10 years ago. Jim invited several literacy professors in North Carolina to take part in a panel for a meeting of the North Carolina Research Association. He asked us to predict 10 years into the future, to identify salient issues we thought we would be facing in the field of literacy education. Ironically, we

Reprinted from *Celebrating the Power of Literacy*, pp.2-9, by J. R. Dugan, P. E. Linder, M. B. Sampson, B. Brancato, & L. Elish-Piper, Eds., 2004, Commerce, TX: College Reading Association.

were making predictions at that meeting for the present, and I do not recall our predictions being anywhere close to the recent truths.

In an effort to try another round of predicting the future, this time of the organization, I thought it would make good sense to look at past events that have shaped the current state of the College Reading Association (CRA). A benefit of predicting the "whether" is that no one can accurately dispute your predictions. After 10 years, it is likely that most have forgotten the predictions. So, in an age of accountability, I have found a way to escape the bean counters; my goal is to give this prognostication my best shot, and not worry much about the accuracy. At least the predictions will not be much worse than those of professional weather forecasters.

I would like to divide my paper into three sections. First, I would like to re-count influential past events of the College Reading Association. In other words, I would like to examine events that likely shaped where the organization finds itself today. In addition, I would like to highlight comments made by past CRA Presidents who identified timely issues during their terms of office. This section will make up the bulk of my remarks. Second, I would like to reflect briefly on where I think the organization stands today. Finally, I would like to offer several "best guess" predictions about where the organization might be headed.

The Past

The College Reading Association was founded in 1958 by 10 or so college teachers from Pennsylvania, who met at Temple University in Philadelphia. They identified themselves as the Committee for a College Reading Association, which they envisioned as an organization for professional educators living in the Northeastern and Mid-Atlantic states who were interested in promoting college reading programs.

The first formal conference of the new organization was held at LaSalle College, also in Philadelphia, on October 11, 1958. About 50 participants re-presenting 30 schools attended the meeting. The second conference was held the following May at Lehigh University, where the group adopted the first constitution and by-laws, written by Al Mazurkiewicz. Bruce Brigham was elected the first President of the new organization, but he resigned after four months. Mazurkiewicz became the new president, and served in that role for the following 3+ years. At this second conference, the registration fee was $1.00, and membership dues were set at $3.00/year.

The College Reading Association now has a number of standing committees and commissions, but the first was the Commission on the Use of Paperbacks, chaired by Jerry Weiss, who served 22 years in this position. The first newsletter was funded and edited by Al Mazurkiewicz, and was published in February of 1961. The first journal, *Journal of the Reading Specialist*, came out in September of 1962, with Al Mazurkiewicz as the first editor. He continued in that role until

1969. The journal title was later changed to *Reading World* in 1969, and then in 1985 to *Reading Research and Instruction.*

The organization was formally chartered in Northampton County, Pennsylvania on November 18, 1963. The charter was signed by John E. Daniel, Albert J. Mazurkiewicz, Charles J. Versacci, Clay A. Ketcham, and Paul N. Terwilliger. In 1968, the first recognition award was given to A. B. Herr, a past Secretary-Treasurer of the organization from Rochester Institute of Technology. Later, in 1972, the A. B. Herr Award for Outstanding Professional Service (service to the organization, research, teaching, professional activity and other professional contributions) was given for the first time to Uberto Price. The following year, the Award was split in two, as it remains today. The A. B. Herr Award is now given for outstanding contributions to the reading education profession, while the Special Services Award (later renamed the Albert J. Mazurkiewicz Special Services Award) is given for service to the organization. The first Master's Thesis Awards were given in 1978 to Patricia Fisher, Ernest Balajthy, and Sara Strous. In 1982, the first Dissertation Awards were given to Mary Ann Medley and Daniel Pearce. The Laureate Award was given for the first time in 1996 to the person who has documented an influence on other reading professionals through mentoring and teaching, longevity as a CRA member, research and publications with students, and participation at CRA conferences, on the Board of Directors, and on committees. Lillian R. Putnam was the first winner of this award.

Alexander and Strode (1999) divided up their CRA history into five-year time increments, and it is interesting to see how they identified the "hot topics" in each of those time periods. This is especially important in terms of seeing where we now stand. At the end of each five-year period, here are the timely issues that concerned CRA members:

1968—i.t.a. (Initial Teaching Alphabet), Words in Color, the Joplin Plan, individualized reading, grouping practices

1973—phonics, linguistic readers, programmed instruction, mechanical and electronic apparati, team-teaching, non-grading, diversity in content and illustrations, compensatory teaching for disadvantaged children

1978—responding to NAEP evidence on "Why Johnny Can't Read," criticism of "anything goes" in the classroom, criticism for accepting non-standard English in the classroom

1983—Right to Read, Back to the Basics movement, instructional time vs. achievement, comprehension, reading-writing connection, theoretical frameworks, discourse analysis, schema theory, guided writing, metacognition, computers in reading

1988--declining availability of grant money in reading, staff cuts, teacher education reform, qualitative research methodologies

1993—continuing classroom cutbacks, low morale, pedagogy under attack

1998—assessment, continuing accountability, deprofessionalization of reading education

Since Alexander and Strode's (1999) reporting ended in 1998, I would like to take the opportunity to offer these "hot topics" from the past 5 year period:

2003—No Child Left Behind, performance-based assessment, paper-and-pencil tests, lateral entry teachers, alternative licensure, "evidence-based/science-based" funding formulas, scripted reading lessons.

What is immediately noticeable from examining the past issues is that many of the topics on the current list have been building up over the past 20 years. These are not new issues. Concerns about the deprofessionalization of our field have been voiced since the mid-1970s. In 1992, CRA President Norm Stahl urged members, in his Presidential Address, to build well-coordinated, ongoing offensives, including building professional alliances, to create a united front to criticisms of higher education. With the recent debates in Washington over the reauthorization of the Higher Education Act, his advice continues to be timely a dozen years later.

Along with timely issues from the past, I would like to conclude this section with advice given by two CRA Past-Presidents during their terms of office. Bert Price, who was CRA President in 1970, listed the following critical areas that he felt needed to be addressed by members:

- Teacher training institutions need to prepare candidates more thoroughly
- We need to narrow the gap separating research and practice
- We should teach reading in a more serious manner
- We need more research on how people learn
- We need more information about the nature of reading and language
- We must match methods, materials, and techniques to the needs of learners

Price's recommendations continue to hold true to this day, especially in light of all the recent interest in "science-based instruction."

In a similar way, President George Mason, in 1984, issued the following challenges to the CRA divisions:

- Teacher Education—take a stand, draft resolutions, seek media coverage, express position on concerns about budget cuts in K-16 schools
- College—undertake a campaign to increase professional stature of its members in order to secure more support for needed college programs

- Clinical—college reading clinics are facing extinction, so prepare convincing justifications in the face of looming budget cuts
- Adult Learning—mount campaigns to educate the public on their programs

His advice to the organization still holds true today, as we struggle for credibility at the local, state, and national levels.

The Present

Currently there are many questions about what works in the literacy classroom. While bureaucrats debate science, teachers and children are left to sort it all out. I have a photograph from the Charlotte Observer, our local daily newspaper, showing a student who had a Roman numeral 4 shaved into his head. This brash act was in anticipation of taking the annual "end-of-grade" test, in which the goal of all students was to score a 4, the highest grade possible. While the newspaper reporter focused on the lengths that teachers and students went to in order to prepare and motivate themselves for the test, the fact that young children take the act of testing so seriously is concerning. Another reporter did a follow-up report on the negative stressors that result from high-stakes assessments.

One of my personal heroes is Ernest Boyer. Boyer used to be the Commissioner of Education under President Jimmy Carter, before this position became a Cabinet post. He was also the former President of the SUNY system. At the time of his death in 1995, he was the Director of the Carnegie Foundation for the Advancement of Teaching in Princeton. Boyer, based on his vision of what a school should be, developed the "Basic Schools" model, introduced in his book of the same name (1995). Boyer expressed concern that, for many children, school was becoming the "pursuit of trivial pursuit," with the focus on learning isolated facts. His vision for a Basic School was a place where kids made connections to the real world, where the goal was not a test score but a coherent view of knowledge. He was concerned that, for many students, clichés become substitutes for reason. I share this same concern about adults. Certainly no one would argue that some children should be left behind, just as you cannot argue that there should be no family values. But this polar distinction between the good guys and the bad guys is, unfortunately, skewed by politics; so that the cliché becomes the political focus rather than what is actually happening with real people in real classrooms. The challenges issued by George Mason 20 years ago are still timely!

The leaders of CRA have been engaged in discussions with leaders in other national literacy organizations, most notably the International Reading Association and the National Reading Conference, to try to present the united alliance Norm Stahl suggested over a decade ago. Some important questions, however, remain.

Boyer, in a speech to the Association of Supervision and Curriculum Development a dozen years ago, suggested several important questions, which should guide us in setting a national agenda for K-12 education. First, to give us an outline for where we need to focus our efforts in education, we should ask, "What is an educated person?" Boyer suggested that an educated person is well informed, acts wisely, continues to learn, and discovers the connectedness of things. Second, we should ask, "What is a good teacher?" He suggests that a good teacher is knowledgeable, relates information to students, promotes active learning, and is an authentic and open human being. Interestingly, Boyer never stated that an educated person is one who scores well on multiple-choice tests. If you asked the average person who they identified as the smartest person alive, I doubt that they would mention someone who was a noted test taker. I would guess they would likely mention divergent thinkers and problem solvers like Albert Einstein or Bill Gates. The scripted lessons I see in many of today's classrooms seem to take the human, creative element from students. I have heard about one local school principal who formally observes teachers by going into their classrooms with a script and a stopwatch, criticizing teachers for being a minute or more off of the script. All this is done, with good intentions, in the name of science. The basal used in that school touts itself as being based on scientific evidence, so the principal assumed that deviating from the script at all would contaminate the researched methodologies. Good teachers are leaving these schools, where they are most needed. Are children the benefactors of this "science" or are they quietly being left behind? Bert Price's suggestions are as real today as they were 35 years ago.

The Future?

So, we have a sense of time and place, based on our past as an organization. We have heard (but have we listened?) to advice from former leaders. Most would agree that our field is in a state of chaos today. So, is it possible to even predict the "whether," knowing the uncertainty of education today. I think so, since there is no immediate penalty for me suggesting where it is we may be headed. Honestly, I have no scientific evidence to support any of my predictions!

Can we learn from past lessons? Plutarch suggested that history repeats itself. If true, it may be helpful to look at where we have been, where we are not, and think ahead to where we may be headed. Here are my ideas.

First, I think we need to heed the advice of George Mason, and respond to criticisms from within and outside the profession, advancing our own rich long-standing store of "scientific evidence" for how reading works and the best ways to teach it. Almost 100 years ago, Huey (1908) discussed the psychology and pedagogy of reading. Since then, a strong line of research has informed our field of reading. To ignore the best thinking of our forebears for practices forged in other arenas is to ignore the past. The fact is that kids did learn using whole language, that kids did learn using direct instruction, and kids did learn using eye movement pacing machines. On the flip side, there are, of course, children who did not learn to read using each of these methods. I would rather rely on an educated and informed teacher's methods than on a script written by someone who has never seen the community, the school, or the child. A script cannot react to a child who looks puzzled. It cannot make creative, informed decisions when things go awry. A book can never replace a good teacher. Ask any parent or child who has ever been in a classroom with an outstanding teacher, and they will tell you this.

Second, we need to be flexible rather than defensive. While we certainly can boast a rich history in literacy education, we must be flexible enough to recognize the efforts of others with a similarly rich research tradition, in areas such as special education and educational psychology. While using different paradigms, their research, blended with our own, can forge new pathways to learning that will benefit children. Rather than arguing about who is right, we need to put forth our best cooperative efforts at synthesizing the information that we know and how best to apply it to the classroom and to the community.

Third, we need to train and mentor the leaders of tomorrow, and foster in them the knowledge, skills, and dispositions to become outstanding and educated persons, who seek lifelong learning. We need people who do not over commit or shirk their responsibilities, and who will get things done. I am convinced that a major characteristic of most leaders in the field is not that they are incredibly smart (although many are!) or that they are incredibly organized (although some are!), but that they get things done when they agree to get them done. Those who talk the most about being incredibly busy often spend too much effort talking rather than doing. I don't know about you, but I'll take a doer every time!

Fourth, we need to connect with the media. I have certainly been guilty of avoiding the limelight. When called on to meet with a newspaper or television reporter, it is easy to discover schedule conflicts. However, who will best make our case? Who will be remembered when policies and legislation are being considered, the person who agreed to the radio interview or the person who hid? In a similar way, we need to connect with legislators, for the same reasons. I once went to a conference on how to be a department chair, and had breakfast with the Dean of Education at a major university. He said that the best move he made as a new dean was to go to his state capital with a bag full of stuffed university mascots. He scheduled meetings with any state legislator who agreed to meet with him. He asked for 30 minutes of their time, and awarded them with a stuffed dog at the end of the meeting. But what he found, and the reason he told the story to me as a new department chair, was that he became the "go to" person when education issues were brought before the state legislature. Rather than calling for the expert advice of someone else, the legislators with whom he met asked their secretaries to call "that guy who brought the dog" to seek his opinion, since he seemed to know a lot about education. In a similar way, we need to figure out how to be the "go to" person for our local and state legislators and media.

Fifth, we need to share, rather than hide, the good things (as well as the bad things) about the profession. There seems to be a conspiracy mentality in the general population today regarding teachers, including us. The feeling is that we are not doing a good job, but trying to hide this fact by being defensive. Everyone seems to be an expert in education. After all, I have had some people tell me that they went through the school system for 16 years, so why shouldn't they be experts? I wonder if these same folks would allow me to extract a tooth. After all, I have been going to the dentist religiously for over 40 years, so I surely should be an expert in dentistry by now, right?

The bottom line, I think, is that we need to be collaborators as much as we are allowed to collaborate. In spite of the fact that we are being told we don't know how to teach and that we should blow up the colleges of education, the fact is that many, many people were well taught, did learn, and are now successful in their jobs. Why not share some credit along with the blame?

References

Alexander, J.E., & Strode, S. L. (1999). *History of the College Reading Association*, 1958-1998. Commerce, TX: College Reading Association.

Boyer, E. L. (1995). *The Basic School: A community for learning*. Princeton, NJ: Carnegie Foundation for the Advancement of Teaching.

Huey, E. B. (1908). *The psychology and pedagogy of reading*. Cambridge, MA: M.I.T Press.

Mentoring Reading Colleagues In Higher Education: Paving The Path To Success

Wayne M. Linek

Texas A&M University-Commerce

Presidential Address
College Reading Association
2004

Introduction

The College Reading Association (CRA) is known as a mentoring organization. It is one of the reasons I thoroughly enjoy being an active member. Although the focus of this speech is on mentoring your reading colleagues, I hope to provide insight and stimulate your thinking about mentoring in a variety of contexts. To accomplish my purpose, I'll begin my talk with my own mentoring experiences. Then I will speak about changes in the concept of mentoring. Next, I'll explain why I see mentoring as a balancing act. After that, I'll discuss the critical aspects of mentoring. Finally, I'll conclude with my view of mentoring as a two way street.

My Background and Experiences

I've discovered over the years that many new faculty are hired who have received minimal mentoring during their doctoral studies. Until I made this discovery, I didn't realize how lucky I had been. When I decided to pursue full time doctoral studies at Kent State University, I was hired as a graduate assistant. I met with Joann Vacca, the department head, and was assigned to the team of Rich Vacca and Tim

Reprinted from *Building Bridges to Literacy*, pp.2-9, by P. E. Linder, M. B. Sampson, J. R. Dugan, & B. A. Brancato, Eds., 2006, Commerce, TX: College Reading Association.

Rasinski as advisors. My first semester, I got to work for Joann, Rich, and Tim as a graduate assistant. Little did I know at the time that I had been given a gift. Not only were these professors highly respected and well known in the reading world, they also knew how to be outstanding mentors. One of the first things they did when I arrived on campus was to introduce me to Nancy Padak. Luck was on my side when Nancy agreed to do an independent study during my second semester so that I could get up to speed on "Whole Language Philosophy."

This team of four consummate professionals included me in their writing, research, and teaching as if I were already a colleague. I became a co-author with Rich, a co-researcher and presenter with Tim and Nancy, and an editorial assistant with Joann. All were exceptional and unique models of teaching, scholarly activity, and service who knew how to hold my feet to the fire when it was necessary. It is easy to see reflections of them in my work. When I advise students and help them realize the power of their own decision-making, Joann is there. When I respond to student writing and ask questions, Nancy is there. When I model strategies for students and provide choice in assignments, Rich is there. When I structure a doctoral seminar and make sure students see that I am only human, Tim is there. Sixteen years later, I still strive for the high standards I saw my mentors model.

I was also blessed with a variety of peer mentors during my doctoral studies and my first tenure track position. Although I cannot begin to mention all of my peer mentors, fellow doc students Betty Sturtevant and Olga Nelson worked with me on conducting research, preparing presentations, and learning how to write professionally. We spent lots of time figuring things out together. At Texas A&M-Commerce, Mary Beth Sampson, LaVerne Raine, Pat Linder and I have supported each other through grant work, teaching, developing programs, high stakes teacher testing, and a myriad of service responsibilities. These colleagues serve as friends, but also as "agitators" when it comes to designing research and collecting/analyzing data. We keep each other going in symbiotic peer mentoring relationships to scaffold our work.

Although my university mentoring team introduced me to CRA, I immediately received mentoring from CRA members. Although there are more than I can possibly mention, I will give a few examples. Estill Alexander served as a mentor when Betty Sturtevant and I first applied to be *CRA Yearbook* (*CRAYB*) editors—and again when I helped Estill with publication of the CRA History. Bill Henk, who chaired the publications committee, mentored the new *CRAYB* editors when Betty and I put together our first peer review board. Bob Rickelman mentored me as CRA President Elect when I didn't have a clue about how to put together a conference. Suffice it to say, in my experience, CRA truly has been an organization of mentors.

Now I have the luxury of serving as a mentor to doctoral students and new colleagues. There are many here today that I've had the pleasure of guiding along the way. They have taught me as much if not more than I have taught them as we have collaboratively researched, presented, edited, and written. They serve as the wind beneath my wings and keep me stimulated and focused as I have become one of the "Old Codgers."

I've reflected on my mentoring experiences, now I'd like you to take a minute and reflect on positive mentoring experiences you have either received or given as a reading professional. [Pause] Now think about what you had to learn "the hard way" when mentoring would have helped. [Pause] Now think about a situation where you served as a mentor and didn't feel particularly successful. What was that like? How could it have been different? [Pause] Before I talk about the balancing act one must engage in as a mentor and the critical aspects of mentoring, let's consider how the concept of mentoring has changed.

Changes in the Concept of Mentoring

Mentors and mentoring are currently perceived as popular and powerful means for people to learn professional and personal skills. In fact, mentoring may be one of the oldest forms of teaching and influence. Popular literature attributes the origin of the term to the ancient Greek storyteller, Homer. In his story of the Trojan War, the King of Ithaca asks Mentor to take care of his son Telemachus while he goes to war. Yet African scholars note that mentors were common in Africa long before the civilization of the ancient Greeks. The modern concepts of mentors and mentoring most likely come from the work of Fenelon, an 18th century French writer and educator (Retrieved from: HtmlResAnchor http://www.mentors.ca/mentor.html).

Although the basic concept of mentoring is ancient, the formal definition of the word mentor has expanded in the past 30 years. For example, the 1970 unabridged *Webster's New Twentieth Century Dictionary of the English Language* does not include the word mentee and lists the following finite definition for the word mentor.

> Mentor, n. [from *Mentor*, the friend and counselor of Odysseus and Telemachus.] a wise and faithful counselor.

On October 25, 2004 a Google search on the term mentee yielded 88,400 hits and the term mentor yielded 4,390,000 hits. These hits range from the homepage of the *National Mentoring Partnership* to advertisements for "breast augmentation" and "erectile dysfunction." Regardless of pop culture usage of these terms, most reading professionals can identify someone who has had a significant and positive influence on their lives. Typical mentors include professors, doctoral peers, and colleagues. Although one usually thinks of mentors as older or more experienced, a mentor can be anyone who serves as a role model, advisor, consultant, tutor, coach, or guide. The days of students sitting at the feet of the wise sage are gone. Our understandings of the social construction of knowledge, coupled with modern technology, provide opportunities for us to serve as mentors any time, anywhere. For example, although traditional mentoring can occur within doctoral programs, with students and colleagues in our own institutions, and at conferences; modern mentoring can occur via technology such as email, list serves, chat rooms, or in any context where scholarly work, teaching, or professional service is the focus.

Mentoring as a Balancing Act

Mentoring our reading colleagues is important because we want to keep the flow of knowledge going in our field. It is also important because we must develop scholars, teachers, and partners who recognize the potentials and pitfalls of teaching, research, and service.

Successful mentoring is not simple or easy, and countless false perceptions about mentoring exist because we have fantasies about the ideal mentor. Although reflecting on our personal experience is important, it is not enough as we may remember only bits and pieces that were designed to be helpful to us, but may not appropriately scaffold the learning of our colleagues. For example, a person who had good research and writing skills but was afraid of taking risks in presenting or submitting manuscripts for publication in their doctoral program may have experienced a mentor's nurturing and encouragement to enhance their self efficacy. Nurturing and encouragement are important, but they can also be problematic when used at the wrong time or for the wrong reason. Likewise, a person who was overconfident when they started their doctoral program may have experienced lots of hard questions or criticisms to mold their professional character. Once again, hard questions and criticism are important, but can be problematic when used at the wrong time or for the wrong reason.

The tightrope one walks as a mentor consists of processes that develop a relationship, scaffold learning, and empower students and colleagues to become independent and successful. But each mentee is different and there are many ways in which one can lose their balance when walking the mentoring tightrope.

Critical Aspects of Mentoring

Critical aspects of mentoring include: listening, commiserating, nurturing, encouraging, scaffolding, asking hard questions, giving critical feedback, helping mentees learn how to deal with dissonance from a metacognitive perspective, recognizing opportunities and options, developing realistic expectations, and learning from our mentees. Let's examine some of these critical aspects.

A mentor must consciously listen to and commiserate with a colleague, but a mentor who focuses on nurturing rather than assessment of the situation and planning how to get past a barrier doesn't provide an opportunity for metacognitive empowerment. For example, sometimes friendly and well-meaning researchers will listen to colleagues talk about how frustrating the research process is. Listening is important, but helping a less experienced researcher see that dissonance is typical when researching and writing—is equally important. The senior researcher who only nurtures and commiserates forgets the goal of mentoring while running the risk of increasing emotional turmoil without helping their colleague learn how to work through dissonance.

Likewise an experienced researcher who tells the junior researcher to "just suck it up" or "things will get better with time" also does a disservice by not helping the colleague understand that this type of dissonance is normal and gives no clue about how to monitor and self regulate. In this instance, a true mentor might listen, commiserate by sharing their own experience, help the colleague assess specifically what the source of the dissonance is, pull options from the mentee or give suggestions for dealing with the situation, then empower the mentee by having them decide on their own plan for resolving the situation. This process should help your colleague keep both short-term and long-term goals at a level of conscious awareness.

Remember that the purpose of mentoring is to help mentees become independent in the analysis and use of their knowledge, skills, and abilities. A mentee may not be able to engage in creative problem solving and make good professional decisions if the mentor does not hold high expectations, help them view expectations realistically, make criteria explicit, and provide critical feedback. Those mentors that mainly tell and give in to colleagues' pleas of "Just tell me what to do" may be imparting knowledge, but they are not serving as mentors.

Thus, it is important that the mentor teaches the ideal, but makes explicit that *it is the ideal* when mentoring scholarly activity and teaching. Sharing one's own failed attempts and taking the time to share thinking processes and procedural knowledge that lead to success helps colleagues develop a sense of self efficacy and perseverance.

If our goal is to model and teach only the ideal, our colleagues may walk away with distorted perceptions and set unrealistic expectations for themselves. This may result in newly hired faculty members trying to start their scholarly careers with extensive studies that require significant amounts of external funding. A junior researcher may give up on a study if their first or second grant proposal is not funded—or if their manuscript is rejected because they can't meet their own unrealistic expectations. In fact, it has been my experience as an editor that some inexperienced writers are disappointed when they receive an adjudication of *revise and resubmit*—because they initially interpret it as disparagement rather than an opportunity to refine their writing for publication. The same is true for teaching, expecting to be perfect and liked by everyone is not a realistic expectation. And completing detailed journal responses for every student every class period will leave little time for the service responsibilities that all good colleagues must share.

Mentors may give colleagues opportunities to collaborate on research projects. However, just having them help collect or analyze data doesn't give them the insight into how to create, implement, and carry their own literacy research through to publication. Consider pushing your mentees to understand the underlying thought processes at work, provide critical feedback, engage them in reflection, and discuss their reflections to help them learn how to become independent.

Mentors can help colleagues become independent by engaging them in the articulation of criteria for teaching, research, and writing. Having mentees self assess, then giving critical feedback on their self assessments and encouraging them to develop options to deal with a variety of situational barriers will help them develop conditional knowledge. In my experience, sharing criteria for grants or manuscripts I am reviewing, then discussing a completed review provides a good model for those who have not experienced reviewing or grant writing in their doctoral studies. After an initial sharing, I have my mentee complete a review for me and I critique the review. Then I encourage them to become reviewers for journals or conference proposals.

Junior colleagues are often initially overwhelmed by combined loads of teaching, research, and service. It is hard to hit the ground running with your research agenda if you have not taught higher education classes or have not carried service responsibilities in your doctoral program. In this case, we can help new colleagues by exploring research possibilities in what they are already doing and by getting things in the pipeline. For example, in higher education a junior faculty member often teaches education or reading classes that have a field component. This field component can be an opportunity to complete a case study or to have preservice teachers help collect data. This type of research provides data for publishable manuscripts and gives novice researchers the practice and experience necessary to become experts. Once the Institutional Review Board (IRB) approves the research and data collection has begun, mentors can encourage colleagues to submit program proposals for research in progress. Having a proposal accepted for a national conference builds self-efficacy as a researcher and provides motivation to complete the study. The following year the completed research can be submitted for a paper presentation and a new study can be undertaken that can be submitted as research in progress. After completing a paper presentation, the manuscript can immediately be revised based on audience feedback and submitted for publication to get things into the pipeline. Once this basic process is internalized and new colleagues become more adept at teaching and juggling their load, the mentor can encourage them to plan more extensive research projects and write grant proposals.

Within our own institutions it is critical for senior faculty members to mentor new colleagues into the culture of the institution because newer employees are often unclear about the criteria for promotion and tenure and are therefore hesitant to say "No" whenever approached with an opportunity or assignment. This lack of clarity is due in part to the fact that criteria for promotion and tenure vary with the culture of the institution, and the culture of the institution changes as people in leadership positions change. For example, a primary investigator or program director may be faced with assigning extra service responsibilities or teaching loads in conjunction with a grant and may ask a junior faculty member to take on the responsibility to solve the immediate need. This solution, however, may create a long-term problem when junior faculty members are evaluated for merit, promotion, and tenure. Senior faculty can serve as good mentors by clearly articulating criteria for promotion dictated by the culture of an institution and by keeping these criteria in mind when making decisions about offering opportunities, making assignments, and giving advice.

Mentors can also periodically monitor mentoring partnerships and gain insight by having short discussions about the success of the mentoring that is occurring. For example, simply asking:

- What's going well?
- What's not going well?
- What do you need that you are not getting?

These questions open the door for mentees to talk about problems that they might not feel comfortable bringing up on their own. Mentee answers to these questions provide opportunities for encouragement and critical feedback. They also provide the context for confronting problems with hard questions if a new colleague is unable to identify what is not going well.

Another way for successful reading scholars to mentor junior faculty members is to help them understand that time must be consistently dedicated to research and writing—and imparting conditional knowledge about when it is okay to say, "No" to *"opportunities."* For example, most higher education institutions want faculty members to procure external funding. When opportunities arise administrators may present them to junior faculty. However, if the culture of the institution is such that peer reviewed research publications are the main criteria for promotion and tenure, a mentor should help a junior faculty member understand that requests for proposals are opportunities, but not required for initial promotion and tenure. In this situation the mentor can help the mentee reflect and initially focus their energy on smaller research projects that will lead to publications—or figure out how to break up an extensive research project into multiple publications. Conversely, some institutions may require grant writing, publishing a book, taking on extra teaching assignments, or providing significant service to become the valued faculty member that receives tenure. So helping new colleagues understand the values of the institution and how to balance their load is crucial.

Finally, regardless of the stage of your career, look for a variety of mentors both within your institution and outside of your institution. CRA and other professional conferences are excellent places to meet mentors. At CRA we are all here to help each other, that's one of the benefits of belonging to this organization. You don't have to be a famous name to work on committees or form partnerships. However, you will work side by side with leaders in our field. Within your institution, it is important for junior faculty members to form a relationship with a senior faculty member who understands the culture. Yet, remember junior faculty can also serve as excellent mentors.

Mentoring as a Two Way Street

I perceive mentoring as a reciprocal relationship. Whenever I assume the role of mentor, I also assume the role of learner. Thus, I am constantly learning new teaching strategies, becoming aware of new research that I haven't had time to read, and being intellectually stimulated in a way that gets me to look at issues in new ways.

The bottom line is that mentoring is a two way street that goes beyond simplistic individualized instruction and nurturing. A successful mentor understands that the relationship built between mentor and mentee is as important as the learning that takes place. This relationship is built on mutual respect, mutual trust, and ethical behavior. Once mutual respect and trust are established, the key to successful mentoring as a teaching/learning process is in the assessment with, transaction with, reflection with, and empowerment of both parties.

In closing, remember that as teachers many of us have nurturing and care giving personalities; so we have to be careful that mentoring does not become an "enabling" or "one-way" relationship with one person doing all the giving. But when we successfully balance caring and mutual respect with sharing responsibility and ethical behavior, the result is a long-term collegial relationship that flourishes well beyond the initial period of mentoring.

References

Mentoring Rationale, Examples, and Our Expertise. (n.d.). Retrieved November 28, 2005 from http://www.mentors.ca/mentorrationale.html

Webster's New Twentieth Century Dictionary of the English Language (Unabridged, 2nd ed.) (1970). New York: The World Publishing Company.

ANOTHER POTHOLE IN THE ROAD: ASSERTING OUR PROFESSIONALISM

Jon Shapiro

The University of British Columbia

Presidential Address
College Reading Association
2005

Being back in Savannah is a nostalgic moment for me. My high school experiences were certainly not the "glory days" of my life. Early one morning over 40 years ago, I climbed out of my bedroom window, took my father's car even though I had no license and drove to the nearest Long Island Rail Road station. I took a train into Manhattan and got a one-way ticket on a Greyhound bus for as far away from home as my paperboy-earned dollars would allow. That ticket took me here to Savannah. I can tell you that that was a scary trip for a short, "shop in the husky department," timid kid. However, most of all it was an eye-opening trip to the horrible absurdities of segregation. Once the bus arrived at the Maryland border I was startled to see separate water fountains and washrooms even though I had read about them in my textbooks. It was shocking to see the nice bus station luncheonettes for whites and the run-down eating areas for African-Americans.

The differences between what we hold dear, such as the values of a nation and what we do in various walks of life, including education, are intriguing, sometimes incredibly frustrating, and often extremely troublesome. For example, it may be amusing that professionals with one set of beliefs about reading hold low levels of opinion about colleagues with contrary views since their arguments often have political overtones. Recall that proponents of whole language have been viewed as the New Left while skills-based proponents were painted as right-wing conservatives. And recently we have witnessed the attacks on and by the members of the National Reading Panel and their colleagues in literacy

Reprinted from *Multiple Literacies in the 21st Century,* by M. B. Sampson, P. E. Linder, F. Falk-Ross, M. Foote, S. Szabo. Eds., 2007, Commerce, TX: College Reading Association.

education. While this may be ironic, it is really quite sad, quite silly, not at all helpful to the dialogue that must take place about reading development and reading instruction, and it is also really absurd.

Actually, I think many of my perspectives center around absurdities. Some are humorous, like the fact that dentists expect you to carry on a conversation while their fingers and tools are in your mouth. But many absurdities are not so humorous. Is it not absurd that in the midst of calls for evidence-based research in education the latest Bible-curriculum adopted by some 317 school districts in 37 states asserts that the Constitution of the United States is based on holy scriptures (Blumenthal & Novovitch, 2005)? This claim flies in the face of the fact that the Founding Fathers whose forebears were escaping religious persecution were explicit in their views regarding the separation of church and State.

Is it not absurd that under "No Child Left behind" the government will shut down schools, ostensibly due to poor teaching but then might disperse these teachers to other schools? Is it not absurd that our Colleges of Education are being criticized for being too philosophical and not practical, but the government is willing to allow individuals into classrooms after being fast-tracked by organizations like Teach for America and by "for-profit" companies that will train people solely over the Internet? Is it not absurd that the latest trends in teaching with later test results in mind, like the balanced literacy script being used in New York City, are known as "backward design" (Chan, 2005).

Yes, we do some absurd things in education and some of these relate to attitudes toward reading and to oneself as a reader; areas that I first began researching 28 years ago. One of the most important attributes that we say we try to foster in children is a love for reading and we hope that many children will become life-long readers. Many teachers and teacher educators say that these are worthy and important goals. In fact, in a survey of over 50,000 IRA members, this area was the fifth most frequent area of interest. But the reality is that there really has not been much attention paid to the affective domain in our professional publications or in our teacher education programs. This should seem absurd considering that a taxonomy of the affective domain was produced over 40 years ago (Krathwohl, Bloom & Masia, 1964) and almost 30 years ago Irene Athey (1976) decried the lack of research paid to this area.

In the past 40 years of *The Reading Teacher* there have been less than 30 or so articles, approximately 1% of the total articles about the affective domain. While teachers are interested in the affective domain, literacy educators who write for the profession and reading researchers virtually ignore the affective aspects of reading and reading instruction. And I am not so sure that many of us include it in our classes or if school board members and other politicians are even aware of its importance.

When it comes to affect and reading, the influential reports of our profession from *On Becoming a Nation of Readers* to the latest handbooks on research have hardly mentioned these factors. When they do, they speak of motivation and engagement but with the focus on the improvement of test scores **not** the development of positive attitudes or the reading habit.

My position is that children's attitudes toward reading and how instruction impacts on their attitudes, their interests, and other affective aspects of their personalities such as self-esteem and self-efficacy **should** be critical areas of concern for reading researchers, teacher educators, and those who work with readers of all age levels, especially those experiencing difficulties. And, even though, many teachers identify this as an important area, what they do in practice tells us that it is not a priority. According to studies by Gerry Duffy (1987, 1992, 2002), teachers' instructional behaviors are governed by the commercial materials that are mandated in the district or state **not** by theoretical considerations or their knowledge of children or their professional judgement. His findings indicate that the formats of reading instruction have not really changed much in over fifty years. Reading textbooks and seatwork predominate and actual instruction in how to read is lost to time spent emphasizing accuracy and in testing children. While some might argue that the advent of balanced reading instruction has made such observations obsolete, visits to many current classrooms would indicate that not much has really changed. In the present era, we may blame the lack of change on the political interference that we have witnessed in education (McGill-Franzen, 2000), the narrowing of the literacy curriculum, the strict control of reading materials—events that Diane Ravitch claims has led schools to become "empires of boredom" (2003, p.162).

In a recent *New York Times* letter-to-the editor (Phillips, 2005), the writer wrote, "In the name of No Child Left Behind and high stakes testing we are turning teachers into machines; robots who must follow scripted curriculum, use mandated lesson plans, teach from restricted lists of books and teach formulaic patterns to match to the demands of test makers." The same narrowing in England has led their Office of Standards in Education to conclude from a five-year research study that children are spending less time reading for pleasure due to the narrowing of the curriculum and the tests that accompany it, which have "squeezed storytelling and joy of reading out of schools" (Cassidy, 2005).

The research literature tells us that formats of reading instruction and the materials that we use to teach can have a profound effect on the way children view reading and the attitudes they have about reading. Researchers have found that young children at school entry do not possess a clear concept of reading. Over time, their concepts become more refined and are influenced by reading instruction. Considering the nature of most of today's "scientifically-based" reading practices, is it any wonder that young children tend to provide very narrow definitions of reading?

It is clear that one of the key perspectives that informs my thinking and work is that what we do in the name of improving reading ability often works against the promotion of positive attitudes toward books, toward reading, and toward oneself as a reader. And it is not as if we are blind to these problems. Many teachers have negative feelings toward the reading instruction that they provide. A teacher once responded to a question on her teaching of reading,

> Well, I just seem to have this conflict about what I think about reading. I mean that these kids are just getting started in reading and that it ought to be a lot of fun, and they ought to be real enthused about this. Its real stiff and structured and the kids don't have freedom. And neither do I because it has to be a certain way and it just goes on and on with exactly the same kind of pattern all the time, and again its real boring for all of us. I guess normally, when we are doing our reading, it is more like a business arrangement that everybody has to endure. Reading shouldn't be like that". And teachers in the U.K. study told inspectors "teaching reading has lost its fun. (Cassidy, 2005)

I believe that we must bring the individual child and the individual teacher back to center stage as it was from the 1870s until the onset of the industrial revolution. Since that time, we have let standardized, controlled reading materials and the accompanying teacher's manuals, the supposed scientifically supported materials and methods, rule our classroom behaviors. They have **ruled** teacher behaviors even though they may have grown uncomfortable delivering that form of instruction. **Ruled** their behaviors even though we may have recognized that there is an assumption that the materials teach reading. **Ruled** their behaviors even though they may have become alienated from the reading instruction that they provide.

We cannot break away from these forms of instruction because teachers are not allowed to teach in a manner consistent with what is known about child development and children's social and emotional growth. And increasingly, teacher educators are being limited in what we present to future teachers in our university classrooms.

It seems to me that reading programs in many classrooms of North America have become similar to other dysfunctional systems. The truth of this dysfunction resides in my first perspective, the absurd things we do in our classrooms. While I will not repeat some of those absurdities I will ask just one question: If we accept the fact that children may acquire the same abilities and skills around the same time, but not as if they had identical learning strengths and styles, why do we expect them to learn to read or learn any reading skill or strategy the same way, at the same pace, or with the same materials? Doing this is absurd, why if we had the same expectations for walking, talking, or potty training we'd create remedial walkers, talkers, and poopers!

You know, when I was in elementary school I was a short, fat kid. I took a lot of teasing. I felt a great deal of shame and, in reality, a great deal of pain. I would cringe when I heard the mocking chant of "shapippo the hippo" or even the more moderate version of "shapips the hips" used by my friends. I think that pain sensitized me to some of the other kids who were suffering. Suffering in reading group when they stammered over words or when they could not answer the teacher's question. Suffering the pain when other kids in the group, waiting like vultures, would cry out the familiar but taunting refrain, "Ooh, ooh teacher I know it."

I have to admit that I also felt the same pain later on in high school. Unable to comprehend certain mathematic relationships I sat cringing in my seat trying to elude being spotted by the teacher. I cringed before my father when he saw my mark on the New York State Regent's exam. I got a six and he said he could have lived with a zero since that would have shown I did not try, but a six just showed how stupid I was! I didn't think much about that pain when I did my teacher training. I didn't hear my professors talk about how kids might feel in the classroom, so I went out and began teaching. But you know what? I met the pain again when I started my career and even later, while on leave from the University of British Columbia, when I spent a year as a Resource Room teacher. I saw the kids who dreaded coming to school each day. The children who learn to be on automatic pilot, their eyes open and nodding that they understand but actually with their cognitive systems shut down in a desperate but often unsuccessful attempt to save their egos. The children no longer willing to try because the classroom is not a risk-free environment for them. I recognized a lot of the pain in their avoidance behaviors. The behaviors that were so familiar to me.

I do not think we can expect kids to not develop avoidance behaviors or negative attitudes when instruction does not meet their needs, abilities or interests. Can we expect anything else when we have absurd entrance and exit criteria even for kindergarten? When politicians maintain that there have to be certain levels of improvement in high stakes test scores regardless of the background and experiences of the children?

It seems to me that we are pretty successful in teaching kids to read even though many choose not to. We seem to have one constant in reading and that is our success to failure ratio. No matter which source you refer to, you read that we successfully teach 75-80% of children to read fluently and with comprehension. That is an amazing figure that few in other endeavors could claim. Why if you were an athlete you would make millions of dollars a year for that level of success. But let's turn that figure around. About one in four to five kids is not successful. In North America that amounts to millions of children. Millions of our future generation dreading coming to school!

The negative feelings of self that result from difficulties in learning to read last a lifetime. I still remember mine. In Peter Johnston's (1985) award winning research with adult non-readers, the longevity of these feelings is confirmed. One of his subjects said:

> What it is, it's the old feelings. It's like, y'know, well…something will
> trigger it. Like when I was a kid in school and they would ask me the first

day, I would be in a first...say, a new class, and they would ask me to read, and the teacher didn't know that I couldn't read. Well, those feelings still can come back to me, and it's like a feeling...never...I can't begin to explain. It's like you completely feel isolated, totally alone, and when that sets in...course, I don't get it now like I did then...but it's still that quaint feeling will come over me, and if I...it overwhelms me...it...it...it takes you right up...you know, and you do, you shut right down. (p. 167)

I wish these kinds of stories were anomalies, isolated events, but I've been in schools in many states and provinces and in virtually every class where teachers are **mandate**d to follow very **prescribed** ways of teaching with materials of **little interest** or **inappropriate** to the abilities of the students, I see children avoiding meaningful participation.

As an individual trained in early childhood education and development, I had real hope for many of the instructional strategies developed in the 1980's and 1990s. I had this hope because these strategies and the teachers that implemented them took into account the individual child. We relied on the teachers' professional abilities and judgement to be aware of individual differences that children brought into their classrooms. In Canada, we trust our teachers to make important decisions about formats of instruction and often in selecting appropriate material, and to be involved in creating the curriculum, something that Diane Ravitch called for in her book, *The Language Police: How Pressure Groups Restrict What Children Learn* (2003). Teachers who are well trained and treated as professionals also tend to be intuitively aware of the psychosocial needs of the children. What are these needs? Well, you may remember that Erik Erikson (1963) postulated psychosocial developmental phases. Even though some of these phases occur in early childhood, I have recast them for the elementary school years.

The first phase is about acquiring a sense of basic trust rather than developing mistrust. Erickson referred to this phase as the realization of hope. In infancy, developing a sense of trust requires physical comfort and a minimum of experiences of fear or uncertainty. If these are assured, trust will be extended to new experiences. A sense of mistrust arises from unsatisfactory physical and psychological experiences and leads to fearful apprehension of future situations. What happens in the "infancy" of a child's school career? The child enters kindergarten and must establish trust in the teacher, as well as in his or her own ability to fit in socially and, in today's kindergartens, academically. What happens to children who are not socially or emotionally or cognitively or developmentally ready to handle situations or tasks in kindergarten? Or for that matter, in any grade? The result is usually a retreat from involvement, loss of trust in the teacher, and the beginnings of doubt in one's own ability.

Phase 2 revolves around acquiring a sense of autonomy rather than feelings of doubt and shame. In early childhood, the acquisition of a sense of autonomy requires the ability to prove one's independence. A sense of doubt and shame arises when the child continues his or her dependency. Children who are successful in their initial instruction in reading and develop fluency in and enjoyment of reading realize that independence. What happens to those children who falter, either only slightly or by quite a bit? Initially, the child starts to doubt his or her own ability to actually progress in reading. Many express the belief that they cannot read. In the worst cases, the children develop pervasive doubt in their abilities and shame about themselves. As one begins to doubt, one begins to withdraw mentally from instruction.

Phase 3 is about acquiring a sense of initiative and overcoming a sense of passivity. As a child assumes more independence and responsibility for herself, she enters a stage of energetic learning. The child realizes a sense of purpose. She enters into her various worlds with all of her inquisitiveness and "adventuresomeness" intact. She may seek out reading experiences and challenges. She can interact with the author, text, and teacher. On the other hand, the child who has experienced frustration and even failure becomes increasingly passive and interaction with books and reading is avoided. Ultimately these children leave school with reading problems, poor attitudes, poor self-concepts, and often knowledge gaps since reading is still the primary means of acquiring information.

I believe very strongly that reading instruction which ignores the psychosocial, developmental needs of young readers **or** reading instruction that causes pain or shame **or** reading instruction that develops boredom or complacency in children is dysfunctional. When we can see the absurdities and the pain from outside the system but become enmeshed with certain methods and materials when inside the system, we are acting in ways that are parallel to what occurs in dysfunctional families. Often times in dysfunctional systems, there is the loss of ability to make choices. There is engagement in behaviors that do not allow us to see the folly of the behavior nor the pain it causes in others. In dysfunctional systems, there is the minimizing or denying of one's own feelings. And the end products of dysfunction are pain, shame, and blame.

I've spoken of the pain of children who are not progressing in reading. There is also pain for parents and teachers: teachers who wish to be good at their jobs but are confronted with the reality that not all of their children are moving ahead in reading; parents who see their children's attitudes toward school change for the worse. And we can sense the shame of children who are not meeting the expectations of their parents and teachers, the significant adults in their lives. These episodes of pain and shame ultimately lead to blame. Some educators blame the child: "He is lazy," "She is an underachiever." Some blame the parents: "What can you expect, his father was the same way." Children, seeing others succeed come to blame themselves. More recently, politicians are blaming teachers and now, teacher educators!

Dysfunctional systems survive in climates where we do not talk and do not trust. The overriding law of the educational system seems to me to be, "Do not allow talk about the real issues." I would say to you that high stakes test scores and grade equivalents are not the real issues. The issues should be whether teachers are allowed to teach in ways that recognize and respect the individuality of the learner and foster their own professionalism? Are children reading? Do they like to read? Do they know how to read for informational purposes? Are teacher educators allowed to exercise their professional expertise over the curricula in their reading education classrooms? Will government-funding agencies give serious consideration to research proposals that do not adhere to the government's agenda?

We also do not trust. Classroom instruction that continues to be difficult for children is rationalized away. The ability to invest confidence, reliance, and faith in children as learners has been lost. We have learned to not trust children to learn unless they are receiving direct instruction. We do not trust teachers to make instructional decisions and to select appropriate materials. And today we no longer trust teacher educators to develop future teachers who know the practical skills of teaching but also the reasons why these methods and strategies are appropriate.

These are harsh words and beliefs and they might even be offensive, but educators at various levels are now being **coerced** by a political movement to engage in curriculum delivery, choices of materials, and forms of evaluation that are extremely rigid, diminish their professionalism, and cause alienation. How do we promote the examination of pedagogical decisions in light of their impact on the quality of all of the children's experiences in school, not just on test scores? Should we be asking those with political power, if we are to choose between approaches or methods of instruction do we choose methods that ignore individual differences?; that do not promote positive attitudes toward reading?; that do not promote the most accurate conceptions of the reading process?; that may harm one's self-esteem?; that reduce the act of teaching to assembly-line behavior? that alienate teachers from their own instruction and vocation? **OR,** Do we choose approaches and methods that are beneficial to all children and, in a wider sense, move beyond test scores and, at the same time provide professional growth and fulfillment for teachers?

To accomplish this in our roles as teachers of reading and teachers of reading teachers, we may sometimes need to strive to break the bonds of custom or policies that are imposed on us. This will not be easy to take on politicians and State departments of education, indeed the federal government is an enormous and daunting task. Certainly it is hard to visualize that single individuals can have much of an impact. Alone a David and Goliath outcome is never going to occur. However, what is the alternative? After all, conviction without action should have no meaning for us.

Back in the 1950s during the frightful time of Joseph McCarthy and his House Un-American Activities Committee, the cartoonist Walt Kelly, through his character "Pogo", wrote "We have met the enemy and he is us." Kelly's message was that in a democracy, those who do n't think their voice matters or who procrastinate in making their voice heard have no one to blame for the situation but themselves (Kelly and Couch, Jr. 1982).

If we do not begin to raise our voices and become public academics, we who are the supposed experts, what hope is there for change? Has it been the case that our most learned colleagues in literacy education and, in fact, all literacy educators, have been disregarded or marginalized by those who control the public forum? Or has it been the case that we are too half-hearted or feel we will not have an impact to bother to be heard in the public forum? I would suggest to you that we, as an organization and as some of the most knowledgeable individuals about reading education, have an obligation to make public our ideas; not just to each other in our journals and at our conferences, but to the general public as well as to those who develop or shape educational policy.

I often think of a poem I read, "There's a hole in my sidewalk: An autobiography in five chapters" (Nelson, 1994).

Chapter I
I walk down the street.
There is a deep hole in the sidewalk.
I fall in.
I am lost...I am helpless.
It isn't my fault.
It takes forever to find a way out.

Chapter II
I walk down the same street.
There is a deep hole in the sidewalk.
I pretend I don't see it.
I fall in again.
I can't believe I'm in the same place, but it isn't my fault.
It still takes a long time to get out.

Chapter III
I walk down the same street.
There is a deep hole in the sidewalk.
I see it is there.
I still fall in. It's a habit.
My eyes are open.

I know where I am.
It is my fault.
I get out immediately.

Chapter IV
I walk down the same street.
There is a deep hole in the sidewalk.
I walk around it.

Chapter V
I walk down another street.

While the title of my speech uses "potholes" rather than holes in the sidewalk, the message is still the same. It is time for CRA to be a leader, to facilitate and assert our collective professionalism in finding a new way around the potholes that compromise the growth in reading and the enjoyment of reading for the various levels of readers that we focus on in this wonderful organization. As Marilyn Cochran-Smith (2005) stated in her Presidential address for the American Educational Research Association, we "...must also be public intellectuals using our expertise, our evidence, and our freedom to challenge a system that does not serve the interests of many students and to lead the way in another direction for the best" (p. 15).

References

Athey, I. (1976). Reading research in the affective domain. In H. Singer & R.B. Ruddell (Eds.), *Theoretical models and processes of reading* (pp. 352-380). Newark, DE: The International Reading Association.

Blumenthal, R., & Novovitch, B. *Bible course becomes a test for public schools in Texas.* The New York Times (nytimes.com), August 1, 2005. *http://www.nytimes. com/2005/08/01/education/01bible.htm?th=&em*

Cassidy, S. *Tests blamed for decline of reading for pleasure. The Independent* (online edition) October 12, 2005. *http://education.independent.co.uk/news/articles317219. ece*

Chan, S. *By the script.* The New York Times (nytimes.com), July 31, 2005. *http://www. nytimes.com/2005/07/31/education/edlife/chan31.html?p*

Cochran-Smith, M. (2005). The new teacher education: For better or for worse? *Educational Researcher, 34*(7), pp.3-17.

Duffy, G., Roehler, L., & Putnam, J. (1987). Putting the teacher in control: Basal reading textbooks and instructional decision making. *Elementary School Journal, 87,* 357-366.

Duffy, G. G. (1992). Let's free teachers to be inspired. *Phi Delta Kappan, 73,* 442-447.

Duffy, G. G. (2002). Visioning and the development of outstanding teachers. *Reading Research and Instruction, 41,* 331-343.

Erikson, E. H. (1963). *Childhood and Society,* 2nd Edition. New York: W.W. Norton.

Johnston, P. H. (1985). Understanding reading disability: A case study approach. *Harvard Educational Review, 55,* 153-177.

Kelly, Mrs. Walt, & Couch, Jr., B. (Eds.) (1982). *The Best of Pogo.* New York: Simon & Schuster.

Krathwohl, D. R., Bloom, B. S., & Masia, B. B. (1964). *Taxonomy of educational objectives, Handbook II: Affective Domain.* New York: David McKay.

McGill-Franzen, A. (2000). Policy and instruction: What is the relationship? In M. Kamil, P. Mosenthal, P.D. Pearson, & R. Barr (Eds.), *Handbook of Reading Research, Vol. III* (889-908), Mahwah, NJ: Erlbaum.

Nelson, P. (1994). *There's a hole in my sidewalk: The romance of self-discovery.* Hillsboro, OR: Beyond Words Publishing.

Phillips, S. (2005) Letter to the Editor, *New York Times,* July 20.

Ravitch, D. (2003). *The language police: How pressure groups restrict what students learn.* New York: Alfred A. Knopf.

THE FUTURE OF WRITING

Karen Bromley

Binghamton University (SUNY)

Presidential Address
College Reading Association
2006

Karen Bromley is a Distinguished Teaching Professor in the School of Education at Binghamton University (SUNY) where she teaches courses in literacy instruction and assessment, children's literature and writing. She was a third grade teacher and a K-8 reading specialist in New York and Maryland. She has written several books for teachers, most recently Stretching Students' Vocabulary *and* 50 Graphic Organizers for Reading, Writing and More.

This speech explores the future of writing by discussing four predictions: the notion that pens and pencils will be collectors' items, the idea that writing will be electronic and we will read only digital text, the certainty that writing will be more challenging to learn and teach, and the idea that speech will replace writing. The audience was left with questions: What will be lost if these predictions become reality? What will be gained? How will curriculum, instruction, and assessment in schools, clinics, and higher education change to reflect these changes in writing?

First, thank you all for coming to the 50th annual Legislative Assembly. I thank you loyal members who never fail to attend, and you newer members who want to learn more about CRA.

In preparation for giving this Presidential speech, I did some *reading* and *thinking* about the history of writing and the changes I have witnessed in writing during my lifetime. I also did some *remembering*—I remembered Jon

Reprinted from *Navigating the Literacy Water: Research, Praxis, & Advocacy*, pp. 2-10, by M. Foote, F. Falk-Ross, S. Szabo, M. B. Sampson, Eds., 2008, Commerce, TX: College Reading Association.

Shapiro's presidential speech last year in Savannah and Wayne Linek's the year before that one. They were both personal and inspiring. My memory fails me beyond those two years except for Tim Rasinski's hilarious presidential speech several years earlier in which he talked about his dog, Ginger, and it being too dark inside a dog to read. I want to warn you however—today's speech will be a yawner compared to previous speeches!

I am not an expert on the future of writing. In fact, I probably know less about it than many of you. But I chose to talk about this topic to learn more myself. In a chapter I wrote recently called "Technology and Writing" for *The International Handbook of Literacy and Technology* (Bromley, 2006), I stopped short of predicting the future. I wrote about how technology has changed our ways of writing and communicating. I wrote about the benefits of combining paper and pencil with technology. I wrote about electronic journals augmenting paper journals and texts. I wrote about how conventions have been affected by technology, but I did not look into the future. So, today I will go beyond that work and offer you four ideas that may make you think differently about writing—an addiction many of us have or should have as academics.

What initially piqued my interest in the future of writing was a visit to my local Barnes and Noble bookstore last summer. As I browsed the children's book section, sipping a cup of Starbucks Hazelnut decaf, words Patrick Shannon would categorize as "pedagogy of consumption," two titles caught my eye. The first was *ttyl* (Myracle, 2004) and the second was *ttfn* (Myracle, 2006). I know *ttyl* in IM (instant messaging) language stands for "*talk to you later*." But I didn't know what *ttfn* stands for. Do you know? When a quick scan of the book didn't uncover the meaning, and feeling foolish, I asked a young girl who stood nearby reading. She said *ttfn* means "*ta ta for now*." Both books by Lauren Myracle are about the friendship of three teenage girls and are written entirely in IM.

The titles reminded me of what a middle-school teacher friend told me recently. She is frustrated because her students use IM in their writing, and she can't tell what they are saying. As well, they defend it when she tells them it is not standard English. This also made me wonder about the future of writing. How has it changed over time? What will it be like in a decade or two or three? How has technology shaped writing? So, here are my four ideas about the future of writing:

Idea #1: Pens and Pencils Will Be Collectors' Items

This idea should not surprise us when we think about how writing has changed over the years. Pre-empted by pictures drawn on cave walls, the first written language, *cuneiform,* was invented 5,000 years ago by the Sumerians who inscribed it on clay tablets (*World Book Encyclopedia,* 2006). Later, the Egyptians used a picture alphabet called *hieroglyphics* written on *papyrus.* The Greeks and Romans developed alphabets and used scrolls and wax tablets. The Chinese made paper in 200 B.C. and used carved blocks of wood for printing.

Movable clay type was first invented in 1000 A.D. by the Chinese and later movable metal type was invented by the Koreans. In Europe, Gutenberg's mechanical press was followed 300 years later by steam-powered presses, and monotype and linotype typesetting machines introduced in the late 19th century.

Tools for handwriting have changed, too. Pencils and quill pens led the way to ink pens and ball point pens. (An interesting aside here—in Budapest this summer for IRA's World Congress, I learned that the ball-point pen was invented in Hungary by Josef Biro in 1938). Felt-tip markers emerged and of course typewriters and computer keyboards. In the 1980s, laser printers and personal computers began to support desktop publishing. Today, our *cyber writing* is digital and includes word processing, e-mail, and text messaging on the Internet, cell phones and PDAs (professional digital assistants) like the Blackberry.

This abbreviated history illustrates dramatic changes in writing in a relatively short time (and, dramatic changes in the vocabulary associated with writing, e.g., *pen, pencil, journal, typewriter, manuscript, cursive* [Does anyone even teach it anymore?], *book, magazine, etc.—word processor, MSWord, IM, pda, email, web, keyboarding, cursor, blog, weblog, blogosphere, hypertext, e-book, e-zine, cyberspace*). Writing has not been a static practice. In a way it is like photography. Some of you, like me, have used a Brownie box camera, a single lens reflex camera, a Polaroid, and now I use a digital camera.

Whether we like it or not, digital text is our future. So, picture a world without pens and pencils where we download our Sudoku and crossword puzzles and use the keypad of a cell phone or PDA to do them. According to the Pew Internet and American Life survey (2006), 73% of adults use the Internet today as compared to about 20% ten years ago (http://www.pewinternet.org/trends/ Internet_Adoption_4.26.06.pdf). And, some experts believe, for example Lasica (2005), author of a book about the digital generation "...we are only 2% of the way into what the internet has to offer" (p. 260). I wonder what the remaining 98% has in store for us. Lasica also predicts the coming of super broadband that will be 100 times faster than today's internet services.

Today computers are replacing pens, pencils, and humans in the newsroom. A U.S. news service, Thomson Financial, uses computers to automatically generate news stories reporting that a company has done better or worse than expected (Van Duyn, 2006). How long do you think it takes to generate these stories? It takes .3 of a second after a company makes results public for a story to be created. Reuters also does this and Bloomberg is not far behind. This scenario in the news is rather frightening for what it promises for other types of writing. I'd like to see some authors publish more quickly, e.g., Lemony Snicket, Tony Hillerman, and Elizabeth George, but, the Captain Underpants books already come out way too often for my taste.

Picture a world where pens and pencils will soon be collector's items, and where every K-12 student will have a laptop or wireless device for writing. I suggest we sell our stock in Cross and Bic and buy stock in a broadband company like Comcast or Time Warner. We no longer live with *Generation X*...this generation is *Generation Text* (Dunnewind, 2003), and who knows about *Generation Next*?

Idea # 2: Writing Will Be Electronic and We Will Read *Only* Digital Text

We already read digital maps on our cars' navigation systems and on our golf carts. In some churches, people read words to the hymns they sing from a screen, not a hymnbook. We already read and write electronically to shop, order food and prescriptions, and pay bills on the Internet. So, picture a world in the not too distant future where our offices and homes are nearly paper-free. We'll spend more and more time in cyber-networking environments like Craigslist, Angelaslist, or Google-Youtube, and much of our writing may be in the blogosphere. We'll submit our scholarly manuscripts online and read journals and books online. A trip to the library to leisurely leaf through a paper copy of a journal will no longer happen. We'll read everything online. We'll miss the chance to serendipitously discover ideas and information when we browse a paper journal. We'll be known as *mouse-potatoes*, as well as the *couch-potatoes* some of us are already!

Picture a world where the community of readers and writers has expanded dramatically. With a mouse click it will be easier to reply online to authors we know and those we don't know. One of my colleagues told me recently that she has had more responses to her article published by *Educational Leadership* in a special online issue, than to any other article she published previously in a paper journal. This makes tremendous possibilities for dialogue, collaboration, and the generation of new knowledge. But, what else will it do? It will also cause us to be even more overloaded and stressed as we are bombarded with even more electronic input.

Picture a world where we read only e-books. Today, Project Gutenberg and World e-Book Library have made hundreds of thousands of scanned books available on the Internet. As well, Google and other Internet providers have plans to digitize more library books. The prediction is that by 2020 there will be 10 million e-books on the Internet (Carpenter, 2006; http://gutenberg.org). A recent article in *The Chronicle of Higher Education* reports that scholars are "...beginning to question whether the printed book is the best format for advancing scholarship and communicating big ideas," (Young, 2006, p. A21). Some forward thinkers believe books should be dynamic rather than fixed and they should be sites for conversation. Young describes an example of open review on the Internet by those who read a professor's scholarly book. The feedback was from colleagues and those who didn't know his field. One person gave him valuable ideas for revising. Guess what another reader who didn't know the field said, "This doesn't have substance. Take some time off, teach a little" (p. A21). So, receiving similar feedback on a book in draft form is in the near future for us as authors.

This process is called *open-source development* and three other quick examples of it point to our future as academic writers. First, *Wikipedia* (http://www.wikipedia.org/) the online public encyclopedia available in several languages that anyone can contribute to, has made us rethink authorship, collaboration, text format, and access. Second, the journal, *Nature,* this summer began making submitted articles available immediately for electronic review by anyone (Young, 2006). The standard review process is also used, but authors can receive online comments from the public as well. Third, this fall, Rice University began the first all-digital university press as a model for other universities faced with increased costs of scholarly publishing. The Rice press will include multimedia features and online discussions of its e-books (Young, 2006).

Picture a world where these types of public collaborations in cyberspace affect all kinds of writing, not just academic writing. Wittenberg (2006) in a recent article in *The Chronicle of Higher Education* suggests that the publishing world is at a "cross-roads." She says "We know users are becoming used to communicating in sophisticated, interactive, and collaborative online environments, and the traditional forms of publishing are at risk of becoming irrelevant if they do not evolve" (p. B20). If the lines between scholarly and commercial publishing are blurring, then libraries, books, magazines, and newspapers are poised for drastic makeovers.

And, what will happen to all the written text we produce? The digital information we create is fragile. It exists as "…magnetic pulses or microscopic pits on a disk" (Carlson, 2004, p. A25). Documents saved in the 1980s on a floppy disk may be unreadable now, but Emily Dickinson's poetry locked away in a box for decades can be found, read, and reproduced. Future historians will need to know how to use software programs and machines that no longer exist. So, the $100 million digital-archiving program the Library of Congress has undertaken will be critical to us and historians (Carlson, 2004; p. A27).

But, to say unequivocally that writing will be electronic and we will read *only* digital text is to forget some past predictions. What happened when we were told the U.S. would "go metric," that ITA would solve children's reading problems, and that the Edsel was the car of the future? We *can* say though that writing as we know it today will certainly change.

Idea # 3: Writing Will Be More Challenging to Learn and Teach

As a graduate student at the University of Maryland years ago, I remember what Bob Wilson, my adviser said about how to write for publication. He said

"Read other articles written in the style and voice you want to use." And that won't change, I hope. We will still read widely before and as we write. Later, at Binghamton, I remember writing my first article for *Language Arts* using a pencil and yellow legal pad. And, for some of us this still works today! I think the department's secretary, Lucille, who retyped many revisions for me on her trusty Remington typewriter, was happier than I was when it was finally accepted 6 months later in a snail-mail letter. In contrast, last week I finished the tenth revision, at least, of a manuscript using MS Word. Then, I navigated the online submission process at IRA's website and sent it electronically to *The Reading Teacher.* I'll get reviews and a decision electronically in less than three months. That contrast between writing 20 years ago and writing today is quite amazing!

There are those who believe that computers and technology have not only caused *more* writing, but have caused more *bad* writing (Grow, 2006; Leibowitz, 1999). It does seem though that the changes I have talked about will make writing more challenging to learn and teach in the future. And, issues that plagued us in the past will be even more critical. Picture a world where plagiarism is rampant. A recent article in *The Chronicle of Higher Education* (Wasley, 2006) describes the plagiarism unearthed at Ohio University by a graduate student in mechanical engineering. He discovered 39 plagiarized theses with material copied from textbooks, other theses, journal articles, and the Internet. Sometimes the copied material was as much as 14 identical pages, including flow charts, data tables, and narrative - with typos and misspellings, as well! The 39 theses were removed from the library and the degrees confirmed are in question. All but a few cases involved international students who may not understand standard citation practices. This plagiarism has prompted discussions at many institutions and it should alert us all to the need for teaching better writing skills, and also to Internet sites like Turnitin, *www.turnitin.com,* the service that helps identify plagiarized work.

Picture a world where researchers, teachers, and students routinely collaborate, discuss, and create multimedia projects with *hypertext*. While the images and sounds of hypertext are sometimes easier and more interesting to read, they also require special skills. We will need to teach these special skills which include how to select and evaluate Internet sources. As Monaghan (2006) says, "...students must be able to interpret not just words, but still and moving images, understanding how they are constructed, how they create meaning and how they can deceive" (A33). Critical literacy and visual literacy will be paramount in all walks of life.

Picture a world where courses like "Writing With Video" take the place of "Freshman Composition 101" which has happened at the University of California (Monaghan, 2006). Teaching multimedia literacy will undoubtedly be a routine part of the general education requirement at all colleges and universities in the future.

In thinking about the difficulty of teaching writing, Sonn (2006) observes in his book *Paradigms Lost: The Life and Deaths of the Printed Word,* that "people have spontaneously and accidentally created what amounts to a new printed medium" (p. 343). It has no real usage rules, and as "great megabyte mountains of information" are created by more people, there is a collapse occurring in grammar and language" (p. 343). This is the relevance problem my middle-school teacher friend faces that I mentioned earlier. It is something we, as teacher educators and researchers, face now and will face in teaching writing in the future.

I've just talked about three ideas that relate to the near future of writing. Fourth and last, please consider a revolutionary idea for the far-distant future.

Idea #4: Speech Will Replace Writing

We will use speech-to-text conversion programs with our laptops, PDAs, and other newly invented writing devices. The act of writing on a keyboard will disappear. Picture a world where your fingers no longer touch keys on a keyboard, but your voice activates and produces digital print. Picture a world where high stakes tests are taken electronically, and students use speech-to-print programs to respond. The need for thinking skills will outweigh the need for keyboarding skills. The art and craft of thinking with speech-to-text writing as an outcome is difficult, and we will need to teach it well.

In his essay "The Future of Writing," Sperber (2002) says "... the revolution in information and communication technology may soon turn writing into a relic of the past" (p. 2). He predicts that with the speech-to-print capability of computers, speech may well displace the activity of writing. "Once it will be possible to by-pass writing, many people may come to realize what a source of discomfort it always was to them" (p. 20). It will be much quicker than handwriting or keyboarding because we speak more quickly than we write. It will free us from the muscular tension of writing, and once we are over the awkwardness of speaking into a machine, it will be freeing. But, reading computer encoded print will still be necessary, and we will need to be competent, creative, cyber-savvy users.

The last stock tip I have is to buy shares in a speech-recognition software company. I should tell you though, my husband is wary of my investment ideas. I wanted to buy Martha Stewart stock a few years ago, just before she was sent to the "gray-bar hotel" in West Virginia. Today though, you can bet I remind him of where her stock is now!

The beauty of giving a speech and having a time limit is that a speaker can omit topics, ignore issues, and leave out expert opinions. I admit I have done that. But, certainly we can agree that writing will not remain a static practice—pens and pencils will slowly disappear, more writing will be electronic, writing will be challenging to learn and teach, and writing will be accomplished more often through speech.

In conclusion, here are some questions to consider. What will be lost if these four predictions become reality? What will be gained? And, how will curriculum, instruction, and assessment in schools, clinics, and higher education need to change to reflect changes in writing? i lv u with ?s 2 pndr

Last, here is a peek at a new book on writing that we literacy educators will want to read, *Beating the Odds: Getting Published in the Field of Literacy* (Wepner & Gambrell, 2006).

References

Bromley, K. (2006). Technology and writing. In M. McKenna, L. D. Labbo, R. D. Kieffer, & D. Reinking (Eds.), *International handbook of literacy and technology (Vol. 2)*. Mahwah, NJ: Lawrence Erlbaum (pp. 349-355).

Carlson, S. (2004, January 30). The uncertain fate of scholarly artifacts in a digital age. *The Chronicle of Higher Education*, pp. A25-26.

Carpenter, D. (2005, October 20). Project to give free web access to books. *Binghamton Press and Sun Bulletin*. Binghamton, NY.

Dunnewind, S. (2003, June 11). 'Generation text': Teens' IM lingo evolving into a hybrid language. *The Seattle Times*. Retrieved July 8, 2006, from http://seattletimes.nwsource.com.

Grow, G. How computers cause bad writing. Retrieved Jul 7, 2006 from http://www.longleaf.net/ggrow/computerbad.html.

Lasica, J. D. (2005). *Hollywood's war against the digital generation*. Hoboken, NJ: John Wiley & Sons.

Leibowitz, W. R. (1999, November 26). Technology transforms writing and the teaching of writing. *Chronicle of Higher Education*. Retrieved July 8, 2006, from http://chronicle.com/free/v46/i14/14a06701.htm.

Monaghan, P. (2006, July 14). More than words. *The Chronicle of Higher Education*, A33.

Myracle, L. (2006). *ttfn*. New York: Amulet Books.

Myracle, L. (2004). *ttyl*. New York: Amulet Books.

Pew Internet and American life Project. Retrieved September 2, 2006 from http://www.pewinternet.org/trends/Internet_Adoption_4.26.06.pdf.

Project Gutenberg. Retrieved August 26, 2006 from http://gutenberg.org.

Scanlan, C. The web and the future of writing. Retrieved July 7, 2006 from http://www.longleaf.net/ggrow/computerbad.html.

Sonn, W. (2006). *Paradigms lost: The life and deaths of the printed word*. Lanham, MD: Scarecrow Press.

Sperber, D. *The future of writing*. Text written for the virtual symposium *text-e*. Retrieved July 7, 2006, from http://www.dan.sperber.com/future_of_writing.htm.

Turnitin. Retrieved September 7, 2006, from http://www.turnitin.com/static/home.html.

VanDuyn, A. (2006, August 18). Need for speed sees computers writing the news. *The financial times*. (p. 1).

Wasley, P. (2006, August 11). The plagiarism hunter. *The Chronicle of Higher Education*, A8-A11.

Wepner, S. B., & Gambrell, L. B. (Eds.) (2006). *Beating the odds: Getting published in the field of literacy*. Newark, DE: International Reading Association.

Wittenberg, K. (2006, June 16). Beyond Google: What next for publishing? *The Chronicle of Higher Education,* B20.

World Book Encyclopedia. Retrieved August 27, 2006 from http://www.worldbook. com.

Young, J. R. (2006, July 28). Book 2.0: Scholars turn monographs into digital conversations. *The Chronicle of Higher Education,* LII (47), A20-A23.

Traditions, Storying, and Crossroads

Ellen Jampole

SUNY-Cortland

Presidential Address
College Reading Association
2007

Ellen Jampole has taught literacy meth-ods, children's literature, measurement and evaluation, and history of education classes at SUNY Cortland since 1990. She has served as department chair and as the Interim Director of Graduate Studies. Ellen has been active in CRA since 1991. She also taught at LSU and prior to that, she was a regular classroom teacher (high school and elementary levels) as well as a reading specialist (grades K-6, 9-11). She loves reading and does so constantly.

Abstract

My presidential address theme came from being Southern, a teacher, and having a love of reading. I have a fondness for Southern writers, humorous writ-ers, and women writers, specifically, funny Southern women writers. I judge a book by its cover. If the title sounds interesting or if there's a catchy picture, then I am most likely hooked. I couldn't resist Jill Conner Browne's The Sweet Potato Queens' Book of Love. It has a great title and a hilarious picture of "royalty" in hot pink and green and big hair. All Southerners have observations about life which we share in a round-about way, making them into elaborate stories. Some observations/stories are quite fitting for us as educators and researchers; as we are at a crossroads in literacy. So, I'll share a few stories with you and give you my interpretation and advice.

Reprinted from *Literacy Issues During Changing Times: A Call to Action.* pp. 3-9, by F. Falk-Ross, S. Szabo, M. B. Sampson, M. M. Foote, Eds., 2009, Commerce, TX: College Reading Association.

This speech is all Linda Gambrell's fault. I met her (and Pat Koskinen) at my first CRA meeting, the 1991 conference at Crystal City, VA; both of them befriended me. Later, after the conference, Linda called me and asked if I'd be interested in applying for the coeditor position for *The Reading News*...I was so excited that I babbled on and on to my department chair (a science educator so he had NO clue of who THE LINDA GAMBRELL IS)...the rest is history.

Historically, as one of the last duties, the CRA president gives an address—and traditionally sweats for a couple of years about the address (which in many ways is harder than planning the conference). My first thought after finding out I won the election was "I can't believe they elected me; OH GOOD GRIEF, I HAVE TO PLAN A SPEECH." Planning this talk has made me crazy (and that's such a short trip). I lost sleep, said some CHOICE cross words; went up several crossroads...then I hit on a ROYAL idea, which I'll explain in a bit, after some background. I really wanted this speech to be finished early, so I could put my mind at ease, but I worked on it the day before I left for the conference (and even the morning I gave it).

I thought about the conference theme and started to tie in with a speech along the lines of: This year we are again at a crossroads in literacy and education. This crossroads is likely to stay for a long time, but we need to do as much as possible to make sure the road chosen is the right one for all children. While I believe we are at a juncture in education (and told Ray Reutzel in an email in September or October, 2007 to deliver me from people who feel balanced literacy is under-cover whole language), that speech wasn't me. Besides I couldn't wear my queenly regalia and talk totally seriously—the two just don't go together.

At the 2006 conference, in the J. Estill Alexander Forum, Allen Berger said writing a good sentence is hard to do...he is so right. Therefore, it follows that writing a good speech is practically IMPOSSIBLE, at least for me, so I will just talk from my heart.

I am from North Carolina, a proud Southerner. As such, I am steeped in manners, traditions, stories, and history. Judy Richardson dressed as a witch to give her presidential address. Tim Rasinski told us he learned everything from his dog. In 2006, Karen Bromley told us about the future of writing. All told great stories, very personalized to their interests.

I was my department's interim chair this past spring—since I wasn't the real chair, I decided I was other furniture...an ottoman...if I was an ottoman, well, I would just be the Empress. So, I decided to keep the theme of being a royal figure for my presidential address.

Harper Lee, Eudora Welty, William Faulkner, Skip Fretwell, Charlotte Simpson, Celia Rivenbark, and Jill Connor Browne, great Southern storytellers all. Who are these last four people? Rivenbark is a writer for the Myrtle Beach Sun Times (newspaper) and has written several books. She is a self described "tarnished Southern belle" with a keen eye and a sharp wit. Browne is a Sweet

Potato Queen, writer, and actually the boss queen—she began the Sweet Potato Queens (SPQ) in 1982. She said that nobody else can be a Sweet Potato Queen, but we can be queens and boss queens of whatever we want. The SPQ as a group are rowdy women; they have adopted Laura Thatcher Ulrich's slogan "well behaved women rarely make history." (I highly recommend ALL the books Rivenbark and Browne have written.)

At Cortland, in the School of Education, I am known as the APA Queen, but I didn't pick that queendom. I picked to be the Boss Queen of CRA—technically, I reckon, y'all picked me, but you didn't know you picked me to be queen. To finish the list of Southern storytellers, Skip is my cousin and Charlotte was my mother.

I hope to tell you a story . . . I hope to share traditions. And, as any Southern mama worth her salt does, I will give you some advice you should follow just because I said so.

My queenly edict is: y'all listen and listen good . . . if you go to sleep, make sure you are in the back few (about the last two-thirds of the room) rows as I can't see what you're doing there.

All Southerners have observations about life. Of course we are really, really willing to share and in a long, round about way. As Rivenbark (2000) says, "We Southerners believe a simple yes or no has a certain harshness in it that could be construed as, horror of horrors, rude. We never answer a question simply. It just isn't in us" (p. 36). We don't share things quickly; we make them into elaborate stories.

Some observations/stories are quite fitting for us as educators and researchers, so I'll share a few of them with you and give you my interpretation and advice as the Boss Queen of CRA.

But, first . . . I thought some more and maybe this speech is really Robert Tate's fault. You see, I always wanted to be a teacher, from when I was a little girl and taught my younger brother to spell his name F   ED. (His name is Fred.) In the sixth grade, I was in school with Robert and Isaac. All three of us were from dysfunctional families. Robert and Isaac hated school; they hated to read. I loved to read—it was such an escape—I believed everybody should love to read. I don't know what happened to Isaac, but Robert and I were in social studies/language arts together in 7th grade. Our teacher, Mrs. Page, gave us an assignment, to read a two-page Mark Twain piece. Mrs. Page came over to me (Robert sat beside me in our grouping) and told me to get busy. I said I'd read it; Mrs. Page did not believe me. Now, this was the dark ages . . . Robert told Mrs. Page he knew I'd read the piece and that she could ask me any question she wanted to and I'd be able to answer it—he so hated to read that he had watched me read. Robert cemented my desire to be a teacher.

Back to current time. Some of the life observations are contradictory—always wear clean underwear when you are going out and never wear panties to a party. Does that mean you only have a party at your house? Beauty is as beauty does; beauty is only skin deep . . . I suppose contradiction is fitting, since teaching and research are filled with diverging points of view!

LIFE OBSERVATIONS	HOW THEY FIT EDUCATORS & RESEARCHERS
What's so special about being a Southerner? Well, just everything that's all. (Rivenbark, 2000, p. XV).	What's so special about being a teacher educator and researcher? Well, just everything that's all.
A closed mouth gathers no feet (Charlotte Simpson, personal communication all my life).	There is always a time for listening—to others as well as ourselves. Listen to students. Listen to government. Listen to what's going on world-wide, to be well-informed. Listen to your heart.
There are five men a woman needs—dancer, fixer, lover, the purchaser of everything we want and nothing we need, and finally the man we can talk to (Browne, 1999, pp. 105-111). (According to Bill Engvall, a man's needs are much more simple—and there are only three—beer, food, sex.)	There are five teachers every learner needs **and has a right to. The fixer,** who teaches strategies so the learners become skilled. **The encourager,** who cheers on each learner's success. **The task-master,** that keeps each earner honest and has high standards. **The passionate one,** who loves what he or she is doing and loves learning. **The knowledgeable one,** the one who has kept on learning, even though he or she has multiple degrees; the one David Pearson told us about Friday (November 2, 2007) that has the disposition to inquire and learn. The one who develops professionally. All of these together sound to me like an effective teacher. (Learners' needs are more complex than men's, it seems.)
Stop dressing your six-year old like a skank (Rivenbark, 2006, p. 27). You know, like the Britney Spears du jour. She goes on to say that the "7-16 girls' department offerings are no different than that of the juniors' department and beyond" (p. 30).	Don't jump on every (or even any) tacky bandwagon that comes around. Staying off bandwagons is akin to wanting to keep Peter Pan collars and cotton for our little girls instead of low-cut spandex with "sexy chick" on the front—do what's right for learners. We need to have a decent foundation to build on. Plutarch is still relevant; Dewey (1938) said we need to keep the old that we know is good and incorporate good new into the curriculum. We need to get the facts right, as Michael Tunnell tole us Thursday (November 1, 2007) meaning we need to get teaching right.
You better have a good defense (Browne, 1999, p. 95).	The best offense is a good defense, right? As Gerald Coles (2006) asked, what needs to be done to ensure that all children learn to read and write? We need to have a good defense to teach all learners to be literate—and our defense will come from research: knowing what works best for each earner. Pearson (November 2, 2007) said we need to be reflective, analytical, and organized. We need to know what works, what doesn't—and why it does or doesn't.

Read like your life depends on it (Skip Fretwell, personal communication, all my life).	Your professional life does depend on it. Be critical literates; know the subtext. Know theory. Know what you believe and why you believe the way you do. Read to stay current. Read to know things, professional and personal. As Rasinski (2002, p. 11) said, "there is a solid theoretical basis for reading as a necessary condition for improving reading achievement and…you cannot become a good reader without widely and regularly reading." Love reading for pure pleasure (Besides your life may depend on it, given the recent parasites and outbreaks!)
Make new friends, keep the old, one is silver and the other is gold.	Mentor new people in CRA, keep up with your old buddies. We all need support and we can all give support. Linda Gambrell at the newcomers' luncheon said some of the best friends she's made have been through CRA.
Never wear panties to a party.	Do the unexpected. Liberate yourself and your students. Teach them to be thinkers.
Do what makes your heart sing.	Without passion, the singing of the heart, nothing great is accomplished. You have to love what you do to be great at it. You need to have the right disposition.
Be prepared.	Prepared: ready, set, equipped, organized, and primed. In the 1960s, the thought was that teaching was a subversive activity. It should be subversive— and effective. There are five mainstays of effective instruction—teacher knowledge, assessment, effective practice, differentiated instruction, and family-school connections (Reutzel & Cooter, 2008, p. vi-vii). Be primed to do the best for students of all ages. Be set to take action. Do your best; be equipped to be effective; be organized active thinkers; be ready, subversive do-ers. As MaryEllen Vogt told us earlier this morning (November 3, 2007) go beyond the basal as it's not enough. Your students' and their students' lives depend on it.
Be p'ticklar (Browne, 1999, p. 59).	I could have started with this and just stopped because, as Browne says, this is the best advice in the whole history of the world. Be p'ticklar (be particular) covers EVERYTHING. We need to be p'ticklar in how and what we teach. There is no one right way to teach. Just like clothes, no matter what they say, are not one size fits all. Be p'ticklar in what you choose to teach with and about—select the best of the best. As Reutzel and Cooter (2008) remind us, it is the teacher who makes the difference. Take it to another level: from an excellent teacher and researcher to an expert teacher and researcher (MaryEllen Vogt, November 3, 2007).

My queenly attire during this conference has been a reflection of what I believe we collectively are—quirky, proud, a little off-beat yet classy, colorful, sparkly, blinding, noisy . . . whatever you want to call it. I'd like to change Ulrich's statement a bit to "well behaved literacy professionals rarely make history." I believe we members of the College Reading Association (to be the Association of Literacy Professionals and Researchers) have made history and will continue to make history.

References

Browne, J. C. (1999). *The Sweet Potato Queens' book of love*. New York: Three Rivers Press.

Coles, G. (2006). *Advancing children's literacy requires starting with the right questions in the debate over literacy*. Awards Breakfast Speech. Pittsburgh, PA. College Reading Association.

Dewey, J. (1938/1963). *Experience and education*. New York: Collier Books.

Pearson, P. D. (2007). *The Knowledge to Support the Teaching of Literacy*. General Assembly Speech. Salt Lake City, UT. College Reading Association.

Rasinski, T. (2002). Effective reading instruction: What we know, what we need to know, and what we still need to do. In P. Linder, M. B. Sampson, J. A. Dugan, B. Brancato (Eds.), *Celebrating the Faces of Literacy: The 24th yearbook of the College Reading Association* (pp. 10-19). Readyville, TN: The College Reading Association

Reutzel, D. R., & Cooter, R. B. (2008). *Teaching children to read: The teacher makes the difference* (5th ed.). Upper Saddle River, NJ: Prentice Hall.

Rivenbark, C. (2000). *Bless your heart, tramp and other Southern endearments*. New York: St. Martin's Press.

Rivenbark, C. (2006). *Stop dressing your six-year-old like a skank: A slightly tarnished southern belle's words of wisdom*. New York: St. Martin's Press.

Tunnell, M. (2007). *Children of Topaz*. Author Presentation. Salt Lake City, UT. College Reading Association.

Vogt, M. E. (2007). *When the teacher's edition is not enough . . . Preparing tomorrow's teachers*. Awards Breakfast Speech. Salt Lake City, UT. College Reading Association.

Other Books by Browne and Rivenbark

Browne, J. C. (2008). *The Sweet Potato Queens' guide to raising children for fun and profit*. New York: Simon & Schuster.

Browne, J. C., & Gillespie, K. (2007). *The Sweet Potato Queens' first big ass novel: Stuff we didn't actually do, but could have, and may yet*. New York: Simon & Schuster.

Browne, J. C. (2005). *The Sweet Potato Queens' wedding planner/divorce guide*. New York: Crown Publishers.

Browne, J. C. (2004). *The Sweet Potato Queens' field guide to men: Every man I love is either married, gay, or dead*. New York: Three Rivers Press.

Browne, J. C. (2003). *The Sweet Potato Queens' big-ass cookbook and financial planner*. New York: Three Rivers Press.

Browne, J. C. (2001). *God save the Sweet Potato Queens*. New York: Three Rivers Press.

Rivenbark, C. (2004). *We're just like you, only prettier*. New York: St. Martin's Press.

So What's in a Word?
The Power of Words

D. Ray Reutzel

Utah State University

Presidential Address
College Reading Association
2008

Ray Reutzel has been an active member of CRA/ ALER since 1985. He has served the organization in many ways, including as editor of Reading, Research and Instruction *(now the* Literacy Research and Instruction*) and as Chair of the Research Awards Committee and former Board of Directors member. In 1999, CRA recognized Ray's numerous accomplishments selecting him as the recipient of the* A.B. Herr Award *for Outstanding Research and Published Contributions to Reading Education.*

He has authored more than 175 refereed research reports, articles, books, book chapters, and monographs and has been published in Early Childhood Research Quarterly, Reading Research Quarterly, Journal of Literacy Research, Journal of Educational Research, Reading Psychology, Reading Research and Instruction, Language Arts, Journal of Adolescent and Adult Literacy, *and* The Reading Teacher, *among others. Ray was the co-editor of* The Reading Teacher *from 2002-2007 and served as a member of the IRA Board of Directors from 2007-2010. In addition, he has received more than 5.5 million dollars in research/professional development funding from private, state, and federal funding agencies. Currently, Ray is the* Emma Eccles Jones Distinguished Professor and Endowed Chair of Early Childhood Education *at Utah State University.*

This presidential address asserts that words are central to the work of becoming literate. Words are not the only but surely among the most meaningful building blocks of language and literacy. Words are powerful. In this address, the focus is upon the power of six words in our lives—*paradox, teacher, change, label, laugh, and reading.*

As I have prepared for this speech over the past few months, I have reflected back upon the many erudite, insightful, moving, and entertaining CRA Presidential addresses given in the past. Last year, Ellen Jampole wowed us as she brought her southern wit along with her personal Sweet Potato Queen support group, and her CRA Boss Queen Wig and Tiara to the Crossroads of the West as we met in Salt Lake City. So, it seems only fair that I should bring the wit and wisdom of the west, my Jeff Foxworthy Redneck support group, and my Cowboy hat to the south as we meet here in Sarasota, Florida. So as the new self-declared CRA TRAIL BOSS, I declare this to be the final roundup of the College Reading Association after 50 wonderful years.

My talk today is entitled, "*So What's in a Word? The Power of Words.*" Words are central to the work of becoming literate. I am one of those people who when they get a new copy of *Reader's Digest* immediately turns to the long running and ever popular "Word Power" feature each month. Words are not the only but surely the most meaningful building blocks of language and literacy. Words are powerful. Today I want to just focus upon a few words, just eight words, seven if we don't count "the," as demonstrations of the power of words in our lives. So for a moment today, let us get carried away by the words. Years ago, Emily Dickinson (1924) wrote poignantly about the power of words in this poem:

> He ate and drank the precious words,
> His spirit grew robust;
> He knew no more that he was poor,
> Nor that his frame was dust.
> He danced along the dingy days,
> And this bequest of wings
> Was but a book. What liberty
> A loosened spirit brings!

The image of that young man in the picture, pouring over the words in a book is powerful. You and I, as literacy professionals, weave artfully the tapestry of literacy word by word.

So, let us begin our journey of words with a short story from one of my favorite books, *The Weighty Word Book*, by Levitt, Berger and Guralnick (1985), Professors of English at the University of Colorado, yup that's right, a western university! This wonderful book contains 26 stories that explain the meanings of 26 weighty words, one each for each letter of the English alphabet. The story I am about to share with you is the "P" word story. It is your job now, to see if you can figure out the "P" word before I reach the end of the story.

Paradox

Have you truly considered the power of the word—*paradox*? In a world, even a universe, composed of seemingly divinely or cosmically appointed opposites, how does considering the meaning of paradox help us live more wholly, peacefully, and joyfully? Parker Palmer, a Quaker Spiritualist, writer of such books as *To Know as We are Known: Education as a Spiritual Journey* (1993) and *The Courage to Teach: Exploring the Inner Landscape of a Teacher's Life* (1998) writes penetratingly about the concept of a paradox.

He reminds us of the dangers brought on by embracing and nurturing a polarizing culture. He reminds us that our Western commitment to thinking in polarities elevates disconnection "into an intellectual virtue." Palmer suggests, "Truth is not approximated best by splitting the world into endless *either-ors* but by embracing the world as a place of *both-and*." Palmer argues that, "We need to argue for the paradoxical—the joining of apparent opposites. We must very often learn to embrace opposites as one. Paradoxes need not be esoteric or exotic. They are found in our everyday living" (Palmer, 1998 p. 63).

Take, for example, breathing. Indeed, breathing itself is a form of paradox, requiring inhaling and exhaling to be whole. Imagine a vitriolic debate about the relative importance of exhaling and inhaling among respiratory therapists? Yet as a literacy profession, we often find colleagues forcefully representing either phonics or whole language as the cure for what ails kids in learning to read. As I have contemplated the notion of the joining of opposites such as we find in paradox, I find myself recently more of a mind to find the "win-win"; more willing to seek that place of wholeness in the joining of opposites as represented by the single word—paradox.

Teacher

Now onto the second word—*teacher*. I don't remember exactly when the moment came that I felt called to teach. Was it when I played school in the basement of our home where my mother had created a little school room complete with desks, bookshelves, and chalkboard? I am not sure? But I do remember a profound feeling that this was to be my life's vocation and avocation.

Frederick Buechner (1993) offers a generous and humane image of one's vocation as "the place where your deep gladness and the world's deep hunger meet" (Buechner, 1993, p. 119). Those of us in this room have chosen to make our contribution to alleviate the world's hunger through teaching the world to read and write, listen and hear, see and express. I also know that I did not find literacy as the focus of my teaching life, rather literacy found me. Parker Palmer (1998) in the *Courage to Teach* illustrates the power of the subject upon the teacher when he wrote:

> Knowing begins with our intrigue about some subject, but that intrigue is the result of the subject's action upon us: geologists are people who hear rocks speak, historians are those who hear the voices of the long dead, writers are people who hear the music of the words. (p.105)

Thus the teacher of literacy gladly feeds the world's deep hunger by helping others feel, hear, and sing the music of the words. A poem authored by Brod Bagert (1999. p. 8-9) in a book entitled, *Rainbows, Headlice, and Pea Green Tile: Poems in the Voice of the Classroom Teacher*, brings home this point far better than I. In his poem, *The Answer Machine*, Brod relates how a veteran teacher, one who was wondering about her life and calling as a teacher noticed the light flashing on her answering machine, and remembered why she had spent a lifetime teaching children to read.

Change

The next word on our journey of words is *change*. I was, truthfully, a bit hesitant to select this word since it has been so thoroughly used and abused in the recent presidential campaign by both sides. But if there is one constant in our lives as educators and researchers, it is embodied in the word—change. Last summer I was introduced to the contents of a book while attending the 3rd Annual Institute of Education Sciences Research Conference in Washington, D.C. The luncheon speaker was talking about the concept of "best practice" and how this idea had influenced the medical profession and was now creeping gradually into the education profession. The book, *Better* (2007) was authored by Atul Guwande who has also authored the book, *Complication: A Surgeon's notes on an Imperfect Science*. In the opening section of this book, entitled, "Diligence," Guwande details the difficulties of promoting change in the medical establishment. He writes about Dr. Ignac Semmelwies, who in 1847, deduced that by not washing their hands consistently or well enough, doctors and nurses were causing childbed fever in hospitals. Remember this was well before we knew about things called germs. Semmelwies had noted that 600 of 3000 women, 20%, who came to the hospital died after childbirth whereas women who remained at home to give birth died much less often, 30 women out of 3000, or 1%. He was determined to implement the "best practice" of hand washing in his hospital. He did so using somewhat dictatorial techniques which eventually cost him his job. But after a year of "diligence" in using the best practice of hand washing, Semmelwies had successfully lowered maternal death rates in the hospital to 30 women in 3000 or just 1%. Coupled with the later discovery of bacteria and viruses, one would expect that the medical profession would submit to the evidence-based practice of diligently washing its collective hands. But this is not the case. We read in Guwande's (2008) book that, "Our hospital's statistics show what studies everywhere else have shown—that we doctors and nurses wash our hands one-third to one-half as often as we are supposed to" (p.15). Change does not come easily in a profession. Like medicine, education is changing to make diligent use of effective, evidence-based practices in teaching literacy that will eventually become common place in classrooms.

And sometimes, change isn't all that transformative! In the writings of the western cowboy poet, Wallace McRae (1992), in his book entitled, *Cowboy Curmudgeon*, McRae writes of the changes associated with reincarnation.

Label

Our next word on the journey of words is *label*. Consider with me for a moment the power of labels—simple little words printed on a variety of goods and services we select or refuse every day. What is the difference between the labels—Cadillac and Yugo? Substantial, right. But how do labels work their magic upon our thinking? Take for example this box and label, Milkbone™ Crunchy Original Dog Treats. The label says—dog treats—which of course would never allow us, as people, to reach into this box and have treat. After all, it says dog food. I have here a new, unopened box of Milkbone™ Crunchy Original Dog Treats. Would you please open this new box for the others to see that it is indeed new and the contents are in fact dog treats? Thank you.

Would anyone like to join me in eating a dog treat? Why won't you eat one? Do you see how the label is limiting your thinking? Ah, the power of a label, just one little word, "dog" when attached to treats and we won't eat. Labels often obfuscate important details that are often over looked or outright dismissed. Labels tend to stop our thinking, obstruct investigation, and close down dialog. Once we label something or someone, it's as if the discussion has ended, the debate terminated, and the investigation ended. So, let's have a deeper look beyond the label. Let's examine the ingredients. Let's read and talk about them as I offer them again to you as the audience....

I often wonder how the power of labels act to constrain our thought rather than to liberate it. If it can be labeled, it can often be dismissed. How do the labels of disability or gifted or failing constrain our thought, limit our investigation, and cause us to refuse to see what lies beneath the surface of the label. We must be cautious so that we are not taken in by the mischief of words when masquerading as labels. Mahatma Gandhi reminds us that:

> Your beliefs become your thoughts. Your thoughts become your words. Your words become your actions. Your actions become your habits. Your habits become your values. Your values become your destiny. ((Gandhi, 1927)

Remember this demonstration of the power of labels. Think beyond the labels we put on things, ideas, people, beliefs, etc. For, if we are not vigilant about our use of labels, they may close our minds to beckoning possibilities and burgeoning human potential.

Laugh

Our next word along the road of our journey of words is, *laugh*. Laughter has often been referred to as the most powerful medicine known to humanity. In the spirit of this final CRA Western Reading Roundup where I am the CRA Trail Boss, we turn our attention to my fractured attempts at humor. As a westerner, we are often thought of as "rednecks" by those who live outside our region. Foxworthy offers many examples of Rednecks to define this particular human species more colorfully. For example, you might be a Redneck if....You burn your yard rather than mow it.

So in the spirit of Jeff Foxworthy, today I unveil a new form of Literacy humor in the genre of a true western Redneck. This new literacy form of humor should become known far and wide as "READNECK" jokes. Please note on the Redneck book cover the black editor's carrot indicating a change to the word Redneck to a new word—READNECK. To help you come to a more complete appreciation of the definition of the word, READNECK, let me offer a few examples for your sophisticated literary consumption....

You might be a READNECK if...
Your idea of a good read is the menu at the local diner.
You might be a READNECK if...
You read 20 minutes a day to your huntin' dog.
You might be a READNECK if...
When you're pregnant you get a tattoo on your belly that says—
READ TO YOUR BABY!
You might be a READNECK if...
You put a book in front of your TV and try to read it with the TV remote.
You might be a READNECK if...
You are caught reading a steamy romance novel in your driver's license photo.
You might be a READNECK if...
You expect to receive a Pan Pizza certificate from Pizza Hut when you return
your books to the public library.
You might be a READNECK if...
You put your copy of *Field and Stream* inside your Bible for readin' at church.
You might be a READNECK if...
You carry a canvas tote full of books for protection when rushing into
the exhibit hall opening at an IRA conference.

Reading

Now we move onto the one word we all came here to celebrate at this 50th Anniversary of CRA, read. To this end—*reading* and the teaching of *reading*, we here in this room have devoted a considerable portion of our lives. When I was in Canada this past winter speaking for a couple of days on an IRA Board assignment, I was told the following amusing anecdote about a young reader named Jake and his early reading experiences.

Learning to Read

Jake is 5 and learning to read.
He points at a picture in a zoo book and says,
"Look Mama! It's a frickin' Elephant!"
Deep breath…. "What did you call it?"
 "It's a frickin' Elephant, Mama! It says so on the picture!"
And so it does…..

A F R I C A N ELEPHANT

The word *read*, Ah, the mere thought of it conjures up such transformative and liberating power. Oprah Winfrey writes and talks frequently about her love of reading. She says,

"Reading opened the door to all kinds of possibilities for me. I loved books so much as a child, as they were my outlet to the world" (Winfrey, para. 5).

I love the music of the word—read as captured in the exceptionally well crafted story of Booker T. Washington by Marie Bradby (1995) in the children's book entitled, *More than Anything Else*. Frederick Douglass once observed as did Booker T. Washington, "Once you learn to read you will be forever free" (Douglass, 2008). Reading is truly the *hinge upon which the gate of social justice swings*!

And now, the two words for which you have more than likely patiently waited…the end. Indeed it is the end, then end of an era. At this meeting we say good-bye to an old friend—the name of the College Reading Association—a name that has come to represent, for many of us, an association of welcoming, nurturing, and friendly literacy colleagues. But alas, with every passing, there is a new birth. So in the spirit of our Western Reading Roundup, let's whoop and holler a bit for our new beginning as the Association of Literacy Educators and Researchers.

My time as President of this organization has drawn to a close and fortunately for you, my speech as well. So I close in the words of Wallace McRae (1992) in his western cowboy poem entitled, *Requiem*.

Thank you so much for the honor of serving you and this exceptional organization for the past several years—an organization which by any other name still smells as sweet!

References

Bagert, B. (1999). *Rainbows, head lice, and pea-green tile: Poems in the voice of the classroom teacher*. Gainesville, FL: Maupin House Publishing, Inc.

Beuchner, F. (1993). *Wishful thinking: A seeker's ABC*. San Francisco, CA: Jossey-Bass.

Bradby, M. (1995). *More than anything else*. New York: Orchard Books.

Dickinson, E. (1924). *Part One: Life, XXI. Complete Poems*. Retrieved January 19, 2010 from   http://www.bartleby.com/113/1099.html

Douglass, Frederick (2008). Quote taken from Abilene Christian University Archives. Retrieved January 20, 2010, from http://www.acu.edu/academics/library/reference/quotes.html

Foxworthy, J. (2008). *You might be a redneck if 2008 calendar*. Kansas City, MO: Andrews McMeel Publishing, LLC.

Gandhi, M. K. (1927). *An autobiography, or the story of my experiments with truth*. Ahmedabad, India: Navajivan Press.

Guwande, A. (2007). *Better: A surgeon's notes on performance*. New York: Picador.

Guwande, A. (2002). *Complications: A surgeon's notes on an imperfect science*. NY: Henry Holt & Co, LLC.

Levitt, P. M., Burger, D. A., Guralnick, E. S. (1985). *The weighty word book*. Longmont, CO: Bookmakers Guild, Inc.

McFeely, W. S. (2006). *Fredrick Douglass*. New York: W. W. Norton & Co., Inc.

McRae, W. (1992). *Cowboy curmudgeon and other poems*. Layton, UT: Gibbs Smith Publisher.

Palmer, P. J. (1993). *To know as we are known: Education as a spiritual journey*. San Francisco, CA: Jossey-Bass.

Palmer, P. J. (1998). *The courage to teach: Exploring the inner landscape of a teacher's life*. San Francisco, CA: Jossey-Bass.

Winfrey, O. (1991, February 21). Quote taken from her interview for the American Academy of Achievement. Retrieved from http://www.achievement.org/autodoc/page/win0int-

KEYNOTE ADDRESSES

INTRODUCTION TO KEYNOTE SPEECHES

Wayne M. Linek

Texas A&M University-Commerce

In order to capture trends in the field of reading and literacy, some keynote speeches presented at the annual CRA conferences are reprinted here. The speeches begin with Linda Gambrell's keynote presented at the 1994 CRA conference in New Orleans, Louisiana, titled, "Motivation Matters." Those who were present for keynote speeches over the years will fondly recall instances such as Wayne Otto's cutting humor as he said, "If the horse is dead, get off" when referring to ten dead (or should be dead) horses in the field of reading and literacy. Other notable inclusions are: Jeanne Chall's reflections on her life in reading, Susan Neuman's social constructivist view of family literacy, and Pat Edwards' reflections on her personal journey.

For those who prefer investigating political trends and issues, be sure to read Rona Flippo's call for finding consensus in our field to limit political and media attacks, Jim Hoffman's defense of teacher education and call for empirical research, and last but not least, Gerald Coles' treatise on asking the right question in the political debate over literacy. Coles' speech occurred during the highly charged political times of the George W. Bush presidency and some of the audience members walked out of the presentation. Coles' speech focused on his perception that educational forces associated with the Bush administration bound public figures and the general public in simplistic debates in order to deflect the real issues of the day. To give readers further insight into the nature of the political environment, Coles' speech was not published in the CRA Yearbook for fear of political reprisal. However, this keynote provides an historical perspective that was present during the CRA conference in Pittsburgh, Pennsylvania and across the nation in 2006.

Next, take some time to compare Donna Alvermann's 1998 predictions about politics, mentoring, motivation, and an organizational name change for CRA by the year 2020 to the reality of the Association of Literacy Educators and Researchers (ALER) of today. Finally, as with the presidential addresses, these keynote speeches are presented in chronological order so that readers can analyze them for trends over time.

MOTIVATION MATTERS

Linda B. Gambrell

University of Maryland
National Reading Research Center

Keynote Address
College Reading Association
1994

In recent years motivation has gained promi-
nence in numerous models of learning in an at-
tempt to explain why *different students expend*
different amounts of time and effort on academic
tasks (Borkowski, Can, Rellinger, and Pressley,
1990; Iran-Nejad, 1990; Pintrich and DeGroot,
1990; Prawat, 1989; Pressley, Borkowski, and
Schneider, 1987). Research supports the notion
that the depth and breadth of literacy learning
is influenced by a variety of motivational factors
(Ford, 1992; McCombs, 1991; Oldfather, 1993).
Currently, there is great interest in exploring mo-
tivational factors that are specifically associated
with reading motivation in both classroom and home contexts so that motivating
contexts for literacy learning can be created. In this paper a brief summary of
historical views of motivation is presented, followed by a review of current views
of motivation and discussion of some of the dilemmas associated with research
on reading motivation. This is followed by a discussion of a recent study, con-
ducted at the National Reading Research Center, focusing on elementary school
children's reading motivation (Gambrell, Palmer, and Codling, 1995).

The work reported herein is a National Reading Research Project of the
University of Georgia and University of Maryland. It was supported under the
Educational Research and Development Centers Program (PR/AWARD No.
117A20007) as administered by the Office of Educational Research and Im-
provement, U.S. Department of Education. The findings and opinions expressed

Reprinted from *Generations of Literacy.* pp. 2-24, by W. M. Linek and E. G. Sturtevant,
Eds, 1995, Commerce, Texas: College Reading Association

here do not necessarily reflect the position or policies of the National Reading Research Center, the Office of Educational Research and Improvement, or the U.S. Department of Education.

M otivation is currently acknowledged in the educational literature as a powerful and useful construct (Csikszentmihalyi, 1991; Ford, 1992; Mc-Combs, 1991; Wigfield and Asher, 1984). Teachers have long recognized that motivation is at the heart of many of the pervasive problems we face in educating today's youth. Research during the past two decades indicates that teachers rank *motivating students* as one of their primary and overriding concerns (O'Flahavan, Gambrell, Guthrie, Stahl, and Alvermann, 1992; Veenman, 1984). There also is abundant research to support the contention that motivation plays a major role in learning (Deci and Ryan, 1985; Dweck and Elliott, 1983; McCombs, 1989). It appears that there is an almost universal consensus that motivation matters. Motivation often makes the difference between learning that is superficial and shallow and learning that is deep and internalized. Clearly, we need to direct our efforts to more fully understanding how children acquire the motivation to develop into active, engaged readers (Guthrie, Schafer, Wang, Afflerbach, 1993; Oldfather, 1993).

The construct of motivation has numerous and competing conceptualizations. For example, Kuhl (1986) used the term to designate all latent and aroused goal states which drive, orient, and select behavior at any given point in time. Wittrock (1986) defined motivation as the process of initiating, sustaining, and directing activity. Maehr (1976) focused on the concept of *continuing motivation*, which he defined as the tendency to return to and continue working on tasks away from the instructional context in which they were initially presented. Most motivational theorists identify two types of motivation: extrinsic and intrinsic (Deci and Ryan, 1985; Lepper, 1988). Behavior is said to be extrinsically motivated when it is done to satisfy some external goal, such as doing well on a spelling test in order to earn the privilege of a Saturday outing. Intrinsically motivated behavior, on the other hand, is characterized by a desire to engage in an activity because doing so brings personal satisfaction.

Researchers have recently begun to view motivation as a phenomenon of "thinking" (Corno & Snow, 1986; McCombs, 1991; Weiner, 1985; Winne, 1985). This conceptualization of motivation focuses on how children think about themselves as readers, how they think about the reading task, and their reasons and purposes for engaging in reading tasks and activities.

Psychologists, researchers, and educators have long been interested in the role of motivation in learning. The early psychoanalytic theorists, such as Freud (1901/1951), posited that motivation is related to basic biological drives or instincts that cause individuals to behave in certain ways. The basic tenet that internal forces influence human behavior is still recognized in contemporary theories of motivation (Ford, 1992). Behaviorists, such as Skinner (1953), later viewed individuals as "blank slates" on which experiences (external events) conditioned and shaped behavior. While this theoretical view is behavioral in orientation and does not recognize cognition and affective experience, it does highlight important principles about how feedback to the learner can influence the selection of goals and the means used to attain those goals. Later, psychologists such as Rogers (1961) and Maslow (1970) put forth the view that individuals have an inborn propensity for growth that is fostered through learning, natural development, and significant others. These theorists focused attention on motives associated with learning, and their work resulted in the development of "self" theories which emphasize the strong and pervasive human need for positive social- and self-evaluations. Recently, cognitive, socio-cognitive, and social theorists have extended and refined these earlier theories and more integrative conceptualizations of motivation have emerged in the literature (Ford, 1992; McCombs, 1989).

A number of contemporary theories of motivation emphasize the importance of self-perception in learning (Dweck, 1986; McCombs, 1989; Weiner, 1990; Wigfield, 1994). Motivation is viewed as a function of the individual's *learned* beliefs about his or her worth, abilities, or competencies. A vast body of research (Bandura, 1989; Covington, 1985; Dweck, 1986; Eccles et al.1983; Weiner, 1990; Wigfield, 1994) supports the contention that learned self-beliefs, expectations, and goals are critical factors that affect motivation and performance.

Ford's (1992) motivational systems theory centers on three aspects of motivation: personal beliefs, emotional processes, and personal goals. *Personal beliefs* are reflected in capability beliefs and context beliefs. Capability beliefs are self-evaluations about whether one has the capabilities needed to attain a goal, while context beliefs are evaluations of whether the environment or context will facilitate goal attainment. Taken together, capability beliefs and context beliefs provide the individual with information that guides decisions about initiating, maintaining, or avoiding learning activities.

According to Ford (1992), *emotional processes* provide an individual with evaluative information about personal values. Emotional processes result in an "energization" of behavior that is reflected in what "turns someone on" or "turns them off," what one likes or does not like, what one *values* or does not *value*. The clarity and saliency of personal values influences what is learned and remembered.

Personal goals represent desired future learning outcomes. The term "personal goal" is emphasized because the goals that direct an individual's activity are *always* within the person (Weiner, 1990). An individual's goals or *reasons* for engaging in an activity are often contextual in that people will adopt many of the goals shared by other individuals in their environment as well as those assigned by authority figures or significant others such as parents or teachers.

In summary, Ford's (1992) motivational systems theory suggests that people will always try to attain goals they value within the limitations of what they think they can achieve based on their capability and context beliefs. This notion is consistent with Winne and Marx's (1982) assertion that a positive state of motivation is a necessary condition for learning. In keeping with Winne's (1985) theory of motivation, the "idealized" reader feels competent as a reader, values reading, chooses to read, and engages in reading activities with intensity.

A number of these current theories suggest that self-perceived competence and task value are major determinants of motivation and task engagement (Eccles et al.1983; Pintrich & Degroot, 1990; Wigfield, 1994). Eccles and colleagues (1983) and Wigfield (1994) have advanced an "expectancy-value" theory of motivation that posits that motivation is strongly influenced by one's expectation of success or failure at a task as well as the value or relative attractiveness the individual places on the task. The expectancy component of this expectancy-value theory is supported by a number of research studies that suggest that students who *believe* they are capable and competent readers are more likely to outperform those who do not hold such beliefs (Paris & Oka, 1986; Schunk, 1985). In addition, there is evidence to suggest that students who perceive reading as valuable and important and who have personally relevant reasons for reading will engage in reading in a manner that includes more planning and effort (Ames & Archer, 1988; Dweck & Elliott, 1983; Paris & Oka, 1986).

While it is a generally accepted notion that motivation plays a central role in reading development, a review of the *Annual Summary of Investigations Relating to Reading* (International Reading Association,1985-1992) revealed relatively few studies related to motivation and reading development. While motivation was not listed as a descriptor in the *Summary,* studies related to motivation were found under related descriptors. From 1985 to 1992, the mean number of studies of motivation was only 9 studies per year. Given the vast amount of research on reading, it appears that relatively little attention has been devoted to the topic of motivation to read.

Framing a Study to Explore the Reading Motivation of Elementary Students

Prior research on the reading motivation of elementary students has focused more generally on attitudes toward reading and specific variables such as gender differences, grade level differences, and to a lesser extent, differences according to reading proficiency level. A number of studies have revealed that girls have more positive attitudes towards reading than do boys (Anderson, Tollefson, & Gilbert,1985; Hansen,1969; Johnson,1973; Greaney & Neuman,1990; Ross & Fletcher,1989; Stevenson & Newman,1986) and that younger children have more positive attitudes toward reading than do older students (Anderson, Tollefson, & Gilbert, 1985; Greaney & Neuman, 1990; Ishikawa, 1985; Parker & Paradis, 1986; Saracho & Dayton, 1991). In addition, recent research by McKenna, Kear, and

Ellsworth (in press) reveals that while above average and average ability readers' attitudes toward reading remain fairly stable, the attitudes of below average readers steadily decrease as they progress through the elementary grades.

Roettger (1980) conducted one of the few studies in the literature specifically designed to explore complex relationships between attitude and reading achievement. The study revealed that high attitude/low achievement students had different expectations of reading when compared with the low attitude/high achievement students. The high achievement/low attitude students viewed reading as a means of gaining information to help them get good grades and perform well in school, while low achievement/high attitude students viewed reading as a way of pursuing specialized personal interests.

During the past four years my colleagues and I have been involved in a series of studies designed to explore elementary students' motivation to read. The studies were framed within the expectancy-value theory of motivation (Eccles et al.1983; Wigfield, 1994) and were designed to explore the roles of self-concept and value in motivation to read as well as more personal dimensions of motivation as reflected in specific reading experiences.

The methodology employed in the primary study was designed to overcome some of the limitations of existing motivational research. First, most of the research to date on literacy motivation has consisted of a single interview procedure. This is not a trivial concern given that motivation to read may be influenced by a large number of variables which may fluctuate across time and context. In this study both a Likert-scale Reading Survey instrument and two Conversational Interviews were used to collect data. One interview focused on narrative reading experiences, while the other focused on reading informational text. Our review of the research on reading motivation confirmed that prior research has primarily focused on motivation as it relates to the reading of narrative text, and few studies have specifically explored the role of text type in the reading motivation of elementary age children.

Another problem inherent in most of the motivation research in reading is that reading ability is a confounding variable, and as such, in research designs "highly motivated" readers are typically identified as proficient, higher ability readers, while "less motivated" readers are identified as less proficient, lower ability readers. We know that this conceptualization is inaccurate (Roettger, 1980), and that there are proficient readers who are not motivated to read, just as there are less proficient readers who are highly motivated to read.

The methodology we employed in this study for exploring young children's motivation to read was guided by the work of Burgess (1980) and his conceptualization of unstructured interviews as conversations and Silverman's (1993) theory of interactionism. According to Burgess (1980) interviews are encounters between human beings trying to understand one another. In his view, conversational interviews should be treated as social events based on mutual participation by the interviewer and the informant. One reason for using conversational interviews is that they can provide greater depth of information than other techniques (Burgess, 1980). In this study, both a survey instrument and conversational interviews were used to collect data.

Participants and Setting

The students who participated in this study were third- and fifth-graders from 4 schools in two Maryland counties. All teachers and third- and fifth-grade students in the 30 classrooms were invited to participate. Data from 3 classrooms were omitted from the final analysis because guidelines for administration of the Reading Survey were not followed. The final sample consisted of 330 third- and fifth-grade students from 27 classrooms who responded to the Reading Survey and 48 students, drawn from the larger pool of subjects, who participated in the two Conversational Interviews.

One county was described by the participating school principals as agriculturally-based with growing bedroom communities. The other county was described as a growing metropolitan area by one principal and as rural, with pockets of bedroom communities, by the other principal. Though school principals indicated a range of socioeconomic levels was represented, every school was described as middle class, with approximately 23% of students eligible for the federal free-lunch program. All four schools housed grades K-5, but student populations ranged in number from 340 to 820. There were 8 third-grade classrooms and 9 fifth-grade classrooms in the two schools in one county; 7 third-grade classrooms and 6 fifth-grade classrooms in the two schools in the other county. Schools in both counties were predominantly Caucasian, with a minority population of approximately 30% in one county and 9% in the other county.

During the sixth week of school, teachers were asked to provide information about their reading program and students. With regard to the reading program description, teachers were provided with a list of seven descriptors (Gambrell, 1992) and were asked to indicate which descriptor best matched their reading program. If the basic program was supplemented in some way, teachers indicated the way in which they individually modified their program. The majority of the fifth-grade teachers (8/13) reported that basals served as the core of reading instruction with supplemental use of children's literature. The remaining fifth-grade teachers reported that children's literature served as the core material used in reading instruction. The majority of the third-grade teachers (10/14) reported that children's literature was at the core of their reading instruction. The remaining third-grade teachers reported using basals as the core material for reading instruction.

The use of teacher ratings of students' reading proficiency and motivational levels was an important feature of this study. According to Marsh, Smith, and Barnes (1983) these ratings are reasonable indicators of student performance and motivation because elementary classroom teachers

(a) spend the entire school day with their students and therefore have considerable contact with them,

(b) are exposed to a wide variety of children, usually in heterogeneously-grouped classrooms, as was the case in this study,

(c) have experience in making professional judgments about individual students; and

(d) are likely to have a variety of opportunities to observe behaviors relevant to both reading achievement and motivation to read. There is a considerable body of recent research that indicates that classroom teachers are reasonably accurate and reliable in estimating student achievement (Coladarci, 1986; Egan & Archer, 1985; Hoge & Butcher, 1984). In addition, prior research has provided evidence of substantial agreement between teacher ratings of students' self-concepts and self-reports by students (Perkins, 1958; Phillips, 1963).

At the conclusion of the sixth week of the academic year teachers were asked to indicate the reading proficiency level of their students (above-grade, on-grade, and below-grade level) and, within each reading proficiency level, to identify two motivated and two unmotivated students. Throughout this paper we use the terms "highly motivated" and "less motivated" in keeping with McCombs (1991) theoretical position that all students are motivated and that it is the *relative strength* of the motivational state that is of interest. Informal conversations with teachers in the participating schools suggested, however, that for the purposes of this study the terms "motivated" and "unmotivated" would be less ambiguous and more useful in making judgments about students' motivation to read. Teachers in this study did not report any concerns about making these judgments.

From the teacher-generated lists, a subset of 48 students was randomly selected to participate in conversational interviews about motivation to read. Equal numbers were drawn from each of the following subgroups for both grade levels and both counties: Motivated Above-Grade, Motivated On-Grade, Motivated Below-Grade, Unmotivated Above-Grade, Unmotivated On-Grade, and Unmotivated Below-Grade. In one county, however, teachers were unable to initially identify any fifth-grade students as below-grade level motivated readers. One month later (mid-November) a follow-up letter was sent to these teachers requesting the identification of any motivated, below-grade level readers in their classrooms. As a result three students were identified, but only one had parental permission to participate in the study. A motivated below-grade level student was then identified from the other county, resulting in a stratified random selection of 24 highly-motivated readers and 24 less-motivated readers across the three reading levels.

Materials

The *Motivation to Read Profile (MRP)* was developed for this study (Gambrell, Palmer, Codling, & Mazzoni, in press). The MRP consists of two parts:

the *Reading Survey* and the *Conversational Interview.* The *Reading Survey* is a 20-item, 4 point Likert-type response scale designed to assess self-concept as a reader (10 items) and value of reading (10 items). The *Conversational Interview* is a scripted, open-ended instrument designed to tap information related to the reading of narrative and informational text and a range of personal factors related to reading motivation. (For a complete description of this instrument see Gambrell, Palmer, Codling, & Mazzoni, 1995).

The internal consistency of the *Reading Survey,* using Cronbach's alpha statistic, was calculated for grades 3 and 5 (Cronbach, 1951, 1988). Cronbach reliability coefficients for the third grade and fifth grade were as follows: Self-Concept as a Reader, third grade = .70, fifth grade = .74; Value of Reading, third grade = .69, fifth grade = .77.

In an additional step to validate the *MRP,* questions which tapped similar information on both the survey instrument and the interview were identified. There was corroborating information available from interview items for 55% of the items on the *MRP.* The responses of two motivated and two unmotivated students at each grade level were randomly selected for analysis to determine consistency of responses between the survey and the interview. Two raters independently compared each student's responses to related items, with an interrater agreement of .87. Consistency was measured by comparing the consistency of the students' response on the *MRP* items and their responses on the interview between the *MRP* and the interview. The consistency across the two measures was .70.

Procedure

Data were collected for the study at three points across the school year using the *Motivation to Read Profile.* The *Reading Survey* was administered in the late fall to 330 third and fifth grade students in 27 classrooms. The *Conversational Interviews* were conducted in early winter and in the spring with a stratified random sample of 48 third and fifth grade students. Each student participated in two interviews.

Data Analysis

The analysis conducted on the Likert-scale Reading Survey instrument reflected a 2 (self-concept, value) x 3 (reading level) x 2 (gender) factorial design. Analysis of variance procedures, t-tests, and chi-square analyses were used, and where appropriate, Tukey post hoc analyses were conducted.

Three separate and distinct analyses were conducted with the interview data. All protocols were transcribed by question so that responses to each question could be scrutinized for patterns and themes. First, the interview data were analyzed with regard to responses that were relevant to the three constructs measured by the *Motivation to Read Profile* (self-concept as a reader, value of reading). Second, where appropriate, responses were tabulated and frequencies were calculated in an attempt to reveal patterns of responses. Third, the constant comparative method of analysis (Strauss and Corbin, 1990) was used for conceptualizing and categorizing data through open coding. Two researchers read all responses to each question and identified emerging patterns and categories of responses.

Results and Discussion

The findings of this study were derived from analyses conducted on student responses to the *Motivation to Read Profile (MRP)*. First, the results relative to performance on the *Reading Survey* (Likert-scale instrument) will be presented, then the results of the analyses of the interview responses will be described.

What the Results of the Motivation to Read Profile
Reveal About Elementary Students

Our analysis of the MRP was guided by a number of questions about young children's motivation to read. In this next section I discuss our findings with respect to our guiding questions.

What do elementary students feel most competent about with respect to reading? Not surprisingly, the results of the analysis of the items related to self-concept as a reader revealed that third and fifth grade students reported feeling most competent about their ability to understand what they read and their ability to figure out unfamiliar words. When we looked at the items that were rated lowest by students, an interesting pattern emerged. Students reported feeling less competent with respect to social interactions and public displays of their reading competence. For example, responses at both grade levels revealed that students feel less competent about discussing their reading with others and their oral reading performance.

What do elementary students value most with respect to reading? One interesting finding with respect to the value of reading was that both third and fifth graders placed a high value on receiving books as gifts and having access to lots of books at home and school. On the other hand, students did not perceive their peers as valuing reading.

How are third and fifth-graders similar and different with respect to motivation to read? As revealed in prior research (McKenna, Kear & Filsworth, in press) the third graders were more positive than the fifth-graders; however, the pattern of responses was remarkably similar with respect to their responses about self-concept as a reader. Our analysis did, however, reveal some interesting differences in the pattern of responses across grade levels with respect to value of reading. For example, third graders were more positive than fifth graders with respect to choosing reading as a pleasure activity, viewing people who read often as interesting people, and spending time in the library.

Does motivation to read differ by reading ability groups? When we looked at responses by reading ability level (above grade level, on grade level, and below grade level) there was a statistically significant difference among the reading ability groups with respect to self-concept as a reader. Responses of students reading below grade level in both third and fifth grade were lower in self-perceived reading competence. In addition, at the third grade level, there were ability level differences with respect to self-perceived competence relative to peers, decoding ability, oral reading, and responding to questions about reading, with the below grade level students reporting lower self-perceived competence compared to the on grade level and above grade level groups. There were no statistically significant differences among reading ability groups with respect to value of reading. This finding raises some interesting questions with respect to the expectancy-value theories of motivation. Perhaps self-concept is a more critical factor in the motivation of children than is the construct of value. In this study, elementary students, in general, seemed to place a high value on reading; however, significant differences in motivation were apparent across reading ability groups with respect to self-perceived competence.

What the Results of Conversational Interviews
Reveal About Motivation to Read

Forty-eight third- and fifth-grade students, 22 males and 26 females, were selected as key informants who participated in two in-depth, conversational interviews. Student responses to the questions posed during the Conversational Interview revealed information about text, school, and home influences on motivation to read.

What children told us about reading narrative text. When we asked the children in our study to tell us about "the most interesting story/book you have read this week," 3 third-grade students were unable to describe a narrative reading experience; however, all fifth-grade students were able to do so. Two of the fifth-graders reported they had not read any stories/books "this week" but they were able to discuss reading done during the previous week.

In response to the request to tell us about the most interesting story/ book they had read, 45 of the 48 students were able to describe in detail something they had read that they found interesting. Of the stories mentioned, 25% were series books. In the course of telling about the story/book, 13% of the children spontaneously mentioned teacher influence (teacher had read the book aloud, teacher mentioned the book, etc.). Several children also spontaneously mentioned liking adventure, mysteries, and series books. When asked about why the particular story/book they identified was "most interesting," children responded in terms of personal interest (25%), story action (23%), and one child mentioned the writing style of the author.

When the children were asked about their "most interesting" story/book, 88% reported that they self-selected the book. Over 60% of these children reported that they chose the book from the classroom or school library. The primary reasons children offered for choosing the particular story/book were personal interest (15%), someone recommended it (10%), interest in a particular genre (10%), and fondness for series books (6%). Interestingly, only 10% reported that the "most interesting" story was one that had been assigned by the teacher.

Over 78% of the children reported having an "all time favorite book." Over 10% of the children mentioned series books as "all time favorites." Over 63% of the children were able to name and discuss a favorite author's book or books. Additionally, 25% of the children named authors of series books as their "favorite author." Only 12% were able to name and discuss the work of a favorite illustrator.

When asked, "Do you know about any books or stories you would like to read?" approximately 70% of the children were able to tell about such books. When asked why they wanted to read these books, 46% mentioned interesting titles, 14% of which were series books. Children reported that they found out about these books from family members (19%), teachers (4%) and friends (4%), by reading other titles by the same author (13%), and from browsing in the classroom or school library (8%).

What children told us about reading expository text. In response to the initial probe to "tell about a time that you read to learn or find out about something . . . something important that you learned recently, not from your teacher and not from television," 5 of the 24 third-grade and 2 of the 24 fifth-grade children were unable to provide a description of a reading experience of an informational nature. One third-grade and one fifth-grade student initially responded with renditions of narrative reading experiences. Of most interest was the finding that 5 third-grade and 6 fifth-grade students could not think of any expository reading they had done recently; however, they responded with references to expository reading they had done in the previous grade, with one third-grade student referring to something he read in kindergarten.

Approximately 40% of the children were able to provide general information about their informational reading, while only 30% were able to provide specific in-depth information about what they had read. Children reported that the informational reading they had done was of interest to them because it was about animals (30%), science/environment (20%), history (17%), and hobbies or sports (10%). Children reported reading primarily informational trade books (77%), encyclopedias (10%), and one child reported reading the newspaper.

When asked how they found out about their "most interesting" informational book/material, 62% reported they self-selected the reading material, while 18% reported it had been assigned by the teacher. Children who self-selected the book/material reported the material was chosen because of interest in the topic (27%), it was important to learn the information (17%), or it was a required assignment (4%).

Home Influences on Young Children's Motivation to Read
When asked about where they read their "most interesting" story/book, children reported that they did the reading at home (56%), school (27%), and

library (4%). When asked where they did most of the reading of their "most interesting" informational book/material, 50% of the children reported they read the informational book/material at home and 35% reported they did the reading at school.

Approximately 65% of the children reported that their favorite place to read at home was in their bedroom, and 80% of these children reported keeping books on a shelf or in a drawer in their bedrooms. When children were asked about how they acquired the books they own, 65% reported they received them as gifts, 16% received them through a book club, and only 10% reported buying books with their own money.

In response to the question, "Did you read anything at home yesterday?," 28 out of 48 children (58%) answered "yes." Of these 28 children, 25 were able to give specific titles or information about their home reading. Fifty-six percent of the children reported spending time reading homework assignments, and approximately 45% of the children reported that they read for pleasure before going to bed at night.

Seventy-five percent of the children reported talking to family members about their reading. Parents were mentioned by 69% (with the mother being mentioned in the overwhelming number of cases), siblings by 15%, others, such as grandparents and caregivers were mentioned by 15%. Over 80% of the children indicated that they were reading a book at home for fun at the time of the interview. Only one child reported owning no books or magazines at home, while 20% reported owning over 100 books, 42% reported owning more than 20, and 35% reported owning fewer than 20. Seventy-seven percent of the students reported owning magazines.

When asked about "good memories about learning to read" children told about pleasant and supportive reading experiences with parents (60%), teachers (21%), and others such as grandparents and caregivers (10%) and siblings (6%). When asked about "unpleasant memories about learning to read" children shared experiences involving parents (10%) and teachers (4%). Finally, when asked "Who gets you excited about reading books and stories?" children identified parents (60%), teachers (23%), others such as grandparents and caregivers (27%), siblings (15%), and friends (15%). Approximately 12% reported that there really wasn't anyone who got them excited about books or stories.

School Influences on Young Children's Motivation to Read

Most children (73%) indicated that they talked with someone at school about the books/stories they read. Of the 35 children who reported talking with others at school about reading, 69% indicated they talked with friends, 15% talked with teachers, and 4% reported talking with others such as the principal and parent volunteers.

When asked, "Do you have any books in your desk right now at school that you are reading for fun?" over 70% of the students responded positively. All of the children were able to name the title of the book or provide specific information about it. Twelve of the children reported having more than one book in their desk for personal reading and five children specifically mentioned series books.

When asked about the reading of their "most interesting" informational books/materials, most of the children reported finding the book/material in the classroom or school library (63%). When asked to describe the reading they did throughout the school day, the children reported reading in the following areas: language arts/reading (75%), math (39%), science (23%), social studies (23%) and other areas such as music, physical education, art (22%). When asked about reading during the school day, children reported that reading math (19%) and social studies (13%) texts was the most boring. The finding that children in this study perceived that math was second only to reading and language arts with respect to time being spent on reading was somewhat surprising, as was their report that reading in math was the most boring.

Over 20% of the children reported that there was time to read in the morning before school work was started, and 8% of the students reported that they had time to read when their work was finished. Most importantly, 88% of the children reported that there was some time during the school day when they could read whatever they wanted to read. Only 2 children reported doing reading in the school library during the previous day.

This study explored elementary students' motivation to read with respect to self-concept as a reader, value of reading and personal dimensions of reading as revealed in conversational interviews about reading. One of the major findings derived from this study is that there was abundant confirming information across the results of the *Motivation to Read Profile (Reading Survey* and *Conversational Interview)* with respect to young children's motivation to read. Approximately 50% of the items on the *Reading Survey* were probed during the interview sessions. An analysis of the consistency of the children's responses revealed that in 70% of the cases, consistent information was provided across the two measures. While the *Reading Survey* provided basic information about elementary students' self-concepts as readers and the value they place on reading, the interviews provided richer and fuller descriptions of the motivational reading experiences of elementary school students.

Self Concept as a Reader

Self-perceived competence is thought to be a critical factor in learning (Bandura, 1989; McCombs, 1989, 1991). The results of the Self-Concept as a Reader Scale indicated that while most elementary students in this study reported that they are "very good readers" (47%), significant numbers of students do not perceive themselves as competent readers. For example,

- 45% reported, "I worry about what other kids think about my reading almost every day."
- 17% reported, "When I read out loud I feel embarrassed/sad."
- 17% reported, "I am an OK/poor reader."

Value of Reading

The results of the Value of Reading Scale suggested that, in general, elementary students view reading as being of high value, as revealed in the following responses:

- 84% reported, "Knowing how to read well is very important."
- 82% reported, "People who read a lot are interesting."
- 68% reported, "I talk to my friends about good books I read."
- 65% reported, "I would like for my teacher to read out loud to the class every day."
- 61% reported, "When someone gives me a book for a present I feel very happy."

Several responses on the Value of Reading Scale, however, pointed to the fact that, for some children, reading is not viewed as a positive activity or as an activity of high priority, as revealed in the following responses:

- 14% reported, "I will spend very little/none of my time reading when I grow up."
- 10% reported, "People who read are boring."
- 10% reported, "My best friends think reading is no fun at all."
- 8% reported, "Libraries are a boring place to spend time."

The conversational interviews yielded several additional insights about elementary children's motivation to read. Four powerful influences on elementary children's motivation to read were revealed—repeated experiences with books, social interactions about books, book access, and choice.

Repeated Experiences with Books

The importance of repeated experiences with books was revealed throughout the interviews as children talked about why they engaged in reading. Children described reading books previously read aloud by parents or teachers, reading books they had seen on television and in the movies, and reading series books which provide a particular kind of repeated reading experience. These repeated experiences may be closely linked to self-perceived competence in that they provide essential scaffolding necessary for successful reading experiences (Feitelson, Goldstein, Iraqi, & Share, 1993; Vygotsky, 1978). The following examples of children's comments reveal the significance of repeated experience with text, even for older students:

"...I like the Little Mermaid (movie) and I like reading it (the book)."

"...I saw it on *Reading Rainbow...*"

"...I read it after the teacher read it aloud..."

"...I've been reading a book for November and I'm going to still read it for December and it's called *Mouse and the Motorcycle...* we read it in school before...and my mom bought it (from book club)."

"...I want to read *Stuart Little*...my mom read it to us..."

"...I'm rereading that book *(White Fang)* and the bird book."

"...I heard it on tape...my Uncle brought it for me."

One of the most frequently occurring themes throughout the interviews was the compelling nature of series books, which provide repeated experiences of a special nature with characters, setting and general story structure remaining consistent and providing familiarity, while the plot provides new and challenging information. The following comments reflect the highly motivating quality of these books.

"...Well, I'm reading *My Teacher Glows in the Dark* and it's really cool cause he's telling his friend what happened when his teacher took him to outer space...it's good and it's the sequel to *My Teacher is an Alien* and *My Teacher Fried My Brain.*"

"...third one I've read out of 15."

"...they have a whole bunch of these books out like Kristen, Molly, and *Samantha* [American Girls series] . . . I really like reading those books..."

"...I like the Babysitter's Club books . . ."

"...I have a whole set of them [referring to a series]..."

"...I want to read more Boxcar children...I got the first one at the book fair."

"...there's four to the series...I'm on the second..."

"...my sister had a set (of the series) ..."

Social Interactions about Books

The interviews revealed that children place a high priority on social interaction associated with reading books and talking about them with friends, parents, and teachers. The interviews also supported the primary influence of social interaction on young children's motivation to read (Guthrie, Schafer, Wang, & Afflerbach, 1993). Throughout the interviews children talked about hearing about books from teachers, friends, and parents, as the following examples show.

"...my friend Kristin was reading it and told me about it and I said, Hmmm, that sounds pretty interesting."

"...my friend told me about it."

"...I got interested in it because the other group, I'm in the lower reading group and I heard the other group reading it so I checked it out in the library."

"...I want to read [those books]...my teacher told me about them."

"...I heard about them from my teachers...they read good books to us..."

Book Access

Both the survey and the interviews pointed to the importance of book access and book ownership in motivation to read. Having many opportunities for book borrowing and having personal libraries at home appear to be important influences on motivation to read. Recent research by Elley (1992) supports the strong link between reading achievement and book access.

Book Borrowing. Book access for the children in this study was primarily through borrowing from their classroom libraries, pointing to the importance of providing book-rich classrooms (Fractor, Woodruff, Martinez, & Teale, 1993; Morrow, 1992). Children also mentioned a number of other important avenues for obtaining books as the following responses illustrate.

"...I got it from the YMCA bookmobile."

"...got it from the school library."

"...my teacher got books and she asked me to pick one."

"...I got it from the reading specialist...picked it from her collection of Bill Peet books."

Books as Gifts and Book Ownership. All but one of the children in this study reported having their own personal libraries at home. When children were asked how they accumulated their personal libraries, the overwhelming majority reported that they received books as gifts from a wide range of individuals, primarily parents, but almost as frequently mentioned were aunts, uncles, and grandparents, as the following examples illustrate:

"...they were gifts from family members."

"...I beg my Grandma [to buy them]...as gifts"

"...gifts from my uncle and grandfather..."

"...I got them as gifts for Christmas and birthdays..."

On the survey instrument the responses of both third- and fifth-graders indicated that receiving books as gifts was highly desirable. The interviews also revealed that children's book ownership is closely linked to receiving books as gifts. This finding suggests that there is a need for future research to explore incentive programs that give books as a reward (e.g., the 1st grade "Running Start Program" sponsored by Reading is Fundamental) and ways that schools can promote book ownership.

In addition, two children reported having books "handed down" to them by older siblings or cousins. One child said, "I trade with my brothers and people at school...I take anything I can get my hands on!" Another child reported, "My cousin had to move...she handed them down to me."

Book Clubs. Book clubs and incentive programs were also mentioned by a number of children who reported owning larger numbers of books in their personal libraries.

"...I got them from the Troll Book Club ..."

"...I got them from Book It ..."

"...I get 2 or 3 books from Troll Book Club each time."

Choice

The role of choice in motivation in general and reading motivation in particular is well recognized (Spaulding, 1992). In the present study, the survey and the interviews conducted consistently revealed that children are more motivated to read when they choose their own reading materials. For third graders and fifth graders, in particular, self-selection was revealed to be a significant positive factor on the Reasons for Reading Scale. When telling about the "most interesting" narratives and informational texts they had read, children consistently reported they had *chosen* the books. Over 25% of the children indicated that they had selected a book because a teacher or friend had recommended it, told them about it, or the teacher had read it out loud to the class. Children's responses in this study suggest an important relationship between self-selection (choice) and social interaction about books.

The results of this study suggest that there are important differences between children's motivation to read narrative and expository texts. First, almost every child in this study responded immediately and enthusiastically to the request to tell about "the most interesting story/book you have read this week." This was not the case when asked to tell about reading that was informational in nature. Many students had difficulty thinking of anything they had read recently that was informational and a large percentage could only refer to reading that had been done in previous years.

Many of the children who responded readily to the request about informational text were excited and interested in sharing this information. When describing the pleasure and excitement she experienced from reading about a topic in an encyclopedia, one student said, "I don't know why, but I've always been the kind of person to want to, at the flash of a moment, get information...I just crave for information." Other students linked their informational reading to their narrative reading on particular topics. For example, one child described her reading about World War II in the encyclopedia and then proceeded to tell about a related book she had read. She commented, "...and I found out, more from a child's point of view [by reading the narrative book, as compared to the informational text],...her best friend is Jewish and they're trying to get her away from the soldiers . . . you could see how the times were complicated...it was,...I don't know how to say it,...it was just tragic, you know? I like reading about characters and how the authors take real life and put it into their own fiction."

In an earlier study, Leal (1992) reported that elementary children found "infotainment" books—books that are both informational and entertaining— more engaging than either narrative or expository texts. Recently, Pappas (1993) reported that even kindergarten children demonstrated a preference for informational books. The reluctance with which children in the present study responded to the interview questions about informational texts suggests that future research is needed that will focus on motivational aspects related to young children's reading of expository texts.

Perhaps the most interesting and most significant finding from this study was revealed in our analysis of the data from the 48 children who served as key informants by participating in the conversational interviews with the researchers. These 48 children represented differing reading ability groups (above grade, on grade, and below grade level) and different motivational levels (motivated and unmotivated). We expected to find that children who were rated as highly motivated, good readers would have remarkably different responses than would poor readers who were rated as unmotivated. What we found, however, was in keeping with McComb's (1991) position that motivation to learn is a human state and that everyone is motivated to some extent. Our interviews with third and fifth grade students provide compelling evidence that all the children in our study were motivated to read; however, some were more motivated than others.

One truly remarkable finding from our study was that good and poor readers were motivated by the same environmental and social factors. When we asked children questions about personal dimensions of motivation (i.e.,"What have you read lately that was really interesting?" "Where did you get the book?" "Why did you choose that book?" "Who gets you excited about reading?"), their answers were far more similar than different. In other words, good and poor readers appear to be motivated by the same factors: an abundance of available books; opportunities to choose their own reading materials; and time to share and discuss books with others.

One underlying assumption in this study was that interest is a key factor in motivation and that interest would be reflected in the books and stories children chose to talk to us about. Numerous recent studies have documented that interest fosters depth of processing and enhances learning (Alexander, Kulikowich, & Jetton, 1994; Hidi, 1990). Another related factor that has not been as extensively researched with respect to reading is that of curiosity. In our analysis of the responses of children across all interview questions we discovered an interesting link between book familiarity and curiosity. It appears that young children want to read and are curious about books that are somewhat familiar. Across the interview questions, children mentioned that they had read or were interested in reading a book because someone had talked with them or mentioned the book to them or they had seen someone else reading the book. This relationship between familiarity and curiosity was also revealed in children's frequent discussions of series books where the characters and setting are familiar, yet the plot is unique. It appears that children want to read and are curious about books they know something about; this suggests that reading motivation may be effectively fostered by book sharing activities that familarize children with a variety of books. This finding reinforces the notion that social interactions about books and providing opportunities for children to share books may be important considerations in developing motivating instructional contexts for literacy development.

Taken together, the findings from this study make a convincing case that we can help children develop the reading habit and an intrinsic desire to read by creating motivating instructional contexts for literacy learning. The very basic considerations for creating motivating contexts appear to be the following: book-rich classroom and home environments, opportunities for children to engage in self-selecting reading materials, and time to socially interact with peers and others about personally interesting books, stories, and texts. While these considerations are basic, it is important to remember that they are not always easy to implement in the classroom. That *is* our challenge as we work toward helping all children develop into active, engaged readers.

I would like to thank the following members of the NRRC Literacy Motivation Research Team for their significant insights and contributions to the research described in this paper: Rose Mare Codling, Mary Graham, Aileen Kennedy, Mona Mitchell, Barbara Palmer, and Susan Mazzoni.

References

Alexander, PA., Kulikowich, J.M., & Jetton, T.L. (1994). The role of subject matter knowledge and interest in the processing of linear and nonliear texts. *Review of Educational Research, 64,* 210-253.

Anderson, M. A., Tollefson, N. A., & Gilbert, E. C. (1985). Giftedness and reading: A cross-sectional view of differences in reading attitudes and behaviors. *Gifted Child Quarterly, 29,* 186-189.

Ames, C., & Archer, J. (1988). Achievement goals in the classroom: Students' learning strategies and motivation processes. *Journal of Educational Psychology, 86*(3), 260-267.

Bandura, A. (1989). Human agency in social cognitive theory. *American Psychologist, 44,* 1175-1184.

Borkowski, J. G., Carr, M., Rellinger, E., & Pressley, M. (1990). Self-regulated cognition: Interdependence of metacognition, attributions, and self-esteem. In B. Jones & L. Idol (Eds.), *Dimensions in thinking and cognitive instruction* (pp. 53-92). Hillsdale, NJ: Erlbaum.

Burgess, R. (1980). *Field research: A sourcebook and field manual.* London: Allen and Urwin.

Colardarci, T. (1986). Accuracy of teacher judgments of student responses to standardized test items. *Journal of Educational Psychology, 78,* 141-146.

Como, L., & Snow, R. E. (1986). Adapting teaching to individual differences among learners. In M. C. Wittrock (Ed.), *Handbook of research on teaching* (3rd ed.). New York: Macmillan.

Covington, M. V. (1985). The motive for self-worth. In C. Ames and R. Ames (Eds.), *Research on motivation in education: The classroom milieu* (pp. 77-113). New York: Academic Press.

Cronbach, L. J. (1951). Coefficient alpha and the internal structure of tests. *Psychometrika, 16*, 297-334.

Cronbach, L. J. (1988). Five perspectives on the validity argument. In H. Weiner and H. Broun (Eds.), *Test validity.* Hillsdale, NJ: Erlbaum.

Csikszentmihalyi, M. (1991). Literacy and intrinsic motivation. In S. R. Graubard (Ed.),*Literacy: An overview by fourteen experts.* New York: Farrar, Straus and Giroux.

Deci, E., & Ryan, R. (1985). *Intrinsic motivation and self-determination in human behavior.* New York: Plenum.

Dweck, C. S. (1986). Motivational processes affecting learning. *American Psychologist, 41*, 1040-1048.

Dweck, C., & Elliott, E. (1983). Achievement motivation. In E. M. Heatherington (Ed.), *Handbook of child psychology; Vol. 4, Socialization, personality, and social development* (pp. 643-691). New York: Wiley.

Eccles, J., Adler, T. F., Futterman, R., Goff, S.B., Kaczala, C. M., Meece, J., & Midgley, C. (1983). Expectancies, values and academic behaviors. In J. T. Spence (Ed.), *Achievement and Achievement Motives,* W. H. Freeman, San Francisco:

Egan, 0., & Archer, P. (1985). The accuracy of teachers' ratings of ability: A regression model. *American Educational Research Journal, 22*, 25-34.

Elley, W. B. (1992). *How in the world do students* read? Hamburg, Germany: International Association for the Evaluation of Educational Achievement.

Feitelson, D., Goldstein, Z., Iraqi, J., & Share, D. L. (1993). Effects of listening to story reading on aspects of literacy acquisition in a diglossic situation. *Reading Research Quarterly, 28*(1), 71-79.

Fractor, J. S., Woodruff, M. C., Martinez, M. G., & Teale, W. H. (1993). Let's not miss opportunities to promote voluntary reading: Classroom libraries in the elementary school. *The Reading Teacher, 46*, 476-485.

Ford, M. E. (1992). *Motivating humans.* Newbury Park: Sage.

Freud, S. (1901/1951). *The psychopathology of everyday life.* New York: New American Library. (Original work published 1901).

Gambrell, L. B. (1992). Elementary school literacy: Changes and challenges. In M. J. Dreher & W. H. Slater (Eds.), *Elementary school literacy: critical issues*(pp. 227-239). Norwood, ME: Christopher-Gordon.

Gambrell, L. B., Palmer, B. M., & Codling, R. M. (1995). In their own words: What elementary students have to say about motivation to read. *The Reading Teacher, 48*, 176-178.

Gambrell, L. B., Palmer, B. M., Codling, R. M., & Mazzoni, S. A. (in press). *Assessing motivation to read.* University of Georgia-University of Maryland, National Reading Research Center.

Greaney, V., and Neuman, S. B. (1990). The functions of reading: A cross-cultural perspective. *Reading Research Quarterly, 253*, 172-195.

Guthrie, J. T., Schafer, W., Wang, Y., & Afflerbach, P. (1993). Influences of instruction on reading engagement: An empirical exploration of a social-cognitive framework of reading activity. *Research Report #3.* Athens, GA: National Reading Research Center.

Hansen, H. S. (1969). The impact of the home literacy environment on reading attitudes. *Elementary English, 46*, 17-24.

Hidi, S. (1990). Interest and its contribution as a mental resource for learning. *Review of Educational Research, 60*, 549-571.

Hoge, R. D., & Butcher, R. (1984). Analysis of teacher judgments of pupil achievement levels. *Journal of Educational Psychology, 76*, 777-781.

Iran-Nejad, A., (1990). Active and dynamic self-regulation of learning processes. *Review of Educational Research, 60,* 573-602.

Ishikawa, K. (1985). Developmental study of school children's attitudes toward reading. *The Science of Reading, 29,* 89-98.

Johnson, D. D. (1973). Sex differences in reading across cultures. *Reading Research Quarterly, 9,* 67-86.

Kuhl, J. (1986). Introduction. In J. Kuhl and J. W. Atkinson (Eds.), *Motivation, thought, and action* (pp. 1-16). New York: Praeger.

Leal, D. J. (1992). The nature of talk about three types of text during peer group discussions. *Journal of Reading Behavior, 24,* 313-338.

Lepper, M. R. (1988). Motivational considerations in the study of instruction. *Cognition and Instruction, 5,* 289-309.

Maehr, M. L. (1976). Continuing motivation: An analysis of a seldom considered educational outcome. *Review of Educational Research, 46*(3), 443-462.

Marsh, H. W., Smith, I. D., & Barnes, J. (1983). Multitrait-Multimethod analyses of the self-description questionnaire: Student-teacher agreement on multidimensional ratings of student self-concept. *American Educational Research Journal, 20,* 333-357.

Maslow, A. H. (1970). *Motivation and personality*(2nd ed.). New York: Harper and Row.

McCombs, B. L. (1989). Self-regulated learning and academic achievement: A phenomenological view. In B. J. Zimmerman and D. H. Schunk (Eds.), *Self-regulated learning and academic achievement: Theory, research, and practice* (pp. 51-82). New York: Springer-Verlag.

McCombs, B. L. (1991). Unraveling motivation: New perspectives from research and practice. *The Journal of Experimental Education, 60,* 3-88.

McKenna, M. C., Kear, D. M., & Ellsworth, R. A. (in press). Children's attitudes toward reading: A national survey. *Reading Research Quarterly.*

Morrow, L. M. (1992). The impact of a literature-based program on literacy achievement, use of literature, and attitudes of children from minority backgrounds. *Reading Research Quarterly, 27,* 250-275.

O'Flahavan, J., Gambrell, L. B., Guthrie, J., Stahl, S., & Alvermann, D. (1992). Poll results guide activities of research center. *Reading Today*(p. 12). Newark, DE: International Reading Association.

Oldfather, P. (1993). What students say about motivating experiences in a whole language classroom. *The Reading Teacher, 46,* 672-681.

Pappas, C. C. (1993). Is narrative "primary"? Some insights from kindergarteners' pretend readings of stories and informational books. *Journal of Reading Behavior, 25,* 97-129.

Paris, S. G., & Oka, E. R. (1986). Self-regulated learning among exceptional children. *Exceptional Children, 53,* 103-108.

Parker, A., & Paradis, E. (1986). Attitude development toward reading in grades one through six. *Journal of Educational Research, 79,* 313-315.

Perkins, H. V. (1958). Teachers' and peers' perception of children's self-concepts. *Child Development, 29,* 203-220.

Phillips, B. N. (1963). Age changes in accuracy of self-perception. *Child Development, 64,* 1041-1046.

Pintrich, P. R., & DeGroot, E. V. (1990). Motivational and self-regulated learning components of classroom academic performance. *Journal of Educational Psychology, 82*(1), 33-40.

Prawat, R. S. (1989). Promoting access to knowledge. *Review of Educational Research, 59,* 1-42.

Pressley, M., Borkowski, J. G., & Schneider, W. (1987). Cognitive strategies: Good strategy users coordinate metacognition and knowledge. *Annals of Child Development, 4,* 89-129.

Roettger, D. (1980). Elementary students' attitudes toward reading. *The Reading Teacher, 33,* 451-453.

Rogers, C. R. (1961). On *becoming a person: A therapists' view of psychology.* Englewood Cliffs, NJ: Prentice-Hall.

Ross, E. P., & Fletcher, R. K. (1989). Responses to children's literature by environment, grade level, and sex. *Reading Instruction Journal, 32,* 22-28.

Saracho, 0. M., & Dayton, C. M. (1991). Age-related changes in reading attitudes of young children: A cross-cultural study. *Journal of Research in Reading, 14,* 33-45.

Schunk, D. (1985). Self-efficacy and school learning. *Psychology in the Schools, 22,* 208-223.

Silverman, D. (1993). *Interpreting qualitative data: Methods for analyzing talk, text and interaction.* London: Sage.

Skinner, B. F. (1953). *Science and human behavior.* New York: Macmillan.

Spaulding, C. L. (1992). The motivation to read and write. In J. W. Irwin & M. A. Doyle (Eds.), *Reading/writing connections: Learning from research* (pp. 177-201). Newark, DE: International Reading Association.

Stevenson, H. W., & Newman, R. S. (1986). Long-term prediction of achievement and attitudes in mathematics and reading. *Child Development, 57,* 646-657.

Strauss, A., & Corbin, J. (1990). *Basics of qualitative research.* Newbury Park Sage.

Veenman, S. (1984). Perceived problems of beginning teachers. *Review of Education Research, 54,* 143-178.

Vygotsky, L. S. (1978). *Mind in society: The development of higher psychological processes.* Cambridge, MA: Harvard University Press.

Weiner, B. (1985). An attributional theory of achievement motivation and emotion. *Psychological Review, 92,* 548-573.

Weiner, B. (1990). History of motivational research in education. *Journal of Educational Psychology, 92*(4), 616-622.

Wigfield, A. (1994). Expectancy-value theory of achievement motivation: A developmental perspective. *Educational Psychology Review, 5,* 49-78.

Wigfield, A., & Asher, S. R. (1984). Social and motivational influences on reading. In P. D. Pearson (Ed.), *Handbook of reading research* (pp. 423-452). New York: Longman.

Winne, P. (1985). Steps toward promoting cognitive achievements. *Elementary School Journal, 85*(5), 673-693.

Winne, P., & Marx, R. (1982). Students' and teachers' views of thinking processes for classroom learning. *Elementary School Journal, 82,* 493-518.

Wittrock, M. C. (1986). Students' thought processes. In M. C. Wittrock (Ed.), *Handbook of research on teaching* (pp. 297-314). New York: Macmillan.

FUTURE CONTROVERSIAL ISSUES IN LITERACY: THE SAME OLD STUFF OR A WHOLE NEW BALL GAME?

William A. Henk

Pennsylvania State University, Harrisburg

Keynote Address
College Reading Association
1996

In 1996 William A. Henk served as Director of the School of Behavioral Sciences and Education, and as Professor of Education and Reading at Pennsylvania State University, Harrisburg. Although his duties were primarily administrative in nature, within the education programs he taught courses in elementary level and diagnostic reading as well as in measurement and evaluation, reading psychology, curriculum integration, and current issues in education. He was the recipient of the College's Outstanding Teaching Award for 1991, the Distinguished Service Award of Phi Delta Kappa Harrisburg Chapter in 1996, and co-recipient of the Pennsylvania Educational Research Association's Outstanding Paper Award in 1997. Dr. Henk has written extensively in the areas of reading comprehension, instruction, and assessment as well as educational technology, having published in most major literacy journals.

G enerally speaking, predicting the future is risky business. Any individual foolhardy enough to propose a vision of the unknown runs the risk of being revealed as woefully shortsighted or laughably bold. In the field of literacy, the perils of prediction in this day and age are especially acute. That is, although

Reprinted from *Exploring Literacy.* pp. 63-73, by W. M. Linek and E. G. Sturtevant, Eds, 1997, Commerce, Texas: College Reading Association literacy's traditional controversies tend to be longstanding, the advent of text-related computer technologies could completely revolutionize our current thinking about reading and writing. With these risks squarely in mind, I offer one tentative vision of six major future controversial issues in literacy, half of which relate directly to technology, while the remainder center on issues of the present that will almost certainly persist.

The Impact of Technology

Text-related technologies have realized an unprecedented evolution in recent years. This emergence is not at all surprising. Advances in the capabilities of computer hardware occur so rapidly that newly purchased CPUs and peripherals no sooner arrive than they become relegated to yesterday's news. Likewise, new software emerges at an astounding rate as developers attempt to corner still another lucrative piece of the seemingly endless applications market.

Reading as Writing

One major outcome of the avalanche of more powerful and sophisticated technologies is that the *distinction between reading and writing processes will become profoundly blurred*. In short, electronic texts will serve to make reading more constructivist in nature by providing readers with numerous presentation options. Most significantly, the expanded memory capabilities of personal computers will allow an even greater range of *hypertext* links to be embedded in otherwise traditional texts. Using hypertext, readers can go beyond the linear text material on the page to access additional textual, graphic, auditory, animated, or quick time movie information. This non-linear "writing" will be accomplished by uniquely accessing the multimedia links which define, describe, illustrate, demonstrate, and elaborate upon the meaning of unknown or interesting words, difficult concepts, and confusing text propositions. In effect, readers will literally be able to construct (or write, if you will) their own personalized texts in this digital post-typographic era (Reinking, 1995).

The continuing proliferation of computer-assisted *interactive fiction* will contribute further to making reading and writing processes more nearly alike. In interactive fiction, readers are given options at key points in a story, which allow the plot to proceed in several possible directions. Readers can traverse a story repeatedly, taking a different pathway of events nearly each time. As with hypertext, the reading is non-linear and dynamic so that, in effect, readers construct the equivalent of custom texts, which conform to their various episodic preferences.

A related, constructivist text-reading opportunity made possible by technology is the notion of *multiple perspectives* (Bolter, 1991). These texts can be read from the respective viewpoints of different characters in the story. Readers may elect to read a narrative told exclusively by one character through the entire text, or they could choose to switch among the full range of varying characters' perspectives that have been provided by the author. Imagine, for instance, being able to experience scenes through the sensory, perceptual, cognitive, and emotional lenses of any major character. Obviously, the original writing of such a text would be enormously time consuming; however, I suspect that, in the future, authors will invite readers to construct novel character perspectives that could become part of a virtual living text.

One final way that reading and writing processes are becoming ever more similar is through the use of *multimedia* courseware. This powerful combination of visual, auditory, kinetic, and mixed modes of delivery demands a deeply thoughtful presentation of concepts in which authors anticipate the whole spectrum of necessary textual aids that diverse readers will require, expect, or desire. Multimedia texts represent an extremely formal approach to delivery that should clearly abide by the principles of effective instructional design. As such, multimedia authors must configure their software with the greatest care and effort.

For that matter, the branching capabilities made possible by the other technologies discussed thus far (hypertext, interactive fiction, and multiple perspectives) also make extensive demands on the author. Trying to anticipate the possible preferences for plot options and character perspectives, not to mention the specialized learning needs of a universe of readers, represents a daunting task for writers, even with very user-friendly development software.

Another intriguing issue related to the technologies discussed thus far revolves around how reading comprehension can be validly assessed. On one hand, tracking the routes of readers through these malleable texts will be relatively easy for the computer. Still, one wonders how the tensions between reading efficiency, depth of understanding, and reading appreciation will ultimately be reconciled.

These technologically delivered texts truly stretch the limits of constructivist learning and, as such, present reading educators and researchers with a wealth of altogether new possibilities and challenges. Some authorities have gone so far as to suggest that the interactive capability of electronic texts signals the eventual demise of books as the primary written communication medium (Reinking, 1995).

The Diminishing Importance of Reading?

A second major controversial literacy issue of the future is that reading could become less of a priority. On the surface, this assertion would seem to run counter to repeated warnings about the increased literacy demands of an advanced technological society. Surely, the demands will be different. Locating and managing information (using electronic dictionaries, encyclopedias, the World Wide Web, databases, spreadsheets) and an ability to decipher procedural texts that facilitate the use of the technologies will almost surely gain in importance and promote greater amounts of specialized reading. However, the demands need not necessarily overwhelm the reader. Although hardware configuration remains a mystery to most of us, many software applications are sufficiently user friendly that reading the documentation becomes an option rather than a necessity. This increased ease is made possible largely by the ascendancy of non-verbal elements (e.g., icons, drawings, photos, animation) in cutting edge microcomputer software.

Advanced technologies might also have the dual effects of (1) making the reading process less challenging and/or (2) subverting reading in favor of visual literacy. With regard to reducing the challenges of reading, technologies such as *reading machines* and *voice recognition-activated word processors* have already exerted an impact on the importance of reading. For example, the Kurzweil Reading Machine, originally developed for use with blind individuals, can accurately pronounce the overwhelming majority of words that appear on nearly any page of English text (Rickelman & Henk, 1990). Put another way, the Xerox-like machine or its hand-held equivalent can convert practically any text from a reading to a listening exercise, even for sighted users. Given the popularity of books on tape with commuters, one wonders how the potential general availability of reading machine technology might affect the priority status reading currently enjoys.

The voice-activated word processors could also devalue the reading process, but in a different way. Using this software, writers will tend to focus on the auditory component of the message rather than its visual characteristics because the latter will be provided for them automatically. Admittedly, if the writer must reread the text for the purposes of revision, the re-inspection demands would promote literacy acquisition. However, the newer software will have a "reverse" capability, like the reading machine, to read the text back to the author orally. The point here is that the reading growth that would naturally occur as individuals, especially children, engage in conventional writing activities might be circumvented almost altogether if they opt to use voice recognition word processing technology. In short, both the reading machine and the voice-recognition writing programs beg the question, "Will children engage in the act of reading if it can just as easily be avoided?"

Two other threats to the significance of reading stem from society's increasing fascination with *visual literacy* and the emergence of *virtual reality* technologies. Each day it seems that we are bombarded with increasingly seductive visual messages through the media which, in turn, may render print contexts boring, particularly in the eyes of our youth. Television broadcasting, including high tech advertising and music videos, is ever-present; movie theaters sell out with the release of each new blockbuster; and video games and movie rentals have become a pervasive leisure option in our society. Collectively, great effort is devoted to shaping viewing contexts that garner and maintain the public's attention because the potential commercial rewards are staggering. In turn, this new visual literacy possesses the potential to undermine the appreciation of literature in the minds of our most impressionable factions of society.

Virtual reality, although in its infancy, could become another major competitor for the relatively high status that reading has held over the years. At present, virtual reality creates the impression in users of being immersed in a fairly authentic, albeit imaginary, context. Through the use of various viewing and kinetic devices that are networked interactively with an executive control computer, this technology permits users to experience a powerful set of sensations and perceptions in response to their actions in the virtual world. These simulations have the potential to compete with and ultimately surpass the vicarious experiences readers enjoy when engaged with even the most riveting of texts. This multifaceted technology will ultimately allow users to experience simulations of reality across the entire sensory spectrum. Taken to its extreme, virtual reality augmented by the holographic technologies of the future (similar to those portrayed on the Holodeck of *Star Trek's* Starship Enterprise) will permit "readers" to forego the written word altogether. Virtual reality "readers" could experience text worlds so directly and completely that they will move from the role of interested lexical bystanders to that of nearly full participants.

Technology and Ethical Dilemmas

A third set of future controversial issues derives from the notion that *technology could create additional ethical problems in literacy*. The majority of my concerns here focus on the capacity of technology to manage information in an unjust manner. Technologies such as e-mail will invariably become susceptible to tampering and violations of confidentiality. Electronic messages can be altered or attributed in a fraudulent but convincing manner, and the consequences for the victim could be severe. There is also a distinct possibility that technology will encourage and facilitate plagiarism and other forms of *academic dishonesty*. I fear that the now infamous web site "School Sucks" which provides users with already written term papers is just the tip of the iceberg. It's true that the papers at that site are substandard, but I doubt such resources will always be low in quality. Moreover, I presume that competitors for this ignoble trade will proliferate once services are made to be more profitable and essentially untraceable. To make matters worse, the *integrity of copyrights* and the concept of *ownership of ideas* are clearly in jeopardy in a dynamic electronic literacy environment.

Perhaps the most dangerous dimension of technology's impact on literacy is *privileged access*. Our society is decidedly culpable for already having created a literacy chasm between dominant and subordinate social and economic classes, races, and cultures. Unfortunately, technology may serve to exacerbate the situation. Here the potential for another kind of Matthew Effect is ripe; that is, those rich in literacy stand to get richer by virtue of technology access, while those poor in literacy will be left even further behind. It is imperative, therefore, that every conceivable effort be made to ensure equal access to technology for all citizens. Anything less is unconscionable, albeit likely.

Chronic Literacy Controversies

In speculating about future controversial literacy issues, one experiences a curious irony. On one hand, the probability that technology will exert an extraordinary impact stands in sharp contrast to the equally distinct possibility that many of today's most divisive literacy issues will continue to be debated indefinitely. This latter prospect looms large because the history of education as a discipline has been marked by a remarkable resistance to true change; unfortunately, its concomitant controversies tend to be equally resilient.

Innovative Instructional Literacy Practices Under Siege

The formidable resistance to holistic forms of literacy instruction leads me to believe that *political pressures for instructional conservatism will persist*. In particular, whole language has been, and will continue to be, under relentless attack from the conservative right. To some extent, the opposition seems warranted. Numerous educational communities bought into whole language without a solid understanding either of its tenets or its eventual implementation obstacles (Walmsley & Adams, 1993). Even in the absence of an agreed-upon operational definition of whole language (Bergeron, 1990), many educators accepted the philosophy on the basis of intuition rather than on scientific evidence. From a pragmatic standpoint, most would-be whole language school districts hastily mandated implementation without providing the types of professional development opportunities that teachers needed to be successful. It is not surprising, then, that the reviews on whole language are mixed (Stahl, McKenna, & Pagnucco, 1994), causing many avid supporters to consider the more moderate literacy instruction associated with transitional, balanced, literature-based, or eclectic approaches (McIntyre & Pressley, 1996; Routman, 1996).

Despite these criticisms, there are a host of extremely commendable features of holistic literacy instruction that warrant continuance (e.g., authentic texts, relevant tasks, self-evaluation, cooperative learning, thematic curricula). Unfortunately, these elements may fall prey to a general political siege on whole language that has been masterfully orchestrated by its right-wing opponents. The most radical adversaries (Blumenfeld, 1996) suggest that society will be thrown into utter chaos if progressive whole language advocates (i.e., elitist reading professors) have their way. In effect, they charge that whole language endeavors to impose a socialistic agenda on the country by purposely limiting the literacy acquisition of children. The reasoning follows that these illiterate children will be far more susceptible to the pagan, Marxist political agendas of the left. While this logic is so absurd as to be laughable on one hand, it is downright offensive to the countless educators who have committed their very lives to the betterment of children. To suggest that teaching professionals at any level would intentionally prevent children from realizing their full intellectual potential is patently outrageous. Sadly, the propagandistic properties of the attack on holistic literacy instruction are sufficiently well disguised that an uninformed lay public might just embrace this rhetorical drivel.

The Assessment Debate Wages On

A second chronic literacy controversy for the future is that the *debate over the use of standardized tests versus authentic assessments will almost certainly endure*. For years, advocates of more innovative types of literacy instruction have claimed that standardized measures are wrong minded (Valencia, Hiebert, & Afflerbach, 1994). These authors suggest that the norm-referenced approach simply fails to resonate with the progressive nature of the instruction and therefore cannot hope to assess its impact. Moreover, they argue that standardized assessments provide little useful instructional information, lack a sensitivity to small yet important changes in performance, and ultimately mislead parents, teachers, and administrators alike (Goodman, Goodman, & Hood, 1989). Traditionalists, on the other hand, tend to dismiss the value of authentic assessment on the grounds that it is unscientific (i.e., subjective and soft). They contend that global indicators of reading and writing achievement in the form of standardized tests are absolutely necessary for determining how children, their teachers, and their schools are performing. In this sense, they claim that, in the absence of norms, there is no reliable way to evaluate the general effectiveness of literacy instruction on an inclusive basis. To their way of thinking, all of the school's constituencies (parents, school boards, communities, legislators) deserve the quality control that standardized testing allows.

Regrettably, little hope for timely compromises appears to exist. The competing philosophies that under gird this assessment conflict are held with the firmest of resolves by their respective camps. Holistic educators resent having their orientations being held to an inappropriate benchmark of accountability, and they rail loudly about nearly any type of normative assessment. They believe that comparisons between groups of children do nothing to advance the literacy attainment of an individual child. Conversely, the more conservative educational element maintains that school districts must be held up to a set of verifiable standards, and that it is their duty to share the results with their constituencies. Their belief is that accountability will be a strong incentive for school systems to perform at the highest levels, and in turn, children will be the beneficiaries of the increased public vigilance.

In my opinion, education as a whole would be better served if we viewed both authentic and standardized assessments in their proper perspectives. Let's face facts. There will always be a need for schools to demonstrate their competency to the societies they serve. The key here is that this evidence can take disparate forms. Personally, I adhere to the philosophy that standardized tests represent merely one indicator of a child's literacy achievement. These normative results should be viewed in concert with the multiple measures that emerge naturally from the literacy instruction itself. This approach, while hardly original, strikes me as being concomitantly reasonable, realistic, and responsible. Yet, resistance to this kind of compromise is formidable in some literacy circles, which leads me to believe that the controversy will probably endure for years to come.

I am hopeful, though, that new assessment instruments can be developed which might appease both camps in the future. These instruments would revolve around literacy tasks that are essentially authentic, yet allow for the construction of norms. Some noteworthy headway has been made in this regard. In particular, newer commercial reading inventories like the *Qualitative Reading Inventory-II* (Leslie & Caldwell, 1995) and the *Basic Reading Inventory* (Johns, 1996) emphasize versatile usage and include more authentic texts, retelling rubrics, think aloud provisions, and prior knowledge and strategy assessments, while offering some degree of comparative possibilities.

In addition, some affective dimensions of literacy like reading attitude and literacy self-perceptions, which are important considerations in holistic instruction, have been shown to be amenable to standardized assessment. In particular, instruments like the *Elementary Reading Attitude Survey* (McKenna & Kear, 1990), the *Reader Self-Perception Scale* (Henk & Melnick, 1995), and the *Writer Self-Perception Scale* (Henk, Bottomley, & Melnick, 1996) have shown promise in the affective domain. Perhaps over time, these instruments and others yet to come can help to bridge the current enormous assessment void.

The Persistence of the Paradigm Wars

A final literacy controversy of the future is that the unfortunate paradigm wars in literacy research of the present are unlikely to abate any time soon. As others have noted (Kamil, 1995), the rift between experimental and ethnographic researchers runs very deep and seems to be growing ever larger.

This philosophical polarization over what represents truth in research has festered for a number of years, but has proliferated of late (see Edelsky, 1990; Grundin, 1994; McKenna, Robinson, & Miller, 1990a, 1990b; Stanovich, 1993; Taylor, 1994; West, Stanovich, & Mitchell, 1993) despite calls for a cessation of hostilities (Stanovich, 1990). And as Ray Reutzel argues so eloquently (this volume), the accompanying discord threatens the integrity of the field as a whole. Sadly, the struggles go well beyond mere disagreement. The dialogues between quantitative and qualitative researchers often degenerate into disrespectful, personal attacks that intentionally or otherwise belittle the belief systems of other literacy professionals. Such combative language has been termed by some as a "discourse of derision." Frankly, the purpose of these mean-spirited missives eludes me.

Besides a general preference for civility, why should we be bothered by this research chasm? Among other things, I don't believe that literacy educators can afford to air their dirty laundry publicly. Education is under fire generally. Providing our critics with additional ammunition diminishes us all and reduces our chances of acquiring and maintaining necessary resources. Moreover, the profession has reached the point where the individuals we prepare in higher education don't know what to believe any more. In some contexts, I am fearful that the pressure to be indoctrinated into one perspective or the other will prevent both preservice and inservice teachers from taking a broader, more inclusive view of literacy research and pedagogy.

In large measure, my fear of indoctrination stems from the fact that literacy represents a truly multifaceted construct. Viewed in this way, it seems extremely peculiar to me that any single research perspective could be viewed as ultimately and exclusively valid. I believe that literacy researchers would do well to examine phenomena using as many different appropriate lenses of inquiry as possible, to aggregate and synthesize the data, and to draw maximally informed interpretations. In my opinion, the usefulness of many quantitative studies would be enhanced if subsequent qualitative inquiry were done with outlier subjects. Likewise, numerous qualitative studies lend themselves to quantitative follow-ups that would yield a more complete picture of the phenomena under study and lend credence to proposed category trends. Surely a middle ground exists in which quantitative and qualitative research paradigms can share a complementary coexistence. At the same time, as Kamil (1995) points out, this middle ground needs to extend well beyond mere detente. The warring factions cannot simply go about their business, co-existing by essentially ignoring each other or adhering to the concept of incommensurability. All parties must participate actively in the debate or we will not move forward as a field. However, I share Kamil's belief that by failing to enter into a productive, courteous dialogue, researchers will fall short of remedying the plight of those whom we profess to serve.

A Final Word

Only time will tell if any of the predictions made in this paper will ring true. Perhaps technology will fail to exert as dramatic an impact on literacy as proposed here. By the same token, innovative literacy instruction might withstand the intense political pressure it labors under; authentic and standardized assessment indicators could be utilized in a complementary fashion; and the factions favoring disparate research paradigms could seek a mutually beneficial collaboration. At the risk of being naive, I believe literacy educators and researchers can resolve their differences with good faith dialogues within a climate of respectfulness. I also feel that we have the expertise and wherewithal to harness the power of technology for the common good. At any rate, literacy professionals need to anticipate several possible futures to prepare for the numerous challenges and opportunities that lie ahead. The very quality of our children's lives hangs in the balance.

References

Bergeron, B. (1990). What does the term whole language mean? *Journal of Reading Behavior*, 22, 301-329.

Blumenfeld, S. (1996). *The whole language/OBE fraud*. Boise, Idaho: The Paradigm Company.

Bolter, J. (1991). *Writing space. The computer; hypertext, and the history of writing*. Hillsdale, NJ: Erlbaum.

Edelsky, C. (1990). Whose agenda is this anyway? A response to McKenna, Robinson, and Miller. *Educational Researcher*, 19, 7-11.

Goodman, K., Goodman, Y., & Hood, W. (Eds.). (1989). *The whole language evaluation book*. Toronto, Ontario: Irwin.

Grundin, H. (1994). Who's romanticizing reality? A response to Keith Stanovich. *Reading Teacher*, 48, 8-9.

Henk, W., Bottomley, D., & Melnick, S. (1996). Preliminary validation of the *Writer Self-Perception Scale*. In E. Sturtevant & W. Linek (Eds.), *Growing literacy, Eighteenth yearbook of the College Reading Association*, (pp. 188-199). Harrisonburg, VA: College Reading Association.

Henk, W., & Melnick, S. (1995). *The Reader Self-Perception Scale* (RSPS): A new tool for measuring how children feel about themselves as readers. *The Reading Teacher*, 48, 470-482.

Johns, J. (1996). *Basic reading inventory* (6th ed.). Dubuque, IA: Kendall-Hunt.

Kamil, M. (1995). Some alternatives to paradigm wars in literacy research. *Journal of Reading Behavior*, 27, 243-261.

Leslie, L., & Caldwell, J. (1995). *The qualitative reading inventory* -IL Glenview, IL: Scott, Foresman.

McIntyre, E., & Pressley, M. (Eds.). (1996). *Balanced instruction: Strategies and skills in whole language*. Norwood, MA: Christopher-Gordon.

McKenna, M., & Kear, D. (1990). Measuring attitude toward reading: A new tool for teachers. *The Reading Teacher*, 44, 626-639.

McKenna, M., Robinson, R., & Miller, J. (1990a). Whole language: A research agenda for the nineties. *Educational Researcher*, 19, 3-6.

McKenna, M., Robinson, R., & Miller, J. (1990b). Whole language and the need for open inquiry: A rejoinder to Edelsky. *Educational Researcher*, 19, 12-13.

McKenna, M. C., Stahl, S. A., & Reinking, D. (1994). A critical commentary on research, politics, and whole language. *Journal of Reading Behavior*, 26, 211-233.

Reinking, D. (1995). Reading and writing with computers: Literacy research in a post-typographic world. In K. Hinchman, D. Leu, & C. Kinzer (Eds.), *Perspectives on literacy research and practice, Forty-fourth yearbook of the National Reading Conference*. Chicago, IL: National Reading Conference.

Rickelman, R., & Henk, W. (1990). A machine that "reads." *The Reading Teacher*, 44, 512-513.

Routman, R. (1996). *Literacy at the crossroads: Crucial talk about reading, writing, and other teaching dilemmas*. Portsmouth, NH: Heinemann.

Stahl, S. A., McKenna, M. C., & Pagnucco, J. R. (1994). The effects of whole- language instruction: An update and a reappraisal. *Educational Psychologist*, 29, 175-185.

Stanovich, K. (1990). A call for the end of the paradigm wars in reading research. *Journal of Reading Behavior*, 22, 221-231.

Stanovich, K. (1993). Romance and reality. *Reading Teacher*, 47 280-291.

Taylor, D. (1994). The trivial pursuit of reading psychology in the "real world", A response to West, Stanovich, and Mitchell. *Reading Research Quarterly*, 29, 276-289.

Valencia, S., Hiebert, E., & Afflerbach, P. (Eds.). (1994). *Authentic reading assessment: Practices and possibilities.* Newark, DE: International Reading Association.

Walmsley, S. A., & Adams, E. L (1993). Realities of whole language. *Language Arts, 70,* 272-280.

West, R., Stanovich, K., & Mitchell, H. (1993). Reading in the real world and its correlates. *Reading Research Quarterly, 28,* 34-50.

CONTROVERSIAL PATHWAYS TO LITERACY: THE PRESENT

D. Ray Reutzel

Brigham Young University

Keynote Address
College Reading Association
1996

In 1996 D. Ray Reutzel was a Karl G. Maeser Distinguished Research Professor and Associate Dean of Teacher Education in the David 0. McKay School of Education at Brigham Young University (BYU). Dr. Reutzel is the author of more than 90 articles, books, book chapters, and monographs. He has published in, Journal of Reading Behavior, Journal of Literacy Research, Journal of Educational Research, Reading Psychology, Reading Research and Instruction, Language Arts, Journal of Reading, Reading World, *and* The Reading Teacher, *among others. He was the Editor of* Reading Research and Instruction *and a co-author of* Teaching Children to Read: From Basals to Books, *2nd Edition, published by Prentice-Hall/Merrill. He was a program author and consultant for Scholastic Incorporated's* Literacy Place® *school reading program.*

S ince Dr. Estill Alexander called to ask if I would participate in this panel today, I have mulled over many controversial issues in literacy, ranging from the politics and power of literacy, to privilege and access, to literacy knowledge, skills, and strategies. The more I considered the possibilities, the greater became my anxiety. I have genuinely worried about which controversial issues to select as exemplars of the diverse voices and multiple perspectives within our literacy community. After considerable inward turmoil, I selected two issues, not for the issues themselves, but for deeper, perhaps more troubling and

Reprinted from *Exploring Literacy.* pp. 56-62, by W. M. Linek and E. G. Sturtevant, Eds, 1997, Commerce, Texas: College Reading Association vexing contradictions nested deep within these exemplar controversies. The two issues I have chosen are these: 1) the paradigm wars in reading research; and 2) the continuing chasm between the university literacy researcher and the classroom literacy practitioner. Please be reminded, I chose these two controversies primarily as exemplars of deeper, more problematic dilemmas, not necessarily for the controversies themselves.

Continuing Paradigm Wars in Reading Research

The paradigm wars in literacy research are in themselves a lesson in paradox. Amid the admirable and persistent calls within the literacy community for greater cooperation, collaboration, and appreciation of a broader range of voices and methods in literacy research, there is also an increasing invidious incivility in our discourse that attacks the very heart of our community. Kamil (1995), in an article entitled "Some Alternatives to Paradigm Wars in Literacy Research," asks:

> What went wrong with [these] debates? When the idea for intellectual exchanges about literacy issues was conceived, it was thought they would promote productive dialogue about substantive issues. We have seen little of the sustained, productive dialogue that literacy researchers and practitioners would have desired. (p. 244)

Rather than making clear the benefits, possibilities, and opportunities new research paradigms offered us as a community, we have diffused much productive effort in polarizing the debate, pointing out the flaws and limitations of others' research paradigms, and sprinkling our debates with printed and verbal invectives.

John Ruskin (1976) once declared, "Education does not mean teaching people to know what they do not know; it means teaching them to behave as they do not behave" (p. 75). As the destructive diatribe of the research paradigm wars continues to descend upon our literacy community, the need for "education" as Ruskin describes it seems to be increasingly evident. Of all communities of intellect, those of us who love literacy and aspire to prepare classroom teachers of literacy should evidence refinement and civility in our conversations.

In an April 1996 article in the *U. S. News and World Report* (Marks) entitled, "The American [un]civil wars: How crude, rude, and obnoxious behavior has replaced good manners and why that hurts our politics and culture," the lack of civility was identified as a national phenomenon that is clearly denigrating our ability to effectively communicate and threatening our ability to maintain a sense of community. In fact, this recent article asserts a strong connection between incivility and increasing violence in our nation. Ninety percent of U.S. citizens polled believe that incivility contributes to the increase of violence in the country and 85% believe incivility divides the national community. As has recently been observed in the May/June, 1995 *Royal Bank Letter of Canada*,

> People might think of a civilized community as one in which there is a re-fined culture. Not necessarily; first and foremost it is one in which the mass of people subdue their selfish instincts in favor of a common good. (p. 2)

Kamil (1995) points out further that our arguments about research paradigms and methods have been made personal rather than professional. He notes that the goal of this controversy has been "winning," not the discovery of knowledge or insight.

When our intellectual discourse turns divisive and our dialogue becomes discourteous, this bespeaks a dim future for a community commonly united in a desire to privilege everyone—every individual, regardless of age, gender, race, creed, color, religion, etc.—with the dignity and self-esteem that flows from equal access to literacy and learning. In short, our debate over research paradigms bespeaks anything but civility and productivity. Rather, it speaks of crudeness, rudeness, and a total insensitivity to the feelings and rights of others. The controversy over research paradigms could be largely resolved by listening, respecting, and privileging diverse voices through cooperative and caring conversation. We can, will, and must have vigorous and rigorous disagreements, but must we be utterly disagreeable in so doing? I hope the College Reading Association will never lose the atmosphere of caring collegiality we have all enjoyed prior to this current divisive and ultimately destructive debate. There is enough room in CRA for all voices to be heard.

It is incumbent upon each of us to be intellectually honest about the limitations of our own preferred research paradigms and methods with others and ourselves. No one research method is sufficient to answer all research questions. We must openly admit the limitations of the research paradigms or methods we choose as well as defending their proper application, understanding, and benefits. If we do this, we will continue to experience the reasons we come each year to CRA, as they are so well described by Dinah Maria Mulock (1976).

> Oh, the comfort, the inexpressible comfort, of feeling safe with a person, having neither to weigh thoughts, nor measure words—but pouring them all right out—just as they are—chaff and grain together—certain that a faithful hand will take and sift them—keep what is worth keeping—and with the breath of kindness blow the rest away. (p. 165)

A Continuing Chasm Between the University Literacy Researcher and the Classroom Literacy Practitioner

Now, the second controversial issue—the continuing chasm between university literacy researchers and classroom literacy practitioners. Several years ago, I was attending the National Reading Conference in New Orleans. As I rode the elevator to my room, which was near the top floor of the hotel, a family entered the elevator on the second floor. The father looked at my name tag which indicated the name of the conference. He inquired, "I see you along with many others are here for a reading conference. What do you do at a reading conference? Do you read?" Taken a bit by surprise, I replied, "Well, yes, but actually this is a group of university researchers interested in reading and literacy. We are here to learn about each other's research studies." He responded quickly to me, "Oh, I see. You guys study how to teach people to read and write better, huh?" I replied, "Yes, but that isn't all. We study how teachers feel about themselves as readers, how they feel about teaching reading, and how students feel about reading." He seemed perplexed and even a little put off: "Well, I suppose that's important, but as a parent I would want to know how I can help my children become avid and capable readers. They need to learn the skills and dispositions of good reading. Kids these days can feel good about knowing little or nothing. I've read about kids who graduate from high school today who can't tell you where Washington, D.C., is on a map. They don't know famous inventors like Eli Whitney. They don't seem to know much, but they feel good."

By his comments, the vocabulary, and the concerns of my elevator acquaintance, I knew this fellow was no rube. He had a command of the language and of thought that was obviously above average. I felt a bit rebuked by his candid observations. He was clearly pointing to a need for researchers and literacy research to be relevant to the needs of real children, teachers, families, and taxpayers.

Walter E. Williams (1996), an Associated Press writer for the *Washington Post*, wrote recently:

> American students rank No. 1 in the world in how good they feel about their math skills, but a 1992 international study by the Educational Testing Service (ETS) showed American students ranking last in math achievement (behind Slovenia). Research surveys show self-esteem levels at least as high among black students as white students, but a majority of either of them are unable to write a persuasive letter, date the Civil War, or calculate simple interest. (p. 13A)

For over a decade I have worked with classroom teachers in workshops, seminars, graduate classes, and research meetings. I frequently share with them published research articles. These classroom practitioners often groan when they read the tides, questions, and findings of these articles and remark something like this: 'When are they going to study something real, relevant, and important to us? Why don't they ask us what the issues are that need to be researched?" These students are much like our university students, and seem to be suggesting that researchers are missing the significant issues associated with real students and real teachers, however they are defined in published research.

Kamil (1995) puts it this way:

> Although literacy researchers merrily engage in sophistry, nothing is done to help advance the plight of those for whom we profess to have concern. This profession should be about research in how to teach children to read. It should be about research in how best to equip workers to read informative manuals for their jobs. It should be about research in how individual speakers of one language learn to read in another . . . It should be about making certain that what we do is useful and applicable to real world contexts. (p. 244)

I admit Kamil may be slightly overstating his case, but I ask, do his observations deserve our careful attention as researchers and teacher educators?

Ken Zeichner, well known teacher education researcher, writes in a 1995 article entitled, "Beyond the Divide of Teacher Research and Academic Research":

> Despite the fact that many of my colleagues are known throughout the world for their research related to issues of equity, social justice, and schooling, these teachers [Zeichner's students] did not feel connected to this body of scholarship including his own and did not see it as offering them much guidance in dealing with their daily struggles to educate all students to high academic standards. (p. 159)

Richard and Joanne Vacca, longtime members of CRA, wrote a commentary years ago in the *Reading Research Quarterly* entitled "Two Less Than Fortunate Consequences of Reading Research in the 1970s" that may bear repeating today. They wrote, "Nevertheless, despite all that was good about reading research in the past decade, some of its broad social and political consequences may indeed have a deleterious effect on present and future inquiry in the field" (1983, pp. 382-383). Two of these consequences are interrelated and come to mind quickly:

Consequence #1: The de-valuing of reading instruction research
Consequence #2: The squeezing out of the reading educator

Vacca and Vacca continue:

> As reading researchers move squarely into the 1980's we hope that they do not work apart from one another; that the classroom teacher [and other stakeholders] play an integral role with researchers in determining what

we should get smart about, that interdisciplinary teams continue to inquire into reading and its instructional implication and applications. (1983, pp. 382-383)

We cannot afford to exclude the voices of teachers, parents, and policy makers from our research. Failure to demonstrate relevance to these audiences may at some future time spell the diminution or outright dismantling of our literacy research community. Exclusivity in research paradigms, methods, or questions will no doubt lead most assuredly to the extinction of our community as it did to the dinosaurs of ancient date.

Consider the following poem concerning the need for relevant scholarship:

Today a professor in a garden relaxing
Like Plato of old in the academe shade
Spoke out in a manner I never had heard him
And this is one thing that he said:

Suppose that we state as a tenet of wisdom
That knowledge is not for delight of the mind,
Nor an end in itself, but a packet of treasure
To hold and employ for the good of mankind.
A torch or a candle is barren of meaning
Except it give light to men as they climb,
And thesis and tomes are but impotent jumble
Unless they are tools in the building of time.

We scholars toil on with the zeal of a miner
For nuggets and nuggets and one nugget more,
But scholars are needed to study the uses
Of all the great mass of data and lore.
And truly our tireless and endless researches
Need yoking with man's daily problems and strife,
For truth and beauty and virtue are
Confirmed by their uses in practical life.

[Anonymous]

As we consider these exemplars of controversy, I express a heartfelt plea that we, as CRA members, make a genuine effort to span the chasm between interested external stakeholders beyond the boundaries of our current literacy community and draw them into our circle of friends as colleagues in a caring conversation.

References

The duty of civility. (1995, May/June). *Royal Bank Letter of Canada*, 76 (3), 2.

Kamil, M. L. (1995). Critical issues: Some alternatives to paradigm wars in literacy research. *Journal of Reading Behavior*, 27, 243-261.

Marks, J. (1996). The American [un]civil wars. *U.S. News and World Report*, 120 (16), 66-73.

Mulock, D.M. (1976). In R. L. Evan (Ed.), *Richard L. Evan's quote book*. Salt Lake City, UT: Publishers Press.

Ruskin, J. (1976). In R. L. Evan (Ed.), *Richard L. Evan's quote book*. Salt Lake City, UT: Publishers Press.

Vacca, R. T., & Vacca, J. L. (1983). Guest editorial: Two less than fortunate consequences of reading research in the 1970s. *Reading Research Quarterly*, 28, 382-383.

Williams, W. E. (1996, September 13). U. S. students may feel good, but they still lack vital skills. *Deseret News*, p. 13A.

Zeichner, K. M. (1995). Beyond the divide of teacher research and academic research. *Teachers and Teaching: Theory and Practice*, 1, 153-172.

IF THE HORSE IS DEAD, GET OFF

Wayne Otto

Professor Emeritus
University of Wisconsin

Keynote Address
College Reading Association
1996

Wayne Otto, a former US Marine and high school English teacher, earned his doctorate from the University of Wisconsin-Madison in 1961. He taught at the University of Oregon for three years, the University of Georgia for one year, then joined the faculty of the Department of Curriculum and Instruction at the University of Wisconsin-Madison and served there until 1995. He coauthored several books, one which was moderately successful (Corrective and Remedial Teaching, *three editions), and contributed to the development of instructional materials including the* Wisconsin Design for Reading Skill Development. *He wrote a monthly column for the* Journal of Reading *(which is now called something else) from 1985 to 1995, when he retired at the end of the spring semester. He was the major professor of 62 doctoral students, a few of whom have subsequently become good friends, and a whole bunch of master's degree students, some of whom still send an occasional Christmas card. As a Professor Emeritus he now spends his time watching tapes of* Northern Exposure, *live trapping raccoons, raising hostas and lilies, reading lots of really good books, and wondering why we keep making this learning-to-read-thing so difficult for kids.*

U sed to be that all I had to do was walk across the street when troubles troubled me. Over to the Old Style place. There amongst frosty mugs of diet Dr Pepper, Willie singing sad songs soft and sweet, and dreamy ambiance,

Reprinted from *Exploring Literacy,* pp. 37-49 by W. M. Linek & E. G. Sturtevant, Eds, 1977, Commerce, TX: College Reading Association

I'd spend a couple hours telling Jimmy and be healed. Go in with blue eyes cryin' in the rain and come out back on the road again.

But now that I'm retired, living in the country, the Old Style place and Jimmy are a trip to town away. Out of sight and almost out of mind because out here the closest thing to trouble is when the heifers get out and trample the lilacs. Excitement is maybe burning some brush in the driveway. But that was before I heard from Marino.

When I heard from Marino, what I told him was that, sure, I could be at the next College Reading Association meeting and how pleased I was to be asked. It seemed like an okay idea at the time, there at the American Reading Forum annual meeting on Sanibel Island in December. Must have been the surfeit of sunshine, Dove bars, and grits that had got me feeling so euphoric. Besides, who could pass up a trip to Charleston, jewel of the Atlantic seaboard?

Of course I was feeling different by the time I got back to the cold reality of December in Wisconsin, after the customary delays at the Detroit airport. I've always looked forward to making formal presentations with about as much gusto as cleaning behind the kitchen stove or passing a kidney stone, so the prospect of coming out of retirement for a rare public appearance made me wish I'd asked Doc Crocker to renew my Prozac prescription. I asked Diane if she thought Marino would believe it if I told him my Pacemaker was on the blink and just didn't show up.

She said I could suit myself, but she was going to Charleston. Not only that, she said, but she'd be taking a side trip to Savannah to check out that garden of good and evil that's been haunting the best seller list for the past three years or so.

So I did what I'd always done when troubles troubled me. I waited until the township's crack snow removal team had knocked over our mailbox, I blew the biggest drifts out of the driveway, and then I drove to town.

Jimmy seemed a little bit distracted when he slid my diet Dr. Pepper down the bar, kept edging over toward the book he'd just put down. But true to the high traditions of the fraternity of barkeeps, he pulled up a stool when I started pouring out my pitiful tale of woe. When I got to the part where I wondered what I could say to such a distinguished group of colleagues, he stopped me with a gesture and he said, "Don't you big shot perffessers ever read any books?"

He popped me another diet Dr Pepper and he showed me his book. It was Kinky Friedman's *Elvis, Jesus, and Coca Cola* (1993). (I knew about Kinky Friedman. I'd seen him on the Stephanie Miller Show. He's not merely a guitar playing country and western singer and band leader of considerable repute; he is also the author of quite an impressive string of mystery novels that have earned him more than just passing critical acclaim. And he earned my admiration and respect after Stephanie schmeikled him about all the subtle meaning his fans keep finding in his works. Kinky replied that people seem to be able to get a lot more out of his books than he puts into them. That's a degree of insight and candor seldom seen in my line of work.) I leaned forward in anticipation.

Jimmy opened his book, told me listen to this, and quoted me a line where Kinky is addressing his associate, Ratso, as follows: "We have another wise old saying in Texas, Ratso . . . When the horse is dead, get off' (Friedman, 1993, p. 36).

Jimmy let that sink in for a while. Then he said, "You reading people got lotsa dead horses cluttering up your field. That's bad. What's worse is that you people just keep on riding the dead ones."

After he'd let that sink in for a while, he said, "Talk about the horses." And then, before I could ask which horses looked deadest to him, he said, "Now get outta here; I gotta finish this book before the after-work crowd comes barging in." He smiled when he said it.

Naturally, I called Fats Grobnik, my confidant and seer, to see what he might say about the dead hoses. Seemed like a good idea to him, he said, but he couldn't talk because he just happened to be right in the middle of *Armadillos and Old Lace* (Friedman, 1994), another of Kinky's creations, and he had to find out if the butler did it, and he hung up.

Which was okay with me, because I was pretty sure by then that there would be enough dead horses out there to last me at least an hour. I pawed the turf and got set to break out of the starting gate.

But then I remembered a little ritual that Diane started years ago. On Derby Day she always makes us a couple of mint juleps and we watch the annual running of the Kentucky Derby. It isn't the race, it's the juleps that bring me back year after year; but I have learned one thing from watching. And that's that picking the right horses is no easy task.

So I got to thinking that I'd better be careful not to talk about just any old horses—not sick ones or wounded ones or three legged ones, not even little dead ones. I should talk about the really big ones—Morgans and Clydesdales—and the really dead ones. I reined in my urge for a quick breakaway and e-mailed out a call for help.

I told a very select few of my most trusted colleagues about Kinky's words to the wise and I asked them to tell me about their dead horses. I told them that I wanted to know what reading practices and programs and rituals and tribal behaviors they thought were the biggest and the deadest of the dead horses that reading professionals continue to ride.

My esteemed colleagues' responses were enthusiastic, even passionate. They told me they were seeing lots of dead horses being ridden out there; and judging from their language, some of them were pretty upset about it. It was reassuring to know that it isn't just Jimmy, Fats, and me who see dead horses when we survey the field of reading. And it was challenging to see that their responses were diverse—they were seeing some horses that I'd missed. And they were calling some horses that I HAD seen by entirely different names. That was disconcerting.

I could see that I'd need to do some serious sifting and winnowing in order to find the biggest and deadest horses that reading professionals continue to try to ride. What I finally came up with is my personal Top Ten list of dead horses, which I shall momentarily submit for your scrutiny. But first, take that moment to think what horses would be on your personal list if you were, perchance, to make one. My guess is that your list wouldn't be very different from mine. We'll see. Meanwhile, no wagering, please.

Top Ten

10. **Early, Intensive Teaching of Phonics.** If this horse isn't dead, it ought to be; but what with people like Phyllis Schlafly glued to the saddle, I doubt that the people who are riding it can be persuaded to get off. I think it was Mike Royko who called Schlafly "the national nag." Which brings to my mind an intriguing picture: the national nag riding the national nag.

I truly believe that some people are born with a phonics gene and some are not. People with the phonics gene are irrefutably convinced that they themselves can recognize words effortlessly, spell flawlessly, and understand perfectly everything ever written by Plato, Shakespeare, and Newt Gingrich because they were taught (they never say they learned, they always say they were taught) phonics early and well. And they all believe that everyone else should be—or should have been—taught the same phonics in the same way that they themselves were taught.

People without the phonics gene generally seem to think that a little phonics isn't likely to do serious harm; and many of them actually think a balanced diet that includes some phonics can be quite nutritious.

I place myself in the latter group, the balanced diet group. So while I'm hoping that the phonics nag will finally be abandoned, I'm also hoping that it manages to leave a few of its genes behind to enrich the pool.

Now let me add another short parenthetical observation. When I read E. D. Hirsch's new book, *The Schools We Need and Why Don't We Have Them* (1996), I sort of expected him to be an early, intensive phonics nut. So I was pleased when he took what I just called a balanced diet position instead. Hirsch laments the unproductive polarization that results when the "phonics approach" is characterized as "conservative, hickory stick, and Republican" and the "whole language approach"—generally identified as the antithesis of phonics—is characterized as "liberal, wishy washy, and Democratic." And then he says that in the heat of battle, few have wanted to listen to Chall and Adams, who found that middle of the road approaches, including phonics and whole-language, are the most effective. I'm not sure I agree with his choice of exemplary middle-of-the-roaders, but I can't hate a guy who is willing to take a balanced, commonsense position regarding phonics instruction.

Which brings me to my next dead horse....

9. **(Capital W) Whole (Capital L) Language.** This was a pretty good horse until it got the big WL branded on its flank. After that, lots of folks apparently failed to notice that what had been a perfectly sensible collection of ideas had deteriorated into effete rhetoric and bumper sticker slogans, so they continued to climb onto that poor horse until it died. Died of mismanagement and abuse. And that's a crying shame, because a dead horse makes an awfully easy target for all the slings and arrows that professional education critics care to hurl its way.

Again, I think we had a good horse here before it got branded and ridden to death by people who lacked the good sense to keep it up and running. Like the phonics horse, I hope it left some genes in the pool.

8. **Explicit Instruction Is Bad.** I approach this horse with some trepidation; I'm not so sure I want to declare it dead. No doubt about it, there's a lot of ill-conceived and poorly-executed explicit instruction going on out there, and it's bad. Still, on the other hand, there is a widely held belief in certain education circles that any and all explicit instruction is bad—that it's unnatural. I'm not certain where such a belief originated, but in reading education it has been broadcast and strengthened by pronouncements from WL gurus. To be fair, some of those pronouncements have been vastly over interpreted by zealous disciples, but that only adds to the mystique.

Personally, I'm satisfied with the abundance of common sense evidence to show that while some learning occurs as a function of holistic activity, other learning does indeed proceed from direct instruction. I have heard that Courtney Cazden, for example, talks about the "Peekaboo" and "Bye-Bye" metaphors for learning (and teaching). Infants learn to play peekaboo by playing it. On the other hand, most parents spend a fair amount of time and effort teaching their children the appropriate way, place, and time to say bye-bye. I think if we'd introspect for a moment, each of us could think of some instances where *Holistic Learning* and other instances where *Direct Instruction* is the more effective in helping people learn to read.

So do you see what I mean about approaching this horse with trepidation? To declare *Explicit Instruction is Bad* a dead horse is to suggest that explicit instruction is good. Which it is—sometimes. But other times it isn't. So there's your dilemma. Of course it could easily be resolved with the application of a little common sense. But ours is a field where the application of common sense is singularly uncommon. Hence, my trepidation.

7. **Programs and Models.** This is the Wonder Horse. It's the deadest of the lot, so I wonder why so many people keep trying to ride it. I wonder why well read, deeply insightful, perfectly sensible people keep skulking around publishers' displays and rushing off to visit far-away sites in search of better ways to teach reading. That the horse is dead is amply demonstrated by the

fact that programs and models for teaching reading come and go as regularly as the seasons change. Yet multitudes keep to the saddle, looking to strangers for answers to questions that only they, themselves, can answer.

Personally, I'm convinced that the Programs and Models Horse has always been propped up mainly by charlatans and self-serving schemers—and, yes, a few sincere but misguided dreamers. I'm in no position to cast stones because I, myself, have—in a previous incarnation—participated in a large scale program/model development project. I, of course, see myself as one of the few misguided dreamers; but the fact is that the Wisconsin Design for Reading Skill Development, in spite of (or possibly to a great extent because of) good intentions, proved to be a dismal failure. As I experienced it, the failure wasn't due to shoddy construction; it was due to the fact that the people who attempted to adopt the developed program hadn't had the experience of participating in its development. Trying to make it work was like trying to run a marathon in somebody else's shoes. I don't think that experience was unique. I think that somebody else's program will always turn out to be a poor fit.

So our landfills are full of ill-fit programs that failed. Small wonder, though, that the pursuit of canned programs and models persists: It's good for business. When a program dies, all the so-called experts on the chicken and peas banquet circuit simply change their banners and start selling another brand of snake oil. Nice work if you can stand it.

Neil Postman makes a relevant observation in his 1995 book, *The End of Education.* He says, "There was a time when educators became famous for providing reasons for learning; now they become famous for inventing a method" (p. 26).

I think that the poor Programs and Models horse may have done itself in. Just couldn't bear the embarrassment any longer.

6. **Study Skills.** I know that the old proverb says it doesn't pay to beat a dead horse; but I like to beat this one just for the pure pleasure of it. Common sense has always told us—and the preponderance of available research is in agreement—that if you don't know what in hell is going on before you start to study, you won't know what in hell is going on after you've studied, no matter how snappy the acronym for your study skill may have been. Nevertheless, study skills continue to be taught in content-free environments. And, worse, study skills continue to be taught with a kind of "one size fits all" assumption that displays a glib disregard for differences in individuals' background knowledge or for personal needs, aspirations, and style. I want to kick this dead horse because it continues to attract so many determined riders.

Mitchel Resnick makes a couple of points in *Turtles, Termites, and Traffic Jams* (1994) that I think we reading teachers ought to keep in mind when we think about ways to enhance our students' learning. He happens to be talking specifically about the teaching of geometry, but the points are valid across the curriculum. He says that we shouldn't be looking for the best way to do geometry; we should be looking for MORE ways of doing (and thinking about) geometry. Two reasons:

First, "Different people find different approaches more accessible....Too often, schools give special status to particular ways of thinking about mathematical and scientific ideas. By privileging certain types of thinking, they exclude certain types of thinkers" (p. 103). Second, "Everyone can benefit from learning multiple ways of thinking about things....Understanding something in several different ways produces an overall understanding that is richer and of a different nature than any one way of understanding" (p. 103). Those statements are as relevant, I think, for teaching, say, history and literature as they are for teaching geometry.

Privileging certain types of thinking and limiting ways of understanding: That's what killed the Study Skills horse a long, long time ago. Time to get off and move upwind.

5. **Getting It Right.** Here's a dead horse that I might have missed if it hadn't been for the wisdom that Barry Sanders shares in a splendid book titled *A Is For Ox* (1994). This is what he says:

> Given the way that most schools currently teach reading and writing—the primary, traditional tools for knowing and reasoning—an observer might readily conclude that fiction has developed out of a spirit of determined seriousness, and that teachers have quite naturally committed themselves to continuing that somber tradition. But history actually reveals quite the contrary: the roots of storytelling lie buried deep in play and joking, a fact that the majority of teachers appears to have forgotten....Schools draw on an opposite scenario. Young children give up the freedom and formlessness of play, and struggle to "get it right" in reading and writing. (pp. 79-80)

Small wonder, then, that so many people leave school not only unwilling ever to read again, but also perfectly willing to pay Hallmark three bucks a pop to express their innermost musings for them in writing. Sanders has lots more to say about the traditions of playfulness and the need for teachers to be playful in their approaches to reading and writing. He's happily offering us a horse of another color. Let's get on it and go!

4. **Reader Response.** It's a crying shame, but this once magnificent steed was ridden to death by riders who just never bothered to get to know their animal. Sadder still, it looks to me as if good intentions contributed heavily to its demise; I think lots of people who did manage to get off the dead *Getting It Right* horse and the dead *Study Skills* horse climbed onto the ***Reader Response*** horse and rode off at full gallop—in the wrong direction. Poor horse may have dropped dead of a broken heart.

It was a good thing to acknowledge that texts may have multiple meanings and that readers always bring very personal and sometimes quite idiosyncratic meanings to written words. It was good to see the privileged ways of thinking that follow from teacher-dominated interpretations of texts move away from center stage and to see multiple ways of understanding move a little closer to the limelight. It was a good thing to view students as active meaning makers rather than passive recipients of knowledge. But it was not a good thing to push the author far from the limelight, or, as some zealots would have it, off the stage entirely. To do this is, as Michael Smith (in press) so nicely puts it, to deny the intelligence that created the text in the first place.

When the Reader Response horse started pulling a bandwagon, too many people jumped onto one side and the wagon lost its balance. Maybe that's what killed the horse.

We educators have never been very good at striking balances. But we're real good at killing off promising horses.

3. **Teacher Training in Reading.** You say you're surprised to see a horse with so much life left in it on this Top Ten list? That's not what surprises me. What surprises me is that it's still got so much life left in it. And what irritates, agitates, and dismays me is that so many so called teacher education programs always have been, still are, and are likely to remain teacher *Training* programs—particularly in reading.

Now I'm not just quibbling over a trivial semantic point here. I mean to be saying that there is a vast difference between teacher training and teacher education; and the difference is exacerbated in the field of reading education because reading is generally approached as "method," not as "content"—or as anything else that has any inherent substance or value. Barry Sanders speaks to this point in *A Is For Ox* (1994). Sanders talks about

> ...the critical difference between understanding literacy as inseparable from the cognitive development of the self and literacy as an externally measured set of skills—a commodity that can be quantified, packaged, and delivered by professionals. Reading and writing turn into literacy by measuring them through statistics—levels of reading skills, rates of comprehension, and so on. Reading and writing are being lost as activities that transform a person into an entirely different creature, a person who has the capability of making continual discoveries about himself or herself. They are being lost as activities through which one finds constant surprises in sentences—both written and spoken—and in the self. (p. 200)

Personally, I'm convinced that another major reason why reading and writing are being lost as activities that transform, surprise, and delight readers and writers is that prospective teachers of reading and writing continue to be trained. They are trained to be efficient users of so-called achievement measures and diagnostic tests and enthusiastic pushers of whatever instructional materials got the most visibility at the last IRA convention.

One fundamental problem, I think, is that we reading teachers have always given far too much attention to *how,* and far too little to *who, what, when, where, and why.* We could take a lesson from Anne Lamott. The subtitle of her bestselling book, *Bird by Bird* (1994), is "Some Instructions on Writing and Life." She's talking education, not training. And so is Sven Birkerts, in a book that's titled and subtitled *The Gutenberg Elegies: The Fate of Reading in an Electronic Age* (1994). A reviewer for *The New York Times* says Birkerts' writing about reading "makes you want to go and do it." When's the last time you felt that way after reading a reading methods text?

Another fundamental problem, I think, is that we teachers of reading teachers have gotten carried away in our quest for self-importance. Richard Dawkins, the famed evolutionary biologist, sums up the problem quite nicely in a passage from a challenging book, *The Third Culture* (1995), edited by John Brockman:

> P. D. Medawar said that there are some fields that are genuinely difficult, where if you want to communicate you have to work really hard to make the language simple, and there are other fields that are fundamentally very easy, where if you want to impress people you have to make the language more difficult than it needs to be. And there are some fields in which—to use Medawar's lovely phrase—people suffer from 'physics envy.' They want their subject to be treated as profoundly difficult, even when it isn't. Physics genuinely is difficult, so there's a great industry for taking the difficult ideas of physics and making them simpler for people to understand; but, conversely, there's another industry for taking subjects that really have no substance at all and pretending they do—dressing them up in a language that's incomprehensible for the very sake of incomprehensibility, in order to make them seem profound. (p. 200)

Call me an unrelenting curmudgeon if you must; but, let's face it, we teachers of reading teachers are so smitten by physics envy that our affliction has reached the delusional stage. How else could we manage to stay on this long dead Teacher Training horse?

2. **Guess What I'm Thinking.** Michael Smith (in press) has another name for this horse; he calls it Keeping Secrets. By any other name, though, the horse is unmistakable: It's the one that has the answers to all kinds of questions, but seldom or never lets students in on how—or why—those particular answers were obtained.

Michael argues that teachers ought to be able to share their secrets, to tell their students how they, as experts, engage in reading and to explain how experts come up with all those answers. As it is, teachers are inclined to try to enlighten their students by giving them answers, but to leave them in the dark about finding answers on their own. What reading teachers need to do, Michael says, is to study their own behaviors to determine what their personal secrets are, because secrets that haven't been articulated can't be shared. The goal is not to encourage novices to copy experts, but to help novices understand what experts do.

Personally, I've long been troubled by how uncommunicative we ostensible "reading experts" are about how we ourselves tackle various reading tasks. Like Michael, I think the main reason is that most of us haven't done a very thorough job of articulating what goes on when we, ourselves, read. We reading teachers are much more inclined to look to strangers for descriptions of effective reading behaviors than to trust our own insights. So we tend always to be in the position of peddling second hand goods. Second-hand Roses, that's us.

We reading teachers need a better sense of where we are as readers and sufficient self assurance to talk openly about our own insights into the complexities and wonders of reading. There's a fresh horse waiting. We ought to ride it.

1. **Being Digital.** Okay, I admit it; I'm being defensive here, giving my Number One Dead Horse the same name that MIT's Media Lab founder Nicholas Negroponte gave his bestselling book, *Being Digital* (1995). I just don't want you to think that I'm an old fogy so ignorant of stuff like Negroponte's book that I simply knee-jerk reject anything and everything that smacks of high tech. In fact, it was Negroponte himself who convinced me that, insofar as the field of reading education is concerned, this horse is dead.

Of the three reasons he gives for choosing the old-fashioned book rather than a more exotic, multimedia format to describe the future, the third is the "more personal, slightly ascetic" (p. 8):

> Interactive multimedia leaves very little to the imagination. Like a Hollywood film, multimedia narrative includes such specific representations that less and less is left to the mind's eye. By contrast, the written word sparks images and evokes metaphors that get much of their meaning from the reader's imagination and experiences. When you read a novel, much of the color, sound, and motion come from you. I think the same kind of personal extension is needed to feel and understand what "being digital" might mean to your life. (p. 8)

And then Negroponte, a self-described dyslexic, adds, "You are expected to read yourself into this book. And I say this as somebody who does not like to read" (p. 8).

The media wizard, it seems to me, has a finer grasp of the essence of reading—and of what ought to be important to those of us who profess to teach reading—than far too many reading experts, whether they be certificated or self proclaimed.

I'm tempted, now, to shower you with quotations from the authors I've been mentioning—Sanders, Birkerts, Lamott, Resnick, Smith, Postman—to bolster my proclamation that the digital horse is dead. But then you could say I protest too much, particularly since I've already told you that I'm being defensive here. So I'll simply leave you in the company of these authors—including Negroponte—to contemplate the horse.

You may conclude that insofar as reading education is concerned, the Digital horse was stillborn, that it never got a chance to show how it might have run. You may even conclude that there is reason to hope that in the fullness of time there will be a resurrection.

And I wouldn't disagree.

Some Spare Horses

When I finished my Top Ten list, I did what I always do when I finish writing something: I faxed it to Fats, who has his finger on the pulse of America. I knew he'd know if I'd managed to pick the biggest and the deadest of the horses that lie dead in the field of reading education.

The next day I called. "Hey, Fats," I said, "what do you think?"

"I think we ought to go fishing," Fats said. "I heard that the bluegills are biting in Partridge Lake." And then he told me about his new Winnebago—two bedrooms, four baths, and a walk-in cooler—and that we could park over by the river in Fremont and he'd pick me up in the morning. Finally, just as I was about to abandon hope, he said, "Oh yeah, about the horses. Those buggers look really dead to me . . . and big. But you might want to round up a couple of extras, just in case you don't manage to use up your whole hour."

And he was gone, no doubt to start stocking the walk-in cooler.

Which was okay with me, because with a few well chosen words he had, as usual, managed not only to put his finger on the pulse of a possible problem, but also to embolden me to do what I really wanted to do. Which was to have at least twelve horses on my Top Ten list.

So here's another one.

Remedial Reading

No question about this one: It's a real horse and it's really dead. The only reason it didn't make my Top Ten list is that I was too embarrassed to put it there after having taught the course for years and years. Because it is our bread and butter, we remedial reading teachers try to convince a gullible public that we possess magical potions and incantations that can transform late bloomers, listless dullards, the linguistically deprived, and the ineptly taught into successful and enthusiastic readers. Of course we've never been able to deliver on most of the promises we make, but never mind. We've come up with such good excuses that we've almost come to believe them ourselves.

It seems clear to me that it was never very sensible to get that poor old Remedial Reading nag up and running in the first place. If all the resources that have gone into remedial reading had been given over to sound instruction the first time around, we'd be riding a horse with a decent chance of finishing in the chips.

I don't think we ever really thought that Remedial Reading would win any races. But hey, we're human; we make mistakes. So let's admit that we made one. The horse is dead. We finished it off. Now let's get off.

Now here's the last one. I saved the best 'til last.

Research

My first impulse was to put Reading Research at the very top of my Top Ten list of dead horses. That's because after more than three decades in the business, I'd be hard pressed to say what positive effects have come out of all the so-called reading research that's gone on. Of course there have been some changes from time to time, but I'm inclined to argue that they haven't been very widespread and they haven't been really substantive. In any event, it seems to me that what changes there have been have come as a result of political and philosophical shifts, not research.

It was hard for me to see a horse for all the riders; but I figured if the Research horse wasn't going anywhere, it must be dead.

Still, I decided to take a closer look, and do you know what? I never did find a corpus delicti. I finally realized that I couldn't find a dead horse because there wasn't any horse. All those riders were just piled up on top of each other, so busy posturing and proclaiming that they didn't even notice that they weren't going anywhere. Worse yet, they were so happy strutting and showing off for each other that they couldn't care less about missing the horse.

So I'm pretty sure there's a perfectly sound Research horse out there someplace, fresh and waiting to be ridden. In this case, it isn't the horse that needs changing, it's the riders.

The underlying problem, I'm convinced, is that in reading research and in the larger enterprise of reading education, it isn't a search for truth that drives our efforts and defines our aspirations, it's a desire to be on the winning team. We reading educators have chosen to engage in a political struggle—to hell with truth and decency. Wendy Kaminer (1995), who happens to be one of my most treasured personal heroes, says that truth in a political struggle is dependent upon politics and is primarily ideological rather than factual in correctness.

Small wonder, then, that so many of us continue to ride dead horses. It isn't the horse that matters. It's the brand on its flank.

References

Birkerts, S. (1994). *The Gutenberg elegies: The fate of reading in an electronic age.* New York: Fawcett Columbine.

Brockman, J. (1995). *The third culture.* New York: Touchstone Book/Simon & Schuster.

Friedman, K. (1993). *Elvis, Jesus, and Coca Cola.* New York: Simon and Schuster.

Friedman, K. (1994). *Armadillos and old lace.* New York: Simon and Schuster.

Hirsch, E. D., Jr. (1996). *The schools we need and why we don't have them.* New York: Doubleday.

Kaminer, W. (1995). *It's all the rage: Crime and culture.* Reading, PA: Addison Wesley.

Lamott, A. (1994). *Bird by bird: Some instructions on writing and life.* New York: Anchor Books/Doubleday.

Negroponte, N. (1995). *Being digital.* New York: Vintage Books/Random House.

Postman, N. (1995). *The end of education: Redefining the value of school.* New York: Knopf.

Rabinowitz, P., & Smith, M. W. (in press). *Resistance and respect in the reading of literature.* New York: Teachers College Press.

Resnick, M. (1994). *Turtles, termites, and traffic jams: Explorations in massively parallel microworlds.* Cambridge, MA: Bradford Book/MIT Press.

Sanders, B. (1994). *A is for ox: The collapse of literacy and the rise of violence in an electronic age.* New York: Vintage Books/Random House.

My Life in Reading

Jeanne S. Chall

Harvard University

Keynote Address
College Reading Association
1997

In 1997, Jeanne S. Chall, was emeritus professor at Harvard University, Graduate School of Education where she founded and directed the graduate program in reading, language and learning disabilities. She has written widely. Among her books are Learning to Read: The Great Debate, Stages of Reading Development, The Reading Crisis: Why Poor Children Fall Behind, Creating Successful Readers, Readability Revisited and the New Dale-Chall Readability Formula, *and* Qualitative Assessment of Text Difficulty.

She is a member of the National Academy of Education and the Reading Hall of Fame and has served on the Board of Directors of the International Reading Association and the National Society for the Study of Education. She is also a member of the Orton Dyslexia Society Council of Advisors. She has received many awards, including the Edward L. Thorndike award from the American Psychological Association for distinguished psychological contributions to education and the American Educational Research Association's award for significant contributions to educational research. She has received the Samuel T Orton Award from the Orton Dyslexia Society, as well.

I taught my first class as a student teacher in New York City's Taft High School in 1941. I had looked forward to teaching, having been an education major. I was introduced to educational research a year later at Teachers College, Columbia University. My love for educational research was unexpected and came

Reprinted from *Literacy and Community,* pp. 12-24, by E. G. Sturtevant, J. R. Dugan, P. Linder & W. M. Linek, Eds., 1998. Commerce, TX: College Reading Association.

as a complete surprise. I had no idea that one could work in education doing research. Nor do I recall that any of my instructors in education were engaged in research. If they were, I was not aware of it.

Within a few days at the Institute of Psychological Research at Teachers College I was smitten as I observed such notable researchers as Irving Lorge and Sophia M. Robinson. My role was to keep notes and to calculate means, standard deviations, and correlations—it was before computers. But it seemed that I could not find a more exciting way to spend my time and with a more exciting group of people. They were helping children and furthering knowledge in a disciplined way. I knew, then, that I wanted to do the same.

Thus, I came to my two loves in education early—my love of teaching and educational practice and my love of inquiry. Although research and practice are often seen as different pursuits, I found that, for me, they had great similarities and were intimately related to each other.

At Teachers College, the project with which I assisted sought workable solutions to one of the great pressing educational problems of that time and today—how best to educate juvenile delinquents and to prevent delinquency—whether to place delinquents in separate schools or to provide them with psychological services and an improved curriculum in regular schools. Among the findings, which are still being found today, 50 years later, were that psychological services (counseling and social services) and a curriculum that had a better match with students' achievement were effective in decreasing the number of delinquents in the regular schools—more effective than special schools. I realized early how practical research can be.

Several years later I learned a similar lesson at Ohio State University as Edger Dale's research assistant. Our task was to assist the National Tuberculosis Association by finding ways to make their pamphlets and other print media more readable for the layman. This very practical mission led to basic research on readability and vocabulary; the Dale-Chall Readability Formula was developed to help assess the difficulty of the pamphlets. It also led to the development of a manual on clear and simple writing. Research and practice were intimately related—with research leading to good practice and real problems leading to useful research.

Throughout my long career I have engaged in both practice and research, usually at the same time. Since educational practice does not leave tracks as does educational research, I should like to mention at least some of the practice I have engaged in.

I have taught students of all ages for more than a half century. Much of it was at the college and graduate level, but much, too, has been with students at all levels who needed special help with their reading.

I have also worked as an advisor and as a consultant on a variety of educational projects, including children's encyclopedias, an educational comic book, computer programs, and the Children's Television Workshop's "Sesame Street" and "The Electric Company." I have consulted with schools and school systems to help them ask and answer educational questions.

These practical assignments helped me gain perspective on the important questions being asked in education—by teachers, administrators, educational publishers, and the media—and they kept me from being too theoretical, too removed from reality. I learned to make the most out of the knowledge that existed and not to resort, unless absolutely necessary, to the use of "we need more research" as an answer to questions. I realized early that even the most theoretical studies ultimately boil down to a yes or no response. Is this or that idea more useful? Should this or that be done? If neither, what should be done?

I was a member of various investigative and policy making committees and commissions organized by professional associations, state and national departments of education, and also a member of the boards of directors of various professional groups. Thus, I had further opportunity to blend research and practice and to broaden my educational perspective.

Focus on Reading

Most of my work—research and practice—has focused on reading. From time to time I have wandered off to mathematics, or to the non-print media, but I soon came back to reading. It offers a broad panorama and great challenge—vast and almost endless issues for research and practice. At the same time, I found reading to be very basic, very much like the bread and butter of education. It is the oldest and most enduring of subjects taught in schools. It is an essential foundation for learning almost all other school subjects—literature, social studies, science, math. It is essential for most jobs in an advanced, technological society.

When reading does not develop as it should, when it lags behind the age and cognitive development of the individual, it brings serious personal frustrations and loss of confidence. It brings equally serious losses to society. In fact, the importance of reading for society and the individual seems to have grown even during the years I have studied it. We are reminded almost daily by leading economists in the United States that we may slip from our status as a world class nation if our work force does not achieve a higher level of literacy. They remind us that when we were a manufacturing nation fewer people needed to be highly literate. But a high-tech society—one that produces and disseminates knowledge and symbols—needs more people who are highly literate. There seems to be a growing mismatch between workers and jobs—with jobs that cannot be filled because workers are not literate enough. But it is not for work alone that there is a mismatch. Responsible citizenship also requires higher literacy, and personal literacy needs seem also to grow with time. The labels on food and medicine packages require considerable reading ability. Add to this the growing numbers of children reported to have reading and learning disabilities, and the low levels of literacy found among minority students. Further, if one considers the low reading scores on the National Assessment of Educational Progress and the failure to significantly raise the verbal scores on the Scholastic Assessment Test, it is not difficult to see why I have stayed with reading and literacy.

There is still one other reason. The field of reading is so rich and varied that I have been able to change my focus within it, making it ever more interesting and challenging.

Studies in Readability

My first research efforts were in readability and in vocabulary, an interest I acquired from Edger Dale, my teacher and mentor at the Bureau of Educational Research at Ohio State University. I worked with him on the development of the Dale-Chall Readability Formula and on various studies of vocabulary during the four years of my graduate study at Ohio State. These formative years were followed by nearly forty years of collaboration on research and writing. In fact, one of our works, *Readability Revisited and the New Dale-Chall Readability Formula* (Dale & Chall), was published in 1995.

I found readability a fascinating subject for research and for application. It was an excellent vehicle for studying reading development—through the changes that take place in the texts that can be read by readers of growing proficiency.

Readability drew its knowledge from many disciplines—the humanities, psychology, statistics, language, semantics—and in turn could be applied to textbooks, newspapers, and magazines, comic books, radio, and so forth.

The four years of working closely on readability and vocabulary with Edgar Dale also taught me lessons about research that still remain with me.—One of these first lessons was the value of past research—why it is important and how to use it.

After a year as research assistant, Dale suggested that I write an article on readability, a review of research. Although I had been assisting him for a year, I did not feel quite ready to write such an article. To be more accurate, I was terrified. I protested that I didn't know enough. "That is why you should write it," he said. "You will learn from your writing."

I started the research with much anxiety, fear, and agony. "Why should I do this?" I thought. Reviewing the past research is not original. I wanted to get on with the new. But after all the fussing, I finally finished it and had to admit it had been a good assignment after all. I gained familiarity with the past research on readability and an ease in working with the ideas of earlier researchers. I gained different viewpoints on the topic—some that were unpopular at the time they were first proposed were later accepted and became the dominant view. I felt

I knew the researchers whose work I reviewed, and I knew how they thought. When I met several of the researchers during the ensuing years, I felt that we had been friends for many years.

I had beginner's luck with that first article. "This Business of Readability" was reprinted in two digest journals (Chall, 1947). But more valuable was the taste for historical synthesis that I developed. My love for this style of research lead to my books, *Readability: An Appraisal of Research and Application* (Chall, 1958), *Learning to Read: The Great Debate* (Chall, 1967), and *Stages of Reading Development* (Chall, 1983). Each received strong research reviews. When I undertook *The Great Debate* (1967), many of my colleagues were skeptical. The research I planned to review was so confused, they said, how could I find anything by going over it again? But I had confidence, from my earlier experiences, that if I stuck with it and found a structure, I would find something useful. Syntheses of past research were out of fashion for a long time but have recently come back in favor. *Becoming a Nation of Readers* (Anderson, Heibert, Scott, & Wilkonson, 1985) is a more current research synthesis by a commission, of which I was a member.

Dale knew that one has to know what scholars of the past knew on a subject if one is to make useful contributions to that subject. He never assumed that what was done in the past was no longer useful or worth knowing. He also knew that the new research does not always clear up all the problems of the past research. Indeed, the results of the new can be more confusing than the old.

Knowing the past research keeps one from being too much within the current fashion. One can see trends in ideas in a field only from a deep grounding in its past theories, research, and writing. It is sad, therefore, to see that current publications tend to refer only to recent writings, omitting even the classic research on a topic (Herber, 1988).

Have we decided to lose our past? If we do not know the past, and if we do not use it well in formulating practice and new research, are we not in danger of repeating the past—the bad as well as the good?

I learned another important lesson from Edgar Dale—the importance of knowing the related research from fields other than one's own. When we planned a project he asked if I had checked it out with the psychologists, the statisticians, the sociologists, and the linguists. Before sending out an article for publication he asked again if I had checked with those in other disciplines who might pick up inconsistencies, conflicts, and errors.

Today, there seems to be little reference in the field of reading to the work of those rooted in other disciplines. This is not difficult to understand, for the reading field is rich in research and writing—richer perhaps than any other field in education. No one person can keep up with all of it.

In the reading field, we seem to have at least five bodies of research—basic research (usually done by educational researchers, cognitive psychologists, and linguists); research on reading methods, materials, and classroom procedures (usually done by educational psychologists, reading specialists, and teachers); research on reading difficulties (by psychologists, neurologists, and special educators); research on the relationship of literature, writing, and reading (by linguists and students of literature and English language arts); and research on reading tests (by psychometricians). There seems to be a tendency for individuals in each of these groups to talk almost exclusively with, and to write for, others within their own field. Seldom does one group refer to the work from the others.

Recently I read an excellent longitudinal study of children's reading in grades 1 to 4. The authors reported that phonemic development was of first importance in early reading without referring to similar findings by leading researchers on language and learning disabilities at least 15 years earlier; and by educational psychologists in the 1930s for beginning reading.

Ignoring the relevant research of others is not uncommon in other areas of education. Can we afford to repeat research studies when our funds are so limited, unless of course the research is a deliberate replication? And can we afford to ignore the relevant research that exists in our field and other disciplines?

Another important lesson I learned from Edgar Dale was to ask for whom one does educational research. For Dale the answer was always clear. All of his studies, including his most theoretical, were designed to be useful in the practice of education—in schools and out of schools. I remember vividly how he helped me realize this. It was after I had written one of my early research reports. He read it, made several editorial suggestions, then said, "Very nice Jeanne. It is very scholarly. What do you think it will mean to the superintendent in Winnetka, the fifth-grade teacher in Oklahoma City, the English teacher in Cleveland?" I knew then that I was far from finished. I had much rewriting to do.

This incident served almost as an imprinting. No matter how theoretical or statistical the research study may be, I try to write it also for teachers, administrators, and others who practice.

Reading Difficulty and Its Prevention

In 1950, when I joined the faculty of the City College in New York, my focus shifted from the readability of texts, in relation to readers' abilities, to the study of the readers, in relation to the texts they read. For 15 years, my interests were concentrated on the teaching of reading and ways of assessing it. I also examined the causes and treatments of those who experience special difficulties in spite of their adequate intelligence—about 10 to 15 percent of the population.

In collaboration with my colleague and Director of the Reading Center, Florence Roswell, I carried out numerous research and development projects. The projects concerned auditory blending and its effects on reading achievement, and why children of low-income families have difficulty and what could be done to remediate their difficulties. We developed tests to help teachers adjust instruction to students' needs. Similar to my collaboration with Dale, Roswell and I have continued our collaboration to the present.

It was at The City College in 1950 when I started to concentrate on the diagnosis and treatment of children, young people, and adults with reading problems. It has continued until today. Indeed, the time I have spent diagnosing and treating individuals with reading problems, and teaching and supervising teachers in this work, has been extremely absorbing and enriching. It influenced not only my teaching and research on reading difficulties, but most of my other research, particularly the research I undertook in the early 1960s on beginning reading methods. Concerned with prevention of reading problems, I sought to find whether there was any evidence that certain beginning reading methods produce better results and help prevent reading failure. This research, which was carried out when I was at The City College, became the book *Learning to Read: The Great Debate* first published in 1967, and later updated in second and third editions in 1983 and 1996.

The study, funded by the Carnegie Corporation, had many facets. It was a synthesis of the past research on beginning reading from the classroom, the laboratory, and the clinic. I also analyzed more than 20 beginning reading programs, including the two most widely used basal readers and their teacher's manuals. I interviewed authors and editors of various reading series. I observed in hundreds of classrooms and talked to as many teachers and principals. I was fortunate again, as I had been with my first synthesis article on readability, to get an almost immediate response. Although many of the reviews in the reading journals were not favorable, most that appeared in the general educational and scholarly journals were very favorable. Even more satisfying was the study's early acceptance by educational publishers in revising their reading programs and its appearance on required reading lists for courses on methods of teaching reading and reading research. Twenty years later the satisfaction was mixed with pain. Despite the fact that my update in 1983 confirmed my earlier conclusions and that my findings were confirmed by the research of linguists, cognitive psychologists, and child development specialists (Adams, 1990). misunderstandings and an attack on its findings and conclusions appeared (Carbo, 1988; Chall, 1988).

My 25 Years at Harvard University's Graduate School of Education

My move to Harvard in 1965 was marked by another shift in my concerns with reading. Much of my attention was focused on building and directing a graduate program for master's and doctoral students which had a dual purpose—training in scholarship and in practice. The Harvard Reading Laboratory was established as a training, research, and service center.

My teaching reflected the dual concerns of the program—research and practice. Through the years I taught the doctoral seminar on reading research—a historical overview of the research on reading and practice. I also taught the courses in the diagnosis and treatment of reading disabilities and,—with the assistance of doctoral students, supervised the testing and teaching in the Harvard Reading Laboratory. I taught a general course on reading for non-reading majors that focused on social policy and, in earlier years, taught the general course on the teaching of reading, as well.

I have also had the great pleasure of directing and advising the dissertations of doctoral students and of directing the research training of the many doctoral and master's students who worked with me on various research projects.

My research continued to be concerned with issues of theory and practice, but it moved over, somewhat, to theory and social policy. Among my studies of reading and social policy was the one commissioned by the Panel on the SAT Score Decline and the College Board on the relationship of textbooks to SAT scores, published in 1977 (Chall, Conard, & Harris, 1977). It was extended to a larger study, *Should Textbooks Challenge Students: The Case for Easier or Harder Books* (Chall & Conard, 1991). My interests in the medical aspects of reading failure became even stronger. I attended lectures at Harvard Medical School on neurology and language, and I edited, with Allan Mirsky, the National Society for the Study of Education Yearbook, *Education and the Brain* (Chall & Mirsky, 1978).

The unanswered questions in *The Great Debate* brought me to a theoretical study of the reading process, *Stages of Reading Development* (Chall,1983, 1996), a work on how reading changes qualitatively as it develops. This was an important study for me since many of the controversies on methods and materials seemed to stem from two theories of the reading process—a single-stage theory or a multi-stage theory. From my synthesis of the relevant theory and research on how reading develops and from my—experience in teaching reading at all levels, I concluded that a developmental multi-stage theory fit the data better and was instructionally more useful. In *The Reading Crisis: Why Poor Children Fall Behind* (Chall, Jacobs, & Baldwin, 1990), we attempted to find out why the literacy of low-income children begins to decelerate around grade 4 and how the deceleration can be prevented. The theoretical basis for the study came from my *Stages of Reading Development.* The work was further enriched by collaboration with linguists, faculty, and graduate students at Harvard.

My interests in social policy brought me to studies of the trends in the reading scores on the National Assessments of Educational Progress. I have tried to explain these trends by relating them to methods and materials used in the schools and to community support for reading (Chall, 1989).

As I reflect on my various professional interests and activities, I am aware of different concentrations at different times. During my early years I concentrated on psychology, statistics, and research design—on objectivity in searching for knowledge about reading. Later, I focused on problems in learning to read and took on the concerns of the teacher and clinician—why certain individuals had difficulty, how to help those individuals learn, and how to prevent such problems. Thus my concerns with the science of reading turned to teaching and healing, and I delved into the neurosciences as well as into the art of teaching. More recently I have been concerned with the broad social, cultural, and educational issues that are related to our reading problems and to their solution and prevention.

Examples of this concern are found in my research on textbooks and publishing, on the trends in scores on the national assessments of reading and writing, and on the methods and materials that work with children from low-income families.

I have gained much from the people I have met and worked with. I have gained great satisfaction from my teaching and have reached the age when my former students are now full professors with students of their own. I have especially gained from my work in the diagnosis and treatment of reading disabilities. Helping children, young people, and adults overcome their reading difficulties has always given me direct and immediate rewards which are especially welcome when the research on which I work reaches a frustrating point. While one cannot always move ahead in research and writing, one can always help a child learn to read.

Current Concerns

In the more than 50 years of my work in the field of reading, I have observed much growth in research and in professional activities. The public has become more conscious about the importance of literacy, for children and for adults.

With these advancements have come many problems. The reading achievement of too many children, young people, and adults is not up to what it should be. This has been reported by the National Assessment of Educational Progress, by the College Board for SAT verbal scores, by school systems throughout the nation, and by industry, which has long complained that employees are lacking the literacy skills needed for work.

I recognize that this sad state is not the sole responsibility of the reading field or of teachers, yet our efforts, particularly those concerned with the methods and materials of reading instruction, may not be fruitful because we are paying too little attention to our hard-won knowledge and experience. We seem to be so pressed by the low literacy achievement of the nation that many of us tend to drop those procedures that are backed up by research and experience for largely untested solutions.

There also seems to be less confidence now than in the past in the power of research and analysis to find better solutions. A single case study or a classroom observation or a "bright idea" is often considered equal or superior to the hard-won knowledge from research and experience.

There is also a loss of confidence in how we can best assess and evaluate reading achievement and progress, thus making it still harder to base practice on objective evidence. Often it seems as if the tests are being criticized because the results are not those we hoped for. Thus, we seem to kill the messenger, hoping it will turn the bad news to good. While there is a need for better assessment instruments, it is hard to believe that better assessments will find that the state of literacy in the United States is substantially better than it is now being reported.

Perhaps my concerns are colored by my long, positive experiences with the power of research to inform and serve practice. Do I see the past in a more ideal state? Perhaps, but I think we are going through a less analytic time at the present and that it may in the long run lead to even lower levels of reading achievement. Many of the proposals for educational reform are made with little evidence of their probable success based on theory, research, and practice. Indeed, many of the proposed changes have been used in the past, under different labels, and were found wanting.

With the loss of confidence in research has come a heightened emotionality and stridency in the dialogues among teachers, parents, and researchers. The education journalists may have caught the essence of the rhetoric by the label "reading wars." The "wars" have spilled over to teachers, to parents, and to the press who oppose and accuse each other about the uses and non-uses of best methods for the benefit of children. The rhetoric seems more heated than what I had experienced during earlier debates and controversies. There have been differences of opinion about reading instruction during the 50 years of my life in reading. But the almost religious fervor of the present rhetoric seems to go beyond what existed in the past. One asks how it is possible, when the research in reading has grown so considerably. Perhaps this vast research base, while contributing to better practices, has also contributed to the loss of faith in its use. Perhaps it is too vast and confusing and not sufficiently interpreted and synthesized.

It is sad to think that we go through the same debates over and over again and that we seem to learn so little from the past. The tendency of researchers to use ever new labels for old concepts also seems to cut us off from the tested knowledge of the past. Thus the research and writing on phonological awareness seems to cut itself off from the earlier research on phonics. Adult literacy seems to cut itself off from child and adolescent literacy, and emergent literacy is cut off from the vast knowledge and experience on reading readiness. Why, one wonders, do we need to "invent" new terms for existing and valid ideas? It may earn immediate attention and interest, but it cuts one off also from teachers who are urged to do the "new" thing when they may already be doing it, but under an old label.

Where Do We Go From Here?

My present concerns, which are many, have not shaken my strong commitment to research and theory, to the value of analysis, and to experience. In the long run, the methods and materials that will prove to be most effective will be in line with research, theory, and experience. In the meantime, many children, particularly those at risk—the children of low-income families and children of all social levels who are predisposed to having reading difficulty—are not doing as well as they can. Such children benefit most from a reading program that has been proven over the years. They need excellent teachers. They need extra help when they fall behind (Chall, Jacobs, & Baldwin, 1990). Children of middle class families are not affected as much by the reading methods and materials used by their teachers since their parents often supplement their child's reading instruction by their own teaching or by obtaining a private tutor.

To improve reading achievement I would hope that we can look more to what we know works and apply it wisely and well. For the past decades, study after study has found that certain classroom practices produce significantly better results—e.g., high expectations and books that challenge, frequent assessment and instruction based on it. A strong beginning reading program that includes systematic instruction in the alphabetic principle, and attention to word meanings in the intermediate grades and later are also important (Chall, 1987).

Unfortunately, some in the reading field act as if the solutions to our pressing problems lie mainly in changing the old, usually tested methods to untested methods—with their ensuing debates and polarities. One wonders why we do not invest that energy and time into doing better, and more widely, what does work. Indeed, research study after research study has found that students need to read widely to grow in reading. Why then don't we put our energies into better school, classroom, and community libraries? Indeed, these services seem to be declining nationally. Also, while we gain ever stronger evidence that extra instruction keeps children from falling ever more behind, the schools tend too often to underfinance this special service. There is also considerable knowledge about the kinds of programs that are effective with kindergarten and first grade children that help prevent low achievement and reduce reading problems. Why do we not look to broad applications of these programs to improve the reading of our children and young people instead of seeming always to be on a search for a single, charismatic solution?

Teachers need to know and understand this body of knowledge in reading and how it is best implemented. But much of it they already know and need only the resources and encouragement to use it.

There is also a need to look into the education of our researchers. If learning to do research is learning more than knowledge and skills, if it consists also of attitude, values, and commitments learned from an experienced researcher, which I think it does, then we must improve how we educate the next generation of researchers.

There is a need, also, for a greater simplicity in what we do. Our theories, research, and practice are becoming more complex and technical, requiring more explanations to translate to other researchers and teachers. The manuals of the major basal reading textbooks, for example, keep getting larger and heavier, suggesting that the teaching of reading to 6-year-olds requires ever more exacting directions and guidance. And the many suggestions made regularly to differentiate instruction for most children make one wonder whether it is humanely possible for a classroom teacher to carry them out.

With all of these growing complexities, one wonders how a teacher can survive. Even more, one wonders how it was possible for anyone to have learned to read before all the new methods and materials were invented. Indeed, we may ask, how did Thomas Jefferson, Abraham Lincoln, or John Dewey become such superb critical readers and writers? I think those of us who are professors, scholars, and researchers of reading must try to simplify it so that it can be understood and used.

And finally, who is to bell the cat? Who is to be responsible? Can teachers use whatever procedures they prefer without being accountable for the results they produce? If the results of standardized tests are not to be accepted, what other objective devices can be used in their place?

What is the responsibility of textbook publishers? They work in a highly competitive atmosphere, but does that mean they can use any procedures and materials that sell?

To what extent should professional organizations take responsibility? And, perhaps foremost, what is the responsibility of the scholar? Is it toward searching for new basic knowledge about the reading process? Or should it also include the responsibility of helping to solve the grave literacy problems facing us today?

An earlier version appeared in D. Burleson (Ed.), Reflections. *Bloomington, IN: Phi Delta Kappa, 1991.*

References

Adams, M. (1990). Beginning to read: Thinking and learning about print. Cambridge: MIT Press.

Anderson, R. C., Heibert, E. H., Scott, J. A., & Wilkinson, I. A. G. (1985). *Becoming a nation of readers: The Report of the Commission on Reading.* Champaign: University of Illinois, Center for the Study of Reading.

Carbo, M. (1988). Debunking the great phonic myth, *Phi Delta Kappan, 70,* 226-240.

Chall, J. S. (1947). This business of readability, *Educational Research Bulletin, 26,* 1- 13.

Chall, J. S. (1958). *Readability: An appraisal of research and application.* Columbus: Ohio State University Press.

Chall, J. S. (1987). The importance of instruction in reading methods for all teachers. In R. Bowler (Ed.), *Intimacy with language: A forgotten basic in teacher education.*

Baltimore: The Orton Dyslexia Society.

Chall, J. S. (1988).Learning to read: The great debate 10 years later—a response to 'Debunking the great phonics myth,' *Phi Delta Kappan, 70,* 521-538.

Chall, J. S. (1989). Could the decline be real? Recent trends in reading instruction and support in the U. S. In Haertel, E., et al, *Report of the NAEP Technical Review Panel on the 1986 reading anomaly, the accuracy of NAEP trends, and issues raised by state level NAEP comparisons* (pp. 61-74). Washington, DC: National Center for Education Statistics and U.S. Department of Education.

Chall, J. S. (1996). *Learning to read: The great debate (3rd ed.).* Fort-Worth, TX: Harcourt Brace.

Chall, J. S. (1996). *Stages of reading development* (2nd ed.). Fort-Worth, TX: Harcourt Brace.

Chall, J. S. & Conard, S. S. (1991). *Should textbooks challenge students? The case for easier or harder textbooks.* New York: Teacher's College Press.

Chall, J. S., Conard, S. S., & Harris, S. H. (1977). *An analysis of textbooks in relation to declining S.A.T. scores.* New York: College Entrance Examination Board.

Chall, J. S., Jacobs, V. A., & Baldwin, L. E. (1990). *The reading crisis: Why poor children fall behind.* Cambridge: Harvard University Press.

Chall, J. S., & Mirsky, A. F. (Eds.) (1978). *Education and the brain.* Chicago: University of Chicago Press.

Dale, E. & Chall, J. S. (1948). A formula for predicting readability, and instructions. *Educational Research Bulletin 27,* 11-20, 37-54.

Dale, E. & Chall, J. S. (1995). *Readability revisited and the new Dale-Chall Readability Formula.* Cambridge, MA: Brookline Books.

Herber, H. (1988, May). *The heritage of our profession.* Paper presented at the Reading Hall of Fame, International Reading Association Annual Conference, Toronto, Canada.

FINDING COMMON GROUND: A REVIEW OF THE EXPERT STUDY

Rona F. Flippo

Fitchburg State College

Keynote Address
College Reading Association
1997

In 1997, Rona F. Flippo was Professor of Reading Education at Fitchburg State College, in Massachusetts. She has authored six books and numerous articles. She was an active member in the International Reading Association, the National Reading Conference, and the Massachusetts Association of College and University Reading Educators. She served on the editorial advisory boards of The Reading Teacher, Reading Psychology, and the Journal of Adolescent & Adult Literacy.

Rona was working on several new books: the Handbook of College Reading and Study Strategy Research: What Do the experts Say?, Contexts and Practices for Classroom Reading, *and* Reading Researchers in Search of Common Ground.

Rona indicated that in retrospect, "I've been speaking out and writing for more rationality in what we do or mandate in schools to children and to teachers for a good portion of my professional life. Now, I'm writing about the need for some common ground in the reading profession in response to the ridiculous policies, mandates, and decisions we've all seen in our legislatures and media." Rona's expression of this need and her "expert study" was the topic of her Keynote Address at the College Reading Association's conference in 1997. Pulling ideas from her publication in the Phi Delta Kappan *(Flippo, 1997), "Sensationalism, politics, and literacy: What's going on?" Rona asks us to continue to seek a "common ground" and to share our agreements publicly.*

Reprinted from *Literacy and Community,* pp. 31-38, by E. G. Sturtevant, J. R. Dugan, P. Linder, & W. M. Linek, Eds., 1998, Commerce, TX: College Reading Association.

When I was a young child, growing up in Brooklyn, NY, there were certain words that I wasn't supposed to say; if I did say them, I was told that my mouth might be washed out with soap (this was a common threat to children in that culture and time). The bad words then, in my "home community" on East 48th Street, were very different from the words some thought were bad when I presented my study (December, 1996) in my "professional community" at the National Reading Conference. The really bad word there was "consensus." Because I was admonished by some for use of "the word," I intentionally tried not to use it during my next presentation of this study at the International Reading Association (IRA) Convention (May, 1997a), and I left it out entirely from the title of this College Reading Association presentation, as well as out of the papers and book proposals I subsequently wrote about my study.

The argument against "consensus" was that it would dampen the combustive sparks of intellectual discourse and intellectual growth and that it could squelch productive debate and discussion.

Now, after almost one year, I'm gratified to see that others in our reading community are beginning to call for some "consensus" or common ground. For example, in this month's *Reading Today* (October/November 1997), I noted that Jack Pikulski, IRA's new President, is warning that the very persistent Reading War is getting "dangerous," and the field does need to engage in discussion that achieves some "consensus," of some kind, soon.

Just listen to some of these headlines which I'll highlight from my Kappan article (Flippo, 1997b, pp. 301-302) to remind you about what has been going on in the media and in the political arena:

- "The Great Debate Revisited" (Levine, 1994, December, *Atlantic Monthly),*
- "As Reading Scores Plummet, States Get Hooked on Phonics" (Walters, 1996, April 18, *Christian Science Monitor),*
- "Parents Report on America's Reading Crisis: Why the Whole Language Approach to Teaching Has Failed Millions of Children" (Levine, 1996, October, *Parents Magazine),*
- "Phonics Boom: Proponents Say Any Other Approach to Reading Only Spells Trouble" (Kastor, 1996, November 15, *Washington Post),*
- "Why Kids Can't Read in California" (Saunders, 1996, January 12, *San Francisco Chronicle)* (of course they don't mention that as of 1990, more than 137 different languages were represented in California, see California Commission on Teacher Credentialing, 1996, as cited in Flippo, 1997b),
- "California Leads Revival of Teaching by Phonics" (1996, May 22, *New York Times),*

- "State Embraces Phonics in Approving New Texts" (Colvin, 1996, December 13, *Los Angeles Times*), and, I love this one:
- "State Rejects 2 Texts; Citing Phonics Law" (Gunnison, 1996, December 13, *San Francisco Chronicle*).

And within the reading community things are equally as volatile. If you don't think so, take a look at this month's *Reading Today* (October/ November 1997), where many IRA members respond to Dick Allington's commentary "Overselling Phonics," which appeared in the August/September 1997 issue.

What started out as a mostly intellectual, research question to find some areas of agreement in our field (because I saw a need for some common ground eleven years ago when I started my study), has obviously tapped into a raging battle within our profession and amongst the media, politicians, and public. Because of this, the political implications of the study are now as important as the data and the findings themselves. Therefore, much of what I'm going to talk about tonight will reflect this political tone (or tenor).

Basically, it appears that reading instruction has moved from "a concern" amongst interested parents, teachers, administrators, and others interested in education, to a "big" ticket item. In my December 1997 *Kappan* article, I point out that, in essence, the politicians have seized upon the ongoing reading debate (within our profession) as an opportunity to promote their positions and to draw attention to themselves as leaders of educational reform.

In fact, I believe that the political interest and "fire" behind the reading debates have actually further fueled "the fires" to the point that many within our profession are debating in a warlike manner—*attack, defend position, attack again.*

Rather than continue to polarize ourselves by continually focusing on our disagreements, I feel it is time to stop and really focus on the agreements that we do share as a profession. That is what I tried to do with my study.

So, where can we start? Maybe with an answer to the question, "What do reading researchers know?" We know that decisions about reading instruction should not be set up as extreme "either/or" positions. We know that phonics and other necessary skills instruction can be taught by teachers who have whole language philosophies. We also know that neither "phonics" nor "whole language" is a method, and we know that teachers should not be required to teach by one approach alone (Flippo, 1997b, pp. 302-303).

Finally, we know that even though each of us has an individual set of beliefs and philosophies regarding teaching, most of us would agree with certain practices and contexts concerning learning and environments for learning. In the remainder of this presentation I wish to report some major agreements among experts in the field of literacy and reading research. I suggest that these agreements, which span philosophies, and others we will find if we look, rather than the much publicized disagreements, should be considered by state boards and politicians as they propose, shape, and mandate their legislation (Flippo, 1997b, p. 303).

My study of experts spanned ten years. To gather these data I employed a Delphi technique, which involved asking selected reading experts, who represented the major schools of thought in literacy education, to specify what they believed teachers "should do" and "shouldn't do" in their classrooms to promote reading development. Each of the selected experts generated his or her own list of items anonymously, and the remaining experts agreed or disagreed, again anonymously, with each item on these lists. Each round was followed up with queries and interviews as needed (Flippo, 1997b, p. 303).

The experts involved in my study include Richard Anderson, Brian Cambourne, Edward Fry, Yetta Goodman, Jane Hansen, Jerome Harste, Wayne Otto, Scott Paris, P. David Pearson, George Spache, and Rand Spiro.

After four complete rounds, I found that there were 33 practices and contexts that the experts agreed would tend to make learning to read difficult for children; they also agreed on 19 things that teachers might do to facilitate the children's learning to read (Flippo, 1997b, p. 303). Please note that this is not about getting agreement on any "method"! This is about finding out what people would agree to—people from many different philosophies.

For the first round of the study, I sent the experts Frank Smith's (1973) list of "Twelve Easy Ways to Make Learning to Read Difficult," and the experts responded to those, either agreeing or disagreeing, or editing. The experts also then began to develop their own lists during this first round. Smith's list of statements had been cited fairly often in the literature, and it seemed to furnish an adequate starting point to stimulate interest and discussion among the experts.

The lists of agreements are lengthy, and some seem more important and central to the current hot issues than others. Therefore, for this presentation I will highlight the findings and generalize the agreements that seem most significant to the debates reported in the media and to what the state boards and legislatures have been acting on.

Practices that the experts agree would tend to make learning to read difficult for students include:

- emphasizing only phonics instruction,
- drilling children on isolated letters or sounds,
- making sure that children do it correctly or not at all,
- focusing on the single best answer,
- making word-perfect oral reading the prime objective of your classroom reading program,
- focusing on reading skills rather than on interpretation and comprehension,
- using workbooks or worksheets with every reading lesson,

- grouping readers according to ability,
- following a basal program without making modifications,
- teaching letters and words one at a time and making sure each new letter or word is learned before moving on to the next letter or word, and
- expecting students to be able to spell correctly all the words they can read.

Practices that experts agree would tend to facilitate learning to read include:

- bringing opportunities for reading, writing, talking, and listening together so that each feeds off and into the other,
- talking about and sharing different kinds of reading,
- focusing on using reading as a tool for learning,
- making reading functional and purposeful,
- developing positive self-perceptions and expectations concerning reading,
- using a broad spectrum of sources and a variety of real books for student reading materials,
- providing multiple and repeated demonstrations of how reading is done or used, and
- using silent reading whenever possible and whenever appropriate to the purpose (Flippo, 1997b, p. 304).

Some have criticized my study, saying that these items are too simplistic—"too common sensical," or "too non-common sensical," depending on whether you're talking about the desirable or undesirable contexts and practices—so that, they say, the conclusion that there is some agreement is flawed.

I'm not saying that these items aren't simplistic, and I'm not saying that they are necessarily the most important ones to focus on, but this study does clearly show that experts from different camps can agree on practices that are at the very least, related to teaching reading. And some of them are very important and relevant. Additionally, I think that these agreements are very important because people in the media, people in state legislatures, and even some of those in our field, espousing one position or another, do not think there is anything that all camps do agree on.

Here's another criticism: others have criticized my study, saying that it isn't possible to discuss these practices and contexts across philosophies, because these experts come from different discourse communities and really speak different languages. For instance, the critics say, these experts would define "reading" differently, so how can they even approach the idea of consensus on anything?

I say, if we can't even agree on a common language, how can we communicate with other people outside the field of reading about what we are talking about? How can we expect politicians, parents, teachers, and the media to understand us? Are they (the critics) trying to say that our differing philosophies limit us so much that we can't understand each other and others really cannot understand us? Frankly, I find this criticism as even more evidence that we must seek some common ground.

Even men and women these days are learning to speak the others' language, as books like *Men Are from Mars, Women are from Venus* (Gray, 1992) have shown us. And we better learn to speak the same language soon, to intelligently discuss our agreements, or here's what can happen: A recent article in the *U.S. News & World Report* (Toch, 1996) illustrates how we are perceived by the media and the real need we have for more professional unity and political awareness:

> In the reading debate, as in other school reform issues, many progressives and traditionalists seem more eager to fight than to find common ground, routinely misrepresenting each other's views and needlessly polarizing debates at students' expense. It is left to the rest of us to break through the overheated rhetoric, finding in both sides important pieces of a national solution. (p. 64)

Do we really want the media and politicians to piece together *their* solutions because we're fighting and arguing so much with each other that we can't "get it together"?

By the way, did you take notice, as I did, of the study done by Cassidy and Wenrich, reported in the February/March 1997 issue of *Reading Today?* They researched the "hot" and "not hot" topics today in reading research, and found that "hot" topics—in other words, topics that are receiving current, positive attention—are phonics, phonemic awareness, and skills instruction. But, listen to this, the "not hot" topics (the ones that are receiving negative or little attention) are *comprehension, schema theory,* and *word knowledge/vocabulary!* This is, of course, the result of what has been going on politically inside and outside our field.

Here's more Brooklyn street culture: We, my friends and I, boys and girls alike, were very protective of our street. We lived on East 48th Street between Avenues L and M. If any other kids ever set foot on our block, we aggressively protected our turf, even if we had to throw stones, rocks, and bricks at them to scare them away. Such has also become the custom among those of us who protect turf in our field. Because people seem afraid that agreement and consensus may weaken or neutralize the power of their ideas, many don't want to allow anyone else on their block. They would resort to the old Brooklyn way of throwing rocks to prevent it, even if this behavior causes the neighborhood to get a bad reputation.

Let's stop throwing rocks at each other. Let's "hang together" in our literacy neighborhood. I think we can take these agreements and other agreements that the reading community will hopefully generate in the near future from across philosophies and say to the media and politicians that the field of reading professionals are standing on a common ground, and we do not believe that the political solutions now being pushed are good for children or conducive to reading development. In fact, if you carefully review these agreements among these diverse experts, you will see that the political solutions offered in California and other states where politicians are jumping on the "back to phonics" bandwagon are often counter to what literacy experts across philosophies believe to be facilitative practices and contexts (Flippo, 1997b, p. 304).

I believe we need balance between agreement and disagreement, just like we need a balance of reading approaches. Since all we've focused on in the past is the disagreements, it is the model we've become most familiar with in our field. I feel that we need to begin looking at agreement in some way very soon.

And, for those of you who feel that we've seen the worst, and surely things will get better; Nicholas Lemann in the new *Atlantic Monthly* (November 1997) article, entitled "The Reading Wars" predicts that (a) efforts to establish greater quality control in public education (translating to "more central authority") will go on constantly for the next few decades, (b) schools all over the country will be hard pressed by parents and politicians to move toward imparting skills, without considering development of a joy of learning, and (c) as long as the US continues in its current prosperous and peaceful condition, the more the politicians and the press will keep school curricula issues in the fore of American politics.

In closing, and on a more positive note, I do want to say that since doing my last presentations, I do now see evidence that more people are talking more about the need for "common ground." Whether we call it "common ground," "agreement," or yes, that bad word "consensus," others now seem to be looking for it, and I applaud that idea.

We don't give up anything by being a respectful community. Growth in our field will not be sacrificed or diminished just because we aren't arguing publicly with each other. And, we don't need to agree on everything either. We already acknowledge our differences. Now, let's acknowledge some common ground.

References

Allington article draws praise, nays. (1997, October/November). *Reading Today, 15*(2), 17.

Allington, R. L. (1997, August/September). Overselling phonics. *Reading Today, 15*(1), 15-16.

California Commission on Teacher Credentialing (1996). *Standards of program quality and effectiveness for professional teacher internship programs for multiple and single-subject teaching credentials with a (bilingual) cross-cultural, language, and academic development (CLAD/BCLAD) emphasis.* Sacramento, CA: California Commission on Teacher Credentialing, State of California.

California leads revival of teaching by phonics. (1996, May 22). *New York Times,* p. B8.

Cassidy, J., & Wenrich, J. K. (1997, February/March). What's hot, what's not for 1997. *Reading Today, 14*(4), 34.

Colvin, R. L. (1996, December 13). State embraces phonics in approving new texts. *Los Angeles Times,* p. A1.

Flippo, R. F. (1996, December). *"Seeds of consensus" : The beginnings of professional unity.* Paper presented at the annual meeting of the National Reading Conference, Charleston, SC.

Flippo, R. F. (1997a, May). *Reaching consensus: Findings from the expert study.* Paper presented at the annual meeting of the International Reading Association, Atlanta, GA.

Flippo, R. F. (1997b). Sensationalism, politics, and literacy: What's going on? *Phi Delta Kappan, 79*(4), 301-304.

Gray, J. (1992). *Men are from Mars: Women are from Venus.* New York: Harper Collins.

Gunnison, R. B. (1996, December 13). State rejects 2 texts, citing phonics law. *San Francisco Chronicle,* p. A1.

Kastor, E. (1996, November 15). Phonics boom: Proponents say any other approach to reading only spells trouble. *Washington Post,* p. Dl.

Lemann, N. (1997, November). The reading wars. *Atlantic Monthly, 280,* 128-130, 132-134.

Levine, A. (1994, December). The great debate revisited. *Atlantic Monthly, 274,* 38-44.

Levine, A. (1996, October). Parents report on America's reading crisis: Why the whole language approach to teaching has failed millions of children. *Parents Magazine, 71*(10), 63-68.

Pikulski, J. J. (1997, October/November). Beginning reading instruction: From "The Great Debate" to the reading wars. *Reading Today, 15*(2), 32.

Saunders, D. J. (1996, January 12). Why kids can't read in California. *San Francisco Chronicle,* p. A23.

Smith, F. (1973). Twelve easy ways to make learning to read difficult. In F. Smith (Ed.), *Psycholinguistics and reading* (pp. 183-196). New York: Holt, Rinehart, and Winston.

Toch, T. (with Daniel, M.). (1996, October 7). Schools that work. *U.S. News & World Report, 121*(14), *58-64.*

Walters, L. S. (1996, April 18). As reading scores plummet, states get hooked on phonics. *Christian Science Monitor,* pp. 1,4.

A SOCIAL-CONSTRUCTIVIST VIEW OF FAMILY LITERACY

Susan B. Neuman

Temple University

Keynote Address
College Reading Association
1997

Susan B. Neuman is an Associate Professor in the department of Curriculum Instruction and Technology in Education at Temple University. She is Coordinator of the Reading and Language Arts Graduate program. She received her doctorate at the University of the Pacific in Stockton, California. Dr. Neuman's research focuses on literacy and technology, family literacy and early literacy development. She has studied the relationship between television and reading for many years, documenting this work in Literacy in the Television Age.

Her most recent co-edited book is Single-Subject Experimental Research: Applications for Literacy. *In addition, she has co-authored* Language and Literacy Learning in the Early Years: An Integrated Approach *and has over 50 articles in* American Education Research Journal, Reading Research Quarterly, Reading Teacher, and Early Childhood Research Quarterly. *In addition, Susan has been co-editor of the* Journal of Reading Behavior. *Her newest co-edited book is* Children Achieving: Instructional Practices in Early Literacy *to be published by International Reading Association.*

R esearch supporting the crucial role of the family and early literacy experiences on children's later success in reading and writing has led to an increasing number of programs conceptualized around the family as a unit (Connors, 1993; Shanahan & Rodriquez-Brown, 1993; Winter & Rouse, 1990). Known widely as intergenerational or family literacy, these programs have been designed to improve

Reprinted from *Literacy and Community.* pp. 26-30, by E. G. Sturtevant, J. R. Dugan, P. Linder, & W. M. Linek, Eds, 1998, Commerce, Texas: College Reading Association the education of the mother or other caregivers in order to improve the quality of family life and the achievement of the child. Though varying in design and form (Nickse, Speicher, & Buchek, 1988), programs focus on training parents in literacy and effective parenting skills, assisting children in reading and writing skills, and providing opportunities for parent-child experiences. Consequently, these programs address not only the parent or the child as literacy learners, but the parent-child relationship. It is presumed that the skills learned and practiced by the adult and the child produce an intergenerational and/or reciprocal transfer of skills.

A primary challenge for family literacy researchers, however, has been to understand the process of transmission of behaviors from parent to child and child to parent, particularly as it applies to families from diverse economic, educational and cultural backgrounds (Connors, 1993). For example, although many program developers support a "family strengths model" which recognizes the importance of respecting cultural differences in child-rearing practices (Darling, 1989), Auerbach (1989) has argued that these programs continue to perpetuate a "transmission of school practices model." She suggests that the unifying assumption underlying these programs is school-based: parents are taught to transmit the culture of school literacy through the vehicle of the family.

Yet what characterizes the homes of successful literacy learners, both middle and lower income, is the sheer range of opportunities to use literacy-related practices as an integral part of daily family life (Anderson & Stokes, 1984; Auerbach, 1989). Children and adults experience reading and writing not as isolated events but as part of the social activities with family and friends in their homes and communities. Literacy-related activity, therefore, often occurs in cultural contexts for action that is constructed by people in interaction with one another (Laboratory of Comparative Human Cognition, 1983). Teale's ethnographic study (1986), for example, reported that for almost 90% of all reading and writing activities observed in 22 households, the focus of the activities was not on literacy itself; rather, literacy occurred as aspects of activities which enabled family members to organize their lives.

I argue that family literacy programs should be viewed within the cultural context, a way of thinking, behaving and responding to one's environment. Consequently, this article will show that there is great variability among programs reflecting the specific needs of the participants and the community. Several key features, however, appear common to each of the three following models.

Three Models
A Community-Based Program:
Family Intergenerational Literacy Lab

The Family Intergenerational Literacy Lab (FILL) is a community-based program in Alabama designed to serve families with an average income of $4500.

The program aims at moving away from the traditionally General Equivalency Diploma (GED) or child-centered focus of many family literacy programs to one that is more holistic. Typically, reading instruction for adults is centered on the goals established by each individual. For the first two hours of the day, children attend a preschool program while parents attend classes which focus on the ability to solve problems through reading and writing skills and strategies. Time is set aside each day for parents and children to spend time together, working on computers, playing games, and making snacks for the children in preschool. The program also focuses on common family activities such as trips to grocery stores, pharmacies and the library, and social activities like musical plays and performances.

FILL is the product of a dynamic collaboration among community organizations. Vista volunteers help to recruit and organize activities. The local bookstore donates books. Other agencies conduct workshops, with the transit system providing tokens for all to attend in various locations. The senior center helps by supporting child-care and making meals for special occasions. In this small Alabama town, family literacy has become a community effort bringing people from businesses, schools, and agencies together.

A Head Start Family Literacy Program: The Ramah Navajo Family Literacy Pilot Project

In this isolated area of the Navajo nation, the Ramah Head Start program has set out to establish a program that strengthens both the native language and traditions of families as well as English language literacy skills. Sensitive to the Navajo tradition, family literacy sessions begin with a 'talking circle,' a custom during which people articulate family and community concerns and arrive at decisions that benefit both families and the community. These concerns form the basis for a participatory reading curriculum, which involves parents and extended family members in using literacy to solve community concerns. In addition, on a regular basis, project leaders provide informational workshops ranging from "How to be your child's advocate in the school/service agency system," to making "toys from junk around the house." Traditionally, families join together with project staff for meals and social occasions.

Since the Navajo tradition gives childrearing roles to the extended family, the family literacy team developed a mobile lending library with multicultural books, toys, and developmentally appropriate learning materials. These materials provide opportunity for all those involved in the young children's lives to participate in playing, talking, and teaching in the context of family life. The project has appeared to lay a firm foundation for continuing family literacy approach in the larger community, creating greater awareness and knowledge about holistic approaches to family and early childhood development.

A School-Based Program:
Parents and Children Reading Together

The Book Club (Neuman, 1996) is a weekly get-together of parents from early childhood classrooms to talk about and read children's storybooks. Designed to be a meeting place for conversations about children's books and a time for parents and children to read together, book clubs are held weekly at schools for about 12 weeks. Sessions follow a similar format and are co-facilitated by a parent leader and a bilingual teacher from the community. Parents are free to select either an English or Spanish version of the story.

Each week begins with a choral reading of a children's book. The facilitator dramatizes the action, emphasizes repetitive phrases, and sometimes stops to ask questions as she reads. Following the reading, the facilitator then engages parents in a discussion of the story, focusing on three key questions:

1. What would you want your child to take away from this book? Acting as a recorder, the parent leader lists common themes, distinctive qualities about the book, descriptive phrases, and unusual vocabulary.

2. What kinds of questions or comments would you use to stimulate a discussion of the story? Various question types, (e.g., recall, prediction, and questions that related to other experiences), and other books are recorded.

3. How would you help your child revisit this book? Parent suggestions like rereading or activity extensions such as visiting a zoo, making cookies, or going for walks together are described.

Conversations are designed to engage parents in analyzing events and ideas presented in the story, relating stories to their own personal experiences as well as helping to bridge these experiences to their children's early educational needs. In this respect, the discussion format assumes that parents had rich experiences to share with others that could be applied to children's literature selections.

Library pockets and small index cards are provided so that parents can write down questions they believe most useful for guiding discussions with their children. Following the discussion of approximately 40 minutes, parents then visit their child's classroom and read their new book together for about 15 minutes, depending on the level of interaction. For those less proficient parent readers, they may read the story to their child, or ask him or her to pretend to read it to them; or they may tell the child the story as they remembered it using the pictures as guides. Parents are given a new book each week to add to their home libraries.

Pre- and post-test scores for children in these Book Clubs compared with a control group indicate their effectiveness in enhancing children's concepts of print and receptive language skills. These results provide strong support that smaller-scale, as well as comprehensive family literacy programs, can enhance children's achievement in schools.

Common Features of Programs

Although each of these models approach family literacy differently, there are several common features. For example, these programs:

1. Offer literacy instruction to families, broadly defined, to include parents, caregivers, siblings, extended family and young children,

2. Include strong participant involvement in curriculum planning and development,

3. Create a supportive environment, where achievements (both short and longer-term) are recognized and celebrated,

4. Provide opportunities for family and social networks to be formed through activities in classrooms and communities, and

5. Know the community, its resources and seek active collaborations with other social and educational services.

Providing educational support to families is an awesome challenge. In the process of seeking the mechanisms for supporting literacy development, researchers have redefined literacy as a far more complex process than was ever conceived in the past. The challenge facing us today is to understand how we can help to support collaborative relationships among schools, families and communities to aid children's literacy development.

References

Anderson, A. & Stokes, S. (1984). Social and institutional influences on the development and practice of literacy. In H. Goelman, A. Oberg, & F. Smith (Eds.), *Awakening to literacy* (pp. 24-37). Portsmouth, NH: Heinemann.

Auerbach, E. R. (1989). Toward a social-contextual approach to family literacy. *Harvard Educational Review, 59*, 165-181.

Connors, L. J. (1993). *Project Self Help: A family focus on literacy* (No. 13). Center on Families, Communities, Schools & Children's Learning.

Laboratory of Comparative Human Cognition. (1983). Culture and cognitive development. In W. Kessen (Ed.), *History, theory and methods*. Vol. 1 of P.H. Mussen (Ed.), *Handbook of child psychology*. New York: Wiley.

Neuman, S. B. (1996). Children engaging in storybook reading: The influences of access to print resources, opportunity and parental interaction, *Early Childhood Research Quarterly, 11*, 495-514.

Nickse, R., Speicher, A. M. & Buchek, P. C. (1988). An intergenerational adult literacy project: A family intervention/prevention model. *Journal of Reading, 31*, 634642.

Shanahan, T. & Rodriquez-Brown, F. (1993). Project FLAME: *The theory and structure of a family literacy program for the Latino community*. Paper presented at the American Educational Research Association Conference, Atlanta, GA.

Teale, W. H. (1986). Home background and young children's literacy development. In W. H. Teale, & E. Sulzby (Eds.), *Emergent literacy* (pp. 173-206). Norwood, NJ: Ablex.

Winter, M. & Rouse, J. (1990). Fostering intergenerational literacy: The Missouri Parents as Teachers program. *The Reading Teacher, 43*, 382-387.

Are We Trend Spotters or Tale Spinners? A Report from the Field

Donna E. Alvermann

University of Georgia

Keynote Address
College Reading Association
1998

In 1998, Donna E. Alvermann was a University of Georgia Research Professor in Reading Education. Her most recent research explored the potential of feminist pedagogy and poststructural theory for interpreting gendered literacy practices in middle school, high school, and college level classrooms. Having minored in history throughout her undergraduate and graduate programs, she was particularly interested in tracing personal experiences and theoretical underpinnings that guided her present research.

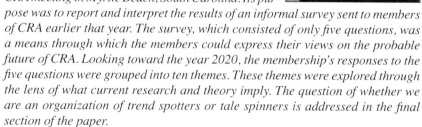

This paper was a keynote address for the 1998 CRA meeting in Myrtle Beach, South Carolina. Its purpose was to report and interpret the results of an informal survey sent to members of CRA earlier that year. The survey, which consisted of only five questions, was a means through which the members could express their views on the probable future of CRA. Looking toward the year 2020, the membership's responses to the five questions were grouped into ten themes. These themes were explored through the lens of what current research and theory imply. The question of whether we are an organization of trend spotters or tale spinners is addressed in the final section of the paper.

W hen Nancy Padak invited me to speak on a topic of my choice at the 1998 annual meeting of the College Reading Association, my first inclination

Reprinted from *Advancing the World of Literacy.* pp. 8-25, by J. R. Dugan, P. E. Linder, W. M. Linek, & E. G. Sturtevant, Eds., 1999, Commerce, TX: College Reading Association.

was to focus on some aspect of literacy that would involve all of us in thinking about reading, literacy, and CRA in the new millennium. Then I recalled Bill Sheldon's advice (Bill was on my doctoral committee at Syracuse University). He advised staying as far away from crystal ball gazing as possible. So, I compromised and made only one of the five questions that I posed on a mail survey distributed during the summer of 1998 pertain to crystal ball gazing. Briefly, these were the five questions I asked:

1. If you could begin your career anew in reading and literacy education, what would you likely choose as your dissertation topic, and why would this be your choice of topics?

2. What do you want the students whom you teach and advise to say about you after they have completed their programs?

3. If you had to give assistant professors in the field a few words of advice, what would they be?

4. As you look into your "crystal ball" toward the year 2020, what do you see in store for CRA?

5. What additional questions/issues do you think I should address in my talk this Fall?

Participants

With Gary Shaffer's assistance, I obtained a complete mailing list of all CRA members as of May 1998. This list was used in distributing the survey. Eight surveys were returned because of no forwarding address, and several graduate students who received the survey indicated that they felt the questions did not pertain to them and hence chose not to respond. A return rate of approximately 25%, which, while not statistically valid[1] for representing the membership, was considered acceptable for the purpose of this paper—to determine if we, in CRA, are *trend spotters* or *tale tellers*.

Demographically speaking, those who completed the survey represented a broad cross-section of CRA's membership. The northeastern and southeastern sections of the United States accounted for 70% of the returned surveys, with each of these sections representing 35%. The midwestern states (with 14%) and the southwestern states (with 11%) accounted for the next largest group of returned surveys. The northwest (with 3%) and Canada (with slightly less than 2%) accounted for the smallest group of returned surveys. This distribution is fairly representative of the membership of the College Reading Association at large.

Analysis and Results of the Survey

In analyzing the results of the survey, I used a constant comparative method that involved rereading the responses to each of the five questions and then coding them according to key words used by the respondents. This method of analysis allowed me to retain the actual language of those who responded and to find themes within the overall data set. For example, the term *balance* was implied or appeared verbatim in responses to questions about what people would change about their dissertation topics, what they wanted their students to say about them, what advice they would offer new assistant professors, and what they believed is in store for CRA by 2020. Three other themes, *intellectual pursuits, practical matters,* and *teacher education,* were also implied in the responses to the first four questions. The term *technology* appeared in response to the question about what respondents would choose as a topic if they were to re-do their dissertations today, as well as to the question about what they saw in store in for CRA by the year 2020.

In all, ten themes were identified across the first four questions on the survey. These themes included: a balancing act, intellectual pursuits, matters of reading, mentoring and modeling, motivating factors, political issues, practical matters, professional organizations, teacher education, and technology.

The responses to question 5 (What additional questions/issues do you think I should address in my talk this Fall?) were so variable that they defied easy classification. For example, some respondents indicated that they had "no other ideas" (with one person adding, "I'm sure you will have more than you can address!"), while others wanted me to provide an "overview of where we have been as well as where we are going" in the literacy field. One person wanted me "to take a stand on phonics and its role in meaningful reading instruction" while another requested that I "provide leadership in determining the focus of the profession." As you can well imagine, I had difficulty deciding how to code the diversity of responses I received to question 5. Many respondents simply omitted answering the question, while a number suggested that I answer the same questions I asked everyone else. This latter suggestion seemed one way of addressing question 5 while at the same time providing a way out of the problem I had in classifying people's varying responses to the question. I will share my responses to the first four questions after providing a brief summary and interpretation of the data survey data.[2]

Interpretation of Data from Survey
A Balancing Act

The notion of seeking balance in one's professional life was a major theme. This showed up in respondents' choices in alternative dissertation topics. For example, one person said she would choose to do a dissertation this time around on the "use of informational text in K-2 because the focus is presently on narratives." Another person would study adolescent literacy "because [it] is being overlooked in the current focus on early literacy."

The importance of balance was reflected, as well, in how professors said they wanted to be remembered by their students. They would prefer to be remembered for loving both their students and their subject area, for focusing on both reading and writing, for being well informed about both theory and practice, and for being tough but fair.

CRA members also had words of advice for new assistant professors that echoed the need for balance in one's professional life. For example, they recommended helping undergraduates and graduate students understand theory while concentrating on the practical, balancing university commitments with civic responsibilities, researching and writing both collaboratively and independently, and striving for diversity since "specialization is for insects." Managing stress on the job was a big factor in the balancing act. One respondent advised CRA members to remember that in interacting with new assistant professors, "a little kindness, support, and humor can go a long way in easing stress," while another believed that the key to stress management was learning how to handle the wearing of many hats with many different demands.

In terms of balance and the future of CRA as an organization, one person saw growth in the organization as "both a curse and a blessing," while another sought a more geographically balanced membership, brought about perhaps by holding the annual conference "in different locations, like the Midwest." Still another remarked that CRA "needs to become less of an Eastern U.S. organization."

Intellectual Pursuits

This theme was marked by comments having to do with the inquiry process. For instance, one respondent, if given the opportunity to change dissertation topics, would choose to do a study that explores students' inquiry processes. Most professors wanted to be remembered for challenging students to think critically. They also wanted students to examine their own beliefs about literacy, teaching, and learning. Two respondents specifically noted that they wanted to be remembered as active learners who are always learning new things. Others wanted to be remembered for helping students stretch their thinking in new and complex ways.

As for how new assistant professors might invest in worthwhile intellectual pursuits, the respondents focused on inquiry processes that involve researching, writing, and publishing. For example, several people advised that new assistant professors develop a program of research and establish a reasonable agenda for publishing. Others were more specific about how younger faculty might engage in intellectual pursuits. One respondent, for example, advised new assistant professors to read John Dewey, while others advised them to "spend time in the library" and "join a writing group."

Intellectual pursuits involving inquiry also figured into people's crystal ball gazing about CRA's future. One person wanted to see more collaboration among CRA members, particularly in the area of inquiry. Another person predicted that by the year 2020, "CRA will be encouraging of creativity, inquiry, invention, and the reconstruction of knowledge in schools."

Matters of Reading

When it comes to matters of reading, a number of respondents would not change a thing about their dissertation. Citing reasons such as, "I'd focus on early intervention because first grade reading instruction continues to interest me," or "I'd choose the same topic-narrative text analysis—because I still find it fascinating," these respondents were adamant that their first choice would not change. Others were not so sure, however. For instance, one person noted that phonological awareness would be a good topic to explore "because the phonological deficit hypothesis is all the rage in the LD area." Another person would choose a topic related to "the role of women in the field of reading instruction." Some would choose topics that they deem worthy of making a difference, such as studying emergent literacy and "turning kids at-risk on to reading because it is this population that often drops out."

CRA members want their students to say the following things as a result of having taken classes with them: that they enjoy reading and that they metacognitively know what to do as readers. In terms of the role CRA is likely to play in matters of reading in the year 2020, respondents said they saw "a renewed interest and appreciation for reading specialists" and "a need to incorporate worldwide literacy issues into our definition and vision of literacy."

Mentoring and Modeling

Although no one mentioned mentoring and modeling as a topic they would choose to study if they were to do another dissertation, they did mention this topic when they responded to the question about what they would like their students to recall about them. Generally, CRA members want to be remembered as caring, having the time to listen, being supportive, and practicing what they preach. Their advice to new assistant professors includes choosing with care the faculty members who will be their mentors, and working closely with their mentors "to learn the what and how about all university requirements."

Overall, CRA is perceived as continuing its mentoring role well into the year 2020. Respondents predicted that the organization will "keep its congenial, family atmosphere," will continue to be "a nurturing environment," and will remain "a friendly, collegial organization that welcomes new members...[especially] a lot of newer, younger faces."

Motivating Factors

After reading as a topic, the largest number of changes in dissertation topics came from respondents who said that if they were to begin their careers anew, they would choose to do a study that involved some type of motivating factor. For example, several mentioned doing studies on the affective dimensions of life-long reading. Specifically, there was interest in studying the attitudes of under-prepared community college readers, the decline of interest in reading at the middle and high school levels, and the building of self-esteem in multiethnic settings.

Motivation plays a major role in terms of what CRA members would like their students to say about them as a result of taking their classes. Expressions of enjoyment, encouragement, and confidence building were among the major motivating factors mentioned by respondents. For instance, one person wanted to be remembered by her students for turning them on to literacy; another, for motivating them to do well by pointing them in the right direction; and still another for helping them think about new options.

As for motivational advice to new assistant professors, the word from CRA members was to "reject the medical model; you're not here to heal or fix problems, but to help readers discover their own success." Another member advised, "If you don't enjoy what you're doing, find something else to do, or go somewhere else; life's too short to be miserable."

Political Issues

Two respondents were explicit in their desire to incorporate the political in any new dissertation that they might write. As one of them noted,

> Back in the '60s when I, as so many others, was a political activist, I never saw politics as affecting literacy and school practices. Thus, I put my interest and enthusiasm for politics aside in the '70s and concentrated on teaching methods and materials. Only in the '90s did I realize the synergistic relationship between politics and education, specifically literacy education. Hindsight is always 20/20, but I wish I had stayed politically active in combination with "literacy active."

Advice to new assistant professors was also explicitly political. For example, respondents urged people new to the field to "try to reclaim in our various states the generation of reading specialists we seem to have lost," "stay away from the negative people; learn how to find 'the high road' of professional conduct by associating with professionals already on that road," and "keep a low profile if your senior faculty are at war over philosophical differences."

Hope was expressed that CRA would become more politically active by the year 2020 by speaking up "for what we know to be best practices" and by focusing on "new ways to voice our position on educational issues." One respondent worried, however, that CRA, while continuing to be supportive, would not be strong enough to affect federal policy.

Practical Matters

How to organize and manage language arts instruction and how to teach learning disabled youngsters in the college-prep classroom were practical questions that respondents posed as alternative dissertation topics. One person stated that for practical purposes "[she] would still probably pick a topic that would make an 'easy-to-complete' dissertation." She believed that the process of writing a dissertation was more valuable than the actual content, and that "the important thing is to finish it."

CRA members would like to be remembered for being "realistic, connected to the real classroom," for teaching practical material that can be applied in the classroom, and for providing "real-life experiences that enable [their students] to become better teachers and diagnosticians." This same emphasis on the practical is echoed in the respondents' advice to new assistant professors. For example, academics new to the literacy field are advised to "spend time in schools and keep current," to "coordinate classes so that projects and experiences relate to each other," and to "select service and teaching opportunities closely related to [their] research interests." Other words of advice include being organized, staying calm, doing "a solid job of teaching," saying no to a multitude of committee assignments, and being disciplined enough to spend time at the word processor writing for publication.

The practical also entered into respondents' predictions about what is in store for CRA twenty years hence. For instance, one person wrote, "I see the literacy field as we know it becoming increasingly classroom and teacher focused.... We will become even more applied in our research than we are now."

Professional Organizations

With the exception of one person who predicted that by the year 2020, CRA will be "bigger and better, always involved in growth," respondents focused almost exclusively on what they perceived to be a *decline* in CRA's membership. Comments such as "CRA will have fewer members as travel funds continue to dwindle," "I'd like to see CRA grow; it qualifies now as a best kept secret," and "I hope it has found new life (it seems to be fading a bit now)" are representative of the respondents' concerns. Suggestions for how CRA might revitalize itself included the following: reshape the organization's mission to appeal to practitioners, change its name to be more representative of its membership, do a better job of publicizing itself, increase its emphasis on diversity, and participate in activities with other professional organizations that have literacy as a focus.

As for CRA members' advice to new assistant professors in terms of joining professional organizations, the recommendation is to become involved early and participate actively. In one respondent's words, "Link with the field quickly and frequently." Another person mentioned the importance of working hard at local and state levels.

Teacher Education

CRA members who would change their dissertation topics if entering the field initially at this point in time and who wanted to focus on teacher education said they would investigate the quality of the educational experiences students receive in their undergraduate programs. For example, one respondent would study whether or not more reading courses and higher standards in teacher education programs would lead to a higher quality of graduates. This person believed that "currently public schools seem to shoulder the responsibility of providing basic knowledge about reading instruction." Another respondent would investigate a similar topic—undergraduates' insecurity when it comes to providing reading instruction, while another would explore the impact of feedback on preservice teachers' ability to implement reading instruction. Only one individual expressed an interest in studying instruction cross-culturally.

Generally, respondents would like their former students to say that they felt prepared to teach reading as a result of having had their classes. In one respondent's words "that they left our program with confidence." Another person wanted students to see a relationship between methods courses and field placement, while another wanted students to be able "to teach reading to every child and feel comfortable discussing methodologies with parents."

Looking into their crystal balls at CRA's role in teacher education in the first two decades of the next millennium, the respondents were in agreement that CRA will increase its focus on reading teacher education. The organization will do this by becoming "a strong and forceful voice for teacher educators," by "continuing to support the professional development of literacy educators through strong publications and annual meetings," and by "focusing on best practices." Although one respondent predicted that CRA will become increasingly influential in the field of reading teacher education, another person was not as optimistic about this possibility, noting that the only change she saw coming "is the unwillingness of younger people to become involved in professional organizations."

Technology

If respondents were to enter the literacy profession anew, a number of them would change their dissertation topics to reflect their current interests in technology. They listed topics that ranged from studying the impact of hypertext and hypermedia on literacy development and comprehension to looking for new ways that technology might be used to develop students' critical thinking. The rationale they gave for wanting to study technology in relation to literacy education was the sense they had of its potential impact on students' ability to meet the challenges of a highly technical world. One respondent, who had initially focused on technology as a dissertation topic, put it this way: "I'd still focus on technology because it represents the most significant change in literacy in several hundred years." Another person noted that she would study students' comprehension of multiple texts "because it's the kind of reading challenge that we're faced with increasingly as we become 'Internet literate'."

By far, technology was the theme that surfaced most often in relation to CRA's status in the year 2020. Some individuals saw technology as a way to increase CRA's visibility in the field, while others believed it might lead to isolationism and a drop in conference attendance. A few wondered if CRA will become a "virtual" organization that conducts all its business (e.g., publishing and conferencing) on line. One respondent even posed the possibility that CRA may come to stand for "computer reading association." Generally speaking, respondents to the survey viewed technology as a tool to be used by teachers and a new generation of students who have grown up with the idea of a "virtual" world.

My Responses to the Survey Questions

If I were to begin my career anew, I would change my dissertation topic. This time around I would study some aspect of critical media literacy as it pertains to adolescents in non-school settings, such as public libraries, teen clubs, and so on. This topic interests me because I wonder to what extent teenagers, who are deemed at risk of dropping out of school, will engage in literacy activities involving print and nonprint popular culture texts. In terms of what I would like former students and advisees to say about me, it would be that we collaborated on projects of mutual interest, and that I helped them think critically about what is said and done in the name of literacy research and instruction. In a somewhat related vein, my advice to new assistant professors would be to turn a critical eye to what they otherwise might not question about their teaching and research. The very things we take for granted—the "just because they are" sort of phenomena—are what we need to question the hardest. Finally, what do I see in store for CRA by the year 2020? An organization that has changed considerably to keep pace with the changing technologies, and increasingly, an organization that addresses issues of vital importance if we are to grow as a profession—issues such as the politics of literacy and a more visible presence of underrepresented populations, both in the CRA membership and its publications.

Trend Spotters or Tale Spinners

This section of the paper was the most challenging to write. I relied on the current literature to gain a sense of whether or not the responses to the survey questions were more in the realm of trend spotting than tale spinning, or vice versa. In the end, of course, it was a judgment call, but I offer here some current thinking about the themes that I identified in the responses to the survey. This thinking is based on the work of numerous scholars who are writing in three general areas: the interface between literacy and social change, the critique of constructivist pedagogy, and the promises and dangers of new communication technologies. After considering what the literature has to say about issues that are presently on the minds of a number of CRA members, I conclude by answering the question, so, are we trend spotters or tale spinners?

Interface Between Literacy and Social Change

Currently, there is much attention given to the social character of reading and writing and to the embeddness of these literacy practices in the larger social milieu. Less than two decades ago, reading and writing were seen as psychologically motivated and largely cognitive in nature. Today, as Colin Lankshear and his colleagues (1997) have noted, literacy studies encompass far more than the private internal cognitive states and events that were the focus of reading researchers in the 1970s and '80s. In their assessment of where the field of literacy is on the eve of a new millennium, Lankshear et al. describe it as framed within a sociocultural perspective:

> Within this frame, questions of power and the role of literacies as social practices within social productions and distributions of power [are] foregrounded, and "the politics of literacy" has emerged as a well-subscribed focus of theoretical attention....And most recently, those who adopt a sociocultural approach to literacy have begun to address in earnest the implications of current developments in electronic technologies, which threaten to move us from print to post-print text cultures. (p. 3)

Personally, I think it is important to bear in mind that conceptions of literacy as critical social practice do not deny the cognitive or behavioral aspects of reading and writing; instead, they portray them as attendant processes in a much larger social context, one that is institutionally located in the political structures of society where power is at stake in people's social interactions on a day-to-day basis. Issues of race, class, gender, age, sexual orientation, and other identity markers are historically part of these interactions (Luke & Freebody, 1997).

This change in the way literacy researchers and practitioners are thinking about print and nonprint text-mediated practices[3] is reflected in a number of recently published books, several of which have been edited by members of the College Reading Association—e.g., *Handbook of Literacy and Technology: Transformations in a Post-Typographic World* (Reinking, McKenna, Labbo, & Kieffer, 1998); *Learning from Text Across Conceptual Domains* (Hynd, 1998), and *Reconceptualizing the Literacies in Adolescents' Lives* (Alvermann, Hinchman, Moore, Phelps, & Waff, 1998). What each of these books has in common is a focus on changing literacies, and to varying degrees, the embeddedness of these literacies in a sociocultural framework.

Literacy educators are just beginning to make practical connections between popular culture texts of all types (e. g., print, CDs, videos) and students' motivations to read. Lorri Neilsen's (1998) and David O'Brien's (1998) chapters on how adolescents connect popular culture texts to the realities of their lives, Cynthia Lewis's (1998) article on horror fiction in the classroom, and Anne Haas Dyson's (1996) book on young children's writing about their superheroes are just a few of the recent publications by well-known literacy researchers. Although generally opposed to the mindless insertion of popular culture texts into school curricula, Michael Apple (1996) does acknowledge that such texts have a place if the intent is to teach toward a more socially just society by connecting students' real life experiences to school learning. What Apple (1996), writing as a critical theorist, and Neilsen (1998), O'Brien (1998), Lewis (1998), and Dyson (1996), writing as literacy educators, seem to agree on are the important social and political uses that can be made of popular culture in the curriculum. Teachers who neither disparage students' choices in reading materials nor look the other way when students bring their everyday life outside the classroom into school stand a good chance of helping them understand why reading is always a social practice.

Critique of Constructivist Pedagogy

A constructivist teacher is a facilitator, not a transmitter, of knowledge. That is what Mary Klein (1997), a preservice teacher educator at James Cook University in Australia, saw herself, as someone who helped undergraduates in mathematics education personally construct their own meanings of the content they would teach through problem solving, exploration, and collaboration.[4] Only after taking a hard look at what was largely unexamined about her constructivist practice was Klein able to understand how her modeling of preferred pedagogical methods served to maintain the status quo. This discovery about herself and the pitfalls associated with the rhetoric of constructivist pedagogy were made visible when Klein used Australian theorist Bronwyn Davies' (1994) notion of positioning.

Briefly, *positioning* is a poststructuralist term for describing how members of any discourse group (e.g., teachers, students, and so on) speak themselves and others into existence through everyday talk. This talk varies, of course, in relation to the discourses available to the group members, especially in terms of who is doing the speaking, from what position of authority (or lack of authority), in what context, and with what gain in mind. In Klein's (1997) case, she was speaking from her position as an adult, a teacher, a giver of grades, and an expert in her field. Klein's students, on the other hand, were speaking as novices, as undergraduates who depended on her to prepare them for the real world of primary school teaching.

What Klein (1997) discovered was that through her modeling of strategies in what she supposed was a supportive environment, she in fact was sending a message that there is really only one way to teach young children—and that is through modeling. In Klein's words:

> Modeling may become a problem because every possibility cannot be modeled. I later realised that I was modeling not only authoritative and immutable content, but also a given and supposedly unquestionable process or method of teaching.... On occasion students would express some concerns they had with constructivist practice. This occurred most frequently when engaged in discussion with me on a one to one basis. One such encounter is produced [below]:
>
> **Student:** This "constructivism," that's just another angle isn't it, I mean it's not the way you've got to go?
>
> **Klein:** Well it's not the way you've got to go ... you have to decide which way you want to go. It's kind of the theory behind the sourcebooks and the syllabus.... But you've got to decide where you are going to fall between the traditional, which was how I was taught at school and the constructivist ideas ... (pp. 280-282)

As Klein (1997) went on to note, by reminding the student of the theory and authority behind the constructivist approach, she left little room for experimenting with alternative methods. In her words:

> There was little ambiguity concerning to which end of the continuum I felt this student should aspire in her teaching, and of course in any assessment connected with the subject. Thus the discourse becomes regulatory in that it sets up a discursive framework into which student talk and writing must be fitted if it is to be heard. (p. 282)

While it is certainly the case that not all constructivist teaching ends up positioning students in the manner just illustrated, the literature on modeling (especially when the modeling is done by a mentor teacher) suggests that it is the rare student who questions or resists what he or she sees being advocated.

Constructivist pedagogy has also come under critical scrutiny of late for its tendency to focus on the creation of activity-based, problem-solving contexts for students' learning rather than on the inquiry processes students actually use in thinking about course-specific content in new and meaningful ways (Ball, 1992; Bonnett, 1995). For example, the premise that literacy teacher educators will improve preservice and inservice teachers' instructional performance by helping them acquire research-based knowledge about print-rich environments is suspect. Instead, what the literature on the value of educational research for professional development suggests is that teacher educators are most effective when they support preservice and inservice teachers "in building relationships between research-based models of children's thinking, their own students' thinking, and how they can interpret the models in light of their own students and classrooms" (Rhine, 1998, p. 29). As Deborah Ball's work (cited in Rhine, 1998) has demonstrated,

> Teachers are usually not prepared to transform rich environments into rich learning. Activities can be devoid of meaning unless the teacher is capable of providing students with appropriate challenges and helping the learner bring the meaning out of the activity. (p. 27)

The implications of this critique of constructivist pedagogy for literacy teacher educators are perhaps best understood when considered in terms of professional development initiatives. For these initiatives to result in the changes envisioned, service providers will need to engage teachers in inquiry-oriented instruction that moves beyond increasing their knowledge base about strategy instruction to orienting them toward inquiring into their students' thinking about specific content.

Promises and Dangers of New Communication Technologies

One of the most intriguing questions educators are asking on the eve of the new millennium is whether or not technology is changing family, community, and workplace structures. David Hakken, a professor of anthropology and director of the Policy Center at the State University of New York Institute of Technology, believes the answer is no, or at least not to the degree that was predicted. Speaking at a special congressional seminar sponsored by the Consortium for Social Science Associations on social changes attributed to the new communication technologies, Hakken (cited in Sroufe, Wurtz, & Maher, 1998) contended that "despite the belief that we are currently in the midst of a profound transformation to a new way of life brought about by computer technology, many early predictions have not come about" (p. 11).

A second speaker, Jan English-Lueck, an associate professor of anthropology at San Jose State University, took a slightly different view. As a result of studying the impact of computer technology on family life in Silicon Valley, English-Lueck (cited in Sroufe, Wurtz, & Maher, 1998) concluded that while there have been no changes in basic family patterns, the new communication technologies have led to our spending "a great deal of supposedly free time...thinking about work-related issues" (p. 12). This change is reflected in the increased number of separate rooms set aside in people's homes for computers and work-related tasks. The intrusion of computer technology into nonwork settings, then, is currently the only major trend that has been spotted by scholars studying the social impact of communication technologies on families, communities, and the workplace.

An area that promises to be the site of several new trends in technology for the next decade or two is the school. In fact, studies of how the new communication technologies are being used to realize certain societal expectations in schools are already the focus of several international scholars' collective writings on language, literacy, and the new work order (e.g., Gee, Hull, & Lankshear, 1996; Lankshear & Knobel, 1998). Briefly, the *new work order* refers to a new form of capitalism—what some (e.g., Drucker, 1993; Peters, 1992) might call a kinder, gentler capitalism, at least rhetorically speaking.

However, as James Gee and Colin Lankshear (1997) have pointed out, the new work order and its attendant genre of "fast capitalist texts" are best understood in relation to how they are changing and shaping the face of education. Fast capitalist texts comprise an emerging genre of business texts that attempt to explain a global, hyper-competitive "new capitalism," which Gee (1998) describes as a "non-authoritarian hierarchy, a fitting oxymoron for our new age" (p.387). An example of a fast capitalist text is Peter's (1992) book, *Liberation Management*, in which he applies Bakhtin's notion of "carnival" to describe new capitalism and to call for business leaders who are adept at using new imagery—the language of which has often been used in the past to critique capitalism and Western hegemonic practices. According to Gee and Lankshear, this literature has helped to forge school reform movements organized around such motifs as preparing students to engage in "higher order thinking, real understanding, situated expertise ... [and] learning to learn" (p. 86) activities. Spurred on by the highly competitive global economies of new capitalism, these fast capitalist texts have a darker side to them—a side which—we, as educators, might want to investigate more thoroughly before endorsing wholesale their implications for school literacy reform.

What is important here is the connection between these new work order texts and the communication technologies on which they depend As Colin Lankshear and Michele Knobel (1998) have pointed out, "this 'new frontier' can be a dangerous space.... [Dangerous because] the issues attending the introduction of new technologies have far-reaching and often invisible implications, which present worthy subject matter for practices of critical literacy" (p. 5). As literacy educators we have the responsibility, then, of teaching our students how to read critically the texts of these new technologies so that they become opportunities for liberation rather than openings for oppression.

Conclusion

So, are we trend spotters or tale spinners? Judging from what I could find in the education research literature that was relevant to the survey themes described earlier, I tend to think we qualify more often as trend spotters than tale spinners, and for these reasons. First, those who responded to the survey indicated a substantial interest in the sociocultural, both in the changes they would make in their dissertation topics and in the issues they saw in store for CRA by the year 2020. This focus on the sociocultural is in line with the increased attention being paid to the interface between literacy and social change in the research literature.

Second, the constructivist model of teaching and learning seemed well ingrained in the survey respondents' written responses to the question, "What do you want the students whom you teach and advise to say about you after they have completed their programs?" Certainly, the research literature suggests that constructivist thinking is very much in vogue right now. However, the literature also suggests that there is a growing critique of certain aspects of constructivist pedagogy. Specifically, there is concern over how we position students in our classrooms and in our relationships with them as their advisors. There is also some question about the degree to which inquiry-oriented instruction actually takes into account preservice and inservice teachers' expertise in inquiring into their own students' thinking processes and linking that inquiry with what the research literature has to say about children's literacy acquisition and development.

Finally, the respondents to the CRA survey were definitely trend spotters when they consistently pointed out the need for balance. Whether describing how they would change their dissertation topics, how they want to be remembered by their students, what advice they would offer new assistant professors, or what they predict lies in store for CRA in the next millennium, the respondents were clear in their call for balance. The education research literature also reflects a field caught up in the balancing act. Even the critique of the constructivist model of teaching and learning could be viewed as one way of addressing the imbalance some scholars see in that model.

In terms of tale spinning, it occurs to me that the survey responses suggested far more radical changes in the structure of CRA as an organization than might be supported in the literature that I read. For instance, I did not locate any studies that predicted professional organizations, such as CRA, are on the road to becoming "virtual" organizations. In fact, the report recently issued by the Consortium for Social Science Associations (Sroufe, Wurtz, & Maher, 1998) would suggest just the opposite.

Finally, as an organization we seem pretty adept at offering practical advice when it comes to helping new assistant professors make their way up the career ladder. Whether this advice is more tale spinning than trend spotting is difficult to say. Although a relatively large body of research exists on mentoring in general, that which pertains to mentoring colleagues in our own field of literacy education, especially in the academy, is virtually uncharted territory (Alvermann & Hruby, 1998). And, interestingly enough, none of the survey respondents listed it as a possible dissertation topic. Perhaps this is an area that members of our profession might consider exploring in a collaborative project that involves cross-institutional participation.

Author Notes

[1]According to Mangione (1995), response rates on mail surveys that fall below 50% are not scientifically acceptable. In Mangione's words, "If the only thing you did was to put a questionnaire in an envelope and ask people to fill it out, it would be common to see response rates in the 20% range, and it would

not be surprising to see them in the 5% range" (p. 62). To have obtained a higher response rate, I would have needed to supply potential respondents with a self-addressed postage-paid envelope and to follow up with a second-wave mailing reminder. Due to time constraints and budgetary concerns, I did neither. Justifications aside, the 25% return rate was at the upper end of what Mangione (1995) would have predicted, and more importantly, it did provide me with some direction for the keynote talk that inspired the use of a survey in the first place.

[2]A complete listing of all themes with their supporter descriptors for questions one through four is available from the author at the University of Georgia, College of Education, 309 Aderhold Hall, Athens, GA 30602 or dalverma@ arches.uga.edu

[3]The New London Group (1996) has also written extensively on the impact of digital texts on our thinking about text-mediated practices.

[4]An example from mathematics education is included here because little research has been conducted on modeling the constructivist approach in literacy teacher education. What has been conducted is typically presented at annual meetings of various professional organizations but not written up for publication. Interestingly enough, even fewer studies have been published on the role of mentoring among literacy faculty.

References

Alvermann, D. E., Hinchman, K A., Moore, D. W., Phelps, S. E, & Waff, D. R. (Eds.). (1998). *Reconceptualizing the literacies in adolescents' lives.* Mahwah, NJ: Lawrence Erlbaum.

Alvermann, D. E., & Hruby, G. G. (1998, April). A *survey of literacy teacher educators' mentoring relationships.* Paper presented at the annual meeting of the American Educational Research Association, San Diego, CA.

Apple, M. W. (1996). *Cultural politics and education.* New York: Teachers College Press.

Bonnett, M. (1995). Teaching thinking, and the sanctity of content. *Journal of Philosophy of Education, 29,* 295-309.

Carr. D. (1995). Is understanding the professional knowledge of teachers a theory-practice problem? *Journal of Philosophy of Education, 29,* 311-331.

Davies, B. (1994). *Poststructural theory and classroom practice.* Geelong, Australia: Deakin University Press.

Drucker, P. F. (1993). *Post-capitalist society.* New York: Harper.

Gee, J. P. (1998). On mobots and classrooms: The converging languages of the new capitalism and schooling. *Organization, 3*(3), 385-407.

Gee, J. P., & Lankshear, C. (1997). Language, literacy and the new work order. In C. Lankshear (with J. P. Gee, M. Knobel, & C. Searle). (1997). *Changing literacies* (pp. 83-102). Buckingham, UK: Open University Press.

Gee, J., Hull, G., & Lankshear, C. (1996). *The new work order: Behind the language of the new capitalism.* Boulder, CO: Westview Press.

Hynd, C. R. (Ed.). (1998). *Learning from text across conceptual domains.* Mahwah, NJ: Lawrence Erlbaum.

Klein, M. (1997). Looking again at the "supportive" environment of constructivist pedagogy: An example from preservice teacher education in mathematics. *Journal of Education for Teaching, 23*(3), 277-292.

Lankshear, C. (with J. P. Gee, M. Knobel, & C. Searle). (1997). *Changing literacies.* Buckingham, UK: Open University Press.

Lankshear, C., & Knobel, M. (1998, April). *Critical literacy and new technologies.* Paper presented at the annual meeting of the American Educational Research Association, San Diego, CA.

Lewis, C. (1998). Rock 'n' roll and horror stories: Students, teachers, and popular culture. *Journal of Adolescent and Adult Literacy, 42,* 116-120.

Luke, A., & Freebody, P. (1997). Critical literacy and the question of normativity: An introduction. In S. Muspratt, A. Luke, & P. Freebody (Eds.), *Constructing critical literacies* (pp. 1-18). Cresskill, NJ: Hampton Press.

Mangione, T. W. (1995). *Mail surveys: Improving the quality.* Thousand Oaks, CA: Sage.

Neilsen, L. (1998). Playing for real: Performative texts and adolescent identities. In D. E. Alvermann, J. P. Young, K. A. Hinchman, D. W. Moore, S. F. Phelps, & D. R. Waff (Eds.), *Reconceptualizing the literacies in adolescents' lives* (pp. 3-26). Mahwah, NJ: Lawrence Erlbaum.

New London Group (1996). A pedagogy of multiliteracies: Designing social futures. *Harvard Educational Review, 66,* 60-92.

O'Brien, D. G. (1998). Multiple literacies in a high-school program for "at-risk" adolescents. In D. E. Alvermann, J. P. Young, K. A. Hinchman, D. W. Moore, S. F. Phelps, & D. R. Waff (Eds.), *Reconceptualizing the literacies in adolescents' lives* (pp. 27-50). Mahwah, NJ: Lawrence Erlbaum.

Peters, T. (1992). *Liberation management: Necessary disorganization for the nanosecond nineties.* New York: Fawcett.

Reinking, D., McKenna, M. C., Labbo, L. D., & Kieffer, R. D. (Eds.), (1998). *Handbook of literacy and technology: Transformations in a post-typographic world.* Mahwah, NJ: Lawrence Erlbaum.

Rhine, S. (1998). The role of research and teachers' knowledge base in professional development. *Educational Researcher, 27*(5), 27-31.

Richards, C. (1998). Popular culture, politics, and the curriculum. *Educational Researcher, 27*(5), 32-34.

Sroufe, J., Wurtz, S., & Maher, B. (1998, August/September). Is technology changing society? *AERA Research Policy Notes (OIA Info Memo),* 11-12.

TEACHER DECISION MAKING IN LITERACY EDUCATION: LEARNING TO TEACH

Gay Su Pinnell

The Ohio State University

Keynote Address
College Reading Association
1999

In 1999, Gay Su Pinnell's professional work focused on the literacy education of young children and on ways to support teachers of reading, writing, and language arts. An experienced elementary teacher, she has been instrumental in investigating, implementing, and developing the Reading Recovery program that resulted in the application of research to practice in helping over 500,000 initially struggling children become independent readers and writers. In addition, she has completed several large investigations which have influenced research in the field of literacy education and has produced numerous books and articles, notably  Guided Reading: Good First Teaching for all Children, Word Matters: Teaching Phonics and Spelling in the Reading/Writing Classroom, Voices on Word Matters: Learning About Phonics and Spelling in the Literacy Classroom, Help America Read: A Handbook for Volunteers, A Coordinator's Guide for Help America Read, *and* Matching Books to Readers, *all of which she co-authored with Irene Fountas. Co-authored with Irene Fountas and Andrea McCarrier is* Interactive Writing: Bringing Language and Literacy Together, K-2. *Her newest book, co-authored with Carol Lyons, is* Learning to Make a Difference: A Practical Guide for the Improvement of Literacy Teaching. *Her research was recognized by the International Reading Association in 1991 when she received the Albert J. Harris Award. In 1989, she received the Ohio Governor's award for*

Reprinted from *Literacy at a New Horizon*, pp. 10-26, by P. E. Linder, W. M. Linek, E. G. Sturtevant, & J. R. Dugan, Eds., 2000, Commerce, TX: College Reading Association.

outstanding service to the State of Ohio in education and she has also received the Ohio State University Distinguished Teaching Award. In 1993 she received the Charles A. Dana Award which is presented for Pioneering Achievements in Health and Education. She is a member of the Reading Hall of Fame.

A persistent question in literacy education is: What do teachers need to know and be able to do to assure successful literacy for students? The reason this question reoccurs is that the answer is complex. As literacy researchers, we investigate aspects of teaching and learning. We examine evidence of student learning and construct assessment procedures. We look at text resources and observe how children interact with them while reading. We look at teacher-student interactions and analyze how they support learning. We are always seeking to put together the information that will provide a way for teachers to become more effective in teaching children to write and read.

Teachers' decision making is the foundation of effective teaching. Professional development provides demonstrations of instructional approaches. It is not unusual for a school staff to be bombarded with eight to ten "training" sessions over a school year. Sometimes approaches are part of a coherent plan; often they are not. We can access a plethora of guides, instruction books, and "how to" manuals. Reading teachers are even going on the Internet to share and capture ideas. But the critical difference lies in *how* teachers select and apply the ideas and methodologies they learn.

Likewise, assessment data are available now as never before. In addition to the enormous growth in standardized testing, teachers in many school districts are required to apply observational assessments in a systematic way. These individualized measures yield important data; but, again, how teachers access, interpret, and apply information to teaching makes the critical difference.

Typically, instructional improvement is sought through acquiring new materials. As teachers and researchers in literacy, we are also concerned with text resources. Instructional materials, including books, are available in abundance. We can purchase good texts from publishers if we have the resources. There are "kits" and "reading systems" available to support students. Yet, it is the teachers' ability to analyze and select materials in the light of individual students' needs that makes all the difference. And, many of these decisions are made "on the run" while teaching and, in fact, managing a class of 20 to 30 young children. Others, must be made in the interstices of the day—before school, recess, lunch, planning periods, and evenings. Teachers seldom get long periods of time to reflect. They must react on the spot to individual students' responses; and even if they have a weekly plan, which is usually required, they must replan every day to maximize their effectiveness tomorrow.

At any moment in time, with reference to the individual child, the teacher's decision making process might simultaneously address questions such as these:

- Based on my assessment and the sum total of my experience with him, what does this child know?
- What can he do without help?
- What can he do with my help?
- What does he need to know next?
- Why is this new learning important at this moment in time?
- What kind of help will be most effective for him?
- What kinds of texts can he read independently?
- What kinds of texts will support his learning more?
- How can I assure that he is constructing knowledge of a *process* that he can apply in many other situations?
- Does he understand what I am asking him to do in this instructional situation?

Now, multiply those decisions by the number of children in the group or class. The teacher might be asking:

- What strengths are common across this group or class?
- What do *most* of the children need to learn next?
- Do I need to form groups with similar behaviors? Or, can I work with the whole class to teach a certain skill?
- How can I structure the social context so that learning is maximized?
- What can children do independently that will result in productive learning [so that I can work with an individual or small group]?
- Should I provide demonstration or direct instruction; or should I structure the context so that children make their own discoveries?
- What kinds of texts will support all the children in the class?
- How can I make my instruction efficient so that I can support all students in the class?
- How can I interact with the class, groups, and individuals to assure that students learn *processes* that they can apply in many other situations?

The questions above reflect only a portion of the decisions that teachers make on a daily basis. I have not even mentioned the management of schedules, materials, and record-keeping, nor the interactions and negotiations with other adults that are required. It is no wonder that new teachers are so often overwhelmed. The decision making is constant and demanding.

Guided Reading

To examine teacher decision making, I have selected one instructional context—guided reading. I have chosen guided reading because it is an intensive instructional setting in which teachers become highly aware of their own decision making processes. I'll define and describe that context and then discuss some of the critical decisions teachers make. Finally, I'll describe what we have learned about supporting teachers in their decision making.

First, guided reading is situated within a comprehensive literacy program, of which it is only one component. For about 10 to 30 minutes per day, a child participates in *small group* reading instruction that is organized, structured, planned, and supported by the teacher. Children in the group are similar in their reading behaviors and read about the same level of text.

During the rest of the day, that same student will participate in whole-group, small-group, and individual activities related to a wide range of reading and writing, almost all of which involve children of varying experience and abilities.

Guided reading is an integral component of a rich language and literacy instructional support system. The system includes experiences with literature through shared reading, hearing stories and informational pieces read aloud, and supported study. It includes workshops and projects, shared writing, and word study through phonics and spelling. The components are not separate elements but are linked together by:

- the oral language that surrounds, supports, and extends all activities; and,
- the content or topic of focus.

Children need to read and write about something interesting to them. After all, prior experience is, perhaps, *the* important factor in reading comprehension. So, students need experiences that help them store knowledge of their world as well as literary knowledge. Guided reading makes the whole process come alive with purpose because it involves teacher support to help students access and use personal, world, and literary knowledge. There is a dynamic and ongoing connection between the broader literacy curriculum, skills instruction, and the guided reading lessons that are taught every day.

Second, guided reading matches books to readers. Young children are building the network of understandings that make up a reading process. Children develop successful processing strategies as they learn to read for meaning. When children are reading books they *can* read, they are able to use many different sources of information in a smoothly operating system—doing all of those things that good readers do.

Terms like "hard" and "easy" are always relative. Using observation and assessment, we learn to know the readers, so any text can be hard, easy or just right. Our goal is the "just right" text. If a text is too hard, children struggle. They lose meaning and may conclude that reading just doesn't make sense. If their reading doesn't sound like language, they may begin to think that reading is just saying one word after another. Laborious reading is difficult to listen to, frustrates children and teachers, and promotes children's practicing ineffective and inappropriate reading behaviors.

What about books that are easy? They have a place in the literacy curriculum. We need easy books to promote enjoyment, practice, and fluency. Easy reading gives children "mileage" as readers and builds confidence; they can automatically, or almost automatically, use their current skills. But expanding their skills—"upping the ante" in reading—requires engaging in some problem solving. That means reading books that provide just the right amount of challenge—not too easy and not too hard. For guided reading, we need books that are "just right." The reader must be able to process or read the text well:

- Using knowledge of what makes sense, sounds right, and looks right simultaneously in a smoothly operating system.
- Knowing or solving most of the words quickly with a high level of accuracy.
- Reading at a good rate with phrasing and intonation (that is, putting words together in groups so that the reading sounds like language).

Matching books to readers means finding texts that provide just enough challenge to engage readers to work out problems or learn new strategies. The goal is not just to learn new words and add them to a reading vocabulary, although that will inevitably happen. It's about the processing, the "working out," that helps readers learn the skills and strategies that will make them gain independence—strategies that they can apply again and again as they read other texts. The "just right" book provides the context for successful reading and enables readers to strengthen their "processing power."

Third, guided reading helps children use what they know about letters, sounds, and words. Readers use visual analysis to solve words, and they can do so in isolation, but that is not how it happens in reading. Readers work on words embedded within continuous text. Word solving involves the orchestration of complex strategies that access many different kinds of information. It is not simply a process of looking at individual words in a string and solving one at a time. The words are part of a language system that involves meaning, world experience, grammar, or syntax, as well as visual patterns and their relation to sound and meaning. Our task as teachers is to help readers coordinate these understandings and behaviors while reading continuous text.

Fourth, guided reading provides the opportunity for systematic, organized teaching and learning.

1. Children are organized into small groups who demonstrate similar reading behaviors and who read about the same level of text. This grouping makes it possible to select the right text and teach effectively.

2. Books are selected from a collection organized into a gradient of difficulty. Teachers can select the right level and, within that, select texts that support their teaching. The gradient of difficulty moves:
   • from fewer lines of text, large print, and very clear space, to more lines with smaller print and smaller spaces;
   • from a few easy, high-frequency words, to a more difficult and wider range of high-frequency words, to complex sentences with all categories of words in the language;
   • from many phonetically regular words to irregular words with more difficult spelling patterns;
   • from words with fewer syllables to texts with many more multisyllable words; and,
   • from simple, everyday concepts to more specialized words, often used figuratively, with many meaning connotations, or connected to a kind of technology that requires specialized knowledge.

3. The teacher introduces the text, providing a framework of meaning, language, and visual information to help students successfully process the text, which is new to them. The book introduction usually includes some attention to the visual information in words.

4. The children read the whole text or a unified part of a text softly to themselves rather than in unison. In guided reading, each group member reads it all; and, over time, that means that everyone reads a lot. This reading involves processing a text in a way that helps to build effective strategies. The teacher observes and supports reading in a way that reminds students to use effective strategies such as searching for meaning, taking words apart, and so on.

5. After the children finish reading, the teacher revisits the text to make some brief teaching points directly related to reading the text. This teaching might be related to any aspect of reading—comprehension, fluency, self-monitoring, or self-correcting. Teachers reinforce effective strategies or teach new skills that children can use while reading more books.

6. Additional time (about a minute or two) is spent on extended letter and/or word work that has nothing to do with the text read in the lesson but is connected to principles students need to learn. Explicit word work is a temporary measure for specific groups of children, who need more help in word solving. The teacher uses magnetic letters, dry-erase board, and/or easel and paper.

7. Often, the teacher engages children in follow-up activities that help them use print in different ways—using writing or art. This follow-up extension is an ideal way to help children develop skills of summarizing, extending meaning, analyzing aspects of text, interpreting text, using graphic

organizers to discover the structure of text—all skills that are essential and also are tested on those proficiency exams.

Fifth, guided reading gives young readers the chance to explore a wide range of texts that they will enjoy and be able to read. In reading, experience counts; and experiences you enjoy count the most. As we struggle to provide intensive skills instruction, we cannot forget that we learn more through meaningful and enjoyable experiences. The work is not necessarily easy. Meeting a challenge makes for better learning.

Most early books in a guided reading collection are not recognized literature because we have been careful to provide support for children's learning high frequency words. These books support beginning readers. These books are childlike and accessible; they start young readers along the way.

As readers build strength, they encounter a wider variety of texts. A good guided reading program will include fantasy, realistic fiction, biography, autobiography, history, science, and other genres. All the time, children are learning "how to" read this wide variety of text. Some selections will be "short reads" (articles or short stories). We also may include complex, hard-to-read picture books, the equivalent of short stories for elementary age children. There's an opportunity in guided reading to teach children how to look for plots within plots, literacy devices such as flashbacks, how authors use paragraph organization and side headings, and how to read diagrams and charts. Some are much longer "chapter books" that will build readers' stamina.

The teacher's goal in teaching is to help children learn generative processes that they can apply in many ways. They do acquire specific pieces of information—letter-sound relationships, words, characteristics of genre—but at the same time, they must be "learning how to learn." We can not directly teach the "in-the-head" strategies that we want the learner to develop; but our interactions with children can support this kind of generative learning (Clay, 1991).

In guided reading, the teacher is constantly balancing the difficulty of the text with the way he or she supports children in reading the text. A text is selected for a small group of children who are similar in their reading behaviors at a particular point in time. In general, the text is about right for children in the group. The teacher introduces the story to the group, supports individuals through brief interactions while they read, and guides them to talk together afterwards about the ideas and words in the text. In this way, teaching works to refine text selection and help individual readers, through their reading, to move forward in the development of a reading process. A key to supporting reading is the selection of books that are not too easy, yet not too hard, and that offer a variety of challenges to help readers become flexible problem-solvers.

Teacher Learning

Go back to the complex series of decisions presented earlier and then map those decisions onto an instructional context like guided reading. You will come up with a challenging task for the teacher. How do teachers acquire complex understandings about the learning and teaching processes and learn to use their knowledge effectively? For every learner, systems are connected. As we acquire new knowledge, we build a network of understandings to support the new learning. That is true of our students as well as ourselves. We constantly use our prior knowledge to make sense of and acquire new knowledge.

Teacher education starts young teachers on their way, but it would be impossible to design an educational program that would enable every individual to effectively accomplish superb teaching. In saying this, I realize that there will be exceptional individual new teachers who have had extensive experiences in working with people—both children and adults—and have developed some of the cognitive processes necessary for effective teaching. Most new teachers, however, continue to need support as they acquire the experience and knowledge essential for good teaching.

Starting them on their way and supporting their continuing development means enabling teachers to learn from their own teaching. A young child approaching a literacy task such as writing a story, for example, may compose using oral language knowledge and familiar experiences. The child will then be faced with the task of writing words. In the process of writing a message, the child must remember what he wants to say while attending to the construction of words. He may use letter-sound knowledge; he may connect the word he wants to write to words he already knows. The process requires him to keep the message in mind while shifting down to the word and to the letter-sound level. Writing the word requires even more skill as he has to remember the directional movements required to write the letters in a word, one after another.

Through all of this processing, teachers are carefully observing and analyzing behavior. The process is not linear; thinking is going on at many levels. Here are some of the actions involved (also see Lyons & Pinnell, 1999):

- *Observe.* The teacher's most powerful tool is observation of students' behavior. This observation is strengthened by systematically applied assessments, and learning to use such procedures is a staple of teacher education and professional development. The key to effective teaching, however, is the internalization of observation skills. Assessment is ongoing as an integral part of teaching. Teachers are always thinking about alternative explanations for children's behavior, and this thinking helps to build a theory of learning. Through observation, the teacher continues to test theory against the specific behaviors of the children. For example, a teacher observing children's reading behavior might notice whether the child makes attempts at words and what kinds of information the reader is using in those attempts.

- *Probe.* Interacting with students is the way to gather more information about their processing. Internalizing observational techniques equips teachers with the kinds of questioning skills that will help them learn more about children's thinking. It is possible to generate alternative hypotheses. For example, the teacher might question the child during reading, asking, "why did you stop?" Or, "what would make sense there?" The child's responses provide more information.
- *Select hypotheses.* Based on background experience, teachers narrow the focus to probable explanations for students' behavior. For example, the teacher might decide that the child is neglecting visual information or needs to check letter-sound information against meaning.
- *Test hypotheses.* Teachers interact with students based on the theory of behavior. It takes time for young teachers to amass the background experience necessary to interpret students' behavior and interact in a way that would take them further in building a reading process. If reflection is a regular part of teaching, experience will help build the individual repertoire.
- *Reassess.* Observational skills are essential to tell us as teachers whether or not instructional interactions were effective. For example, a teacher who interacts with students to support fluency and phrasing in reading will expect a shift in the reader's behavior and will observe for the effect. An important teaching skill is observing to detect whether or not the child is engaging in the learning process. If not, the whole cycle of observation and hypothesis testing would begin again.

This process becomes even more complex when applied to work with groups of children. In guided reading, for example, you may have several observations of the children in the group. You may know the kinds of texts they can read (level of difficulty) as well as the typical kinds of behaviors they exhibit. Will they be exactly alike? Certainly not, but there will be similarities. You need to think about what they know as you select a text that you think will be within their control with the support of an introduction. In selecting the text, you are thinking about the supports and challenges in the text. You will have some ideas about what the children in the group need to learn at this moment in time, and you will be thinking about how you can call examples to their attention. The introduction and the moment-to-moment interactions provide the support readers need not only to read *this* text, but to learn something about the reading process that they can apply to the reading of other texts.

An Example

Janet was working with a group of first graders in April. She had observed that as a group, these students

- could recognize and use repeating elements of story structure;
- readily became engaged in a story;
- knew many high frequency words;
- could recognize and use part of words such as endings;
- could apply knowledge of letter-sound relationships to solving words; and
- knew how to use punctuation such as quotation marks.

She wanted her students to follow a story over a longer, more complex text. She selected *The Hole in Harry's Pocket* (Bloksberg, 1995). She also knew that there would be new words to solve. While she expected students to use pictures as a way of extending meaning, it was clear that this text was far too complicated for the children to rely on pictures for information as to the precise words and message of the text.

In this story, a little boy is sent to the store to get some milk. He takes the money his mother gives him and puts it in his pocket, along with some other treasures, such as a lucky ring, a toy car, and a whistle. On the way, he jumps over curbs and counts cracks in the sidewalks. When he gets the milk, however, he discovers that his money is missing. Retracing his steps, Harry finds some of the articles that were in his pocket, along with the money. Overjoyed, he runs home to his mom, who asks, "Where's the milk?"

This humorous story requires the reader to remember at least some of the articles in Harry's pocket, follow the sequence of events that takes him to the store and on the path back home, predict that he would find the money, and realize that he ran home without the milk. Readers are always, as Adams (1990) says, reading and thinking. The text has some challenges in terms of word solving; for example, words like *lucky, whistle, cracks, shiny,* and *tightly* would likely be new to first graders and could be the subject of some brief lessons on how to take words apart. Our ultimate goal, however, in a story like this one would be that young readers would be engaged in this humorous story. They would understand Harry's consternation at losing the money, predict that when he found the first object (from his pocket) that he might find the money, and laugh because they knew that Harry had forgotten the milk. Let's look at Janet's introduction to *The Hole in Harry's Pocket*. Janet's goal for each teaching move is written in **bold** above the teacher's words. The whole interaction has a conversational quality, but it truly is intentional instruction.

Introduction *to The Hole in Harry's Pocket*
Introduces main idea and character. Draws attention to illustrations.
Teacher: This is a story about a boy named Harry. There he is on the cover of the book. He's reaching in his pocket and looking surprised. The title of this story is *The Hole in Harry's Pocket.*
Sherri: He's got a hole?

Invites children to predict based on the title and cover.

Teacher: Yes, he has a hole in his pocket and you know what can happen if you have a hole in your pocket.

Andy: You can lose your money.

Sherri: He's got shorts so it could fall right through.

Provides information.

Teacher: Well in this story, his mom sends him to the store for some milk, and he puts it in his pocket.

Andy: Does he lose it?

Introduces title and draws attention to concepts that provide foundation for construction of meaning.

Teacher: Look at the title page. It says *The Hole in Harry's Pocket. You see some things in this picture that Harry has. What are they?*

Sherri: A car.

Jenny: A whistle.

Andy: Is that a ring and there's his money?

Uses specific vocabulary of the text. Provides information essential to the plot:

Teacher: Yes, he might have put some of these things in his pocket—there's a toy car, a whistle, a shiny ring, and the money. Turn the page. There's Harry looking in the refrigerator, and on the next page, there's his mom giving him the money to go to the store. She's telling him something about the money.

Jenny: To take care of it and not lose it!

Teacher: It could be. Turn the page. He's putting the money in his pocket and some other things...

Andy: Like his ring!

Teacher: Yes, and on the next pages, he walks to the store. He's hopping up and down on the curb on this page. On the next, he's looking at the cracks in the sidewalk. Maybe he's counting them.

Jenny: That page is like the cover.

Invites personal response.

Teacher: Yes, he got the milk but then he discovered that the money was gone! So what would you do?

Andy: Go look for it.

Jenny: I'd go back home and tell my Mom.

Sherri: He could have dropped it and then he could go back all the places he was and look for it.

Confirms predictions. Draws attention to word structure.

Teacher: That's just what he does. He goes back home and on the way, you'll see that he finds some things. Turn to page 9. There's something on the sidewalk that looks shiny. What would you expect to see at the beginning of the word *shiny?*

Sherri: Like my name!

Teacher: Yes. . . .

Andy: Sh . . .

Models checking visual information with meaning.

Teacher: That's right. Put your finger under the word shiny.

Does it look kind of shiny in the picture?

Several children: Yes.

Andy: It's the ring.

Uses vocabulary from the story and draws attention to visual information. Connects words to meaning.

Teacher: Yes, the ring is made of *silver,* like this one I have. Two words tell you what the ring is like—*shiny* and *silver.* Find them. Children locate *shiny, silver.*

Teacher: He thinks that ring is lucky for him, so he is really glad to find it.

Sets the task for the readers.

Teacher: Now you can get started reading this story to find out whether he really got the milk for his mom. You might find something that is pretty funny in this story.

Janet planned to watch carefully to see children's response to this story. She hoped that they would be quick to realize that Harry had forgotten the milk. As she observed, she was pleased to see that children in the group were reading most of the words accurately and that nonverbally they were showing interest in the story. Several students were reading with phrasing, slowing down to problem-solve. One student was reading word by word, and she made a note to work with him on fluency.

She interacted briefly with Sherri to work out the word *lucky.* She showed Sherri the word *luck,* and the child worked out *lucky* by noticing the *y.* She supported Andy's reading of a long, compound sentence, "He held the money tightly and ran the rest of the way home." Andy knew all of the words except *tightly,* but as he stopped to solve the word, he lost the momentum of the sentence and became dysfluent. Janet encouraged him to start again at the beginning of the sentence and read it again, pausing slightly after the word *tightly,* and reading the rest of the sentence all at once. That was the page at which several of the children laughed.

After all the children had read the story, Janet invited them to talk about it. They entered into a conversation in which several children mentioned their own experiences in forgetting or losing something. Janet went back to the word *tightly,* helping children connect it with *night* and to notice the *ly* ending. She used a small dry-erase board to illustrate:

night

tight

tightly

They ended by talking about when they realized Harry had forgotten the milk. Three children said it was when he got home and two said it was when his mom asked him. Janet demonstrated how she was thinking about the milk on page 13, when the text said that Harry ran home, *holding the money tightly.* She also pointed out how the comma helped her know how to read the text in an interesting way and also to realize that the author was setting an important piece of information that would help her in understanding the text. Janet was helping the students learn how to comprehend a text *while* reading it. She was showing her young students that comprehension doesn't happen at the end of the story; understanding is constant during the act of processing print.

Reflecting on the lesson afterwards, Janet commented that this group of children were just beginning to read and understand more complex texts. She wanted them to follow the events of the story while simultaneously remembering what Harry put into his pocket. She also wanted them (simultaneously) to meet the challenges in word solving that the text offered. Each reader would need to "take apart" several words (not the same for all of them).

Janet had a lesson plan in her mind, although she did not preplan or script her interactions with students. She wanted to observe students using a range of word solving strategies, for example, using letter sound information, noticing letter clusters and word parts, and connecting known with unknown words. She wanted the students to be able to slow down to problem solve and then speed up again to read with some phrasing and fluency. She had in mind some actions that she wanted to demonstrate. Because she knew her students well, she could select a text that would provide powerful examples for her teaching.

Supporting Teacher Development

The example I have presented shows the delicate balance between observation, direct teaching, and encouraging students to bring their own thinking to a text. How does a teacher educator help a developing teacher refine his/her skills and ability to think about teaching? In my experience, training sessions can provide valuable input, but coaching is the real key to learning (Joyce & Showers, 1980, 1982). Not surprisingly, coaching is the context that staff developers find most difficult. The coach (staff developer) must be just as alert as the teacher to seize the moment and the example that will be most helpful. Coaching sessions can not be totally preplanned or scripted, but there are some general principles that can be followed. These principles might be similar to those described for teachers' looking at children's' learning, although more "layers" of complexity are involved.

- *Observe.* As teacher educators, we observe classroom lessons, noting children's and the teacher's responses, each in relationship to the other. We look for evidence of learning on the part of the children and connect that evidence to teaching moves. We have a kind of road map in the head that represents our understanding of teaching and learning. Observation is the key to what we might bring to the attention of the teacher to help him/her learn from teaching.

- *Probe.* Conversation with the teacher provides the support that helps her/him put reflections on practice into words. The descriptions that arise help both teacher and staff developer to identify the factors in the lesson that make it effective.

- *Select hypotheses.* Together, the coach and the teacher draw inferences about what will support learning for these children. They explore the decisions of the lesson—text selection, introduction, prompting children while reading, discussion, and word study. They analyze children's behavior and hypothesize what would have made the lesson more successful and/or what the teaching decisions should be in tomorrow's lesson. The coach provides feedback for the teacher's *own* analysis; that is, the goal is not so much to tell the teacher what to do as to provide support for thinking.

- *Test hypotheses.* The coach and teacher agree on some actions to take the next day or over the next few days. Typically, interactions would take place fairly frequently over an extended period of time, so that there would be ongoing discussion of teaching moves and students' responses.

- *Reassess.* The coach and teacher are working together in an investigative process, one that results in multiple levels of learning: the children, the teacher, and the coach. As new learning takes place on all levels, the interactions change. The teacher is discovering how children learn, while the teacher educator is learning how to support teachers in analyzing and improving their teaching.

The goal is to help the teacher become conscious of the examples that arise daily in classroom settings. From these examples, teachers learn how to teach and continuously build their own theories of learning (Lyons & Pinnell, 2001).

Principles to Guide Effective Teaching Education

We have learned over the past decade from our work with teachers and staff developers that there is no one way to help teachers learn. Inservice sessions can be good stepping-off points because they provide valuable information and sometimes demonstrations of new approaches and techniques.

In-class coaching provides the support and feedback that makes it possible for teachers to put ideas into action and then to reflect on them. Colleague support is vitally important in the entire process. Conversation among teachers can be highly productive and supportive of learning. A process of change, which all learning involves, will not last unless there is the community support of colleagues who are mutually committed to the goals and who support each other (Darling-Hammond & McLaughlin, 1996). Teacher education is effective when:

- there is a balance between demonstration of specific teaching approaches and the reflection and analysis needed to build the process of thinking about teaching;
- complex ideas are experienced, analyzed, and discussed across a variety of learning contexts—guided reading, writing workshop, reading aloud, etc.
- it is grounded in the practice of teaching children;
- it involves learning conversations surrounding specific acts of teaching; and
- it is supported by a learning community that shares a language for talking about complex ideas related to teaching and learning.

As teachers share experiences and they talk, listen, and examine teaching together, they are building the community that will sustain their efforts over time (L. Lambert, Walker, Zimmerman, Cooper, M. D. Lambert, Gardner, & Slack, 1995; Lieberman, 1996; Schon, 1983).

Good teaching is not a program you can buy or legislate. It can not be handed down by decree or forced by high stakes testing (Bradley, 1998). Development takes place at the school and classroom level as teachers work out their daily problems. If we, as teacher educators can get next to those problems, give real assistance in solving them, and prompt learning in the process, we will have a chance of making the real difference in children's literacy learning.

References

Adams, M. J. (1990). *Beginning to read: Thinking and learning about print.* Cambridge, MA: MIT Press.

Bloksberg, R. (1995). *The hole in Harry's pocket.* Lexington, MA: D. C. Heather & Co.

Bradley, D. H. (1998). Addressing school reform: What's essential and what's not. Forum in *Reading Today.* Aug./Sept. 18.

Clay, M. M. (1991). *Becoming literature: The construction of inner control.* Portsmouth, NH: Heinemann.

Darling-Hammond, L. (1996). What matters most: A competent teacher for every child. *Phi Delta Kappan, 78,* 193-200.

Darling-Hammond, L., & McLaughlin, M. (1996). Policies that support professional development in an era of reform. In M. W. McLaughlin & I. Oberman, (Eds.), *Teacher learning: New policies, new practices* (pp. 202-218). New York: Teachers College Press.

Fountas, I. C., & Pinnell, G. S. (1996). *Guided reading: Good first teaching for all children.* Portsmouth, NH: Heinemann.

Joyce, B., & Showers, B. (1980). Improving inservice training: The message of research. *Educational Leadership, 37,* 379-385.

Joyce, B., & Showers, B. (1982). The coaching of teaching. *Educational Leadership, 40,* 4-10.

Lambert, L., Walker, D., Zimmerman, D., Cooper, J. Lambert, M., Gardner, M., & Slack, P. J. (1995). *The constructivist leader.* New York: Teachers College Press.

Lieberman, A. (1996). Practices that support teacher development: Transforming conceptions of professional learning. In M. W. McLaughlin & I. Oberman, (Eds.) *Teacher learning: New policies, new practices,* (pp.185-201). New York: Teachers College Press.

Lyons, C. A., & Pinnell, G. S. (2001). *Learning to make a difference: A practical guide for the improvement of literacy education.* Portsmouth, NH: Heinemann.

Lyons, C. A., Kerbow, D., Pinnell, G. S., Manning, C., & Watson, V. (1999). *Understanding literacy coordinators' reasoning and actions while coaching primary classroom teachers.* The National Reading Conference Annual Meeting. Orlando, Florida.

Pinnell, G. S., & Lyons, C. A. (1999). *Literacy coordinator as instructional leader: The development of technical knowledge and skill.* Paper presented at the American Educational Research Association. Toronto, Canada.

Schon, D. (1983). *The reflective practitioner.* New York: Basic Books.

Vygotsky, L. S. (1978). *Mind in society.* Cambridge, MA: Harvard University Press.

STORIES THAT CAN CHANGE THE WAY WE EDUCATE

Patricia A. Edwards

Michigan State University

*Keynote Address
College Reading Association
2001*

Pat Edwards is a Professor of Language and Literacy and a Senior Researcher at the National Center for the Improvement of Early Reading Achievement at Michigan State University. She is also the recipient of the prestigious Michigan State University 2001 Distinguished Faculty Award. She holds a Doctorate in Reading Education from the University of Wisconsin-Madison and is the author of two nationally acclaimed family literacy programs: "Parents as Partners in Reading. A Family Literacy Training Program" and "Talking Your Way to Literacy. A Program to Help Nonreading Parents Prepare Their Children for Reading." She was a member of the Board of Directors of the International Reading Association from May 1998 to May 2001. Also, she participated in the UNESCO World Symposium on Family Literacy as one of 50 researchers contributing to the development of world policy on family literacy. Dr. Edwards has served as an advisor to the First National Goal "Readiness for School," and the Michigan State University Institute for Families, Youth, and Children. Numerous foundations and organizations have recognized her research. Dr. Edwards is on assignment with Heinemann Speakers Bureau and she has held workshops, inservice training sessions with school districts nationwide and abroad.

Dr. Edwards has taught in public schools and universities for twenty-five years has published books and articles focused on family/multigenerational literacy and emergent literacy: Her research has been published in such journals as. Yearbook of the National Reading Conference, Theory into Practice, Teaching

Reprinted from *Celebrating the Faces of Literacy*, pp. 20-30, by P. E. Linder, M. B. Sampson, J. R. Dugan, B. Brancato, Eds., 2002, Commerce, TX: College Reading Association.

Education, Educational Policy *and many others. She is the author of* A Path to Follow: Learning to Listen to Parents *(Heinmann, 1999). She is also the author of two forthcoming books.* Examining Dialogues Used in Parent-Teacher Conferences *(Heinemann) and* Children's Literacy Development: Making it Happen Through School, Family and Community Involvement *(Allyn & Bacon).*

When Dr. Jane Mantanzo invited me to speak at CRA in March 2001, I wondered how I would address the four divisions of CRA: Teacher Education (the largest), Clinical, College Reading, and Adult Literacy. As I struggled with my talk for this occasion, it led me to reflect on my career that I found touched these four divisions in one way or another. As a graduate student at Duke University, I worked in the reading clinic and at Louisiana Tech University, I coordinated the Reading and Study Skills program. While I witnessed much success working in the Duke University reading clinic and in coordinating the reading and study skills program at Louisiana Tech University, my stories as a teacher educator and my work in adult literacy are stories that I feel have changed the way we educate children in this country. Therefore, I have decided to share these stories with you.

Beginning the Story

When I entered college I knew automatically that I was destined to become a teacher, simply, because I had been told all of my life that teaching was a good career for women, especially African American women. I attended a small African American teachers' college in the South (Albany State College, now Albany State University located in Albany, Georgia) and was constantly reminded of how important my role would be as an African American educator in the lives of boys and girls of color. My undergraduate professors often informed me that African American students needed to see positive role models in the classroom. Specifically, they needed teachers who understood something about their cultural heritage as well as their learning styles in order to assimilate education with the family and community life.

My teaching career would begin within a new integrated system of education and this caused concern for my undergraduate professors about the problems I might encounter as an African American teacher in a school with a majority White population. These professors agonized with me over the challenges for me as a minority teacher given the fact that I might end up in contexts where I could be the only minority teacher in the school setting. The existence of this possibility prompted them to suggest I attempt to play an informal role in helping my White colleagues understand the African American culture, while utilizing my White colleagues to assist me in understanding theirs. Despite this, however, my professors' attention to the need for creating relationships that promoted understanding between the home and school cultures were nonexistent. In fact, they provided no training or guidance as to how I could best interact with the families of the students in an integrated school setting. Further, I had no formal guidance in understanding and appreciating the home literacy environments of my newly diverse population of students or knowledge of whether their culture did or did not resemble my own, and if this would make a difference in my ability to work with the families of my students. My professors apparently were unaware that my lack of knowledge about home literacy environments could cause me to unknowingly alienate my students and their families, thus negatively affecting their quality of education.

Perhaps my undergraduate professors assumed that I would discover how to work with families based on "gut reaction" or "instinct" or that what I needed to know I would be able to infer easily from general descriptions of family life for a particular cultural group. However, these assumptions have serious limitations and in fact offer further problems for helping teachers to understand the families of their students.

As a masters student at North Carolina A&T University, I was involved in an innovative program designed to increase the number of minorities in higher education. Consequently, I began my joint college and classroom-teaching career at North Carolina Central University that was a rare and wonderful experience. I coordinated the Pre-Student Teaching Program and taught in the public schools in Durham, Raleigh, and Chapel Hill. Because of my unusual experience of serving both as a college and classroom teacher simultaneously, I can comfortably say that I began my academic career by trying to understand how to teach myself as well as helping preservice teachers learn to teach in a variety of teaching situations, i.e., team teaching, self-contained, non-graded, open classroom, multi-aged grouping, etc. I explored, along with my students, the knowledge and skills necessary to teach in these situations. I also began to examine the impact of these new organizational patterns on parents and children.

During this same period of time, I was enrolled in an educational specialist program at Duke University. At Duke, I spent a lot of time working as a reading clinician. I then decided to go the University of Wisconsin-Madison to work on my doctorate in reading education.

After completing my doctorate, I accepted a position at Grambling State University, a small, southern black university located in a rural, northern Louisiana community (Grambling, LA). This experience allowed me to share some of the frustrations black teacher educators at primarily black colleges/ universities are facing, i.e., declining enrollments in teacher preparation programs, large numbers of students failing teacher competency tests, and weaker students choosing to become teachers. I addressed in my seminar class the issue of families and children because my students expressed to me that their parents had struggled with the "system" to get them through it, and after getting through it, they still felt that they had been "dealt a bad deal," so to speak. For example, one student named Cassandra told a chilling story of how her parents had to fight with the principal, teacher, and supervisor when she was in fourth grade to prevent them from putting her in a special education class. Angela, another student in the seminar class, commented that she and her parents experienced teachers quickly giving up on her and wanting to track her into lower sections or special education classes. Several other students agreed with Cassandra's and Angela's past encounters and indicated that their parents had fought similar battles. Intrigued by these revelations, I began to explore with my students the possibilities of what it would mean to improve the "system" that they said had not served them and their families adequately.

While teaching at Louisiana Tech University, a predominately White southern university located in a rural, northern Louisiana community (Ruston, LA), I was faced with another challenging situation. My White students often complained that "our teacher training program has not done a very good job in showing us how to work with families, especially families different from us, and we desperately need to know how to do this."

As a teacher trainer and reading educator, I have always been interested in the family's ability to support its children's development as readers and writers. In 1983 I got an opportunity to develop this interest that later evolved into the *Parents as Partners in Reading* program. In the spring of 1983, I received a W. K. Kellogg National Fellowship. As part of the Fellowship, I decided to focus on family involvement through employing multiple lenses, which draw from educational, psychological, sociological, cross-cultural, and policy perspectives. Over the three-year fellowship period, I visited over fifty agencies, organizations, and institutions of higher education throughout the United States and abroad. This opportunity gave me the distinct opportunity to communicate with many noted experts who addressed family issues from multiple perspectives. Some of these experts included: Joyce L. Epstein, Oliver Moles, Dorothy Rich, Shirley Brice Heath, Valora Washington, Dorothy S. Strickland, David L. Williams, Jr., Barbara Rogoff, Eugene Garcia, Vincent Greaney, and Moncrieff Cochran.

After studying work on family involvement from various perspectives, I began thinking about how I could utilize the information I had gathered to both help my own community of Ruston, Louisiana, where I was living and working at the time, as well as fulfill the goals of the fellowship. It was at this point that I decided to volunteer to be a parent consultant at the local Head Start Center in this small rural northern Louisiana community. My goal was twofold: (1) to increase the families' awareness of the importance of supporting their children's educational development; and (2) to assess how low SES parents interpreted the request from teachers to read to their children (Edwards, 1989). What I found was that the ways parents interpreted the teacher request to "read to their child" was often quite divergent to the goals and practices intended by the teachers. Also, I discovered that while teachers thought that their requests for parent involvement was quite clear and specific, parents in fact where often confused or uncertain about what "read to your child" entailed. Additionally, I found that there was little evidence that the teachers' requests acknowledged the enormous challenges faced by parents on a daily basis. Requests to "read to your child" or "come to school" did not account for the high illiteracy rate of parents or the difficulty poor parents' face in arranging time away from a low paying job or in finding child care for younger siblings.

After a successful year at the Head Start Center, I moved to Louisiana State University where I continued my research on parent-child book reading. I organized the *Parents as Partners in Reading Program* at Donaldsonville Elementary School located in Donaldsonville, Louisiana, a small, rural southern community. The Learning Together Company in 2003 will publish an updated and revised version of the *Parents as Partners in Reading Program*. My goal was to train parents to participate in effective book-reading interactions with their children. It involved defining for parents the participatory skills and behaviors found in effective parent-child reading interactions. The most effective reading interaction techniques were also modeled for the parents.

Over ten years ago, I met with a group of low-income mothers with marginal reading skills in the school's library at Donaldsonville Elementary School for two hours once a week for twenty-three weeks. In these sessions, the mothers learned how to share books with their children. The book-reading intervention (*Parents as Partners in Reading,* see Edwards, 1993) fell into three phases: coaching, peer modeling, and parent-child interaction. Each phase was approximately the same length (6 or 7 weeks). The first phase, coaching, consisted of me modeling book-reading behaviors (i.e., previewing books, asking questions, varying voice, pointing to pictures/words, permitting the child to explore book, linking text-to-life, and life-to-text connections, etc.).

The second phase of instruction, peer modeling, focused on promoting parents' control of the book-reading sessions and strategies. In this phase, parents began to direct the book-reading strategies sessions themselves, focusing on modeling particular book-reading strategies for the group and practicing the targeted strategies with one another. More specifically, one or two parents each week would model how they would read a book to their child for the entire group, and the other parents would provide feedback and coach one another in the use of the strategies. My role in the phase was supportive and served to: (a) guide parents' participation in book-reading interaction with each other, (b) find connections between what the parents already knew and what they needed to know, (c) model effective book-reading behaviors for the parents when such assistance was needed, and (d) provide praise and support for their attempts.

During the final phase, parent-child interaction, I ceded total control to the parents and functioned primarily as a supportive and sympathetic audience: offering suggestions to the mothers as to what books to use in reading interactions with their children; evaluating the parent-child book-reading interactions; and providing feedback or modeling. In this final phase, parents actually brought their own children to the sessions and used the strategies directly with them.

In addition to learning how to share books with their children, parents were acquainted throughout the year with the various types of literature (e.g., Mother Goose, poetry books, board books, pop-up books, flap books, cloth books, plastic books, alphabet books, wordless picture books, predictable books, easy to read books, picture storybooks, and folk and fairy tales). They were also acquainted with the types of skills stressed in the various children's books. For example, parents were informed that cloth, toy, and vinyl books help children identify colors, sounds, and familiar objects in the environment. Board books will build their children's vocabularies, and increase their awareness of numbers, colors, shapes, and seasons. Alphabet and counting books focus on development of specific skills, such as learning to count sequentially from one through ten and learning to identify the letters of the alphabet. Concepts books will help their children understand easy concepts as well as abstract ones. Easy concepts included colors, such as red or blue, and shapes such as circle or square. The more difficult books may introduce opposite concepts such as fast or slow.

I spent a great deal of time with the parents focusing on words found in basic concept books (see Jett-Simpson, 1984). The concepts addressed included: position concepts, time concepts, size and weight concepts, distance and height concepts, speed concepts, number/amount concepts, color concepts, and shape concepts.

The parents were also shown what to look for in books for children. For example, they were encouraged to ask themselves the following types of questions:

1. Are the illustrations colorful and appealing?
2. Is the size of the book comfortable for your child to hold?
3. Can the print be easily read?
4. Is the language natural and appealing?
5. Is the story or information worth reading?
6. Is this a book both my child and I will enjoy?

Lastly, the parents were encouraged to tap other sources for guidance in book selection. I suggested that they tap one or all of the following sources for guidance in book selection:

1. Ask other parents what books they are reading to their children.
2. Ask librarians to suggest the more popular books.
3. Ask bookstore sales people what books are best sellers.
4. Ask your child to name a book he or she likes, then try to find a similar

one or one written by the same author.

Recruiting Parents

Some of the critics of programs designed for low-income families have said that parents will not attend because they are simply not interested in helping their children. This is not true. Laurea (1986) and Obgu (1974) found that non-mainstream parents who lack knowledge do not necessarily lack interest in their children's schools or in learning how to help their children. In order to dispel this belief when implementing my program, I asked for community support in recruiting parents for the book-reading program. I contacted an unlikely group of community leaders who knew the parents in other contexts outside of school—a bar owner, bus driver, grandmother, the ministerial alliance, and people sitting on street corners.

The ministers agreed to preach from their pulpits about the importance of parents helping their children learn to read and especially the importance of parents attending the weekly book-reading sessions. After my first meeting with the ministers, a priest of a predominately African-American Catholic Church urged parents to participate in the book-reading program, noting in a sermon that literacy was an important tool of faith and that children needed to be able to read the confirmation requirements. Both Black and White ministers delivered similar messages urging parents to attend the program and to help their children in school weekly.

The owner of a local bar surfaced as a strong supporter of the program. He attended all of the book-reading sessions and told the mothers who patronized his establishment that they no longer would be welcome unless they put as much time into learning how to read to their children as they spent enjoying themselves at his bar. He transported mothers to and from the sessions, working with the social services department to secure babysitters for parents who otherwise would not have come.

The bus driver offered to drive parents to the program each week. The grandmother organized a telephone campaign that involved calling program participants each week. Lastly, the people sitting on the street corners began to talk about the program and encouraged all the parents they came in contact with to attend.

Reactions to and Support of the Book-Reading Program

For these parents, the school library became a place for gathering socially to talk about literacy and to exchange ideas—a kind of family gathering place. The library atmosphere helped the parents to relax and to enjoy learning how to help their children. The parents came to understand that abundant experiences with simple books, and repeated readings of familiar books and stories would benefit both them and their children. Parents who feared coming to school because of their own past experiences now enjoyed coming and could actually laugh about the experiences they were encountering. Several parents expressed that they were having the opportunity to relive in a positive way their school experiences through their children and they loved every moment.

Recognizing the need for helping marginally literate parents help their children, the school media specialist redefined the role of the school library by making it accessible to these new clients. For example, she taught the parents how to be library assistants. She showed them how to reshelve books in their proper place, how to use the card catalog, and how to be of assistance to other parents if she was not available. Further, the media specialist designed a computer program, which listed the names of each child whose parents were participating in the book-reading program. The parents were able to check books out under their child's name. She kept a computerized list of the types of books the parents were checking out. This information was shared with the child's teacher and me.

The school media specialist assisted me each week in selecting the books correlated to the topics that were being addressed in the book reading sessions. She also assisted me in selecting books that the parents could understand. The school media specialist commented that the library had become one of the busiest and most productive places in the school. She expressed amazement that showing parents how they can help their children can change parents' views about the school as well.

Concluding Comments about the Donaldsonville Story

The Donaldsonville parent story greatly impacted me and it also greatly impacted our nation. A new field of study emerged from this research called "family literacy." Former First Lady Barbara Bush is a big supporter of this new field of study.

I strongly believe that parents want a better life for their children than for themselves. Education is part of that better life. Most of us would agree that when semiliterate, functionally illiterate parents are educated with their children, they are better able to work productively themselves, and they are better able to provide the atmosphere that will nurture the intellectual development of their children. And their children in turn are more likely to lead more productive lives.

Another Story to Tell

When I moved to Lansing, Michigan in 1989 to teach at Michigan State University, I continued my research on families and children. I always wondered if there were other stories that parents needed to "tell" and teachers needed to "hear." Therefore, in the fall of 1995, I met with a group of twelve first-grade teachers in Lansing, Michigan. The teachers in my research study group represented eight of thirty-three elementary schools in Lansing, and the schools in which they teach are located in very diverse communities culturally, economically, and ethnically. I asked the teachers to identify a pool of students who were having difficulty learning to read and write, and who were at-risk of failing first grade.

As a consequence, I interviewed the parents of the children that the teachers identified as being at-risk of failing first grade to learn about their stories of their children's early literacy beginnings. I called these stories, "parent stories" of early literacy. I define parent "stories" as the narratives gained from open-ended conversations and/or interviews. In these interviews, parents respond to questions designed to provide information about traditional and nontraditional early literacy activities and experiences that have happened in the home (see Edwards, et al., 1999). According to Vandergrift and Greene (1992) "every parent has his or her own story to tell" (p. 57). Coles (1989) contends, "one's responses to a story is just as revealing as the story itself" (p. 18). Victoria Purcell-Gates (1995) states, "When we seek to understand learners, we must seek to understand the cultural context within which they have developed, learned to interpret who they are in relation to others, and learned how to process, interpret, or decode, their world" (p. 5). Courtney Cazden (1988) supports Purcell-Gates contention by arguing that: "Teachers, like physicians and social workers, are in the business of helping others: But as a prerequisite to giving help, we have to take in and understand" (p. 26). I, too support the notion of taking in and understanding the world of others. This is certainly practiced in other professions. For example, when a parent takes their child to the doctor, the doctor is very dependent on the parent's history of their child's illness. Unfortunately, very few first grade teachers have a history of a child's literacy development from the parent's point of view.

I firmly believe that teachers are professionals who can master the challenge of working with and relating to families, not just children. Unfortunately, there are few guidelines or standards for teachers as they attempt to involve the whole family in a child's education. This contrasts with other professionals in the United States, starting with medicine, and continuing through law, architecture, engineering, and nursing that are characterized by a specialized knowledge base, a commitment to client welfare, and the definition and transmission of professional standards (Darling-Hammond & Cobb, 1996).

I suggest that parent stories could serve as one common mechanism for teachers to draw on when they seek to involve parents in their child's education. It is common practice for professionals like doctors, lawyers, and architects to collect information, which gives them particular insights about their patients/ clients. Teachers are often criticized for not living in the neighborhoods in which they teach, but rarely do doctors, lawyers or architects live in the neighborhoods in which they practice their professional craft. Instead these professionals rely on collecting information as a way of developing a professional interaction with their patients/clients. I approach parent involvement in the same way.

Concluding Comments about Parent Stories

Parent stories offer a route out of the blame cycle and the justification teachers sometimes give for not successfully teaching children labeled at-risk. Parent stories allow teachers to identify what it means, specifically, when we use the words "home literacy environment" to talk about students' success or lack of success in school. By using parent stories in this way, teachers are able to look at specific issues, problems and strengths of homes, which influence the literacy development of students. This is the first step towards making connections between parent stories and how they can be used to better educate every child.

Also, parent stories have the potential to alter teacher's own dispositions and practice. The concept of parent stories is supported by work of Taylor and Dorsey-Gaines (1988). Taylor and Dorsey-Gaines stated:

> If we are to teach, we must first examine our own assumptions about families and children and we must be alert to the negative images in the literature. Instead of responding to 'pathologies,' we must recognize that what we see may actually be healthy adaptations to an uncertain and stressful world. As teachers, [administrators] researchers, and policymakers, we need to think about the children themselves and try to imagine the contextual worlds of their day-to-day lives. (p. 203)

In my opinion, parent stories should prompt the investigation and redirection of current "parent-involvement," "parent-teacher communication," and "creation of home-school connections" initiatives. It is also my opinion that parent stories underscore the importance that society must begin to really listen to all parent voices and value their information about their children without prejudice, judgment, or apathy. If we can do this, we will embrace the multiplicity of experiences that parents have and can bring to the educational adventures of their children.

References

Cazden, C. B. (1988). *Classroom discourse: The language of teaching and learning.* Portsmouth, NH: Heinemann.

Coles, R. (1989). *The call of stories.* Boston: Houghton Mifflin.

Darling-Hammond, L., & Cobb, V. L. (1996). The changing context of teacher education. In F. B. Murray (Ed.), *The teacher educator's handbook: Building a knowledge base for the preparation of teachers* (pp: 14-62). San Francisco: Jossey-Bass Publishers.

Edwards, P. A. (1989). Supporting lower SES mothers' attempts to provide scaffolding for book reading. In J. Allen & J. M, Mason (Eds.) *Risk makers, risk takers, risk breakers:*

Reducing the risks for young literacy learners. Portsmouth, NH: Heinemann.

Edwards, P. A. (1993). *Parents as partners in reading: A family literacy training program.* Second Edition. Chicago: Children's Press.

Edwards, P. A., Pleasants, H. M., & Franklin, S. H. (1999). *A path to follow: Learning to listen to parents:* Portsmouth, NH: Heinemann.

Jett-Simpson, M. (1984). *Parents and beginning reading.* Atlanta: Humanics Limited:

Laurea, A (1986). *Social class differences in family-school relationships: The importance of cultural capital.* Unpublished manuscript, Department of Sociology, StanfordUniversity:

Ogbu, J. (1974). *The next generation.* New York: Academic Press.

Purcell-Gates, V. (1995). *Others people's words: The cycle of low literacy.* Cambridge: Harvard University Press.

Taylor, D., & Dorsey-Gaines, C. (1988). *Growing up literate: Learning from inner-city families.* Portsmouth. NH: Heinemann.

Vandergrift, J. A., & Greene, A. L. (1992). Rethinking parent involvement. *Educational Leadership, 50*(1), 57-59.

WHAT RESEARCH REVEALS ABOUT LITERACY MOTIVATION

Linda B. Gambrell

Clemson University

Keynote Address
College Reading Association
2001

In 2001 Linda B. Gambrell was Professor and Director of the School of Education at Clemson University. Prior to coming to Clemson University, she was Associate Dean for Research at the University of Maryland where she taught graduate and undergraduate reading and language arts courses. She began her career as an elementary classroom teacher and reading specialist in Prince George's County, Maryland. She has written books on reading instruction and published articles in journals such as Reading Research Quarterly, The Reading Teacher, Educational Psychologist, *and* Journal of Educational Research.

From 1992-97, she was principal investigator at the National Reading Research Center where she directed the Literacy Motivation Project. She has served as an elected member of the Board of Directors of the International Reading Association, National Reading Conference, and College Reading Association. She served as President of the National Reading Conference and the College Reading Association. From 1993-96, She was co-editor of The Journal of Reading Behavior, *Publication of the National Reading Conference. She has received professional Awards including the 1998 International Reading Association Outstanding Teacher Educator in Reading Award, and the 2001 National*

Reprinted from *Celebrating the Faces off Literacy,* pp. 32-42, by P. E. Linder, M. B. Sampson, J. A. R. Dugan, & B. Brancto, Eds., 2002, Commerce, TX: College Reading Association.

Reading Conference Albert J Kingston Award. Her current interests were in the areas of reading comprehension strategy instruction, literacy motivation, and the role of discussion in teaching and learning.

This paper is based on an invited address at the first Estill Alexander Leaders in Literacy Forum at the 2001 College Reading Association annual conference in Orlando, Florida. It is an honor and privilege to be invited to deliver this address. Dr. Alexander had a very positive influence on my professional life as a colleague and a scholar. He was well known for his contributions to the field of reading motivation. His pioneering work in this area was influential in my own work, and it is fitting that at this first forum named in his honor that I address recent advances in the field of reading motivation. Dr. Alexander was indeed a scholar and a gentleman who embodied the best of what our field has to offer. He was committed to furthering the goal of literacy for all, was a dedicated member of CRA, and was a friend and mentor to many CRA members. I know that Dr. Alexander would be pleased to be remembered by his many CRA friends and colleagues every year at this forum in his honor.

My topic is motivation—specifically literacy motivation. Motivation has long been recognized in the educational literature as a powerful and useful construct. Researchers and teachers have become increasingly aware of the importance of literacy motivation in literacy development. Positive literacy motivation has been associated with a number of desirable outcomes including higher reading achievement, deeper cognitive processing, greater conceptual understanding, and willingness to persevere (Allington, 1986; Anderson, Wilson, & Fielding, 1988; Hidi, 1990; Tobias, 1994).

In this paper I will explore what research reveals about effective literacy motivation, as well as what we need to know more about in order to create classroom contexts that foster motivation to read. We know that some students expend great time and effort on academic tasks such as reading, while other students do not. One of the lingering questions is why different students expend different amounts of time and effort on such tasks. Such differences are often explained as motivational in nature. Some students are more highly motivated to read than others. During the past decade there has been increasing interest in motivational factors that are specifically associated with reading motivation. Because of the powerful relationship between motivation and achievement, it is important that we come to a fuller understanding of the role of motivation in literacy learning.

Simple Definitions for a Complex Construct

My view of literacy motivation has been strongly influenced by the research of motivational theorists such as Ford (1992) and Winne (1985). Their work is grounded in the expectancy-value theory, which emphasizes the roles of self-concept and value as critical constructs of motivation. The self-concept component is supported by a number of research studies that suggest students who believe they are capable and competent are more likely to outperform those who do not hold such beliefs (Paris & Oka, 1986; Schunk, 1985). There is also evidence to suggest that students who perceive reading as valuable and important, and who have personally relevant reasons for reading, will engage in reading in a more planful and effortful manner (Paris & Oka, 1986).

The motivational systems theory developed by Ford (1992) maintains that people are motivated to attain goals they value and perceive as achievable. Similarly, Winne (1985) views the "idealized reader" as one who feels competent and perceives reading as being of personal value and practical importance. The work of Wittrock (1986) has also been particularly influential in my own thinking about what constitutes motivation. According to Wittrock, motivation is the process of initiating, sustaining, and directing activity. In the research to date on literacy motivation far more attention has been devoted to what initiates engagement, while very little of the research has explored the nature of sustained engagement in reading. Maehr's (1976) research, for example, defines motivation as the tendency to return to and continue working on tasks. In my view, continuing and sustaining engagement in reading/literacy activities is clearly the heart of true motivation.

Some Things We Know and Some Things We Think We Know About Literacy Motivation

Research to date has revealed insights about the role of gender and grade level on literacy motivation. First, there is ample evidence that motivation to read decreases from grade 1 to grade 6 (McKenna, Kear, & Ellsworth, 1995), and that girls are more motivated to read than boys (Askov & Fischbach, 1973; McKenna, et al., 1995; Parker & Paradis, 1984). Recent research, however, suggests that perhaps we should not take these findings at face value. For example, while the research of McKenna, Kear, and Ellsworth (1995) documents a decline in reading motivation as students go up the grade level, recent research suggests that there may be variations in the motivation of students, especially in the early grades as reading competence is being developed. A cross-cultural study conducted by Mazzoni, Gambrell, and Korkeamaki (2000) found that motivation to read increased during first grade on fall-to-spring measure and began to decline during second grade for both Finnish and U.S. students. Because American students begin first grade at age 6 and Finnish student begin first grade at age 7, this study documented a schooling rather than age effect on reading motivation. This finding suggests that first grade may be a very critical time in the development of motivation to read and that there are variations in motivation that have not been fully accounted for in the prior research that has suggested a linear decline in motivation from grades 1 through 6. Clearly, additional research is needed that will explore critical dimensions of motivation during the early developmental period of literacy acquisition.

Second, a number of studies have suggested that girls possess more positive attitudes about reading than boys (Askow & Fischbach, 1973; McKenna, et al., 1995; Parker & Paradis, 1983). This research is fairly consistent, except in the case of Finland, where 9 year old boys rated themselves as better readers than girls (Elley, 1994). However, in the cross cultural study by Mazzoni, Gambrell, and Korkeamaki (2000) with first grade students (US, age 6; Finland, age 7) and second grade students (US, age 7; Finland, age 8), US and Finnish girls reported more positive attitudes toward reading than boys at both grade levels. It should be noted that the finding reported by Elley (1994) was based on self-report on a single question that was used to infer children's self-perception of reading ability, while the results of the Mazzoni, Gambrell, and Korkeamaki (2000) study were based on a multiple-item motivational survey:

The general finding in the research literature that girls are more motivated to read than boys seems clear and straightforward. However, in reviewing the research on motivation and gender, several concerns arose. Most of the motivational research to date has focused on school or textbook reading and the reading of narrative. What has been neglected is information about the motivation of both boys and girls to read informational text. In a study by Gambrell, Codling, and Palmer (1996), third and fifth grade students were asked to tell about a story (narrative) they had recently read. For the third graders, 21 out of 24 students were able to tell about a story they had read recently, while all 24 fifth graders were able to do so. What was most telling in this study was the fact that when the third and fifth grade students were asked to tell about an informational text they had recently read, 5 out of 24 third graders could not remember reading any informational text, while 6 out of 24 fifth graders could not do so. There are obvious differences in the exposure and experiences students have in reading informational text that may be associated with literacy motivation. It may well be that these differences may also be related to gender. There are many questions that have not yet been fully explored with respect to findings about the role of gender in literacy motivation.

What Do We Know About Creating Motivating Contexts for Literacy Learning?

In Flippo's (2001) study of reading experts there was compelling agrement on the importance of literacy motivation. Many of the points of agreement among the literacy experts in Flippo's study were grounded in the belief that motivation is an important outcome of instruction. There appears to be congruence across theoretical perspectives, research findings, and literacy experts that the following classroom characteristics foster motivation to read: access to reading materials, opportunities for self-selection, and social interactions about books.

Access to reading materials

During the past decade, a number of studies documented that when students have classroom environments that are book rich, the motivation to read is high (Allington & McGill-Franzen, 1993; Elley, 1992; Gambrell, 1995; Guthrie et al., 1996; Lundberg & Linnakyla, 1993; Morrow, 1992; Neuman & Celano, 2001; Neuman & Roskos, 1993; Purcell-Gates et al., 1995). Being surrounded by an abundance of high quality, high interest reading materials is critical to the development of reading motivation. Availability of books and other reading materials encourages students to engage in reading in a voluntary and sustained manner: However, one caveat is worth noting with regard to access to books. It is not just having books available that is important—rather it is how the books are made accessible to students and what teachers do to promote engagement with books and reading materials. We know, for example, that books that are displayed or featured in some way by the teacher are the books that students gravitate toward. It is also true, that students want to reread books that the teacher has read aloud. It seems that having books available and having a teacher who promotes reading in interesting and exciting ways creates a motivating context for literacy learning.

Opportunities for self-selection

Perhaps one of the most robust findings in the psychological literature is that choice is related to motivation. Consequently, it is no surprise that self-selection of reading material is strongly linked to motivation to read. The research supports the notion that the books and stories that students find most interesting are those they have selected for their own reasons and purposes (Gambrell & Morrow, 1996; Palmer, Codling, & Gambrell, 1994). Schiefele's (1991) research revealed that students who were allowed and encouraged to choose their own reading material expended more effort in learning and understanding the material they read.

Research suggests that providing students with time to engage in self-selected reading promotes literacy motivation. Wiesendanger and Birlem (1984) analyzed eleven research studies on self-selected reading and reported that nine of these studies presented evidence that students were more motivated to read as a result of participating in self-selected reading. Increases in motivation to read have also been reported for a range of students who engaged in self-selected reading, including remedial readers (Mayes, 1982) and adolescent students with discipline problems (Coley, 1981). These studies also suggest that motivation to read is linked to spending more time reading, thereby helping students gain much needed practice and experience.

Social interactions about books

Theories of motivation and reading emphasize that learning is facilitated by social interactions with others. Several studies have documented that social interaction promotes achievement, higher-level cognition, and intrinsic desire to read (Almasi, 1995; Guthrie, Schafer, Wang, & Afflerbach, 1995). A number of studies have also shown that a classroom environment that fosters social interaction is more likely to foster intrinsic motivation than more individualized, solitary learning environments (Ames, 1984; Deci & Ryan, 1985; Guthrie, Schafer, Wang, & Afflerbach, 1995). Guthrie et al. (1996) found that students who had opportunities to interact socially with peers during literacy activities were more intrinsically motivated to read, and they read more widely and more frequently than students who were less socially interactive. The National Assessment of Education Progress (NAEP), reporting on trends in academic progress, found that students who engaged in frequent discussions about reading with friends and family were more motivated to read, and had higher reading achievement scores, than student who did not have such interactions (Campbell et al., 2000).

Sharing ideas with others about books, stories, and information is an important factor in developing engaged and motivated readers. There is ample research evidence that social interactions about what one has read has a positive influence on reading motivation and achievement. In Flippo's (2001) study, there was agreement among literacy experts about the importance of the role of social interaction in reading. Specifically, there was expert agreement that children should be encouraged to talk about and share the different kinds of reading they do in a variety of ways with many others. Taken together, research studies and literacy experts place a high priority on social interactions associated with discussions about text, and that motivation is enhanced when students perceive the leaning context to be socially supportive.

Intrinsic and Extrinsic Motivation:
It's Not a Question of One or The Other

Perhaps the thing that all literacy researchers and teachers would agree upon is that we would like for all of our students to find reading personally rewarding. We want all of our students to be intrinsically motivated to read—we want them to read when no one is looking, when no one is offering candy or pizza. We want them to want to read because we know that literacy is one of, if not THE, cornerstone of academic success and good citizenship.

When students are intrinsically motivated, they engage in reading because they want to do it. On the other hand, if a student engages in reading only because they will receive a reward, we say that the student is extrinsically motivated. Extrinsic rewards can be either tangible (such as stars or candy) or can be intangible (praise from the teacher, feedback on performance). The question that has intrigued teachers and researchers for decades is "Should we use extrinsic rewards to encourage children to read?" While most of us would agree that teacher praise and teacher feedback are desirable, many would not agree that candy and stars are appropriate.

Fawson and Fawson (1994) explored the effects of tangible extrinsic reward for reading. They investigated a program that offered elementary children an incentive (a popular food) for reading a certain number of books. They compared the incentive group with the control group and found that intrinsic motivation to read did not increase as a result of the incentive program. Other researchers have reported results that suggest that if you reward a student who enjoys reading with an extrinsic reward, such as points, food, or money, the student may choose to read less frequently once the incentive is discontinued (Deci, Valerand, Pelletier, & Ryan, 1991). The concern then is that extrinsic rewards may have a detrimental effect on the intrinsic motivation to read.

Cameron and Pierce (1994) conducted a meta-analysis of the research on rewards. They concluded that extrinsic rewards do not necessarily have a negative impact on intrinsic motivation with respect to attitude, time on task, and performance. A number of studies have shown that, under certain conditions, rewards can enhance motivation. In these studies, students who were given an incentive (promised a reward for certain behavior) showed an increase in intrinsic motivation compared to students who were not offered an incentive (Brennan & Glover, 1980; Karnoil & Ross, 1977). On the other hand, other researchers have reported a negative effect on intrinsic motivation when incentives were promised for a specified level of performance (Deci, 1975; Lepper, Greene, & Nisbett, 1973):

As you can tell, the controversy around intrinsic and extrinsic motivation continues. Much of the research in the past has pitted intrinsic motivation against extrinsic motivation. During the past decade my views about intrinsic and extrinsic motivation have changed dramatically. While I firmly believe that intrinsic literacy motivation is the ultimate goal of reading instruction, I now believe that there is a complex and not fully understood relationship between extrinsic and intrinsic motivation.

For example, there is evidence that suggests that we are motivated by the reward itself (Deci, 1975). If we are paid to do a task such as reading, it may result in a decrease in our desire to read; however, being paid may be very effective in motivating us to make money. In other words, we tend to view the "reward" as desirable and valuable. Therefore, if we want to develop the intrinsic desire to read, books and extra time to read are probably the most effective rewards.

Research in the past has neglected to take a good look at the relationship between the extrinsic reward and the desired behavior. I have to admit that observations in the classroom of a truly outstanding teacher influenced my thinking about extrinsic and intrinsic motivation more than reading the existing research literature. In this classroom the teacher used primarily intangible extrinsic rewards, along with some tangible rewards to motivate students to engage in academic learning. For example, after a reading skill group where all children were able to demonstrate mastery, she rewarded the students with 10 extra minutes of free reading time. Following a math lesson, she rewarded the third grade students with the opportunity to take home a 4th grade math worksheet . . . if they wanted to. All students were eager to assume this challenge and every child in the class took that 4th grade math for homework. After another whole class lesson, the teacher rewarded the class by saying, "You all did such great work! I'm going to read two chapters to you during teacher read-aloud time today." Basically, what this teacher did was to demonstrate every day the value of literacy and other academic tasks. Her rewards were always linked to literacy and academic activities. In the literacy research, we have scant information about how reading related rewards influence intrinsic literacy motivation. Our observations of this outstanding teacher led us to develop what we call the "reward proximity hypothesis." This hypothesis posits that the closer the reward (books, reading time, etc.) to the desired behavior (engaging in independent reading) the greater the likelihood that intrinsic motivation will increase (Gambrell & Marinak, 1997).

Summary

I think we can all agree on the importance of literacy motivation. I believe that the central and most important goal of reading instruction is to foster the love of reading. Knowing **how** to read is not sufficient. Students must have both the skill and the will to read.

Students who are motivated to read will spend more time reading. There is clear evidence from reading research that the amount of time spent reading is the major contributor to reading proficiency (Allington, 1983; Stanovich, 1986). According to Cunningham and Stanovich (1998), reading has cognitive benefits beyond getting meaning from the page. Their research indicates that the very act of engaging in reading can help students compensate for modest levels of cognitive ability by increasing their vocabulary and general knowledge. Perhaps the most important finding from the research of Cunningham and Stanovich (1986) is that ability is not the only variable that counts in the development of intelligence. Their research supports the notion that students who read a lot will enhance their verbal intelligence. They found that this was true for all students—those of all ability levels. Everyone benefited from time spent reading, but struggling readers benefited most. In other words, reading makes a person smarter. Students who are motivated to read will make time for reading, will read more, and as a result are likely to increase their intelligence. Current research supports the notion that motivation should be a central and significant consideration in the literacy curriculum. There are many issues related to reading motivation that will require our attention in the future in order to understand how children acquire motivation to read. We will need creative research designs and methodologies to explore the ever-expanding questions about the role of motivation in literacy learning.

References

Allington, R. L. (1983). The reading instruction provided readers of differing reading ability. *Elementary School Journal, 83*, 549-559.

Allington, R: L: (1986). Policy constraints and effective compensatory reading instruction: A review.: In J: V: Hoffman (Ed:), *Effective teaching of reading: Research and practice* (pp: 261-289): Newark, DE: International Reading Association:

Allington, R. L., & McGill-Franzen, A. (1993, October 13). What are they to read? Not all children, Mr. Riley, have easy access to books. *Education Week, 26.*

Almasi, J. F. (1995). The nature of fourth graders' sociocognitive conflicts in peer-led and teacher-led discussions of literature. *Reading Research Quarterly, 30*, 314-351.

Ames, C. (1984). Achievement attributions and self-instructions under competitive and individualistic goal structures. *Journal of Educational Psychology, 76*, 478-487.

Anderson, R. C., Wilson, P. T., & Fielding, L. G. (1988). Growth in reading and how children spend their time outside of school. *Reading Research Quarterly, 23*, 285-303.

Askov, E. N., & Fischbach, T. J. (1973). An investigation of primary pupils' attitudes toward reading. *Journal of Experimental Education, 41*, 1-7.

Brennan , T. P., & Glover, J. A (1980). An examination of the effect of extrinsic reinforcers on intrinsically motivated behavior: Experimental and theoretical. *Social Behavior and Personality, 8*, 27-32.

Cameron, J., & Pierce, W. D. (1994). Reinforcement, reward, and intrinsic motivation: A meta-analysis. *Review of Educational Research, 64*, 363-423.

Campbell, J. R., Hombo, C. M., & Mazzeo, J. (2000). NAEP 1999 trends in academic progress: Three decades of student performance. *Education Statistics Quarterly, 21*, 31-36.

Coley, J. D. (1981). *Non-stop reading for teenagers: What we have learned and where we go from here.* Paper presented at the annual meeting of the College Reading Association, Louisville, KY: (ERIC Document Reproduction Service No. ED 211951)

Cunningham, A. E., & Stanovich, K. E. (1998). What reading does for the mind. *American Educator*, Spring/Summer, 8-15.

Deci, E. L. (1975). *Intrinsic motivation.* New York: Plenum Press.

Deci, E. L., Valerand, R. M., Pelletier, L., & Ryan, R. (1991). Motivation and education: The self-determination perspective. *Educational Psychologist, 26*, 325-347.

Deci, E., & Ryan, R. (1985). *Intrinsic motivation and self-determination in human behavior.* New York: Plenum Press.

Elley, W. B. (1992). *How in the world do students read?* Hamburg, Germany: International Association for the Evaluation of Educational Achievement.

Elley, W. B. (1994). *The IEA study of reading literacy: Achievement and instruction in thirty-two school systems.* Exter: BPCC Wheatons.

Fawson, P. C., & Fawson, C. (1994, May). *Conditional philanthropy: A study of corporate sponsorship of reading incentive programs.* Paper presented at the meeting of the International Reading Association, Toronto, Canada.

Flippo, R. F. (2001). *Reading researchers in search of common ground.* Newark, DE: International Reading Association.

Ford, M. E. (1992). *Motivating humans.* New York: Sage.

Gambrell, L. B. (1995). Motivation matters. In W. M. Linek & E. G. Sturtevant (Eds.), *Generations of literacy: Seventeenth yearbook of the College Reading Association* (pp. 2-24). Harrisonburg, VA: College Reading Association.

Gambrell, L. B., Codling, R. M., & Palmer, B. M. (Winter, 1996). *Elementary students' motivation to read.* (Reading Research Report No. 52). Athens, GA: University of Georgia-University of Maryland, National Reading Research Center.

Gambrell, L. B., & Marinak, B. A. (1997). Incentives and intrinsic motivation to read. In J. T. Guthrie & Al. Wigfield (Eds.), *Reading engagement: Motivating readers through integrated instruction* (pp. 205-217). Newark, DE: International Reading Association.

Gambrell, L. B., & Morrow, A. M. (1996). Creating motivating contexts for literacy learning. In L. Baker, P. Afflerbach, & D. Reinking (Eds.), *Developing engaged readers in school and home communities* (pp. 115-136). Hillsdale, NJ: Erlbaum.

Guthrie, J. T., Schafer, W., Wang, Y., & Afflerbach, P. (1995). Relationships of instruction to amount of reading: an exploration of a social, cognitive, and instructional connection. *Reading Research Quarterly, 30,* 8-25.

Guthrie, J. T., Van Meter, P., McCann, A. D:, Wigfield, A., Bender, L., Poundstone, C. C., Rice, M. E., Faibisch, E. M., Junt, B., & Mitchell, A. M. (1996). Growth of literacy engagement: Changes in motivations and strategies during concept-oriented reading instruction. *Reading Research Quarterly, 31,* 306-325.

Hidi, S. (1990). Interest and its contribution as a mental resource for learning. *Review of Educational Research, 60* (4), 549-571.

Karnoil, R., & Ross, M. (1977). The effect of performance relevant and performance irrelevant rewards on children's intrinsic motivation. *Child Development, 48,* 482-487.

Lepper, M. R., Greene, D., & Nisbett, R. E. (1973). Undermining children's intrinsic interest with extrinsic reward. *Journal of Personality and Social Psychology, 28,* 124-137

Lundberg, I., & Linnakyla, P. (1993). *Teaching reading around the world.* Hamburg, Germany: International Association for the Evaluation of Educational Achievement.

Maehr, M. L. (1976). Continuing motivation: An analysis of a seldom considered educational outcome. *Review of Educational Research, 46,* 443-462.

Mayes, F. J. (1982). U.S.S.R. for poor readers. *Orbit, 13,* 3-4.

Mazzoni, S. A., Gambrell, L. B., & Korkeamaki, R. L. (2000). A cross-cultural perspective on early literacy motivation. *Reading Psychology, 20,* 237-253.

McKenna, M. C., Kear, D. J., & Ellsworth, R. A. (1995). Children's attitudes toward reading: A national survey. *Reading Research Quarterly, 30,* 934-956.

Morrow, L. M. (1992). The impact of a literature-based program on literacy achievement, use of literature, and attitudes of children from minority backgrounds. *Reading Research Quarterly, 27,* 250-275.

Neuman, S. B., & Roskos, K. A. (1993). Access to print for children of poverty: Differential effects of adult mediation and literacy-enriched play settings on environmental and functional print tasks. *American Educational Research Journal, 32*, 801-828.

Neuman, S. B., & Celano, D. (2001). Access to print in low-income and middle-income communities. *Reading Research Quarterly*, 36, 8-26.

Palmer, B. M., Codling, R. M., & Gambrell, L. B. (1994). In their own words: What elementary children have to say about motivation to read. *The Reading Teacher, 48*, 176-179.

Paris, S. G., & Oka, E. R. (1986). Self-regulated learning among exceptional children. *Exceptional Children, 53*, 103-108.

Parker, A., & Paradis, E. (1984, October). *The second year of an examination of attitude development toward reading in grades one through six.* Paper presented at the Annual Meeting of the Northern Rocky Mountain Educational Research Association, Wyoming.

Purcell-Gates, V., McIntyre, E., & Freppon, P. A. (1995). Learning written storybook language in school: A comparison of low-SES children in skills-based and whole language classrooms. *American Educational Research Journal, 32*, 659-685.

Schiefele, U. (1991). Interest, learning, and motivation. *Educational Psychologist, 26*, 299-323.

Schunk, E. (1985). Self-efficacy and school learning. *Psychology in the Schools, 22*, 208-223.

Stanovich, K. E. (1986). Matthew effects in reading: Some consequences of individual differences in the acquisition of literacy. *Reading Research Quarterly, 21*, 360-401.

Tobias, S (1994). Interest, prior knowledge, and learning. *Review of Educational Research, 64* (1), 37-54.

Wiesendanger , K. D., & Birlem, E. D. (1984). The effectiveness of SSR: An overview of the research. *Reading Horizons, 24*, 197-201.

Winne, P. (1985). Steps toward promoting cognitive achievements. *Elementary School Journal, 85*, 673-693.

Wittrock, M. C. (1986). Students' thought processes. In M. C. Wittrock (Ed.), *Handbook of research on teaching* (pp: 297-314): New York: Macmillan.

Effective Reading Instruction: What We Know, What We Need to Know, and What We Still Need to Do

Timothy V. Rasinski
Kent State University

Keynote Address
College Reading Association
2001

In 2002 Timothy Rasinski was a professor of education in the Department of Teaching, Leadership, and Curriculum Studies. Dr. Rasinski taught graduate and undergraduate courses in literacy education. His major interests included working with children who find reading difficult, phonics and reading fluency instruction, and teacher development in literacy education. He has published over 100 articles and 10 books on various aspects of reading education.

A past editor of The Reading Teacher, *the most widely read journal in reading education in the world, Dr. Rasinski was an editor for the* Journal of Literary Research. *Rasinski has served as president of the College Reading Association and he served on the Board of Directors of the International Reading Association. He earned bachelor degrees in economics and education at the University of Akron and the University of Nebraska at Omaha. His master's degree in special education also comes from the University of Nebraska at Omaha. Dr. Rasinski was awarded the PhD from The Ohio State University.*

Reprinted from *Celebrating the Faces of Literacy,* pp. 10-19, by P.E. Linder, M.B. Sampson, J. R. Dugan, & B. Brancato, Eds, 2002, Commerce, TX: College Reading Association.

It's not often that I am offered the opportunity to act as an expert in front of my own colleagues and given freedom to espouse my own beliefs about how the world should be. But when those opportunities do come along I relish them because they allow me, or should I say force me, to move outside the narrow and confined world I live in and think more freely and expansively about how an ideal world might look. In this case the world I refer to is the world of reading, and in particular the world of reading instruction.

What We Know

We do know a lot about reading and how reading instruction can be most effective–for struggling readers and for all readers. Despite the criticism aimed at it, I think the National Reading Panel (2000) did identify some critical components of literacy learning that need to be addressed in any effective reading curriculum and program for the primary grades—phonemic awareness, phonics or word study, reading fluency, vocabulary, comprehension, teacher development, and technology. I think we can all agree that these areas do have the potential to impact children's development as readers. From my perspective as a reading clinician, I find children coming into our reading clinic usually are impeded in their reading development by one or more of these concerns—decoding, lack of fluency, inadequate vocabulary and background, passive approaches to constructing meaning. Intensive, engaging, authentic, and regular instruction in those areas of concern usually results in generalized improvement in reading.

Unfortunately the National Reading Panel did not specifically endorse reading itself as a key provision in successful reading programs. I am among many others who feel that this is a gross oversight. Although there may not be a sufficient number of experimental studies that have demonstrated the effects of student reading on reading development and achievement, there is a solid theoretical basis for reading as a necessary condition for improving reading achievement and a number of correlational studies that have demonstrated fairly convincingly that you cannot become a good reader without widely and regularly reading. All of the recent National Assessment of Educational Progress studies (e.g., Donahue, et al., 1999) as well as the International Association for the Evaluation of Educational Achievement study (Postlethwaite & Ross, 1992) have found that reading achievement is closely connected to the amount of reading students do.

If we accept the idea that reading volume is critical to reading achievement, then motivation for reading must also be recognized as a key factor for success in teaching reading. Certainly, two major characteristics of struggling readers are their lack of reading and their lack of motivation for reading.

I think we have also come to the conclusion that balanced and integrative reading instruction is a key to success. You just can't teach phonics, and you just can't teach in literature study groups. Students need it all, delivered in a regular, intense, and engaging manner.

Our current understanding of reading has also lead us to a recognition of the importance of early reading intervention. The best time to correct a problem in reading is as early as possible. This not only means early intervention such as Reading Recovery and other such programs, it also means early detection of reading difficulties, which can be a tough sell to parents or teachers who don't wish to burden their child with a label so early in their lives. Nevertheless, when effective early identification and intervention occur, children are more likely to be successful in the long run.

So these are some of the known in our field–what is truly important in teaching reading:

- Volume of reading and volume of reading instruction
- Motivating students to read more
- Early assessment and intervention (as well as instruction in phonemic awareness)
- Instruction in phonics and decoding
- Instruction in reading fluency
- Instruction in vocabulary
- Instruction in comprehension.

To be perfectly honest, the list offered above provides little in the way of new or unusual information. Reading educators and scholars have been aware of these issues for decades. Nevertheless, it is always wise to affirm for ourselves from time to time what is known in the way of effective instruction for children.

What We Need to Know and Do

I'd like to switch now to the second and more speculative part of my title— what is it that we don't know about effective reading instruction, what is it that we don't know enough about, and what is it that we wonder about? This is my chance to speculate about reading–what questions do we need answers to in order to make reading instruction more effective for all students, especially those who struggle so much in learning to become literate. For the large part, my questions and wonderings revolve not so much around the big ticket items that we seem to reaffirm for ourselves over and over again, but more about the nitty gritty items within those big pictures–we know phonics is important, for example, but we still need to know how to make phonics instruction work successfully for students. This is a question that needs to be answered through classroom-based, in-the-trenches research, or as we say in my hometown, Akron, where the rubber meets the road. This is where we often find our work being co-opted by others—others who are not guided so much by the well-being of students, but by the quick buck, the easy fix, the one-size-fits-all type program developed by people whose knowledge of readers and reading instruction is limited at best.

Science and Art of Reading Instruction

It is in this gulf between theory and research and actual practice that the science of literacy instruction must make room for the art and poetry of literacy instruction. It is where I find myself situated professionally and it is where I find so many of my College Reading Association (CRA) colleagues situated. More than most other professional literacy organizations, I believe, the College Reading Association and its members work to make those theoretical constructs and those grand research results come to life in the classrooms of teachers and in the lives of kids—especially kids who struggle in reading.

One of the big ideas in literacy education that we have known for a long time is the importance of time—instructional time and time engaged in authentic reading. Theoretical models of reading and research into reading achievement have noted that time is truly important. But the theories and research offer little in ways that time for reading and reading instruction can indeed be maximized. We need to find ways to maximize time—how can this actually be done?

Expanding Literacy Instruction at Home and in the Community

If the school day is filled to capacity, we need to think about the home—getting parents and families more involved in the reading program. The little known Even Start (ES) programs offer wonderful examples of trying to increase achievement through family involvement. Nancy Padak and other CRA members have reported numerous times at this conference about family literacy programs, especially Even Start. In ES programs, parents of young children who are working on their GEDs and improving their own literacy skills are given assistance in helping their preschool and early childhood children move toward literacy development.

The Fast Start program that I have reported on at previous CRA meetings provides parents of kindergarten and first grade children with materials and specific and proven methods for helping their children get off to a solid and early start in their reading. Parents are asked to spend no more than 15 minutes per day reading to, reading with, and listening to their children read short poems and then engaging in a few word games and activities.

Bruce Stevenson's (2001) recently completed dissertation at The Ohio State University found that a three-month implementation of Fast Start had a profound and positive effect on children identified as most at risk. Regular use of Fast Start by parents resulted in gains in reading achievement that approached an effect size of approximately two standard deviations over a control group of similar children not in the Fast Start program. Imagine the possibilities if children had the opportunity to engage in Fast Start for their entire kindergarten and first grade years.

Consider the role of the community in expanding time for reading. Susan Neuman spoke at this very conference four years ago in Boston to inform us of ways that communities, even in the most impoverished parts of large urban areas, can be empowered to deliver powerful and caring instruction and opportunities to read for children.

Expanding Literacy Instruction in the School

Consider the role of the school and teachers in expanding reading instruction: Is it possible to change the nature of schooling to increase instruction? I think it is possible, but we need to go beyond the simple solutions of lengthening the school day or the school year. Belinda Zimmerman and her colleague Tracy Foreman reported at this conference a few years ago about their Reading Workshop Program (Zimmerman, Foreman, & Rasinski, 1996). Belinda and Tracy are first grade teachers who were able to expand the school day for their most at-risk children by extending the school day by 45 minutes three days per week for the lowest quartile of students in their classrooms. Each Tuesday, Wednesday, and Thursday they would begin their school day 45 minutes before the beginning bell and provide the four or five lowest students in their classrooms with intensive and direct instruction on reading that correlated perfectly with what they were teaching in reading during the regular school day.

Zimmerman et al. (1996) found that the students they worked with made greater gains than children who were receiving Title I assistance. Moreover, they found anecdotally that the children who went through their morning workshop programs were doing very well in their subsequent grade levels. It has always been a mystery why their local school district was unwilling or unable to support these two innovative teachers in the remarkable and groundbreaking work they were doing or to expand the program to other classrooms.

We viewed another approach to maximize instructional time in school just this past year in the primary grades in Tallmadge, Ohio. This school system had adopted a guided reading approach to literacy instruction. Small groups of children met with their teacher for approximately 20 minutes per day for direct instruction in reading. One of the problems with this approach has always been what do the other students do while the teacher works with the one group. In many cases the other students are given assignments by their teachers to do independently, but are more often than not off task during this time, engaged minimally in productive reading behavior.

The Tallmadge school system overcame this problem with what they called their reading SWAT teams or Circle Reading Program. During the 30 minutes or so that a teacher had allotted for guided reading, her room would be "invaded" by the school reading coordinator, the Title I teacher, and a couple of trained reading tutors or instructional assistants. Each adult would work with 4-5 students in her or his assigned group for the entire 30 minute period. Thus each child had a maximum amount of direct guided reading instruction in small groups for a total of 30 minutes per day and the teacher still had another

90 minutes remaining for self-selected reading, writing, word study, and other literacy based instructional activities.

These are but a few examples of instructional innovations that are actual elaborations of the more general theories and research into reading. This is the kind of research that is really needed to move our field forward. We already know what the big ideas are. Our next step is to find and document ways to flesh out those big ideas in the lives of teachers and students.

Phonics Yes, But What Kind of Phonics?

In a similar vein, it is well known that instruction that focuses on words, fluency, vocabulary, and comprehension is essential to reading success. The National Reading Panel has told us this. But the equally important question we are left with is what does effective instruction in these areas look like? The National Reading Panel, for example, found that phonics instruction was important, but it was unable to indicate if a particular form or approach to phonics instruction was more effective than another:

If we don't show teachers and teachers-in-training specific and effective ways to develop instruction in phonics or other key areas of literacy instruction, others will. Indeed, our history as a profession is replete with examples of "educational gurus" who often come from fields unrelated to education with some "guaranteed" instructional approach that is touted to be effective but that is based on little research and even smaller amounts of classroom and clinical application. Such programs are, at best, questionable in their approach and effectiveness and, at worst, actually harmful to students' development.

Again, I think this area of bringing life to the general theories, principles, and research into literacy is where College Reading Association members flourish. Let me offer one more personal example. Ruth Oswald and myself (Oswald & Rasinski, 2001) have reported at CRA meetings our work with a word decoding activity called *Making and Writing Words*, an elaboration of Cunningham and Cunningham's (1992) *Making Words*. Implementing this approach in Ruth's second grade classroom over two years, we found substantive and significant improvements in students' ability to decode words when compared with more traditional approaches to word study. The big theory (e:g. National Reading Panel, 2000) tells us that phonics and decoding instruction are important. Our research indicates that Making and Writing Words appears to be one effective approach for fleshing out and bringing to life phonics and decoding instruction in real classrooms.

Just What is Guided Reading?

Let me offer a few other big ideas that need fleshing out. Comprehension instruction has been identified by the National Reading Panel as a critical ingredient in successful literacy education programs. In many schools the comprehension portion of the curriculum has been translated into guided reading.

In my work with schools over the past several years, I have discovered that there is a great deal of confusion in what is meant by guided reading. Some schools adhere to the Cunningham, Hall, and Defee (1998) approach to guided reading. Others have Fountas and Pinnell (1996) in mind when speaking of guided reading. Still others refer to Opitz and Ford's (2001) conception of guided reading. In many schools comprehension instruction has been reduced to a few models of implementation. Are any of these models more effective than any other? Is there evidence that these models are more effective than other models that are developed by well-informed teachers developing their own form of comprehension instruction? These are the types of questions that need to be asked and answered. Certainly, comprehension instruction is important, but what does effective comprehension instruction look like and how is it actually implemented in classrooms?

Questions About Assessment

In terms of instructional reading level, it is well known that we learn best when the learning task presented before us is challenging but not frustrating. Too hard and we give up, get frustrated, and learn to avoid a particular task. Too easy and we simply cover what we already know and learning is less than optimized. One of our tasks as reading educators is trying to find that material that is "just right" or as Vygotsky might call it—the Zone of Proximal Development. Do we know how to determine instructional level in children? We have some idea by using information such as decoding accuracy and comprehension.

But where does fluency fit in the mix of determining instructional level? Are there good standards for determining instructional level based on fluency norms? Can 6 to 10 questions per passage in an IRI provide an adequate and valid measure of comprehension? What about quality of miscues students make while reading in determining instructional level? Where does self-efficacy fit into the determination of instructional level?

Even the concept of instructional reading level is getting muddied. Not long ago I saw a report of a standardized reading test that gave results in terms of reading grade level, instructional grade level, and ZPD (Zone of Proximal Development) grade level. I had thought these were essentially the same concept, but this particular test gave three different scores. What is a teacher to do with these scores? Here's another example, I think, of a test maker benefiting commercially by misinterpreting important ideas and, in the long run, making things less clear and less easy for all of us.

The reason we are so interested in readers' instructional level is so that we can match the reader to an appropriate text. This requires an ability to estimate the reader's reading level *and* the reading level of the text to be read. But do we really have a good handle on that big idea called readability? Are we truly able to provide good clear estimates of reading difficulty based on a comprehensive range of factors beyond word and syntax? What we seem to have gotten in recent years is a much less clear picture of readability with the addition of other concepts such as lexile scores, reading recovery levels, Fountas and Pinnell levels, and other material leveling systems.

We all know that continuous assessment and diagnosis is important. But how do we do it? Can we assess validly and in ways that minimize valuable time that should be used for instruction? I think approaches like the one-minute probes in which students read texts for 60 seconds offer wonderful ways for measuring fluency and decoding quickly and validly. But what about assessing comprehension? Is it possible to assess comprehension in a way that is quick and valid?

I think informal assessment is much more effective and comprehensive than standardized assessments that attempt to minimize the role of the teacher. I am a firm believer in the Informal Reading Inventory (IRI). Yet I am finding that IRIs differ greatly in the scores that can be obtained. Not long ago I had graduate students administering two different IRIs to students. They found that the two different IRIs give radically different measures of students' overall reading proficiency. On one third grade passage, for example, a third grader read with 99% accuracy and 100% comprehension. The third grade passage from another IRI administered to the very same student resulted in 88% accuracy and 40% comprehension. That same trend was found on other passages and with other students. When this happens, which IRI performance is the valid one? How can assessment ever be made valid when the reliability and consistency of the scores we obtain have such great variance?

What Kind of Professional Development?

The National Reading Panel has told us that teacher professional development in literacy is a critical factor to reading success. But again, while the big idea is certainly evident, what does this mean for schools? Is there a place for one-shot professional development? Most people would say no, but we do it quite often, and I know of many teachers who decided to get more involved in their own professional development after attending a single in-service session.

If long-term professional development is the goal, what should effective professional development look like? This is an issue that absolutely needs to be addressed. Do we have good models of successful professional development approaches?

I think the model offered by the Benchmark School in Media, Pennsylvania offers a good way to think about the professional development of teachers. Under the leadership of school principal Irene Gaskins, the faculty chooses a topic to explore, define, develop, and translate into curriculum and instruction each year. It is the faculty itself that is empowered by choosing its own problems and investigating them on their own, calling in consultants when needed.

So how do we go about developing and testing models of instruction that are based on the more general research and theories of literacy? I believe that members of the College Reading Association are in a unique position to make this happen. We may not be the basic researchers who do the more general research and form the fundamental theories of our profession. We are not the teachers who work with children on a daily basis. We are the "tweeners," those who are the bridges between the big picture, big research, big theories from the National Reading Panel and other such organizations, and actual classroom practice.

We understand those big ideas and theories and we can put them into meaningful models of practice and evaluate them. One of the great needs in our field are more literacy scholars, like those in CRA, who feel at home both in the world of research and theory and in the world of classroom and clinical practice—a group of educators who can take the more general findings of the National Reading Panel and develop ways for implementing those findings in real classroom settings. It is in the gulf between theory and practice that members of the College Reading Association can make, and have made significant contributions to the field of literacy education. Interestingly, even the title of our own publication, *Reading Research and Instruction* is suggestive of the model of connecting theory and practice, researchers and practitioners. Our newest journal, *Literacy Cases Online,* provides us with another powerful tool for adding flesh and bones and life to the more broad theories of effective literacy instruction that currently guide literacy education policy in the United States.

We know a lot about what works in reading education. That is, we have a good general picture of effective literacy education. For that general picture to come to life in our country's classrooms, we need scholars who are willing and able to develop specific models of instruction that apply those general theories and broad understandings into actual classrooms and with real teachers. This is a critical need. Members of the College Reading Association, I believe, are some of the best-suited scholars to make that happen.

References

Cunningham, P. M., & Cunningham, J. W. (1992). Making Words: Enhancing the invented spelling-decoding connection. *The Reading Teacher, 46,* 106-115.

Cunningham, P. M., Hall, D. P., & Defee, M. (1998). Nonability-grouped, multilevel instruction: Eight years later. *The Reading Teacher, 51,* 652-664.

Donahue, P. L., Voelkl, K. E., Campbell, J. R., & Mazzeo, J. (1999). *NAEP 1998: Reading report card for the nation and the states.* Washington, DC: U. S. Department of Education.

Fountas, I. C., & Pinnell, G. S. (1996). *Guided reading: Good first teaching for all children.* Portsmouth, NH: Heinemann.

National Reading Panel. (2000). *Teaching children to read: An evidence-based assessment of the scientific research literature on reading and its implications for reading instruction: Reports of the subgroups.* Washington, DC: National Institute of Child Health and Human Development.

Opitz, M. F., & Ford, M. P. (2001). *Reaching readers: Flexible and innovative strategies for guided reading.* Portsmouth, NH: Heinemann.

Oswald, R. A., & Rasinski, T. (2001). Making and Writing Words in a second grade classroom. In W. Linek, E. Sturtevant, J. Dugan, & P. Linder (Eds.), *Celebrating the voices of literacy: The 23rd yearbook of the College Reading Association* (pp. 108-116). Readyville, TN: The College Reading Association.

Postlethwaite, T. N., & Ross, K. N. (1992). *Effective schools in reading.* Hague: International Association for the Evaluation of Educational Achievement.

Stevenson, B. (2001). *Efficacy of the Fast Start parent tutoring program in the development of reading skills by first grade students.* Unpublished doctoral dissertation. Columbus, OH: The Ohio State University.

Zimmerman, B., Foreman, T., & Rasinski, T. (1996). Reading Workshop: An early intervention approach for at-risk students. In E. Sturtevant & W. Linek (Eds.), *Growing literacy: Yearbook of the College Reading Association* (pp. 159-169). Harrisonburg, VA: College Reading Association.

LATINO CHILDREN'S LITERATURE *IS* MAINSTREAM

Becky Chavarría-Cháirez

Keynote Address
College Reading Association
2003

Becky Chavarría-Cháirez is the author of Magda's Tortillas ~ Las tortillas de Magda, *and* Magda's Piñata Magic ~ Magda y la piñata mágica, *fully bilingual children's picture books published by Arte Público Press/Piñata Books. Becky Chavarría-Cháirez, also is owner of Chameleon Creek Press, a literary and arts communications group serving aspiring to accomplished writers. Based in New Mexico, the award-winning broadcast journalist, freelance writer, playwright, speaker and multiculturalist, can be reached at www.chameleoncreekpress.com or chameleoncreek@aol.com.*

The children's book genre has come a long way in recent years, as children's literature has broadened its reach to speak to and about the infinite rainbow of readers. For those of us who care about and promote literacy, this is the time many of us have been waiting for. And, for me, this is what my life has prepared me for.

Consider, we live in a nation where all are afforded the promise of inalienable rights; individual freedoms, democratic principles, and ideals that sustain and bind us. Among the mix is the diversity of American life and culture, which ensures our ever-changing cultural landscape, will need and seek multicultural, multilingual stories to mirror the lives of our American children.

Reprinted from *Celebrating the Power of Literacy*, pp. 36-43, by J. R. Dugan, P. E. Linder, M. B. Sampson, B. Brancato, Eds., 2004,Commerce, TX: College Reading Association.

The American melting pot remains on simmer. This will likely be present throughout our lifetime and the lives of generations to come. Due to our geographic kinship to *las Américas* in this hemisphere, war, disease, political change and the desire for the American dream, these factors will ensure that our American culture and literature will continue evolving and that the need for Latino/Hispanic-themed and bilingual children's books will grow. And, for children's book authors and illustrators, this means our artistic assignment will be to capture this dynamic trend and accurately reflect our ever-shrinking planet for the children. This situation is precisely why I began writing for children about Latino children, their families, and many blendings of culture wrapped in universally understood terms *AND* in two languages, the two most spoken languages in the United States. This is not a prediction for the future, because the future *IS* now!

Each one of you here today has seen it, and at the very least, has certainly read about this American shift. And, the publishing industry and literary community have taken notice of this reality. Nearly everything Latino/Hispanic is influencing and flavoring our pop culture in many genres—from Hollywood, art, music, culinary trends, and the media; the children's book market is no exception.

Diversity is here. Diversity matters. Diversity is no longer a foreign notion, neither misunderstood nor underrated. In my life, diversity has been a way of life. Diversity has been a cornerstone of what I consider life's university without walls.

Let's flash back to my upbringing. I grew up in one of America's most unique cities, San Antonio—home of sun, salsa and Cisneros, as I say. San Antonio offered an environment where my culture was dominant and in constant interaction with many cultures and peoples in the city which I lovingly refer to as the "military melting pot," a southern cousin to Ellis Island. But, unlike Ellis Island, San Antonio is just a few hours north of the U.S.-Mexico border.

In my old neighborhood, beyond each front doorstep, there were many worlds to discover. My old neighborhood, barrio or as I like to imagine, my own Ellis Island, was one residential block of 20 single-family dwellings. It was a place where Korean, German, Italian, Irish, Sicilian, Mexican-American, Polish, Czech, Scottish, French—and most likely a few others—interacted and blended in the simplest and yet most profound ways.

Across the United States, many cities much further from San Antonio, cities located in North Carolina, Georgia, Oregon, Arkansas, and virtually every state in the union, are absorbing Latino culture. My San Antonio roots have traveled far and adopted many other Latino cultures along the way—through war, economic hardship, and the quest for the American dream.

Let's further consider the numbers and the outlook: **The majority of Hispanic children in the United States were born here to U.S. citizens of Hispanic origin.** I am the offspring of U.S.-born, Mexican-American parents, whose parents came into the U.S. soon after the Mexican Revolution and the flu pandemic that killed untold millions.

The majority of Hispanic children in the U.S. are predominantly English speakers and yet, the continuous arrival of immigrants from Latin American countries coupled with the growing need for the practical use of Spanish in the workplace, and the desire of many Latinos to preserve culture through language, further ensure that there always will be a need for children's books, educational materials and *THEN SOME* in Spanish.

In recent years, Hispanic newspapers and magazines have begun featuring more advertising for Spanish-language audiences.

In the '80s and '90s, major U.S. cities like Dallas, Houston and San Antonio became one-newspaper towns—and those are just the ones in Texas. But, now, in the 21st century, Dallas and Fort Worth each have another daily paper. No, these are not new English-language dailies in direct competition—these are new dailies published in Spanish. The largest Spanish-language—newspaper dailies in North Texas are in Dallas/Fort Worth—*Al Día,* which is owned by The Belo Corporation and *Diario La Estrella,* which is owned by the Fort Worth Star-Telegram. Both are corporate-owned, not a mom-and-pop periodical, like the majority of Latino publications that have been in existence.

Discount stores like Wal-Mart, Target, and Toys Я Us have expanded their book inventories to include Spanish and bilingual titles.

For those of you who own a DVD player - - - - (that reminds me...I have a knock-knock joke that I'm saving to tell you all later, be sure to remind me).

DVD's are making a tremendous impact on the exchange of cultures and languages. One can select from numerous options. You've probably noticed that now you can opt to view a DVD program/movie and supplemental features, activities, and games in several languages.

Now if we turn on the tube to watch television, haven't you noticed some commercials in Spanish are being aired on English-language television? And, I'm not talking, "Yo *quiero Taco Bell.*" The first time I saw these Spanish-language ads, I checked to see who flipped the channel and then, I realized it was *intentional* on the advertisers' part, if not inevitable. Spanish is creeping into the workplace and marketplace. Notice how often you now see signage and advertising in Spanish. Next time you step into your shower, take a close look at the product labels for your shampoo or look in your medicine cabinet and read the side panels on your over-the-counter medications.

Tune in your AM/FM shower radio and you will likely hear Latino rhythms and Hispanic recording artists spicing up the pop music charts. I haven't done a complete inventory, but I think all of the daytime soaps have their Latino characters and they aren't just maids and gardeners anymore.

In the classroom, bilingual education programs are also diversifying. Recently, dual-language programs in schools allow children to learn all subjects in English and Spanish, putting the languages to simultaneous use. Currently, the United States has more than 31 million Hispanics, making it or rather, *us—nosotros,* the fifth largest Spanish-speaking country in the world. *¿Qué?* you may be asking yourselves. Listen carefully and let this sink in.

This is not only happening in the southwest region of the United States. For example, the 2000 census found that North Carolina's Hispanic population registered a 394 percent increase in population, making North Carolina one of the fastest-growing states with a growing Hispanic population. **By 2010, it is projected that only Mexico will have more Spanish-speakers.** (Yes, let's stop and allow me to repeat that sentence again. Write this down.) And by 2050, Hispanics will number 96 million, approximately 24% of the overall U.S. population. Before you attempt to fully fathom that estimate, consider the likelihood that this government projection may be somewhat conservative. So, why not round that up to 100 million!

Now for those of you who savor politics in America, the political parties are allocating additional funds and outreach efforts to court the growing Hispanic vote in several states, including Georgia, and Arkansas, not to mention in those states generations ahead in that trend. On a recent ABC news show, George Stephanopoulos predicted that there is no turning back. Every future presidential candidate's political future will greatly benefit from the candidate's ability to speak Spanish and know how to court the many sectors in the Pan-Hispanic community.

Coming full circle—returning to the literary scene. More publishers will be publishing bilingual books and stories based in Hispanic culture or featuring Latino characters. Bilingual books are versatile and user-friendly, not only serving a greater number of readers, but also reaching across generations and their language proficiencies within extended Hispanic families. In some homes one parent or an entire generation may speak Spanish and the other parent may prefer English. And, in some, as my family—TEX-MEX or *Spanglish* was forbidden.

Publishers no longer ask if they should venture into the Hispanic book market. Some are sorry they hesitated entering the market, but can console themselves in knowing that the genre will remain in demand.

As more students enroll in dual-language programs, they will seek Spanish titles to reinforce their new language usage.

Perhaps one of the unexpected benefits of writing bilingual children's books is that my books and those of many other Latino children's book authors are not just for kids. Adults use them, too! English-as-a-Second Language students and Latinos who are learning to read in their native language, Spanish, and then bridging from their native language to English are taking these early steps into literacy and bilingualism with children's books. It makes sense—Absolutely, *¡Claro que sí!*

Teachers and librarians affirm that the bilingual children's book genre with Hispanic-themed stories is on target. Their enthusiastic acceptance and usage of these books in their libraries and classrooms is helping Hispanic children's books become instant classics.

Diversity begets more diversity. Perhaps diversity is universal. Looking within the Latino demographic, there is much to consider beyond language— there are *other* nuances of culture to capture. But, this is not an easy task. There is immense diversity within this diverse ethnic group. For publishers and writers, this means they must carefully edit books that present this Pan-Hispanic rainbow in its many dimensions.

Hispanics are not from one country and they do not all share the same customs and language preferences. For that matter, they may be from one or more racial groups. And, not all Latin Americans speak Spanish. In South America, Brazilians speak Portuguese. One Central American country's official language is English. Which one? Belize.

Tortillas are considered Hispanic, but are not traditionally served in every Latin American country. The same goes for tamales, tacos, even chips and salsa—the spicy condiment that has been outselling catsup in the United States. Salsa is something you eat but is it also a style of music and a dance style popularized in the Caribbean, a musical mélange of Afro-Cuban and Latino rhythms. *Mariachi* music is not universally played either. Did you know the *mariachi* is something the Mexicans borrowed from the French?

Book publishers—the mainstream, multi-cultural and Hispanic houses—have all taken notice. The surge in dual-language programming in the Southwest and other regions where the influx in Hispanic populations continues, further fuels this demand. Several Latino writers—myself included—decided to write children's books to meet their personal desire for stories which mirror the real-life cultures and traditions of Latino children in the U.S. In fact, this is the mission of my publisher, Arte Público Press and Piñata Books, its children's imprint.

Some of the best selling Spanish children's books are not written by Hispanics and they aren't about Hispanic children, i.e. *Clifford Barney™, Curious George™, Madeleine™* (well, okay, Pepito is Madeleine's *amigo*, a Spaniard) and others, yet they have universal appeal to youngsters. But, the real growth market and demand is for books for and about Latino characters and themes.

If you are interested in writing for the Latino market, keep in mind these criteria that most publishers want to see in their titles:

- Authentic characters, setting,—even in fiction, situations are and should be true to life, easy for Hispanic as well as all young readers to relate to.
- Positive portrayal of Hispanics as leaders, teachers, role models. Biographical books about Hispanic leaders are much needed as schools seek Latino heroes, writers, sports stars, artists, politicians, educators and others to focus on the contributions of Latino society in the U.S.
- Correct use of language, spelling, grammar, and the text should be impeccably translated. Children's books are not just for entertainment. They can reinforce proper usage of Spanish. In bilingual books, the reader should receive a clear and easily understood message in either text. Translation is a fine art of utmost importance.

- The absence of stereotypical images. Not all Hispanics are short, dark-skinned, with black hair and use burros for transportation. These images were common in the earliest portrayals of Hispanics. Stereotypes are to be avoided in all depictions of Latino culture and lifestyles. Avoid stereotypical messages and images regarding economic, cultural, religious, and lifestyle diversity to illustrate and model whom Latinos really are.
- Realistic portrayal of cultural issues, traditions to instill ethnic pride and cross-cultural awareness are desired in varying degrees.

Just as every child is individual and unique, the same is true of the Hispanic/Latino child. There is what I call "The Latino Melting Pot" to consider. While the majority of Latinos in the Southwestern United States are from Mexico, there are Latinos from dozens of Latin-American countries. It is important to remember, each Latino child is part of a unique family with his or her cultural fingerprint. More and more of these children are being born into multi-ethnic homes to Hispanic and non-Hispanic parents.

Keep a watch on the bookstore and library shelves; diversity in Latino-themed children's books will evolve into another literary trend. As children's stories explore the basic elements of Latino cultures with themes about holidays, celebrations, food and traditions, folklore, history and more this is only the beginning. Given the multitude of Hispanic groups and the number of blended Latino and non-Latino cultures, diversity in Latino books will be the next wave, or, rather a permanent fixture in American children's literature; an accurate reflection of the many peoples who make up Hispanic life in the U.S. and the greater Americas.

As publishers expand the scope of their stories and cultural situations, we will likely begin seeing more children's books featuring blended Latino families. Part of the American experience is the continual melting pot within our borders. Stories about how a Latino/Hispanic family must familiarize itself with another Latino's customs, foods and other ethnic/cultural traditions are important because mommy is Puerto Rican and daddy is Mexican. Grandma is German but Grandpa is Cuban. These are more common now. And, let's check out reality television—like it or not.

Recently, in the weeks before this conference, I have, like many of you, been watching *The Bachelor*. Quickly, tell me, there are three eligible ladies left in "Roseland"…Who are they? I am most intrigued by the dynamics and interaction millions witnessed a few nights ago with Bachelorette Mary and her Cuban-American family in Miami, Florida. All along, I thought that Mary was Latina, but since the girls' surnames are never given I wasn't sure.

Then Mary brings Bachelor Bob to her folks home to meet all her *hermanas* and her *padres*. A family member translates for Bob and the millions of viewers. And the body language: Did you notice how Bob was surrounded by Mary's relatives who talked to him well within his personal space? Well, I got a big kick out of this…This is happening all over the US. Couples like Mary and Bob are marrying, having children, and adding to the need for bilingual children's books.

It used to be the old fables taught us how to act and behave and there were those nursery rhymes, fairy, and moralistic tales. Today's children's books provide guidance on a whole new level. These stories will help families build understanding, mutual respect and find, if not foster, common ground—the stuff that binds families together. As different ethnic groups neighbor one another in the American landscapes, expect to see their stories side by side, sharing shelf space in bookstores and libraries. Beyond telling stories to entertain, they can enlighten and help draw families together, Hispanic-themed children's books. . . . are part of the literary melting pot. Hispanic-themed books help demonstrate empathy, appreciation, and respect for our differences. It is not an act of political correctness, it is the right thing to do—I consider it just another dimension to what we call the all-American experience.

Now children's books like those in my Magda Madrigal series feature adventures that tell their stories, although fiction, they are reality-based.

Parents who just over a decade ago were wanting their children to learn Japanese, now realize there is a much greater likelihood that the next generation will be doing more business with the extended American family—the ones who share our hemisphere and speak Spanish. I would even venture to say that Arabic will be the next language wave. It will be a necessity for national security and building cultural bridges.

Teachers can attest that their Hispanic youngsters derive a greater sense of belonging and gain a higher self-esteem when Latino children are not just viewed as "an other," but as another in the American family, this has a vitally visceral and visible impact. I get the biggest kick out of reading my books to Hispanic children. I love watching the students' body language. They become fully entranced by Magda making tortillas or creating piñata magic for her little brother and hearing how the characters can speak both languages. The body language is strong: kids' pupils dilate and they hang onto every word. For Hispanic children, these stories validate who they are and will build their cultural self-awareness and boost their personal self-esteem. Who knows, this new genre in children's books could be the supplemental link that educators have needed to help Hispanic students stay in school and celebrate who they are. We won't know right away, but this book genre is something to experience. *Vamos a ver.* We shall see.

Lastly, for non-Hispanic children, I want them to discover the universal themes and emotions—Hispanic children have stories to tell about their first day at school, losing a pet, moving to a new house, having a new baby brother or sister. The situations are similar and the subtle differences in the details are only minor, not differences, just the details—the details of life.

My character, Magda Madrigal is like millions of Latino children in the U.S. and accurately captures a glimpse into their lives including their Spanish language, family traditions, and food customs—the universal elements of culture. Magda's stories underscore the universal connections we all share. Family, home, love, compassion, problem solving, and always, with a generous helping of adventure!

So, stay tuned and watch the bookshelves in your local libraries and bookstores. The first Latino U.S. president is probably in diapers right now. Oh, and don't touch that dial because Bachelor Bob will soon choose his bacherlorette. If it's Mary—the family will deal with questions of language, race, perhaps religion, customs, traditions, and blend every aspect of their lives as their hearts may intertwine. And, if Bob chooses Mary, we know the family WILL be able to do some things together—watch the same DVD's.

Which brings me back to my joke:

Knock-knock . . . or *'Tan-Tan'*
Who's there? *¿Quén es?*
DVD/DVD who. . . .? *¿Quién?*
DVDDVDVDVD—That's all folks!

Preparing Elementary Teachers in Reading: Will University-Based Programs Move Forward or Be "Left Behind"?

James V. Hoffman

The University of Texas at Austin

Keynote Address
College Reading Association
2003

In 2003, James Hoffman was Professor of Language and Literacy Studies at the University of Texas at Austin. He taught graduate courses and directed the undergraduate reading specialization program. Jim is a Past-President of the National Reading Conference and a former editor of the Reading Research Quarterly. *He served as editor for the* Yearbook of the National Reading Conference. *His research interests include texts, teaching, and teacher preparation.*

Just one week after the closing of the College Reading Association's annual (2003) conference hosted in Corpus Christi, the Texas State Board of Educational Certification (SBEC) approved a procedure for certifying virtually anyone with a bachelor's degree in a relevant area to teach at the high school level. This procedure requires that the candidate pass a test but it does not require the completion of any accredited academic preparation program, nor does it require any practicum experiences as conditions for certification. The governor

Reprinted from *Celebrating the Power of Literacy,* pp. 24-35, by J. R. Dugan, P. E. Linder, M. B. Sampson, B. Brancato, & L. Elish-Piper, Eds., 2004, Commerce, TX: College Reading Association.

of Texas was not the only source of support for this initiative. The proposal was also supported by the State Association of School Boards in Texas. Teacher unions, professional associations for teachers, and teacher educators spoke in opposition to the proposal but fell short in their goal to block the action. The media tended to characterize the opponents of the proposal as "turf-protecting." The State Board of Education approved the new procedures in March of 2004 (Hoffman & Sailors, in press).

What motivated this action? Certainly some of the credit (or blame) falls on the federal *No Child Left Behind (NCLB) Act* of 2001 (United States Office of Education, 2003) that requires states to ensure that all teachers are highly qualified in every subject they teach by the end of the 2005-06 school year. It is left to the individual states to determine what counts as "highly qualified." Currently, the number of "highly qualified" teachers in most states, particularly in low-income areas, falls well short of the targets set by NCLB. The action taken by SBEC, and no doubt the source of support from the State Association of School Boards, was argued for explicitly in terms of NCLB and teacher supply. But clearly, this is not the only motivating factor. Public schools have been exposed in Texas over the past decade to the "high-stakes" testing movement. Schools portrayed as failing by politicians are vulnerable to radical reform. With the economy stalled and unemployment high even among the college educated, teaching now stands as a viable short-term option for employment. Finally, the tax-base for schools has shrunk with the economy. The choice between "opening doors" to all (a no-cost option on the front end) and investing in teacher education has become a point of deliberation. Policy makers are reluctant to invest in the same teacher education that has been characterized as the source of the problem with low performing schools.

Are the policy initiatives underway in the state of Texas an anomaly? Or, are these actions part of a national trend to "leave behind" traditional forms of preservice teacher preparation? Will the "open-door" policy be restricted to the certification of secondary teachers? Or, will it be extended to all levels?

I believe there is sufficient evidence to suggest that the actions taken in Texas are indeed part of an effort that is national in scope to dismantle teacher preparation programs. Decisions made and actions taken over the next several years, as with the SBEC plan for certification, may well shape teaching and teacher education far into this millennium. Teacher education is "at risk" of being left behind in the face of such initiatives. As teacher educators concerned with the preparation of teachers in the area of reading, we cannot ignore this movement or its ramifications. How can educators, government officials, and the public ensure the high qualifications of all who teach reading in all elementary and secondary public schools? What is the best way to improve the quality of teacher preparation and increase the numbers of qualified teachers to the levels needed? How can we insure that teachers who are qualified and prepared in the area of reading will take and keep positions in high-poverty schools? How can teacher education regain the trust of the public?

This address explores these key questions with a particular focus on teacher preparation in reading. I have organized this report around the work of the International Reading Association's National Commission on Excellence in Teacher Preparation in Reading. I will offer a summary of the Commission's research and the findings. Most of these findings have been published previously in the research literature and will be referenced accordingly. The goal here is to bring together the total work of the Commission as a way of both addressing the concerns of the moment as well as setting an agenda for the future. I will use the findings from this research to frame a positive role for reading educators to take in addressing the challenges of public trust and public policy. I use the personal pronoun "we" throughout the manuscript. This usage acknowledges the contributions of the many educators, cited in the references, who contributed to the work of the Commission. I also use the term "we" to situate myself with the community of reading teacher educators. This is my identity. While I cannot assume to speak for this community, I choose to speak from within it.

The Work of the Commission

In the spring of 1999 the International Reading Association (IRA) established a National Commission on Excellence in Teacher Preparation in Reading. The Board of Directors charged the Commission with developing and executing a program of research that would lead to the identification of the qualities of effective teacher preparation programs with a specific focus on reading. The work of the Commission was to focus on programs of initial teacher preparation offered in the context of four-year, university-based baccalaureate programs. The Commission organized a program of research around three distinct but interrelated studies.

Study 1: Preservice Teacher Preparation in Reading

A national survey of teacher education programs was conducted to determine the "status-quo" of teacher preparation programs across the United States (Hoffman & Roller, 2000). The national survey was designed to assess the status quo for reading teacher preparation programs and practices across the United States. Through this survey descriptive data on existing programs and program features as well as data on the judgments of quality were gathered. Over 900 reading teacher educators from across the United States, representing a wide variety of institutional contexts, responded to this survey. The major findings from this IRA Commission survey study included:

- The average number of semester course hours in the area of reading was greater than six (two+ courses).

- Despite recent trends toward 5-year and fifth-year programs, 84% of the respondents described the 4-year baccalaureate as available to students.
- Undergraduate reading specializations were available in over 40% of the programs, with an average of 16+ semester hours required in these programs.
- Descriptions of course textbooks and course topics suggested that a comprehensive and "balanced approach" to reading was represented in most programs.
- Extensive field experiences in teaching reading prior to student teaching (supervised and connected to course content) were commonplace.
- The vast majority of the teaching faculty had both classroom experience in teaching, as well as advanced degrees in the area of reading.
- Teaching diverse learners was identified as a major focus in many programs.
- Over 85% of the respondents rated their programs as "very good" or "outstanding."

Clearly, teacher preparation in the area of reading is receiving greater attention today than in any previous period (Austin & Morrision, 1963; Hoffman & Pearson, 2000). However, variation within the IRA survey data suggests that the range in program characteristics and program quality is great. The results of this survey are useful in interpreting the findings from the other studies conducted by the Commission.

Study 2: Critical Features of Excellence in Teacher Preparation Programs

The second study focused on the identification of program features associated with "excellent" reading teacher preparation programs (Harmon, et al. 2001; Hoffman, Roller, & The National Commission on Reading Teacher Preparation, 2003). The selection panel worked to identify a set of excellent programs of teacher preparation in reading that could become the focus point for the identification of the critical features of programs. Through a competitive application process, a panel of prominent reading educators selected eight sites they judged to have outstanding preparation programs graduating excellent beginning teachers of reading. Twenty-eight colleges and universities applied to participate in the study, providing detailed descriptions of their programs, vignettes of classroom teaching, documentation of learning by recent program graduates, and critiques of these vignettes by program faculty and students and by public school principals and teachers. Some of the applicants nominated their entire teacher preparation programs for consideration, while others submitted just their reading specialization programs. In addition to the criterion of excellence in preparation, the panel also took into consideration the diversity of public and private institutions, large and small, in communities across the United States. The review panel identified eight programs. These were not the "eight best programs," but rather these were eight excellent programs representative of the many that exist in the country. Three of the programs offered undergraduates a choice of a "reading specialization." Only these reading specialization programs were studied. At the other five institutions the emphasis on reading was program wide. At the point in time when these programs were identified, the program directors and other interested faculty became part of the IRA Commission and full collaborators in the research effort.

The Commission looked across these eight sites to identify critical program features using qualitative methods. In site visits, structured interviews, and small group meetings with program faculty, the Commission gathered data about each of the eight programs. The eight common features of excellence identified by the Commission through this qualitative analysis were:

- *Content.* Teacher educators engage preservice teachers with a comprehensive curriculum and guide them toward the development of a cohesive knowledge base for effective teacher decision-making.

- *Apprenticeship.* Teacher Educators engage their preservice teachers in a variety of course-related field experiences where they have opportunities to interact with excellent models and mentors.

- *Vision.* Teacher educators center their program around a vision of literacy, quality teaching, and quality teacher education.

- *Resources and Mission.* The teacher education program has sufficient resources (intellectual, financial, and professional) to support the mission for quality teacher preparation.

- *Personalized Teaching.* Teacher educators value diversity and are prepared to offer their preservice students responsive teaching and an adapted curriculum.

- *Autonomy.* Teacher educators are active in adapting and negotiating with their institutions to make sure their students receive the most effective preparation possible.

- *Community.* Teacher educators work to create an active learning community that includes the faculty, their students, and mentor teachers.

- *Assessment.* Teacher educators continually assess their students, their program, their graduates, and themselves to guide instructional decision-making and program development.

Study #3: Investigating the Experiences and Practices of Commission Program Graduates: A Longitudinal Study

In the third and final line of research, the Commission followed a group of graduates from these "excellent" programs through their first years of teaching. This third study in the Commission research program was guided by two questions: (1) How do the graduates of IRA Commission programs transition into full-time teaching responsibilities? and (2) How effective are graduates of IRA Commission programs in teaching reading? We adopted both quantitative and qualitative research methods to explore these basic research questions. The study was a longitudinal comparison study spanning a three-year period of data collection.

The research perspective for the first year of the longitudinal study was qualitative. In large part the decision to adopt a qualitative perspective for Year 1 was based on the nature of the research question. We were interested in understanding the experiences of the first year teachers as interpreted by them and the ways in which these experiences connected to their preservice preparation. There were 101 participants in Year 1 of the study. Forty of these participants were graduates of the three IRA Commission sites who had completed a reading specialization. Thirty-three of the graduates had completed one of the Commission's five reading embedded programs. Twenty-eight additional graduates were identified for participation in the study to serve as comparison teachers. These comparison teachers were graduates from the three Commission institutions that offered a reading specialization. However, these twenty-eight comparison teachers had completed a "general" program and not the specialization.

Structured telephone interviews were conducted at three points in the beginning teachers' first year of teaching (September, January, June). Inductive data-driven analyses yielded 4 overarching themes—instructional decision-making, negotiations, community, and valuing of teacher preparation—that distinguished the responses of graduates of the IRA exemplary programs from those of graduates of general education programs.

Instructional decision-making. Commission teachers reported creating learning experiences and alternative structures that reflected mindful and purposeful planning, such as flexibly grouping students, providing a range of reading material, and offering individual tutoring in response to varying student needs.

Negotiations. Commission teachers were more likely to mention specific actions or decisions taken by them to meet students' needs. These actions were often in the form of supplements to the curriculum but at times were even at odds with the prescribed program within the school where they were working.

Community. Graduates of the Commission programs, in large part reported seeking out learning communities, drawing from their school community, as well as colleagues and peers from their teacher preparation programs.

Valuing Teacher Preparation. Finally, Commission teachers viewed their teacher preparation positively and related it to their current classroom practices. Commission graduates reported valuing a variety of features of their teacher preparation programs including college classroom practices, field experiences, and the knowledge base gained from course work.

These four themes revealed stark contrasts between graduates of Commission programs and the graduates of the general education programs. The beginning teachers' from the specialization programs definitive talk about valuing teacher preparation combined with their informed, knowledgeable talk of teaching and learning in their classrooms indicate a likely connection between quality reading teacher preparation and subsequent teaching (A complete report of findings from the first year of the study can be found in Maloch, et.al, 2003).

The methodology for Years 2 and 3 was expanded to include data collection on the classroom environment and classroom teaching that was descriptive and quantitative in nature. We also expanded the participant group to include teachers in the same schools as the Commission graduates. This addition was made to better ground the comparison of Commission teachers with other teachers in a context that was similar. The research questions for Year 2 were focused on a description of the teaching practices of Commission graduates and comparing these practices to other teachers: (1) What are the teaching practices associated with graduates of the Commission sites? and (2) How do these teaching practices compare to other teachers? All of the program teachers included in Year 1 of the study who were teaching in self-contained K-5 classroom settings were invited to continue participation, as were all of the original comparison graduates. Forty-six of the Commission graduates meeting these criteria agreed to continue into Year 2. All of the original program comparison teachers who participated in Year 1 were invited to continue in the study (These were the graduates of the three Commission sites who had completed a general program and not the reading specialization). Eleven of these original program comparison teachers agreed to continue participation. To augment the number of comparison teachers with the same years teaching experience, we actively recruited participation of teachers with the same years teaching experience in the same schools where the Commission gradates were teaching. Seventeen additional teachers meeting these criteria were identified through this process. Combining these two groups we created a group of 28 second-year comparison teachers. A second comparison group was added for Year 2. This group consisted of experienced teachers, matched as close as possible to the Commission teachers' grade level and recommended by the school principals at the Commission teachers' sites as being "excellent." Seventeen of these experienced (nominated as excellent) teachers were successfully identified and agreed to participate in the study following this procedure. The average years teaching experience for this group was thirteen years. We refer to this group as the "site-based experienced teacher" group. The total number of teacher participants for the second year of the study was 92.

For Year 3 of this study we expanded the data collection in participating classrooms to include more frequent observations. We also expanded our data collection to include direct measures of student reading achievement with pre (early fall) and post (late spring) standardized testing. All of the program teachers included in Year 2 of the study were invited to continue participation into Year 3. Comparison teachers (same years experience and same grade levels as program teachers) and site-based experienced teachers at the same grade level (recommended by principals as excellent) were recruited. We were able to collect complete data, including student achievement, during Year Three on eighteen program teachers and fifteen "same years" comparison teachers.

Classroom teaching during years 2 and 3 was examined using the TEX-IN3 observation instrument (Hoffman, 2001). This instrument was selected because of its comprehensive focus on effective reading and literacy practices. The TEX-IN3 is focused on the literacy environment of the classroom. It is specifically designed and validated for use in self-contained elementary classrooms. The TEX-IN3 has three major components: a text Inventory; a text-In-use observation; and a series of text Interviews. The instrument has demonstrated excellent reliability and validity characteristics. The major components of the TEX-IN3 have been validated in terms of student achievement growth in reading (Hoffman, Sailors, Duffy, & Beretvas, in press). Our focus on the literacy environment as a window to examine teacher effectiveness is consistent with a highly productive line of research into the teaching of reading and reflects findings from a number of studies that have shown the literacy environment created within the classroom is a critical feature of effective teaching. Data collection with the TEX-IN3 was conducted once during Year 2 and three times during Year 3 in all participating classrooms. Observers were trained to high levels of reliability on the TEX-IN3. They were "blind" to the status of the teachers they observed. We analyzed the data from the TEX-IN3 following the same procedures used in Year 2 to compare Program and Comparison Teachers (same years experience) classrooms.

I will share with you only selected findings from Year 2 and 3 observations. There was a statistically significant effect for Teacher Group (F=4.8, $df=2$, p<.01) on the ratings of teachers on the Holistic Text Environment. These ratings represent the average score on a 1 through 5 rubric with one the lowest score possible and five the highest. Post hoc analysis revealed the difference between the Commission program graduates and the Same Years teaching group was statistically significant (p<.01) and the difference between the Commission program graduates and the experienced teachers was not (p=.23).

The analysis of the data related to the observations of student engagement with texts in the classroom was restricted to the data gathered during the observations focused on reading instruction time (as designated by the classroom teacher). The snapshot QTE observation score is focused on the entire class. The snapshot differences were statistically significant (F=4.867, $df=2$, p<.01). Post hoc analysis revealed statistically significant differences favoring the Commission graduates over both the same year and site-base experience comparison groups (p<.05). The average student sweep QTE scores were also statistically significant (F=.5066, $df=2$, p<.01). Post hoc analysis revealed statistically significant differences favoring the Commission graduates over the same years comparison teachers.

The evidence gathered during Years 2 & 3 suggests that the graduates of high quality preparation programs continue to maintain their advantage over the "same years" comparison teachers that was documented in Year 1. The patterns of statistical significance are noteworthy given the power limitations associated with the relatively small numbers of teachers included in the study. Just as important, though, are the consistent patterns in the differences examined across the two years of data collection with the TEX-IN3. A complete report of the findings from the Years 2 & 3 follow-up study can be found in Hoffman, J. V., Roller, C. M., Maloch, B., Sailors, M., Duffy, G. G., and Beretvas, S. N. (2004) and The National Commission on Excellence in Elementary Teacher Preparation for Reading (2003).

Discussion

The evidence gathered through the work of the Commission suggests that participation in a high quality teacher preparation program that focuses specifically on the teaching of reading has a positive influence on the experience of the teachers entering the profession, and on the quality of and engagement with the literacy environment they create within their classrooms. These claims rest on both the qualitative data gathered in Year 1 and on the observational findings from Years 2 and 3 of the study. While these findings may come as no surprise to teacher educators, they offer scientifically based research evidence for the impact of the quality of teacher preparation on entry into teaching and classroom teaching practices. I am not aware of any study of reading teacher preparation that has followed this large of a sample of teachers over a period of three years with careful attention to the interpretive experiences of the participants and the direct observation of teaching practices. Of the eleven studies included in the NRP report on preservice teacher preparation in reading, the majority was limited to 4 to 6 weeks of data collection. None of the studies reviewed followed graduates into classrooms.

Reactions and Responses

Already, there have been attempts to discredit the work of the Commission. Susan Neuman, in Education Weekly, was reported to have called the work of the Commission as "invalid" because the selection of Commission sites was not random. This criticism itself is invalid since there never was an attempt to generalize to all teacher education programs. The sample selection was purposeful.

Some reading teacher educators have criticized the report arguing that the programs were not the "best" programs. There was never an intention to identify the best programs, only to identify a set of quality programs that represent the diversity of programs in country. We could replicate this study tomorrow. We could cast the net again. If we did I suspect we would identify 8 different programs, but the findings related to features and the impact would be similar and that is the crucial test of scientific inquiry.

The research has been criticized for the lack of a theoretical framework. This research was never conceived as a test of a theory. It is an empirical study designed to provide the data that could become the basis for building a theory. It is research grounded in the reality of what exists. Our goal is to reveal and then explain. This is theory building. This is no different from what was so successful in the research in teaching literature for over two decades. This is not a study to answer questions but a study that should be useful in formulating theories and framing future research.

The work has been criticized from a "what's new" perspective. True, the findings are aligned with IRA/NCTE and even NCATE standards. However, we cannot assume anything that is obvious to reading educators as good teaching or teacher education will be accepted and supported without "scientific" support. There has been no research base for the IRA/NCTE standards for teacher preparation in reading until now. We are not surprised that complexity and "good practices" shine in this study. We were not in search of a "silver bullet" solution. What is important to note in the findings is the significant discrepancy between most teacher education programs, as represented in the survey study, and the features of excellence. This is not said to discredit or devalue what we do but to inspire and direct our resolve to move forward.

Why the effort to discredit the research of the Commission? Could it be that the findings that suggest an investment in quality teacher preparation as a promising path are at odds with the current policy environment designed to dismantle teacher preparation programs? The work of the Commission suggests strongly that an investment in teachers and teacher education will have a positive impact on teaching and students. I began this address with a report on an effort in the state of Texas that would begin the dismantling of teacher preparation programs. I argued that this kind of effort is part of a larger national effort to discredit teacher preparation. If we remain passive we will be left behind. If we dig in our heels and become defensive, we will be dismissed as turf protecting by the public and the policy-makers. To move forward in reading teacher preparation, we must advocate for a positive agenda for reform that builds on the findings of the Commission on the one hand and supports future efforts for research into effective practices on the other. The work of the Commission provides a sound base to launch this effort. The choice is simple. It is move forward or be left behind. There is no in between position. The public will not tolerate nor should we tolerate "business as usual." The challenge is an individual one for each of us as teacher educators to make changes. It is also the responsibility of organizations like the College Reading

Association (CRA), the International Reading Association (IRA), and the National
Reading Conference (NRC) to assume a key role in supporting our efforts.

References

Austin, M. C., & Morrison, C. (1962). *The torch lighters: Tomorrow's teachers of reading.* Cambridge, MA: Harvard University Press.

Harmon, J., Hedrick, W., Martinez, M., Perez, B., Keehn, S., Fine, J. C., Eldridge, D., Flint, A. S., Littleton, D. M., Bryant-Shanklin, M., Loven, R., Assaf, L., & Sailors, M. (2001). Features of Excellence of Reading Teacher Preparation Programs. In J. V. Hoffman, D. L. Schallert, C. M. Fairbanks, J. Worthy, & B. Maloch (Eds.), *Fiftieth yearbook of the National Reading Conference.* Chicago: National Reading Conference.

Hoffman, J. V. (2001). *The TEX-IN3: Text inventory, text in-use, and text interview observation system.* Unpublished manuscript. University of Texas at Austin.

Hoffman, J. V., & Pearson, P. D. (2000). Reading teacher education in the next millennium: What your grandmother's teacher didn't know that your granddaughter's teacher should. *Reading Research Quarterly, 35*(1), 28-44.

Hoffman, J. V., Roller, C. M., & The National Commission on Excellence in Elementary teacher Preparation for Reading Instruction. (2001). IRA excellence in reading teacher preparation: Current practices in reading teacher education at the undergraduate level in the United States. C. Roller (Ed.), *Learning to teach reading: Setting the research agenda* (pp. 32-79). Newark, DE: International Reading Association.

Hoffman, J. V., & Sailors, M. (2004). Those who can't teach can: Assessing the impact of *No Child Left Behind* on the teacher education. In K. Goodman, P. Shannon, and Y. Goodman (Eds.) *Saving our schools, (*pp. 137-150). Berkeley, CA: RDR Books.

Hoffman, J.V., Sailors, M., Duffy, G.G., & Beretvas, N. (2004). The effective elementary classroom literacy environment: Examining the validity of the TEX-IN3 Observation System. *Journal of Literacy Research, 36*(3), 303-334.

Hoffman, J. V., Roller, C. M., Maloch, B., Sailors, M., Duffy, G. G., & Beretvas, S. N. (2004). Teachers' preparation to teach reading and their experiences and practices in the first three years of teaching. *The Elementary School Journal, 105*(3), 267-288.

Maloch, B. et al. (2003). Understandings, beliefs, and reported decision making of first-year teachers from different reading teacher preparation programs. *Elementary School Journal, 103,* 431-458.

The National Commission on Excellence in Elementary Teacher Preparation for Reading Instruction. (2003). *Prepared to make a difference.* Newark, DE: International Reading Association.

United States Office of Education. (2003). *Inside No Child Left Behind.* Retrieved March 25, 2003 from http://www.ed.gov/legislation/ESEA02/pg2.html#sec1119

Fast Start: Successful Literacy Instruction that Connects Schools and Homes

Nancy Padak
Tim Rasinski

Kent State University

Keynote Address
College Reading Association
2003

In 2003 Nancy Padak and Tim Rasinski were professors of literacy education at Kent State University. Their research interests focused on fluency and family literacy. Each is a Past-President of CRA; they also edited the CRA Yearbook, The Reading Teacher, *and the* Journal of Literacy Research. *The program described in this paper is available from Scholastic (2005).*

Reading more often leads to reading better. Moreover, children who come to school having been read to typically have an advantage over their peers who did not have such preschool experiences. Both of these assertions, long accepted as givens in the literacy community, speak to the importance of engaging children in reading outside of school. Yet the unfortunate truth is that most students do very little reading out of school. The home can help here. Parental involvement in reading is an untapped source for increasing the sheer amount that students read, which in turn will increase children's proficiency in reading.

Parental involvement can significantly influence children's learning in general and reading achievement in particular. Ann Henderson (1988; Henderson & Berla, 1994), for example, concluded that parent involvement leads to improvements in student achievement, grades, test scores, and overall academic performance. Results from nearly every National Assessment of Educational

Reprinted from *Celebrating the Power of Literacy*, pp. 11-23, by J. A. R. Dugan P. E. Linder, M. B. Sampson, B. Brancato, and L. Elish-Piper, Eds., 2004, Commerce, TX: College Reading Association.

Progress have indicated that students who are regularly involved with their families in literacy-related activities have higher levels of reading achievement than students whose parents are not actively involved in their reading. Similarly, an international study of reading instruction found that the "degree of parental cooperation" was the most potent of 56 significant characteristics of schools most successful in teaching reading (Postlethwaite & Ross, 1992).

Experimental research results likewise point to the value of parental involvement in children's reading. Children whose parents engage them in family literacy activities have accelerated oral language development (e.g., Senechal, LeFevre, & Thomas, 1998), greater phonemic awareness and decoding ability (e.g., Burgess, 1999; Purcell-Gates, 1996), and higher overall reading achievement (e.g., Cooter, Marrin, & Mills-House, 1999; Foertsch, 1992; Morrow & Young, 1997) compared to peers without such opportunities.

Unfortunately, ongoing and consistent efforts to involve parents in children's reading have proven difficult to sustain. Many teachers we know have described unsuccessful and unrewarding experiences when working with parents. Others believe they don't have time or energy for such a program when they seldom get release time, remuneration, or recognition. Most parent involvement programs in reading tend to be one-shot affairs such as talks by local experts in reading, "make it and take it" workshops, pre-packaged commercial programs, or short-term incentive programs. These approaches have little effect on students' reading achievement or attitudes, particularly for children who struggle with reading (Padak, Sapin, & Baycich, 2002).

We believe that Fast Start (FS), the parental involvement program we describe in this article, offers an alternative to typical approaches to parental involvement. The principles on which FS is based are described below. We then explain the program itself and finally share research results based on several trials in public schools.

Characteristics of Successful Parent Involvement Programs

Successful parent involvement in reading programs share several attributes (Rasinski & Padak, 2004). These characteristics provide the basis for FS. They can also be used as guidelines for teachers and schools to design their own programs to meet specific needs or to design evaluations of existing programs.

Use Proven and Effective Strategies

Parents often have limited time to devote to working with their children. Therefore, at-home activities must be based on proven and appropriate methods for achieving success in reading. Too often, at-home activities have questionable value for improving academic performance. Drawing and coloring pictures or cutting out photographs from magazines may not be the best use of parents and children's time together at home.

Provide Training, Communication, and Support

Most parents are not teachers. They need good and understandable training that includes demonstrations and opportunities for discussion and questions. Someone who is enthusiastic about and committed to parent involvement should provide the training.

Teachers need to understand the realities of busy family life and be sensitive to educational barriers that may impede parent–child reading activity. Some parents may feel uncomfortable reading aloud to their children because of their own real or perceived lack of reading ability. Parents of English Language Learners may not themselves be fluent readers of English. Parents whose own educational experiences were negative may hesitate to attend school functions. Yet all these parents want to help their children succeed. The teacher's challenge, then, is to find meaningful ways for all families to be involved in home reading activities. Making books on tape available is one way to promote all families' involvement. With some thought, resourceful teachers can find many more.

Continuing communication and support can provide parents with timely feedback about their questions and concerns and can encourage persistence with the at-home reading activities. Support can be in the form of a regular informative newsletter, monthly sessions in the school, or offers of personal contact by phone or email. Ongoing communication and support build bonds between home and school and demonstrate to parents that other people care about their children's reading growth.

Real Reading

One of the best things that parents can do for children of any age is to read to them. Reading aloud provides children with a model of fluent reading and offers parents natural opportunities to point out text features for young children. Similarly, when parents read with their children or listen to their children read, children grow as readers. Texts for these activities should be authentic (e.g., poems, song lyrics, jokes, jump rope rhymes); children should be able to read them successfully with enough support from parents. These simple activities— read to, read with, and listen to children—are powerful ways to promote student growth in reading.

Some parent involvement plans fail because parents lack appropriate texts or the time or resources to acquire them. Although periodic trips to the public library are advisable, requiring them as a condition of participation in at-home reading activities might discourage parental involvement. The easiest solution is to provide parents and children with reading materials. When the materials are provided, parents are more likely to remember to do the activities with their children. The materials themselves act as reminders to parents to get the job done.

Make Activities Easy, Consistent, and Enjoyable

Parents tell us that parent involvement activities don't work if they are too complex, take inordinate amounts of time, or change from day to day or week to week. They say it's hard to develop a routine of working with their children under these conditions. Therefore, at-home reading activities need to reflect this reality. At-home activities for young children should be relatively brief (10-15 minutes several times each week), simple routines with some variation to keep interest high. Such activities make it easier for parents and children to develop predictable, time-efficient routines. These, in turn, increase the likelihood that the at-home activities will be conducted regularly and successfully.

Consistency is important as well. Once an effective instructional routine is introduced, major changes or disruptions in the parent-child routine should be avoided. Rather, families should be able to develop a level of comfort with the routines. Variety can be introduced by changing the texts and the ways in which parents and children respond to what they read.

For parents and children to persist in academic tasks over the long term, the instructional activities must be enjoyable for everyone. A sense of informality and playfulness infused into the activities can help achieve this goal. Parents should be reminded to be enthusiastic, provide positive encouragement, and support their children's attempts to read. Allowing children some control over activities also lends enjoyment to the sessions. If the reading is followed by some word games, for example, children can choose the games as well as the words to include.

Provide Ways to Document Home Activities

Documenting at-home activity permits teachers and schools to monitor parent—child involvement and evaluate the program's success in achieving its goal. More important, perhaps, documentation gives parents tacit encouragement and reminds them to continue reading with their children. Parents can use a log sheet to record their work with their children over a specified period of time. Parents tell us that posting the sheet in a prominent place reminds them to do the activity. At the end of the time period the log sheets are returned to the school.

We used these guidelines to develop FS. Teachers or school administrators can also use them to design other programs for parent involvement in reading. When home and school collaborate to provide enjoyable and authentic reading experiences, students benefit because they have multiple daily opportunities to grow as readers.

Fast Start in Reading

FS is a program we developed at Kent State University for involving parents of young readers (kindergarten through Grade 2) and struggling readers. In FS parents read short, highly predictable passages with their children. We have found that rhyming poetry, nursery rhymes, jokes and riddles for children, and short vignettes work very well. Each day parents and their children spend about 15 minutes on one of the passages. What we ask parents to do is specific and based on effective instructional principles:

1. The parent reads the passage to the child, and they talk about its content.

2. Parent and child read the passage together until the child is able to read it alone.

3. The parent listens to the child read and gives encouragement, support, and praise.

4. Parent and child select and then play several short word games from a menu of ideas.

These word games are generic and grouped to provide developmentally appropriate support for children. Group A activities (see Appendix) concentrate on concepts about print. Group B activities focus on phonemic awareness, and Group C activities are for children who are beginning to read independently. Teachers tell parents which group of activities to use for the word games.

School personnel invite parents to attend FS training sessions at the beginning of the school year. Several sessions are offered, morning and evening, so that parents can choose which session to attend. Sessions are typically led by children's teachers. Parents leave the sessions with informational packets (see Appendix), enough passages for one month, and log forms for recording their work with their children. Each month from October through May, teachers send home new sets of readings and new log sheets. The program is relatively inexpensive and time efficient. The major cost is duplication, and the major time commitment for teachers is in the initial training sessions.

Parent participation in FS has been exceptionally high, and student growth in reading is apparent and significant, especially among children who are most at risk for reading problems.

Kent State's Summer Reading Program

An adapted version of FS has been an integral part of Kent State's summer reading program, a five-week clinical tutoring program for children experiencing significant difficulty in learning to read. During the first week of the program parents are asked to attend an orientation session during which they are introduced to the adapted version of FS (adapted for children in intermediate and middle grades as well as primary grade students), provided with material (or it is provided by individual tutors on a daily basis), and asked to engage in FS tutoring daily. We have found a strong relationship ($r = .60$ to $.79$) between the parents' level of participation in FS tutoring with their children and their children's reading growth (word recognition and reading fluency) over the course of the brief summer reading program (Rasinski, 1995).

Fast Start in Worthington, Ohio

School psychologist Bruce Stevenson (2002) implemented FS over a three-month period with beginning first-grade students. Parents worked with their children on the program for a relatively short period of time—about ten minutes per day. Nevertheless, he found that FS had a statistically significant and substantial effect on the reading growth (letter and word recognition, reading fluency) of the lowest achieving first-graders, those who would normally he considered most at-risk for academic success. FS students made nearly twice the gain as a control group doing more traditional parent involvement activities in letter and word recognition and reading fluency. Moreover, he found that parents found the program easy to implement and valued the opportunity to employ it with their children.

Fast Start in Akron and Canton, Ohio

A couple of years ago we were talking about parental involvement and FS at an in-service session for teachers. After the session, Sharon Davis, a first-grade teacher at Seiberling School in Akron, indicated an interest in implementing FS at her school. Consequently, we worked with eight first-grade teachers and a kindergarten teacher to implement FS in 2001-02. We analyzed results of the Seiberling implementation in summer 2002 and shared them with Canton teachers early in the 2002-03 school year. As a result, Canton implemented FS in grades K and 1 in its 18 elementary schools during the 2002-03 school year.

Our evaluation of FS focuses on children's achievement as well as children's, parents', and teachers' perceptions. To evaluate achievement, we use the tests and measures currently in place in the schools. Perceptions are obtained through surveys (for parents and teachers) and interviews (with children) developed especially for this research. Interested readers may contact either of us for copies of these survey and interview instruments.

Analysis of children's reading achievement data for both K and 1 and in both school systems was based on a 2 time] X 3 level of involvement] design. The time variable was beginning and end of the school year. For level of involvement, we asked teachers to mark class rosters indicating whether students were actively involved in FS, somewhat involved in FS, or not at all involved in FS.

Kindergarten assessments in Canton are based on Clay's *Observation Survey* (2002). Analysis of these assessments showed that children who were involved in FS:a) had significantly greater word vocabulary growth ($p < .05$), b) attained concepts about print more quickly (p < .05), and c) learned to identify upper and lower case letters more quickly (p < .05) than their non-FS counterparts.

K indergartners in Akron and first graders in both school systems are assessed with the *Developmental Reading Assessment* (Beaver, 1997). Analysis of scores for these children showed that students who were at least somewhat involved in FS significantly outperformed their non-FS counterparts (p < .01). Taken together, these results show that the FS program was effective in increasing children's reading abilities, regardless of their measured ability at the beginning of the year. Being "somewhat" involved in FS was enough to lead to achievement gains.

Children who participated in FS were overwhelmingly positive about the experience (see Table 1). When commenting on the poems, in addition to general positive comments, children noted that they liked the content of the texts and that they enjoyed working with family members. Regarding content, for example, one child said, "I liked the rhyming words and they were funny." Another commented, "The poems were not hard or easy—they were just right." Children also enjoyed the word play activities. Sample comments show this: "They help you read a lot"; " 'cause I can learn stuff—how to do the sounds and how to make all the letters"; "because I got to play with my dad." The few children who had negative perceptions commented that the work was too hard or boring.

Table 1. Children's Perceptions*

	Yes	A Little	No
Like poetry reading?	129 (91%)	9 (6%)	3 (2%)
Like word activities?	126 (89%)	10 (7%)	5 (4%)
Did (adult) enjoy?	127 (90%)	11 (8%)	3 (2%)
Did FS make you a better reader?	138 (98%)	1 (1%)	2 (1%)

141 individual interviews at Seiberling (spring, 2002, N=25) in Akron and 4 elementary schools (spring, 2003, N=84; spring 2004, N=32) in Canton.

As Table 1 shows, children firmly believed that FS helped them become better readers. Their reasons for this belief centered in three areas:

- Challenging content: "Because they had lots of words I didn't know"; "the words were hard but now I'm reading."
- Encouraged reading development: "The harder it gets, the better you get"; "because I couldn't read that much before and now I'm reading a lot of stuff"; "because they have hard words, and the more I read, the more I know."
- Encouraged interest in reading: "because all of a sudden I sat down and started reading"; "I read them every day after school. Sometimes I write poems myself."

Parents' perceptions about FS were also very positive (see Table 2). Many parents commented positively about their children's and their own reaction to

FS: "The one-on-one time was nice"; "It gave him something to look forward to every night"; "I have always loved poetry. I see the same excitement in [my child] now"; "brought us closer together." The few negative reactions centered in difficulty maintaining the child's interest and the parent or child believing FS was a "chore."

In general, parents were also very positive about the impact that FS had on their children's reading ability and on whether the time they devoted to FS was well spent. With regard to the former, parents commented, "[Child] is eager to read now and without assistance"; "it seemed to help him with his fluency and expression"; "it has helped him recognize words and build confidence in reading." And about spending time in FS, sample parent comments were "To see your child read and want to read is priceless"; "this is a nice way for the family to spend time together"; "allows for quality time."

Table 2. Fast Start: Parents' Response*

	YES	SOMEWHAT	NO
Child enjoyed sessions	357 (66%)	152 (28%)	31 (6%)
Parent enjoyed sessions	369 (68%)	134 (25%)	36 (7%)
Child enjoyed poems	436 (80%)	94 (17%)	18 (3%)
Child enjoyed word play	224 (73%)	96 (31%)	17 (6%)
Made a difference in child's reading	303 (57%)	177 (34%)	47 (9%)
Time well spent	439 (83%)	60 (11%)	27 (5%)

Seiberling parents, 2001-02 (N=31) and Canton parents, 2002-03 (approximately 275) and 2003-2004 (approximately 225).

Teacher responses to the FS survey are summarized in Table 3. In general, teachers believed that FS time was well spent and that their students enjoyed the activity. Teachers were less sure about academic benefits or about parents' responses. We found it intriguing that of the three groups surveyed/interviewed, teachers' perceptions of FS were the least positive. Although we have no explanation for this finding, we are planning further research to learn more about teachers' ideas about FS.

Table 3. Teachers' Perceptions of Fast Start*

Among active participants:
- Reading improved (38%)
- No difference in reading ability (38%)

Among "somewhat active" participants:
- Reading improved (24%)
- No difference in reading ability (35%)

Parent response:
- Positive (39%)
- Negative (39%)
- Mixed (20%)

Student response:
- Liked (86%)
- Disliked (5%)

Time well spent?
- Yes (64%)
- No (13%)

selected responses from teacher surveys in Akron and Canton

Conclusion

Fast Start has demonstrated to us that parents really do want to help their children in reading. In many cases they just don't know what to do or what materials and programs to choose. When schools get parents involved in a systematic way, using effective methods of instruction and providing support, materials, and communication, children make substantial and significant progress as readers.

Although parent involvement may not be a cure-all for every difficulty that children encounter in reading, we know that it does make a difference—in some cases, a huge difference. Our experiences lead us to recommend that all education professionals try and try again to involve parents actively in children's literacy development. The potential benefits are simply too great to pass up.

References

Beaver, J. (1997). *Developmental reading assessment.* Upper Saddle River, NJ: Pearson.

Burgess, S. (1999). The influence of speech perception, oral language ability, the home literacy environment, and prereading knowledge on the growth of phonological sensitivity: A 1-year longitudinal study. *Reading Research Quartely, 34,* 400-402.

Clay, M. M. (2002). *An observation survey of early literacy achievement (2nd ed.).* Portsmouth, NH: Heinemann.

Cooter, R., Marrin, P., & Mills-House, E. (1999). Family and community involvement: The bedrock of reading success. *The Reading Teacher, 52,* 891-896.

Foertsch, M. (1992). *Reading in and out of school: Factors influencing the literacy achievement of American students in grades 4, 8, and 12 in 1988 and 1990.* (ERIC Document Reproduction Service No. ED 341 976)

Henderson, A. (1988). Parents are a school's best friends. *Phi Delta Kappan, 70,* 148-153.

Henderson, A., & Berla, N. (Eds.). (1994). *A new generation of evidence: The family is critical to student achievement.* Washington, DC: National Committee for Citizens in Education. (ERIC Document Reproduction Service No. ED 375 968)

Morrow, L., & Young, J. (1997). A family literacy project connecting school and home:
Effects on attitude, motivation, and literacy achievement. *Journal of Educational Psychology, 89,* 736-742.

Padak, N., Sapin, C., & Baycich, D. (2002). *A decade of family literacy: Programs, outcomes, and the future.* Columbus, OH: ERIC Clearinghouse on Adult, Career, and Vocational Education.

Postlethwaite, T. N., & Ross, K. N. (1992). *Effective schools in reading: Implications for educational planners.* The Hague: International Association for the Evaluation of Educational Achievement.

Purcell-Gates, V. (1996). Stories, coupons, and the TV Guide: Relationships between home literacy experiences and emergent literacy. *Reading Research Quarterly, 31,* 406-428.

Rasinski, T. V. (1995). Fast Start: A parental involvement reading program for primary grade students. In W. Linek & E. Sturtevant (Eds.), *Generations of literacy. Seventeenth yearbook of the College Reading Association* (pp. 301-312). Harrisonburg, VA: College Reading Association.

Rasinski, T., & Padak, N. (2004). *Effective reading strategies: Teaching children who find reading difficult* (3rd ed.). Upper Saddle River, NJ: Pearson.

Senechal, M., LeFevre, J., & Thomas, E. (1998). Differential effects of home literacy experiences on the development of oral and written language. *Reading Research Quarterly, 33, 96-116.*

Stevenson, B. (2002). *The efficacy of the Fast Start parent tutoring program in the development of reading skills of first grade students.* Unpublished doctoral dissertation, The Ohio State University, Columbus.

Appendix: Daily Fast Start Lesson

Fast Start

FAST START has two parts—reading the poem or passage and playing with the words. Here are directions for each part. A FAST START session should take about 10-15 minutes. Please do FAST START at least 5 times each week.

Reading the Poem or Passage

1. Sit next to your child.

2. Hold the poem so both of you can see it.

3. Read the poem **to** your child. Do this two or three times. Read it slowly and expressively. Point to the words as you read.

4. Read the poem **with** your child. Do this two or three times. Again, read slowly and expressively. Point to the words as you read, or let your child point as you read.

5. Listen to your child read the poem by himself or herself. Do this two or three times. Have your child point to the words as he or she reads and be sure to tell your child what a good reader he or she is!

   Remember: Read to . . . read with . . . listen to your child read.

Playing With the Words

Your child's teacher will tell you which group of word games you should use. Pick an activity or two from your child's group. Do different activities on different days so your child will enjoy the word work. Be sure to tell your child what a good job he or she is doing.

Group A

1. Ask your child to count the lines in the poem. Ask him or her to point at each line as it is counted.
2. Have your child count the words in the poem. Ask him or her to point to each word as it is counted.
3. Ask questions about the words—How many words are in line 1? Show me the third word in line 2. Which line has the most words? Which line has the fewest words?
4. Say a letter of the alphabet. Ask your child to find all the times that a particular letter is used in the poem. Repeat for several other letters.
5. Point to a word. Ask your child to tell you the letter that begins the word. Then ask him or her to tell you what letter ends the word. Repeat with several words.
6. Give your child a pencil or marker. Say a word from the poem and have your child find it and mark it some way—circle it, underline it, highlight it, etc.

Group B

1. Say two words from the poem. Ask your child to tell you if the words rhyme with one another. Repeat with several other pairs of words.
2. Find a word from the poem that is a simple rhyming word. Ask your child to say some words that rhyme with the word you chose. Write all these words in a list on the poetry sheet.
3. Say a word from the poem. Ask your child to say the word by breaking it into sounds. (For example, you might say "bat," and your child would say "buh—a—tuh.")
4. Do the opposite of #3—you say "buh—a—tuh" and ask your child to tell you what word it is: "bat." Then ask your child to find the word in the poem.
5. Say two words from the poem. Ask your child if they start with the same sound. Repeat several times. (Choose some words that do start with the same sounds and some that don't.)

Group C

1. Use the word cards. Ask your child to select a word or two from the poem to put on the cards. You also select a word or two.
2. After you have gathered 10-12 words over several days, play with them. If you make a duplicate set of cards, you can play "Concentration" or "Go Fish."

3. Find words from the poem that all have the same vowel. Put the words on word cards. Ask your child to sort the cards into categories according to the sounds that the vowel makes in the words.

4. Ask your child to sort the word cards into categories according to the consonant sound that is found in the word. For example, sort your words into all the words that begin with the "buh" sound. Or, sort your words into all the words that end with the "kuh" sound.

5. Select a word from the poem. Play guessing games with the word. For example, with the word "hat," you could ask, "What word would we have if we changed the /h/ to a /p/?" "What word would we have if we put an /e/ on the end?"

6. Ask your child to read the words as you flash them to him or her. Challenge him or her to read them as quickly as possible.

WRITING FROM THE HEART

Joyce Sweeney

Keynote Address
College Reading Association
2004

In 2004 Joyce Sweeney was the author of 12 novels for young adults, the latest of which, Takedown *(Sweeney, 2004) was nominated by The American Library Association as a Best Book for Reluctant Readers.* Players *(Sweeney 2000) was chosen as a Top 10 Sports Book for Teens by* Booklist *and as a Top 10 Book for Teens by* Working Mother Magazine. *Joyce was also a writing teacher and conducts an ongoing workshop in Fort Lauderdale, which had so far produced 11 published authors. She has published short stories and poems in numerous journals and anthologies.*

I've done a lot of speaking but I've never been asked to be a keynote before. I want you to know I took that responsibility very seriously. I'm wearing pantyhose tonight!

It's a pleasure to be here with you, preaching to the choir. I gave a lot of thought to what would be good to talk about tonight. Actually I thought a lot about what wouldn't be good to talk about. I mean, yes we could talk about reaching out to teen readers by writing good books and how important and at risk those teen readers are, and how if we lose them in those years, we lose them forever...but I have a feeling you've heard that speech before. Actually, most of you have probably given that speech before.

So I thought tonight I would talk about something you don't know about, something you couldn't know about because it's personal to me. I want to talk about my personal creative process because I think it's fascinating how writers really work; it's a magical process to me and it amazes me that it produces these

Reprinted from *Building Bridges to Literacy,* pp.12-17, by P. E. Linder, M. B. Sampson, J. R. Dugan, & B. A. Brancato, Eds., 2006, Commerce, TX: College Reading Association useful objects—the books—that you teach and work with. A lot of authors don't tell the truth about what that process is like. They want to get up and say, "I felt kids should read a book about blah, blah, blah" and they act like it was an intentional thing they were in control of. I'm here to tell you it's not. It's a weird, unfathomable personal thing. These books just come up out of us, like ... vomiting ... and low and behold it's a useful, marketable thing. I have a good friend who's a therapist and she works with dreams a lot. And we've talked a lot about how storytelling and dreaming are extremely similar. When you dream, your unconscious puts together all sorts of scraps from things you've been thinking about and tells you a story that helps you or soothes you or expresses what you need to express. Writing stories is the same thing, only you do it consciously, or actually semi-consciously.

So to illustrate, I want to talk about the two books we have here, *Takedown* (Sweeney, 2004) and *Waiting for June* (Sweeney, 2003) and walk you through some of what was going on with me and how that all comes together to make a book.

Alright, before I start we have to get one big confession out of the way. I'm a pro-wrestling fan. I'm not a little fan; I'm a big fan. I go to arenas and I'm on the Internet. I've loved wrestling since I was five years old. I used to watch it with my grandfather and I got hooked when I was too young to do anything about it. So there it is, now you know the worst about me.

Okay, with *Takedown* (Sweeney, 2004), the genesis was Lionel Tate, do you remember who he was? It was all over the news down here. He was a thirteen-year-old boy who murdered a little girl and when he killed her, he was doing a wrestling throw. And then the media went into a frenzy that wrestling desensitizes kids to violence; it makes them violent, etc. etc. And as a wrestling fan, I knew this wasn't true and in fact, I knew there was some kind of positive, valuable aspect to wrestling. I didn't know what the heck it was, but I got it in my head that I could write a book that would somehow explore that.

So I was ruminating on that and I was out walking one day, and a sort of scary looking guy started walking kind of parallel to me. And I went through the usual thought process you go through ... what will I do? Am I imagining this? Should I run? All the stuff you say to yourself when you feel threatened. I realized I had a key ring in my hand and I thought to myself, well, if he gets any closer, I'll close my fist over this key ring and hit him in the head with it. And I realized, hey! I got that from wrestling! If you hit someone with a foreign object, it makes your punch stronger! And I thought, well, that's nice, but I don't think that's enough to make a book. The guy ended up being harmless and I still didn't have an idea for my book.

But that event made me remember another event that had happened a few years back. I was riding on a bus with my mother and a guy stepped on and he had a gun, very visible, in his waistband. And the driver said right away, "Get off!" I guess that's the training bus drivers get, to just yell "Get off" but anyway the guy didn't budge. And then a really interesting thing happened. About half the people on the bus jumped up, pushed past the guy with the gun and ran off the bus. And the other half, including me and my mom stayed where we were. Now it turned out alright, the driver must have signaled the police in some way because they came right away and dragged the guy off. But I was left with this thought...there was no way to know what was the right thing to do. The people that pushed past the guy might have guessed wrong. What if that made him mad and he just started shooting them one by one? Or what if we were wrong, to freeze and stay there? The others got away. We were still there in the dangerous situation. You like to think in every emergency, there's a right thing to do that will save you and a wrong thing to do that will hurt you. But I realized, you never know!

And the next thing that totally rattled me was Andrew Cunanan. He was the man accused of murdering Gianni Versace and for weeks he was on the loose down in Fort Lauderdale. He was on the run and desperate and he killed a guy to get his car.

That led to the media terrifying us by saying how clever and desperate he was, how he could pop up anywhere at any time, how ruthless he was. He was supposedly sighted in the area where I was teaching a night class every Thursday, and we'd go out to the parking lot and actually look around...is he here? Is that guy him?

So I started toying with the idea that maybe some kids who are wrestling fans run across this desperate gunman? Will there be anything of value in what they know from wrestling? Or will it have made them think violence is all a game and make them more vulnerable?

Then, there's always a little gift you get from the universe when you're planning a book. I went to the Mystery Writers conference and I was just there to mentor some of my students, so I could attend any seminar I wanted and just have fun. So they had a module that was given by an FBI agent who was on a Special Response Team...a SWAT team. And he started talking about hostage negotiations and what they do and how they handle it. And I was totally fascinated and realized if my crazed gunman got into a house and the police came right away, it could turn into a hostage situation. So I raised my hand and asked him, "Do you do things differently if there are kids in the house?" And he said, "Oh, yes, I would do a lot of things differently if there were kids." And so for the next 30 minutes I took over the whole question and answer period with him, ruining it for all the other people, plotting and researching my novel. And I got his card and called him later and asked some more questions.

I still didn't know what being wrestling fans had to do with it or how I was going to vindicate wrestling, but I had enough to start a book and writers know that you just trust the process once it gets going and let it take you. So I set up this story, where I have a thirteen-year-old boy who begs his mother to let him have friends over when she's not there and he finally gets her convinced that it's safe to do, and mean old me, I send the crazed gunman over there, the police come and the kids—all wrestling fans—are in a hostage situation. There were lots of surprises along the way, for one thing, several of the kids got out. I didn't expect that. It was like the bus story. One kid just made a run for it and it worked. And at one point in the story, my main character got the chance to get out and he *stayed*. He didn't want to leave his friends behind.

So he's plotting and planning and trying to get himself and his friends out and of course the whole situation is making him go crazy…and guess what he does? He turns to his wrestling hero in his mind. He calls on him and starts asking him for advice.

And then I had it. I understood why wrestling means so much to me and why I think it means so much to other kids. I grew up without a father. You're always sort of trained to say, it isn't a big deal, I'm fine, my mom does a great job. But you know something is missing. You want that big, larger than life, heroic man who always knows what to do, who role models being brave and strong, that protector. Look at the characters and storylines in wrestling. These guys are defending womanhood, sticking up for America, punishing cheaters and cowards—they are upholding exaggerated male values! And we need male values, all of us. In a dangerous situation, or in a time when we want to be ambitious and strong, we all need that "inner dad" to tell us what to do.

My wrestling hero is Ric Flair. I discovered Ric Flair at a time when my writing career was at an all-time low. Ric Flair is a larger than life, cocky, flashy guy who was a child prodigy and who clearly loves to perform. He wears sparkly clothes and he struts down that aisle with all the lights shining on him. People who want to be writers have that inner performer. Even though we're usually shy, we dream of walking that aisle, having the applause and the attention, being great. So I was feeling down and I'd watch Ric Flair and say to myself, "yeah, work it, baby!" But as I got to be more and more of a fan I learned a lot about Ric Flair, the real person. His career was a lot like my career. You get pushed and promoted, then maybe you get ignored for a while. You get applauded but you also get rejected and beat up and tired. His company got new management that didn't like him. That had happened to me! His company went bankrupt. That happened to me! And I learned from him, just by watching that he kept going, kept trying, just waited for the next opportunity. He started as a very shallow, silly role model but he turned into a true hero.

And I realized that all of us fatherless kids have to have someone like that—so when we're in a tough situation we can call on that image and say, what would he do? And that's what the main character in *Takedown* (Sweeney, 2004) does and that's what saves him.

And then, just before I move on to *Waiting for June* (Sweeney, 2003), one more thing. Remember when I said storytelling was like a dream? That it's some kind of unconscious metaphor for what's going on in your life? After it was written I realized why I was so interested in heroism and danger and life and death that year. It was a year when I had had some very weird medical symptoms and it led to me having repeated tests for cancer. I didn't have cancer and I'm fine, but being tested for it over and over was so scary every time I had to wait for lab results. And I realized that was the gunman. Death can come to anyone's house and hold a gun on them, even mine. And that fear was what gave the energy to the story.

Okay, *Waiting for June* (Sweeney, 2003). Very different kind of book. The genesis of this book was just pure serendipity. I was teaching a writing class where I was giving prompts. And sometimes, you know, you write along with the class just to pass the time or see if the exercise is any good. And I gave the prompt: Write about something that will never happen. And the wag that I am, since I had a tubal ligation when I was 26, I thought, I'll write about being pregnant. Because, believe me, that will never happen! So I took the voice of a pregnant teenage girl and this is what I wrote:

> I'm in my third trimester now, when dreams are supposed to be especially vivid. Lately, I've been dreaming bout whales, pale and bloated; drifting in a murky sea. They're always on the edge of my visual horizon, sometimes moving out of sight, which panics me. I don't know if I'm supposed to be human or another whale, left behind by the pod; but it seems important to catch up, and I never do. The memorable part of this dream is the sound, the whale songs that rollover me in the water, so my body feels the sound and knows its shape. The whales cry in pulses, the most comforting sequence of beats imaginable. Not fast, like a heartbeat. Not even the pace of breathing. Slow, like the rhythm of someone stroking a cat.

Well, I don't know how many of you are writers, ladies and gentlemen, but when you accidentally write a passage that good, you're stuck with it. I remember showing it to my friend on the way home that night saying, I have to do something with this!

So then I say to myself. Oh, great, I have to figure out how to write a pregnant whale book!

Now obviously I need to figure out how to get the whales in here. I don't want to deal with the obvious, that she feels big or it's something about sonograms or anything like that. So I started looking at it as something magical, some kind of magical message. I had read an article that stayed with me that said that in the third trimester, there may be some way that the baby can communicate feelings and even thoughts to the mother. I mean, obviously not word thoughts, but what about images and ideas? What about dreams?

I'm very interested in Native American religions and so I thought, well, what if the father of the baby is Native American and whales are sacred in his culture and so the baby knows this and is sending this to the mother? Well, I had a problem right away with that. I like to set my books locally, it just solves so many problems, but I thought oh, shoot, now I have to research the Pacific Northwest and find some Indians with whale totems and I hate doing research! So I was very annoyed but felt like I should take the assignment I was given.

Well, I'm right on the verge of doing that—and this is again where I find the process very magical—and there's this big article in the *Sun Sentinel* about the Tequesta Indians and how they were whale hunters and the whale was their tribal totem and on and on. It was such a gift! I didn't know there were whales off the coast of Florida! And I certainly didn't know they were important to the local Indians. And the article went on to say that the Tequesta didn't stay here, that most of them left and migrated to Cuba and that some Cubans secretly keep the Indian ways alive.

How perfect was that? Sophie's baby could have a Cuban father who doesn't even know his culture, maybe his parents know it but he doesn't know it and he passes it all on to the baby and she's communicating it to Sophie. And I felt this rush of excitement because this is something that I find so exciting, how a child can be the product of so many cultures coming together.

And I know why that is so exciting to me. All of my relatives on my father's side died young. So I never really had the opportunity to know them. And I always had a feeling, from some pictures of my father and his mother, that there might be an African American ancestor there somewhere. And there were little things for me...things about my medical history, things about my hair...that would sort of bear that out. Well at one point I found a family history that had been written by my great aunt, my grandmother's sister, and it said that their parents operated a flatboat on the Mississippi River . . . I know, you're already seeing scenes from *Showboat,* aren't you? But here was this weird footnote in the family history. It said that there was a black man who worked with my great grandparents, and that he saved my great grandmother from drowning and that he was an important friend of the family. My grandmother was the youngest child, born later than all the rest. She looked very different from her sisters. So all of this made me think, maybe my theory wasn't so crazy after all.

And I realized why I had set up my book the way I had, where the father of Sophie's baby is a mystery and Sophie's mother wants to keep her father's identity a mystery. Because all of us might be the product of who knows what powerful, magical culture and a baby is always a culmination of all these talents and gifts and abilities that might have come from anywhere.

What I've been trying to illustrate with all this is that if you want to connect with kids on the emotional level, you have to write on the emotional level. I wrote some novels when I was younger that came all from the head and they weren't that successful. You have to go into your fears and your fantasies and you have to use your heart and your gut to write a book that kids will respond to, because they know. They always know if you're faking or if you're insincere. So if you don't give them something that is soulful and meaningful for you, it won't resonate for them. That's what I've learned in these 20 years I've been writing—that when I really express myself, that's when I can make the connection.

References

Sweeney, J. (2000). *Players*. New York, NY: Winslow Press.
Sweeney, J. (2003). *Waiting for June*. Tarrytown, NY: Cavendish Children's Books.
Sweeney, J. (2004). *Takedown*. Tarrytown, NY: Marshall Cavendish.

Content Area Literacy: The Spotlight Shifts to Teacher Educators

Donna E. Alvermann

University of Georgia

Keynote Address
College Reading Association
2005

Changing instruction in ways that produce genuine, wide-spread improvements in literacy and comprehension is no simple task for a society. Ideas do not flow effortlessly from teacher to teacher or from research to practice.
> Ronald F. Ferguson
> John F. Kennedy School of Government
> Harvard University, January 2004

Written as part of the foreword to Dorothy Strick-land's and my co-edited book, Bridging the Literacy Achievement Gap, Grades 4-12, *this statement by Ron Ferguson, a Harvard professor who works with school districts to close achievement gaps, signals the complexity of making instructional changes. As teacher educators, we know this in our bones. If pressed, we'll even admit to being part of the problem at times. Challenges to the status quo affect us just as they do the teachers we teach. And that's not to say that we (and they) don't change. It's how that change comes about in the age of new media and informa-*

Reprinted from *Multiple Literacies in the 21st Century,* pp.-14-19, by M. B. Sampson, P. E. Linder, F. Falk-Ross, M. Foote, & S. Szabo, Eds., 2007, Commerce, TX: College Reading Association.

tion communication technologies that interests me here. Specifically, I want to focus on how the literacies of a new generation of youth, sometimes collectively referred to as Digital Natives (Prensky, 2001), work to create openings in one or more of our largely unquestioned teacher education practices. But first, what do I mean by Digital Natives and to which unquestioned practices am I pointing?

Digital Natives

Referring to the youth of today as Digital Natives—that is, 'native speakers' of the digital language of computers, video games, and the Internet,—Prensky (2001) goes on to contrast their several years of practice at parallel processing and multitasking to the rest of us so-called Digital Immigrants, who like all immigrants retain to some degree our "accent," that is, our foot in the past. In Prensky's words,

> the 'digital immigrant accent' can be seen in such things as turning to the Internet for information second rather than first, or in reading the manual for a program rather than assuming that the program itself will teach us to use it (n. p).

The importance of distinguishing between digital natives and digital immigrants for those of us in education, he adds, is this:

> Digital Immigrants don't believe their students can learn successfully while watching TV or listening to music because they (the Immigrants) can't. Of course not—they didn't practice this skill constantly for all of their formative years. Digital Immigrants think learning can't (or shouldn't be) fun. Why should they—they didn't spend their formative years learning with Sesame Street.

> Unfortunately for our Digital Immigrant teacher, the people sitting in their classes grew up on the 'twitch speed' of video games and MTV. They are used to the instantaneity of hypertext, downloaded music, phones in their pockets, a library on their laptops, beamed messages and instant messaging. They have little patience for lectures, step-by-step logic, and 'tell-test' instruction. (n. p.)

From Norton-Meier's (2005) perspective on how she, the mother of two video-game playing adolescents, experiences the different worlds of digital natives and digital immigrants, it is a matter of how information is processed that sets the two apart. Whereas digital immigrants tend to process information methodically, often in a linear fashion, digital natives are given to multitasking and the integration of words, images, and sounds as they make lightning-quick decisions in interactions with others. For digital natives, "Graphics come *before* texts. . . . They play the game first and then read the manual for information or clues to solve the next problem or adventure" (Norton-Meier, p. 430).

Unquestioned Practices

The notion that pictured information might be preferred to printed text when it comes to learning new skills and content would likely come as a surprise to most digital immigrants. In a print-centric world, the practice of expecting students to acquire knowledge primarily from words and only secondarily from visuals such as photographs, charts, and other graphic images is for the most part unquestioned. The superiority of print-based learning is taken for granted, so much so in fact that visual literacy is largely ignored by today's advocates of "scientific" reading instruction.

But print-centric practices are not the only ones to dominate the literacy teacher education scene. Those of us who teach preservice and inservice courses in colleges of education in the United States frequently assume that traditional schooling practices (e.g., attending classes in regularly defined spaces and places for a set number of hours) are preferable to credit-bearing courses built around on-the-job training, long-distance learning, and the like. Although the increasing popularity of online courses, with their flexibility in space, place, and time, would seem to afford college level students more choices in how they learn, the actual content of the courses offered may not vary much from that which would be offered in more traditional settings.

This adherence to the "tried and true" in academic offerings has been described elsewhere as the Institution of Old Learning (IOL)—a tongue-in-cheek term coined by O'Brien and Bauer (2005) to denote the rigidity of certain historically situated practices and organizational structures in U. S. schools. Predating the federally legislated No Child Left Behind Act (2001) and scientific reading instruction by nearly a hundred years, the IOL attempts to fit new information communication technologies into its century-old rigid structures and practices. Unfortunately, while it is easy to critique the IOL in relation to newer literacies and technologies, it is quite another matter to loosen its stranglehold on the mindset of U.S. educators at large.

Using Youth Literacies to Create Openings

Given the Web's capacity for mingling words, images, and sound bytes, as well as a growing trend for digital natives to find their own reasons for taking on certain literate identities—reasons that include but also go beyond reading and writing to acquire school knowledge of academic texts—it is tempting to suggest that youth literacies may very well play a significant role in opening up the Institution of Old Learning (O'Brien & Bauer, 2005). How might this be done, and what would it look like?

First and foremost, an undertaking such as this would necessarily involve teacher educators finding ways to become grounded in young people's perceptions of their literate identities. Recently, Sarah Jonas, Director of Education

Services for The Children's Aid Society in New York, and I decided to do just that. Sarah interviewed Ariel Steele and Eric Washington, two youths who participate regularly in out-of-school time programs at The Children's Aid Society's Dunlevy Milbank Center, nearby where they live in Central Harlem (Alvermann, Jonas, Steele, & Washington, 2006). Piecing together interview transcripts, Sarah and I discovered that a great deal can be learned from carefully listening to young people talk about how they identify with particular reading and writing practices both in- and out-of-school. For example, consider the following things that Ariel and Eric wished their teachers knew about them as readers and writers.

Ariel wished her teachers knew how much she disliked having to wait while others finished reading something in class: "Actually, I just wish, you know, that if a group of people finish a book in class, we shouldn't be penalized to wait for the rest of the group to finish. They [teachers] should allow us to do a report on the book for extra credit or something, or maybe just let us start a new book on our own." To Sarah and me, Ariel's comment is reflective of what Prensky (2001) meant when he observed the following about digital natives:

> They grew up on the 'twitch speed' of video games and MTV. They are used to the instantaneity of hypertext, downloaded music, phones in their pockets, a library on their laptops, beamed messages and instant messaging. They have little patience for lectures, step-by-step logic, and 'tell-test' instruction. (n. p.)

Both Ariel and Eric spoke about the importance of text messaging and instant messaging to their identities as writers. Neither thought their teachers appreciated fully the value of either form of messaging. Ariel said she and her friends text message and IM all the time, even sometimes during school when it is technically not allowed. When asked what young people their age find so appealing about text messaging and IMing, both Ariel and Eric stressed that it's easier, often, than talking. To back up this claim, they said they knew plenty of people their age who strongly dislike writing in school, and never write (pencil to paper) outside of school, but who think nothing of writing entire paragraphs while text messaging. Ariel also described a friend who creates alternate (screen) identities for herself when IMing in chat rooms, which Ariel described as being akin to writing a story. Yet this friend, Ariel explained, would never think of herself as a writer and does not enjoy writing stories in or out of school.

Text messaging as a popular form of writing recently surfaced as one of the major findings in a study I am presently analyzing that involves struggling middle school readers. Repeatedly, I hear the same refrain: "It's easier than talking." When asked what is meant by "easier than talking," a typical answer involves something along these lines: "you can think about what you say and change your mind before blurting it out." One young man stated that text messaging helped him to feel better about himself because he didn't have to risk looking at a person's face if he had unintentionally insulted that person. Another said that he didn't want his friends to know how much their kidding bothered him—and that they wouldn't know this if they didn't have a chance to see his face or hear his voice. Although it's difficult to say what is behind different youths' motivations for text messaging and IMing, one thing seems clear—writing about one's ideas and feelings carries less risk than expressing them orally. The implications of this for content area teachers bent on holding class discussions are worth exploring.

Under the Spotlight's Glare

Although these examples are but a few of the many that I could have called on to illustrate my point about the importance of staying grounded in young people's literacies, they represent what I see as a first step toward creating openings in the Institution of Old Learning. As teacher educators, we will do well to remember that while operating at "twitch speed" may be well nigh impossible for digital immigrants, it is still the case that the digital natives in our classes (and in the classes that our students teach) will be every bit as anxious as Ariel for some kind of individualized assignment that will let them escape the lockstep nature of traditional instruction.

It is also the case that we would do well as teacher educators to remind the preservice and inservice students in our content area classes of the importance of taking seriously what young people can tell us about text messaging and IMing. Speed of communication aside, these two forms of writing would seem to afford certain students—especially those whose self-efficacy may not be as high as others in their peer group—a sense of security and accomplishment. And this is not simply the perception of a few students whom I interviewed. For in a recent review of the experimental and quasi-experimental research on classroom-based literacy interventions taught by content area teachers in classes they were regularly assigned to teach, my co-authors and I (Alvermann, Fitzgerald, & Simpson, 2006) found that there is research to support teachers capitalizing on young people's interests in socializing with their peers by building into the school day opportunities for collaborative reading and writing activities. Such activities are thought to foster engagement by helping students make connections between literacies they value outside of school and those they are expected to apply in their content area classes.

Of course, the use to which this information is put will depend to a large degree on the reception it receives in teacher education circles. If we turn our backs on ideas that seem too far outside the Institution of Old Learning—especially ideas that challenge the status quo—then we end up with a pedagogy that is one-sided where teaching in relation to learning is viewed as causative rather than contextual. Nearly a decade ago, Green (1998) warned our field against just such a move for the following reasons:

On the one hand, an important shift is underway from canonic forms and orders of knowledge, culture and textuality to what can be called the realm of the techno-popular. In terms of English teaching, this means shifting from literature to media, and hence from literary culture to popular culture as the focus for curriculum practice.... On the other hand, new and different formations of subjectivity are arguably emerging among young people ... as they are characteristically immersed in new intensities of media culture, the flow of images and information, and their associated forms of life.... Taken together, these aspects of difference represent significant challenges for educational theory and practice. (p. 180)

In a nutshell, then, where are we, and more importantly, where are we going? Is it feasible to think that young people and their literacies might serve as guides of one kind or another on our quest to update our instructional practices? As teacher educators, are we willing to entertain the possibility that the students in our classrooms may one day decide that transforming the Institution of Old Learning is insiders' work—that they can do it without us? And, as a closing thought, just who is us?

References

Alvermann, D. E., Fitzgerald, J., & Simpson, M. S. (2006). Teaching and learning in reading. In P. Alexander & P. Winne (Eds.), *Handbook of educational psychology* (2nd ed., pp. 427-455). Mahwah, NJ: Lawrence Erlbaum Associates.

Alvermann, D. E., Jonas, S., Steele, A., & Washington, E. (2006). Introduction. In D. E. Alvermann, K. A. Hinchman, D. W. Moore, S. F. Phelps, & D. R. Waff (Eds.), *Reconceptualizing the literacies in adolescents' lives* (2nd ed., pp. xxi-xxxii). Mahwah, NJ: Lawrence Erlbaum Associates.

Ferguson, R. F. (2004). Foreword. In D. S. Strickland & D. E. Alvermann (Eds.), *Bridging the literacy achievement gap, grades 4-12* (pp. vii-viii). New York: Teachers College Press.

Green, B. (1998). Teaching for difference: Learning theory and post-critical pedagogy. In D. Buckingham (Ed.), *Teaching popular culture: Beyond radical pedagogy* (pp. 177-197). London: UCL Press.

No Child Left Behind Act of 2001. PL 107-110, 115 Stat.1425, 20 U.S.C. 6301 *et. seq...*

Norton-Meier, L. (2005). Joining the video-game literacy club: A reluctant mother tries to join the "flow." *Journal of Adolescent & Adult Literacy, 48*, 428-432.

O'Brien, D. G., & Bauer, E. B. (2005). New literacies and the institution of old learning. *Reading Research Quarterly, 40*, 120-131.

Prensky, M. (2001). Digital natives, digital immigrants. *On the Horizon, 9* (5). Retrieved November 1, 2005 from http://www.marcprensky.com/writing/default.asp

Thinking About Our Future as Researchers: New Literacies, New Challenges, and New Opportunities

The New Literacies Research Team

Jill Castek   Julie Coiro

Douglas K. Hartman   Laurie A. Henry

Donald J. Leu   Lisa Zawilinski

University of Connecticut

Keynote Address
College Reading Association
2005

A perfect storm is taking shape in reading research and instruction. This storm is not over the horizon, it is not even on the horizon. Instead, as new technologies transform the nature of literacy, it confronts us on a daily basis, impacting every student, every teacher, every teacher education program, every assessment instrument, and every state's reading standards. Ironically, most of us are not aware of the storm that rages around us as new technologies redefine what it means to be literate in the 21st century.

Why has this storm appeared now? Events have conspired to simultaneously bring together three challenges that we must recognize and begin to address. Each profoundly impacts our ability to prepare students for the reading and writing demands that will define their future.

Today, we would like to outline those challenges. Then, we will explore several opportunities that can help us to weather this storm, should we take advantage of them. Finally, we will outline steps that we might take together to advance our research field in order to better serve the literacy needs of teachers, students, parents, and our increasingly global community.

Reprinted from *Multiple Literacies in the 21st Century,* pp.-31-50, by M. B. Sampson, P. E. Linder, F. Falk-Ross, M. Foote, & S. Szabo, Eds., 2007, Commerce, TX: College Reading Association.

In a world in which the Internet has become this generation's defining technology for literacy and learning, we will require bold new thinking to re-conceptualize our field. We hope to initiate that process.

Three Challenges that Confront Reading Research

The Challenge of Capacity

The National Research Council (1999, 2000, 2002) has recently concluded that a century of educational research has yet to produce an adequate research base to systematically, cogently, and consistently inform instruction, public policy, teacher education, and assessment in our nation. The lack of a research base is driven by the lack of adequately trained young researchers. Our graduate programs have not yet produced sufficient numbers of doctorates in education who have been adequately trained to make research and development their primary activity in the academy (National Occupational Research Center, 2004). According to survey data collected by the National Opinion Research Center, only seven percent of doctorates in education list research and development as their primary postdoctoral activity (Hoffer, et al., 2004).

The capacity challenge we see in education, generally, appears even more profoundly within the specific area of reading research, the area in education which many might suggest has the longest and richest historical tradition of research (Chall, 1965; Gates, 1921; Gray, 1984; Huey, 1908; E.L. Thorndike, 1917; R. L. Thorndike, 1973-74). One has only to observe the firestorm that recently erupted around the report of the National Reading Panel (National Institute of Child Health and Human Development [NICHD], 2000) to suggest that our research base in reading is not yet adequate to consistently inform instruction.

As in the general field of education, the lack of an adequate research base specifically in reading education is driven by the lack of adequately trained young researchers. Despite its central role, reading research produces relatively few doctorates and channels the fewest number of those who complete the doctorate into research and development activities (National Occupational Research Center, 2004). As a result, we face a shortage of new colleagues entering our research ranks.

In the 2003-2004 academic year, for instance, there were 645 university faculty positions advertised in the U.S. that required expertise in the conduct of reading research as a job requirement, but only 84 doctorates were awarded that year with a reading research focus (Hartman, 2004). The pattern in preceding and subsequent years has been similar: the U.S. has a critical shortage of highly qualified reading researchers.

Today, intense global economic competition (Friedman, 2005) makes learning to read and use information sources more important to success than ever before, yet we have an inadequate research base on which to make public policy decisions and a desperate shortage of new doctoral students to remedy the situation. Our research capacity is woefully inadequate, just at the time when we require it the most.

The Challenge of Change

The challenge of capacity is complicated by the challenge of change. New technologies for information and communication regularly redefine what it means to be literate. Despite increasing recognition that the Internet will be central to our lives in the 21st century (Hartman, 2000; Partnership for 21st Century Skills, 2003), we have hardly any research into the nature of online reading comprehension and communication. Indeed, despite both informed speculation (Coiro, 2003; Henry, 2005; RAND Reading Study Group [RRSG], 2002; International Reading Association [IRA], 2002) and evidence to the contrary, (Coiro & Dobler, in press; Coiro, 2007; Henry, 2006; Leu, Castek, Hartman, Coiro, Henry, Kulikowich, & Lyver, 2005), our field often assumes that online reading comprehension is isomorphic with offline reading comprehension (Leu, Zawilinski, Castek, Banerjee, Housland, Liu, & O'Neil, in press). Most importantly, we seldom prepare new scholars to study the new dimensions of reading that take place online.

Why should this be an important area of research? Put simply, the nature of reading comprehension has changed and we have little research to direct either our instruction or our understanding of this area. The RAND Reading Study Group (2002) has summarized the issue:

> … accessing the Internet makes large demands on individuals' literacy skills; in some cases, this new technology requires readers to have novel literacy skills, and little is known about how to analyze or teach those skills. (p. 4)

The issue is not unimportant. More than one billion individuals have Internet access (de Argaez, 2006; Internet World Stats: Usage and Population Statistics, n.d.). One-sixth of the world's population is now reading and writing online, redefining what it means to be literate in an online world.

These Internet readers construct meaning from their reading experiences on the Internet in ways that differ from how reading takes place within the pages of a book; additional skills and strategies are required (Leu, Zawilinski, Castek, Banerjee, Housland, Liu, & O'Neil, in press). We know little about these differences but, if you have any doubt that online reading differs from offline reading, simply view the videos we have placed on the Internet of three different readers reading on the Internet. These are available at: http://www.newliteracies.uconn. edu/reading.html. The online videos illustrate the new strategies readers require as they make choices about where to go and what to believe, constructing meaning during online reading.

We can see the changes talking place in reading reflected in data on Internet use within school settings, homes, and the workplace:

- In 1994, only 3% of all K-12 classrooms in the U.S. had Internet access; today 93% do (Parsad, Jones, & Greene, 2005).

- In 2004, nearly 75% of all households in the U.S. had Internet access (Neilson/Net Ratings, 2004).
- Eighty-seven percent of all students between the ages of 12 and 17 in the U.S. report using the Internet; nearly 11,000,000 do so daily (Pew Internet and American Life Project, 2005).
- More than 90% of students between the ages of 12 and 17, with home access to the Internet, report using the Internet for homework and over 70% used the Internet as the primary source for information on their most recent school report or project (Pew Internet & American Life Project, 2001).
- In 2005, 93% of workers in the U.S. in companies with more than 100 employees reported using the Internet and other online information resources in the workplace (Harris Interactive Inc., 2005).

It is clear that the Internet has become a vital new dimension of reading (International Reading Association, 2002; Lebo, 2003; Parsad, Jones, & Green, 2005; U. S. Department of Commerce, 2002).

Despite this recognition, there is relatively little understanding of, or consensus about, how reading comprehension instruction should be conceptualized or conducted in relation to online information (Coiro, 2003; RRSG, 2002). As a result, little instruction in the new demands of online reading comprehension takes place in schools (Karchmer, 2001; Leu, 2006). This shortcoming is due in large measure to two related observations: (a) we know little about the new reading comprehension skills and strategies that are required on the Internet (International Reading Association, 2002; RRSG, 2002) and (b) there is little research on instructional methods dedicated specifically to enhancing comprehension of informational texts on the Internet (Coiro, 2005).

While we are beginning to establish a research base in the reading of traditional texts (NICHD, 2000; Biancarosa & Snow, 2004), there is hardly any research, yet, on the nature of reading comprehension and learning on the Internet and with other information and communication technologies (ICTs). While we have few, new, reading researchers graduating each year with doctorates who seek careers that focus on research and development, we have even fewer researchers prepared to investigate how to best integrate the new reading skills required on the Internet into classroom instruction, assessments, or public policies (Coiro, 2003; Leu, 2006; Leu, Kinzer, Coiro, & Cammack, 2004; Partnership for 21st Century Skills, 2003).

That failure has important consequences for education in the twenty-first century because academic achievement is dependent on the ability to read, comprehend at high levels (Alexander & Jetton, 2002; Bransford, Brown, & Cocking, 2000), and solve problems (Dochy, Segers, Van den Bossche, & Gijbels, 2003) as the Internet is an increasingly important source of information (Lyman & Varian, 2003). Most importantly, students with limited reading comprehension skills struggle with learning in school and are more likely to drop out (Finn, 1989, 1993; Wylie & Hunter, 1994) thus limiting their ability to fully seize life's opportunities for themselves and limiting their contributions to society (Thompson, Mixon, & Serpell, 1996). That challenge may increase as reading on the Internet becomes increasingly important and if we continue to fail to support students with online reading.

There can be little doubt that the Internet has rapidly become an important part of our daily lives (Lebo, 2003; Leu, Kinzer, Coiro, & Cammack, 2004; U.S. Department of Commerce, 2002). Reading on the Internet appears to require new skills and strategies, yet we know far too little about them. We believe that we must begin to confront the challenge of change with an intensive research agenda to study online reading comprehension.

The Challenge of Those Who Need Our Help the Most

The challenge of capacity and the challenge of change are important elements of the storm that has hit our shore. The greatest challenge of all, however, may be the challenge of those who require the most support with online comprehension in schools because they have access to the Internet at home the least.

In an age of No Child Left Behind (No Child Left Behind Act of 2001, 2002) and increased attention to reading, our assessments of reading achievement in the U.S. have not kept up with the reading skills required by the Internet. Not a single state reading assessment required by No Child Left Behind measures students' ability to read search engine results; not a single state measures students' ability to read online to locate information; not a single state measures student's ability to critically evaluate information on the internet; not a single state measures students' ability to synthesize information online from disparate sources; and not a single state allows all students to use a word processor for their state writing assessment (Coiro, 2005; Leu, 2006; Leu, Ataya, & Coiro, 2002).

The compounded result is that few students are being supported in developing the new literacies of online reading comprehension in school classrooms (Karchmer, 2001; Leu, 2006). The problem is greatest in our poorest school districts, the ones under the greatest pressure to raise reading test scores on assessments that have nothing to do with the Internet.

Because of traditionally low patterns of reading performance, poor urban and rural school districts face enormous pressure to achieve adequate yearly progress on print-based reading skills required by No Child Left Behind legislation (No Child Left Behind Act of 2001, 2002). As a result, schools most at risk must focus complete attention on the instruction of more traditional reading experiences, abandoning any instruction in the skills required for reading online: asking essential questions, searching for online information, critically evaluating online information, synthesizing online information, or communicating online. *It is the cruelest irony of No Child Left Behind that students who need to be prepared the most at school for an online age of information, are precisely those who are being prepared the least.*

This challenge is not inconsiderable. Eight million U.S. adolescents are considered illiterate (Biancarosa & Snow, 2004). Almost a third of adolescents cannot read at basic levels (National Center for Educational Statistics, [NCES], 2003). Moreover, nearly twice the number of white, economically advantaged students perform above the basic level as their economically disadvantaged peers, those with the least Internet access at home. Moreover, this gap is increasing over time (NCES, 2003).

With the new reading skills that the Internet requires, the reading achievement gap will only get larger as online reading experiences become more central to our literacy worlds. In the end, we appear to spend, know, and do little to help readers most at risk of dropping out of school, those in poor urban and rural school districts. Most importantly, we have not yet prepared a generation of highly trained researchers to focus their attention primarily on pursuing studies required to inform classroom reading instruction in ways that prepare our most economically challenged students to read and learn effectively in an age of global communication and online information.

New Opportunities

It is ironic that the U.S., arguably the nation with the most advanced Internet infrastructure, is far behind other nations with integrating the new reading skills required on the Internet into classroom instruction, public policies, or assessment (Leu, 2006; Leu & Kinzer, 2000). New Internet technologies have leveled the playing field for economic competition among nations in ways not previously possible. Countries like Ireland, China, Finland, Japan, Canada, Australia, India, The Republic of Korea, and others understand this and are much farther along than the U.S. in establishing public policies to prepare their students for the new reading and writing demands of the twenty-first century (Bleha, 2005; Friedman, 2005). Their students are being prepared for the reading comprehension demands of workplaces in a globalized, information economy, often more thoroughly than we have considered preparing students in our own nation (Leu, 2006).

Despite the leveling of the global arena, itself presenting us with additional challenges to consider in the U.S., we see some opportunities in the current state of research in our field.

The Emergence of New Theoretical Perspectives

One opportunity we have consists of growing work in the development of better theories that will help us to better understand the questions we should ask. A number of different research communities have begun to explore the changes that new technologies, and the social practices they engender, bring to literacy. Scholars from disciplines such as cultural anthropology (Markham, 1998; Street, 2003; Thomas, forthcoming), sociolinguistics (Cope & Kalantzis,

2003; Gee, 2003; Kress, 2003; Lemke, 1998), cognitive science (Mayer, 2001), and information science (Bilal, 2000; Hirsch, 1999) have identified changes to literacy as they study the consequences for their individual areas of study. These fields are developing new ways of looking at the problem. As this takes place, a new perspective about the nature of literacy is beginning to emerge. This perspective, often referred to as "new literacies," is still in its initial stages but it is clear to most that it will be a powerful one, redefining what it means to be literate in the 21st century (Lankshear & Knobel, 2003; Leu, Kinzer, Coiro, & Cammack, 2004).

"New literacies" is highly contested space however; the construct means many different things to many different people. To some, new literacies are seen as new social practices (Street, 1995; 2003) that emerge with new technologies. Some see new literacies as important new strategies and dispositions required by the Internet that are essential for online reading comprehension, learning, and communication (Coiro, 2003; Leu, Kinzer, Coiro, & Cammack, 2004). Others see new literacies as new Discourses (Gee, 2003) or new semiotic contexts (Kress, 2003; Lemke, 2002) made possible by new technologies. Still others see literacy as differentiating into multiliteracies (The New London Group, 2000) or multimodal contexts (Hull & Schultz, 2002) and some see a construct that juxtaposes several of these orientations (Lankshear & Knobel, 2003). When you combine these uses of "new literacies" with terms such as ICT Literacy (International ICT Literacy Panel, 2002) and informational literacy (Hirsch, 1999; Kuiper & Volman, in press; Webber & Johnson, 2000), the construct becomes even more challenging to understand. However, most would agree there are at least four defining characteristics of an emerging new literacies perspective.

First, new technologies for information and communication and new envisionments for their use require us to bring new potentials to literacy tasks that take place within these technologies. While they may differ on the construct they use, each set of scholars would probably agree that the Internet and other new ICTs require new skills, strategies, and dispositions for their effective use.

Second, new literacies are central to full civic, economic, and personal participation in a globalized community. As a result, they become important to study so that we might provide a more appropriate education for all of our students.

Third, new literacies are deictic (Leu, 2000); they regularly change as defining technologies change. The new literacies of the Internet and other ICTs are not just new today, they will be newer tomorrow, even newer next week, and continuously renewed on a schedule that is limited only by our capacity to keep up. Of course, literacy has always changed as technologies for literacy have changed (Manguel, 1996). What is historically distinctive is that by definition, the Internet permits the immediate, nearly universal, exchange of new technologies for literacy. With a single click, a new technology such as Wikipedia can be distributed to everyone who is online.

Finally, new literacies are multiple, multimodal, and multifaceted (Kress, 2003; Lemke, 1998). Thus, they increase the complexity of any analysis that seeks to understand them and will benefit from analysis that brings multiple points of view to understand them (Labbo & Reinking, 1999). It may also suggest that the area is best studied in interdisciplinary teams as questions become far too complex for the traditional single investigator model (Coiro, Knobel, Lankshear, & Leu, in press).

We are using this emerging notion of new literacies as we conduct work on the nature of the new literacies of online reading comprehension, especially in classroom contexts for learning. To guide our work, we have been using this theoretical definition:

> The new literacies of the Internet and other ICT include the skills, strategies, and dispositions necessary to successfully use and adapt to the rapidly changing information and communication technologies and contexts that continuously emerge in our world and influence all areas of our personal and professional lives. These new literacies allow us to use the Internet and other ICT to identify important questions, locate information, analyze the usefulness of that information, synthesize information to answer those questions, and then communicate the answers to others. (Leu, Kinzer, Coiro, & Cammack, 2004, p. 1570)

Within this perspective, new literacies of online reading comprehension are defined around five major functions: (a) identifying important questions, (b) locating information, (c) analyzing information, (d) synthesizing information, and (e) communicating information. These five functions contain the skills, strategies and dispositions that are both transformed by online reading comprehension while, at the same time, appear to somewhat overlap with offline reading comprehension. What is different from earlier models is that online reading comprehension is defined around the purpose, task, and context as well as the process that takes place in the mind of a reader. Readers read to find out answers to questions on the Internet. Any model of online reading comprehension must begin with this simple observation.

Initial studies, now beginning to emerge, are beginning to define a rich and complex picture of online reading comprehension. One study, among highly proficient sixth grade students (Coiro & Dobler, in press), found that online reading comprehension shared a number of similarities with offline reading comprehension but that online reading comprehension also included a number of important differences. A second study (Leu, et. al, 2005), found no significant correlation, among seventh grade students, between performance on a measure of offline reading comprehension and a measure of online reading comprehension (ORCA-Blog) with good psychometric properties. These results also suggest that new skills and strategies may be required during online reading. A third study (Coiro, 2007), using a regression model, found that while offline reading comprehension and prior knowledge contributed a significant amount of variance to the prediction of online reading comprehension, additional, significant variance was contributed by various aspects of students' online reading comprehension ability. The results of this study are also consistent with the belief that new skills and strategies are required during online reading comprehension.

Additional research is taking place on several, federally funded research grants in the U.S. One of these, the Teaching Internet Comprehension to Adolescents (TICA) Project (Leu & Reinking, 2005), explores the skills and strategies that proficient online readers at the seventh grade level report during online reading comprehension. The project website is available at: http://www.newliteracies. uconn.edu/iesproject/. Another, funded by the Carnegie Corporation (Hartman, Leu, Olson, & Truxaw, 2005), studies how best to integrate the new literacies of online reading comprehension and learning into the preparation of new secondary teachers in math, science, and English education. This project website is available at: http://www.newliteracies. uconn.edu/carnegie/index.html. Initiative like these, and others, are likely to provide a clearer picture of how online reading comprehension differs from offline reading comprehension.

New Definitions of Doctoral Preparation

We have been discovering a second promising opportunity in a somewhat new approach to doctoral preparation. Centered in the New Literacies Research Lab at the University of Connecticut is the New Literacies Research Team. This is a continually evolving consortium of professors, graduate researchers, school districts, organizations, policy makers, teachers, and school leaders who seek to prepare students for the new learning and literacy skills required by the Internet and other information and communication technologies. We engage in systematic study to define what students need to learn to use the Internet effectively for literacy and learning. We also study how best to assess and teach these new skills. What defines us is our extraordinary collaborative approach, our high standards, and our commitment to K-12 schools.

To be admitted, doctoral students must have previously taught in K-12 classrooms and must publish, or have a peer-reviewed article accepted in an important educational journal during their first year of doctoral study. We work as colleagues, recognizing the valuable insights that each person brings to the inquiry process. Professors, graduate researchers, teachers, school leaders, and others work shoulder-to-shoulder, equally contributing to the inquiry process and respecting one another as colleagues. Our team currently includes eight doctoral students, four professors, three undergraduates, one project coordinator, five urban school districts in Connecticut, and an extended set of partner organizations, policy makers, teachers, and school leaders who seek to prepare students for the new learning and literacy skills required by information and communication technologies such as the Internet.

The results of our highly collaborative style and high standards for one another has been extraordinary. In the last two years, our three advanced doctoral students have authored one book, twenty-one peer-reviewed articles or book chapters, delivered nineteen invited addresses and forty-eight conference papers, and provided thirty days of professional development to schools, universities, and states departments of education around the nation. They have been invited to institutes at the Universities of Oxford (UK) and Berkeley, served as reviewers on major journals and conferences, and held positions on major committees in reading research organizations. Moreover, during these two years, they have secured nearly $100,000 in research grants and their work has contributed to securing nearly $2,000,000 more. The effects of establishing very high standards, supporting students in reaching them, and working within a collaborative, empowerment model has been stunning. We believe our experience holds great promise as we consider how to better prepare the next generation of researchers that we require.

The Potential of Collaborative Effort
Within Our Larger Research Community

We suspect that the lessons we have learned about collaboration may point to an opportunity today for our larger research community to improve the collective impact of our work. It seems to us that the problems within the study of online reading comprehension and literacy, in a broader sense, are far too complex for any single investigator to fully understand or effectively study. Instead, it has become very clear to us that the study of the more complex issues we face in the study of online reading, writing, and communication demands teams that bring multiple perspectives (Labbo & Reinking, 1999) to the investigation. We believe that we will see increasing numbers of collaborative teams form to study the complicated nature of literacy in an online world that continuously changes as new technologies repeatedly emerge, requiring even newer literacies to fully take advantage of their potential for reading, writing, and communication.

The online tools that have been emerging recently such as blogs, wikis, and other social network tools, as well as the even newer ones that are yet to come, may permit us to bring our collective insights, from many different points of view, to the study of these critical issues. Of course, these new tools will also require each of us to acquire new literacies so that we might benefit from such an online, collaborative approach. We believe that greater collaboration that takes place online will be required if we hope to provide direction to schools and teachers during an age in which the very nature of reading continually changes.

Moving Forward: An Action Plan

We are convinced that we are in the midst of a perfect storm, driven by a constellation of forces that have come together to present our field with a series of important challenges. The most consequential aspect of this convergence is that, at a time when public policy appears to be focused on supporting our most challenged readers, it is actually preventing those readers from being prepared for their reading future. Students in our most economically challenged schools should be receiving the most instruction in the new literacies of online reading comprehension since they often have little opportunity to acquire these at home. Instead, the pressure to achieve Adequate Yearly Progress (No Child Left Behind Act of 2001, 2002) on assessment instruments that have nothing to do with online reading comprehension pressures teachers into abandoning instruction in how to read and comprehend information on the Internet.

What steps might we take within our research community to improve opportunities for all of our students? We believe that a way out of our situation may be found in some of the steps that follow.

Preparing More, And Better Trained, Doctoral Students

Recent statistics reflect the lack of doctorates in reading research who seek careers in research (Hartman, 2004). Our searches for new assistant professors force all of us to live this reality each year. Advertisements for new positions have appeared earlier and earlier until this year when we saw our first search advertised before the fall semester even began. There is intense competition for the very few, highly-trained, doctoral students who seek a career in university research. And, within this group there are even fewer who have been adequately prepared for both quantitative as well as qualitative research methods, something that will be increasingly required if we expect to raise the level of our doctoral preparation programs. Our field would benefit from having higher standards and far greater financial support to recruit the finest young educators into a life of research at a university. This is likely to require financial support that exceeds the limited resources available within universities, schools, and departments. Currently, this often comes from federally funded research grants. It may need to come in the form of a federal initiative to support doctoral students if we are serious about preparing, to a very high level, a new generation of literacy researchers.

Mentor Doctoral Students Within Collaborative Research Teams

If we acknowledge that research questions are now so complex that they can best be studied within collaborative research teams, then we must prepare doctoral students for these types of scholarly collaborations. It would be incongruous to prepare them for a world in which there is increasing collaboration with programs still based on the single investigator model. Doctoral programs need to be viewed as a rich collaborative effort, with scholarship taking place collaboratively, often with multiple major advisors and multiple students in place of a single advisor working closely with a single student.

Take Advantage of Online Social Networking Tools to Strengthen Our Research Community

To attack the most pressing and complex research questions that we face will require greater collaborative efforts within our research community. To advance this agenda, we will need to take greater advantage of social networking and communication tools that exist online and new ones as they appear. This will require each of us to become more proficient with the new literacies that we study. This may seem complex and challenging to those of us unfamiliar with the new literacies of online communication.

The nature of the problem may be seen in the examples of good colleagues who regularly post email replies to individuals on listservs, flooding hundreds of inboxes with personal messages. Simple mistakes like this cost time, especially when listservs have large numbers of subscribers.

Those who advance beyond email and listserv technologies to other forms of social networking tools may be rewarded with the potential to increase the significance of the issues that they study and to learn from colleagues who bring new insights to the collective work. They will bring new meaning to the ancient aphorism, "Many hands make light work."

Such a development, of course, will require universities, traditionally based on the single investigator model, to change their reward system away from favoring only single-authored publications to those, such as this article, that results from joint, collaborative contributions.

Study Online Reading, Writing, and Communication in School Settings

We have gained greatly from important work on students' use of new technologies for literacy in out-of-school settings (e.g. Alvermann, 2002; Chandler-Olcott & Mahar, 2003). We now require an intensive agenda on how best to support students with the new literacies of the Internet within school settings. We need to know how best to organize instruction in these new literacies so that those who do not have access to important new ICTs outside of school receive the best possible instruction within school on their effective use. We have far more research on out-of-school use of new literacies and far less on in-school use. We need to reverse that situation, mindful of the knowledge that we have already acquired from out-of-school contexts.

Recognize the Issue As Systemic

If we seek to fully integrate the new literacies of the Internet and other ICTs into the classroom, we must begin to understand that the problem will not be solved simply with research. Research will be important, but the challenge we face, like every aspect of school change, is systemic. Since change does not take place in schools without school leaders with the vision and capacity to lead, we must help school administrators to understand the nature of the issue and the solutions we have found. It will also require fundamental change in state standards, so that new literacies appear within the set of reading and content area standards, not in newly emerging technology standards. It is far too easy for teachers to see technology standards as the responsibility of others, something that happens once a week, down the hall, in a computer lab. Defining the problem as a reading issue will ensure that all teachers see it as part of their responsibility. It will also require these new literacies appear as a central component of our teacher education programs in reading and literacy. Finally, it will require new curricular materials to support teachers' instruction in the classroom. All levels of the educational system must adjust to the new realities of new literacies required to use the Internet and other ICTs effectively.

Focus Considerable Research Effort on Changing Both the Content and the Nature of Assessment

A critically important aspect of the systemic change we require consists of changes in our assessment instruments. None of the skills of online reading comprehension are currently assessed by state reading tests (Leu, Ataya, & Coiro, 2002). Teachers and school leaders will have a hard time teaching online reading comprehension skills and strategies unless the effects of that instruction will be recognized by assessments that measure growth and diagnose needs. Some initial models are appearing in measures (See, for example, Educational Testing Services, 2005). We require much more, however, as well as assessments that evaluate students' ability to read in the unbounded context that the Internet is, not artificial contexts intended to partially replicate the Internet.

Invest in Professional Development

Another critically important aspect of the systemic change we have to negotiate will be the important professional development that must take place in every school. Teachers will have to become newly literate with new ICTs if we expect them to pass these along to their students. They will also benefit from an understanding of new instructional models that take full advantage of the Internet such as Internet Workshop (Leu, 2002), Internet Project (Leu, Leu, & Coiro, 2004), inquiry models (Eagleton, Guinnee, & Langlais, 2003; Milson & Downey, 2001), and Internet Reciprocal Teaching (Leu & Reinking, 2005). Acquiring new literacies and learning how to integrate them into the classroom will take considerable time and resources. Schools must be prepared to invest in both.

Understand that New Literacies are Both Multiple and Deictic

Forward movement will also require us to recognize that new literacies do not replace traditional literacies; they transform them, creating new, multiple forms of literacy that must be acquired. Moreover, we will need to also recognize that these new literacies are deictic (Leu, 2000), they continually change as even newer technologies appear, requiring even newer literacies for their effective use.

The Internet ensures that any new technology for information and communication will rapidly spread. This creates an important challenge: How does one keep up with all the new literacies that continually emerge? The answer to this question is not yet clear. It may be that students will increasingly need to be prepared to learn how to learn continuously changing literacies from continuously changing technologies, rather than to simply master a fixed set of literacies. Learning how to learn may generalize far better to a landscape of continuous change in technologies and the literacies they require to effectively use them.

Take a Calculated Risk

What we see as necessary will not be easy to accomplish. It requires new ways of thinking, new ways of working, and new ways of teaching. As we have seen, it also requires extraordinary effort from all of us. Most importantly, it will require a calculated risk from you; we need each of you to bring your expertise to the study of online literacy. It will not be possible if the only ones who make the effort are a small handful of scholars who look at literacy and technology issues. These changes involve all of us. Regardless of what you study in your own work, we require your expertise to help define the future.

The Future of Reading Research Will Be Defined by the Choices We Make Today

Some might argue that the changes we have outlined in this paper run great risks. We would argue, however, that not making the changes creates far greater risk. If we do not change, literacy researchers will become increasingly marginalized during the important public policy debates that lie ahead, losing the opportunity to influence events that will take place in school classrooms. Others, outside the literacy research community, will fill the vacuum and define online reading, writing, and communication for us and without us. Research communities in assessment (International ICT Panel, 2002), library and media studies (American Association of School Librarians & Association for Educational Communications and Technology, 1998), educational technology (International Society for Technology in Education, n.d.), and learning research communities (Partnership for 21st Century Skills, 2003) are already beginning to do so. If this trend continues, we will be left alone to study reading issues defined by our past, not our future and, once again, the reading research community will be left out of important public policy decisions that affect classrooms, teachers, and students.

Authors' Note

[1]The New Literacies Research Team is a continually evolving consortium of professors, graduate researchers, school districts, organizations, policy makers, teachers, and school leaders who seek to prepare students for the new learning and literacy skills required by the Internet and other information and communication technologies. We engage in systematic study to define what students need to learn to use the Internet effectively for literacy and learning. We also study how best to assess and teach these new skills. What defines us is our extraordinary collaborative approach, our high standards, and our commitment to K-12 schools. Jill Castek and Laurie Henry are currently doctoral candidates in Educational Psychology; Julie Coiro is Assistant Research Professor in Education; Douglas K. Hartman is Professor of Education; Donald J. Leu is the John and Maria Neag Chair of Literacy and Technology; and Lisa Zawilinski is a doctoral student in Curriculum and Instruction.

[2]Portions of this material are based upon work supported by the Institute for Education Sciences and the U.S. Department of Education under Award No. R305G050154, the North Central Regional Educational Lab/Learning Point Associates, and the Carnegie Corporation. Opinions expressed herein are solely those of the author and do not necessarily represent the position of either the U.S. Department of Education, the North Central Regional Educational Lab, or the Carnegie Corporation.

References

Alexander, P. A., & Jetton, T. L. (2002). Learning from text: A multidimensional and developmental perspective. In M.L. Kamil, P. Mosenthal, P.D. Pearson, & R.Barr (Eds.). *Handbook of reading research, (Vol. 3)* (pp. 285-310). Mahwah, NJ: Erlbaum.

Alvermann, D. E. (Ed.). (2002). *Adolescents and literacies in a digital world.* New York: Peter Lang.

American Association of School Librarians and Association for Educational Communications and Technology. (1998). *Information power: Building partnerships for learning.* Chicago: American Library Association.

Biancarosa, G., & Snow, C. (2004). *Reading next: A vision for action and research in middle and high school literacy, A report to the Carnegie Corporation of New York.* Retrieved November 2, 2004 from http://www.all4ed.org/publications/ReadingNext/

Bilal, D. (2000). Children's use of the Yahooligans! Web search engine: Cognitive, physical, and affective behaviors on fact-based search tasks. *Journal of the American Society for Information Science, 51,* 646-665.

Bleha, T. (May, June, 2005). Down to the wire. *Foreign Affairs.* Retrieved December 15, 2005, from http://www.foreignaffairs.org/20050501faessay84311/thomas-bleha/down-to-the-wire.html

Bransford, J. D., Brown, A. L., & Cocking, R. R. (2000). *How people learn: Brain, mind, experience, and school* (expanded edition). Washington, DC: National Academy Press.

Chall, J. S. (1965). *Learning to read: The great debate.* New York: McGraw-Hill.

Chandler-Olcott, K., & Mahar, D. (2003). "Tech-savviness" meets multiliteracies: Exploring adolescent girls' technology-mediated literacy practices. *Reading Research Quarterly, 38,* 356-385.

Coiro, J. (2003). Reading comprehension on the Internet: Expanding our understanding of reading comprehension to encompass new literacies. *The Reading Teacher, 56*(6). Retrieved November 11, 2005 from http://www.readingonline.org/electronic/rt/2-03_column/index.html

Coiro, J. (2005). Making sense of online text. *Educational Leadership, 63*(2), 30-35

Coiro, J. L. (2007). *Exploring changes to reading comprehension on the Internet: Paradoxes and possibilities for diverse adolescent readers.* Doctoral dissertation. The University of Connecticut.

Coiro, J., & Dobler, E. (in press). Exploring the online reading comprehension strategies used by sixth-grade skilled readers to search for and locate information on the Internet. *Reading Research Quarterly.*

Coiro, J., Knobel, M., Lankshear, C., & Leu, D. J. (in press). *The handbook of research in new literacies.* Mahwah, NJ: Lawrence Erlbaum Associates.

Cope, B., & Kalantzis, M. (2003). *Text-made text.* Melbourne, AU: Common Ground.

de Argaez, E. (January, 2006). *Internet world stats news, 14.* Retrieved February 1, 2006 from http://www.internetworldstats.com/pr/edi014.htm#3.

Dochy, F., Segers, M., Van den Bossche, P., & Gijbels, D. (2003). Effects of problem-based learning: A meta-analysis. *Learning and Instruction, 13,* 533-568.

Eagleton, M., Guinnee, K., & Langlais, K. (2003). Teaching Internet literacy strategies: The hero inquiry project. *Voices from the Middle, 10,* 28-35.

Educational Testing Services. (2005). *Measuring College-level information and communication technology proficiency.* ETS: Princeton, NJ. Retrieved November 22, 2005 from http://www.ets.org/Media/Tests/ICT_Literacy/pdf/ICT_Measuring_College_Info_and_Comm.pdf

Finn, J. D. (1989). Withdrawing from school. *Review of Educational Research, 59,* 117-142.

Finn, J. D. (1993). *School engagement and students at risk.* Washington, DC: U.S. Department of Education, National Center for Education Statistics [On-line]. Available at: *http://nces.ed.gov/pubsearch/pubsinfo.asp?pubid=93470.*

Friedman, T. L. (2005). *The world is flat: A brief history of the twenty-first century.* New York: Farrar, Straus & Giroux.

Gates, A. (1921). An experimental and statistical study of reading and reading tests. *Journal of Educational Psychology, 12,* 303-14.

Gee, J. P. (2003). *What video games have to teach us about learning and literacy.* New York: Palgrave Macmillian.

Gray, W. S. (1984). *Reading: A research perspective, 1881–1941.* Newark, NJ: International Reading Association.

Harris Interactive Inc. (2005). *Web@work survey 2005.* Retrieved March 13, 2005 from http://www.websense.com/company/news/research/webatwork2005.pdf

Hartman, D. K. (2000). What will be the influences of media on literacy in the next millennium. *Reading Research Quarterly, 35,* 280-282.

Hartman, D. K. (2004). *An analysis of the employment opportunities for reading, language arts, and literacy faculty in higher education during the 2003-2004 academic year.* A research paper presented at the 54th Annual Meeting of the National Reading Conference, San Antonio, TX.

Hartman, D., Leu, D. J., Olson, M. R., & Truxam, M. P. (2005). *Reading and writing to learn with the "new literacies": Preparing a new generation of teachers and research-*

ers to develop literate American adolescents. Grant proposal funded by Carnegie Corporation of New York.

Henry, L. A. (2005). Information search strategies on the Internet: A critical component of new literacies. *Webology, 2.* Retrieved November 15, 2005 from http://www.webology.ir/2005/v2n1/a9.html

Henry, L. A. (2006). SEARCHing for an answer: The critical role of new literacies while reading on the Internet. *The Reading Teacher, 59,* 614-627.

Hirsh, S. G. (1999). Children's relevance criteria and information seeking on electronic resources. *Journal of the American Society for Information Science, 50,* 1265-1283.

Hoffer, T. B., Sederstrom, S., Selfa, L., Welch, V., Hess, M., Brown, S., Reyes, S., Webber, K., & I. Guzman-Barron, I. (2003). *Doctorate Recipients from United States Universities: Summary Report 2002.* Chicago: National Opinion Research Center.

Huey, E. B. (1908). *The psychology and pedagogy of reading: With a review of the history of reading and writing and of methods, texts, and hygiene in reading.* New York: Macmillan.

Hull, G., & Schultz, K. (2002). *School's out! Bridging out-of-school literacies with classroom practice.* New York: Teachers College Press.

International ICT Panel (2002). *Digital transformation: A framework for ICT literacy.* Princeton, NJ: Educational Testing Service. Retrieved December 5, 2005 from http://www.ets.org/research/researcher/ICT-REPORT.html.

International Reading Association. (2002). *Integrating literacy and technology in the curriculum: A position statement.* Newark, DE: International Reading Association.

International Society for Technology in Education. (n.d.). *National foundation standards for all students.* Retrieved December 5, 2005 from http://cnets.iste.org/currstands/cstands-netss.html.

Internet world stats: Usage and population statistics. (n.d.) Retrieved October 25, 2005 from http://www.internetworldstats.com/stats.htm.

Karchmer, R. A. (2001). The journey ahead: Thirteen teachers report how the Internet influences literacy and literacy instruction in their K–12 classrooms. *Reading Research Quarterly, 36,* 442–467.

Kress, G. (2003). *Literacy in the New Media Age.* London & New York: Routledge.

Kuiper, E., & Volman, M. (in press). The web as a source of information for students in K-12 education. In J. Coiro, M. Knobel, C. Lankshear, & D. Leu (Eds.), *Handbook of research on new literacies.* Mahwah, NJ: Lawrence Erlbaum Associates.

Labbo, L. D., & Reinking, D. (1999). Negotiating the multiple realities of technology in literacy research and instruction. *Reading Research Quarterly, 34,* 478-492.

Lankshear, C. & Knobel, M. (2003). *New Literacies.* Buckingham: Open University Press.

Lebo, H. (2003). *The UCLA Internet report: Surveying the digital future.* Los Angeles UCLA Center for Communication Policy. Retrieved May 12, 2003 from http://www.ccp.ucla.edu.

Lemke, J. L. (1998). Metamedia literacy: Transforming meanings and media. In D. Reinking, M.C. McKenna, L. D. Labbo, & R.D. Kieffer (Eds.), *Handbook of literacy and technology: Transformations in a post-typographic world* (pp. 283-301). Mahwah, NJ: Erlbaum.

Leu, D. J., Jr. (2000). Literacy and technology: Deictic consequences for literacy education in an information age. In M. L. Kamil, P. Mosenthal, P. D. Pearson, & R. Barr (Eds.) *Handbook of Reading Research, Volume III* (pp. 743-770). Mahwah, NJ: Erlbaum.

Leu, D. J., Jr. (2002). Internet workshop: Making time for literacy. *The Reading Teacher. 55,* 466-472.

Leu, D. J. (2006). New literacies, reading research, and the challenges of change: A deictic perspective. In J. Hoffman, D. Schallert, C. M. Fairbanks, J. Worthy, & B. Maloch (Eds.) *The 55th Yearbook of the National Reading Conference* (1-20). Milwaukee, WI: National Reading Conference. Video available: http://www.newliteracies.uconn. edu/nrc/don_leu_2005.html

Leu, D. J., Ataya, R., & Coiro, J. (December, 2002). *Assessing assessment strategies among the 50 states: Evaluating the literacies of our past or our future?* Paper presented at the National Reading Conference. Miami, FL.

Leu, D. Castek, J., Hartman, D., Coiro, J., Henry, L., Kulikowich, J., & Lyver, S. (2005). *Evaluating the development of scientific knowledge and new forms of reading comprehension during online learning.* Final report presented to the North Central Regional Educational Laboratory/Learning Point Associates. Retrieved May 15, 2006 from http://www.newliteracies.uconn.edu/ncrel.html.

Leu, D. J., Jr., & Kinzer, C. K. (2000). The convergence of literacy instruction and networked technologies for information and communication. *Reading Research Quarterly, 35*, 108-127.

Leu, D. J., Jr., Kinzer, C. K., Coiro, J., & Cammack, D. (2004). Toward a theory of new literacies emerging from the Internet and other information and communication technologies. In R. B. Ruddell & N. Unrau (Eds.), Newark, DE. International Reading Association: *Theoretical Models and Processes of Reading, Fifth Edition* (1568-1611). Retrieved October 15, 2005 from http://www.readingonline.org/newliteracies/ lit_index.asp?HREF=/newliteracies/leu

Leu, D. J., Jr., Leu, D. D., & Coiro, J. (2004). *Teaching with the Internet: Lessons from the classroom*, 4th Edition. Norwood, MA: Christopher-Gordon Publishers, Inc.

Leu, D. J. & Reinking, D. (2005). *Developing Internet Comprehension Strategies Among Adolescent Students At Risk to Become Dropouts.* Proposal submitted to the U. S. Department of Education, Institute of Education Sciences. Washington, D.C.

Leu, D. J., Zawilinski, L., Castek, J., Banerjee, M., Housand, B., Liu, Y., & O'Neil. M (in press). What is new about the new literacies of online reading comprehension? In A. Berger, L. Rush, and J. Eakle (Eds.). *Secondary school reading and writing: What research reveals for classroom practices.* National Council of Teachers of English/ National Conference of Research on Language and Literacy: Chicago, IL.

Lyman, P. & Varian, H. R. (2003). *"How Much Information 2003?* Berkeley: University of California, Berkeley. Available at http://www.sims.berkeley.edu/research/projects/ how-much-info-2003/

Manguel, A. (1996). *A history of reading.* New York: Viking.

Markham, A. (1998). *Life online.* Walnut Creek, CA: AltaMira Press.

Mayer, R. (2001). *Multimedia learning.* Cambridge, UK: Cambridge University Press.

Milson, A. J., & Downey, P. (2001). Using Internet Resources for Cooperative Inquiry. *Social Education, 65*, 144.

National Center for Education Statistics [NCES]. (2003). *The nation's report card: Reading highlights 2003.* Washington, DC: U.S. Department of Education. Retrieved October 15, 2004 from http://nces.ed.gov/pubsearch/pubsinfo.asp?pubid= 2004452

National Institute of Child Health and Human Development [NICHD]. (2000). *Report of the National Reading Panel. Teaching children to read: An evidence-based assessment of the scientific research literature on reading and its implications for reading instruction.* (NIH Publication No. 00-4769). Washington, DC: U.S. Government Printing Office.

National Occupational Research Center (2004). *Survey of earned doctorates.* Washington, D.C., NORC. Retrieved on July 1, 2006 from http://www.norc.uchicago. edu/issues/ docdata.htm

National Research Council. (1999). *Improving student learning: A strategic plan for education research and its utilization.* Committee on a Feasibility Study for a Strategic Education Research Program. Commission on Behavioral and Social Sciences and Education. Washington, DC: National Academy Press.

National Research Council. (2000). *How people learn: Brain, mind, experience and school.* Committee on Developments in the Science of Learning. J. Bransford, A. Brown, & R. Cocking (Eds.). Committee on Learning Research and Educational Practice. S. Donovan, J. Bransford, and J. Pellegrino (Eds.). Commission on Behavioral and Social Sciences in Education. Washington, DC: National Academy Press.

National Research Council (2002). *Scientific research in education.* Committee on Scientific Principles for Education Research. R. J. Shavelson & L. Towne (Eds.). Center for Education. Division of Behavioral and Social Sciences and Education. Washington, DC: National Academy Press.

Nielsen/NetRatings (2004). *Three out of four Americans have access to the Internet, according to Nielsen/NetRatings.* Retrieved March 18, 2004 from http://www.nielsen-netratings.com/pr/pr_040318.pdf.

No Child Left Behind Act of 2001, Pub. L. No. 107-110, 115 Stat. 1425 (2002). Retrieved December 10, 2003, from http://www.ed.gov/policy/elsec/leg/esea02/index.html

Parsad, B., Jones, J., & Greene, B. (2005). *Internet access in U.S. public schools and classrooms: 1994-2003.* U. S. Department of Education. Washington, D.C.: National Center for Educational Statistics. Retrieved October 15, 2005 from http://nces.ed.gov/pubs2005/2005015.pdf

Partnership for 21st Century Skills. (2003). *Learning for the 21st Century.* Washington, DC: Partnership for 21st Century Skills. Retrieved October 15, 2005 from http://www.21stcenturyskills.org/images/stories/otherdocs/P21_Report.pdf

Pew Internet & American Life Project. (2001). *The Internet and education: Findings of the Pew Internet & American Life Project.* Retrieved October 15, 2005 from http://www.pewinternet.org/report_display.asp?r=67.

Pew Internet & American Life Project. (2005). *Teens and technology.* Retrieved April 15, 2006: http://www.pewinternet.org/topics.asp?c=4.

RAND Reading Study Group [RRSG]. (2002). *Reading for understanding: Toward an R&D program in reading comprehension.* Santa Monica, CA: Rand.

Street, B. (1995). *Social literacies: Critical approaches to literacy in education, development and ethnography.* London: Longman.

Street, B. (2003). What's new in new literacy studies. *Current issues in comparative education*, 5(2), 1-14.

The New London Group. (2000). *Multiliteracies: Literacy learning and the design of social futures.* London: Routledge.

Thomas, A. (in press). Cyberspace, cybercommunity, cyberculture, cybercitizenship. In J. Coiro, M. Knobel, C. Lankshear, & D. Leu (Eds.), *Handbook of research on new literacies.* Mahwah, NJ: Lawrence Erlbaum Associates.

Thompson, R., Mixon, G., & Serpell, R. (1996). Engaging minority students in reading: Focus on the urban learner. In L. Baker, P. Afflerbach & D. Reinking (Eds.), *Developing engaged readers in school and home communities* (pp. 43-63). Mahwah, NJ: Lawrence Erlbaum Associates.

Thorndike, E. L. (1917). Reading as reasoning. *Journal of Educational Psychology, 8,* 323-332.

Thorndike, R. L. (1973-1974). Reading as reasoning. *Reading Research Quarterly, 9,* 135-147

U.S. Department of Commerce: National Telecommunications and Information Administration. (2002). *A nation online: How Americans are expanding their use of the Internet.* Washington, DC: U.S. Department of Commerce.

Webber, S., & Johnson, B. (2000). Conceptions of information literacy: New Perspectives and implications. *Journal of Informational Science, 26,* 381-397.

Wylie, V. L., & Hunter, W. A. (1994). *The dropout problem: Can schools meet the challenge?* NASSP Bulletin, *78,* 74-80.

LIVING IN THE PROMISED LAND...
OR CAN OLD AND NEW LITERACIES
LIVE HAPPILY EVER AFTER IN THE
CLASSROOM?

Linda D. Labbo

University of Georgia

Keynote Address
College Reading Association
2005

By the year 2007, it is projected that over 1,380 billion instant messages will be transmitted and received.

Retrieved January 5, 2006
<http://www.russellshaw.net/ibdinstantmessage. htm>

More than 2 million American children ages 6 -17 have their own personal websites today—10 percent of the 23 million kids have Internet access from home today—a threefold increase since 2000.

Retrieved October 15, 2003
<http://www.grunwald.com/surveys/cfi/overview. html>

We need to see how much more students will need in the future than we are now giving them. We do not [currently] teach students how to integrate ... archival photo images, video clips, sound effects, voice audio, music, [or] animation [in their writing].

Lemke, 1998, p. 228

Reprinted from *Multiple Literacies in the 21st Century,* pp.-20-30, by M. B. Sampson, P. E. Linder, F. Falk-Ross, M. Foote, & S. Szabo, Eds., 2007, Commerce, TX: College Reading Association.

Many educators are grappling with how to effectively use computer technologies for literacy instruction because the goal for doing so is not clear. Questions teachers ask during staff development training, conference presentations and graduate courses indicate the breath and depth of teachers' concerns in this regard. Should I focus on using computers mostly to support my second graders' print-based literacy development? Should I be using the computers in my classroom to help my third graders make better scores on standardized tests? Should I be introducing my fifth graders to new strategies, like searching the Internet or critically reading the information they find on the Internet? How can I realistically add computer activities to an instructional day that is already full? None of my curricular resources have any suggestions for using computers. How can I fit computer activities into the literacy curriculum when the teacher guide doesn't give me any directions or ideas? These and other questions persistently plague educators who are attempting to identify an appropriate goal for computer use in the classrooms of today and of tomorrow.

It is worth noting that computer technologies, transformative agents in many realms, create change because they help participants meet goals in unique, efficient, and creative ways. In other words, technology has the power to redefine the parameters, nature, and conduct of work mainly because clearly stated goals are interwoven into culturally situated mindsets. The purpose of this paper is threefold:

1. to recommend an appropriate goal for using computer technologies in the literacy curriculum,
2. to provide a brief rationale for the goal,
3. to recommend pedagogical conditions for using computer technologies that accomplish the goal.

An Appropriate Goal for Using Computer Technologies in the Literacy Curriculum

Undeniably, computer technologies are transforming the business world. For example, on a recent trip I observed as my adult son sat in the comfort of his home office and conducted convenient, on-demand, virtual Internet tours of fifteen houses for sale. Doing so saved him countless hours of making phone calls, marking real estate ads in various newspapers from surrounding geographic areas, setting up appointments, driving by potential homes of interest, and visiting every possible house within his price range. The virtual tours gave my son fingertip access to various types of information—electronic slide shows of outside/inside photographs, interactive 360 degree views of major living areas, and links to information that included when the homes were built, annual tax rates, average utility bills, asking prices, and the email address of realtors. In this and other instances, computer technologies are transforming the way work is conducted.

Realtors use Internet sites to advertise in cost-effective ways, target specific audiences, provide visual displays that allow buyers to *step-into* the environment, disseminate specific information, and lay a foundation for a lucrative working relationship with potential home buyers—at least those who can afford to own computer technologies and those who know how to use Online tools. The architecture of the Internet space allowed realtors to accomplish old work in new ways, thereby transforming the culture and practice of home buying for the public. The bottom line is usually economic in the business world. Undoubtedly, the primary goal is leveraging the power of new multimedia technologies to make a profit. The differences between old and new business practices in the realm of real estate are easily identified because the goal is clear and the technology tools utilized align in ways that are specifically designed to accomplish the goal.

However, understanding the unique ways that computer technologies may be used to enhance or transform literacy instruction is a more complex undertaking because, currently the goal appears to be rather schizophrenic—consisting of two discrete purposes that remain separate in the mindsets of many teacher educators, educators, and literacy researchers. For decades, technology has been touted as an educational change agent that will inevitably lead to a utopian school system and a utopian society. For example, after motion pictures hit the entertainment industry in the 1920s, Thomas Alva Edison predicted that they would replace textbooks, and perhaps even teachers, as the primary means of relaying information in classrooms (Tyback & Cuban, 1995). Even though the means of instruction would change, the goal for instruction would remain constant—to educate masses of Americans and American immigrants to be good citizens who are functionally literate. History tells us that Edison's technologically transformative prediction did not come to pass.

The Promised Land

More recently, proponents of computer technologies are likely to adopt the expectation that the classroom should be a Promised Land. In biblical history the Promised Land was a delightful place—flowing with milk and honey (Exodus III: 8). The *Promised Classroom* should also be a delightful place of dynamic learning—flowing with computer hardware, Internet connections, student-centered learning, and self-motivated learners (e.g., Leu & Kinzer, 2000; Labbo, 1996; Reinking, 1994). Furthermore, technology proponents expect that teaching and learning will be positively transformed when computer technologies are present in classrooms and correctly implemented (Cuban, 2001). Students educated in such an environment are likely to be well-prepared for their literacy futures—futures that require highly complex, *new* computer-related literacy skills and strategies that are fundamentally different from *old* or conventional paper and print-related literacy skills and strategies (Leu, 2000).

No Child Left Behind

Recent policies and sources of educational funding in the United States have muddied a utopian, future-seeking perspective because they have focused primarily on how computers can and should be used to help students gain *old* literacy—fundamental, print-related skills (NCLB Retrieved March 1, 2006, http://www.ed.gov/nclb/landing.jhtml) as those skills are assessed on standardized tests. The underlying goal is to use evidence-based instructional approaches to produce evidence on how well students are doing on standardized tests. The unintentional result is that educators and parents may focus on students' test scores as the ultimate educational goal. Thus, educators, policymakers, and researchers receive mixed messages and find themselves pondering about which goal is the most appropriate one to pursue. The time has come to move beyond either/or thinking and to seek a convergence of goals for effective computer technology use in the classroom and literacy curriculum. The time has come to explore a *convergent goal* that recognizes old and new literacies as two sides of the same coin. One side consists of traditional literacy and the other side consists of new literacies.

Rationale for the Goal of Convergence

Venezky (1995) defined literacy as the basic capacity to write and read in a specific language, with an approach to meeting the needs of daily life by applying reading and writing skills. This definition stands the test of time if, and mainly if, the needs of daily life include making meaning with the multimedia symbols, modes, and tools that appear on computer displays. Old or traditional print-based literacy refers to print-based skills and strategies that have been largely taught throughout the years with traditional pedagogical tools and materials that include paper, pencils, blackboards, flash cards, work sheets, writing journals, basal readers, children's literature, textbooks, encyclopedias, and library resources. Using these materials and tools aligned well with the type of literacy activities students encountered when they graduated from school. They could participate in the work place, seek higher education, and use literacy skills to accomplish personal and recreational goals.

Therefore, it follows that if we expand Venezky's definition to include computers as a part of the daily life students currently encounter and will encounter when they graduate, then the goals converge in productive ways. The definition also still works if we expand the notion of reading and writing skills to include not just print based information. "...[o]ne can substitute for 'print' various other sorts of texts and technologies: painting, literature, films, television, computers, telecommunications..." (Gee, 1996, p. 143). Indeed, Gee states that he sees "...no gain from the addition of the phrase 'involving print'...other than to assuage the feelings of people committed to reading and writing as decontextualized and isolable skills" (p. 144). Students who graduate from schools of today and tomorrow should be well equipped to step into work places that demand the ability to use and continue to learn how to apply computer technology skills. They should be well prepared to seek higher education and be upwardly mobile because they are able to make meaning with computer-related interactive, multimedia modes and tools. Finally, students who graduate from schools of today and tomorrow should be able to meet professional, personal, and recreational goals with computer technologies that allow them to enter into various discourse communities. New literacies are multiple in nature and refer to on-screen skills and strategies that include abilities to utilize multimedia resources for various academic, personal, and communicative purposes.

An Example of Convergence of Goals

Consider the following example of goals that converge and yet represent two different sides of the same literacy coin. My mother, who went to school during the Great Depression era in the United States, learned old paper and pencil literacy skills that allowed her to engage in citizenship, economic endeavors, social activities, and personal recreational pursuits. My daughter, who is a new mother, learned a combination of old and new literacy skills throughout her 16 years of schooling within the United States. She also engages in citizenship, economic endeavors, social activities, and personal recreational pursuits. Thus the goals are the same but the avenues of literacy and the skills and strategies required for pursing those literacy engagements are different.

My mother went through schooling at a time when goals were aligned with how they were taught in classrooms. Students were not taught skills primarily so they could demonstrate how well they were doing and achieving on standardized tests that compared their test scores to other students. My daughter went through schooling at a time when testing was used primarily to inform instructional decision making in the classroom. Computer technologies were fairly new to her in a university setting and the literacy skills involved in accomplishing assignments required students to think critically about the multimedia information they assembled and represented from Internet resources.

Figure 1. Convergent Goals

	CONVERGENT LITERACY GOALS BUT DISCRETE LITERACY SKILLS	
GOALS	MY MOTHER	MY DAUGHTER
Citizenship	Read newspaper before voting	Compared Internet campign reports and video linked to statistics on congressional voting record
Economic	Addressed wedding invitations with pen & ink calligraphy as a hobby/vocation by word of mouth	Began an Online purse business with an interactive web page
Social	Wrote & saved ribbon-tied WWII letters from husband	Sent e-newsletters to relatives with video clips, photos, and stories about her new baby
Personal	Wrote poetry journals to reflect on life experiences	Published poetry on the Internet to share, receive feedback, and discuss with other poets in a virtual writing group.

Before her death, my mother observed my daughter navigating through websites and sending e-mail messages. She said the whole thing made her head spin because the literacy strategies required to accomplish goals with the computer where outside of her realms of experience or interest.

Computers Support Old/Traditional Literacy Development

Computer programs can be used to support children's development of specific, traditional literacy skills. Blok, Oostdam, Otter, and Overman (2002) conducted a meta-analysis of over 40 computer assisted programs (CAI) that were designed to support basic literacy skills practice and found that programs that include interactive game playing, decision making, and scaffolding tools (such as intelligent agents that give feedback or directions on students' choices) provide a small, but positive effect size on students' phonemic awareness, spelling, phonics, vocabulary development, and comprehension. For example, computer programs that provide audio support and high levels of interactivity can foster students' phonological abilities (Reitsma & Wessling, 1998). Further-more, studies indicate that when programs utilize digitized speech or provide isolated sounds of language that students blend by moving a computer cursor, their phonological awareness improves.

Creativity and word processing programs also support young students' writing development. For example, Cochran-Smith (1991) found that students who composed with word processing programs were able to write more com-plex passages than they did with paper and pencil because producing text with keyboard typing, revising text by cutting and pasting, and printing out legible text was an easier endeavor. Children's metacognitive discourse, lexical density, and organizational cohesiveness also increased when using a word processing program (Bangert-Drowns, 1989; Jones & Pelligrini, 1996).

Computers Require New Literacies

New literacies involve combinations of symbolic modalities that are situated within specific cultural and social practices (New London Group, 1996). Meaning making with new literacies includes reading and writing in multiple modalities (e.g., graphics, animations, video, audio narration, music, special effects, hyperlinks, search engines, power point presentations, and print) in ways that are significant within cultural groups (Andrews, 2004). Lankshear and Knobel (2005) include the following forms of literacy within a new literacies classification scheme—electronic gaming, mobile communication, weblogs, multimedia text production, scenario planning, Zines, critical literacy, Fan Fiction, Magna/Anime, memes, and Adbusting. Making meaning with computer technologies in the work place, online, and in classrooms requires reading and composing in multiple symbolic modes (e.g., animations, visual graphics, audio narration, video, music, special effects, hyperlinks, search engines, presentation software, and print). New computer technologies and the resulting new forms of electronic texts such as e-mail and multimedia websites require new conceptions and competencies of literacy and literate behaviors (Flood, Heath, & Lapp, 1997; Leu & Kinzer, 2000).

It is evident that computer technologies and high speed Internet access are transforming how and when our students communicate. For example, I observed an undergraduate student at a local coffee shop engage in three different electronic communications within a time span of ten minutes. First, she talked with her roommate over her cell phone about which type and flavor of coffee she would recommend. Next, she sent and received a dozen instant messages over her cell phone. Finally, she opened her lap top computer and sent an e-mail message through the coffee shop's wireless connection. When I asked her to tell me about the messages, she said she was just keeping in touch with a friend and that the email message was a question about an assignment that she sent to a course instructor. The uses of the technologies might seem trivial to a casual onlooker; however, the ease with which the young woman utilized various technology tools for authentic, communicative purposes should entice us to learn more about the role that technology might also play in her university coursework.

Pedagogical Conditions

A basic premise of this paper is that classroom computer transformations will occur when the conditions of teaching spring from the recognition of convergent goals for literacy instruction. I suggest that the following four conditions will serve as guidelines to support teachers' efforts to successfully use computer technologies to transform literacy instruction.

Transformations Occur When Teachers Have Professional Development and On-SiteTechnology Support

Research suggests that teachers do not receive enough support that results in the highest quality of professional staff development (Trotter, 1999). Coiro (2005) relates that a key component of an effective model for staff development for in-service teachers includes utilizing on-the-job study groups that allow teachers to be more directive in the nature and content of training. A key component of effective study groups includes providing technical support so teachers may find a comfort zone and experience success with their first forays into utilizing computer technologies for literacy instruction. Such groups may consist of peer pairs as learners, or communities of teachers as learners (e.g., Lyon & Pinnell, 2001).

Transformations Occur When Computer Technologies are Integrated Throughout the Day

Teachers who model how to use computer technologies to accomplish *functional goals* help students gain both old and new literacies. One way teachers accomplish this objective is to design computer activities that are related to tried-and-true literacy routines. For example, teachers of young children can innovate on morning message, a routine that involves writing down dictation from students about the events for each day, by using a keyboard and a digital whiteboard to model old and new literacies. A digital whiteboard is an electronic dry erase board that serves as an interactive touch screen/monitor when connected to a computer (Solvie, 2003). Children learn concepts about print as they see text appear as it is typed from left-to-right with a return sweep. They may also learn how to use spell and grammar checkers as teachers demonstrate word processing tools. Later in the day, a teacher may model how to check an Internet weather station to decide if students need to wear coats on the playground.

Transformations Occur When Computer Technologies are Integrated Across the Curriculum in Collaborative Ways

E-mail exchanges between students in various geographic regions support students' traditional and new literacies. Email exchanges also create motivating and authentic reasons to communicate (Garner & Gillingham, 1998; Tao & Reinking, 2000). As students exchange electronic messages, they learn the conventions required to communicate (e.g., conversational tone, recursive writing, including previous segments of message to create context).

Transformations Occur When Participants Compose Multimedia Productions that Multiply Meaning (Lemke, 1994)

Creating, representing, and sharing ideas with multimedia resources supercedes the written word. Indeed, Lemke (1998) notes that multimedia work may not be based on an "organizing spine of text" (p. 288). For example, the organizing factor might be a graphic organization of images, video, or audio narratives that connect in unique ways. The larger notion behind multimedia composing with pictures, animation, audio narratives, music, transitional cinematic effects, links, and words expressed in various fonts, is that all of the media sources combine in ways that multiply meaning. In other words, taken together, the combination of media presents a more powerful and potentially deeper meaning construction than would words or images or any of the media resources would if they stood alone.

Concluding Comments

Technology will continue to impact everyday life and the literacy strategies employed to use technology. As the future unfolds, we are likely to experience the results of emerging trends, such as live media events that instantly display in cars, clothing that includes digital components that allow wearers to change the temperature, and the ability to access most of the world's library collections through searchable formats.

How will computer technologies impact the everyday, literacy instructional life of the classroom? The answer is that—it depends. It depends in part on whether educators and researchers will consider seriously how old and new literacies can co-exist harmoniously and convergently in current and future classrooms. Doing so is not just a matter of exclusively using new computer technologies to support old ideas about literacy, with the hope that somehow by using new computer tools that students will incidentally learn new literacies. New literacies demand cultural, pedagogical, and philosophical transformations. "When the only tool you own is a hammer, every problem begins to resemble a nail" jokes Abraham Maslow (jokes2go.com retrieved January 15, 2006). When the only definition you have of literacy focuses on print-based skills, every computer activity you design begins to resemble paper and pencil learning. As teachers, teacher educators, and researchers, our notions about our goals for technology and literacy will determine the focus and nature of our work.

References

Andrews, R. (Ed). (2004). *The impact of ICT on literacy education*. London: Routledge Falmer.

Bangert-Drowns, R. L. (1989). Research on word processing and writing instruction. Paper presented at the meting of the American Educational Research Association, San Francisco, March, 1989.

Blok, H., Oostdam, R., Otter, M. E., & Overmaat, M. (2002). Computer-assisted instruction in support of beginning reading instruction: A review. *Review of Educational Research, 72*, 101-130.

Cochran-Smith, M. (1991). Word processing and writing in elementary classrooms: A critical review of related literature. *Review of Educational Research, 61*, 107-55.

Coiro, J. (2005). Every teacher a Mrs. Rumphis: Empowering teachers with effective professional development. In R. A. Karchmar, M. H. Mallette, J. Kara-Soteriou, & D. J. Leu (Eds.), *Innovative approaches to literacy education: Using the Internet to support new literacies*. (pp. 199-219). Newark, DE: International Reading Association.

Cuban, L. (2001). *Oversold and underused: Computers in the classroom*. Cambridge, MA: Harvard University Press.

Flood, J., Heath, S. B., & Lapp, D. (Eds.). (1997). *Handbook of research on teaching literacy through the communicative and visual arts*. New York: Macmillan.

Garner, R., & Gillingham, M. G. (1998). The Internet in the classroom: Is it the end of transmission-oriented pedagogy? In D. Reinking, M. C. McKenna, L. D. Labbo & R. D. Kieffer (Eds.), *Handbook of literacy and technology: Transformations in a post-typographic world*, pp. 221-231. Mahwah, NJ: Erlbaum.

Gee, J. P., (1996). *Social linguistics and literacies: Ideology in discourses* (2nd ed.). London: Taylor and Francis.

Jones, I., & Pelligrini, A. D. (1996). The effects of social relationships, writing media, and microgenetic development on first-grade students' written narratives. *American Educational Research Journal, 33*(3), 691-718.

Labbo, L. D. (1996). A semiotic analysis of young children's symbol making in a classroom computer center. *Reading Research Quarterly, 31*(4), 356-385.

Lankshear, C., & Knobel, M. (2003). *New literacies: Changing knowledge and classroom learning*. Buckingham, England: Open University Press.

Lemke, J. L. (1994). *Multiplying meaning: Literacy in a multimedia world*. Paper presented at the National Reading Conference, Charleston, SC. (ERIC Document Reproduction Service No. ED 365 940).

Lemke, J. L. (1998). Metamedia literacy: Transforming meanings and media. In D. Reinking, M. C. McKenna, L. D. Labbo & R. D. Kieffer (Eds), *Handbook of literacy and technology: Transformations in a post-typographic world* (pp. 283-301), Mahwah, NJ: Erlbaum.

Leu, D. J. (2000). Our children's future: Changing the focus of literacy and literacy instruction. *The Reading Teacher, 53*, 424-431.

Leu, D. J. (2002). The new literacies: Research on reading instruction with the Internet. In A. E. Farstrup & S. J. Samuels (Eds.), *What research has to say about reading instruction* (pp. 310-336). Newark, DE: International Reading Association.

Leu, D. J., & Kinzer, C. K. (2000). The convergence of literacy instruction with networked technologies for information, communication, and education. *Reading Research Quarterly, 35*, 108-127.

Lyon, G. A., & Pinnell, G. S. (2001). *Systems for change in literacy education: A guide to professional development.* Portsmouth, NH: Heinemann.

New London Group (1996). A pedagogy of multiliteracies. *Harvard Educational Review, 60*(1), 66-92.

No Child Left Behind (Retrieved March 1, 2006), http://www.ed.gov/nclb/landing. jhtml

Osborne, R. J., & Wittrock, M. (1985). The generative learning model and its implications for science education. *Studies in Science Education, 12,* 59-87.

Reinking, D. (1994). *Electronic literacy.* (Perspectives in Reading Research No. 4, National Reading Research Center). Athens: University of Georgia Press.

Reitsma, P., (1988). Reading practice for beginners: Effects of guided reading, reading while listening, and independent reading with computer-based speech feedback. *Reading Research Quarterly, 23,* 219-235.

Reitsma, P., & Wesseling, R. (1998). Effects of computer assisted training of blending skills in kindergarten. *Scientific Studies of Reading, 2*(4), 301-320.

Solvie, P. A. (2003). The digital whiteboard: A tool in early literacy instruction. *The Reading Teacher, 57*(5), 484-487.

Tao, L., & Reinking D. (2000). E-mail and literacy education. *Reading and Writing Quarterly, 16,* 169-174.

Trotter, A. (1999, September 23). Preparing teachers for the digital age. *Education Week, XIX*(4), 37-42.

Tyback, D., & Cuban, L. (1995). *Tinkering toward utopia: A century of public school reform.* Cambridge, MA: Harvard University Press.

Venezky, R. L. (1995). Literacy. In T. L. Harris and R. F. Hodges (Eds.), *The literacy dictionary.* (p. 142). Newark, DE: International Reading Association.

A FEW WORDS ABOUT SENTENCES

J. Estill Alexander
Leaders in Literacy Forum

Allen Berger

Keynote Address
College Readimg Association
2006

Allen Berger is Heckert Professor Emeritus of Reading and Writing at Miami University, Ohio. Prior to that tenured position he was tenured at the Universities of Pittsburgh and Alberta as well as Southern Illinois. He began his career teaching high school in Utica and Rochester, New York.

Allen has written about 400 articles on reading and writing education. In 1982, he and H. Alan Robinson (Past President of IRA) co-edited a new version of previously published (1950s and 1960s) books about what research reveals for teaching reading in high school. An updated, expanded version, titled Secondary School Literacy: What Research Reveals for Classroom Practice, *has been published by NCTE with the endorsement of The National Conference on Research in Language and Literacy. Co-editors with Allen on that publication are A. Jonathan Eakle and Leslie Susan Rush.*

Allen has been active in both NCTE and IRA, chairing committees for both, and serving on the team that developed the national standards for reading professionals. He has won many awards, most recently the CRA Laureate Award (2005); he was named as the Outstanding Literacy Educator by both the Ohio Reading Council and the Ohio English Language Arts Council. He has

Reprinted from *Navigating the Literacy Waters: Research, Praxis, & Advocacy,* pp. 27-31, by M. Foote, F. Falk-Ross, S. Szabo, M. B. Sampson, Eds., 2008, Commerce, TX: College Reading Association.

received the Distinguished Achievement Award for Editorial Writing from the Educational Press Association of America.

Allen studied with and was mentored by William D. Sheldon (Past President of IRA), Margaret J. Early (Past President of NCTE), and Leonard Braam (Past President of CRA) of Savannah, Georgia. He lives in Savannah, Georgia.

Abstract

In his address, Allen Berger discusses ways to write clear, simple sentences, how to choose words for those sentences, how to weave sentences into paragraphs, and how to put paragraphs together, without jargon, into opinion/ editorials for different audiences. He encourages the involvement of students in critiquing a best draft before sending out a final version to the public or profession.

Some of you may recall Eric Hoffer, the bricklayer who in between laying bricks wrote books. Reflecting on his writing life, he stated: "I could hang onto an idea for years. I could chew on a sentence for months. All that I have accomplished is that I have written a few good sentences. The sentences that I have written are going to stay. They have staying power. I love a good sentence." (Eric Hoffer in the 90-minute documentary, *Eric Hoffer: The Crowded Life*, PBS, January 17, 1978)

Why is it so difficult to write a few good sentences? I'm not sure I know the answer to that question. But let me be presumptuous enough to share a few reminders in writing sentences for publication.

Let me interject here, before I continue, a way to focus students' attention on sentences. Ask, how many sentences are in a newspaper paragraph. Few will come up with the answer: one. Explain why the first sentence tells the whole story, the next has a few more details, and so on. You might then provide a few "facts" for a make-believe news story: a car accident, hit a power pole, two people injured, brought to the hospital, etc. Ask students to be reporters and write a news story of one-sentence paragraphs. Remind students that just as the first sentence is the most important, so too is what's at the beginning of each sentence. For instance, some students will begin: Yesterday there was a car crash that injured two people, etc. Ask: which is more important, that it happened yesterday? That there was a car crash? Or that two people were injured? So they will revise their sentence to begin: Two people were injured yesterday when their car crashed into a power pole. The next sentence will give more details, perhaps names, etc.

Back to my main point about reminders. First, it is crucial for writers to remember the audience. Writing for teachers is not the same as writing for researchers. You use different sentences. It's not about talking or writing up or down; it's about communicating.

When I edited NCTE's (National Council of Teachers of English) quarterly *English Education* for seven years, I received many fine articles, but they were for the wrong audience: they were appropriate for *English Journal* or for the *Journal of Reading* (now titled *Journal of Adolescent & Adult Literacy*), both of which were for high school teachers mainly. The journal I edited, *English Education*, was for teachers of teachers; that is, mostly professors (a step away from reality). When I returned such articles I wrote a note suggesting one of the other journals, and often I received a reply letting me know that the articles were accepted.

One of the crucial audiences to write for nowadays is the public. When seminal thinker Louise Rosenblatt addressed researchers when she was 97 or 98 years old at the annual meeting of the National Reading Conference, she told the audience: "Be a good citizen. Write for the public." Yet relatively few researchers know how to write for the public.

Earlier this month, I was at the 50th anniversary of the Reading and Language Arts Center at Syracuse University. The conference concluded with alumni telling what they would like to see in the future. One prominent individual said that he would like students who graduate with a doctoral degree to know how to write for the public. "I have no idea how to write an op/ed," he said.

Writing an opinion/editorial is extremely difficult and, for me, to write the approximate 500 or 600 words takes between 15 and 20 hours.

If you want to improve your sentences, share your writing with your students and others before publication. Here's what I normally do. I run off copies of my next-to-final draft for students and ask them to read and make comments in the margins, with particular attention to clarity. When they finish, we discuss their comments. Then I collect all the drafts. The next morning, when refreshed, I throw away all the pages with no comments on them. Then I concentrate on comments they wrote on page one and maybe incorporate some of their suggestions. Then I do the same with page two until the end. What may appear clear to me may not be clear to readers.

Sometimes students are lifesavers. Once I wrote a piece for *Reading Today*, a publication of the International Reading Association. I titled it "Dead People Who Should be Remembered." I wrote five vignettes (about John Downing, R. Buckminster Fuller, Marion Jenkinson, Eileen Tway, and William D. Sheldon) and shared what I had written with my students. The next day, as I read the student comments, one student—and only one—wrote in the margin at the end of one of the vignettes: Is this person really dead? The person in question and I had been colleagues at the University of Alberta.

I picked up the phone and dialed the number of a former student and colleague who was living in Newfoundland. After a brief conversation I hung up and phoned IRA headquarters and told the editor that one of the people was not dead in the piece I had just faxed. I suggested that he might call the piece "Dear People Who Should be Remembered," or "People Who Should be Remembered," or just get rid of that vignette about Marion Jenkinson, which is what happened. The four vignettes appear under the title "People Who Should be Remembered" in *Reading Today*, June/July 1996.

There are many other values in sharing writing with students prior to publication. They learn valuable lessons through your modeling part of the writing process, which they may emulate in their own classrooms. They also learn the value of ethical behavior in submitting something that is the very best they can do; so that the editors or readers won't have to waste time trying to figure out what you intended.

If you want to shorten a sentence, eliminate unnecessary words. I learned that in grammar school. My teacher used to tell all us little kids to make believe we were sending a telegram and that we had to pay for every word.

To digress again, it's not only important to write good sentences but also to choose right words. You can do this with your students through a cloze technique with poetry. Just have a line or stanza from a poem with a word missing, and ask students to put in a word that continues the flow of rhythm and meaning, and then compare their words with the word the poet chose. When I was a college student, I had the good fortune to study with Norman Nathan, who introduced me to this concept (before cloze emerged in reading research and pedagogy). He and I co-wrote an article that provides more details. Titled "The Building Blocks of Poetry," it appears in the January, 1971, issue of *English Journal*.

Try also eliminating jargon. I once wrote an article titled "Words That Have No Meaning" (Berger, 1994) in which I questioned the sweeping misuse of newer maladies which often shift the blame for poor reading and writing to a mysterious flaw in the brain, when many students so afflicted might profit from a better diet and a good night's sleep. In that article, I poked fun at a commonly used expression: prior knowledge. I naively thought that a person either knew something or didn't know something and, if there is such a thing as prior knowledge, then what's prior to the prior knowledge? A friend told me to knock it off because, even though it's jargon, it's one of the few things we can agree on.

Let's conclude with whether a sentence should be passive or active. When I ask students why they tend to write research and papers in the third person or passive voice, or both, I'm told (that they're told) that it's more objective. I could never figure that out. So, I went to see how Einstein and Newton wrote, and Newton (1704/1952) simply wrote, for examples, "I measured" and "I made a little hole. . . ." (in *Opticks*) and Einstein (1916/1931) cheerfully wrote about "our old friend the railway carriage" (in"*Relativity: The Special and General Theory*). Why then do students and others feel they need to write that "it was found that", or "the investigator measured", or "the data were collected by the investigator", when they're the investigator? Why write convoluted sentences? Surely Newton wouldn't write that an investigator was sitting under an apple tree when an object that looked like an apple appeared to fall or was dropped upon the investigator's head.

References

Berger, A. (1996, June). People who should be remembered. *Reading Today,13*(6), 38.

Berger, A. (1994, Oct.). Words that have no meaning. *Reading Today, 12*(2), 31.

Einstein, A. (1931). *Relativity: The special and general theory.* (3rd ed.; R. W. Lawson, Trans.). New York: Crown. (Original work published 1916)

Nathan, N., & Berger, A. (1971, January). The building blocks of poetry, *English Journal, 60*(1), 42-46.

Newton, I. (1952). *Opticks or a treatise of the reflections, refractions, inflections & colours of light.* New York: Dover. (Original work published 1704)

Advancing Children's Literacy Requires Starting with the Right Questions in the Debate over Literacy

Gerald Coles

Keynote Address
College Reading Association
2006

Educational psychologist Gerald Coles is a full-time researcher, writer, and lecturer on literacy, learning and psychology and is the author of numerous articles and several books including: The Learning Mystique: A Critical look at Learning Disabilities, Reading Lessons: The Debate over Literacy, *and* Reading the Naked truth: Literacy, Legislation and Lies. *Currently he is writing a book on what teachers and parents need to know about the brain and learning to read. Before devoting himself to full-time research and writing, he was on the faculties of the Department of Psychiatry at Robert Wood Johnson Medical School, University of Medicine & Dentistry of New Jersey*  *and the Warner Graduate School of Education and Human Development at the University of Rochester. At the medical school he directed and worked as a clinician in a program for children, young adults and adults with severe reading problems. Consequently, he brings to his writing and research considerable experience as a practitioner of literacy education.*

Gerry has discussed educational issues on national and regional television and radio programs. In 2002, he received a Distinguished Alumnus Award from the University at Buffalo and lives in Ithaca, New York.

He believes the educational forces associated with the Bush administration have succeeded in binding everyone in a very narrow debate over whether "we need to teach sequential skills in order to make children readers." His argu-

ment is that the question needs to be, "What needs to be done to ensure that all children learn to read?" By asking that question we include not only a broader definition of the instructional issue, but all else that affects learning success or failure (housing, health, classroom and school libraries, family income, etc.) something the Bush administration doesn't want to discuss.

Abstract

Instead of asking the question, "What is the best instruction for teaching children to read?," the better question for guiding policy should be, "What needs to be done to ensure that all children learn to read?" The latter question includes the former, while the former excludes the many other influences (nutrition, health, etc.) that contribute to reading achievement. This paper first debunks the scientific evidence used to justify Reading First mandates, and then examines the many additional influences on reading achievement, underscoring the failure during the last six years of the Bush administration to create policy that would address these influences.

The question currently dominating literacy policy in the United States is, "What is the best instruction for teaching children to read?" On the face of it, the question seems sensible for guiding literacy policy, especially because it resonates with the long-standing framing of reading education as "The Great Debate" over teaching methods (Chall, 1967). For many reading educators, moreover, the question seems right because it frames the stock in trade of the reading profession. And if college reading professors had any inclination in recent years to reconsider this question, attacks from such reading luminaries as Reid Lyon, George W. Bush's former "reading guru," had to put many of them on the defensive. Accusing reading professors of being "so wimpy" about using "scientific evidence" and stating that he would like to pass legislation "to blow up colleges of education" because they were not right minded about correct reading instruction (Lyon, n.d.; Benton, 2006), the charge surely compelled many professors to focus even more narrowly on instructional methods.

Despite the importance of the question both for the reading profession and for public policy, I propose that "What is the best instruction for teaching children to read?" is the *wrong* policy question because it is insufficient and misleading, and therefore yields damaging educational consequences, especially for poor children, for whom the policy is supposedly aimed at helping the most. Instead, as I will explain in the pages ahead, the right question should be, "What needs to be done to ensure that all children learn to read?" If we were to ask this question instead, we would be addressing instruction, but would also include all else that contributes to literacy success.

A version of the second question was formulated in the College Reading Association's 2006 conference theme, "Three Rivers of Literacy Knowledge: World, Self, Word" (so named after the rivers—Monongahela, Allegheny, Ohio—that join in Pittsburgh, the conference's venue). These "three rivers" embrace literacy instruction (the "word"); the learner (the "self") in all of her or his facets, not just as a cognitive processor of literacy information; and the "world," which includes the social influences, including political policy influences, that shape the self and the acquisition of the "word." To maximize the likelihood of literacy success among children, all of these points must be addressed.

Reading First

Unfortunately, the nation's chief literacy policy, titled "Reading First" and contained in the No Child Left Behind legislation, only embraces the question "What is the best instruction for teaching children to read?" It then makes matters worse by providing a single answer, "scientific reading instruction," which is a grandiose title cloaking an anemic pedagogy. A stepwise progression from smaller to larger units of language, scientific reading instruction moves the learner step-by-step from phonemic awareness to phonics, then on to fluency, and eventually to comprehension. Yes, there is "comprehension" along the way, but it is always comprehension-lite, starting with the minor role it plays in skills-learning, especially as it appears in phonics-heavy, decodable texts, and continues through reading material for which comprehension means one right answer for one right question, with little invitation to bring different questions and answers to a discussion of text; a model that dovetails well with the testing imperatives of No Child Left Behind. Fastened within heavily scripted, pre-packaged reading programs, comprehension has little wiggle-room to be nuanced, critical, or alternative.

As a recent report of the Department of Education's Inspector General reveals, Reading First pedagogy has been the single form of reading education being rammed into schools that apply for Reading First funding. Presumably, the rammers believe it is the sole, superior scientifically-based teaching, but as the Department of Education Inspector General's critical report suggests, the ramming has also produced personal financial and professional gain. Quoting an email from the Reading First Director, on reading programs that attempted to be "party crashers" to the small, pre-selected group of publications which the overseers of Reading First strongly advocated, the Director (2006) wrote:

> Beat the [expletive deleted] out of them in a way that will stand up to any level of legal and [whole language] apologist scrutiny. Hit them over and over with definitive evidence that they are not [scientifically-based reading instruction], never have been and never will be. They are trying to crash our party and we need to beat the [expletive deleted] out of them

in front of all the other would-be party crashers who are standing on the front lawn waiting to see how we welcome these dirtbags. (Office of Inspector General, p. 27)

For the rammers, evidence for Reading First instruction comes from the National Reading Panel Report (2000), a document cited in Reading First legislation and repeatedly identified as Reading First's gold standard research. For example, as the Department of Education states, "The Reading First initiative builds on the findings of years of scientific research, which, at the request of Congress, were compiled by the National Reading Panel" (U. S. Department of Education, 2006).

Following publication of the National Reading Panel (NRP) Report, I began reviewing the studies used in the Report and eventually read all of them for my book, *Reading the Naked Truth: Literacy, Legislation, and Lies* (Coles, 2003). How was that possible, anyone who has read the publicity on the NRP Report might wonder, given the vast number of studies? For example, answering the question, "What did the National Reading Panel do?" the National Institute of Health, a chief architect of the study, stated that the Panel reviewed "all the research available *(more than 100,000 reading studies)* [emphasis added] on how children learn to read" (National Institute of Health, 2006).

100,000! In fact, the task, while formidable, was a lot less than suggested by this inflated claim. The reality was (National Institute of Health, 2000): 52 studies were used for the section on phonemic awareness, 38 studies for phonics, 14 for fluency, and 203 for 16 categories of comprehension (12 or 13 studies in each category). The alchemy explaining the differences in the numbers is this: although the NRP identified 100,000 studies on reading, almost all were immediately discarded as being of any use because the panel concluded they had nothing to do with its preconceived notion of what it deemed essential for reading acquisition, i.e., the stepwise ingredients beginning with phonemic awareness and moving onward. Thus, for example, there was no review of studies on writing, classroom libraries, critical literacy, teachers' professional competence, families and literacy, motivation, children's interests, etc. (As a personal but significant aside, I need also note that my full reading of the studies seems to be more than most, if not all, of what the NRP members did, partly because of time constraints that required more work from the panel than it could do if it were to meet publishing deadlines.)

From my review of these studies and no others, I concluded in *Reading the Naked Truth* (2003) that not only were all of the Report's conclusions wrong, these NRP studies alone actually provided evidence to support conclusions opposite to those of the NRP's, including those concerning the benefits of the Reading First's reviled foe, literature-based/whole language instruction. In brief (and amply documented in *Reading the Naked Truth*), my conclusions were these:

1. Skills-emphasis instruction is not superior to teaching skills as needed. For example, students learning skills as needed in literature-based classrooms do as well on the skills portion of conventional reading tests as do students in classes that focus thoroughly and heavily on skills: no better, but no worse. Hence, the NRP report offers no evidence that early, intensive skills instruction is necessary for children to get off to a good start in reading.

2. Reading First instruction is not superior for promoting comprehension beyond first or second grade. This conclusion is based on the surprisingly small number of comprehension studies actually used in the NRP Report, a paucity that is one of the hidden secrets of the NRP Report. A related hidden secret is the Report's generally slender definition of "reading." Although the Report makes many claims about "reading," particularly with respect to the positive effects of skills training, the term "reading" refers at one time to performance on a skills test, another time to word identification, elsewhere to success with word sounds. Only rarely does the term "reading" refer to the commonly accepted definition, that is, reading and comprehending sentences, paragraphs, passages, or stories. By never making these differences clear, the Report appears to rely on an illusion to transmit its conclusions about skills and "reading."

3. Nor is Reading First instruction superior to whole language teaching, as judged by conventional reading tests. The comparison studies used in the NRP Report show that on these tests, which also include skills subtests, children in whole language classes do as well as those in Reading First-type classes.

4. Omitted from the Report are the conclusions of the NRP studies themselves that whole language teaching does not diminish the effective use of word skills for obtaining meaning. Children in whole language classrooms use a greater variety of reading information, and, therefore, do rely less on word skills when comprehending text. However, when they employ word skills, they do so with a higher percentage of accuracy than do readers in skills-heavy classes.

5. The NRP studies also suggest that whole language teaching has other benefits not considered in the Report's narrow boundaries: for example, it encourages a more positive attitude and enthusiasm toward reading, and is more likely to include extensive writing, which in turn helps children learn word skills, written expression, and vocabulary.

6. Schools thinking that Reading First instruction would be most helpful for "at risk" children should think again because the Report's evidence

does not support this conclusion. Neither is there evidence that Reading First instruction helps "disabled" readers overcome their problems and become normal readers. Nor does the Report demonstrate that Reading First instruction is superior for poor children.

In other words, every major instructional conclusion in the NRP Report is not supported by its own research evidence, and overall, the Report is one more example of the pseudoscience that has been foisted on the public in recent years; pseudoscience aimed at bolstering preordained policy aims, rather than policy derived from genuine scientific findings (Mooney, 2006).

Finally, if we look beyond the NRP Report, further evidence for appraising the effectiveness of Reading First instruction comes from recent assessments of fourth-grade reading achievement in states and the nation. At the state level, for example, pre-Reading First test gains were 2.6 points. Following Reading First, that score declined to a 1.9 point gain. On the National Assessment of Educational Progress, pre-Reading First gains for fourth-graders were 0.4; post Reading First, there was a -0.2 loss (Bracey, 2006). Putting all this differently, we have in Reading First legislation and mandates the wrong answers to the wrong policy question!

An Historical Perspective

None of this comes as a surprise to anyone with an historical perspective of the precursor to Reading First; that is, the Texas "education miracle" created under Governor George W. Bush and showcased as the centerpiece of his 2000 and 2004 election campaigns. "Key to Success," was the title of a prominent ad in these campaigns, featuring the Governor hugging a school child while a background voice says: "As governor, George Bush enacted education reforms that produced dramatic results" (Factcheck.org, 2004).

And what instruction was responsible for the results? As defined by the Governor in a speech to Texas teachers, his instructional vision meant a return to old-time basics:

> The building blocks of knowledge were the same yesterday and will be the same tomorrow. We do not need trendy new theories or fancy experiments or feel-good curriculums. The basics work. If drill gets the job done, then rote is right. (Bush, 1996, pp. 1-2)

Unfortunately for students, this old-time educational religion actually produced the Texas myth. Students did do much better on the Texas tests, but these "dramatic results" turned out to be a consequence of teachers teaching to the limited test demands, not because of genuine advances in reading. For example, independent evaluations found that the achievement on the Texas tests was not duplicated on national tests. Overall, fourth- and eighth-graders did about the same as students nationally, not worse, but not better. However, most deplorably for minority students, the group Bush's "signature issue" supposedly was to help most, the new curriculum produced a *larger* achievement gap between them and White students! At the high school level, the reality of the "miracle" revealed itself even more: the dropout rate was among the highest in the nation and increased for Black students after the new curriculum was introduced (Coles, 2003, pp. 115-118.)

"Self/World" Under Governor Bush

To understand more fully the cause of these outcomes requires returning to the framework of the 2006 CRA conference, "World, Self & the Word." Texas children faced the damaging effects of a "word" curriculum devised to make them narrow processors of "the building blocks of knowledge." In addition, there were damaging effects to those aspects of the "self" that affect learning outcomes; effects strongly influenced by the social policy in the "world". In this instance, a world strongly shaped by Governor Bush's policy decisions. The following are a few examples (unless otherwise cited, the references for Governor Bush's policy decisions can be found in Coles, 2003).

Hunger in Texas

Fundamental to the learning "self" are children's levels of nutrition and hunger because, as research has well-documented, they are correlated with reading and other academic outcomes (e.g., Dykman, 1999; Meyers & Cahwla, 2000; Pollitt, 1995). The impact of this connection for many Texas children is suggested in the following statistic: under Governor Bush, Texas ranked third in the percentage of malnourished residents, especially children. The governor's response, when given an opportunity to ameliorate the problem, was evident in the following story: when considering a bill that would have taken a minimal step to reduce hunger by coordinating the state's hunger programs, he vetoed the bill! Afterward, replying to a reporter's question about hunger in the state, the baffled governor asked, "Where?" Another policy decision that affected children's hunger was Bush's decision to slash the state's payments for food stamps, an essential program for the poorest of children.

Health in Texas

Another scientifically documented influence on the learning self is health (Gietzen & Vermeersch, 1980; Pateman, 2003). Under Governor Bush, Texas ranked second in the percentage of poor children who lacked health insurance. In 1999, he had an opportunity to address the problem and thereby promote both children's well-being and reading achievement. Yet, while Texas was flush with a budget surplus, he fought to block affordable health care legislation for about 250,000 children. Meanwhile, he declared a legislative emergency to push through a $45 million tax break for oil well owners, saying, "People are hurting out there."

Class Size in Texas

In addition to a child's internal make-up (nutrition, health, etc.), the learning self is also influenced by the "world" context for learning; a good example of which is class size. Smaller classes, especially in the early grades, enable a teacher to be more professionally responsive to individual differences and craft learning according to children's particular needs. This means that the teacher would not be forced to use a one-size-fits-all prepackaged reading program. As Project STAR and related class-size research in Tennessee has documented, small classes (13-17 students), significantly foster reading and math outcomes for minority and poor children (Finn & Achilles, 1990). Yet Governor Bush opposed efforts to reduce class size, arguing that it was "an infringement of local control" (an exceptionally ironic statement, given how No Child Left Behind has obliterated local control!).

Greater Downsizing of the World, Self and Word

The Texas policy used to downsize the learning "self" was expanded at the national level when George W. Bush became president. Along with the Reading First focus on the "word," the assault on children's well-being, particularly on those aspects related to literacy outcomes, has been relentless. In August, 2006, a Children's Defense Fund review of new census data showed that following an historic low in 2000, the number of children living in poverty has grown over the last 6 years by 11.3 percent, and a child's likelihood of being poor has increased by almost 9 percent. Speaking of the assault on "programs that assist poor children who continue to be left behind," Marian Wright Edelman, President and Founder of the Children's Defense Fund, asked, "What kind of country are we?" (as cited in Reid, 2006). The following examples of policy indifference to children's well-being underscore why Edelman posed this question.

Asthma

Asthma is a condition that affects over 5 million children and can hurt reading achievement by interfering with children's sleep, increasing the likelihood that they will miss school and making them less attentive when they do attend. Asthma especially affects children living in poor urban areas, because the greater pollution generally occurring there compounds respiratory problems. As a result, "disabling asthma was 66 percent higher among Black children than among White children, and 46 percent higher among low-income children than among higher-income children. Children with disabling asthma have almost twice as many lost school days as children with impairments due to other types of chronic conditions." (Children's Defense Fund, 2006, p. 24).

Asthma has multiple determinants, but power plants have long been identified as a leading cause, because the sulfur dioxide and nitrogen dioxide they emit are associated with the disease and various respiratory illnesses. Power plants also are a major source of the pollution that produces smog.

None of the dire health and learning consequences of power plant pollution are inevitable, because policy changes could reduce their emissions to next-to-nothing if power plant companies were to employ, or were forced to employ, state-of-the-art technologies. Instead, the Bush administration's legislative response has been "Clear Skies" (better named "Leave No Pollutant Behind"), a policy concerned primarily with the profits of power companies, not public health. The balance between profits and public health can be gleaned in these numbers: by 2020, power companies would save an estimated $3.5 billion under this kind of legislation, while the estimated national health costs by that year would be $61 billion (Waite, 2005)!

Vision

When we ask "What needs to be done to ensure that children learn to read and write?," good vision, another scientifically supported link to literacy outcome, should be at the top of the list. Rick Weissbourd, a lecturer at the Harvard Graduate School of Education, noted at a conference on the impact of vision on literacy achievement, "In my experience, policy makers [concerned with]...reading don't talk about vision much; practitioners do" (Gillespie, 2001). Like most socially created problems of the "self" that are related to literacy outcomes, minority and poor children are especially affected. At the same conference, Antonia Orfield, a Harvard optometrist, discussing "the epidemic proportions of visual problems among urban poor children," reported that 50% or more minority and low-income children have vision problems that interfere with their academic work; twice the normal rate (25%). Contributing to this "epidemic" is a policy indifference to the causes of vision problems; chief among which are inadequate prenatal care, poor parents' inability to afford to pay for their children's lenses, and fewer manipulative toys for poor children to help develop visual skills (Rothstein, 2004).

The first two problems are readily correctable by a good national health care program (one that would duplicate those in every other industrial nation). Solid legislation requiring a living wage (a wage adequate to meet the basic needs of a worker and dependents) could begin to address the problem of access to manipulative toys by providing poor parents with additional income to purchase them. Instead of these measures, under the Bush administration and the previous Republican Congress, the paltry minimum wage (one much below a living wage) has not moved from $5.15 in more than eight years. In 2006, nearly two minimum wage workers were required to match the $9.28 buying power of one minimum wage worker in 1968 (Sklar, 2006).

Lead

Much evidence connects lead toxicity to educational underachievement, especially reading underachievement. Again, poor children, with blood lead levels five times that of middle-class children, were affected most (Lanphear, Dietrich, Auinger & Cox, 2000). Lead toxicity decreased significantly after lead in gasoline was eliminated in the 1970s. However, lead continues to be a problem because it remains in paint chips and dust, particularly in older homes and buildings, and is ingested by young children through hand-to-mouth activity. Although the standard for lead toxicity has been lowered over the years—10 micrograms per deciliter (mcg/dl), about 100 parts per billion is the currently acceptable "safe" standard—lead researchers have determined that there are no safe lead levels for children.

Solutions for removing lead from homes and other environmental sources have long been established and only lack of political will prevents their implementation. Remarkably, but not surprisingly, the Bush budgets have continued to underfund the federal lead poisoning prevention program. For example, the Bush budget proposed reducing fiscal year 2005 funding of the program by 20%, with similar cuts for fiscal years 2006 and 2007 (United States Department of Housing, 2006).

General Health

As the Children's Defense Fund documents, the health and health care needs of poor children are extensive, with "poor and minority children—especially Black and Latino children—continuing to lag behind White and affluent children in almost every health indicator" (Children's Defense Fund, 2006, p. 2). Poor and minority children are more likely to have unmet medical and dental needs and are more likely to miss days of school due to illness or injury.

The connections to school achievement are clear: children in poor health are more likely to miss days of school, and students who miss more than 10 days of school in a 90-day semester have trouble remaining at their grade level" (Klerman, 1988). Moreover, poor children who are ill are not only two to three times more likely to miss school, they are also more likely to be "on the verge of academic failure" (Allensworth, Lawson, Nicholson, & Wyche, 1997), with reading underachievement the core of academic failure.

Again, these academic repercussions could be drastically reduced with federal policy initiatives. Instead, not only is there indifference to national health care, recent Bush budgets propose reducing Medicaid, the chief federal and state program that provides a modicum of health care for poor children, by $45 billion over the next 10 years. Doing so would leave the states the option of raising taxes or cutting benefits. Attempting to divert attention from federal disinterest in the poor, a Bush administration Medicaid "reform" panel recommended in November, 2006, using the traditional conservative "states' rights" ploy, that states have "more freedom" in administering the health program. However, as William Vaughan, a senior policy analyst at Consumers Union observed, this "flexibility" proposal was really code for allowing states to cut eligibility and benefits (Freking, 2006).

Housing-Student Mobility

Frequent housing changes also are related to lower reading achievement, especially for poor children, who are more likely to move from one school to another in rundown neighborhoods. One way to reduce mobility is by promoting affordable housing, such as through Section 8 housing vouchers, a federal subsidy program for renting in privately owned housing. However, rather than strengthening the program, federal funding for affordable housing has been cut repeatedly in recent years, with the Bush administration targeting a $3 billion cut in fiscal year 2006 and more in subsequent years. These cuts would mean that over the next few years, approximately 375,000 families would lose access to affordable housing, a surefire way to intensify reading problems (National Alliance of HUD Tenants, 2006).

Hunger

Hunger, also linked to reading underachievement, affects millions of children living in households categorized as "food insecure," and here too programs meant to address the problem are under attack. For example, one way to reduce hunger is through the Food Stamp Program, which provides nourishment for over 25 million people, mostly households with children. This is a clearly straightforward measure that would contribute enormously to reading achievement, but the Bush FY2006 budget heads in the opposite direction, calling for reducing food stamp funding by $500 million over the next 5 years! Similarly, cuts are to be made in other anti-hunger programs, such as the Emergency Food Assistance Program and the Commodity Supplemental Food Program. No funding at all is proposed for the Community Food and Nutrition Program (Food Research and Action Center, 2006).

On the other hand, the Bush administration appears to have found one way to eliminate "hunger": remove the word from the federal government's vocabulary! In November, 2006, the Department of Agriculture instantly concealed a disturbing reality by issuing a report on hunger that described families who do not get enough to eat as having "very low food security," unlike its previous reports that described these families as having "food insecurity with hunger." As Jim Weill, director of the Washington-based Food Research and Action Center (FRAC), observed, putting the linguistic slight-of-hand in broader terms, "There are 35 million people in this country who are struggling with hunger, no matter what you call it. The technical terms have been revised, but it doesn't change the reality of stagnant wages, rising costs for housing, health and energy, and the resulting squeeze on food. Millions of people don't have enough to feed themselves, their families or their children" (Food Research and Action Center, November 15, 2006).

To help address hunger, FRAC called for: strengthening the Food Stamp Program; connecting more children to child nutrition programs, such as school breakfast, summer meals, child care food and after school snacks and meals; and boosting family incomes through strategies like an increased minimum wage and refundable tax credits for low-income workers. Political leaders truly concerned about reading achievement would rush to transform these recommendations into reality!

What Does It Take to Raise Children?

The aforementioned influences on reading achievement underscore the need to develop and implement policies that address family income, a fundamental requisite for providing children with the cognitive, physical and emotional foundation, as well as parental time and nurturing, to foster reading success. Yet the nation's economic policies have moved in the opposite direction, especially for the poorest of families! For example, although workers have been increasingly productive and business profits have been good, even the conservative American Enterprise Institute has acknowledged, in a comment that sounds as if it came from Karl Marx, "It looks like the gains from the recovery haven't really filtered down. The gains have gone to owners of capital and not to workers" (as cited in Leonhardt, 2005). Hence, real median household income was almost 3% lower in 2005 than in 2000, and the decline in real household income was largest for the bottom 20 percent of households (Joint Economic Committee, 2006).

As a result of this division, many parents who continue to earn low wages have kept their household income from falling in recent years by working more hours. As Dean Baker (2006), co-director of the Center for Economic and Policy Research in Washington, D.C., has written:

> Inequality in the United States has increased hugely over the last quarter century, as there has been a shift from labor income to profits. The benefits of this growth have gone overwhelmingly to the richest 10% of families, and among this group, disproportionately to the richest 1 percent. Most households have had very modest gains in income over this period, and the gains they did experience have been largely the result of the growth in two-earner households. (p. 1)

Has this growing inequality been due to the blind dynamics of the "market?" No, says Baker, "This upward redistribution *has been largely driven by deliberate policy decisions*" (Baker, 2006, p. 1, emphasis added).

Furthermore, lacking a living wage policy, many working families are sinking deeper into poverty, even though they are working more hours; a trend cloaked by the federal government's misleading poverty guidelines. According to these guidelines, the poverty level for a family of four in 2005 was $19,570 (somewhat higher in Alaska and Hawaii), a preposterously low figure, evident to anyone who has been responsible for family expenditures that include those for children, or who contrasts these poverty guidelines with "living wage" standards, defined as a family budget actually required to afford a safe and decent, yet modest, standard of living.

Comparing the differences between federal poverty and living wage criteria underscores the extent of the burden on many families when they try to find the funds to provide children with adequate nurturance for school success. At the "federal poverty level," for example, only about 7.5% of families in the Northeast and Midwest, 8.9% in the West, and 11.8% in the South meet this official criterion. However, by the more realistic "living wage" standard, over 30% of families in most parts of the country fall below poverty level (Economic Policy Institute, 2005)! How are these families going to overcome the financial obstacles that prevent them from providing their children with the time and resources necessary for ensuring reading and academic success?

Education Budget

"Public schools are America's great hope," President Bush has effused on many occasions (Bush, 2002, June 19), a conception included in his explanation of "compassionate conservatism" (Bush, 2002, April 30), and one which might raise the hope that perhaps, despite the indifference in the policy areas I have outlined, he at least supports public schools. Lamentably, the indifference is seamless! During the administration's first years, despite all of its purported focus on educational achievement and being the president's "signature issue," the annual education budget increases were under 1%, (fiscal year 2003 = 0.7% increase; fiscal year 2004 = 0.5%). The single notable increase came for fiscal year 2005, which at the end of Bush's first term just happened to coincide with the 2004 Presidential election campaign! However, once a second term was secured, the education budget began heading south: a decrease of 0.9% was proposed for fiscal year 2006, and a 3.8% cut for fiscal year 2007!

For fiscal year 2006, 48 programs were marked for elimination, including:

1. National Writing Project—The premier effort to improve writing in the nation by providing professional development for teachers to help their students become successful writers and learners. Not a surprising cut, given the President's focus on "reading," not "literacy."
2. Elementary and High School Counseling
3. Dropout Prevention
4. Talent Search—to increase the number of youth from disadvantaged backgrounds to complete high school and attend college
5. All vocational education at the high school level

Beyond diminished support for educational programs, there is the problem of children, particularly poor children, attending physically deteriorating schools that do not provide an adequate infrastructure for educational needs. Currently, an estimated $268 billion is needed for repairs that would simply bring these schools up to basic standards. Yet despite the extent of deterioration suggested by this estimate, the Bush budget for repairing or replacing schools remains at $54 *million*, with no additional funds projected for maintenance and construction (see current and previous budgets and analyses at Office of Budget and Management, 2007)

Social Program Cuts

Overall, Bush's proposed budget cuts to 2010 for social spending, such as Medicaid, housing assistance, food stamps, Head Start, K-12 education, etc. come to approximately $185 billion, or 14%. If we look for an explanation for these cuts, we find that they are primarily due to decreased revenue, because of tax cuts for the rich and increased military spending, particularly for the Iraq debacle. For example, the Center for Budget and Policy Priorities (2005) calculates that the 2001-2005 tax cuts increased the deficit in 2005 by $539 billion. Without these cuts, the nation would have had a surplus that could have been used to *increase* social and educational spending. During the same years, there was a 37% increase due to military spending, which does not include all of the extra appropriations for the Iraq war (Iraq war spending, as of December, 2006, came to approximately $350 billion [National Priorities Project, 2006]). In contrast, to these figures, a relatively smaller percentage increase in domestic program spending, about 15% or $22 billion, such as the kind that helps children, contributed to increasing the deficit.

Although the deficit was reduced in fiscal 2006, the Center on Budget and Policy Priorities calculates that this was a "temporary blip" rather than solid progress, and "the long-term outlook remains bleak." If Bush's tax cuts become permanent, deficits are estimated to total "nearly $3.5 trillion over the next 10 years (2007-2016), surely leaving less and less for children's well-being and certainly further damaging literacy achievement" (Kogen & Horney, 2006).

Three Rivers

If we accept the current standard of "scientifically-based" as the guide for determining policy to maximize students' reading achievement, the array of policy influences on the "self" that I have reviewed surely have ample, scientifically-documented support requiring their inclusion in any genuine policy aimed at promoting literacy. Placing these influences within the College Reading Association's 2006 conference theme, "Three Rivers of Literacy: Knowledge: Word, Self, World," reveals that the Reading First approach is a policy drought focused rigidly, narrowly, and obsessively on a conception of the "self" solely as a cognitive processor of words.

Understanding this drought requires placing it within a larger context that includes growing inequality, a dedication to the well-being of corporations and the rich, an increasing indifference to most Americans, especially the poor, all of which is wrapped up in a pretense of concern, a "compassionate conservatism."

It is a strategy which, while appearing to address social inequities, employs instead a minimalist scheme for focusing narrowly and inadequately on one slice of social inequity: reading. Doing so, the policy includes several callous hoaxes, chief of which is the assumption that reading is the bootstrap that will enable poor children to lift themselves to further academic success, which in turn will lift them to a secure a place in the global economy. The culmination of this hoax supposedly will greatly level the nation's class inequities and elevate the economy. And, yes, as part of this trajectory, good readers will be better shoppers! As Bush wrapped it all in one package, "helping children and adults gain the reading skills they need to succeed in life [will] provide students with the foundation to achieve their dreams," increase their "economic participation," help "create more stable and vibrant economies," and enable "adults to be better consumers" (Bush, September 15, 2006).

To ensure that the "three rivers" do not become the overarching policy approach to reading achievement, compassionate conservatism attacks those who highlight the impact of the entire "self" on literacy acquisition. To talk about the influence of the conditions of poverty on children's literacy outcome, compassionate conservatism insists, is to make "excuses." As the right-wing Heritage Foundation insists in its "no excuses" perspective, with the right [school] principal (who knows how to stretch inadequate funding), high standards, a good curriculum, and common sense, poor children can stay poor yet become academically successful. There is no need for "reducing class size, modernizing school facilities," or employing what Heritage labels as "any of the conventional nostrums for improving public education" (as cited in Carter, 2000, p. 4). All such recommendations are "excuses."

Similarly, Bush has insisted that any talk about the effect of poor children's lives on their learning participates in "the soft bigotry of low expectations," a phrase often repeated in his speeches (Bush, July 20, 2006). Within this compassionate conservative framework, poverty is accepted as a given, while the keys to success are Reading First and "holding schools accountable" through testing (Bush, July 1, 2003). As if to underscore his insistence on the need to eschew language that contains the "bigotry of low expectations," the word "poverty" seems never to appear in any speech the president has given in the poorest of schools; not in the District of Columbia, North Carolina, Mississippi or anywhere else! When the word does appear, as in a 2001 speech announcing the further dismantling of the "War on Poverty" begun during the Johnson administration, the President explained that "much of today's poverty has more to do with troubled lives than a troubled economy." The answer? Faith-based and community initiatives filled with "idealistic Americans" providing "works of compassion" for these troubled lives (Bush, May 21, 2001).

Finally, to frame this policy drought, we need to place it within the context of the nation's labor force. Despite constant cries that reading and additional education are critical for a labor force in an economy at risk, in fact there presently is *no* gap between workers' skills and job demands, nor is there projected to be! As Michael J. Handel concludes in his examination of the issue:

> While most individuals will benefit personally from more education and training, there is little evidence of a large or growing gap between employers' demand for skilled workers and their supply. There is not even any agreement on the specific skills employers are believed to need so badly in such greater numbers. The increasing number of immigrants with limited English language proficiency also contradicts the notion that employers have a problem hiring workers with limited skills. (Handel, 2006)

In other words, from the viewpoint of those making policy on behalf of the nation's business needs, there is little incentive to go beyond the current status quo and provide genuine, full education for all children. The reality, from a cold-blooded profit perspective, is that large numbers of poor people are expendable in relation to business's labor needs. Therefore, if large numbers of poor children do not get very educated, nothing is lost. Putting considerable resources into the lives and education of poor children would increase domestic spending but not produce a profit. Consequently, a policy of pretending to do something for poor children, while doing very little, works well, for profit that is, not for poor children. This division provides another view of the influence of the "world" and raises the question of whose interests does policy serve and ignore?

The grim reality of the combination of Reading First pedagogy, NCLB testing, and "no excuses" reading education requires that college reading curricula go beyond the attenuated "word" framework that drives current policy and, instead, include a full "three rivers" perspective on literacy education. Such a perspective is especially required for teachers to become able not only to appraise the specious Reading First's claims, but to recognize and act upon the reality that successful teaching and learning requires a "three rivers"— world, self, and word—approach. The essential starting question for reaching these rivers remains, "What needs to be done to ensure that children will learn to read and write?"

References

Allensworth, D., Lawson, E., Nicholson, L., & Wyche, J. (1997). Schools and health:

Our nation's investment, National Academies Press, 1997, p. 159.

Baker, D. (2006). Increasing inequality in the United States, *Center for Economic and Policy Research*. Retrieved on December 27, 2006, from http://www.cepr.net/index. php?option=com_content&task=view&id=481&Itemid=8

Benton, J. (2006, May 29). After run of successes in other fields, he sees bright future in for-profit schools. *Dallas Morning News*. Retrieved on December 27, 2006, from http://www.dallasnews.com

Bracey, G. (2006, October). The 16th Bracey report on the condition of public education. *Phi Delta Kappan*, 151-166.

Bush, G. W. (1996). Governor George W. Bush speaks out!" *Right to Read Report*. March-April.

Bush, G. W. (2001, May 21). Remarks by the President in commencement address University of Notre Dame, Notre Dame, Indiana. Washington, D.C.: The White House. Retrieved on December 27, 2006, from http://www.whitehouse.gov/news/releases/2001/05/20010521-1.html

Bush, G. W. (2002, April 30). Fact sheet: Compassionate conservatism. Washington, D.C.: The White House. Retrieved on December 27, 2006, from http://www.whitehouse.gov/news/releases/2002/04/20020430.html

Bush G. W. (2002, June 19). President speaks at White House Conference on Character and Community. Washington, D.C.: The White House. Retrieved on December 27, 2006, from http://www.whitehouse.gov/news/releases/2002/06/20020619-22.html

Bush, G. W. (2003, July 1). President discusses education reform in D.C., Kipp D.C. Key Academy. Washington, D.C.: The White House. Retrieved on December 27, 2006, from http://www.whitehouse.gov/news/releases/2003/07/20030701-3.html

Bush, G.W. (2006, July 20). President Bush addresses NAACP Annual Convention. Washington, D.C.: The White House. Retrieved on December 27, 2006, from http://www.whitehouse.gov/news/releases/2006/07/20060720.html

Bush, G. W. (2006, September 15). Literacy Day, 2006: A proclamation by the President of the United States of America. Retrieved on December 27, 2006, from http://www.whitehouse.gov/news/releases/2006/09/20060915-13.html

Carter, S. (2000). *No excuses: Lessons from 21 high-performing, high-poverty schools*. Washington, D.C.: Heritage Foundation.

Center on Budget and Policy Priorities (2005, January 31). *CBO Data show tax cuts have played much larger role than domestic spending increases in fueling the deficit*. Retrieved on December 27, 2006 from http://www.cbpp.org/1-25-05bud.htm

Chall, J. (1967). *Learning to read: The great debate*. New York: McGraw-Hill.

Children's Defense Fund (2006). *Improving children's health: Understanding children's health disparities and promising approaches to them*. Washington, D.C.: Children's Defense Fund.

Coles, G. (2003). *Reading the naked truth: Literacy, legislation, and lies*. Portsmouth, NH: Heinemann.

Dykman, R. (1999). Infancy to adolescence: Long-term effects of nutrition on growth. In *Breakfast and Learning in Children Symposium Proceedings* (pp. 61-66). Washington, DC: United States Department of Agriculture, Center for Nutrition Policy and Promotion.

Economic Policy Institute (2005, August 31). Economic snapshots. Retrieved on December 27, 2006, from http://www.epi.org/content.cfm/webfeatures_snapshots_20050831

Factcheck.org (2004, May 12). *Bush education ad: Going positive, selectively*. Retrieved

December, 27, 2006, from http://www.factcheck.org/article181.html.

Finn, J. & Achilles, C. (1990). Answers and questions about class size: A statewide experiment. *American Educational Research Journal*, *27*, 557-577.

Food Research and Action Center (2006). Budget Fight FY 2007: Protect Food Stamp and Child Nutrition Programs. Retrieved December 27, 2006, from http://www.frac.org/Legislative/Budget_07/index.html

Food Research and Action Center (2006, November 15). More than 35 million of Americans lived in food insecure households in 2005. Retrieved December 27, 2006, from http://www.frac.org/Press_Release/11.15.06.html

Freking, K. (2006, November 17). Democrats reject changes in Medicaid, Associated Press. Retrieved December 27, 2006, from http://www.wtopnews.com/index.php?nid=106&pid=0&sid=979084&page=2

Gietzen, D. & Vermeersch, J. (1980). Health status and school achievement of children from Head Start and free school lunch programs. *Public Health Reports.* 1980, 95, 362–368.

Gillespie, K. (2001, April 17). How vision impacts literacy: An educational problem that can be solved. *Learning Problems: The Visual Connection.* Harvard Graduate School of Education. Retrieved December 27, 2006, from http://www.optometrists.org/therapists_teachers/Harvard_study_literacy.html

Handel, M. (2006). Worker skills and job requirements: Is there a mismatch? Washington, D.C.: Economic Policy Institute, 2006. Retrieved on December 27, 2006, from http://www.epi.org/content.cfm/book_worker_skills

Joint Economic Committee, Democrats (2006, September 21). Losing ground: The middle class in the Bush economy. *Economic Fact Sheet*. Retrieved on December 27, 2006, from http://www.jec.senate.gov/democrats

Klerman, L.(1988). School absence—A health perspective. *Pediatric Clinics of North America*, *35*, 1253-1269.

Kogen, R. & Horney, J. (2006, October 11). Deficit announcement masks bigger story: Long-term outlook remains bleak. Washington, D.C.: Center on Budget and Policy Priorities. Retrieved on December 27, 2006, from http://www.cbpp.org/10-11-06bud.htm

Lanphear, B., Dietrich, K., Auinger, P., & Cox, C. (2000). Cognitive deficits associated with blood lead concentrations <10 μg/DL in U.S. children and adolescents. *Public Health Reports*, 115, 521-529.

Leonhardt, D. (2005, August 31). U.S. poverty rate was up last year. *New York Times*, 1-14.

Lyon, G. Reid (n.d.). Interview. *Children of the Code*. Retrieved December 27, 2006, from http://www.childrenofthecode.org/interviews/lyon.htm

Meyers, A., & Cahwla, N. (2000). Nutrition and the social, emotional, and cognitive development of infants and young children. *Zero to Three*, *21*, 5-12.

Mooney, C. (2006). *The Republican war on science*. New York: Basic Books.

National Alliance of HUD Tenants (2006). 375,000 families may lose Section 8 under Bush budget proposal for 2006. Retrieved December 27, 2006, from http://www.saveourhomes.org/news/news2.php

National Institute of Health (2006). *National Reading Panel: What did the National Reading Panel Do?* Washington, D.C. Retrieved December 27, 2006, from http://www.nichd.nih.gov/health/topics/national_reading_panel.cfm.

National Priorities Project (2006). The war in Iraq costs! Northampton, MA: National Priorities Project. Retrieved on December 27, 2006, from www.national priorities.org

National Reading Panel (2000). *Report of the National Reading Panel: Teaching Children to Read. Reports of the Subgroups.* Washington, D.C.: National Institute of Child, Health and Human Development.

Office of Budget and Management (2007). Budget of the United States Government. Washington, D.C.: The White House. Retrieved on December 27, 2006, from http://www.whitehouse.gov/omb/budget/

Office of Inspector General (2006, September). *The Reading First Program's Grant Application Process.* Washington, D.C.: Department of Education.

Pateman, B. (2003). Healthier students, better learners. *Educational Leadership, 61*(4), 70-74.

Pollitt, E. (1995, October). "Does breakfast make a difference in school?" *Journal of the American Dietetic Association, 95*(10), 1134-9.

Reid, J. (2006). *New census data shows 1.3 million children have fallen into poverty since 2000,* Washington, D.C., Children's Defense Fund. Retrieved December 27, 2006, from http://www.childrensdefense.org/site/News2?page=NewsArticle& id=7887

Rothstein, R. (2004). *Class and schools: Using social, economic, and educational reform to close the black-white achievement gap.* Washington, D.C.: Economic Policy Institute, 37-38.

Sklar, H. (2006, December 2). Minimum wage breaks no-raise record. Retrieved December 27, 2006, from http://www.commondreams.org/views06/1202-22.htm

U. S. Department of Education (2006). *Reading First, Program Description.* Retrieved December 27, 2006, from http://www.ed.gov/programs/readingfirst/index.html.

United States Department of Housing and Urban Development (2006). Fiscal year 2007 budget summary. Washington, D.C.: United States Department of Housing and Urban Development.

Waite, J. (2005). *Dirty skies: The "Clear Skies Act of 2005" would harm the public, help big polluters and worsen global warming.* U.S. Senate Committee on Environment and Public Works, Hearing on S. 131, the "Clear Skies Act of 2005," February 2. Retrieved December 27, 2006, from http://www.nrdc.org/air/pollution/tjw0205.asp

PEDAGOGIES OF THE OPPRESSORS: CRITICAL LITERACIES AS COUNTER NARRATIVES

Patrick Shannon

Penn State University

*Keynote Address
College Reading Association
2006*

Patrick Shannon is a professor of education at Penn State University. His most recent book is Reading Against Democracy *(Heinemann, 2007). This talk will be the opening chapter of* Pedagogies of the Oppressors.

All institutions present lessons concerning what we should know, who we should be, and what we should value in order to position us. They use specific pedagogical strategies that always involve text, broadly defined, that are supposed to be read in a particular way and that are always political. Regardless of their form, each text is organized through language conventions—they have a code to crack, a grammar to follow, meanings to construct, and intentions to discover. Through a story of a long car ride, I develop an argument for critical literacies to read such texts against their intended meanings.

M y summers are spent driving our kids to one place or another. It used to be short trips to lessons, sporting events or friends' houses. Now it's to and from college campuses with all their stuff in tow or to and from internships in order to study the evolutionary genomics of corn or the contamination transport

Reprinted from *Navigating the Literacy Water: Research, Praxis, & Advocacy*, pp. 2-10, by M. Foote, F. Falk-Ross, S. Szabo, M. B. Sampson, Eds., 2008, Commerce, TX: College Reading Association.

within differing ground systems. None of these activities can take place within 10 driving hours of home. Each must be negotiated singly because they occur in opposite directions from one another. If one goes to the Midwest, the other travels South or to the Northeast. As an aside, Kathleen and I (I'm married to Kathleen) can't quite understand how two tragically hip literacy teachers could raise a couple of nerds with complete pocket protection. When the kids speak to one another in codes that they pretend to be scientific, Kathleen and I know that they are just talking about sex, drugs and rock and roll. After all, they are college students.

At the end of this summer, I drove to Grinnell, Iowa, to deposit our daughter for her senior year. Pointed west, we talked about her plans for this year and next, the curious fact that Indiana has outsourced its part of I 80 to a foreign company, and the inevitable truth that Chicago will never complete its can-of-worms road system in order to permit drivers to get where they want to go without swearing. On the way back, I attended to the public pedagogy of the free radio airwaves. I use the word *free* loosely to mean that I did not have a subscription to private stations. Between belting out oldies lyrics along with the station disc jockeys who populate the dial, I listened to National Public Radio (NPR) in its various forms across two time zones. Within one 13-hour jaunt, I learned four lessons that make me a modern American:

> Lesson One: Consume above all else, consume,
> Lesson Two: Believe experts,
> Lesson Three: Romanticize the past, and
> Lesson Four: Civic life is boring.

Let me stop for a moment to declare my intentions for this talk. I hope to develop the argument for critical literacies as essential elements of reading education at all levels of schooling. They are necessary for citizens to participate in the governing of their lives—be they limited to what the Golden Arches mean, whether to vote for building that new school in your town, or how to understand such terms as *regime change*. My route to that hope has three stops along the way.

The first stop is the notion of public pedagogy—all institutions present lessons to us concerning what we should know, who we should be, and what we should value. They use specific pedagogical strategies that are not always readily apparent, but they are nonetheless there. Sports cars are painted red for a reason, eh? Ministers give sermons. And Bill Gates talks endlessly about innovation.

Second, I'll stop at the notion that the pedagogical strategies always involve texts, broadly defined, that are supposed to be read in a particular way. For example, the texts during my drive were aural, visual, tactile, and even gustatory. That is, I listened to chatter, songs, and reports. I looked at the bumper stickers, lane dividers, and signs. I felt the ripple bumps before the ticket booths, the cold steel of the gas nozzle, and the hot tea (because my dad told me that coffee would stunt my growth). I tasted the sugar-laced foods in Iowa, Illinois, Indiana, and Pennsylvania, but stopped twice for salads in Ohio. I am happy to report that I did not smell Gary, Indiana, as I used to when Kathleen and I worked at Purdue, and we would drive to see the Cubs play at Wrigley Field, although the steel plants are running to some capacity. Regardless of their form, each of the texts was organized through language forms and conventions—they had a code to crack, a grammar to follow, meanings to construct, and intentions to discover.

The third stop will be to acknowledge that pedagogies and texts always represent the ideological struggles to position me and to capture my allegiance. The texts are designed for more than me, but I'll admit that I take them personally. I used to think that taking it personally was a problem, until I recognized that others took it personally too. Our individual issues were really social problems. Now I used what C. Wright Mills (1959) called a sociological imagination.

Think about my choice of radio network—NPR has been on the Bush administration's hit list for 5 years because it is assumed to project a liberal bias. As we all know, only Fox News is fair and balanced. We can examine the slants between the *New York Times* and the *Wall Street Journal* in newspapers. It seems easy to locate political ideologies within media news. It is more difficult perhaps to identify ideologies within other institutions however. Do you think of churches as ideological? Sports? Corporations? Schools? And of course, not all examples within a category fit neatly under an ideological label.

Because of this variation and the fact that these pedagogies, texts and ideologies must rely on language to carry their meanings, they are never complete or unitary. They don't convey a uniform message. Rather, they contain holes and contradictions that permit readers to insert themselves as active participants within the continuous construction of their identities and negotiations of social spaces. That is what makes critical literacies possible. These acts of identifying contradictions, stepping into those gaps, and bending those oppressive intentions are what I mean by critical literacies. I use the plural of literacy here because I recognize that reading and creating different types of texts require different sets of practices that vary across time and place.

Using the texts of my journey home, I hope to demonstrate how the government, courts, media, think tanks, businesses big and small, sports, and even churches use pedagogical strategies in order to re-present the world for me and to teach me my place within it. For example, throughout the day, I passed government texts composed to regulate my driving, positioning me and suggesting to me that I live in a society of laws. The standardization of the signs and the articulation system among signs (shapes, colors, symbol, alphabet) is a pedagogical strategy meant to teach me that I am a subject of the state, equal to all others. If this were not the intent of the authorities behind the signs, then there would be qualifications. And of course, there are some official qualifications marked on signs that split speeds for trucks and cars, assign lanes only to car pools, and divert only certain drivers to be weighed.

Do you see the pedagogy here? Standardization of symbols and grammar is the pedagogical strategy selected to represent equality and uniform expectations. If we teach reading only as breaking codes and following authors' intentions to their ends, then we obscure what's really going on here. These laws (all laws?) are negotiated continuously. By that I mean, no one drove the speed limit, some never left the passing lane, and some cars followed the trucks at the easy on/ easy off rest stops instead of complying with the signs segregating vehicles by size. The negotiations of these law/sign/texts were mediated by patrol cars, horns, hand signals, and wrecks. Officials intended all signs to be read by all drivers, but each sign conveyed more than it stated. For example, what can be made of the 70 miles an hour speed limit in Indiana and Iowa and the 65 law in Pennsylvania, Ohio and Illinois? Is it that life is cheaper near corn?

But there are seamier sides to these negotiations as well. Although the pedagogy of the standardization of symbols is meant to convey uniformity and equality, it actually hides important realities. Minorities and the poor are more likely to be pulled over by the police, they are more likely to be ticketed and more likely to receive punishment—even more severe punishment than other groups. These realities are the social life of the texts/signs—how the signs work in society and for whom. Unless we include pragmatic practices, how the signs position me and others, and critical practices, what the signs hide, within our reading instruction, then the pedagogy of standardization inhibits our recognition and evaluation of that social life. The signs oppress us, some more than others. Does that mean that I am advocating driving on the wrong side of the road? No, it means that we should advocate and engage in teaching reading to others in order that they can identify the contradictions between standardization in signs and preferential treatment in reality.

Let me try to make these points about pedagogy, texts and ideologies clearer with another example. One of the main NPR stories of that day was U. S. District Judge Anna Diggs Taylor's order to halt the National Security Agency's warrant-less wiretapping program that had been secretly authorized by President Bush in 2001. According to Judge Taylor, the President's program violates privacy and free speech rights and the Constitutional separation of powers among the three branches of government. She was quoted as writing: (This is difficult to take down when you are driving).

> It was never the intent of the framers to give the President such unfettered control, particularly where his actions blatantly disregard the parameters clearly enumerated in the Bill of Rights.... There are no hereditary kings in America and no powers not created by the Constitution.

Judge Taylor employed the pedagogical strategy of displacement in which she associates President Bush's actions with those of a king – someone above the law. Clearly her text is meant to teach us that the President has overstepped his bounds as the story of the Constitution taught in all U.S. schools is that it is a document intended to balance powers among branches of government in order to prevent the rise of a monarchy. The immediate response from the White House was to say the words "national security during the War on Terror" and to repeat that phrase several times within three short sentences. This is the pedagogical strategy of euphemization in which the War on Terror is to stand for the warrantless wiretapping, and therefore, to legitimize it by the association. This is a popular pedagogy of the White House as President Bush often uses the phrase "in other words." The oral statement/text was meant to teach listeners that we are at war, that it's a war against terror; and therefore, the experts must take actions that are new and bold.

NPR, for its part, employed the pedagogical strategy of expert commentary to provide what it considers rational grounds for its legitimacy as a source of knowledge, not just of information. Some experts interviewed were elected officials. Democrats applauded the ruling for the most part. Republicans spoke from a news release entitled "Liberal Judge Backs Dem Agenda to Weaken National Security." Other experts were from institutions outside of government: think tanks, advocacy agencies, and universities. For example, Anthony Romero, Executive Director of the ACLU, used the pedagogical strategy of trope to suggest that Diggs' ruling was "another nail in the coffin" of the Bush Administration's anti-terrorism programs. Bobby Chesney, a national security law specialist from Wake Forest University stated, "No question that the ruling is a poorly reasoned decision."

Perhaps the political ideological struggle is apparent within these texts and the pedagogies of the institutions of courts, government, and radio are too. Conservatives might suggest that simply airing Diggs' ruling as news demonstrates NPR's liberal bias because it undermines the war efforts. Perhaps, liberals will frost because the White House was able to present its smoke-and-mirrors justification one more time publicly. But I want to draw your attention to NPR's pedagogy in parading "experts" before the public, as if their statements were the ends of all considerations. What is a national security law specialist? What does the category of *national security* entail? Why is a specialist needed? How does NPR pick specialists? Who gets to pick them? What is the market for specialists? How might that market have an effect on what can be said? These are critical questions left unspoken on NPR that day.

I've mentioned some pedagogies, texts and ideologies in order to whet your appetite for critical literacies. Standardization, displacement, euphemization, expert commentary, rational grounds, and trope are not the usual names reading educators use when talking about pedagogical strategies. As Roger

Simon (2001) explained, the term pedagogy extends the concept of teaching beyond the details of what information is worth knowing, what it means to know something, and what students and others might do together in order to also include the cultural politics that such decisions support. To propose a pedagogy is to propose a political vision. To talk about pedagogical practices is to talk about politics. The strategies I've mentioned so far and the textual means by which advocates within institutions express their visions are pedagogies of the oppressors. All seek to position us in ways that bring both opportunities and limits for our agency. Rarely do institutions announce their intentions directly and the pedagogical strategies they employ help them to legitimize their visions without full disclosure. Public pedagogical strategies put the onus on the learner because school is out, eh? That's what critical literacies can do. They can help us with that burden.

On the road again. Billboards act as the Sirens did for Odysseus on nearly every mile of the highway. "Stop to fill up" they inveigle. Fill up in every way imaginable. The signs compete with each other near (with several alternatives listed on one sign) and far (as some invite you to drive past the close businesses in order to stop at ones distant and more exotic). The signs don't just inform; they create as well. As I drove I felt—not just thought, but felt— that I could use a discount pair of pants or shoes, a Krispy Krème donut, or fireworks! Some signs/texts worked simply from branding. Their logo alone evoked the vision in readers' heads that companies worked so hard to create over time. The green circle with the white queen of beans invited me for a venti chocolate macchiato half decaf, low fat with whip for way too much money. But the pink double D was not enticing enough to stop for a sugar ring. Sometimes logos work strangely over time. In our family's early driving trips, the golden arches meant clean, or at least cleaner, restrooms with changing tables. That story remains clearly in my head. When I see the arches now, I always steer clear. Those days are over—I'm only somewhat happy to say.

Branding and logos are a form of displacement, but they involve a different type of association. Instead of displacing one element for another in order to instantiate a single association, branding seeks to position the reader as the lead in a story of ownership and consumption. In that order, thank you. Buy, then consume, and then buy again. Just like Aldous Huxley envisioned in *Brave New World* —"End not mend" was the official slogan delivered through hypnopedia—one of my favorite terms.

The pedagogical strategy of storying is not the same thing as displacement nor is it the same as George Lakoff's framing. Rather another psychologist is responsible for storying—the randy behaviorist John B. Watson after he left academia for Madison Avenue. Thank Watson for the piles of goodies next to the cash registers in grocery stores because "like rats in the maze, consumers reach for the items within proximity." In 1923, Watson invented program lead-ins when he delivered a 10-minute national radio lecture on the glands that he ended at the mouth, just before his sponsor's commercial for toothpaste. After empirical tests demonstrated that consumers could not choose their brand by senses alone, Watson proposed that Americans "walk a mile for a Camel," "take a coffee break with Maxwell House," and follow the advise of the Queens of Spain and Romania to use Ponds Cold and Vanishing Cream. In each of these "stories" the reader/customer was to see him or her self with the hip, new ways of living, and of course, buy the product. We have not come a long way baby from Watson's invention of market research.

Storying is a powerful pedagogical strategy, and I am using it for this talk, as I channel Charles Kuralt in order to put you in the driver's seat for this trip across America. It's kind of a buddy talk and drive. I'm Thelma, and you can be Louise. We're in this together!

Logos and slogans are supposed to evoke the storying with the least amount of institutional exposure. That happens just as Watson planned with the logo, phrase, brand becoming the stimuli and the pleasant story association resulting as the conditioned response. The S-R chain continues with the story leading directly to purchases. The pedagogical strategy of repetition of the stimulus and response connections works dramatically as we open our wallets to satisfy immediately our desires created and fulfilled by business. This is language that educators understand, but we are never as successful with the stimulus and response strategy as the advertisers who can part a fool and his money—sometimes lots of money—in 30 seconds or less. Buyer beware!

Another NPR story during my trip demonstrated just how wary a buyer must be. U. S. District Judge Gladys Kessler ended a seven-year case against tobacco companies by agreeing with the federal government that the tobacco CEOs had conspired to deceive the public about the health risks of smoking for 50 years. The judge ordered the companies to apologize publicly, admitting their conspiracy to deceive, and to stop using euphemization in order to teach the public that problems with smoking can be abated by smoking "light, low tar, mild, or natural cigarettes." These terms were used to fool the public about what the companies had known since 1954 when CEOs met at a New York hotel to agree to the cover up. The judge described tobacco as, "The highly addictive product that leads to a staggering number of deaths per year, an immeasurable amount of human suffering and economic loss and a profound burden on our national health care system." The Judge stated that new federal law prevented her from fining the companies the $14 billion that the feds sought.

Again NPR trotted out experts to demonstrate their legitimacy. The experts presented a couple of sides to the story. William Corr, the Executive Director of the Campaign for Tobacco Free Kids applauded. Mark Smith, an R. J. Reynolds spokesman, stated, "We're gratified that the court did not award unjustified and extraordinary expensive monetary penalties, but we're disappointed that Kessler found the firms had engaged in conspiracy." Again the expert opinion is a wash, and dare I say uselessly predictable. No expert on NPR mentioned anything about the fact that the government subsidizes tobacco production through the Department of Agriculture, that antismoking education has been effective only with certain segments of the population, and that the required public apologies would bring smoking to the public's attention, and therefore, promote it. Since most people in the United States already know that smoking is hazardous to your health because it kills many, the apology ads will simply sell cigarettes. Although none of these opinions were heard on NPR, each was voiced within the a two minute segment on a CBC broadcast from Windsor Ontario that I caught while rolling past Toledo.

In this example, we encounter the market ideology that brings much of the American right and left political ideologies together in the celebration of capitalism and its right to direct modern, and even, postmodern life. The free market worked for 50 years to the misery of millions of people and the cost of billions (estimated $280 billion in company profits and medical costs of 100s of millions). Without government regulation, even with government support, captains of industry and those who work for them put profit above people's well being. The tobacco companies did not and do not police themselves. Decoding company statements or even the NPR banter would not reveal the deadly consequences of this market ideology; comprehension of companies' and government's purposeful deception makes us dupes. Only reading that would enable us to identify the pedagogical strategies the companies used would prepare us to be agents within the construction of our identities within a living democracy. And those critical reading practices are necessary for kids as well as adults because as we've learned recently—things don't go better with Coca Cola or Count Chocula—even in the school lunch lines.

Without a subscription channel to carry you across the country, a driver must punch the scan button to continue constant aural stimulation. That act brings two distinct, but somewhat overlapping, voices to the driver's ears. Oldies but goodies songs and DJs and Christian preachers seem to rule the airwaves between central Iowa and central Pennsylvania. They are particularly crowded around the 80s and 90s numbers on the dial. I don't want to get in too much trouble here—so I will tread softly.

First, let me say that oldies aren't as old as they used to be. Kurt Cobain and Nirvana do not play oldies—despite what some disc jockeys tell you. Dion and the Belmonts performed oldies. "Well I'm the type of guy, who likes to roam around" is the perfect song for driving home. As I listened to oldies, my rented Hyundai became my parents' Ford 300, and I forgot my present in order to invoke the past. Each song invited me to forget the day's events—29 killed in Baghdad, France balked at leading the peace-keeping force in Lebanon—in order to remember the glories of my youth. Then, life was simple. Shoo doop be do be do, shoo doop be do be do.

The pedagogy of nostalgia is potent. Conservatives hold it as a core value. If the present were like the past, then things would be better, they say without much evidence. Well, my 1950s had American enforced regime changes as well—perhaps you remember Iran in 1953 and Guatemala—one for oil and the other for food. My 60s had American enforced regime changes in Vietnam (South not North) and my 70s had Chile. You get the picture, and remember that those pictures of nostalgia are always air brushed. The pedagogy of nostalgia has the same intention as the magician who points in one direction to hide what she's doing with the other hand. The pedagogy of nostalgia is powerful politically. Think Morning in America (which was President Reagan's campaign theme and is still the title of William Bennett's non NPR talk radio show). The pedagogy of nostalgia works economically as well because it delivers a certain demographic. Perhaps that's why station disc jockeys now date their oldies period for their stations, and my era only gets played before dawn, when men my age have to get up to pee.

Radio ministers evoke nostalgia as well—Gimme that Old Time Religion. They teach reading directly. That is, they name, read, and explain scripture to an audience. They promote reading because Christians must learn to read in order to be saved from a horrid afterlife. Reading reveals God's words, and those words solve the teleological puzzle of human life by giving it purpose. We are here, they say, in order to prepare to live eternally with God's grace. But life on earth is tempting and confusing. So radio ministers help listeners address those temptations and confusions by naming them and locating scripture that provides answers. Because those answers are not transparent, ministers mediate them. The mediations I listened to on my trip were not offered as interpretations, rather the ministers spoke with and from authority. This is the pedagogical strategy of certainty, in which text is treated as if it were closed with a single meaning. Not a meaning reached by negotiation and consensus, mind you, but one that identified truth. We ignore this revealed truth at our peril.

This, I'm sure you will agree, is a bad reading lesson. Our questioning the authority within and behind text should cut deeper than the decades old debate over readers' roles in the construction of meaning from/with text. The new debate should center on the positioning work of texts and the political and economic forces that enable that work to be accomplished. The radio ministers spoke for God. That's a pretty strong authority—even for a lapsed Catholic like me. As a first generation American of Irish decent, however, I know that there are disputes over God's truth, even among different sects of faithful Christians. The ministers of each denomination differ on the meaning of scripture—the word of God. So we have multiple Gods with multiple truths depending on which point on the dial we select. Of course, each God has a differing amount of force behind its authority. Trying to understand how multiple Gods and multiple truths are possible is overwhelming and often sorrowful. But even among the radio stations the problem is clearly before us. And beyond the radio airwaves, Lebanon and Israel had just agreed to a ceasefire and Baghdad was still burning. The problems posed by multiple god authorities and multiple truths are clearly literacy issues with multiple texts, many pedagogical strategies, and several ideologies. Dig in at your own risk.

Truth in our field is set by science. The force behind education science, at the moment, is the federal government's No Child Left Behind and the Education Science Reform Act of 2002, both of which state that scientifically based work is all that matters. I found it interesting, then when NPR reported that day that after seven decades of measurement and testing, scientists were preparing to vote in order to determine if Pluto were to remain a planet. What a great lesson in how language works to change truth and reality to whatever we want it to be. Clarify the definition, vote on truth, and poof Pluto's gone. How do we explain this to children who have been taught only to struggle with the code and meanings of text and not the claims of authority, the effects of genre, and the intentions to maintain order and hierarchies? Can we tell them that science changed its mind?

The entire story revealed science for what it is—BOGSAT—a bunch of guys sitting around a table making decisions based on criteria that they deem to be important. In this instance the question might seem silly because it doesn't appear to harm anyone except the poor shmuck stuck with a warehouse full of nine planet mobiles. But when we think about the practice— BOGSAT—to determine definitions and goals, and then, measure truth accordingly, we might identify problems. Think about the science behind the multiple definitions of reading proficiency across the 50 states. Students can become proficient simply by moving across state lines. Consider whether the NAEP test should be the ultimate truth? We cannot look at the pedagogy of certainty with the same eyes after the Pluto closed plebiscite. Who got to vote is only the tip of the iceberg. Who put the item on the agenda? What was their authority? What were the criteria? What does a split vote mean? Does Pluto become a half planet or a planet only certain days of the week? All that is solid melts into air.

Two stories occupied most of the air-time on NPR and other news networks during my drive. The first story announced the arrest of a suspect in the JonBenet Ramsey case. The second speculated that Tiger Woods was well on his way to winning a twelfth major golf tournament. As you might remember, JonBenet Ramsey was a 6-year-old child beauty queen who was murdered on the day after Christmas in 1996. Perhaps you recall the case and the years of tabloid reporting that followed. The new suspect was arrested while teaching second grade at a private school in Bangkok, and he was to be extradited to Colorado within a week. Sound bites from Mr. Ramsey, two other relatives, the Colorado district attorney, three FBI officials, and a homeland security officer were aired throughout the day as the story grew in size, if not, importance. In effect, the

Reprinted from Navigating the Literacy Water: Research, Praxis, & Advocacy, pp. 2-10, by M. Foote, F. Falk-Ross, S. Szabo, M. B. Sampson, Eds., 2008, Commerce, TX: College Reading Association.the famous are just damn fun to watch and read about. Tiger Woods is a celebrity to be sure, allowing cameras into his house to sell Buicks and watches and whatever. He travels to Dubai just to hit golf balls into the ocean off the world's most expensive hotel island. Behind his celebrity is his golf, and he stays a bright celebrity because he wins. Other celebrities are famous for being famous. All the stories and infotainment that surround them teach us what can happen in America. If you become a celebrity, you can become rich and party like it's 1999. Play golf, confess murder or become the American Idol, it's all the same. Once you get the public eye, you have it made.

The JonBenet and Tiger stories occupied the news like a siege. During the early hours of the day, these stories were small, but as the day wore on (13 hours remember) these stories overtook the rest of the news. The only way out was the unthinkable—turn the radio off—something that a driver can only do on a short trip or in order to listen to a book or A Teaching Company course on CD. I have taken these private routes on occasion, but to stay public on that day was to submit to endless angles on the JonBenet Ramsey case and the possibilities of Tiger's weekend. Their ubiquity set the day's agenda for drivers. We were going to relive spectacle and celebrity through true crime and sports. Try as NPR might, the two verdicts—can you remember them at all after our 15 minutes of fame with JonBenet and Tiger?—pale in comparison. You don't have to be a fan of Paddy Cheyefsky and Sidney Lumet's vision of news in the film "Network" in order to understand the direction of this agenda. Civic life is boring in comparison to crime, celebrity and sports. The daily repetition of this agenda develops expectations and habits of mind and action that severely diminish the roles that literacy could play in our lives, leaving us less powerful in the construction of our identities and in the negotiation of public life.

As I crossed the Ohio/Pennsylvania border between Youngstown and Sharon, I recognized the overall lessons of my day in the one-sided public sphere. I had been taught to consume products, services, and most of all ideologies, through a variety of pedagogical strategies and types of texts. Except for the market for gas which was $3.20 a gallon because of a war, suppressed production, pension fund speculation, and a government that will not challenge the oil industry, no other text asked me what the hell I was doing driving past countless excellent colleges and universities to drop our daughter off in Iowa. Consume, I have been taught that lesson since birth. But should this be the signature American lesson?

Believe experts was the second lesson. If not particular experts, then believe in the idea of expertise. This is the lesson of modernity, eh? We are happy benefactors of this lesson. That is, we are experts on literacy education who believe that we should be consulted when the public considers… well… literacy education. We are puzzled when business or government bypasses our expertise. But remember, expertise is not neutral or innocent or natural as should be apparent from my examples from my day in the car. Expertise is always embedded in ideology, has a political agenda in the questions raised and forgotten, and presents itself as a closed narrative. A consequence of believing experts is a diminished confidence in our abilities to understand complexities.

All day, I was taught to romanticize the past—to long for a simpler life when everything was easier. Tell me, when was that simpler life? How was it simpler? For whom was it simpler? At whose expense? Who made the present what it is? These questions were never posed during my drive.

The most damaging lesson perhaps was the lesson that civic life is boring. My drive taught me to leave making sense of the local and its connections to the regional, national, and global to the experts, while I consume objects and ideas that make me what Nietzsche labeled ''the last man,'' who has no great passion or commitment to anything on earth, who is unable to hope for the future, who merely earns a living and keeps warm. To turn away from civic life in order to crave private comforts is to abandon democracy.

Let me tell you that it's a long way from the border to the exact center of Pennsylvania with those four lessons spinning your thoughts. It's particularly problematic when you believe that you are personally culpable in the teaching surrounding those lessons. I don't mean that I have anything directly to do with the lessons I've used as examples or the composition of the texts that delivered those lessons. While I'll admit that I engage in school and public pedagogies constantly and that my efforts are pregnant with ideologies, I have not sold my services to the airway or roadways. Rather I'm culpable for not preparing people to live in a democracy. That is, I have not worked successfully to expand literacy education beyond decoding and comprehension in order to include the families of practices that enable readers to see how text positions them and how that positioning enables and disables them as citizens charged with responsibilities to negotiate the past, present and future around the fundamental values of freedom and equality. By not articulating ways in which these families of literacy practices are necessary elements of literacy, and not just add-ons required only for the more sophisticated literacies of the intellectual and economic elites, I perpetuate a dismissal of civic responsibilities as boring, too complex, and better left for the experts.

Fortunately, there are others who are several steps ahead of me. George Lakoff struggles with this issue from a cognitivist perspective. *Don't Think About An Elephant* (2004) and more recently *Whose Freedom?* (2006) discuss the instantiation of ideological frames through public pedagogies. Frances Moore Lappe (2006) takes up this topic from a sociological perspective in *Democracy's Edge*, which describes the social practices of living democracy as opposed to the thin democracy that I described today. Kevin Phillips (2006) looks at the subject through political lens in *American Theocracy*. These are not wild-eyed radicals who pose utopian solutions. Rather they are American intellectuals from varying ideological camps who see the need for citizens to navigate institutional pedagogies more astutely or democracy will end. They encourage us to teach reading through coding and meaning resources, but also as pragmatic and critical practices. What they mean by this is that unless citizens recognize how differing types of texts work and for whom they work, the lessons I was taught during my drive will expand to occupy more and more of public space until there is little room for citizens to participate in the decisions that affect their lives.

These writers do not provide a blue print concerning how this expansion of literacy education might happen. They leave that work to us. Allan Luke and Peter Freebody (1997) present a theoretical treatment of a four resources model that connects coding and meaning with pragmatic and critical practices. Others employ various versions of that model in classrooms from preschool to postsecondary. Consider Vivian Vasquez's (2004) work with 4 and 5-year-olds in *Negotiating Critical Literacies With Young Children*. Randy and Katherine Bomer's (2001) work across elementary and secondary grades in *For A Better World: Reading and Writing for Social Action*. The classic work with college students is still Ira Shor's *Critical Teaching and Everyday Life* (1980). Cheryl Dozier, Peter Johnston, and Rebecca Rogers (2005) discuss the education of critical reading teachers in *Critical Literacy/Critical Teaching*. Read the 20th Anniversary Issue of *Rethinking Schools* (2006) for a collection of educators working to expand literacy. Each of these authors remains optimistic about possibilities of literacy within a democracy even within the darkening spaces of public pedagogy. All critique and analyze the institutional intentions to close discussion and to protect and extend the present advantages for the few through thin democracy. They and I invite you to take up critical literacies as counter narratives to our present circumstances. To do so will help citizens participate more actively in the construction of their civic identities and the negotiations of free, just, and equitable social life.

My title is a play on Paulo Freire's *Pedagogies of the Oppressed* (1970). His argument was that society's have-nots have been taught that they are beneath the capabilities to make culture and to shape history. Freire thought that literacy could counteract those lessons in order for individuals to reinvent themselves as agents of culture and history. This he labeled the pedagogy of the oppressed. In this talk, I have attempted to reveal more about the oppressors behind what Freire called the banking theory of learning—in which ideas, values, and interpretations are deposited in readers' minds as facts and truth.

Am I an oppressor? And are you oppressed? I am, only if you accept my words through codes and single meaning without recognizing and evaluating the pedagogical strategies I have employed, the texts I've used to state my case as facts, and the ideology behind my work. We all have the intentions to teach others what knowledge is worth knowing, what's of value, and how to be. We all have a vision of the future and what it should be. I hope that I have left my pedagogy open enough, however, for you to engage my intentions pragmatically and critically. I am only an oppressor if you have limited your literacy practices to codes and meaning, and allowed my positioning and intentions to oppress you. If we hope to end oppression, then we must engage in a social movement to promote critical literacies for all.

References

Bomer, R. & Bomer, K. (2001). *For a better world: Reading and writing for social action*. Portsmouth, NH: Heinemann.

Dozier, C., Johnston, P. & Rogers, R. (2005). *Critical literacy/critical teaching: Tools for preparing responsive teachers*. New York: Teachers College.

Freire, P. (1970). *Pedagogy of the oppressed*. New York: Seabury.

Lakoff, G. (2004). *Don't think about an elephant: Know your values and frame the debate*. New York: Chelsea Green.

Lakoff, G. (2006). *Whose freedom? The battle over America's most important idea*. New York: Farra, Strauss & Giroux.

Lappe, F. M. (2006). *Democracy's edge: Choosing to save our country by bringing democracy to life*. San Francisco: Jossey-Bass.

Luke, A., & Freebody, P. (1997). The Social Practices of Reading. In S. Muspratt, A. Luke & P. Freebody (Eds.). *Constructing critical literacies: teaching and learning textual practices*. Cresskill, NJ: Hampton Press.

Mills, C. W. (1959). *Sociological imagination*. Chicago: University of Chicago.

Phillips, K. (2006). *American theocracy: The peril and politics of radical religion, oil, and borrowed money in the 21st century*. New York: Vintage.

Shor, I. (1980). *Critical teaching and everyday life*. Montreal, QC: Black Rose Publishing.

Simon, R. (2001). Empowerment as a Pedagogy of Possibility. In Shannon (Ed.) *Becoming political too: Readings and writings in the politics of literacy education*. Portsmouth, NH: Heinemann.

Vasquez, V. (2004). *Negotiating critical literacies with young children*. Mahwah, NY: Lawrence Erlbaum Associates.

Teacher Knowledge and Teaching Reading*

Mia Callahan
Vicki Benson-Griffo
P. David Pearson
University of California Berkeley

Keynote Address
College Reading Association
2007

*This paper was based, in part, on the address that Pearson gave at the 2007 annual meeting of the College Reading Association in Salt Lake City. Please note that all three authors contributed equally to the final product and that we determined the order by random draw.

Helping children learn to read may look easy to the uninitiated, but teachers know better. The consummate reading teacher is at once a wordsmith and a meaning maker, a player and a coach, an artist and a technician—moving seamlessly between detail and vision, kindling in students the insights and connections needed to make meaning from print. The masterful reading teacher makes thousands of instantaneous decisions about assessment and instruction each day, some targeted to an entire class, others carefully choreographed for individual students, and all directed at ushering students securely onto the path of literacy and its attendant rewards.

Reprinted from *Literacy Issues During Changing Times: A Call to Action,* pp. 37-59, by F. Falk-Ross, S. Szabo, M. B. Sampson, M. M. Foote, Eds., 2009, Commerce, TX; College Reading Association.

Trying to characterize the nature and development of the complex knowledge base needed for any profession is a challenge, and teaching is no different. To determine the kinds of experiences that children need in order to learn to read and write well, to define the knowledge that teachers need to enable that learning, and then to carefully consider how teacher education can best develop that knowledge is the commitment we make as educators—to society as a whole and to each and every child. The stakes are high in today's policy world. An ever-increasing global economy demands that our nation's children be prepared with competitive skills and knowledge in order to succeed. As more jobs requiring low levels of education move abroad, available domestic jobs demand heightened levels of education (Levine, 2007). Consequently, teachers are faced with increasing demands in training, assessment, on-going professional learning, instructional expectations, and student outcomes. It is our responsibility to provide teachers of reading with the knowledge and skills to meet these extrinsic demands as they focus on fulfilling the intrinsic mission of our profession—helping children become lifelong readers.

Teacher quality has been found to be one of the most consequential school variables affecting students' learning (see, Ferguson, 1991; Sanders & Rivers, 1996; Wright, Horn, & Sanders, 1997; Rivkin, Hanushek, & Kain, 2000). Large-scale longitudinal studies specific to reading achievement have found the same significant teacher quality effects in low-performing schools (Denton, Foorman, & Mathes, 2003; Foorman, Schatschneider, Eakin, Fletcher, Moats, & Francis, 2006; Mathes, Denton, Fletcher, Anthony, Francis, & Schatschneider, 2005). The ascendancy of teacher quality as the main guidepost for educational reform is evident throughout policies such as the No Child Left Behind Act of 2001 (NCLB; U.S. Department of Education, 2002), which mandated that all states supply a "fully qualified teacher" for every classroom by 2007. While no one would argue that the premise of a highly qualified teacher in every classroom is noble and just, the impact and subtext of NCLB has, in actuality, *minimized professional standards* by defining a highly qualified teacher merely as one who has (a) fulfilled the state's certification and licensing requirements, (b) obtained at least a bachelor's degree, and (c) demonstrated subject matter expertise. Although teacher quality may be measured within the law by program and licensure completion, educational research clearly shows that program and test completion *are not* sufficient means for measuring teacher development and quality (Wenglinsky, 2002).

When national policies such as NCLB (2001) rest on the assumption that "scientifically-based" teaching methods and, in turn, quality teaching will alleviate difficulties for struggling students and ultimately close the achievement gap experienced by disadvantaged and minority students, more is required than simply putting certificated teachers into the classroom. To meet both the challenges of today's teaching world and the goal of equitable education for all children, it is our responsibility as researchers and teacher educators to build a more comprehensive framework of teacher expertise—one that acknowledges the reality that new teachers, at the point of initial credentialing, still have much to learn to hone their expertise, and also embraces the expectation that teacher knowledge grows over time through the twin tools of teacher education and professional development. In the spirit of trying to understand the trajectory of teacher development, we set out to achieve several goals in this manuscript. Our first is to present two very different perspectives on teacher development—a marketplace view and a professional accountability view, and dispel some of the myths that have fueled these and other similar perspectives. We then make the case for a developmental perspective of teacher knowledge. Finally, we probe the complex nature of assessing teacher knowledge and the nagging issues that continue to challenge us in this realm.

Contrasting Views of Teacher Development

The question of how to best prepare teachers for the classroom has been vigorously debated by educators and policymakers since the arrival of the common school in the 1830s, when teachers were simply required to have completed the level of schooling they were hired to teach (Labaree, 2008). Today, the debate is alive and well, with numerous studies and opinion pieces questioning the value and role of teacher education (Carnegie Task Force on Teaching as a Profession, 1986; Goodlad, 1990; Holmes Group, 1986; Howey & Zimpher, 1989; Zeichner, 1993). Two opposing perspectives on teacher preparation currently dominate the controversy—the marketplace view and the professional accountability view.

Marketplace View

Chester Finn of the Thomas B. Fordham Foundation advocates a *market vision* of teacher quality—invite all comers, give them the support they need, then use student performance as the sole criterion for weeding out the chaff (Finn, Kanstoroom, & Petrelli, 1999). Fire the teachers who don't produce and close the schools that don't perform. In other words, look for evidence of quality *after* hiring, based solely or primarily on student test score gains. The model works as a strict marketplace economy. Finn and Petrelli (2000) argue that we are using the wrong metaphor for teaching, at least in terms of teacher preparation. Rather than liken teaching to medicine, where the hallmarks of the profession are standards, internships, examinations for licensure, and mandatory professional development, Finn and Petrelli suggest journalism as a more apt metaphor. They propose that in teaching (as in journalism), a degree in the profession *may* be helpful in some instances, but degrees in other areas, such as English, law, or history, can lead to as much, if not greater success. Allow people from a variety of backgrounds to enter the profession of teaching and leave teacher quality and longevity to be judged by student performance.

Professional Accountability View

By contrast, in a professional accountability view (Darling-Hammond, 2006b), the professional community holds itself accountable for ensuring that teachers obtain the best disciplinary and pedagogical knowledge possible. The goal of the professional model is to make sure that standards are in place *before and after hiring*, through licensing, induction, evaluation, and professional development. The inherent promise is the same that any profession makes to its constituents—that its members will know as much as they can about their work. In this model of teacher development, the key is to first specifty the minimal levels of development that are required for a teacher to begin working in his or her own classroom then, recognizing that growth in both content and pedagogical knowledge is expected throughout a career (Pearson, 2001), support continued opportunities for teacher learning.

All that we have learned about the development of teacher knowledge contradicts the *market vision* assumptions and dispels the attendant myths (Darling-Hammond, 2006b) that fuel this and similar perspectives:

Myth 1: Teachers are born, not made.

Myth 2: Teaching is simple—the mere transmission of what you know—therefore subject matter knowledge is all that is required.

Myth 3: Teaching is primarily learned through experience. Effective practice cannot be taught.

Myth 4: Teacher education programs offer little more than esoteric theories that muddy the practical requirements of teaching and may even hinder good teaching in general.

Research over the past 30 years instead supports a *professional vision*, in which teacher effectiveness is shaped by the extent and quality of both teacher education and experience. Reviews conclude that even with the shortcomings of current teacher education and licensing requirements, fully prepared and certificated teachers are generally better rated and produce better student outcomes than unskilled teachers (Ashton & Crocker, 1986; Evertson, Hawley, & Zlotnik, 1985). There is much that teachers need to learn along the way as they move from knowing a few vague principles about how to teach to possessing more specific knowledge about how to improve teaching and learning for specific subjects, skills, and processes. Short-circuiting teacher education short-changes both teachers and students alike.

Understanding the Role of Teacher Knowledge: A Developmental Model

The assumption of professionalism within the teaching profession has waxed and waned over the decades as we have moved between training and learning models of teaching (Hoffman & Pearson, 2000). Teacher education experienced a major paradigm shift from the *training model* of the 1960s and 1970s to the *learning model* that emerged in the 1980s and continues to present day (Cochran-Smith & Fries, 2005; Hoffman & Pearson, 2000). The training model, often associated with the process-product research paradigm that was popular in the 1970s and 1980s, operated from a clear, if naïve, research and policy perspective. It assumed that we could (a) go out into classrooms to find out what teaching behaviors distinguish teachers who promote high achievement and growth from those who do not, and then (b) teach all teachers to use the processes characteristic of the more effective teachers. Teacher training, in turn, focused on equipping teachers with specific behavioral and psychological routines characteristic of effective teachers (see Hoffman & Pearson, 2000, for a full review). Numerous lists of teacher competencies emerged and became integral components of training programs, specifying criteria for teacher behaviors, learning outcomes, learning experiences, and assessment plans. The compelling feature of the training model was its emphasis on student achievement as the screening device for inferring teacher quality and requisite behaviors. As a critical element to teacher improvement, these programs emphasized systematic training of teachers and the learning of instructional routines and procedures. This model gradually atrophied in the mid 1980s when teacher preparation expanded to consider the varying contexts in which teachers worked and the types of knowledge they needed to operate successfully in those contexts. The emerging learning model focused on teacher cognition rather than behavior, aimed to understand the source and development of teacher knowledge, and emphasized flexible application of knowledge in response to the variety of classroom contexts. While many teacher educators work on the assumption that the learning model of teacher development prevails, certain policies and practices, especially those enacted in the wake of the No Child Left Behind (2002) reform movement, would lead us to conclude that the training model is alive and well (Pearson, 2007).

Definitions of Knowledge

Teacher knowledge has been an elusive construct. Several researchers committed to professionalizing the teaching force (and, in the process, championing the learning model of teacher development) have worked to codify a professional knowledge base aimed at producing teachers who could not only enact effective teaching behaviors, but who were empowered learners, leaders, and school reformers in control of their own actions and thinking. Building on a tradition of subject matter knowledge and the rise of pedagogical knowledge, Shulman (1986) noted a "missing paradigm" of knowledge that he coined pedagogical content knowledge—a type of knowledge that extends beyond subject matter into "aspects of content most germane to its teachability" (p. 9). Knowledge has also been subdivided into categories such as declarative knowledge (knowing what to teach), procedural knowledge (knowing how to teach it), and conditional knowledge (knowing why, when, and under what circumstances to teach it) (see Almasi, 2003, pp.108-111). Educational psychology has long explored its own version of conditional knowledge in privileging the idea of metacognitive knowledge. Simply defined as both the knowledge about cognition and regulation of cognition (Flavell, 1979), metacognitive knowledge is the awareness of what is needed to perform effectively and equips teachers with the tools necessary to take control of their own learning, enabling them to handle classroom complexities (Hammerness, Darling-Hammond, & Bransford, 2005). Rowan, Schilling, Ball, and Miller (2001) created a slightly different infrastructure of subdivisions for teacher knowledge, using the labels Knowledge of Students and Content for an understanding of likely concepts, misconceptions, and difficulties that students encounter, and Knowledge of Teaching and Content for an understanding of teaching actions appropriate for various situations. While each of these accounts has proven useful as a heuristic to help us better understand the types of knowledge teachers possess, each falls short of indicating precisely how knowledge matures over time.

What teachers learn prior to entering the classroom is a basis from which to begin, but it cannot, and does not, equip them with the requisite knowledge to apply and integrate learning theories into the myriad of complex classroom situations. We know that knowledge is dynamic and that teachers are made not born; they do, after all, get better over time. In other words, teachers are clearly stepping out of the classroom at the end of their careers knowing a whole lot more than what they stepped in with. The knowledge that evolves is a direct result of teacher education both in and beyond the academy. As teachers make and remake themselves, their knowledge is affected by a host of factors, including experiences prior to entering teaching, the type of training program attended, experiences and support in the classroom, as well as individual differences. The crucial questions in better understanding this journey are, "how do we define what it is that develops," and "how does it change over time"?

Phases of Career Development

A good first step is to consider what it would mean to have a theory of how teacher knowledge develops over time. One way to think about development (see Snow, Griffin, & Burns, 2005) is as a continuum of professional career development, emphasizing the phases teachers pass through and requirements they fulfill, as well as a criterion for knowledge measurement along the way. Across phases, an individual teacher:

1. is inducted into a teacher education program based on academics and ability to work with children,

2. receives preservice preparation in a teacher training program,
3. takes licensing tests based on subject matter and teaching knowledge,
4. receives one to two years of mentoring in early teaching,
5. continues licensing requirements that are based on performance assessments such as portfolios, written evaluations, videotaped lessons, and student work,
6. participates in professional development in and out of the classroom, and
7. receives advanced certification based on performance assessments and examination.

Career progression is only part of the picture, however. Fulfilling accreditation benchmarks such as graduating from a teacher education program and passing state licensure requirements does not guarantee that the teacher will possess the knowledge required for expertise—only that they will have passed through a stage where one would have expected them to have had the opportunity to acquire that knowledge.

A Trajectory of Teacher Knowledge Development

So, what does the changing face of teacher knowledge look like? What difference would it make whether or not it changed over time? How would we know it was changing? There are many accounts of the trajectory that professional knowledge takes throughout a teaching career. Most of these accounts are conceptual rather than empirical—they represent ideal trajectories rather than observed pathways. In this essay, we have privileged the account provided by Snow and her colleagues (2005) to emphasize a trajectory of teacher knowledge development for teaching reading. Their sequential model distinguishes five levels of differentiated and increasingly sophisticated knowledge that layer upon one another like the layers of an archeological dig (see Figure 1), with declarative knowledge at the bottom of the site (representing less mature levels of knowledge) and reflective knowledge nearest the surface (representing the more mature levels, levels that build on and benefit from less mature levels):

- declarative (*knowing what*),
- situated-procedural (*knowing how, but highly strategic in application*),
- stable-procedural (*knowing how, but routinized, almost automatic*),
- expert-adaptive (*knowing how, when, with whom, and under what conditions*), and
- reflective knowledge (*knowing it all, where the potholes are, what needs fixing, what keeps you up at night*).

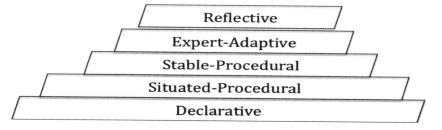

Figure 1. Levels of teacher knowledge building on one another like layers in an archeological dig.

, ,,. These five categories of teacher knowledge vary as a function of program emphasis and coincide with points along the career progression (see Figure 2). For example, declarative knowledge is most emphasized during subject matter and education coursework in a preservice certification program where a teacher in training is learning about topics such as content knowledge, child development, and instructional approaches. During this career point, declarative knowledge dominates professional learning in most programs.

As teachers enter their first-year of teaching, they build on their declarative knowledge base with procedural knowledge on how to plan, organize, and maintain instruction for the majority of the class. While declarative knowledge still constitutes a large piece of the pie, it is not as pronounced. With the beginning teacher, situated- and stable-procedural knowledge become more pronounced. And, reflective and expert knowledge begin to develop also in tandem. During this period, it is important for a teacher to have a reliable set of peer and mentored supports as expert knowledge is still developing. It is important to note that when looking at Figure 2 (the percentages are approximate, included only to indicate relative size), it is tempting to infer that declarative knowledge decreases over time and across stages. It does not. The size of the total pie increases at each level (note the difference in the size of the pie at each point), so that the total amount of declarative knowledge in each stage is larger than it is at an earlier stage, but it appears smaller because it takes up a smaller proportion of a substantially larger pie at later stages, when more mature levels of knowledge dominate.

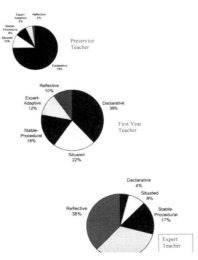

Figure 2

As teachers gain experience and take on a more reflective, metacognitive role, they become more sophisticated in assessing the wide array of student needs and providing instructional strategies based on those needs. Additionally, expert teachers are able to recognize gaps in their knowledge base and seek ways to deepen their understanding. The master teacher is ready to take on leadership roles in the school, such as leading professional development activities and mentoring novice teachers. As this stage, expert-adaptive and reflective-organized knowledge carry a larger proportion of the pie, while the other aspects of knowledge, although larger in absolute size, are a smaller proportion of the total.

This model is not meant to presume that development occurs in a linear fashion across fixed stages. Rather it aligns knowledge growth across a career progression and indicates a trajectory of teacher development that illustrates a professional evolution from novice to expert. As teachers become more ex-

Table 1: Changes in teacher knowledge across a career pathway: Pragmatics

Type of Knowledge	*What knowledge about the pragmatic dimensions of language might look like?*
Declarative knowledge	Teachers at this level understand the fundamental form-function relationship in language use—that writers and speakers use the formal tools and features of text to fulfill different functions and achieve different goals (i.e., to inform, to persuade, to entertain).
	They have a passing acquaintanceship with key terms related to pragmatics—such as discourse, register, genre, textual devices and conventions, voice, style, persona, stance, perspective—but their knowledge is not well-developed or differentiated.
	They understand the social and cultural functions that texts perform in different contexts (school, work, play, home) and ways in which those contexts shape textual use and interpretation.
Situated, can-do procedural knowledge	Teachers possess at least a few routines for addressing these features of language use, such as Questioning the Author, and teach students about how to use genre and register to achieve particular effects on an audience (e.g., persuasion or entertainment). These lessons would be fairly prescribed and circumscribed--the understandings about text developed therein may or may not be applied to reading and writing activities in other classroom contexts.
	Teachers may be more skilled at teaching students the meaning of terms, such as genre, voice, and perspective than helping student to apply these understandings to their reading and writing of texts.
Stable procedural knowledge	At this level, the routines have become more or less automatic for the teachers, and they are beginning to be able to adapt to the performance needs of different groups and individuals. Teachers have acquired additional routines for developing students' understandings of the pragmatic dimensions of text and are beginning to develop approaches for assessing these understandings.
	The teacher's knowledge is becoming increasingly differentiated, as is instruction.

	Instruction may include more explicit attention to the form/function relationship, may include analysis of more subtle stylistic features (e.g., the connotative loading of words and idioms), and may include increasing attention to the ways that societal forces shape authors and texts.
Expert Adaptive Knowledge	At this level, teachers are less reliant on specific routines and are better able to integrate issues of discourse and pragmatics into students' daily interactions with texts. The teachers own understanding of these issues and their application to reading and writing has become more sophisticated. Whereas in the declarative stage, teachers understood the meaning of terms such as discourse, register and genre, they are now able to connect these stylistic variations to the pragmatic/social (and political or ideological) functions of text. Teachers at this level can anticipate and respond to obstacles that their students will confront in applying these understandings to their interpretation and composition of texts.
Reflective, organized, analyzed knowledge	At this level, teachers can use their understandings about the pragmatic dimensions of text proactively and in larger contexts. They can evaluate the effectiveness of programs, routines, and activities designed to develop students' understandings about the pragmatic dimensions of text and their ability to apply these understandings to their reading and writing. These teachers may be involved in developing new approaches to teaching pragmatics at the school or district level.

pert, they know more about specific, particularly advanced, aspects of teacher knowledge.

Table 1 offers an illustration of how teacher knowledge might actually change for a given domain of reading (Cervetti & Pearson, 2005), showing how knowledge of the pragmatic aspects of language would change for each of the five levels of teacher knowledge.

Professional Growth: Preservice Education and Beyond

It is one thing to specify *what* teachers should know, but it is quite another to specify the point in their careers *when* they need to know it and *how* it can best be developed. Teacher education has been called to task even by those within the profession: the Holmes group (1986), the Carnegie Task Force on Teaching as a Profession (1986), and scholars such as Goodlad (1990), Howey and Zimpher (1989), and Zeichner (1993). They have all urged "the redesign of teacher education to strengthen its knowledge base, connections to practice and theory, and capacity to support the development of powerful teaching" (Darling-Hammond, 2006b, p. 20). In order for reforms to have a deep and lasting effect, the fundamental tools that teachers need must be discerned, and a clearer understanding of how to best to help them develop these tools is needed. To create a meaningful career path for teachers—a path that honors the need for continuing development both personally and professionally—we must use our understanding of how teacher knowledge develops at various stages of a teaching career when considering methods of teacher education. Surely, what teachers of reading know when they walk into their very first classrooms will look different from what they know after years of seasoning. How much of this body of knowledge should they learn in preservice programs? What knowledge is better learned while on the job—through mentorship, professional development, or continuing graduate coursework? The abiding questions that should shape any effective model of professional growth for teachers of reading is, "how will teachers best develop essential knowledge for instruction and at what points along the career trajectory do they acquire it?"

Preservice Teacher Training

Data from a number of studies indicate a robust relationship between teacher preparation in reading instruction and student outcomes (e.g., Darling-Hammond, 1999; Fuller, 1999; Hoffman Roller, Maloch, Sailors, Duffy, & Beretvas, 2005; Laczko-Kerr & Berliner, 2002, National Reading Panel, 2000). Not only do teacher preparation and certification predict student achievement in reading, they also are significantly related to teaching practices associated with higher levels of reading achievement (Darling-Hammond, 1999). In addition, "more teacher education appears to be better than less—particularly when it includes carefully planned clinical experiences that are inter-woven with coursework on learning and teaching" (Darling-Hammond, 1997, p.10). Darling-Hammond (1999) also found that "measures of teacher preparation and certification are by far the strongest correlates to student achievement in reading and mathematics, both before and after controlling for student poverty and language status" (p. 4). Laczko-Kerr and Berliner (2002) compared the academic achievements of students in grades 2 through 8 taught by regularly certified school teachers (those who attended accredited universities and met all state requirements for initial teaching certification) to students of undercertified teachers (those who held either emergency, temporary, or provisional certificates, *including* Teach for America teachers). Results of the SAT-9 tests showed that students taught by certified teachers outperformed "precertified" teachers on each of the three subtests (Language Arts, Mathematics, and Reading) by about 2 months on a grade-equivalent scale. In comparing certified and uncertified teachers, the Texas Studies (Alexander & Fuller, 2004; Fuller, 1999) reported a significant, positive correlation between fully-licensed teachers and student passing rate on the state achievement tests after controlling for socioeconomic status, school wealth, and teacher experience.

While not as transparently compelling as the evidence from student performance, many studies also show that teacher education has a significant impact on teachers' personal views about their own preparedness and about teaching in general. On a survey of beginning teachers in New York that compared teachers who had entered teaching through alternative pathways to graduates of teacher-education programs, those who had graduated from teacher-education programs answered that they felt better-prepared to plan instruction, meet the needs of their diverse learners, create positive learning environments, and make subject-matter knowledge accessible to their students (Darling-Hammond, 1999; Darling-Hammond, Chung, & Frelow, 2002).

Simply put, teacher preservice preparation is critical to effective teaching. What teachers bring to the classroom is influenced by what they have had an opportunity to learn. But, even high-quality preservice teacher education cannot adequately prepare teachers for all challenges and complexities of the classroom. Teacher development is a career-long process (as our model of knowledge development implies), and teachers not only develop their knowledge over time, they get better at teaching. Even if we have "modal" or "default" programs, we will always need to promote flexibility and versatility. Settling for scripted programs as a surrogate for teacher education can never address the growing complexities of today's classrooms. Rather, teachers need a deep and broad knowledge base – opportunities to become adaptive experts (Darling-Hammond, 2006b); not only in what to teach, but in how to teach it.

Ongoing Professional Development

Through research, we have learned a lot about how to effectively educate teachers before they enter the classroom, but we are less sure about how to continue the trajectory of professional development over time. A host of training studies emerged in the 1980s and early 1990s, specifically process-product research which demonstrated positive effects for teacher training in effective classroom practices (for a review see Hoffman & Pearson, 2000). For example, comprehension instruction have proved amenable to direct training and also effective in promoting student engagement and growth in student achievement (Rosenshine & Stevens, 1984). In addition, the National Reading Panel Report (2000) documented findings that teachers can successfully learn to implement strategy instruction when offered systematic training and feedback. But other modes of research, emerging in the late 1980s, questioned the efficacy of training, and began to consider teacher education as a more interactive, constructivist, teacher-centered process that situated knowledge and authority within the teacher. Influential studies by Richardson and colleagues (Placier & Hamilton, 1994; Richardson, 1994) demonstrated that as teacher beliefs changed prior to changing practices, they were ultimately reflected in improved student reading comprehension. The Valdez study (1992) is a classic example of this approach, demonstrating that staff development has a positive effect on teacher disposition by promoting continued reflection and an openness toward effective change. This work has been extensively reviewed by teacher education scholars (e.g., Richardson & Placier, 2001; Wilson & Berne, 1999), resulting in a consistent set of conclusions, succinctly summarized by Richardson (2003) into a set of principles.

While combing the research literature to help us rethink what can and should occur during professional preparation and development, Cervetti and Pearson

(2005) uncovered nine fundamental principles specific to professional learning (in most cases, highly overlapping with Richardson's principles):

1. programs addressing the beliefs that teachers bring with them about teaching are more likely to foster openness to new ideas and reflection on personal assumptions;

2. programs that foster the expectation of and skills required for continuous learning are more likely to support the development of career learning paths;

3. programs that ensure the development of a comprehensive and usable knowledge base are more likely to sustain successful initial teaching experiences;

4. programs that help teachers apply what they have learned in teacher education programs to particular contexts and students ease the transition to classroom teaching;

5. programs that promote articulation among standards, coursework, and internship experiences are more likely to help teachers develop a sense of personal efficacy and professional responsibility;

6. programs that stay the course are more likely to succeed than those that change foci frequently;

7. programs that are sensitive to local context are more likely to succeed than generic approaches;

8. programs that encourage careful analyses of teaching and the generation of shared knowledge are more likely to nurture a sense of collective responsibility for instruction; and

9. programs that achieve a balance between school/program needs and the needs of individual teachers are more likely to support teachers' movement along the developmental continuum toward becoming adaptive experts.

Considering these principles, the long-standing tension between top-down (externally imposed) and bottom-up (internally and locally developed) approaches to reform might be resolved in an amalgamation of the two. The top-down approach views knowledge as something to be imported from the external world. Thus, the task is to find that knowledge and those better ideas to implement, and then apply them. The bottom-up approach views knowledge as something that must be catalyzed within a specific teacher learning community. This approach focuses on better assessing the current needs of students and teachers in a particular setting and finding a path to meeting those needs. The essence of the dilemma is that we are quite sure that some level of external intervention (top-down) is required for teacher knowledge to develop fully. We see that not all know, or can easily learn on their own, all they need to know to become a masterful teacher of reading. However, if we deliver this knowledge to teachers on a silver platter, they may either reject it outright or, even worse, engage in mock compliance, hoping that the reform that brought the new knowledge into the school will soon go away. Embedding bottom-up principles within a top-down framework encourages genuine "buy-in" from the teachers by allowing their learning to be activated rather than bound and delivered; privileging interactions with their fellow teachers and, in turn, creating unlimited possibilities for learning; engendering confidence in their decision-making abilities; creating a sense of autonomy along with responsibility for what is happening in their classrooms; and empowering them to make deliberate and thoughtful changes in their classrooms based on their learning (Pearson, Taylor, & Tam, 2005; Richardson & Anders, 1994; Taylor, Pearson, Peterson, & Rodriguez, 2005). In sum, instead of looking at top-down and bottom-up approaches as competing strategies, we should use them both to create a broad framework that outlines the expertise to be developed and sets parameters for how it should be implemented, but allows considerable versatility and flexibility in how one achieves the expertise.

If we are to accept the challenge of the *professional* vision of teaching outlined at the outset of this essay and aspire to this high level of prerogative teachers need to do their job (see Pearson, 2007), we must accept accountability for preparing a diverse candidate pool; for making sure they develop deep and broad knowledge, skills, and dispositions that will prepare them for the classroom and the variety of children they will serve; and to continue to support their personal and professional development as they move through their careers. In order to exercise professional prerogative in response to the increasing demands of the classroom and the varying contexts, teachers need more than a set of prescribed skills. They need an adequately filled toolbox when they head out into the field, and the ability to add to that toolbox throughout their careers with continual learning opportunities. Ultimately, that toolbox should hold a number of tools, mainly types of knowledge layered from declarative to procedural to adaptive to reflective, namely:

(a) an understanding of universal development—both of the child and the reading processes—common to all those taking the steps toward literacy;

(b) an understanding and appreciation of individual differences, both within and without the learner, so that responses to student needs are appropriate, instructive, and constructive;

(c) a deep intimacy with language—its phonology, morphology, etymology, orthography, semantics, syntax, pragmatics, and discourse—and an understanding of how best to develop and use implicit and explicit teaching opportunities that go beyond mere "transmission" of knowledge;

(d) an ability to assess students with multiple indicators of learning progress and use the information in ways that ensure continuous development, including an ability to find alternate strategies to help those students not making good progress; and finally,

(e) an ability to see "competing strategies" (e.g., whole language vs. phonics) as an opportunity to explore when and where each is most effective, based on a strong knowledge base of both the learner and the process of reading development.

When considering *how* teachers best learn, it is important to acknowledge a certain irony. While, as teacher educators, we go to great lengths to make sure attention is given to the research on children, how they learn, and their most optimal learning environments, we sometimes deliver this knowledge base to preservice and inservice teachers in a model that often ignores what we know about adult learning. Through the work of the Commission on Behavioral Social Sciences and Education and the National Research Council (1999), we know that novices differ from experts in how they learn—what they notice, how they organize and interpret their environment, and how they reason and solve problems. We also know that learning is an active process that involves interactions between preexisting competencies and the environment. Unfortunately, in a situation in which teacher knowledge is uneven, we tend to mandate methods for all teachers, *even* for those who have demonstrated that they possess the knowledge required to make differential decisions. One size does not fit all teachers. We know that learning is a time-consuming endeavor, and that people must achieve a threshold of learning that is sufficient to support transfer to new situations. And yet we often touch too superficially on topics of great importance. We need to heed these important truths about learning in general when teaching our teachers. We need, first of all, to think of them as learners and, secondly, as adults with particular learning needs, interests, and preferences. Considering teachers as, first and foremost, learners, seems an appropriate stopping point for this only partially completed journey into the professional development of the teaching profession. One point that needs emphasis as we end this particular journey— nothing could be more important than understanding the nature of professional knowledge and the factors that account for its successful development.

Assessing Teacher Knowledge

As we continue to explore what it is that teachers of reading need to know and be able to do to reach all learners, we are faced with the simultaneous challenge of finding ways to assess that knowledge. It is a challenge fraught with a host of dilemmas, many of which continue to bedevil us. Perhaps in delineating these dilemmas, we will gain a clearer picture of our charge, putting us in a stronger position to resolve them using what we *do* know about effective assessments of teacher knowledge.

Our first dilemma is rooted in the inherent challenge of measuring a construct that is still in the process of being defined. How do we build valid assessments without a clearly specified body of knowledge to assess? To be sure, the domain of teacher expertise for literacy instruction is vast and complex. Of necessity, it would have to include knowledge of:

    1. learners and how they develop,

2. reading acquisition and how it develops,
3. the structure of both oral and written language,
4. instructional techniques that can be tailored to a diverse learners, and
5. ways to monitor and assess children to promote optimal learning and development.

Without a deep understanding of what teachers of reading need to know and be able to do to become masterful in diverse settings, assessing their preparedness remains out of reach. The volume compiled by Catherine Snow and her colleagues (Snow, Griffin, & Burns, 2005) goes a long way in providing a conceptually rich account of teacher knowledge, but it is based on professional consensus, not empirical evidence of the value and efficacy of the knowledge domains outlined. Other things being equal, we would rather rely on evidence than on our best professional consensus about the role of different sorts of knowledge.

A second persistent dilemma in assessing teacher knowledge arises from the difficulty of describing competence. On what basis will teacher proficiency be judged? Cochran-Smith and Lytle (2001) identified three ways that outcomes of teacher education are currently being considered: (a) through evidence about professional performance, (b) through evidence of teacher candidate test scores, and (c) through evidence about impacts of teaching practice on student learning. What does understanding look like in the various domains of knowledge that support the teaching of reading when these alternative criteria of excellence are privileged? How much of a domain should a teacher master before stepping into a classroom?

To further confound the situation, assessment formats matter. Ideally, they should vary according to the domain being measured (Darling-Hammond, 2006a). For instance, a teacher's declarative knowledge might be appropriately assessed with a multiple-choice or constructed-response test such as the Praxis (ETS, 2008), whereas a teacher's situated- and stable-procedural knowledge might be better captured through live or videotaped observation conducted by a literacy expert, and expert and reflective knowledge might more appropriately be measured through teacher-defended portfolios of lesson plans, assignments, and analyses of student work samples. Unfortunately, making principled arguments about what types of tests capture different types of learning, and what represents proficiency on each particular test, require a deeper understanding than we currently have of the knowledge base for the teaching of reading.

Another nagging difficulty stems from the developmental nature of knowledge acquisition. Teacher knowledge develops over time, and mapping out an appropriate timeline of assessment that matches the developmental trajectory of teacher learning is an incredibly complex undertaking. How do we create assessments that not only reflect *what* teachers need to know, but also *when* they need to know it? Would we assess the same knowledge in the same way at the end of a preservice teacher education program as we would after a year of induction into the profession? The knowledge that teachers are expected to have should vary depending on where they fall on the developmental continuum. While the National Board for Professional Teaching Standards (NBPTS) presents a rich model of what expert teaching looks like once it is in place (NBPTS, n.d.), it neglects the matter of development leading to the expertise. Wilson, Floden, and Ferrini-Mundy (2001) underscored the need for a stronger understanding of the *when* aspect of teacher knowledge: "We need more studies that relate specific parts of teachers' preparation (subject matter, pedagogy, clinical experiences) to the effects on their teacher practice, and perhaps on student achievement" (p. iv).

Finally, the dilemma of creating reliable and valid assessments persists. In assessment design, the question of whether the test does the job it is employed to do should always guide development. Many teacher tests have been criticized in the past for yielding insufficient evidence of test validity and reliability (Haertel, 1991; Haney, Madaus, & Kreitzer, 1987; Smith, Miller, & Joy, 1988). What do we know about validly and reliably measuring the knowledge and expertise we deem teachers of reading should to have? Foundations of psychological science indicate the importance of demonstrating assessment reliability; for example, is there evidence of inter-rater consistency, as well as consistency of scores among evaluations of teacher work such as lesson plans, portfolios, and classroom observations?

Of greater difficulty is the task of demonstrating the various and interrelated forms of validity such as criterion, construct, and consequential validity, that serve as an empirical evaluation of the meaning and consequences of the assessment. At a minimum, we must demonstrate two aspects of criterion-related validity: (a) the scores on a candidate assessment predict future success (as in predictive validity), and (b) the scores correlate with some external standard of teacher knowledge (as in concurrent validity). Also at a minimum, the scores ought to generalize to the full construct domain rather than limited aspects of it; in other words, are all aspects of teaching represented?

No task is more daunting than to demonstrate construct validity. We can usually manage to determine whether a measure looks and feels like what we say we are measuring (face validity) and distinguishes between something experts have (or have more of) but novices don't have (or have less of). That is surely a part of construct validation. However, more ambitious construct validation, in which we can validate that our assessment system is consistent with the theory of growth in teacher knowledge upon which the system is built, usually eludes us.

The most recent addition to the validity portfolio is consequential validity, which focuses on the consequences of using any assessment for making real world decisions, such as what happens when teachers either possess the knowledge or don't: do they teach better (different set of practices) and do kids learn more?

Another way of summarizing these dilemmas is to say that assessing teacher knowledge is difficult because we are trying to assess a concept that we have yet to clearly define. The good news is that we are making headway in resolving most of these major dilemmas. Research continues to shed light on the *what, how,* and *when* of the teacher knowledge needed for effective reading instruction and, in turn, elucidate critical information needed for developing good assessments. The light is still dim, but we have available to us a fair amount of relevant information and professional consensus to guide our efforts. We know, for example,

1. that defining and measuring knowledge to support the teaching of reading is an iterative process.
2. that using multiple assessments in multiple formats provides a more stable estimate of knowledge or skill.
3. that performance assessments, content-specific portfolios, structured interviews, and classroom observations provide important complements to paper and pencil tests of basic literacy skills, content knowledge, and pedagogical knowledge.
4. that using student achievement test score gains as a measure of teacher knowledge [the so-called value-added measures (Braun, 2005)] overlook or confound many nonteacher factors (e.g., home background, attendance, mobility, school resources, socio-economic status) that heavily influence student learning. We can hope to tie teacher expertise to student achievement, but for the foreseeable future, we need to be cautious.

We also suspect that viewing teacher assessment in a slightly different role—as a means of fostering ongoing personal and professional growth of teachers—will add value to its fundamental role of maintaining quality and fostering accountability. But admittedly, rarely has the responsibility for assessing teacher knowledge and quality been viewed as a positive phenomenon that is the responsibility, and right, of every teacher.

Different approaches to teacher assessment hold different conceptions of what the process of teaching involves and what knowledge is being invoked. One assessment type does not fit all. Each one is limited and partial. As mentioned earlier, different assessment formats tend to be better-suited to particular kinds of knowledge. We have developed and validated a range of approaches to measure teacher knowledge: paper and pencil tests, either multiple-choice or constructed-response; observations of classroom instruction, either live or via videotape; and reflective portfolios that give teachers an opportunity to explain, defend, and critique their own work. The chart below (see Table 2) suggests how various assessments best align to different knowledge types. Declarative knowledge, for example, is best, or at least most efficiently, assessed via a multiple-choice or constructed-response test. Situated- and stable-procedural knowledge are best captured through live or taped observations reviewed by an literacy expert or a district supervisor, while expert and reflective knowledge can only be assessed

Table 2: Assessing different types of teacher knowledge*	Test it	Observe it	Defend it
Declarative	√	?	
Situated	?+	√	
Stable		√	?
Expert	?-	?+	√
Reflective	?-	?+	√

by asking teachers to analyze their own practice by examining artifacts of their teaching and their students' learning.

*Note: √= yes; ? = not sure; ?+ = maybe; ?- = not likely

As teacher educators, we need to ensure that teachers of reading possess the knowledge, skills, and strategies needed at each step of the way in their teaching careers. We need to pay special attention to the knowledge needed to navigate the dynamics and complexities of diverse learners, something we have clearly fallen short of addressing, given the disproportionate academic underachievement of low-income and ethnic minority students. To do so, we must be able to assess exactly what is in their toolbox, and what is not, at key stages of development—and then provide professional experiences that will allow them to acquire the missing tools. It is our professional responsibility— to both our children and to the teachers we send into the classroom—to build into our profession the expectation that assessing knowledge is a good thing, that it helps us grow and become better teachers of reading. We need to do it as a matter of course, all the while knowing that the ultimate assessment of how well we are doing as teacher educators will not be found in a single multiple choice test or even a carefully wrought performance review. It will be found in the toothless grin of a first grader reading his first book, in the easy exhale of a satisfied teacher, energized by that smile, and by her abiding sense of a job well done. Finding and validating measures that allow us to predict when the easy exhales and toothless grins will occur would be useful.

Some Final Words

As a profession, we are under great scrutiny—some would say attack. Why? Because we have not met our part of the bargain that all professions make with society—to ensure that members of their profession, from novice to expert, possess the very best and most current knowledge available in order to adequately fulfill their professional charge, which, in the case of teaching, is to prepare our student population for productive entry into our civic participation and the economy. We desperately need teachers who can—and are given the prerogative to —apply their craft with great flexibility. Professional knowledge, deep and broad, is the only basis for being granted flexibility of this sort. But, these newfound degrees of teacher freedom come with greater professional responsibility—the willingness to keep knowledge current, as well as a willingness to examine and change practice; in other words, to accept the possibility, indeed the likelihood, that new knowledge will trump old practice, no matter how comfortably the old ways fit (Pearson, 2007). This can only happen if all our teachers possess a disposition to inquire and to learn, to outgrow themselves as professionals. In the words of Cervetti and Pearson (2005), "We cannot ... eliminate the achievement gap in our schools without closing the knowledge gap in our profession" (p. 223). Closing that knowledge gap ought to be the highest priority of teachers and teacher educators.

A final word on the mission of the professional education of reading teachers. We take the education of reading teachers seriously only because it is a means to an end. The goal is not simply increased teacher knowledge and skill, because that is only a means to the greater end of better teaching in our schools. And that, in turn, is but a means to an even greater end—more and better student learning, particularly learning to read and write. And reading and writing performance is useful only because it allows entry into a world of books and print and further learning, that, in turn, is useful to the degree that it improves the quality of life an individual can lead—a life filled with options and opportunities. Thus, we take the teaching and learning of teachers seriously, because it is the first step on our collective journey to greater opportunity for each and every student who enters the doors of our classrooms. That is the prize, the purpose, and the power of teacher education. A noble calling. An awesome responsibility.

References

Alexander, C., & & Fuller, E. (2004 April). *Does teacher certification matter?: Teacher certification and middle school mathematics achievement in Texas.* Paper presented at the American Educational Research Association annual meeting, San Diego, CA.

Almasi, J. (2003). *Teaching strategic processes in reading.* New York: Guilford Press.

Ashton, P., & Crocker, L. (1986). Systematic study of planned variations: The essential focus of teacher education reform. *Journal of Teacher Education, 3,* 73-83.

Braun, H. (2005). *Using student progress to evaluate teachers: A primer on value-added models.* Princeton, NJ: Educational Testing Service.

Carnegie Task Force on Teaching as a Profession (1986). *A nation prepared: Teachers for the 21st Century.* New York: Carnegie Forum on Education and the Economy.

Cervetti, G., & Pearson, P. D. (2005). A model of professional growth in reading education. In C. Snow, M. Griffin, & S. Burns (Eds.), with G. Cervetti, C. Goldenberg, L. Moats, A. Palincsar, P. D. Pearson, D. Strickland, & M. E. Vogt, *Knowledge to support the teaching of reading: Preparing teachers for a changing world* (pp. 201-224). San Francisco: Jossey-Bass.

Cochran-Smith, M. & Fries, M. (2005). Researching teacher education in changing times: Politics and paradigms. In M. Cochran-Smith & K. Zeichner (Eds.), *Studying teacher education: The report of the AERA panel on research and teacher education.* Mahwah, NJ: Erlbaum.

Cochran-Smith, M. & Lytle, S.L. (2001). Relationships of knowledge and practice: Teacher learning in communities. In A. Iran-Nudged & P. D. Pearson (Eds.), *Review of research in education* (pp. 249-305). Washington, DC: American Educational Research Association.

Commission on Behavioral Social Sciences and Education and the National Research Council (1999). *How people learn: Brain, mind, experience, and school.* Washington, DC: National Academy Press.

Darling-Hammond, L. (1997) *The right to learn: A blueprint for creating schools that work.* San Francisco: Jossey-Bass.

Darling-Hammond, L. (1999). *Teacher quality and student achievement: A review of state policy evidence.* University of Washington: Center for the Study of Teaching and Policy: A National Research Consortium.

Darling-Hammond, L. (2006a). Constructing 21st century teacher education. *Journal of Teacher Education, 57*(3), 300-314.

Darling-Hammond, L. (2006b). *Powerful teacher education: Lessons from exemplary programs.* San Francisco: Jossey-Bass.

Darling-Hammond, L., Chung, R., & Frelow, F. (2002). Variation in teacher preparation: How well do different pathways prepare teachers to teach? *Journal of Teacher Education, 53*(4), 286-302.

Denton, C. A., Foorman, B. R., & Mathes, P. G. (2003). Perspective: Schools that "beat the odds": Implications for reading instruction. *Remedial and Special Education, 24*(5), 258-261.

Educational Testing Service (ETS). (2008). *Praxis II: Subject Assessments: Teaching Foundation Tests.* Princeton, NJ. Educational Testing Service.

Everston, C., Hawley, W., & Zlotnik, M. (1985). Making a difference in educational quality through teacher education. *Journal of Teacher Education, 36*(3), 2-12.

Ferguson, R. F. (1991). Paying for public education: New evidence on how and why money matters. *Harvard Journal of Legislation, 28*(2), 465-498.

Finn, C. E., Jr., Kanstoroom, M. & Petrilli, M. J. (1999). *The quest for better teachers: Grading the states.* Washington, DC: Thomas B. Fordham Foundation.

Finn, C.E. Jr. & Petrilli, M.J. (Eds.). (2000). *The state of state standards 2000: English, history, geography, mathematics, science.* Retrieved January 15, 2008, from www. Edexcellence.net/library/soss2000/2000soss.html.

Flavell, J. (1979). Metacognition and cognitive monitoring: A new area of cognitive-developmental inquiry. *American Psychologist, 34,* 906-9.

Foorman, B. R., Schatschneider, C., Eakin, M. N., Fletcher, J. M., Moats, L.C., & Francis, D. J. (2006). The impact of instructional practices in Grades 1 and 2 on reading and spelling achievement in high poverty schools. *Contemporary Educational Psychology, 31*(1), 1-29.

Fuller, E. (1999). *Does teacher certification matter? A comparison of elementary TAAS performance in 1997 between schools with high and low percentages of certified teachers.* Unpublished report. Austin: University of Texas, Charles A. Dana Center.

Goodlad, J. I. (1990). *Teachers of our nation's schools.* San Francisco: Jossey-Bass.

Haertel, E. (1991). New forms of teacher assessment. In C. Grant (Ed.), *Review of Research in Education, 17,* 3-29.

Hammerness, K., Darling-Hammond, L., & Bransford, J. (2005). How teachers learn and develop. In L. Darling-Hammond & J. Bransford (Eds.), *Preparing teachers for a changing world: What teachers should learn and be able to do* (pp.358-389). San Francisco, CA: Jossey-Bass.

Haney, W., Madaus, G., & Kreitzer, A. (1987). Charms talismanic: Testing teachers for the improvement of American education. *Review of Research in Education, 14,* 169-238.

Hill, H. C., Rowan, B., Ball, D. L. (2005). Effects of teachers' mathematical knowledge for teaching on student achievement. *American Educational Research Journal, 42*(2), pp.372-406.

Hill, H. C., Schilling, S. G. & Ball, D. L. (2004). Developing measures of teachers' mathematics knowledge for teaching. *Elementary School Journal, 105*(1), 11-30.

Hoffman, J. V., & Pearson, P. D. (2000). Reading teacher education in the new millennium: What your grandmother's teacher didn't know that your granddaughter's teacher should. *Reading Research Quarterly, 35*(1), 28-44.

Hoffman, J. V., Roller, C., Maloch, B., Sailors, M., Duffy, G., & Beretvas, S. N. (2005). Teachers' preparation to teach reading and their experiences and practices in the first three years of teaching. *Elementary School Journal, 105*(3), 267-287.

Holmes Group, Inc. (1986), *Tomorrow's teacher: A report of the Holmes Group.* East Lansing, MI: The Holmes Group, Inc. (ED 270 454).

Howey, K. & Zimpher, N. (1989). *Profiles of preservice teacher education: Inquiry into the nature of programs.* Albany: State University of New York Press.

Labaree, D. F. (2005). Life on the margins. *Journal of Teacher Education, 56 (3), 186-191.*

Labaree, D. F. (2008). An uneasy relationship: The history of teacher education in the university. In M. Cochran-Smith, S. Feiman-Nemiser, J. D. McIntyre, & K. E Demers, (Eds.), *Handbook of research on teacher education: Enduring questions in changing contexts* (3rd Edition., pp. 290-306). New York: Routledge.

Laczko-Kerr, I. & Berliner, D. (2002). The effectiveness of "Teach for America" and other undercertificated teachers on student academic achievement: A case of harmful public policy. *Educational Policy Analysis Archives, 10*(37). Retrieved October 16, 2008, from http://epaa.asu.edu/epaa/v10n37.

Levine, A. (2007). *Educating Researchers.* Washington, DC: The Education Schools Project.

Mathes, P. G., Denton, C. A., Fletcher, J. M., Anthony, J. L., Francis, D. J., Schatschneider, C. (2005). The effects of theoretically different instruction and student characteristics on the skills of struggling readers. *Reading Research Quarterly, 40*(2), 148-182.

National Board for Professional Teaching Standards. (n.d.) *Standards.* Retrieved October 16, 2008, from http://www.nbpts.org/the_standards.

National Reading Panel. (2000). *Report of the National Reading Panel: Teaching children to read: An evidence-based assessment of the scientific research literature on reading and its implications for reading instruction.* Washington, DC: National Institute of Child Health and Human Development. Retrieved October 16, 2008, from http://www.nichd.nih.gov/publications/nrp/report.cfm.

No Child Left Behind Act of 2001, Pub. L. No. 107-110, 115 Stat. 1425 (2002). Available from http://www.ed.gov/nclb/landing.jhtml.

Pearson, P. D. (2001). Learning to teach reading: The status of the knowledge base. In C. Roller (Ed.), *Learning to teach reading: Setting the research agenda* (pp. 4-19). Newark, DE: International Reading Association.

Pearson, P. D. (2007). An endangered species act for literacy education. *Journal of Literacy Research, 39*(20), 145-162.

Pearson, P. D., Taylor, B. M., & Tam, A. (2005). Effective professional development for improving literacy instruction. In R. Indrisano, & J. R. Paratore (Eds.), *Learning to write, writing to learn: Research and theory in practice* (pp. 221-224). Newark, DE: International Reading Association.

Phelps, G. & Schilling, S. (2004). Developing measures of content knowledge for teaching reading. *Elementary School Journal, 105*(1), 31-48.

Phelps, G. (2004). *Content knowledge for teaching reading: Technical report on reading measures used on the Study of Instructional Improvement teacher questionnaire.* Ann Arbor: University of Michigan.

Placier, P. & Hamilton, M. L. (1994). Schools as contexts: A complex relationship. In V. Richardson (Ed.), *Teacher change and the staff development process: A case of reading instruction* (pp. 135-159). New York: Teachers College Press.

Richardson, V. (1994). *Teacher change and the staff development process: A case in reading instruction.* New York: Teachers College Press.

Richardson, V. (2003). The dilemmas of professional development. *Phi Delta Kappan, 84*(5), 401-406.

Richardson, V., & Anders, P. (1994). The study of teacher change. In V. Richardson (Ed.), *Teacher change and the staff development process: A case in reading instruction* (pp. 159-180). New York: Teachers College Press.

Richardson, V., & Placier, P. (2001). Teacher change. In V. Richardson (Ed.), *Handbook of research on teaching* (4th ed., pp. 905-950). Washington, D.C.: American Educational Research Association.

Rivkin, S. G., Hanushek, E. A., & Kain, J. F. (2000). *Teachers, schools, and academic achievement* (Working paper no. 6691 revised). Cambridge, MA: National Bureau of Economic Research.

Rosenshine, B. & Stevens, R. (1984). Classroom instruction in reading. In P. D. Pearson, R. Barr, M. Kamil, & P. Mosenthal (Eds.), *Handbook of reading research* (Vol. 1, pp.745-798). New York: Longman.

Rowan, B., Schilling, S., Ball, D., & Miller, R. (2001). Measuring teachers' pedagogical content knowledge in surveys: An exploratory study. *Consortium for Policy Research in Education, Study of Instructional Improvement, Research Note S-2.* Ann Arbor: University of Michigan. Retrieved October 19, 2008, from http://www.sii.soe.umich.edu/documents/pck%20final%20report%20revised%20BR100901.pdf.

Sanders, W. L., & Rivers, J. C. (1996) *Cumulative and residual effects of teachers on future student academic achievement.* Knoxville: University of Tennessee Value-Added Research and Assessment Center.

Shulman, L. S. (1986). Those who understand: Knowledge growth in teaching. *Educational Researcher, 15*(2), 4-14.

Smith, G. P., Miller, M. C. & Joy, J. (1988). A case study of the impact of performance-based testing on the supply of minority teachers. *Journal of Teacher Education,*

39(4), 45-53.

Snow, C. E., Griffin, P., & Burns, M. S. (Eds.), with G. Cervetti, C., Goldenberg, L. Moats, A. Palincsar, P. D. Pearson, D. Strickland, & M. E. Vogt (2005). *Knowledge to support the teaching of reading: Preparing teachers for a changing world.* San Francisco: Jossey-Bass.

Taylor, B. M., Pearson, P. D., Peterson, D. S., & Rodriguez, M. C. (2005). The CIERA school change framework: An evidence-based approach to professional development and school reading improvement. *Reading Research Quarterly, 40*(1), 40-69.

Valdez, A. (1992). Changes in teachers' beliefs, understandings, and practices concerning reading comprehension through the use of practical arguments: A follow-up study. Unpublished doctoral dissertation, University of Arizona, Tucson.

Wenglinsky, H. (2002). How schools matter: The link between classroom practices and student academic achievement performance. *Educational Policy Analysis Archives, 10*(12). Retrieved February 27th, 2008, from http://epaa.asu.edu/epaa/v10n12.

Wilson, S. M., & Berne, J. (1999). Teacher learning and the acquisition of professional knowledge: An examination of research on contemporary professional development. In A. Iran-Nejad & P. D. Pearson (Eds.), *Review of research in education* (pp. 173-209). Washington, DC: American Educational Research Association.

Wilson, S. M., Floden, R., & Ferrini-Mundy, J. (2001). *Teacher preparation research: Current knowledge, gaps, and recommendations.* A research report prepared for the U.S. Department of Education. Seattle: Center for the Study of Teaching and Policy, University of Washington.

Wright, S. P., Horn, S. P., & Sanders, W. L. (1997). Teacher and classroom context effects on student achievement: Implications for teacher evaluation. *Journal of Personnel Evaluation in Education, 11*(1), 57-67.

Zeichner, K. M. (1993). Traditions of practice in U.S. preservice teacher education programs. *Teaching and Teacher Education, 9*(1), 1-13.

Getting the Facts Right In Books for Young Readers: Researching *Mailing May*

Michael O. Tunnell

Brigham Young University

Keynote Address
College Reading Association
2007

Michael O. Tunnell teaches children's literature at Brigham Young University. He has published several professional books, including Children's Literature, Briefly *(with Jim Jacobs; 2008) and* The Prydain Companion *(2003)—as well as a variety of journal articles about children's books. He also writes for young readers. Some of his titles include* The Children of Topaz *(1996),* Mailing May *(1997),* Wishing Moon *(2004), and* Moon without Magic *(2007).*

Michael Tunnell was the invited speaker for CRA's Children's Book Author presentation for the first evening of the 51st annual conference. The topic he chose to discuss was the research that goes into the writing of his books for young readers.

I had never been to Grangeville, Idaho, but as I stood gazing down its main street, I was flooded with the strange and thrilling sensation that I'd stood there before. However, this small mountain town was no longer the place I had traveled so far to see. What I really was seeking was the Grangeville of the 1910s. But remnants of bygone days were there to be found, and therefore I

Reprinted from *Literacy Issues During Changing Times: A Call to Action*, pp. 12-22, by F. Falk-Ross, S. Szabo, M. B. Sampson, & M. M. Foote, Eds., 2009, Commerce, TX: College Reading Association.

was feeling the exhilaration recognized by anyone who chases history. It is the rush that comes with standing at the site of a human drama about which you've been reading and studying and dreaming. To be there is often the only way to make your research complete, and when you arrive, the place seems magically familiar. In this case, I had been chasing a very tiny slice of Americana, the story of a 5-year-old Grangeville girl who made postal history in 1914.

My search for May Pierstorff began when I was browsing through a book titled *1910s* (Stewart, 1989, p. 24), a collection of interesting facts about that particular decade, and this brief entry caught my eye: "A 48-POUND BABY CHICK?" But instead of information about giant poultry, I found the story of an Idaho couple who could not afford to send their young daughter by train to visit her grandmother. How did they solve their problem? The Pierstorffs mailed her! Parcel post was new in 1914, but even then regulations prohibited mailing living things, except for queen bees and baby chicks. The limit for a package was 50 pounds, and little May Pierstorff apparently weighed in at around 48. She was classified as a baby chick, and for 53¢ worth of postage—much less than the price of a train ticket—she was loaded on the railroad mail car and then delivered to her grandmother's doorstep later that day.

I smiled as I read this account of May's mailing, but then I came to attention in my chair. I've always wanted to be struck by the muse, and maybe this was as near as I'll ever come. Suddenly, I knew that May's story was just the right stuff for a children's book. However, I needed to know more of May's story. The few paragraphs in *1910s* told me little, and the book did not provide a reference. I decided to start my search by visiting the history librarians at Brigham Young University. When I told them what I was after, I got a response I was destined to hear again and again: "It's probably just folklore," accompanied by pleasant laughter. When absolutely nothing surfaced during our search, it seemed May's story was indeed an urban, or rather, a rural legend.

Nevertheless, the librarians suggested I call the Idaho Historical Society. If there was a shred of truth to the story, someone there should know. But when I got Guila Ford on the phone in her Boise, Idaho, office, she knew nothing of May Pierstorff and, with a pleasant laugh, suggested that the tale might be . . . well, a bit of western folklore. Nevertheless, she was willing to help me find out if this was fact or fiction.

I didn't even know the town in Idaho from which May supposedly was mailed, or her destination, so Guila did a search of the Idaho census looking for Pierstorffs. In a matter of days, I received a letter telling me that the only Pierstorffs in Idaho during the early part of the twentieth century lived in the area around Lewiston. Included were photocopies of the 1920 census reports that listed the family of John E. Pierstorff and his wife Sarah. Though John and Sarah had five children, there was no May. I wanted to believe that their daughter, listed as Charlotte M., had the middle name of May. After all, she was 11 in 1920, which would have made her the right age.

Before I could decide what to do next, serendipity took a hand in my affairs. I was reading the August 2, 1993, issue of *U.S. News* and *World Report*, with no thought of May in my mind, when I ran across a four-page advertisement titled "America's History is in the Mail." It celebrated the opening of the Smithsonian's National Postal Museum and included a timeline of U.S. postal history. Beneath the year 1914 was printed: "Four-year-old Mary Pierstroff is delivered by U.S. Mail to her grandparents, for 53 cents (the chicken rate), because her parents were reluctant to pay the train fare. 'Mailing' children is soon banned by the post office" (*U.S. News and World Report*, 1993, p. 60). If the Smithsonian Institute knew about May (even if they had spelled her first and last names wrong), then not only was her story true, but I also had a solid source of information. I called directory assistance and got a number for the Smithsonian. A few minutes later, after being transferred only once, I was talking to Jim O'Donnell, a Museum Specialist at the National Postal Museum in Washington, D.C. Jim also didn't know May's story but was pleased to engage in researching "this bit of postal history." A couple of weeks later, I received a letter from Jim, who had asked the museum curator where he had found the information for the timeline. The curator thought it came from an old edition of *Postal Life*, but a search yielded nothing. Instead, Jim had found a brief, boxed article titled "The Parcel Post Kid," published in an issue of the *Parade Magazine* that accompanied the *Washington Post* on January 10, 1982. The article offered little new information, except a photograph of May and, of most importance, the points of her departure and arrival: Grangeville to Lewiston.

Now that I knew where May had lived, I zeroed in on the Nez Perce County Historical Society in Lewiston, Idaho. I telephoned and spoke with Lora Feucht, telling her I wanted to learn as much as I could about the little girl who was mailed from Grangeville to Lewiston in 1914. Her response: "That really happened? I've never heard a thing about it." She asked me to give her a week to do some research.

Soon after I received a large, brown envelope from Lora with all the evidence I had hoped for, including confirmation that the child from the 1920 census was the little girl who had been mailed. Lora had located Charlotte May Pierstorff's relatives, who still lived in the area, and from them acquired magazine and newspaper clippings galore, including May's obituary (which told the tale of her being mailed). She died in 1987, and though it was 1993, I felt as if I barely had missed being able to meet her.

In the packet of clippings, I found an article from the *Smithsonian* (Kernan & Lautman, 1993); highlighted for me was a single paragraph telling about May (p. 60). I've wondered since if this was the source the curator of the National Postal Museum had used for his postal history timeline. Other brief accounts of May's adventure also had appeared in *The American Philatelist*, *The National Enquirer* (which, by the way, was as outrageously inaccurate as one might expect), and a variety of newspapers from the northern Idaho and Washington area.

One of the most important items sent to me by Lora Feucht was a photo-copy of the article that appeared in the *Gem State Banner*, one of Lewiston's two newspapers at the time, on February 19, 1914 "SEND GIRL AGED 4 BY PARCEL POST" announced the headline, followed by "Weighs 48 1-2 Pounds and Journey Requires 53 Cents in Stamps" (Gem State Banner). Though the *Banner* got her age wrong (she was 5 months away from being 6), this clipping erased even the slightest doubt about May's story. She indeed had been mailed to her grandmother in Lewiston: "Mrs. C. G. Vennigerholz, 1156 Twelfth Avenue." The event was newsworthy enough to appear in print the very day it occurred, and the article revealed much about what actually happened. For instance, the conductor on the Grangeville to Lewiston line of the Camas Prairie Railroad, Harry Morris, entered the mail car to collect a fare from the "little flaxen-haired miss" only to be shown the "stamps attached to her coat." The article also named Leonard Mochel as the mail clerk who delivered May to her grandmother soon after her arrival.

The news clipping was a valuable discovery, but there was an even bigger find in the materials from the Nez Perce County Historical Society—a typed, two-page account written and signed by Leonard Mochel the railway postal clerk who traveled with May. Leonard revealed he was Sarah Pierstorff's cousin, which meant May had not been abandoned to survive as best she could among letters and packages sorted by a stranger.

Leonard obviously recalled the events of February 19, 1914, years after they happened, for he begins with these words: "This story dates back to the time when the Post Office Department increased the weight of parcel post packages to a limit of fifty pounds." Actually, parcel post within the United States had been initiated on January 1, 1913, only about a year before May was mailed. Before that time, only items weighing 4 pounds or less could be sent by mail. In my further research of the time period, I discovered that the United States government had maintained parcel post agreements with foreign countries long before reasonable domestic service was established. The new domestic regulations allowed 50-pound packages to be sent short distances (short-haul packages) and 20-pound packages to be sent long distances. Leonard made it clear that no one knew quite what to make of the new, hefty weights allowed. "There were numerous speculations as to the various things that could be car-ried by and in the United States mail," he said. "Many jokes about supposed happenings were recounted and several accounts were printed in the newspapers causing much merriment."

Leonard's memory seemed a bit foggy when it came to some of the small details. He can only approximate the year when he helped mail his cousin's daughter, "about 1915." He recalled May's weight (combined with that of her small valise) as 49 pounds and the amount of the postage as exactly 50 cents ("two cents for the first pound and one cent for each additional pound"). And on the topic of where the stamps were affixed, he also disagreed with most other reports. I had read that the stamps were glued to a tag attached to May's person or were glued directly to the back of her coat, but Leonard said they were "affixed to her valise."

Even though Leonard's memories about postage amounts and package weights may not be accurate, he still had the best view of the events of that day. His words offered something unavailable in any other source—a play-by-play, firsthand account. Leonard breathed life into the players of this tiny historical drama, and thus into the whole story. For instance, Leonard made no mention of tight finances as the reason May's parents chose to send her by mail. Instead, he painted the picture of a playful Sarah Pierstorff, who listened to jokes and stories about outrageous items sent by parcel post and decided to test the waters. She knew there would be no risk involved and that her daughter would not be frightened. After all, Leonard stayed with his cousin when in Grangeville, which meant he and May knew one another well. So one morning in February, Sarah stopped her postal clerk cousin before he left for work and asked him to mail a package to her mother. "I was sure flabbergasted," said Leonard, but he consented to give Sarah's idea a try. The postmaster didn't seem to raise much of an objection and "after several witticisms duly weighed her." Besides most living things, postal regulations also prohibited the mailing of smelly items. Though Leonard didn't quote the postmaster's witty comments, I can imagine him sniffing May, laughing, and declaring that she at least passed the smell test.

Leonard's report also gave a more personal look at May herself. For instance, he recounted that May became "dizzy and carsick" during the train ride. When she went to the door to get some air, the conductor, Harry Morris, caught her and "immediately protested that [Leonard] was carrying a passenger and asked for her ticket." When Leonard explained the situation and showed Harry the stamps, the conductor "laughed and remarked that he had seen everything now" and "that this would make an authentic news report." In 1962, when the *Lewiston Morning Tribune* interviewed May (Mrs. Kay Sipes), she wondered if the unsettling train ride in 1914 might have affected her subconsciously ("Girl Sent by Post has Dislike for Trains," 1962). "I love to travel," she said, "but I don't like to ride in trains." She also said she remembered very little about her amazing journey, only that she had to get up early, that it was bitterly cold, and that Conductor Morris looked extremely important "with his gold watch and chain draped across his big tummy."

Harry Morris turned in his news scoop as soon as the train arrived in Grangeville. Leonard thought that the story must have made every newspaper in the country and as a result "we found some of our relatives in the state of New York, and were able to trace our ancestory [sic] to the Mayflower." But the aftermath of May's mailing was not all pleasant. Within days, Leonard heard from his chief clerk, George Addleman, in Spokane, Washington. Mr. Addleman had read about May in the *Seattle Star Mirror* and wanted to know why Leonard shouldn't be given 500 demerits for violating the interstate commerce ruling concerning passengers in mail cars (700 demerits meant dismissal). He insisted that half a fare be paid to the Camas Prairie Railroad. As there were no children's fares at the time, the price of a ticket for May was $1.55. If the Pierstorff's were financially strapped, the 53¢ postage was a real savings. John Pierstorff was a farm laborer, and my research revealed that farm laborers in the Mountain States averaged about $10.00 per week in 1914.

The pressure mounted as other citizens decided to capitalize on the opportunity to use parcel post in creative ways. Within a week, a news article appeared in *The Spokesman-Review* in Spokane. The headline read: "ILLEGAL TO SEND CHILD BY MAIL" (1914). After describing May's mailing and its illegality, the article reported that local postal inspectors were "in receipt of a communication from Priest River from a man who asked permission to send a dog to Spokane. He was informed that the dog was unmailable."

Leonard Mochel received a good scare, but in the end John and Sarah agreed to pay half the fare and Leonard escaped the 500 demerits. Though the article in the *Gem State Banner* (1914) stated that May would be returned to her parents by parcel post, it is a fair bet she wasn't. However, no one, including May's son, Gerald Sipes, seems to know exactly how May got back to Grangeville. Traveling from Lewiston to Grangeville was arduous in 1914, unless you took the train, because the roads were so poor. It is almost certain that May rode the train home as a passenger rather than a package.

Though the train was the easy way to travel, the line between Grangeville and Lewiston wasn't your run-of-the-mill stretch of track. Lora Feucht also sent me information about this segment of Camas Prairie Railroad, including some photographs and a copy of a train schedule with the effective date of February 8, 1914. What I discovered was fascinating. This leg of the Camas Prairie Railroad belies its name—there is nothing prairie-like about the terrain. Though Grangeville sits on what is called the Camas Prairie, comparatively flat farmland nestled among the mountains, the edge of the "prairie" rises to over 3,700 feet above sea level before making a spectacular plunge downward through rugged peaks and cliffs to Lewiston at an elevation of 732 feet. This 3,000-foot drop in elevation occurs on only 77 miles of track. As the crow flies, the distance is a good deal shorter, for the track is replete with switchbacks. In 1914, there were 61 trestles and seven tunnels along the way. The rails clung to steep mountainsides and sailed above dizzying canyon depths atop towers of crisscrossed timbers. "Steel on stilts," folks called it. Little wonder May was carsick.

According to the schedule, Leonard and May pulled away from the Grangeville Depot at 7:00 a.m. Coming down the steep grade, the passenger train averaged 19.2 miles an hour; this included making stops at 14 small towns with names like Cottonwood, Culdesac, Fort Lapwai, and Joseph. Of course, Leonard would drop off and pick up mail at each stop until he made his final drop at 11:00 a.m. in Lewiston.

During my efforts to uncover May's story, I also had the opportunity to speak and correspond with Gerald Sipes. Though I had missed meeting May, talking with her son, and eventually meeting him face-to-face, turned out to be a wonderful substitute. Gerald worked on the Camas Prairie Railroad his entire career as an agent-telegrapher and later as a claim agent-station supervisor. He was there when passenger trains still ran from Grangeville to Lewiston. Therefore, Gerald was able to answer questions about the railroad and about his mother, though he knew few details about the mailing incident. The first time I called Gerald, I asked if he had the photograph of May that I had seen reproduced with several of the magazine articles. If so, I asked, would you have a copy made for me? In 3 days, I found an envelope in my mailbox containing May's photograph and an actual clipping of the February 19 article from the *Gem State Banner* (1914). "Enclosed are all of the clippings and photo [of] when Mom was 4 (1912) that I have left. Please return these as soon as possible so they won't get lost," read the accompanying note. Though we had never met in person, he entrusted me with the only original photograph of the young May that he possessed. When I finally met Gerald and his wife, Shirley, I found them both to be as delightful as my initial impression led me to believe. I also picked up a few more pieces of the puzzle from them, including the newspaper report that appeared on February 20, 1914, in the *Lewiston Morning Tribune*, entitled "Girl Journeys Parcels (sic) Post," that confirmed May's departure and arrival times.

At last, I seemed to have nailed down most of the facts, but I needed more than facts. I needed to share as much of May's experience as possible, duplicate it as best I could. That required a visit to both Grangeville and Lewiston.

Lora Feucht and her colleagues at the Nez Perce County Historical Society hooked me up with two local people who made my visit seem like a step back in time. The first I contacted was Carmelita Spencer, curator of the Bicentennial Historical Museum in Grangeville. Carm, as everyone in Grangeville called her, was the proverbial bundle of energy and knew Grangeville better than I know my own children. Happily, she agreed to show me the sites related to May.

My second important local contact was Jim Morefield. As Supervisor of Maintenance on the Camas Prairie Railroad, Jim literally had the power to recreate the past for me. I wanted to follow May's path from beginning to end, and that meant I had to ride the rails from Grangeville to Lewiston. It was a cold winter day when I called Jim, and he agreed to take me over the route, if I'd wait until April or May. I had more reason to be ecstatic than I realized at the time, for I was about to traverse the trestles and tunnels of what I soon discovered to be one of the last vestiges of old-time railroading.

In late April of 1994, I made the 650-mile drive from Provo, Utah, to Lewiston. Going north from Boise, the winding two-lane highway followed the Salmon and Payette Rivers, curling through canyons and mountain valleys that rival the beauty of any in the Rockies. Finally, after a few scenic hours of driving, I descended onto the high mountain plains of the Camas Prairie and soon was standing on the streets of Grangeville.

I never was able to determine where in the Grangeville area the Pierstorffs had lived, but I knew I could begin May's journey at the old post office. I called Carm Spencer, who appeared almost instantly in a Lincoln Continental that dwarfed her tiny stature. She whisked me away on a tour of the town, including not only the old post office masquerading as the Fireside Lounge but also the site of the old Grangeville train depot. The depot is gone, and I only have a blurry photograph of the small wooden structure that was snapped long after its heyday. Carm tried to locate a better shot, but the photograph files of the local newspaper yielded nothing, as did a search by the Idaho Historical Society.

However, I did see the Schmadeka Building. Erected in 1910, it was one of the few structures remaining that May likely passed on the way to the train station. Carm pointed to the brick building's second story, telling me about Dreamland Hall. There couples twirled away their evenings on Schmadeka's hardwood dance floor. I also saw the site of the Lyric, a silent movie auditorium around in May's time but replaced in the 1930s by the still impressive theater, the Blue Fox. And I was able to stand on the site, now occupied by a new bank, where the major department store sat in 1914. Even though Alexander-Friedenrich burned down a few years before my visit, I created a scene in *Mailing May* that took place inside the store.

With an odd sense of reluctance, I left Carm Spencer and Grangeville in order to make Lewiston by nightfall. Early the next morning Jim Morefield met me at my motel, colorfully named the Sacagawea, and with real anticipation, I climbed into his Ford Bronco turned hyrail (highway/rail vehicle). We headed toward the small town of Spalding (known as Joseph in 1914). Jim needed a railroad crossing in order to drive the hyrail onto the tracks, and Spalding offered the closest and most traffic-free spot.

My major interest, of course, was to experience the route of May's trip, but the moment I crawled out of the Bronco to watch Jim settle it onto the rails, I knew I was now interested in some of the finer points of railroading. For instance, I discovered that a Bronco's wheels are too far apart to sit on the rails until a wheel adapter kit moves them inward to measure 60 inches from center to center. I watched Jim lower and then lever into place the rail gear attached at the front and rear. Steel wheels, miniature railcar wheels with rubber treads, guide the hyrail along the track just like a locomotive, once the Bronco's steering wheel is locked in place. In a few minutes, we were on our way up the mountain to Grangeville.

We were able to enjoy the luxury of stopping whenever we wanted to take a photograph or examine a tunnel, and as Jim explained his railroad, I began to understand that it was virtually no different than it had been 80 years earlier. There were no electrical switches. No high tech computer monitoring. And though diesels had been substituted for steam locomotives, the trestles they passed over were still the same giant turn-of-the-century wooden structures, timbers replaced here and there over the years to keep them intact. But unlike the Durango and Silverton Narrow Gauge Railroad and other lines restored for the tourist trade, the Camas Prairie Railroad still hauled freight up and down the mountains in 1994—a weekly train except during the busier grain-harvesting season.

I was amazed to discover what a gargantuan task it is to keep a rail line maintained in good working order. Railroad ties, for instance, must regularly be replaced as they deteriorate or are "cut in" by the constant pounding weight of the trains—the tie plate holding the rail literally sinks into the wood. Jim saw to the replacement of anywhere from 1,000 to 6,000 ties yearly on the Grangeville line alone, and as we cruised along, he pointed to hundreds marked with florescent paint dots awaiting removal. At 3,000 per mile, the job of checking the ties was no small affair.

Of course, the steel track must be checked and replaced as well. Jim showed me how track may soften or become pitted causing vibration that in turn destroys ties. The joint bars that connect the rails must be checked constantly for loose bolts or cracks. Jim showed me how to listen for loose bolts as the hyrail crossed each joint. Sure enough, just by the sound we discovered a few bolts that needed tightening.

I'm sure May wasn't the least bit concerned with railroad ties and joint bars, but I'm certain she paid plenty of attention to the steep grades and sharp curves, the dark tunnels and the towering trestles. I know I did. Soon after Spalding the hyrail started a sharp ascent with grades as steep as 3% and sharp switchbacks. Forty-one of the 61 trestles still remain, as well as six of the seven tunnels. In Lapwai Canyon, the track makes a complete semicircle as it crosses a curving trestle and runs through Tunnel 1 (a bore of over 800 feet), creating an arc with a diameter of only about 1,000 feet.

The trestles were breathtaking. The longest and tallest spans Lawyer's Canyon. Of steel construction and built in 1908, it is 1580 feet long and 286 feet high. Half Moon Trestle is the tallest wooden structure at 141 feet, and though it is 685 feet long, there are two others that approach 900 feet. Half Moon Trestle contains a million board feet of timber. Throwbacks to the steam engine days still grace these wooden bridges—barrel stands. About every 100 feet a small platform extends outward, designed to hold a barrel of water used to extinguish trestle fires.

We were high up on the side of an Idaho mountain by the time we reached Tunnel 5. As we started through, an owl swooped down from the pilings, flew over us, and then circled back, obviously angry that we'd disturbed his daytime repose. We stopped, and as I stood by the tracks peering at the owl and scanning the panoramic scenery, I felt like I was seeing exactly what May saw. If I turned my back on the hyrail, no signs of the late 20th century spoiled the illusion.

That evening I completed the last leg of May's trip. Back in Lewiston, I found the old Union Pacific Station where May was unloaded and carted with the mail to the Lewiston Post Office. Trains don't come into Union Depot these days. The building is a nicely restored office complex that retains much of the splendid appearance of a substantial railroad station circa 1914. From Union Depot it is only two blocks to the old Lewiston Post Office, a columned edifice similar to many of the larger government buildings of the era. The post office was completed in 1912, ready and waiting for May's arrival. Today Lewiston has a newer, more modern post office, and the city offices reside in the old post office building.

Then I remembered May's mailing label: "Mrs. C. G. Vennigerholz, 1156 Twelfth Avenue." Could the house still be standing? From the post office I drove up into Lewiston's avenues. I felt a chill pass through me as I pulled in front of a corner lot with a house bearing the numbers 1156. Leonard Mochel had walked up those steps to deliver May to her grandmother.

As I was snapping a few pictures, Linda Carlton came out the front door, wondering if she could help me with something. I suppose she was a bit suspicious of a strange fellow photographing her home. But when I told her May's story, Linda took me inside and showed me a large, framed photograph of the Vennigerholz home before the Carltons bought and remodeled it. The house had been slated for demolition more than once; Bob and Linda Carlton saved it from what seemed a certain death.

As I stood outside 1156 Twelfth Avenue, I was warmed by a sense of satisfaction. True, some might think May's story insignificant. But to me, it is a story that epitomizes America and the innovative spirit of her people. Of all the details about May's story that I learned, I suddenly knew that the most important detail had nothing to do with railway schedules or postal rates but rather with the wonderful, creative ways in which ordinary people solve difficult problems.

Before the sun disappeared and darkness took the house, I gazed at it one last time. Though the Carltons had extended and modernized the place, I could still see Mary Vennigerholz opening the front door, a shocked look on her face—for no one had bothered to notify her that her granddaughter was coming, much less coming by parcel post.

References

America's history is in the mail. (1993, August 2). *U. S. News and World Report*, pp. 59-62.

Illegal to send child by mail.(1914). *The Spokesman-Review.*

Girl journeys parcels post. (1914, February 20). *Lewiston Morning Tribune.*

Girl sent by parcel post now has dislike for trains. (1962). *Lewiston Morning Tribune.*

Kernan, M. & Lautman, R. C. Some beguiling mail chauvinism at a brand-new museum. (1993, August). *Smithsonian*, 24(5), p. 76.

The parcel post kid. (1982, January 10). *Parade Magazine.*

Send girl aged 4 by parcel post. (1914, February 19). *Gem State Banner.*

Stewart, G. B. (1989.) 1910s. New York: Crestwood House.

Tunnell, M. O.(with Chilcoat, G. W.). (1996). *The children of Topaz: The story of a Japanese-American internment camp based on a classroom diary*. New York: Holiday House.

Tunnell, M. O. (1997). *Mailing May*. New York: Greenwillow.

Tunnell, M. O. (2003). *The Prydain companion: A reference guide to Lloyd Alexander's Prydain Chronicles*. New York: Holt.

Tunnell M. O. (2004).*Wishing Moon*. New York: Dutton.

Tunnell, M. O. (2007). *Moon without Magic*. New York: Dutton.

Tunnell, M. O., & Jacobs, J. S. (2008). *Children's literature, briefly* (4th ed.). Upper Saddle River, NJ: Allyn & Bacon.

Teachers of English Learners: Issues of Preparation and Professional Development

MaryEllen Vogt

California State University, Long Beach

Keynote Address
College Reading Association
2007

MaryEllen Vogt is Distinguished Professor Emerita at California State University, Long Beach. Dr. Vogt has been a classroom teacher, reading and special education specialist, district reading resource teacher, and university teacher educator. She received her doctorate from the University of California, Berkeley. A co-author of eight books, including Reading Specialists *and* Literacy Coaches in the Real World *(2nd Ed.; 2007) and* Making Content Comprehensible for English Learners: The SIOP Model *(3rd Ed.; 2008), her research interests include improving comprehension in* the content areas, teacher change and development, and content literacy and language acquisition for English learners. Dr. Vogt served as President of the International Reading Association in 2004-2005.

Abstract

Throughout the United States, rapidly increasing numbers of students whose first language is not English are enrolling in our schools. A majority of these students are native-born English learners, while the remainder are foreign born. In order to meet the academic and language development needs of these

Reprinted from *Literacy Issues During Changing Times: A Call to Action*, pp. 23-36, by F. Falk-Ross, S. Szabo, M. B. Sampson, & M. M. Foote, Eds., 2009, Commerce, TX: College Reading Association

students, we must re-think preservice and inservice teacher preparation. This
involves planning preservice and professional development programs that: (a)
focus on the effective teaching practices that result in improved academic and
language proficiency for English learners, and (b) are responsive to teachers'
development over the course of their careers. Progressive Differentiation, as
described by the National Academy of Education's Reading Sub-Committee
(Snow, Griffin, & Burns, 2005), is used as a framework for identifying levels of
development throughout a teacher's career and for considering programmatic
issues related to the education of English learners. Questions to consider and
recommendations for preservice program design are included.

In Mr. Jensen's 8th grade American History class, there is a mix of linguistically diverse students. About half of the students are native English speakers,
while the others have a variety of home languages, including Spanish, Arme-
nian, Farsi, Portuguese, Vietnamese, and French. With this mix of students,
Mr. Jensen feels frustrated when he assesses their understanding of the history
concepts he teaches. Many of the English learners (ELs) have no background in
American history, while others, even those who are native-born, lack the English
proficiency to read and listen with comprehension. Because of the state history
standards he must teach, he feels there is little or no time to stop and reteach
his ELs and other students who may have failed to meet the day's objectives.
He also worries about the students who seem to master history concepts almost
effortlessly. Several of them appear disinterested and bored while he is teaching.
Mr. Jensen frequently feels overwhelmed and at times inadequate to meet the
varied academic and language development needs of his diverse students.

Like Mr. Jensen, many of today's teachers in the United States are challenged
when their language of instruction differs from the home languages of many of
their students. The purpose of this paper is to focus on teacher preparation in the
United States especially as related to English learners, and to examine teacher
development through Progressive Differentiation, as described by the National
Academy of Education's Reading Sub-Committee (Snow, Griffin, & Burns,
2005). Additionally, the purpose is to reflect on our role as teacher educators in
planning undergraduate and graduate programs and professional development
that respond to teachers' developmental career paths.

Background

The number of English learners in our schools continues to grow, with the
rate of growth considerably outpacing that of native-English speaking students.
Limited English proficient (LEP) students (another name for ELs) comprise approximately 10.5 percent of the nation's pre-K –12 school enrollment, up from

5 percent in 1990 (Hoffman & Sable, 2006). The National Clearinghouse for English Language Acquisition (NCELA) reported in 2007 that the following states experienced growth of more than 200 percent in their LEP population between 1994-2005: Nevada, Colorado, Nebraska, Arkansas, Indiana, Kentucky, North Carolina, South Carolina, Alabama, and Georgia (NCELA, 2007). As English learners attend our schools in increasing numbers contributing their talents and cultures, there are also troubling aspects related to their schooling (Short, Vogt, & Echevarria, 2008, p. 6):

1. Only 4 percent of 8th grade English learners and 20 percent of students classified "formerly as EL" scored at the proficient or advanced levels on the reading portion of the 2005 National Assessment of Educational Progress (NAEP; Perie, Grigg, & Donahue, 2005). This means that 96 percent of the eighth-grade limited English proficient students score *below* basic level. This is particularly noteworthy, because NAEP exams often exempt students at the beginning proficiency level of English as a second language (Grigg, Daane, Jin, & Campbell, 2003; Short, Vogt, & Echevarria, 2008).

2. English learners have some of the highest drop-out rates (Steinberg & Almeida, 2004). Since NCLB (No Child Left Behind; U.S. Department of Education, 2002) legislation was enacted in 2001, there appears to be an increase in the number of high school English learners not receiving a diploma, because they failed high-stakes tests, despite fulfilling all other graduation requirements (Biancarosa & Snow, 2004; Center on Education Policy, 2005).

3. Fifty-nine percent of adolescent students identified as Limited English Proficient live in families with incomes 185 percent below the poverty line (2000 U.S. Census; Batalova, Fix, & Murray, 2005).

4. Eighty-nine percent of secondary Hispanic students read below grade level (Perie, Grigg, & Donahue, 2005).

5. A recent five-year, statewide evaluation study found that English learners with 10 years of schooling in California had less than a 40 percent chance of meeting the criteria to be re-designated as fluent English proficient (Perie, Grigg, & Donahue, 2005).

6. Ten percent of young adults who speak English at home fail to complete high school, but the percentage is over three times higher (31 percent) for young adult ELs. If English learners reported speaking English with difficulty on the 2000 U.S. Census, their likelihood of completing high school dropped to 18 percent. However, if they reported speaking English very well, their likelihood of graduating was 51 percent (Klein, Bugarin, Beltranena, & McArthur, 2004).

Diversity among English Learners

Who are the English learners that are experiencing performance gaps? As with all students, ELs are not the same. They differ in their educational backgrounds, culture, socioeconomic status, literacy levels in English, and other characteristics (Short, Vogt, & Echevarria, 2008). For example, along the spectrum of English learners, teachers will find students with limited or no schooling in their primary language (L1), with limited or no literacy in their L1, and who lack experiences that are relevant to U.S. educational contexts. At the other end of the spectrum, teachers will find students with strong academic backgrounds in their first language who are fully literate in their L1 and who have had a wealth of experiences that relate strongly to educational topics and content in this country.

Somewhere in the middle of the spectrum are students who were born in the United States, but their home language is not English. Many of these students have developed some literacy in both English and their home language, but often they lack proficiency in either. Worse, other native-born ELs are illiterate both in English and their home language, and they have been attending U.S. schools since kindergarten.

Currently, in both elementary (Pre-K to Grade 5) and secondary (Grades 6-12) education, there are more English learners in the United States that are native born than are foreign born. In the elementary grades, 24 percent of ELs are first generation Americans, while 44 percent of secondary ELs are foreign-born. The rest of the students classified as LEP are native-born (Capps, Fix, Murray, Ost, Passel, & Herwantoro, 2005).

Of course, at various points along the spectrum there are other students whose profiles may be unique to their personal and educational backgrounds. As you read the following students' profiles (Echevarria, Vogt, & Short, 2008, p. 8), consider their academic and literacy strengths, as well as their English development needs.

1. Muyisa was born in Zaire (now the Democratic Republic of Congo). She spoke Swahili and Lingala as a child, and French while in an international school in Brussels. Her father, a diplomat posted at the embassy in Belgium, was recently assigned to the U.N., and Muyisa is enrolled in a high school ESL program in New York City.

2. Born in the Dominican Republic, Diego came to the U.S. in third grade. He had attended school in his home town and learned to read and write in Spanish. His family settled in northern New Jersey but they have moved frequently. He's now in Union City, NJ and in a bilingual program.

3. Thanh came from a rural area of Vietnam. Through a family reunification plan, she arrived in the U.S. at age 12. She attended school occasionally in her village when she wasn't working in the rice paddies but doesn't read and write Vietnamese well. She will enter a middle school near New Orleans soon.

4. Ignacio was born in Mexico and came to California at the age of four. He speaks Spanish at home and had limited exposure to English before enrolling in preschool in Long Beach last fall.

Each of these students is an English learner and all need English instruction at varying degrees. Additionally, each needs to learn age- and grade-appropriate content concepts in order to make satisfactory progress in meeting academic standards.

Educating English Learners

In recent years, two major syntheses of research on the education of English have been published, both with a focus on academic literacy (Echevarria, Vogt, & Short, 2008, p. 11-12). The first, conducted by the National Literacy Panel on Language-Minority Children and Youth (NLP) analyzed and synthesized research with regard to English literacy attainment. During their review, the panel considered studies on second language literacy development, cross-linguistic influences and transfer, sociolinguistic contexts, instruction and professional development, and student assessment. What follows are the major findings from the NLP report (August and Shanahan, 2006):

1. English learners benefit from instruction in the key components of reading as defined by the National Reading Panel (NICHD, 2000): phonemic awareness, phonics, fluency, vocabulary, and text comprehension.
2. Instruction in these five components is necessary but not sufficient to teach English learners to read and write proficiently in English. Oral language proficiency is needed also, so ELs must have instruction in this area.
3. Oral proficiency and literacy in the student's native language (L1) will facilitate development of literacy in English, but literacy in English can also be developed without proficiency in the L1.
4. Individual student characteristics play a significant role in English literacy development.
5. Home language experiences can contribute to English literacy achievement, but on the whole, the research on the influence of sociocultural factors is limited.

The second major review which yielded some similar findings, was conducted by researchers from CREDE (The Center for Research on Education, Diversity & Excellence), a former federally funded research center. The researchers focused on EL studies about oral language development, literacy development (from instructional and cross-linguistic perspectives), and academic achievement. Findings related to this paper, and that are in addition to the NLP findings, include:

1. Processes of second language (L2) literacy development are influenced

by a number of variables that interact with each other in complex ways (e.g., L1 literacy, L1 oralcy, socioeconomic status, and more).
2. Oralcy and literacy can develop simultaneously.
3. High-quality instruction for English learners is similar to high-quality instruction for other English-speaking students, but ELs need instructional accommodations and support to fully develop their English skills.
4. English learners need enhanced, explicit vocabulary development.

As you reflect on these findings, think about what a teacher would need to know to provide appropriate language and literacy instruction for English learners using the recommendations the research syntheses. Now, read this paragraph about literacy instruction for ELs taken from a recent Reading Teacher column (Manyak & Bauer, 2008, p. 434).

. . . we want to remind readers that code and comprehension instruction represents only one element in our framework for robust literacy instruction for ELs and to challenge teachers to keep in mind a vision of multifaceted instruction that includes not only effective instruction in basic reading elements but also language-rich, socioculturally informed, and additive literacy instruction as well.

At this point, you might be wondering: "Do the teachers with whom I work have this depth of knowledge? Are they prepared to provide the kind of language and academic instruction that English learners need? Is our current teacher preparation program adequately preparing teachers of English learners?"

The Teachers of English Learners

At present, the supply of teachers trained to work with English learners is far below the demand (Echevarria, Vogt, & Short, 2008). In the 1999-2000 Schools and Staffing Survey (NCES, 2002), 41.2 percent of the 2,984,781 public school teachers reported teaching English learners but only 12.5 percent had *8 or more hours of training* in during the past 3 years in how to teach ELs effectively. Now, 6 years after these data were reported, there are only four states that currently require preservice teachers to take coursework in second language acquisition theory, ESL methodology, and cross-cultural communication: Arizona, California, Florida, and New York. Pennsylvania will soon be joining this group by requiring one course for preservice teachers.

To close the achievement gap between English learners and their native-English-speaking peers, we must provide all teachers with effective preparation in teaching linguistically diverse students. This requires that all teachers learn how to teach content concepts and language concurrently, consistently, and systematically (Echevarria, Short, & Powers, 2006; Echevarria, Vogt, & Short, 2008).

Important Questions to Consider

Given the shortage of teachers who are fully prepared to teach English learners (such as those who are ESL-certified), and given the increasing numbers of mainstream teachers who have English learners in their classrooms, among the questions we should be asking are two that are especially important:

1. What do teachers need to know about teaching English learners?
2. At what point in their careers do teachers need to learn and be able to apply this information?

In the early 2000s, I had the opportunity to serve as a member of the Reading Sub-Committee of the National Academy of Education. Our charge was to create recommendations and write a report about how to prepare effective teachers of reading. One of the first discussions in the group included a comment something like, "Oh, no, not another report!" From 1998-2005, at least seven major reports were published on the topic of what teachers need to know to teach reading, and we wondered what we could add that would provide a new or different perspective.

First, the committee decided that the field did not need another list of what teachers should know and be able to do to teach reading. Rather, we focused our literature review and discussions within a developmental view of adult learning that presupposes the creation of structures to support the growth of teachers across their careers. We also wanted to focus on real, practice-based, usable knowledge.

It is beyond the scope of this paper to discuss the entire report (see Snow, Griffin, & Burn, 2005). Instead, I wish to ask you, as the reader, to reflect on the developmental framework created by the committee, Progressive Differentiation, and apply it to the preparation of teachers of English learners. Essentially, the framework responds to three key questions (Snow, Griffin, & Burns, 2005, p. 9):

1. How much knowledge is needed so that novice teachers at a bare minimum do no harm?
2. How much knowledge is needed for a teacher to be in charge of selecting curriculum, and individualizing instruction, independently?
3. How much knowledge is needed for a teacher to be a reliable resource for one's colleagues, or to be the person who evaluates teacher performance, and designs professional development?

In order to begin to answer these questions, we examined a teacher's career progression roughly correlated with the following five points (Snow, Griffin, & Burns, pp. 7-9):

1. Preservice
2. Apprentice
3. Novice
4. Experienced
5. Master teacher

The less mature levels of knowledge of each of these career points underlie the more mature levels. That is, a teacher moves from one level to another, building upon the knowledge and experience gained in the previous levels.

We then postulated that along the continuum of a teacher's career are different and cumulative types of "knowing" (Snow, Griffin, & Burns, 2005, pp. 7-9):

1. **Declarative Knowledge:** This is the "what," representing a teacher's acquisition of a solid foundation of procedural knowledge.
2. **Situated, Can-do Procedural Knowledge:** The teacher can apply knowledge and procedures in normal classroom circumstances.
3. **Stable Procedural Knowledge:** With a reliable set of supports, the teacher can apply knowledge and procedures to situations, conditions, and students that are out of the norm.
4. **Expert, Adaptive Knowledge:** The teacher is able to deal with the full array of instructional challenges, identify problems, seek new research-based knowledge and practices.
5. **Reflective, Organized, Analyzed Knowledge:** The teacher is able to analyze what is read, learned at conferences, and so forth, and evaluate if it is useful or not. He or she can lead professional development and collaborate with university faculty on program design.

The committee's task then was to answer this question for teachers of reading, "What would each component (phonemic awareness, phonics, fluency, vocabulary, comprehension) look like for each point of a teacher's career path and for each level of progressive differentiation?" (See Snow, Griffin, & Burns, 2005, for a detailed answer to this question.)

The Progressive Differentiation framework and an examination of a teacher's career trajectory led me to reflect, and then worry about the preparation of teachers of English learners. For example, within this framework is the assumption that preservice teachers have a solid foundation in declarative knowledge, and the apprentice, novice, and experienced teachers, over time and with experience and effective professional development, cultivate situated, stable, expert, and reflective types of knowing. By the time the teacher reaches the point of master teacher, the dominant type of knowing is primarily reflective with expert, stable, and situated types of knowing about equally represented. Declarative knowledge continues to develop as master teachers add to their knowledge and experiential base.

Why is this worrisome when considering teachers of English learners? The answer to this question leads to another question: What would progressive differentiation look like for preservice, apprentice, novice, experienced, and master teachers, as related to:

1. Understanding and instructional application of theories of second language acquisition;
2. Differentiated instruction for English learners at varied levels of English language proficiency;

3. Assessment of L1 and L2 literacy development;
4. Assessment of ELs' background knowledge, past learning, and funds of knowledge;
5. Lesson design that incorporates both content and language development?

Additional troublesome questions then come to mind:

1. What would progressive differentiation look like for the teachers of Muyisa, Diego, Ignacio, and Thanh?
2. Should their teachers provide the same language and content instruction for them as for their native-English-speaking peers? Will be that be "enough" for them?
3. If not, what are the implications for the professional development of their teachers, so that they can provide appropriate language and content instruction given the students' varied backgrounds and language proficiencies?
4. Is it appropriate that the preparation of teachers who have English learners in their classrooms be "taken care of" in one preservice course (or less) during preservice preparation?
5. As progressive differentiation suggests, should current inservice teachers be expected to develop their knowledge and skills for teaching English learners through professional development? If so, what should this professional development look like?
6. Perhaps most problematic, which teachers (Apprentice, Novice, Experienced, Master) should have the responsibility of teaching English learners, when we acknowledge that the effective teaching of ELs requires deep understandings of second language acquisition and appropriate instructional methods?
7. Finally, what happens to current practices in schools throughout the country where the apprentice and novice teachers, many with no preparation in teaching ELs, are very likely the ones who teach the courses and classes with the highest numbers of English learners?

Implications for Teacher Preparation and Professional Development

At this point, it important to point out that I'm not suggesting that preservice and apprentice teachers should be denied the privilege and responsibility of teaching English learners. Rather, in order for new teachers of ELs to move into the Stable Procedural Knowledge level where they can apply what they know to varied situations and diverse students, additional preservice preparation and ongoing, focused, and relevant professional development is necessary. Further, we need to recognize that while there are instructional practices that are effective for all students, there are specific teaching procedures that when implemented to a high degree, consistently and systematically lead to significantly higher academic gains for English learners (Echevarria, Short, & Powers, 2006; Echevarria, Vogt, & Short, 2008). Many of these teaching procedures are well known to teachers, but it is the combination of them and the consistency with they are used with English learners that appears to influence academic gains.

One required preservice course in "multicultural education," or "second language acquisition," or "Teaching in the 21st Century" is not the answer. It is estimated that by 2025, over 25% of students in U.S. schools will be English learners (www.ed.gov). At present, in some regions of the country, there are districts that already exceed that percentage. Therefore, as teacher educators, we must ensure that all teachers are prepared to meet the academic and language needs of students who first language is not English.

The reading subcommittee of the National Academy of Education concluded the report with recommendations for the preservice preparation of reading teachers titled, "Principles of Professional Learning" (Snow, Griffin, & Burns, 2005, pp. 211-222). I believe these principles are also relevant to preparation programs for preservice teachers who will have English learners in their classrooms. I have included some specific comments regarding English learners in brackets below. The Principles include:

1. Programs that address the ideas and beliefs about teaching that teachers bring with them are more likely to foster dispositions of openness to new ideas and reflection on their own assumptions about effective teaching and learning. [It is not uncommon for preservice teachers to have developed beliefs about ELs, immigration policies, and the responsibility of schools in the education of English learners. These beliefs must be discussed openly and honestly.]

2. Programs that foster the expectation of and skills required for continuous learning are more likely to support the development of career learning paths.

3. Programs that ensure the development of a comprehensive and usable knowledge base are more likely to sustain successful initial teaching experiences [if that knowledge base includes what we know to be effective instruction for all students, plus teaching approaches that are highly effective for teaching content and language to English learners.]

4. Programs that help teachers apply what they have learned in teacher-education programs to *particular contexts and students*, [my emphasis] ease the transition to classroom teaching.

5. Programs that promote articulation among the key components (standards, coursework, and internship experiences) are more likely to help teachers develop the sense of personal efficacy and professional responsibility they will need to achieve an integrated understanding of theory and practice. [If new teachers will be teaching in schools where there

are English learners, the preservice preparation program, including field experiences, must prepare them to do so effectively.]

6. Programs that "stay the course" are more likely to succeed than those that change foci frequently. [Ideally, this mirrors how inservice professional development should be designed and implemented. That is, districts and schools must maintain a long-term focus for professional development and beware of competing initiatives (Echevarria, Short, & Vogt, 2008)].

7. Programs that are sensitive to local contexts [e.g., schools with English learners, from very few to many] are more likely to succeed than generic approaches.

8. Programs that encourage careful analyses of teaching and the generation of shared knowledge are more likely to nurture a sense of collective responsibility for instruction. [This is what is often missing from inservice professional development offerings.]

9. Programs that achieve a balance between school or program needs and the needs and goals of individual teachers are more likely to support teachers' movement along the developmental continuum toward becoming expert, adaptive practitioners. [Inservice professional development should be designed and implemented with this goal in mind.]

It is incumbent on each of us as teacher educators to advocate for effective content and language instruction for English learners, as well as the necessary professional preparation for the teachers who will be providing it. It is not okay for there to be only four states in the US that currently require preservice preparation in teaching English learners. It is also unrealistic to think that one 3-credit course will prepare new teachers to meet the language development and content needs of students acquiring English.

As the numbers of ELs continue to grow, teacher preparation and professional development that focus on research-based instructional models of sheltered instruction must be implemented (i.e., instruction in English targeted to ELs in which language and content are taught concurrently, with instructional practices that have been empirically validated as effective). From our work with the Sheltered Instruction Observation Protocol (SIOP Model), we have found that in those districts and schools where administrators and teachers have focused on the academic and language needs of English learners, as well as the *developmental needs of teachers over time*, the academic and language growth for the ELs has been accelerated (Echevarria, Vogt, & Short, 2008; Short, Vogt, & Echevarria, 2008).

This requires a fundamental shift in educators' beliefs about what constitutes effective teacher preparation and professional development, and an acknowledgement that systemic change requires time, coaching, collaboration, ongoing assessment of outcomes, and a commitment of financial and personnel resources to make it happen. Our future as a nation depends on the appropriate education of **all** of our students, including our many English learners.

Final Thoughts

In late October, 2007, I was working with teachers and administrators in Hazelton, PA. While reading the local newspaper, the *Standard-Speaker*, I came across an impassioned letter to the editor from a woman who resides in Sugarloaf, PA. It was a lengthy letter and because of space limitations, it is excerpted here:

> When I was growing up in Lansford, we had many Polish, Italians, Slovaks, etc., who worked in coal mines. Their native tongue was spoken when the family was together, but not when an English-speaking child was in their home. They knew they were in America—this was our language... All children upon entering school should be proficient in the English language. It should not be the job of kindergarden [sic] and first-grade teachers to teach English...If a child cannot keep up with the work, then they should be held back for a year or two until they are proficient..."

Not surprisingly, I found this to be a disturbing letter, not just because of the sentiments that are expressed, but also because there are other community members who share the belief that English learners should be retained, separated, and denied access to age-appropriate and grade-level subject matter until they have mastered English. For too long, this has been the tradition in American schools, and it is time for us to move past this antiquated and deleterious practice.

Snow, Griffin, & Burns (2005) and the reading subcommittee concluded the report by issuing a challenge to teacher educators. Once again, it is relevant not only to the preparation of reading teachers, but also to the preparation of teachers of English learners:

> We need to engage in a serious self-examination of the challenges of teaching in today's world and the knowledge and skills needed to meet those challenges....We cannot, we believe, eliminate the achievement gap in our schools without closing the **knowledge gap** in our profession. (p. 223)

References

August, D., & Shanahan, T. (Eds.). (2006). *Developing literacy in second-language learners.* Mahwah, NJ: Erlbaum Associates.

Batalova, J., Fix, M., & Murray, J. (2005). *English language learner adolescents: Demographics and literacy achievement*s. Report to the Center for Applied Linguistics. Washington, D.C.: Migration Policy Institute.

Biancarosa, G., & Snow, D. (2004). *Reading next: A vision for action and research in middle and high school literacy.* Report to the Carnegie Corporation of New York. Washington, D.C.: Alliance for Excellent Education.

Capps, R., Fix, M., Murray, J., Ost, J., Passel, J., & Herwantoro, S. (2005). *The new demography of America's schools: Immigration and the No Child Left Behind Act.* Washington, DC: The Urban Institute.

Center on Education Policy. (2005). *States try harder, but gaps persist: High school exit exams 2005.* Washington, D.C.: Center on Education Policy.

Echevarria, J., Short, D., & Powers, K. (2006). School reform and standards-based education: An instructional model for English language learners. *Journal of Educational Research*, 99(4), 194-211.

Echevarria, J., Short, D., & Vogt, M.E. (2008). *Implementing the SIOP Model through effective professional development and coaching*. Boston: Allyn & Bacon.

Echevarria, J., Vogt, M. E., & Short, D. (2008). *Making content comprehensible for English learners: The SIOP Model (3rd Ed.)*. Boston: Allyn & Bacon.

Genesee, F., Lindholm-Leary, K., Saunders, W., & Christian, D. (2006). *Educating English learners: A synthesis of research evidence*. New York: Cambridge University Press.

Grigg, W., Daane, M., Jin, Y., & Campbell, J. (2003). *The nation's report card: Reading 2002*. Washington, D.C.: U. S. Department of Education.

Hoffman, L., & Sable, J. (2006). *Pubic elementary and secondary students, staff, schools, and school districts: School year 2003-2004*. Washington, D.C.: National Center for Educational Statistics.

Klein, S., Bugarin, R., Beltranena, R., & McArthur, E. (2004). *Language minorities and their educational and labor market indicators—Recent trends*. (NCES 2004—009). Washington, D.C.: U.S. Department of Education, National Center for Educational Statistics.

Manyak, P. C., & Bauer, E. B. (2008). Explicit code and comprehension instruction for English learners. *The Reading Teacher*, 61(5), 424-434.

National Center for Education Statistics (2002). Schools and staffing survey: 1999-2000. *Overview of the data for public, private, public charter, and Bureau of Indian Affairs elementary and secondary schools* (NCES2002-313). Washington, D.C.: U.S. Department of Education, National Center for Educational Statistics.

Health and Human Development (NICHD). (2000). *Report of the National Reading panel. Teaching children to read: An evidence-based assessment of the scientific research literature on reading and its implications for reading instruction*. (NIH Publication No. 00-4769). Washington, D.C.: U. S. Department of Health and Human Services

Perie, M., Grigg, W. S., & Donahue, P. L. (2005). *The nation's report card: Reading 2005* (NCES 2006-451). National Center for Educational Statistics, U. S. Department of Education, Washington, D.C.: Government Printing Office.

Short, D., Vogt, M. E., & Echevarria, J. (2008). *The SIOP Model for Administrators*. Boston: Allyn & Bacon.

Snow, C., Griffin, P., & Burns, M. S. (Eds.). (2005). *Knowledge to support the teaching of reading: Preparing teachers for a changing world*. Washington, D.C.: National Academy of Education.

Steinberg, A., & Almeida, C. (2004). *The dropout crisis: Promising approaches in prevention and recovery*. Boston, MA: Jobs for the Future.

HELPING STUDENTS APPRECIATE THE VALUE OF READING

Linda B. Gambrell

Clemson University

Keynote Address
College Reading Association
2008

Linda B. Gambrell is Distinguished Professor of Education in the Eugene T. Moore School of Education at Clemson University where she teaches graduate and undergraduate literacy courses. Prior to coming to Clemson University in 1999, she was Associate Dean for Research in the College of Education at University of Maryland. She began her career as an elementary classroom teacher and reading specialist in Prince George's County, Maryland. From 1992-97, she was principal investigator at the National Reading Research Center at the University of Maryland where she directed the Literacy Motivation Project. She has served as an elected member and President of the Board of Directors of the International Reading Association, National Reading Conference, and College Reading Association.

Her major research areas are literacy motivation, the role of discussion in teaching and learning, and comprehension strategy instruction. Her research has been published in major scholarly journals including Reading Research Quarterly, Educational Psychologist, *and* Journal of Educational Research. *She has served on the editorial review boards for the most prestigious peer reviewed journals in the field of literacy.*

Linda has received professional honors and awards including the College Reading Association A.B. Herr Award for Outstanding Contributions to the Field of Reading, 1994; International Reading Association Outstanding Teacher Educator in Reading Award, 1998; National Reading Conference Albert

J. Kingston Award, 2001; College Reading Association Laureate Award, 2002; and in 2004 she was inducted into the Reading Hall of Fame.

In the area of reading, recent theory and research have focused on understanding the construct of reading motivation and the components of that construct. Motivation to read is defined, for the purposes of this discussion, as the likelihood of engaging in reading or choosing to read. This definition has been used for decades in research conducted by behavioral, humanistic, cognitive and social-cognitive psychologists.

Motivation is central to all stages of reading development. Students who are highly motivated to read will pursue reading, make time for reading, and develop the reading habit. One of the primary reasons motivation is so central to reading proficiency is that the more one reads the better reader one becomes (Cunningham & Stanovich, 1998; Gambrell, 2009). While all students deserve high quality instruction in phonemic awareness, phonics, vocabulary, fluency and comprehension, it is clear that if students are not motivated to read, they will never reach their full literacy potential. Because motivation exerts a tremendous influence on literacy development, it is important for us to consider theory and research on motivation and its influence on our developing understanding of reading motivation.

According to Turner and Paris (1995), motivation does not reside solely in the child; rather it is in the interaction between students and the reading context of the classroom. The role of the teacher in creating a classroom culture that supports and nurtures reading motivation cannot be over-estimated. Alvermann (2008), building on the work of Barton and Hamilton (1998) and Street (1995), defines classroom practice as the "cultural ways in which teachers make sense of what they do, including their interactions with students. These ways involve attitudes, feelings, values, and social relationships, which, while not readily observable, nonetheless serve to regulate who gets to produce or access what textual content, at what point, and for what purposes." The big question, then, is "How can teachers help students' develop an appreciation for the value of reading?"

Three Central Issues in Reading Motivation

Brophy (2008) has urged educators and researchers to focus more specifically on developing students' appreciation for what is taught in school. While he focuses more on content knowledge, there are many insights that can be drawn from his work with respect to reading motivation. According to Brophy, issues in motivation in general fall into three major categories: social context, expectancy, and value. The social context or social milieu is the classroom climate or the context in which the learning takes place. Issues relating to expectancy reflect what is commonly referred to as self-concept of the reader (How do I feel about my chances of being successful at reading?). Issues relating to value reflect the students' appreciation of engaging in reading and the benefits of doing so (Why should I care about this?). Brophy further contests that we know a great deal more about establishing a social context and addressing expectancy problems than we do about helping students appreciate the value of learning tasks such as reading. Brophy (2008) states:

> Work on the social milieu points to the importance of making students feel a sense of belonging and well-being: meeting their needs of autonomy, competence, and relationships (self-determination theory); and maintaining master-goal rather than performance-goal structures (goal theory). Work on the expectancy aspects indicates that the content and learning activities should be at an optimal level of difficulty (neither too easy nor too hard), and the teacher should orient students toward attributing their learning progress to internal and controllable factors (attribution theory), developing positive self-efficacy perceptions (self-efficacy theory), and viewing their abilities as incrementally improvable rather than fixed and limited…Except for difficulty level, these principles do not identify aspects of curricular content domains or learning activities that might affect students' appreciation of their value…Addressing value requires attention to the learners' beliefs and feelings about the content, as well as the processes involved in learning and applying it…Until recently, only a few lines of theory and research did this. (p. 132)

With respect to the motivational aspects of school learning, Brophy (2008) advocates shifting our conversations about motivation away from "intrinsic motivation" to "motivation to learn." Taking a cue from Brophy, I think it may well serve the field of reading to change the way we talk about motivation – moving away from the term "intrinsic motivation" to using the more descriptive and richer term, "motivation to read". At present, reading theory and research do not have much to say about how to help students develop an appreciation of reading and its benefits. Clearly, what is taught must be worth learning, but students may not appreciate the value of reading unless we scaffold instruction in ways that help them to do so.

Motivation to Read: Situational Affordances

In order to fully understand Brophy's emphasis on developing appreciation for what is taught in school, an understanding of situational affordances is needed. We often say that we want students' to be intrinsically motivated to read "for its own sake." This is not truly the case. Highly motivated readers do not engage in reading "for its own sake"—instead they read because it provides some valued benefit—for example, pleasure, satisfaction, or information. These situational affordances carry motivational implications for engagement in reading. The highly motivated reader recognizes the value of reading and the affordances it offers.

In order for reading to hold value for our students it is necessary for students to understand the authentic applications to life outside of school. In most classrooms there are frequent opportunities for students to read both narrative and informational text, however, there is little emphasis on when, where, or why they might use this information in meaningful ways. For reading educators and researchers the challenge is to learn more about the affordances for reading and how we can help students learn to appreciate the value of reading, particularly with respect to authentic applications to life outside of school.

Fostering Appreciation of the Value of Reading with Authentic Literacy Tasks

Embedding instruction in authentic and relevant experiences holds great promise for increasing motivation to read. Situating literacy learning in such tasks allows students to access and apply relevant knowledge (Brophy, 2004; 2008; Cunningham & Allington, 1999; Guthrie, 2008). This notion is perhaps summed up best by Brophy's challenge to researchers and educators to "…learn more about situational affordances for acquiring and using K – 12 content in ways that serve valued human purposes, then develop ways to enable students to exploit these affordances with appreciation of opportunities to engage in worthwhile activities" (2008, p. 136).

Some scholars regard the concept of moving everyday life into schools to reflect more authentic literacy experiences as essential to literacy learning (Brophy, 2004, 2008; Brown, Collins, & Duguid, 1989; Neuman & Roskos, 1997; Scribner & Cole, 1973). Authentic literacy experiences are analogous to those that are encountered in the everyday lives of people, as opposed to school-like activities such as completing worksheets or answering teacher-posed questions. Authentic literacy tasks acknowledge and play into students' needs and desires to do things that are "real life." According to Purcell-Gates (2002), authentic literacy tasks involve meaningful, purposeful, and functional experiences that motivate and engage students.

Authentic literacy has three dimensions: meaning making, purpose, and ownership (Edelsky, 1991). Literacy tasks that encourage purposeful student cognition and result in the construction of new meanings would be considered more authentic than tasks that simply require extraction and recall of information. Authentic tasks, in Edelsky's view, would also provide some personal relevance and require some ownership or control on the part of the learner; a consideration that requires knowledge of what students and society value in terms of literacy events.

Other scholars contend that authentic academic achievement is determined by the extent to which the learner constructs new knowledge, develops and utilizes a cognitive frame for constructing that knowledge, and the value of the newly created knowledge outside of school (Newmann, Marks, & Gamoran, 1996). In their study, Newmann, Marks, & Gamoran (1996) report findings of the School Restructuring Study, a review of the organizational and pedagogical features of 23 recently restructured schools. Although this operational definition appears to involve cognitive elements alone, the researchers acknowledge that the learning they observed was the result of a negotiation of meaning rather than a transmission of information and relied heavily on the student's prior knowledge and the social exchange of ideas.

Street (1995) makes a distinction between autonomous and ideological models of literacy. Autonomous models position literacy as a collection of skills rather than a cultural practice. While skills are necessary for the cognitive process of reading, the practice of reading that prepares students for real world literacy experiences is situated in an ideological model that provides activities and interactions that require meaningful exchanges and responses. Accordingly, Au and Raphael (2000) posit that reciprocity exists between ownership and proficiency, where ownership of literacy learning leads to greater proficiency and proficiency engenders empowerment when faced with authentic, real-life literacy practices.

Authentic Learning and Cognitive Processes

In their commentary on authentic learning activities, Clayden, Desforges, Mills, and Rawson (1994) bring to light the distinction between teaching that is viewed as a transmission of knowledge and teaching that utilizes the social context of learning. Literacy as a socially situated practice involves more than the passing on of knowledge from teacher to student; rather, bodies of knowledge are created through negotiation and interaction of members of a learning community. Knowledge is acquired as the result of social exchanges rather than transmitted in one-way release from teacher to student.

Fisher and Hiebert (1990) found in their investigation of skills-based and literature-based elementary classrooms that lessons planned around literary works rather than skills development involved a greater level of cognitive complexity and allowed for more input and engagement on the part of the students. Cognitive complexity was operationalized in their research as moving along a continuum that progressed from recall of information (low cognitive complexity) to tasks that required the student to synthesize and integrate (moderate cognitive complexity) to learning that resulted in the development of novel constructions of knowledge (high cognitive complexity).

Neuman and Roskos (1997) position their discussion of literacy development with those of Brown, Collins, and Duguid (1989) who describe literacy learning as a process of enculturation into literacy practices. With young children, this involves creating literacy tasks that will prepare them to engage with texts by simulating real life literacies in play settings such as post offices, restaurants and medical offices. In these learning centers, young children have opportunities to engage in literacy activities in authentic contexts of communication and literacy.

Recent Research on Fostering Students' Appreciation for the Value of Reading

In a recent study, reading, writing, and discussion were explored within the context of authentic tasks (Gambrell, Hughes, & Calvert, 2009). Specifically, students read books, discussed their interpretations of the books with others, and engaged in letter writing about the books with adult pen pals. Findings revealed that students' literacy motivation increased for both boys and girls from pre assessment at the beginning of a school year to post assessments at the end of the same school year, and that the increase was particularly salient for boys. In addition, the study found that students engaged in important higher order thinking skills as they talked and wrote about their books.

Several important conclusions can be drawn from the results of this study. First, it appears that authentic literacy tasks support and sustain students' literacy motivation. Evidence of the influence of the nature of the task on student engagement was found in both quantitative and qualitative data sources. The results of the Literacy Motivation Survey (LMS) (Gambrell, Palmer, Codling, & Mazzoni, 1996) revealed that the means of total scores for both boys and girls increased significantly from fall to spring, in contrast to the robust findings in the research that reading motivation declines across the school year and as students progress through the grades (McKenna, Kear, & Ellsworth, 1995).

Of particular interest in this study was the finding that on the pre-intervention administration of the LMS girls had significantly higher scores on value of reading than did boys. This was not an unexpected finding, given that one of the most consistent findings in the motivation literature is that girls have more positive attitudes toward reading than boys (Marinak & Gambrell, in press; McKenna, Kear, & Ellsworth, 1995). However, on the post-intervention administration of the LMS there were no significant gender differences. One possible explanation of this finding is that the authentic and purposeful nature of the pen pal exchange with an adult carried sufficient social value for boys so that they perceived a utility value for engaging in the reading, discussion, and writing activities that would support them in the pen pal exchange. Exchanging ideas with an adult who is personally interested in their ideas may provide a context for scaffolding the school-related tasks of creating, revising, and communicating personal interpretations of a commonly read book. The results of this study suggest that authentic literacy tasks such as book discussions and literacy pen pal exchanges support and sustain literacy motivation.

In another study exploring the reward proximity hypothesis, students reported high motivation while engaged in an authentic reading task (Marinak & Gambrell, 2008). The reward proximity hypothesis (Gambrell, 1996) posits that when there is a close relationship between the reward and the desired behavior (reading) intrinsic motivation is enhanced. In classrooms, both teacher praise and feedback are ideally linked to the desired student behavior. Conversely, extrinsic rewards are usually unrelated to the desired behavior. The reward proximity hypothesis suggests that a student's motivation to read is enhanced when the incentive not only rewards the behavior of reading but also reflects the value of and encourages future engagement in that behavior. In the Marinak and Gambrell (2008) study, students completed an authentic reading task and then received a reward according to treatment condition: book reward, token reward (erasers, rings, charms, etc.), or no reward. The children were asked to browse a selection of newly published books, choose one, read an excerpt, and offer their opinion regarding whether the book should be purchased for their library. After receiving their "reward" (book, token, or no reward) for helping to select books for the library, the students were allowed to choose from three activities to spend the remaining free time: continue reading, do a puzzle, or do a math game. At the end of the period the children were asked, "If your best friend asked you, 'What was the best or most fun thing to do in this room?' What would you tell them?" Every one of the seventy-five children in the study responded that reading or reading the library books was the most fun thing they did in the room that day. Interestingly, this response was given even by children who chose to play the game or complete the math puzzle during their free time. Clearly, the authentic task of reading books to render an opinion about purchase for their school library proved motivating regardless of the reward offered for reading.

Concluding Thoughts

Most educators would agree with the contention that if students are not motivated to read, they will never reach their full literacy potential. Motivation is clearly linked to the notion that the more students read the better readers they become. Students who are motivated to read will make time for reading, will read more, and as a result are likely to increase in both reading ability and intelligence. Just as we must give attention to making sure that students have sufficient amounts of time to read, we must also promote and support classroom cultures that encourage and nurture motivation to read.

In order to increase motivation to read, we must help students develop an appreciation of the value of reading. To do so, we must broaden our definition of reading tasks from one that is school bound to one that is based on real life experiences. Reading instruction needs to be more closely tied to authentic tasks that are connected to real life experiences and context-based problems. According to Neuman and Celano, (2001), a better balance between decontextualized learning and authentic learning may take advantage of what students bring to the academic setting. Neuman and Celano contend that we need to create literacy tasks that engage students in problem-solving activities that reflect the types of real purposes and routines we use in everyday life.

The New London Group (1996), has asserted "…if one of our pedagogical goals is a degree of mastery in practice, then immersion in a community of learning engaged in authentic versions of such practice is necessary" (p. 84). While recognizing that it is not possible for every reading curriculum standard to be easily transposed into a relevant and authentic purpose, if we take the time to know more about our students and their lives, their communities and their interests, connections can be made between learning and living. And if the learning target is not easily tied to some authentic aspect of living in society, perhaps we should question why we must teach it (Malloy & Gambrell, 2008).

References

Alvermann, D. (2008). Why bother theorizing adolescents' online literacies for classroom practice and research? *Journal of Adolescent & Adult Literacy, 52,* 8 – 19.

Au, K. H., & Raphael, T. E. (2000). Equity and literacy in the next millennium. *Reading Research Quarterly, 35,* 170-188.

Barton, D., & Hamilton, M. (1998). *Local literacies: Reading and writing in one community.* London: Rutledge.

Brophy, J. (2008). Developing students' appreciation for what is taught in school. *Educational Psychologist, 43*(3), 132-141.

Brophy, J. (2004). *Motivating students to learn* (2nd ed.). Mahwah, NJ: Lawrence Erlbaum Associates.

Brown, J. S., Collins, A., & Durguid, P. (1989). Situated cognition and the culture of learning. *Educational Researcher, 18,* 32-42.

Cunningham, P. M., & Allington, R. L. (1999). Classrooms that work: They all can read and write (2nd ed.). Reading, MA: Addison Wesley Longman.

Cunningham, A. E., & Stanovich, K. E. (1998). What reading does for the mind. *American Educator,* Spring/Summer, 8-15.

Edelsky, C. (1991).*With literacy and justice for all: Rethinking the social in language and education. Critical perspectives on literacy and education.* London: Falmer.

Fisher, C. W. & Hiebert, E. H. (1990). Characteristics of tasks in two approaches to literacy instruction. *The Elementary School Journal 91* (1), 3-18.

Gambrell, L. B. (2009). Creating opportunities to read more so that our students read better. In E.H. Hiebert (Ed.), *Reading more, reading better* (pp. 251-266). NY; Guilford.

Gambrell, L.B., Palmer, B. M., Codling, R. M., & Mazzoni, S. A. (1996). Assessing motivation to read. *The Reading Teacher, 49,* 2-19.

Gambrell, L. B., Hughes, E., & Calvert, W. (2009, May) *Authentic literacy tasks: Reading, writing, and discussion,* Paper presented at the meeting of the International Reading Association, Minneapolis, MN.

Guthrie, J. (2008). Growing motivation: How students develop. In J. Guthrie (Ed.) *Engaging adolescents in reading* (pp. 99-114). Thousand Oaks, CA: Corwin Press.

Malloy, J. A., & Gambrell, L. B. (2008). New insights on motivation in the literacy classroom. In C.C. Block & S.R. Parris, *Comprehension instruction: research-based best practices*, 2nd ed. (pp. 226-238). New York: Guilford.

Marinak, B., & Gambrell, L. B. (in press). Reading motivation: Exploring the elementary gender gap. *Literacy Research and Instruction*.

Marinak, B. & Gambrell, L.B. (2008). Intrinsic motivation and rewards: What sustains young children's engagement with text? *Literacy Research and Instruction, 47.* 9-26

McKenna, M. C., Kear, D. J., & Ellsworth, R. A. (1995). Children's attitudes toward reading: A national survey. *Reading Research Quarterly, 30*, 934-956.

Neuman, S. B., Celano, D. (2001). Access to print in low-income and middle-income communities: an ecological study of four neighborhoods. *Reading Research Quarterly, 36*(10), 8-26.

Neuman, S. B.,& Roskos, K. (1997). Literacy knowledge in practice: Contexts of participation for young writers and readers. *Reading Research Quarterly, 32*, 10-32.

New London Group. (1996). A pedagogy of multiliteracies: Designing social futures. *Harvard Educational Review, 66*, 60-92.

Newmann, F. M., Marks, H. M. & Gamoran, A. (1996). Authentic pedagogy and student performance. *American Journal of Education, 104*(4), 280-312.

Purcell-Gates, V. (2002). Authentic literacy in class yields increase in literacy practices. *Literacy Update, 11*, 7.

Scribner, S., & Cole, M. (1973). *The psychology of literacy*. Cambridge, MA: Harvard University Press.Street, B. (1995) Social Literacies. London:Longman.

Turner, J.,& Paris, S. G. (1995). How literacy tasks influence children's motivation for literacy. *The Reading Teacher, 48*(8), 662-673.

Speaking the Lower Frequencies 2.0: Digital Ghost Stories

Walter R. Jacobs

University of Minnesota

Keynote Address
College Reading Association
2008

Walter R. Jacobs is an Associate Professor and Chair of the Department of African American & African Studies at the University of Minnesota. A sociologist (PhD, Indiana University, 1999), Jacobs is the author of Ghostbox: A Memoir and Speaking the Lower Frequencies: Students and Media Literacy, *and co-editor of* If Classrooms Matter: Progressive Visions of Educational Environments. *His current research explores personal and social possibilities of students' generation of creative nonfiction.*

Abstract

In Speaking the Lower Frequencies: Students and Media Literacy *Walter R. Jacobs explores how college students can become critical consumers of media while retaining the pleasure they derive from it.* Speaking the Lower Frequencies 2.0: Race, Learning, and Literacy in the Digital Age *builds on its predecessor by examining pedagogy and literacy through theories and practices of digital media making, specifically digital storytelling methods used in a fall 2008 undergraduate class, "Digital Storytelling in and with Communities of Color." Jacobs begins his keynote with the course description and then examines one component of the class project: students' engagement with "social ghosts," the strong but usually hidden and unexamined forces that structure their educational experiences.*

"Digital Storytelling in and with Communities of Color," fall 2008. Storytelling is a tool for preserving memory, writing history, learning, entertaining, organizing, and healing in communities of color. It is in the telling of stories that communities build identities, construct meaning, and make connections with others and the world. In this course we will investigate modes and power dimensions of digital storytelling, analyze the role of digitized media as a method of individual healing, and examine media as tools for community organizing and development. We will explore media making, creative writing, and memoir in both literary and digital writing, and examine the gendered, racialized, and classed dimensions of digital storytelling. We will create projects to tell our stories, examine our social ghosts, and work with community members as part of the 40th Anniversary of the African American and African Studies Department to develop digital stories about Twin Cities communities of color. Students will learn to produce creative work (writing, video, photography, sound, and artwork) and gain technical proficiency in Mac-based editing. Students will produce photographic and video work that will be shared on the course blog. No technical expertise is necessary!
—course description for "Digital Storytelling in and with Communities of Color" undergraduate class, University of Minnesota, fall 2008.

In my 2005 book, *Speaking the Lower Frequencies: Students and Media Literacy*, I investigated strategies for encouraging undergraduate students to become critical consumers of the media without losing the pleasure they derive from it (Jacobs, 2005). Sonia Livingstone, however, notes that in the digital age literacy should provide students with "the ability to access, analyse, evaluate and create messages across a variety of contexts" (Livingstone, 2004, p. 3). In other words, students need to become producers of media content in addition to being critical consumers of media worlds. In my new project I explore this expanded understanding of literacy. *Speaking the Lower Frequencies 2.0: Race, Learning*, and *Literacy in the Digital Age* examines pedagogy and literacy through theories and practices of digital media making, specifically digital storytelling (Jacobs, Raimist, & Doerr-Stevens, 2009). This project is centered on a fall 2008 undergraduate course I co-taught at the University of Minnesota; the epigraph above provides an overview of the main elements of the class. In this chapter I examine one component of the project: students' engagement with "social ghosts," the strong but usually hidden and unexamined forces that structure their educational experiences (Jacobs, Reynolds, & Choy, 2004).

Kristina Woolsey notes,
We are extending infrastructures to support the newest digital technologies that are introduced by industry. However, at the core, we are not focused on learning with technologies. We are supporting students with computers

so that they can better take advantage of an educational system that is at its heart still an idiosyncratic face-to-face, text-based enterprise. (Woolsey, 2008, p. 218)

My co-instructor (Rachel Raimist) and I attempted to challenge this unfortunate reality for many students. In our "Digital Storytelling in and with Communities of Color" class, students learned to use technology to transform their learning experiences, to see themselves as active agents who can use technology in ways not always envisioned by the designers. While the class did employ text-based readings, these were delivered in non-traditional electronic formats. More importantly, the readings provided a foundational structure on which we built the computer-mediated tools and processes that formed the core of the class. Students developed a new paradigm for confronting the many social ghosts fostered by the educational systems they inhabit. I believe that instructors in a diverse array of education locations can deploy technology in ways to facilitate constructive engagement with these ghosts. I present one method here.

Using the Center for Digital Storytelling method

The Center for Digital Storytelling is a California-based non-profit 501(c)3 arts organization rooted in the art of personal storytelling. We assist people of all ages in using the tools of digital media to craft, record, share, and value the stories of individuals and communities, in ways that improve all our lives.

Many individuals and communities have used the term "digital storytelling" to describe a wide variety of new media production practices. What best describes our approach is its emphasis on personal voice and facilitative teaching methods. Many of the stories made in our workshops are directly connected to the images collected in life's journey. But our primary concern is encouraging thoughtful and emotionally direct writing.
—Center for Digital Storytelling website (http://www.storycenter.org/index1.html)

According to Leslie Rule's oft-quoted definition, "Digital storytelling is the modern expression of the ancient art of storytelling. Digital stories derive their power by weaving images, music, narrative and voice together, thereby giving deep dimension and vivid color to characters, situations, experiences, and insights" (Rule, 2009). Such digital stories are both created and shared via the use of computer tools. One of the leading proponents of using Apple Macintosh computer-based products in digital storytelling is the Center for Digital Storytelling (CDS) in Berkeley, CA. As one can readily discern from reading the first page of their website (reprinted in this section's epigraph above), CDS has created a powerful approach to digital storytelling, one that has influenced thousands of individuals and groups.

At the center of the CDS approach to digital storytelling is the 3-day "Basic Workshop." In a setting of 8-12 participants, each student designs and produces an individual digital story. Students are taught to scan and edit images using Adobe Photoshop, craft and record first-person narratives, and use Apple Final Cut Express to combine the elements into a rough draft of a 3-5 minute digital story. After the workshop CDS staff polish the digital story and mail a compact disc (CD) to the participants. The CD contains the final version of the digital story, along with all of the source materials in order to allow students to complete additional edits on their own.

Upon completion of the Basic Workshop students can attend an "Educator Workshop" or a "Facilitator Intensive Training Workshop." The 3-day Educator Workshop is designed to guide K-12 teachers in the practical application of digital storytelling as a classroom program for K-12 age students. The week-long Facilitator Intensive Training Workshop explores curricular and technological issues educators should consider when adapting the CDS digital storytelling process to their own pedagogical environments.

I enrolled in a Basic Workshop in May 2008, and produced a digital story called "Letter to my Mother." (This digital story may be viewed at http://tinyurl.com/JacobsDS/). "Letter to my Mother" is a memorial to my mother, who I believed helped me survive adolescence with an abusive stepmother. It is the digital story manifestation of my memoir *Ghostbox*, in which I explored a life where family problems were blamed on "disrespectful" children who refused to accept "Mom's" authority (Jacobs, 2007). My stepmother is one of my social ghosts, a force that limited my thoughts and decisions until I filled a special shoebox with objects that evoke significant memories: good, bad, and ugly. My "ghostbox" has rendered my stepmother's seething presence benign.

In our fall 2008 "Digital Storytelling in and with Communities of Color" course the students read *Ghostbox* and discussed it with Rachel and me in class. Students also watched and discussed the "Letter to my Mother" digital story. In these discussions students interrogated the social processes of digital storytelling. For example, students learned that it takes courage to share their stories publicly; they risk judgment from others. But once they develop confidence and commitment to the storytelling process, students can generate many new insights. After a thorough analysis of CDS's seven social elements of digital storytelling (Lambert, 2006) we conducted several classes where we taught students the technical skills necessary for creating their own digital stories. These digital stories can be viewed online: http://tinyurl.com/UMstories/.

A digital story on literacy and learning

This is a story examining my time teaching in Brooklyn, New York. Through layering of images, voice, and music, I try to explore my memories as I've stored them in my mind. In many ways my memories are limited, focusing only on certain aspects. This story is an attempt to open up that past and perhaps re-remember these moments in new ways in order to reshape how I view myself now.

—Candance Doerr-Steven's description of her digital story, "White Teacher"

We did not explicitly require students to include social ghosts in the digital stories, but some students did. One student not only produced a story that engaged a social ghost, this social ghost was one explicitly about learning and literacy. Candance Doerr-Stevens' "White Teacher" provides us with a powerful example for rethinking how K-12 educators can view classrooms with diverse student populations. ("White Teacher" may be accessed at http://tinyurl.com/WhiteTeacherDS/).

The fall 2008 "Digital Storytelling in and with Communities of Color" course was a 3000-level class, meaning that it was primarily designed for juniors and seniors. We did, however, enroll several sophomores. Graduate student Candance Doerr-Stevens also enrolled in the class using a graduate directed studies mechanism, given that it fit perfectly with her interests in new media literacies. Rachel and I were so impressed with her early contributions to that class that we invited her to be the third author on our in-progress *Speaking the Lower Frequencies 2.0* manuscript (Jacobs, Ramist, & Doerr-Stevens, 2009).

Candance analyzes "White Teacher" in chapter 6 of the manuscript. She writes,

> I chose to focus on my experience as a fifth grade teacher in Brooklyn, New York, looking specifically at my identity as a White teacher. My choice to revisit this particular memory was inspired by reading Walt's memoir *Ghostbox*. In his book, Walt describes social ghosts as memories from our past that haunt us. Walt proceeds to present the process of creating a "ghostbox," as a space and process through which to re-visit traumatic memories for purposes of "productive haunting." To avoid and forget these memories, Walt argues, is "to let them be born anew in another shape, a form that rots my identity and crumbles my self-worth" (Jacobs, 2007, p. 16).
>
> Wanting to channel some of my own productive haunting, I hoped the process of digital storytelling would help me work through some of the shame and regret I had attached to my memories of teaching in New York City. I decided to revisit this memory through examining the trope of teacher as White savior, looking specifically at how this trope may have influenced my thinking and teaching at the time.

Candance goes on to interrogate dominant discourses that position urban students of color as "downtrodden," "poor and disadvantaged students," or "second class citizens." She was able to present her students less as victims and more as the happy 5th graders that they were; she captured the energetic children who had loving families and enjoyed school. At the same time she avoided representing herself as a villain who did not understand students from a social world that was very different than her own. She posed complex questions about intersections of race, literacy, and learning in public school systems. She shunned easy answers; instead she presented the story as more complicated than "nice White lady goes to Brooklyn." In an age where we are increasingly seeing mainstream commentary such as "The End of White America?" (Hsu, 2009), we need digital stories like Candance's to remind us that race will not go gently into that good night... if ever.

Conclusion

> One way forward for higher education is to nudge more digital content into the open web, combining our honed wariness about privacy and security with our awareness of the full-blown social web. (Alexander, 2008, p. 199)

Bryan Alexander explores ways in which we can integrate social networking tools like blogging and wikis and/or sites such as Facebook and MySpace into collegiate learning environments (Alexander, 2008). An integral component of the "Digital Storytelling in and With Communities of Color" website was for students to post their digital stories to the course blog, http://blog.lib.umn.edu/afroam/storytelling/. In light of issues of privacy and confidentiality (alluded to above by Alexander), Rachel and I allowed students to choose pseudonyms under which they could post their work. Most students used their real names, however, in order to fully create a space where everyone could freely share aspects of their lives, and receive support and encouragement in confronting their social ghosts digitally.

One of the comments posted in response to the "White Teacher" digital story states:

> I enjoyed the mix of images and the music, which was present but not overpowering. Even more, I appreciated the self-critique and the critique of identity in relation to the classroom—both yours and that of your students. Positioning is a powerful factor that often goes unnoticed, unacknowledged.

Indeed, "Digital Storytelling in and with Communities of Color" students explored how "colonized and subjugated people who, by way of resistance, create an oppositional subculture within the framework of domination, recognize that the field of representation (how we see ourselves, how others see us) is a site of ongoing struggle" (Hooks, 2006, p. 389). Students learned to not fear this site of struggle; they discovered how each and every one of us can explore our combination of privileged and disadvantaged identities in a quest to create a more democratic society. "If we want our students to engage the world as critical, informed people, then we need to reshape our plans as that world changes" (Alexander, 2008, p. 200). Digital stories help our students (and ourselves!) confront a world in constant motion by opening windows into spaces we don't know, as well as by guiding us in complicating understandings of contexts we believe that we thoroughly comprehend.

By the end of the semester the students in the fall 2008 "Digital Storytelling in and with Communities of Color" class at the University of Minnesota viewed digital stories as gifts: "Those of us fortunate enough to be able to talk out loud should love our voices, because they tell everyone so much about who we are, both how strong we can be and how fragile" (Lambert, 2006, p. 54). I invite readers from places throughout the educational spectrum to explore how they may similarly help their students develop strong voices and create digital stories as gifts for themselves and others.

References

Alexander, B. (2008). Social networking in higher education. In R. Katz (Ed.), *The tower and the cloud: Higher education in the age of cloud computing* (pp. 197-201). Boulder, CO: Educause.

Hsu, H. (2009). The end of white America? *The Atlantic, 303*(1), 46-55.

Hooks, B. (2006). In our glory: Photography and black life. In L. Wells (Ed.), *The photography reader* (pp. 387-394). New York: Routledge.

Jacobs, W. (2007). *Ghostbox: A memoir*. New York: iUniverse.

Jacobs, W. (2005). *Speaking the lower frequencies: Students and media literacy*. Albany, NY: State University of New York Press.

Jacobs, W., Raimist, R., & Doerr-Stevens, C. (2009). *Speaking the lower frequencies 2.0: Race, learning, and literacy in the digital age*. Unpublished manuscript.

Jacobs, W., Reynolds, T., and Choy, G. (2004). The educational storytelling project: Three approaches to cross-curricular learning. *Journal of College Reading and Learning, 35*(1), 50-66.

Lambert, J. (2006). *Digital storytelling: Capturing lives, creating community* (2nd ed). Berkeley, CA: Digital Diner.

Livingston, S. (2004). Media literacy and the challenge of new information and communication technologies. *The Communication Review, 7*(3), 3-14.

Rule, L. (2009). Digital Storytelling. Accessed January 18, 2009 at http://electronic-portfolios.org/digistory/.

Woolsey, K. (2008). Where is the new learning? In R. Katz (Ed.), *The tower and the cloud: Higher education in the age of cloud computing* (pp. 212-218). Boulder, CO: Educause.

FUTURE OF CRA

THE FUTURE OF THE COLLEGE READING ASSOCIATION

Karen Bromley

Binghamton University-State University of New York

As the College Reading Association (CRA) concludes its first 50 years and looks forward to the future, the good news is that the organization is doing many things well. But, as with any organization, there are often opportunities to change and improve. The purpose of this chapter is to discuss CRA's future in terms of its mission, structure, membership, publications, annual conference and visibility. Portions of this chapter reflect opinions expressed by past presidents of CRA who participated in a session, organized by Dixie Massey and Wayne Linek, titled "Celebrating 50 Years of CRA: Past Presidents Discuss the History of CRA and Reading Research" in 2006. Other past presidents and association members communicated with the author via email.

Topics and issues raised here by past presidents and association members that are related to CRA's future might be addressed in several ways including: the establishment of ad hoc committees that study an issue and report to the Executive Board; discussions by the Executive Board, full Board and the Legislative Assembly; opinion pieces in the newsletter; symposiums at the annual conference; and conversations among members.

Then and Now

CRA was founded in 1958 by several reading educators from colleges in the northeast who began holding annual conferences in Philadelphia, Pennsylvania; Baltimore, Maryland; Bowling Green, Ohio; Jersey City, New Jersey; and Rochester, New York. Since then CRA has grown steadily and today has a membership of 484 educators and researchers representing national and international colleges, universities and private institutions. The majority of conferences have been held on the east coast, but in the last 20 years CRA has started to expand geographically. For example, CRA met in Saint Louis, Missouri in 1992; New Orleans, Louisiana in 1994; Corpus Christi, Texas in 2003; and Salt Lake City, Utah in 2007. There are also plans to meet in Omaha, Nebraska; Dallas, Texas; and to continue to meet in cities in the east, mid-west, and west in the future.

Mission of CRA

CRA's mission is expressed in four goals that appear on the website at www.collegereadingassociation.org and several objectives that appear in the *Constitution and By-Laws*. Today these goals remain as they were first articulated in 1958:

- To promote standards and competency within the profession.
- To stimulate the development and professional growth of teachers and reading specialists at all educational levels.
- To encourage the continuing improvement of college and university curricula and encourage preparation programs for teachers and reading specialists.
- To encourage the continuing improvement of administrative, clinical, diagnostic, and instructional practices related to the learning process. (*Constitution and By-Laws*, 2001, p. 2)

How is CRA accomplishing these goals? In general, CRA does a good job of doing what it set out to do 50 years ago. One of the hallmarks of CRA continues to be its collegiality. Its smaller size allows non-members, new members, and established members to feel welcome and at ease at the annual conference. Bob Rickelman, Past President, notes "CRA has had a consistently welcoming attitude toward doctoral students and new faculty colleagues. I became involved as a committee leader within three years of becoming a CRA member." Judy Richardson, Past President, says CRA "…should continue to promote the sharing of teaching and research between new and more experienced colleagues and nurture members' professional development." John Smith, former Treasurer and Business Manager, believes "CRA should remain a small, close association of literacy professionals with special emphasis on mentoring doctoral students and new faculty members, and continue as a forum for sharing research."

Does the CRA name reflect the goals of the organization and its members? There is concern among some members that the name should change to better reflect the field and a constituency that is broader than "college" and "reading." Other members are happy with the present name and are concerned that CRA will lose members and its identity with a name change. At the 2006 conference, members took a step in the direction of a name change and voted to change the name of the journal from *Reading Research and Instruction* to a more representative name, *Literacy Research and Instruction*. At the conference, members voted to change the CRA name at the 2007 Legislative Assembly. If the name changes, Ray Reutzel, Past President, hopes "…a name change will not alter CRA's identity, focus and mission, and we will continue to focus on and attract teacher educators interested in improving classroom literacy instruction."

Organizational Structure

The organizational structure of CRA appears in the *Constitution and By-Laws* (*Constitution and By-Laws*, 2001) on the website. CRA has four divisions; Teacher Education (404 members), Clinical Research and Practice (124 members), College Reading (120 members), and Adult Learning (55 members). The Executive Board consists of President, President-Elect, Vice President, Treasurer/Business Manager, Executive Secretary, Past President, and Past-Past President. In recent years, the Past-Past President has joined meetings of the Executive Board and full Board to provide advice and counsel. Additionally, the full Board consists of six elected members, division chairpersons, committee chairs, and commission chairs. The Executive Board and full Board meet twice a year, a day before the annual conference and a day before the annual meeting of the International Reading Association (IRA). At other times, the Executive Board is in contact via email and telephone as issues arise. CRA's Legislative Assembly meets annually at the conference at which time all members may voice an opinion and vote on issues.

How effective is this structure? Within CRA many people in different roles have forged a respected professional organization that provides for the advancement of members' scholarship and professional growth. However, it has been suggested that some roles might take better advantage of people's skills and simultaneously tighten CRA's structure. First, the six elected Board members who attend full Board meetings, provide advice and oversight, and vote on CRA activities, could be utilized in other ways. To give Board members a more active role, Ray Reutzel suggests "Some or all committee chairs could be replaced with Board members as chairs who could then more directly link the work of committees to the Board." Second, if co-chairs who serve staggered terms were added to committees with single chairs, increased collaboration and a seamless committee leadership could result. Third, CRA might look to mirror the effective organizational components and the way an organization like the National Reading Conference (NRC) organizes itself and its annual conference. Fourth, the four division structure might be reconsidered and continued only if members support each division and the divisions remain active. However, many CRA members echo Nancy Padak, Past President, who values the divisions. She says "The division structure is one of the things I treasure about CRA because it shows the value we hold for all literacy folks."

Membership

CRA has always been a collegial organization with a collaborative nature that makes it special among other professional organizations. Unlike the International Reading Association (IRA), the National Council of Teachers of English (NCTE), and the Council for Exceptional Children (CEC), CRA's members have been and are overwhelmingly teacher educators involved in teacher preparation. CRA is much like NRC whose members are also predominantly teacher educators but whose main focus is research, while CRA supports applied and practical work as well as research.

Should membership recruitment continue to target teacher educators or should CRA broaden its audience? Feelings are mixed in regard to recruiting a K-12 teacher membership. For one thing, the Thursday evening conference session with a children's book author does attract local teachers. But, CRA's focus on teacher educators is one that many people feel should continue. Norm Stahl, Past President, says "If you have a niche, go with it and build on it. Our niche is teacher educators. We need to identify the things we are good at and drop the rest." Bob Rickelman, Past President, states, "Our challenge is to remain stable and continue to serve the profession by serving a role that is somewhere between what NRC and IRA do. CRA is a way for members to interact closely with some leaders in the field, begin to collaborate and assume leadership opportunities quickly, compared to most organizations, and to foster a sense of community." However, Ray Reutzel notes that "CRA could be healthier financially if membership increased to 800 with 500 attending the annual conference." This would allow for more sessions and other options. It might be accomplished by alternating conference locations among cities in the east, mid-west, and west.

Certainly, CRA needs to work actively to attract colleagues from members' institutions as well as doctoral and masters students. Bill Blanton, Past President, believes "Teacher education is changing. We need to appeal to online masters and doctoral people and those teaching in two-year community colleges who prepare teachers for four year degrees." John Smith notes a pattern of people who join CRA for a year or two and then do not renew. He believes "We need to establish a core of committed CRA members who will become the future leaders of CRA." He wonders if the organization needs to look at the price of membership. "It costs more to belong to CRA than IRA, although the CRA conference is less expensive, as well as shorter and smaller, than IRA."

Publications

CRA has three regular publications. The quarterly journal *Reading Research and Instruction* or *RRI* (soon to be called *Literacy Research and Instruction* or *LRI*) provides CRA's broadest national and international presence. The *CRA Yearbook* is published annually and includes some papers presented at the conference that have gone through another round of blind peer review. The CRA newsletter, *Reading News*, is published electronically three times a year. CRA also occasionally publishes special monographs.

How well do CRA's publications reflect its goals and serve its members? Over time, CRA publications have typically done this well. But, it is critical that editors continue to produce publications that consistently reflect excellence in quality and appearance so that CRA can maintain and gain respectability in the field, satisfy its membership, and attract new members.

The journal, which is well respected in the field, publishes research and scholarly articles written by members and non-members. It is subscribed to by over 600 libraries and all CRA members. It seems to have reflected CRA goals and served membership well over the years. However, the journal can raise its standards. One positive step in this direction is the recent move to a commercial publisher, Routledge, Taylor & Francis, which John Smith believes "…will greatly enhance the professionalism of *LRI*." To increase its citation rates and visibility, Ray Reutzel would like "…to take the journal to an every other month publication and make it available electronically." A format change might be explored, for example, including a section on classroom tested literacy strategies or a column that invites "white papers" on timely topics. However, Maryann Manning, Past President, says "The journal allows us to publish research and there are few outlets for research which is a university requirement for promotion and tenure. So I don't think we want to publish teacher ideas." With some changes however, CRA could print double the scholarly work it does now and increase its visibility in the field as well as its membership.

The yearbook and newsletter are also respected CRA publications that allow members to stay abreast of CRA activities and issues that impact the field. The yearbook prints the best papers presented at the annual conference and needs to continue to be selective in accepting manuscripts. The newsletter has recently become electronic and undergone a format and design change that has made it more reader-friendly and visually appealing.

Of course, the journal, yearbook, newsletter, and occasional monograph can only be as strong and timely as: the quality of articles submitted, the adherence to format guidelines and deadlines by authors, the diligence and skill of editors, and the professional nature of CRA's publisher. These inter-related aspects must mesh well in order for CRA to continue to serve members and the field with the highest quality publications.

Annual Conference

Besides the journal, the annual conference is and probably will continue to be CRA's best opportunity to "showcase" itself. Conferences have been excellent venues over the years for professional growth, collaboration, and friend-making. Clearly, it is critical that CRA continues to invite quality key note speakers with status and visibility in the field who promote debate and discussion related to their work. This is an important way to achieve the organization's goals, provide members with professional development, and attract new members.

Several opinions about the conference suggest it should not change much in the future. Often noted in conference evaluations and comments to the Executive Board is the high caliber of keynote speakers and Awards breakfast speakers.

However, some changes may be warranted. Barb Walker, Past President, likes the fact that CRA has always been "a collaborative kind of organization." She wants "…the roundtable format continued because it is a rich avenue for discussion and collaboration among members." Maryann Manning says "I would like to see us support more doctoral students by encouraging their presentations at the conference. Let's keep the 25 minute session time because it is less threatening for them than a longer time slot."

As with many organizations, CRA can afford to raise its standards. One way to do this that could have multiple benefits begins with the conference. By requiring specific and tighter criteria for proposal submission, the program chair and program committee could be more selective in accepting conference proposals. This then could improve the quality of presentations, which in turn could result in the submission and publication of higher quality manuscripts submitted to the yearbook.

Visibility

There are varying views on how visible and political CRA should be. Marino Alvarez, Past President, created the CRA website in 1997. He says "We need to talk more about what comes out of this organization. We need to educate the public about what we do. For example, tell the world about the Macedonia project and highlight the work of our four divisions." Jon Shapiro, Past President, believes CRA needs to have a political presence. Jon says "We have a unique position as teacher educators that is unlike IRA which is primarily an organization of and for teachers." Norm Stahl echoes this saying "CRA does have political clout. We often send our members forth to be leaders in other organizations. We influence other organizations in this way." Wayne Linek, Past President, adds "We have two committees that have the potential to do more on the political scene, 'Legislative and Social Issues' and 'Public Information.' Although we may not have enough resources to go to Capitol Hill, we could partner with IRA and NRC so that we are visible and have a voice." But, Jerry Johns, Past President, believes politics is not our role. Jerry says "IRA has the size and influence CRA does not possess. CRA is focused on teacher education and we need to present ourselves and our views this way."

While it is not always easy for a small organization to have an impact politically, Judy Richardson says "CRA can show what it believes in by funding awards like the Jerry Johns Promising Researcher Award and the Judy Richardson Literacy as a Living Legacy Award" (found on the website). To this end, Norm Stahl would like to "…encourage divisions and individuals to establish and fund new awards or set up 'foundations' within CRA to fund various worthy activities." Bill Blanton suggests there is "…a need for position statements for newspapers or on the website such as summaries of speaker presentations, descriptions of awards given, and summaries of various teacher education programs." John Smith notes that "I'd like to see the visibility of CRA enhanced, perhaps through more interactions with IRA and NRC."

Conclusion

CRA's smaller size, collegiality and focus on teacher education are clearly assets that other organizations do not offer. Maintaining the friendly atmosphere and focus of the organization, while promoting moderate growth, are surely important goals for the future. Continuity can be a good thing if it is done well. Nancy Padak says "CRA has always been such a welcoming organization. It's a great venue for new scholars to become involved in a professional organization. I hope this continues to be the case, as well. And I suspect that it will because I think it's a value so many of us share."

Bob Rickelman sums up the thoughts of many CRA members when he says "I wonder if maybe we just got lucky, and have been doing some good things for awhile. Maybe our challenge is to remain stable and continue to serve the profession, by serving some important role that is somewhere between that of NRC and IRA. Perhaps CRA provides a way for our members to interact closely with some leaders in the field, begin to collaborate and assume leadership opportunities quickly compared to most organizations, and to foster a sense of community within the organization."

An important role CRA should continue in the future is a venue for teacher educators to share their research and practice as they mentor colleagues, new faculty, and doctoral students. Critical to CRA's successful future is a continual re-examination of its goals, structure, membership, annual conference, publications and visibility for ways to enhance what it stands for and accomplishes. A strong and committed leadership will listen to its members and look beyond to the field itself to determine what it is doing well and what needs to change. Going forward, CRA will need to be vigilant about maintaining and growing the quality of its publications and annual conference, as well as recruiting and keeping new members. The good news is that CRA is one of the top three national literacy organizations for educators and CRA has done a lot of things "right" for the last 50 years. As well, we know what some of our challenges are for the future.

Thanks go to Marino Alvarez, Rita Bean, Bill Blanton, Jerry Johns, Wayne Linek, Maryann Manning, Nancy Padak, Tim Rasinski, Judy Richardson, Bob Rickelman, Ray Reutzel, Vicki Risko, Jon Shapiro, John Smith, Norm Stahl, Maria Valeri-Gold, and Barbara Walker for their input on the future of CRA.

References

College of Reading Association. (2001). *Constitution and By-Laws*. Retrieved January 11, 2010, from the College of Reading Association Web site: www.collegereadingassociation.org

Massey, D. D., & Linek, W. M. (2006, October). *Celebrating 50 years of CRA: Past presidents discuss the history of CRA and reading research*. Symposium presentation at the annual meeting of the College Reading Association, Pittsburgh, PA.

CONCLUSION

CONCLUSION: EVOLVING FROM CRA TO ALER

Wayne M. Linek

Texas A&M University-Commerce

This book has been a labor of love, and that labor is almost finished. As I look back over the Early Leaders' Chapters, Keynote Addresses, Presidential Speeches, Oral Histories, and Future Directions, I am impressed with what our leaders and members have accomplished in the last 50 years. Since Karen Bromley's chapter, "The Future of the College Reading Association" was written, several changes have occurred.

First, the membership voted to change the name of the association from The College Reading Association to The Association of Literacy Educators and Researchers or ALER (pronounced like the word "allure" according to Ray Reutzel). Thus, our final CRA conference was held in Sarasota, Florida in 2008 and the first ALER conference was held in Charlotte, North Carolina in 2009.

Second, the name change precipitated a change in the association's website, from http://www.collegereadingassociation.org/index.html to http://www.aleronline.org/. Although the most current information can be found on the ALER website, the CRA website still exists.

Third, the name change gave rise to a change in the name of the yearbook, from the *College Reading Association Yearbook* to the *Association of Literacy Educators and Researchers Yearbook*. Further, our proprietary publisher, Routledge: Taylor & Francis Group, has provided increased national and international exposure for our journal, *Literacy Research and Instruction*. This shift has worked so well for the journal that ALER leaders are now considering the same shift in publisher for the yearbook.

Fourth, the name change prompted a revision of the *Constitution and By-Laws*. At the time of this writing, the organization is revising these documents to reflect the name change and make pertinent changes in its policies and practices.

All of this change may have some of the members a bit frazzled, but those of you who have been longtime CRA members or served on the board know that a name change has been a bone of contention almost since the founding of CRA. On one side, concern that the name did not truly reflect all divisions of the organization resurfaced yearly at board meetings. Fear that the name limited the interest of potential new members was consistently noted by many members when trying to recruit. Anxiety about lack of university administrators' understanding of the organization's purpose and problems getting funding for travel to CRA was often voiced at the Legislative Assembly. On the other side many members were fearful that changing the name would dishonor tradition and the organization's history. Some were worried that the association would lose name recognition, members, and library subscriptions to its publications.

Sadly, change often has a negative connotation and creates fear—fear that something was wrong with the way things were or fear of the unknown. However, fear that CRA's name change would negatively impact the reputation or recognition of the organization appears to be unsubstantiated. The first ALER conference was well attended and both library memberships and individual memberships have remained steady or increased. Further, concern that a name change would disregard our historical roots appears unfounded with the publication of this monograph. We continue to honor the founders of CRA, its history, its leaders, and its mission as we move further into the 21st Century.

Although not all change is good or necessary, change is a constant in the 21st Century. I prefer to think of change as growth or evolution as these terms tend to have positive connotations. The shift to a new name for CRA demonstrates an evolution that is more in line with current thought, conceptions, and research. However, we know that those who don't heed history are doomed to repeat mistakes and end up in quite a muddle. Therefore, let us look to the knowledge and wisdom provided in this historical monograph to build a future for ALER that will honor the unchanged goals set forth by our early CRA leaders and meet the demands of an ever growing and changing society.

APPENDIX A

Appendix A. Thesis and Dissertation Award Winners

Thesis

1978 Patricia Fisher
Ernest Balajthy
Sara Strous

1979 Concetta G. Hicks
Wendy S. Keeler
Partricia Borowiec

1980 Linda J. Payne
Diane M. LaSorte
Alice R. Edlredge

1981 Margaret B. Robertson
Phyllis Chatlos
Anne Osbourne

1982 Renee Close Goostree
Karen Wood
Dorothy Champlin

1983 Lynn Ellen Keeter

1984 Harvey M. Rubenstein
Judith R Marolf
Janet M. McConologue

1985 Martha W. Johnson

1986 Cynthia M. Battaglia

1987 Mary Jane Pearce

1988 Karen Podey

1989 Delilah Shotts

1990 Lisa H. McGary

1991 Francis K. Hurley

1992 Rebekah E. Legman

1993 None awarded

1994 Randale Reese

1995 Linda B. Hunter

1996 Karen E. Schroeder

1997 Melissa L. Brock

1998 Brenda M. Greene

1999 Elizabeth Kingery

2000 Stephanie Gerdes

2001 Joan Scott Curtin

2002 Cynthia Hayes-Low

2003 Tracy Zimmerman

2004 Susan Barnes Porter

2005 Wendy Warnken

2006 None awarded

2007 Amy Wilson

2008 Susan E. Perkins

Dissertation Winners

1982 Mary Ann Medley
Daniel Pierce

1983 Ernest Balajthy

1984 Robert B. Cooter, Jr.
Sandra U. Gibson

1985 Lynn Smith

1986 Timothy V. Rasinski

1987 K. Roskos

1988 Kathleen Davis

1989 Linda Haren Irwin

1990 Nancy B. Cothern

1991 Patricia L. Schorer

1992 Elizabeth G. Sturtevant

1993 Gaoyin Qian

1994 Victoria Ridgeway

1995 Jan K. Bryan

1996 JoAnn Rubino Dugan

1997 Lawrence R. Sipe

1998 Linda S. Wold

1999 Barbara Abromitis

2000 Christine McKeon

2001 Suzanne Viscovich

2002 Michelle Fazio

2003 Jacqueline Lynch

2004 William Muth

2005 Barbara Ann Marinak

2006 Roberta Linder

2007 Donna Wake

2008 Carla Wonder McDowell
Cheryl L. Potenza-Radis

APPENDIX B

APPENDIX B.
OFFICERS OF THE
COLLEGE READING ASSOCIATION
1958-2008

The Committee for the College Reading Association (Formation Committee)

Bruce W. Brigham, Chairman, Supervisor of Adult, College and Secondary Reading Services, The Reading Clinic, Temple University Philadelphia, PA

Edward Dillon, Secretary-Treasurer, Director of Reading Services, Counseling Center, LaSalle College, Philadelphia, PA

Alberti Mazurkiewicz, Publicity Chairman, Director, Reading and Study Clinic, Lehigh University, Bethlehem, PA

Edward R. Dubin, Institute Staff, The Reading Clinic, Temple Univ., Philadelphia, PA

William A. Gaines, Director, Reading Center, Delaware State College, Dover, DE

Helen M. Hall, Reading Consultant, Swarthmore College, Swarthmore, PA

Mrs. Clay A. Ketcham, Director, Reading and Study Program, Lafayette College, Easton, PA

Mrs. Eleanor M. Logan, Director of Reading Services, Pennsylvania Military College, Chester, PA

Theodore Maiser, Director, Reading Clinic, Muhlenberg College, Allentown, PA

E. Elona Sochor, Director, The Reading Clinic, Temple University, Philadelphia, PA

1958-1959

President, Bruce W. Brigham, Temple University (resigned and was succeeded by Albert J. Mazurkiewicz)

President-Elect, Albert J. Mazurkiewicz, Lehigh University

Secretary-Treasurer, Edward Dillon, LaSalle College

Board of Directors
Mrs. Herbert E. (Clay) Ketcham, LaSalle College
Eleanor M. Logan, Pennsylvania Military College
William A. Gaines, Delaware State College
Edward R. Dubin, Temple University
Thomas Leiper, Pittsburg, Pennsylvania

Conference Coordinator, Edward Dillon, LaSalle College

1959-1960

President, Albert J. Mazurkiewicz, Lehigh University

Secretary-Treasurer, Edward Dillon, Temple University (resigned and was succeeded by Albert J. Mazurkiewicz)

Board of Directors
Mrs. Herbert E.(Clay) Ketcham, LaSalle College
Eleanor M. Logan, Pennsylvania Military College
William A. Gaines, Delaware State College

Edward R. Dubin, Temple University
Thomas Leiper, Pittsburg, Pennsylvania

1960-1961
President, Albert J. Mazurkiewicz, Lehigh University
Secretary-Treasurer, Charles J. Versacci, Lehigh University

Board of Directors
Mrs. Herbert E. (Clay) Ketcham, LaSalle College
Eleanor M. Logan, Pennsylvania Military College
William A. Gaines, Delaware State College

Editor of Proceedings
Mrs. Herbert E. (Clay) Ketcham

*Note: Officer lists are based on what we believe to be the most complete and most accurate information available from published documents for given years. Any errors inherent in these documents will also appear in this Appendix. The Co-Historians acknowledge the assistance of Dr. A. Mazurkiewicz in constructing the first three years of officer lists. Reformatting and word processing by R. G. Brewer.

1961-1962
President, Albert J. Mazurkiewicz, Lehigh University
President-Elect, Mrs. Clay A. Ketcham, Lafayette College
Past President, Mr. Bruce W. Brigham, Temple University
Secretary-Treasurer, Mr. Charles J. Versacci, Lehigh University-IndefiniteAppointment

Board of Directors Directors
William A.Gaines, Delaware St. College
Mr. A. B. Herr, Rochester Institute of Technology
Martha J. Maxwell, University of Maryland
Charles Shinaberry, Slippery Rock St. College
Mr. Paul N. Terwilliger, Gettysburg College
(Sixth director–vacancy)

The following were appointed contributing editors to the Journal of the Reading Specialist
M. Jerry Weiss, English Journal
Clay A. Ketcham, College English
Francis L. Christ, Journal of Developmental Reading
Martha J. Maxwell, Journal of Personnel and Guidance
John E. Daniel, Journal of Experimental Education
Edward R. Dubin, Journal of Clinical Psychology
Charles J. Versacci, Journal of Orthopsychiatry

1962-1963
President, Mrs. Herbert E. Ketcham, Lafayette College
President-Elect, Martha J. Maxwell, University of Maryland
Secretary-Treasurer, Charles J. Versacci, Lehigh University

Board of Directors
A. B. Herr, Chairman, Rochester Institute of Technology
Charles R. Colvin, Gannon College

William A. Gaines, Delaware State College
Paul N. Terwilliger, Gettysburg College
M. Jerry Weiss, Jersey City State College
Past-Presidents: Albert J. Mazurkiewicz, Bruce W. Brigham

The Journal of the Reading Specialist
The Official Organ of the College Reading Association Reading Clinic, Lehigh University
Albert J. Mazurkiewicz, Editor, Lehigh University
Lawrence Charry, Associate Editor

1963-1964
President, Martha Maxwell, University of Maryland
President-Elect, M. Jerry Weiss
Secretary-Treasurer, A. B. Herr, Rochester Institute of Technology

Board of Directors
Phillip Shaw, Brooklyn College
Alvina Burrows, New York University
Charles Colvin, Gannon College
Leonard Braam, Syracuse University
William Gaines, Delaware State College
Marjorie S. Johnson, Temple University
Past Presidents: Mrs. Herbert E. Ketcham, Albert J. Mazurkiewicz, Bruce W. Brigham

1964-1965
President, M. Jerry Weiss, Jersey City State College
President-Elect, Robert C. Aukerman, University of Rhode Island
Secretary-Treasurer, A. B. Herr, Rochester Institute of Technology

Board of Directors
Phillip Shaw, Brooklyn College
Alvina T. Burrows, New York University
Charles R. Colvin, Gannon College
Leonard S. Braam, Syracuse University
Gertrude Williams, D. C. Teachers College
Paul D. Leedy, American University

Past-Presidents
Martha J. Maxwell, Mrs. Herbert E. Ketcham, Albert J. Mazurkiewicz, Bruce W. Brigham

The Journal of The Reading Specialist
The Official Organ of the College Reading Association
Albert J. Mazurkiewicz, Editor, Lehigh University
Leonard S. Braam, Research Abstracts Editor, Syracuse University
Arthur W. Heilman, News, Views, and Review Editor, Penn State University
Lawrence Charry, Associate Editor

1965-1966

President, Robert C. Aukerman, University of Rhode Island
President-Elect, Leonard S. Braam, Syracuse University
Executive Secretary-Treasurer, A. B. Herr, Rochester Institute of Technology

Board of Directors
Phillip Shaw, Brooklyn College Alvina Burrows, New York University
Eleanor M. Logan, Pennsylvania Military College
Gertrude Williams, District of Columbia Teachers College
Paul D. Leedy, American University
Martha Weber, Bowling Green State University
Stanley Weissman, Villanova University

Past-President Directors
M. Jerry Weiss, Jersey City State College Martha J. Maxwell, University of Maryland Mrs. Herbert E. Ketcham, Lafayette College Albert J. Mazurklewicz, Lehigh University Bruce W. Brigham, Temple University

Committee Chairmen
Membership, Phillip Shaw, Brooklyn College
Research, Leonard S. Braam, Syracuse University
Professional Standards and Ethics, Charles R. Colvin, Gannon College
Paper Back Book Commission, M. Jerry Weiss, Jersey City State College
Program, Leonard S. Braam, Syracuse University

Proceedings Editor, Mrs. Herbert E. Ketcham, LaSalle College

Journal Editor, Albert J. Mazurkiewicz, Lehigh University

1966-1967

President, Leonard S. Braam, Syracuse University
President-Elect, William H. Cooper, Ohio University
Past-President, Robert C. Aukerman, University of Rhode Island
Executive Secretary-Treasurer, A. B. Herr, Rochester Institute of Technology

Board of Directors
Gertrude Williams, District of Columbia Teachers College
Paul D. Leedy, American University
Robert M. Wilson, University of Maryland
Martha Weber, Bowling Green State University
Daniel T. Fishco, University of Southern Illinois
Elizabeth Johnson, Diablo Valley College
Uberto Price, Appalachian State Teachers College

Past-President Directors
M. Jerry Weiss, Jersey City State College
Martha J. Maxwell, University of Maryland
Mrs. Herbert E. Ketcham, Lafayette College
Albert J. Mazurkiewicz, Lehigh University

Committee Chairmen
Membership, Philip Shaw, Brooklyn College
Research, Leonard S. Braam, Syracuse University

Professional Standards and Ethics, Charles R. Colvin, Gannon College
Paper Back Book Commission, M. Jerry Weiss, Jersey City State College
Program, William H. Cooper, Ohio University

Proceedings Editor
Mrs. Herbert E. Ketcham, Lafayette College

Journal Editor, Albert J. Mazurkiewicz, Lehigh University

1967-1968
President, William H. Cooper, Ohio University
President-Elect, Roy E. Newton, State University of New York at Albany
Past-President, Leonard S. Braam, Syracuse University
Executive Secretary-Treasurer, A. B. Herr, Rochester Institute of Technology

Board of Directors
Martha Weber, Bowling Green State University
Daniel T. Fishco, University of Southern Illinois
Elizabeth Johnson, Diablo Valley College
Uberto Price, Appalachian State Teachers College
George Schick, Purdue University
Marvin S. Joslow, Reading Institute of Boston
Robert M. Wilson, University of Maryland

Past-President Directors
Robert C. Aukerman, University of Rhode Island
M. Jerry Weiss, Jersey City State College
Martha J. Maxwell, University of Maryland
Mrs. Herbert E. Ketcham, Lafayette College
Albert J. Mazurkiewicz, Lehigh University

Committee Chairmen
Membership, Philip Shaw, Brooklyn College Research,
Leonard S. Braam, Syracuse University
Professional Standards and Ethics, Charles R. Colvin, Gannon College
Paper Back Book Commission, M. Jerry Weiss, Jersey City State College
Program, Roy E. Newton, State University of New York at Albany
Proceedings Editor, Mrs. Herbert E. Ketcham, Lafayette College
Journal Editor, Albert J. Mazurkiewicz, Lehigh University

1968-1969
President, J. Roy Newton, State University of New York at Albany
President-Elect, Uberto Price, Appalachian State University
Past-President, William H. Cooper, Ohio University
Executive Secretary-Treasurer, Leonard S. Braam, Syracuse University

Board of Directors
Elizabeth Johnson, Diablo Valley College
Uberto Price, Appalachian State University
S. Alan Cohen, Yeshiva University
George Schick, Purdue University
Robert M. Wilson, University of Maryland

William Davies, State University of New York at Oneonta
Joseph Nemeth, Bowling Green State University

Past-President Directors
Leonard S. Braam, Syracuse University
Robert C. Aukerman, University of Rhode Island M.
Jerry Weiss, Jersey City State College
Martha J. Maxwell, University of Maryland
Mrs. Herbert E. Ketcham, Lafayette College

Committee Chairman
Constitution, Marvin S. Joslow, Reading Institute of Boston
Elections, Leonard S. Braam, Syracuse University
Membership, William H. Cooper, State University of New York at Albany
Research, William Davies, State University of New York at Oneonta
Professional Standards & Ethics, Robert M. Wilson, University of Maryland
Multi-media Commission, M. Jerry Weiss, Jersey City State College
Program, Uberto Price, Appalachian State University
Publications, William H. Cooper, Ohio University
Procedures & Organization, Bruce W. Brigham, Temple University

Proceedings Editor, Mrs. Herbert E. Ketcham, Lafayette College

Journal Editor, Samuel S. Zeman, Shippensburg State College

1969-1970
President, Uberto Price, Appalachian State University
President-Elect, Robert M. Wilson, University of Maryland
Past-President, J. Roy Newton, State University of New York at Albany
Secretary-Treasurer, *Leonard S. Braam, Syracuse University

Board of Directors
*Martha J. Maxwell, University of Maryland
Daniel T. Fishco, Southern Illinois University
Stanley Krippner, Maimonides Medical Center
Charles R. Colvin, SUNY, Fredonia
*M. Jerry Weiss, Jersey City State College
William Davies, SUNY, Oneonta
Joseph Nemeth, Bowling Green State University
*Robert C. Aukerman, University of Rhode Island
*William H. Cooper, Ohio University
Mary C. Austin, Case Western Reserve University
Paul R. Kazmierski, Lorain Community College
*Ex-President

Editors
Journal, Samuel S. Zeman, Shippensburg State College
Proceedings, Clay A. Ketcham, Lafayette College

1970-1971

President, Robert M. Wilson, University of Maryland
President-Elect, Jules C. Abrams, Hahnemann Medical College
Past-President, Uberto Price, Appalachian State University
Executive-Treasurer, *Leonard S. Braam, Syracuse University

Directors
Stanley Krippner, Maimonides Medical Center
William Davies, Shippensburg State College
Joseph Nemeth, Bowling Green State University
*William H. Cooper, Ohio University
Mary C. Austin, Case Western Reserve University
Paul R. Kazmierski, Rochester Institute of Technology
*J. Roy Newton, State University of New York, Albany
David J. Yarington, University of Massachusetts
Dorothy D. Sullivan, University of Maryland
Esther K. Fox, Silver Spring, Maryland
*Ex-President

Editors
Journal, Samuel S. Zeman, Shippensburg State College
Proceedings, Clay A. Ketcham, Lafayette College

1971-1972

President, Jules C. Abrams, Hahnemann Medical College of Philadelphia
President- Elect, Daniel T. Fishco, University of Southern Illinois
Past-President, Robert M. Wilson, University of Maryland
Secretary-Treasurer, Leonard S. Braam, Syracuse University

Board of Directors:
Mary C. Austin, University of Hawaii
Paul R. Kazmierski, Rochester Institute of Technology
Marvin S. Joslow, The Reading Institute, Boston
Dorothy D. Sullivan, University of Maryland
*Uberto Price, Appalachian State University
David J. Yarington, University of Massachusetts
*J. Roy Newton, SUNY, Albany
Carol O'Connell, Department of Education, State of Ohio
Roy A. Kress, Temple University
George 0. Phillips, Queens College, City University of New York
*Ex-President

Journal Editor, Samuel S. Zeman, Shippensburg State College
Publications Business Manager, James R. Geyer, Shippensburg State College
Membership, Paul R. Kazmierski, Rochester Institute of Technology
Conferences and Special Programs, Dorothy D. Sullivan, University of Maryland

1972-1973

President, Daniel T. Fishco, University of Southern Illinois
President-Elect, George 0. Phillips, Queens College City University of New York
Past-President, Jules C. Abrams, Hahnemann Medical College of Philadelphia
Secretary-Treasurer, Leonard S. Braam, Syracuse University

Board of Directors

   Anthony Amato, Temple University
   Marvin S. Joslow, the Reading Institute, Boston
   Dorothy D. Sullivan, University of Maryland
   *Uberto Price, Appalachian State University
   *Robert M. Wilson, University of Maryland
   David J. Yarington, University of Massachusetts
   *J. Roy Newton, SUNY, Albany
   Carol O'Connell, Department of Education, State of Ohio
   Roy A. Kess, Temple University
   David Wark, University of Minnesota
   Sidney J. Rouch, Hofstra University
   *Ex-President

Journal Editor, Samuel S. Zeman, Shippensburg State College
Publications Business Manager, James R. Geyer, Shippensburg State College
Membership, Paul R. Kazmierski, Rochester Institute of Technology
Conferences and Special Programs, Dorothy D. Sullivan, University of Maryland

1973-1974

President, George 0. Phillips, Queens College City University of New York
President-Elect, Paul R. Kazmierski, Rochester Institute of Technology
Past President, Daniel T. Fishco, Western Illinois University
Secretary-Treasurer, Dorothy D. Sullivan, University of Maryland

Board of Directors

   Carol O'Connell, Ohio State Department of Education
   Barbara M. Klaeser, Milwaukee School of Engineering
   Roy A. Kress, Temple University
   *Robert M. Wilson, University of Maryland
   *Jules C. Abrams, Hahnemann Medical College of Philadelphia
   Mae Johnson, Virginia State College
   Sidney J. Rauch, Hofstra University
   Richard L. Carner, University of Miami
   Gary D. Spencer, Jersey City State College
   *Ex-President

Editor of Journal, Reading World, Samuel S. Zeman, Shippensburg State College
Publications Business Manager, James R. Geyer, Shippensburg State College
Membership Chairman, B. William Gage, Rochester Institute of Technology
Coordinator of Conferences and Special Programs, Janet K. Carsetti, University of
   Maryland

1974-1975

President, Paul R. Kazmierski, Rochester Institute of Technology
President-Elect, Richard L. Carner, University of Miami
Past-President, George 0. Phillips, Sr., Queens College, CUNY
Secretary-Treasurer, Dorothy D. Sullivan, University of Maryland

Board of Directors

   June B. Ewing, Georgia Southwestern College
   Mae Johnson, Virginia State College

B. William Gage, Rochester Institute of Technology
Jules C. Abrams, Halineininti Medical College, and Hospital
Gary D. Spencer, Jersey City State College
*Daniel T. Fishco, Western Illinois University
Barbara Klaesar, Milwaukee School of Engineering
Thomas J. Edwards, SUNY at Buffalo
Carol O'Connell, Department of Education, State of Ohio
*Past President

Editor of Journal, Reading World, Samuel S. Zeman, Shippensburg State College
Publications Business Manager, James R. Geyer, Shippensburg State College
Membership Chairman, B. William Gage, Rochester Institute of Technology
Coordinator of Conferences and Special Programs, Janet K. Carsetti, University of
    Maryland

1975-1976

President, Richard L. Carner, University of Miami
President-Elect, Phillip L. Nacke, University of Kentucky
Past-President, Paul R. Kazmierski, Rochester Institute of Technology
Executive Secretary, June B. Ewing, Georgia South West College
Treasurer, Dorothy D. Sullivan, University of Maryland

Board of Directors:
    *Daniel T. Fishco, Western Illinois University
    Barbara Klaeser, Alvertio College
    Gary D Spencer, Jersey City State College
    Thomas J. Edwards, SUNY at Buffalo
    Carol O'Connell, Department of Education, State of Ohio
    Joseph Brunner, Montclair State College
    Thomas J. Fitzgerald, SUNY at Albany
    Marvin S. Joslow, The Reading Institute of Boston
    * Past-President

Editor of Journal, Reading World, Samuel S. Zeman, Shippensburg State College
Publications Business Manager, James R. Geyer, Shippensburg State College
Membership Chairman, B. William Gage, Rochester Institute of Technology
Co-coordinators of Conferences and Special Programs, Janet K. Carsetti, University of
    Maryland, and Zelda B. Smith, Gables Academies, Miami, FL

1976-1977

President, Phillip L. Nacke, University of Kentucky
President-Elect, Janet K. Carsetti, American Correctional Association
Past-President, Richard L. Gamer, University of Miami
Executive Secretary, June B. Ewing, Georgia Southwestern College
Treasurer, Wallace Miller, University of Southern Mississippi

Board of Directors
    Wallace Miller, University of Southern Mississippi
    B. William Gage, Rochester Institute of Technology
    Carol O'Connell, Department of Education, State of Ohio
    *George O. Phillips, Sr., Queens College CUNY

Thomas J. Fitzgerald, New York State Education Department
Marvin S. Joslow, The Reading Institute of Boston
*Paul R. Kazmierski, Rochester Institute of Technology
Kenneth Bourne, Essex Community College, Chairperson, College Division
*Alberti Mazurkiewicz, Kean College, Chairperson, Teacher Education Division
Marjorie Snyder, Northeast Louisiana University, Chairperson, Clinical Division
Linda B. Gambrell, Hood College
Barbara Klaesek, Alvertio College
*Past-President

Commission and Committee Chairpersons
Historian, Eleanor M. Ladd, Temple University
Media, M. Jerry Weiss, Jersey City State College
Membership, B. William Gage, Rochester Institute of Technology and Portia
    Shields, Howard University
Professional Affairs, Arthur E. Smith, State University of New York, Brockport
Publications, Linda B. Gambrell, Hood College
Publicity, James E. Walker, Northern Illinois University
Research George McNinch, University of Southern Mississippi
Resolutions and   Rules, Dorothy D. Sullivan, University of Maryland
Social Action, Carol O'Connell, Ohio State Department of Education
Conferences and Special Programs, Zelda B. Carver, Gables Academies

Publications Committee Members
Timothy R. Blair, University of Florida
Dolores Dickerson, Howard University
Thomas J. Fitzgerald, New York State Education Department
Linda B. Gambrell, Hood College
Jerry L. Johns, Northern Illinois University

1977-1978
President, Janet K. Carsetti, Read, Inc., Silver Spring, MD.
President-Elect, Thomas J. Fitzgerald, New York State Education Department
Past-President, Phillip L. Nacke, University of Kentucky
Executive Secretary, June B. Ewing, Georgia Southwestern College
Treasurer, Wallace Miller, University of Southern Mississippi

Board of Directors
Marvin S. Joslow, The Reading Institute of Boston
*Paul R. Kazmierski, Rochester Institute of Technology
John Campbell, Howard University
George Mcninch, University of Southern Mississippi
Richard L. Carner, University of Miami
Linda B. Gambrell, University of Maryland
Barbara Macknick, CompPSolv
Rita M. Bean, University of Pittsburgh
James E. Walker, Northern Illinois University
*Past-President

Commission and Committee Chairpersons
Historian, Dolores Dickerson, Howard University
Media, M. Jerry Weiss, Jersey City State College

Membership, Ellen B. Fuchs, Oxford University Press, New York and Portia Shields, Howard University

Professional Affairs, Arthur E. Smith, State University of New York, Brockport

Publications, Linda B. Gambrell, University of Maryland

Public Information, Joan D. Coley, Western Maryland College

Research, Lawrence Kasdon, Yeshiva University

Resolution and Rules, Marvin S. Joslow, The Reading Institute of Boston Social Action, Annie Neal, University of the District of Columbia

Division Chairpersons

Kenneth Bourne, Essex Community College, Chairperson, College Division

Albert J. Mazurkiewicz, Kean College, Chairperson, Teacher Education Division

Marjorie Snyder, Northeast Louisiana University, Chairperson, Clinical Division

Publications Committee Members

Timothy R. Blair, University of Florida

Dolores Dickerson, Howard University

Thomas J. Fitzgerald, New York State Education Department

Linda B. Gambrell, University of Maryland

George McNinch, University of Southern Mississippi

Reading World

Samuel S. Zeman, Reading World Editor, Shippensburg State College

Jerry L. Johns, Reading World Associate Editor, Northern Illinois University

Monograph Series

Robert M. Wilson, Monograph Series Editor, University of Maryland

Jerilyn K. Ribovich, Monograph Series Associate Editor, West Virginia University

Newsletter—Reading News

Jerry B. Zutell, Reading News Editor, Ohio State University,

Jane B. Matanzo, Reading News Associate Editor, Hood College

Conferences and Special Programs

Zelda B. Carner, Miami, FL

1978-1979

President, Thomas J. Fitzgerald, New York State Education Department

President-Elect, William E. Blanton, Appalachian State College

Past-President, Janet K. Carsetti, Read, Inc., Silver Spring, MD

Executive Secretary, June B. Ewing, Georgia Southwestern College

Treasurer, Wallace Miller, University of Southern Mississippi

Board of Directors

*Richard L. Carner, University of Miami

Linda B. Gambrell, University of Maryl and Barbara Macknick, CompPSolv

Arthur E. Smith, State University College at Brockport

Rita M. Bean, University of Pittsburgh *Phillip L. Nacke, University of Kentucky

James E. Walker, Northen Illinois University

Susan Mandel Glazer, Rider College

Lillian R. Putnam, Kean College

*Past-President

Commission and Committee Chairpersons
Historian, Paul R. Kazmierski, Rochester Institute of Technology
Media, M. Jerry Weiss, Jersey City State College
Membership, Ellen B. Fuchs, Oxford University Press, New York, and Dorothy Welle, Kean College
Professional Affairs, Arthur E. Smith, State University of New York, Brockport
Publications, Timothy R. Blair, University of Florida
Public Information, Joan D. Coley, Western Maryland College
Research, Lawrence Kasdon, Yeshiva University
Resolution and Rules, Marvin S. Joslow, The Reading Institute of Boston
Social Action, Annie Neal, University of the District of Columbia

Conferences and Special Programs
Irene Payne, Rochester Institute of Technology

Division Chairpersons
Miriam Chaplin, Rutgers University, Chairperson, College Division
Shirley B. Merlin, Madison College, Chairperson, Teacher Education Division
John J. Pikulski, University of Delaware, Chairperson, Clinical Division

Publications Committee Members
Timothy R. Blair, Chairman, University of Florida
Rita M. Bean, University of Pittsburgh
Lowell D. Eberwein, University of Kentucky
George McNinch, University of Southern Mississippi
William R. Powell, University of Florida

Reading World
Samuel S. Zeman, Reading World Editor, Shippensburg State College
Jerry L. Johns, Reading World Associate Editor, Northern Illinois University

Monograph Series
Jerilyn K. Ribovich, Monograph Series Editor, West Virginia University

Newsletter—Reading News
Jerry B. Zutell, Reading News Editor, Ohio State University
Jane B. Matanzo, Reading News Associate Editor, Hood College

1979-1980
President, William E. Blanton, Appalachian State University
President-Elect, James E. Walker, Northern Illinois University
Immediate Past-President, Thomas J. Fitzgerald, New York State Department of Education Reading Bureau
Executive Secretary, June B. Ewing, Georgia Southwestern College
Treasurer, Wallace Miller, Southwest Baptist College

Board of Directors
Rita M. Bean, University of Pittsburgh
Phillip L. Nacke, University of Kentucky
Lana McWilliams, Memphis State University
Susan Mandel Glazer, Rider College
Lillian R. Putnam, Kean College
Janet K. Carsetti, Read, Inc., Silver Spring, MD
Nancy Dworkin, Center for Unique Learners, Rockville
George E. Mason, University of Georgia

Commission and Committee Chairpersons
    Historian, Paul R. Kazmierski, Rochester Institute of Technology
    Media, M. Jerry Weiss, Jersey City State College
    Membership, Ellen B. Fuchs, Oxford University Press, New York, and Dorothy
        Welle, Kean College
    Professional Affairs, Ernest Dishner, Northern Iowa University
    Publications, Timothy R. Blair, University of Florida
    Public Information, Fred Raetsch, Clemson University
    Research, Lawrence Kasdon, Yeshiva University
    Resolutions and Rules, Marvin S. Joslow, The Reading Institute of Boston
    Social Action, Gary L. Shaffer, James Madison University
    Conferences and Special Programs Irene Payne, Rochester Institute of Technology
        Division Chairpersons
    Miriam Chaplin, Rutgers University, Chairperson, College Division
    Shirley B. Merlin, Madison College, Chairperson, Teacher Education Division
    John J. Pikulski, University of Delaware, Chairperson, Clinical Division

Publications Committee Members
    Timothy R. Blair, Chairman, University of Florida
    Rita M. Bean, University of Pittsburgh
    Lowell D. Eberwein, University of Kentucky
    George McNinch, University of Southern Mississippi
    William R. Powell, University of Florida

Reading World
    Samuel S. Zeman, Reading World Editor, Shippensburg State College
    Jerry L. Johns, Reading World Associate Editor, Northern Illinois University

Monograph Series
    John N. Mangieri, Monograph Series Editor, University of South Carolina
    Jerilyn K. Ribovich, Monograph Series Associate Editor, West Virginia University

Newsletter—Reading News
    Jerry B. Zutell, Reading News Editor, Ohio State University
    Jane B. Matanzo, Reading News Associate Editor, Hood College

1980-1981

President, James E. Walker, Northern Illinois University
President-Elect, Linda B. Gambrell, University of Maryland
Immediate Past-President, William E. Blanton, Appalachian State University
Executive Secretary, June B. Ewing, Georgia Southwestern College
Treasurer, Wallace Miller, Southwest Baptist College

Board of Directors
    Susan Mandel Glazer, Rider College
    Lillian R. Putnam, Kean College
    Janet K. Carsetti, Read, Inc., Silver Spring, MD
    Arthur E. Smith, SUNY at Brockport
    Nancy Dworkin, Center for Unique Learners, Rockville, MD
    George E. Mason, University of Georgia
    Thomas P. Fitzgerald, State Education Department, Albany, NY
    Jerry L. Johns, Northern Illinois University
    Janet Miller, Northern Kentucky University

Commission and Committee Chairpersons
>   Historian, Paul R. Kazmierski, Rochester Institute of Technology
>   Media, M. Jerry Weiss, Jersey City State College
>   Membership, Ellen B. Fuchs, Oxford University Press, NY and Dorothy Welle, Kean College
>   Professional Affairs, Arthur E. Smith, SUNY at Brockport
>   Publications, Timothy R. Blair, University of Florida
>   Public Information, Fred Raetsch, Clemson University
>   Research, Lois A. Bader, Michigan State University
>   Resolutions and Rules, Marvin S. Joslow, The Reading Institute of Boston Social Action, Gary L. Shaffer, James Madison University
>   Conferences and Special Programs, Irene Payne, Rochester Institute of Technology

Division Chairpersons
>   Alice T. Randall, Christopher-Newport College, Chairperson, College Division
>   William H. Rupley, Texas A&M University, Chairperson, Teacher-Education Division
>   Lawrence Kasdon, Yeshiva University, Chairperson, Clinical Division

Publications Committee Members
>   Timothy R. Blair, Chairman, University of Florida
>   Rita M. Bean, University of Pittsburgh
>   Lowell D. Eberwein, University of Kentucky
>   George McNinch, University of Southern Mississippi
>   William R. Powell, University of Florida

Reading World
>   Samuel S. Zeman, Reading World Editor, Shippensburg State College
>   Jerry L. Johns, Reading World Associate Editor, Northern Illinois University

Monograph Series
>   John N. Mangieri, Monograph Series Editor, University of South Carolina

Newsletter—Reading News
>   Jane B. Matanzo, Reading News Editor, Damascus, MD
>   Carol Robeck, Reading News Associate Editor, Texas A&M University

1981-1982
President, Linda B. Gambrell, University of Maryland
President-Elect, Rita M. Bean, University of Pittsburgh
Immediate Past-President, James E. Walker, Northern Illinois University
Executive Secretary, June B. Ewing, Georgia Southwestern College
Treasurer, James R. Layton, Southwest Missouri State University

Board of Directors
>   Nancy Dworkin, Center for Unique Learners, Rockville, MD
>   George E. Mason, University of Georgia
>   Marvin S. Joslow, Reading Institute of Boston
>   Thomas P. Fitzgerald, State Education Department, Albany
>   Jerry L. Johns, Northern Illinois University
>   Janet Miller, Northern Kentucky University
>   William E. Blanton, Appalachian State University
>   Joan D. Coley, Monrovia, MD
>   Walter R. Hill, SUNY-Buffalo, Amherst Campus

Commission and Committee Chairpersons

Historian, Louis A. Oliastro, California State College, PA

Paul R. Kazmierski, Institute of Technology

Media, Sharon V. Arthur, Eastern Connecticut State College, and M. Jerry Weiss, Jersey City State College

Membership, Ellen B. Fuchs, Oxford University Press, NY

Professional Affairs, Arthur E. Smith, SUNY at Brockport

Publications, Ernest K. Dishner, Northern Iowa University

Public Information, Emma Rembert, Florida International University and Fred Raetsch, Clemson University

Research, Betty S. Heathington, University of Tennessee and Lois A. Bader, Michigan State University

Resolutions and Rules, Norman A. Stahl, University of Pittsburgh

Marvin S. Joslow, the Reading Institute of Boston

Social Action, Marino C. Alvarez, Tennessee State University, and Victoria J. Risko, Peabody College of Vanderbilt University

Conferences and Special Programs, Marilyn G. Eanet, Rhode Island College

Division Chairpersons

Alice T. Randall, Christopher Newport College, Chairperson, College Division

William H. Rupley, Texas A&M University, Chairperson, Teacher Education Division

Lawrence Kasdon, Yeshiva University, Chairperson, Clinical Division

Publications Committee Members

Ernest K. Dishner, Chairman, University of Northern Iowa

Reading World

Samuel S. Zeman, Reading World Editor, Shippensburg State College

Jerry L. Johns, Reading World Associate Editor, Northern Illinois University

Monograph Series

David Moore, Monograph Series Editor, University of Kansas

Newsletter—Reading News

Jane B. Matanzo, Reading News Editor, Damascus, MD

Carol Robeck, Reading News Associate Editor, TLC The Learning Center, College Station, TX

1982-1983

President, Rita M. Bean, University of Pittsburgh

President-Elect, Susan Mandel Glazer, Rider College

Immediate Past-President, Linda B. Gambrell, University of Maryland

Executive Secretary, June B. Ewing, Georgia Southwestern College

Treasurer, James R. Layton, Southwest Missouri State University

Board of Directors

Jerry L. Johns, Northern Illinois University

Janet Miller, Northern Kentucky University

William E. Blanton, Appalachian State University

Shirley Merlin, James Madison University

James E. Walker, Northern Illinois University

Joan D. Coley, Western Maryland College
Walter R. Hill, SUNY-Buffalo, Amherst Campus
Irene Payne, Rochester Institute of Technology
John E. Readence, University of Georgia

Commission and Committee Chairpersons

Historian, Frederick J. Fedorko, East Stroudsburg State College
Media, M. Jerry Weiss, Jersey City State College and Maryanne Hall, Georgia State University
Membership, Ora Anderson, Coppin State College
Professional Affairs, Lonnie D. McIntyre, Michigan State University
Publications, Ernest K. Dishner, Northern Iowa University
Public Information, Emma W. Rembert, Florida International University and William A. Henk, University of Georgia
Research, Lois A. Bader, Michigan State University and Betty S. Heathington, University of Tennesse
Resolutions and Rules, Norman A. Stahl, Georgia State University
Legislative and Social Issues, Marino C. Alvarez, Tennessee State University and Victoria J. Risko, Peabody College of Vanderbilt University
Conferences and Special Programs, Marilyn G. Eanet, Rhode Island College

Division Chairpersons

Nancy Dworkin, Center for Unique Learners, Chairperson, Adult Learning Division
Karl Koenke, University of Illinois, Chairperson, Clinical Division
Rhoda L. Ramirez, Lagoven Oil of Venezuela, Chairperson, Teacher Education Division
Dorothy Snozek, Slippery Rock State College, Chairperson, College Division

Publications Committee Members

Ernest K. Dishner, Chairperson, University of Northern Iowa
Donna Alvermann, University of Georgia
Connie Bridge, University of Kentucky
James R. Layton, Southwest Missouri State University
David Moore, University of Northern Iowa
Richard T. Vacca, Kent State University

Reading World

Samuel S. Zeman, Reading World Editor, Shippensburg State College
Jerry L. Johns, Reading World Associate Editor, Northern Illinois University

Monograph Series

David Moore, Monograph Series Editor, University of Northern Iowa

Newsletter—Reading News

Jane B. Matanzo, Reading News Editor, Damascus, MD
Carol Robeck, Reading News Associate Editor, TLC The Learning Center, College Station, TX

1983-1984

President, Susan Mandel Glazer, Rider College
President-Elect, George E. Mason, University of Georgia
Past President, Rita Bean, University of Pittsburgh

Executive Secretary, June Ewing, Georgia Southwestern College
Co-Treasurers, James R. Layton, Southwest Missouri State University, Barbara A. Layton, Springfield, Missouri Public Schools

Board of Directors
Joan D. Coley, Western Maryland College
Walter R. Hill, SUNY-Buffalo
James E. Walker, Northern Illinois University
Irene Payne, Rochester Institute of Technology
John E. Readence, Louisiana State University in Baton Rouge
Linda Gambrell, University of Maryland
Lois Bader, Michigan State University
William R. Rupley, Texas A&M University
Richard Vacca, Kent State University

Commission and Committee Chairpersons
Historian, Frederick J. Fedorko, (Co-chair.) East Stroudsburg State College and Albert Shannon, (Co-chair.) Rider College
Media, M. Jerry Weiss, Jersey City State College and MaryAnne Hall, Georgia State University
Membership, Ora Anderson, Coppin State College
Professional Affairs, Lonnie D. McIntyre, Michigan State University Publications, Ernest K. Dishner, Northern Iowa University
Public Information, Emma Rembert, Florida International University and William A. Henk, University of Georgia
Research, Lois A. Bader, Michigan State University and Betty S. Heathington, University of Tennessee
Resolutions and Rules, Norman A. Stahl, Georgia State University
Legislative and Social Issues, Victoria J. Risko, (Co-chair) Peabody College of Vanderbilt University and Peg Cagney, (Co-chair) Sicklerville, NJ
Conferences and Special Programs, Marilyn Eanet, Rhode Island College

Division Chairpersons
James E. Walker, Northern Illinois University, Chairperson, Adult Learning Division
Karl Koenke, University of Illinois, Chairperson, Clinical Division
Reta Hicks, Western Kentucky University, Chairperson, Teacher Education Division
Dorothy Snozek, Slippery Rock State College, Chairperson, College Division

Publications Committee Members
Ernest K. Dishner, Chairperson, University of Northern Iowa
Donna Alvermann, University of Georgia
Connie Bridge, University of Kentucky
James Layton, Southwest Missouri State University
David Moore, University of Northern Iowa
Richard Vacca, Kent State University
Reading World
Samuel S. Zeman, Reading World Editor, Shippensburg University
Jerry L. Johns, Reading World Associate Editor, Northern Illinois University

Monograph Series
   David Moore, Monograph Series Editor, University of Northern Iowa

Newsletter—Reading News
   Jane B. Matanzo, Reading News Editor, Damascus, MD
   Carol Robeck, Reading News Associate Editor, TLC The Learning Center, College
   Station, TX

1984-1985
President, George E. Mason, University of Georgia
President-Elect, Lois A. Bader, Michigan State University
Past-President, Susan Mandel Glazer, Rider College
Executive Secretary, June B. Ewing, Georgia Southwestern College
Co-Treasurers, James R. Layton, Southwest Missouri State University and Barbara A.
   Layton, Springfield, Missouri Public Schools.

Board of Directors
   Janet Miller, Northern Kentucky University
   Irene Payne, Rochester Institute of Technology
   John E. Readence, Louisiana State University
   Linda B. Gambrell, University of Maryland
   Thomas A. Rakes, Memphis State University
   Richard T. Vacca, Kent State University
   Rita M. Bean, University of Pittsburgh
   Emma W. Rembert, Florida International University
   J. Estill Alexander, University of Tennessee

Commission and Committee Chairpersons
   Historian, Frederick J. Fedorko (Co-chair), East Stroudsburg, State College, Pa.,
      and Albert Shannon (Co-chair), Rider College
   Media, Ceil Mills (Co-chair), North Carolina State University and
      G. Michael Miller (Co-chair), Sam Houston State University
   Membership, Ora Anderson (Co-chair), Coppin State College and Robin
      Alinkofsky (Co-chair), Brooklyn, New York
   Professional Affairs, Lonnie D. McIntyre, Michigan State University
   Publications, Donna Alvermann, University of Georgia
   Public Information, William A. Henk (Co-chair) Penn State University, Capitol
      Campus and Robert J. Rickelman (Co-chair), Millersville State University
   Research, Betty S. Heathington (Co-chair), University of Tennessee and Sharon
   Arthur Moore (Co-chair), Northern Iowa University
   Resolutions and Rules, Norman A. Stahl (Co-chair), Georgia State University and
      William Brozo (Co-chair), Northern Illinois University
   Legislative and Social Issues, Victoria J. Risko, (Co-chair) Peabody College of Van-
      derbilt University and Howard L. Berrent (Co-chair), C. W. Post University
   Conferences and Special Programs, Margaret A. Cagney, Glassboro State Col-
      lege

Division Chairpersons
   Daniel L. Pearce, Eastern Montana College, Adult Learning Division
   Katherine Wiesendanger, Alfred University, Clinical Division
   Rta Hicks, Western Kentucky University, Teacher Education Division
   Laura S. Smith, Silver Spring, Maryland, College Reading Division

Reading World
> John E. Readence, Co-Editor, Louisiana State University
> R. Scott Baldwin, Co-Editor, University of Miami
> Samuel S. Zeman, Executive Consulting Editor, Shippensburg University

Monograph Series
> David Moore, Editor, University of Northern Iowa

Newsletter—Reading News
> Jane B. Matanzo, Editor, Damascus, MD

1985-1986

President, Lois A. Bader, Michigan State University
President-Elect, James R. Layton, Southwest Missouri State University
Past-President, George E. Mason, University of Georgia
Executive Secretary, June B. Ewing, Georgia Southwestern College
Treasurer, Norman A. Stahl, Georgia State University

Board of Directors
> Thomas A. Rakes, Memphis State University
> Richard T. Vacca, Kent State University
> Rita M. Bean, University of Pittsburgh
> Emma W. Rembert, Florida International University
> J. Estill Alexander, University of Tennessee
> Susan Mandel Glazer, Rider College
> Ernest K. Dishner, SW Texas State University
> Betty S. Heathington, University of Tennessee

Commission and Committee Chairpersons
> Historian, Albert Shannon (Co-chair), Rider College and James E. Walker (Co-chair), Texas Woman's University
> Media, Ceil Mills (Co-chair), North Carolina State University and G. Michael Miller (Co-chair), Sam Houston State University
> Membership, Estelle Brown (Co-chair), Glassboro State College and Reta Hicks (Co-chair), Western Kentucky University
> Professional Affairs, Lonnie D. McIntyre, Michigan State University
> Publications, Donna Alvermann, University of Georgia
> Public Information, Sue E Rogers (Co-chair), Averett College and Robert B. Cooter (Co-chair), Bowling Green State University
> Research, Madlyn Levine Hanes (Co-chair), University of South Carolina and Sharon Arthur Moore (Co-chair), University of Northern Iowa
> Resolutions and Rules, Janet Miller (Co-chair), Northern Kentucky University and William Brozo (Co-chair), Northern Illinois University
> Legislative and Social Issues, Larry Kenney (Co-chair), Western Illinois University and Howard I. Berrent (Co-chair), C. W. Post University
> Conferences and Special Programs, Margaret A. Cagney, Glassboro State College

Division Chairpersons
> Daniel L. Pearce, Eastern Montana College, Adult Learning Division
> Katherine Wiesendanger, Alfred University, Clinical Division
> Gary L. Shaffer, James Madison University
> Laura J. Smith, Silver Spring, Maryland, College Reading Division

Reading Research and Instruction
John E. Readence, Co-Editor, Louisiana State University
R. Scott Baldwin, Co-Editor, University of Miami

Monograph Series
David Moore, Editor, University of Northern Iowa

Newsletter—Reading News
William A. Henk, Co-Editor, Pennsylvania State University
Robert J. Rickelman, Co-Editor, Millersville State University

1986-1987

President, James R. Layton, Southwest Missouri State University
President-Elect, J. Estill Alexander, University of Tennessee
Past-President, Lois A. Bader, Michigan State University
Executive Secretary, June B. Ewing, Georgia Southwestern College
Treasurer and Publications Business Manager, Norman A. Stahl, Georgia State University

Board of Directors
Emma W. Rembert, Florida International University
Susan Mandell Glazer, Rider College
Ernest K. Dishner, SW Texas State University
Betty S. Heathington, University of Tennessee
Janet Miller, Northern Kentucky University
Irene Payne, Rochester Institute of Technology
George E. Mason, University of Georgia
Martha D. Collins, Louisiana State University
Marilyn G. Eanet, Rhode Island College

Commission and Committee Chairpersons
Historian, James E. Walker, Texas Woman's University
Media, Ceil Mills (Co-chair), North Carolina State University and G. Michael Miller (Co-chair), Sam Houston State University
Membership, Estelle Brown (Co-chair), Glassboro State College and Reta Hicks (Co-chair), Western Kentucky University
Professional Affairs, Lonnie D. McIntyre, Michigan State University
Publications, Donna Alvermann, University of Georgia
Public Information, Sue E Rogers (Co-chair), Averett College and Robert B. Cooter, (Co-chair), Bowling Green State University
Research, Madlyn Levine Hanes (Co-chair), University of South Carolina and Sharon Arthur Moore (Co-chair), University of Northern Iowa
Resolutions and Rules, Mary M. Brittain, Virginia Commonwealth University
Legislative and Social Issues, Howard I. Berrent, C. W. Post University
Conferences and Special Programs, Margaret A. Cagney, Glassboro State College

Division Chairpersons
Judy Richardson, Virginia Commonwealth University, Adult Learning Division
Madlyn Levine Hanes, University of South Carolina, Clinical Division
Gary L. Shaffer, James Madison University, Teacher Education
Audrey Williams, Baruch College, College Reading Division

Reading Research and Instruction
>   William E. Blanton, Co-Editor, Appalachian State University
>   Karen D. Wood, Co-Editor, University of North Carolina at Charlott

Monograph Series
>   David Moore, Editor, University of Northern Iowa

Newsletter—Reading News
>   William A. Henk, (Co-Editor), Pennsylvania State University
>   Robert A. Rickelman, (Co-Editor), Millersville State University

1987-1988

President, J. Estill Alexander, University of Tennessee
President-Elect, Jerry L. Johns, Northern Illinois University
Past-President, James R. Layton, Southwest Missouri State University
Executive Secretary, June B. Ewing, Georgia Southwestern College
Treasurer, Norman A. Stahl, Northern Illinois University

Board of Directors
>   Ernest K. Dishner, Southwest Texas State University
>   George E. Mason, University of Georgia
>   Betty S. Heathington, University of Tennessee
>   Emma W. Rembert, Florida International University
>   Lois A. Bader, Michigan State University
>   Martha D. Collins, Louisiana State University
>   Marilyn G. Eanet, Rhode Island College
>   Jane B. Matanzo, Damascus, Maryland
>   Victoria J. Risko, Vanderbilt University

Commission and Committee Chairpersons
>   Historian, James E. Walker, Texas Woman's University
>   Media, Margaret A. Cagney, Glassboro State College
>   Membership, Reta Hicks (Co-chair), Western Kentucky University and Estelle J.
>   Brown (Co-chair), Glassboro State College
>   Professional Affairs, Lonnie D. McIntyre, Michigan State University
>   Publications, Richard T. Vacca, Kent State University
>   Public Information, Sue F. Rogers (Co-chair), Averett College and Robert B. Cooter
>   (Co-chair), Bowling Green State University
>   Research, Madlyn Levine Hanes (Co-chair), University of South Carolina and Leo
>   Pauls (Co-chair), Emporia State University
>   Resolutions and Rules, Mary M. Brittain, Virginia Commonwealth University
>   Legislative and Social Issues, Howard I. Berrent, C. W. Post University
>   Conferences and Special Programs, Marion L. Patterson, Coppin State College

Division Chairpersons
>   James R. King, Texas Woman's University, Teacher Education Division
>   Audrey Williams, Baruch College, College Reading Division
>   Judy Richardson, Virginia Commonwealth, Adult Learning Division
>   Madlyn Levine Hanes, University of South Carolina, Clinical Division

Reading Research and Instruction
>   William E. Blanton, Co-Editor, Appalachian State University
>   Karen D. Wood, Co-Editor, University of North Carolina at Charlotte

Monograph Series
 Alan M. Frager, Editor, Miami University, Ohio

Newsletter—Reading News
 William A. Henk, Co-Editor, Pennsylvania State University at Harrisburg
 Robert J. Rickelman, Co-Editor, Millersville University

Publications Business Manager
 Robert B. Cooter, Jr., Manager, Bowling Green State University
 Frederick J. Fedorko, Photographer, East Stroudsburg University

1988-1989

President, Jerry L. Johns, Northern Illinois University
President-Elect, June B. Ewing, Georgia Southwestern College
Past-President, J. Estill Alexander, University of Tennessee
Executive Secretary, Betty S. Heathington, University of Tennessee
Treasurer, Robert B. Cooter, Jr., Bowling Green State University

Board of Directors
 Lois A. Bader, Michigan State University
 Martha D. Collins, Louisiana State University
 Marilyn G. Eanet, Rhode Island College
 Victoria J. Risko, Vanderbilt University
 Jane B. Matanzo American University
 Patricia A. Koskinen, University of Maryland
 Estelle J. Brown, Glassboro State College
 Gary L. Shaffer, James Madison University

Commission and Committee Chairpersons
 Conference, Marion L. Patterson, Coppin State College
 Program, June B. Ewing, Georgia Southwestern College
 Membership, Robin Alinkofsky, Long Island University
 Professional Affairs, Lawrence L. Smith, State University College at Buffalo
 Public Information, Nancy D. Padak, Kent State University
 Awards, J. Estill Alexander, University of Tennessee
 Media, Margaret A. Cagney, Glassboro State College
 Historian, James E. Walker, Texas Women's University
 Research, Leo Pauls, Emporia State University
 Elections, James R. Layton, Southwest Missouri State University
 Resolutions and Rules, Mary M. Brittain, Virginia Commonwealth University
 Publications, Richard T. Vacca, Kent State University
 Legislative and Social Issues, Howard I. Berrent, C.W. Post University

Division Chairpersons
 James R. King, Texas Woman's University, Teacher Education Division
 Marino C. Alvarez, Tennessee State University, College Reading Division

Monograph Series
 Madlyn Levine Hanes, University of South Carolina, Clinical Division
 Antonio Herrara, Grand Valley State College, Adult Learning Division

Reading Research and Instruction
 William E. Blanton, Co-Editor, Appalachian State University
 Karen D. Wood, Co-Editor, University of North Carolina at Charlotte

Monograph Series
>   Alan M. Frager, Editor, Miami University, Ohio

Newsletter—Reading News
>   William A. Henk, Co-Editor, Pennsylvania State University at Harrisburg
>   Robert J. Rickelman, Co-Editor, Millersville University

Publications Business Manager
>   Robert B. Cooter, Jr., Manager, Bowling Green State University Frederick
>   J. Fedorko, Photographer, East Stroudsburg University

1989-1990

President, June B. Ewing, Georgia Southwestern College
President-Elect, Lonnie D. McIntyre, University of Tennessee
Past-President, Jerry L. Johns, Northern Illinois University
Executive Secretary, Betty S. Heathington, University of Tennessee
Treasurer, Robert B. Cooter, Jr., Brigham Young University

Board of Directors
>   Victoria J. Risko, Vanderbilt University
>   Jane B. Mantanzo, American University
>   Patricia S. Koskinen, University of Maryland
>   Estelle Brown, Glassboro State College
>   Lance Gentile, University of Montana
>   Katherine Wiesendanger, Alfred University
>   James R. Layton, Southwestern Missouri State University
>   Audrey Williams, Bernard Baruch College
>   J. Estill Alexander, University of Tennessee

Commission and Committee Chairpersons
>   Conference, Marion L. Patterson, Morgan State University
>   Program, Lonnie D. McIntyre, University of Tennessee
>   Membership, Robin Alinkofsky, Long Island University
>   Professional Affairs, Lawrence L. Smith, Ball State University
>   Public Information, Nancy D. Padak, Kent State University
>   Awards, Jerry L. Johns, Northern Illinois University
>   Media, Margaret A. Cagney, Glassboro State College
>   Historian, James E. Walker, Clarion University
>   Photographer, Frederick J. Fedorko, East Stroudsburg University
>   Research, D. Ray Reutzel, Brigham Young University
>   Elections, J. Estill Alexander, University of Tennessee
>   Resolutions and Rules, Terry McEachern, Nipissing University College
>   Publications, Richard T. Vacca, Kent State University
>   Legislative and Social Issues, Barbara Fox, North Carolina State University

Division Chairpersons
>   Janet Miller, Northern Kentucky University, Teacher Education Division
>   Marino C. Alvarez, Tennessee State University, College Reading Division
>   Rose Anne Khaury, West Chester University, Clinicial Division
>   Antonio Herrara, Grand Valley State University, Adult Learning Division

Reading Research and Instruction
> William E. Blanton, Co-Editor, Appalachian State University
> Karen D. Wood, Co-Editor, University of North Carolina at Charlotte

Monograph Series
> Alan M. Frager, Editor, Miami University, Ohio

Newsletter—Reading News
> Susan Argyle, Co-Editor, Slippery Rock University
> Deborah Wells, Co-Editor, Slippery Rock University

Publications Business Manager
> Robert B. Cooter, Jr., Manager, Brigham Young University
> Frederick J. Fedorko, Photographer, East Stroudsburg University

Yearbook
> Nance. Padak, Co-Editor, Kent State University,
> Timothy V. Rasinski, Co-Editor, Kent State University and John Logan, Co-Editor, Community Consolidated School District 21, IL

1990-1991

President, Lonnie D. McIntyre. University of Tennessee
President-Elect, Norman A. Stahl, Northern Illinois University
Past-President, June B. Ewing, Georgia Southwestern College
Executive Secretary, Betty S. Heathington, University of Tennessee
Treasurer, E. Sutton Flynt, Pittsburg State University

Board of Directors
> Patricia S. Koskinen, University of Maryland
> Estelle J. Brown, Glassboro State College
> Lance M. Gentile, University of Montana
> Katherine D. Wiesendanger, Alfred University
> William A. Henk, Penn State University-Harrisburg
> Marino C. Alvarez, Tennessee State University
> J. Estill Alexander, University of Tennessee
> Margaret A. Cagney, Glassboro State College
> Jerry L. Johns, Northern Illinois University

Committees and Commissions
> Conference, Marion L. Patterson, Morgan State University
> Program, Norman A. Stahl, Northern Illinois University
> Membership, Robin Alinkofsky, Long Island University
> Professional Affairs, Lawrence L. Smith, Ball State University
> Public Information, Nancy D. Padak, Kent State University
> Awards, June B. Ewing, Georgia Southwestern College
> Media, Maria Valeri-Gold, Georgia State University
> Historian, James E. Walker, Clarion University
> Photographer, Frederick J. Fredorko, East Stroudsburg University
> Research, D. Ray Reutzel, Brigham Young University
> Elections, Jerry L. Johns, Northern Illinois University
> Resolutions and Rules, Terry McEachern, Nipissing University College
> Publications, J. Estill Alexander, University of Tennessee
> Legislative and Social Issues, Barbara Fox, North Carolina State University

Division Chairpersons
> Teacher Education, Janet Miller, Northern Kentucky University
> College Reading, Michele Simpson, University of Georgia
> Clinical, Rose Ann Khaury, West Chester University
> Adult Learning, Linda Thistlethwaite, Western Illinois University

Reading Research and Instruction
> William E. Blanton, Co-Editor, Appalachian State University
> Karen D. Wood, Co-Editor, University of North Carolina at Charlotte

The Reading News
> Susan Argyle, Co-Editor, Deborah Wells (Co-Editor), Slippery Rock University

Monograph Series
> Alan D. Frager, Editor, Miami University, Ohio

Yearbook
> Nancy D. Padak, Co-Editor, Kent State University
> Timothy V. Rasinski, Co-Editor, Kent State University
> John Logan, Co-Editor, Community Consolidated School District 21, IL

1991-1992

President, Norman A. Stahl, Northern Illinois University
President-Elect, Victoria J. Risko, Vanderbilt University
Past-President, Lonnie D. McIntyre, University of Tennessee
Executive Secretary, Betty S. Heathington, University of Tennessee
Treasurer, E. Sutton Flynt, Pittsburgh State University

Board of Directors
> Lance Gentile, San Francisco State University
> Katherine Wiesendanger, Alfred University
> William A. Henk, Penn State University-Harrisburg
> Marino Alvarez, Tennessee State University
> Alan D. Frager, Miami University (Ohio)
> Judy Richardson, Virginia Commonwealth University
> Jerry L. Johns, Northern Illinois University
> June B. Ewing, Georgia Southwestern College

Committees and Commissions
> Conference, Marion L. Patterson, Morgan State University
> Program, Victoria J. Risko, Vanderbilt University
> Membership, Donna Mealey, Louisiana State University and Bonnie Higginson, Murray State University
> Professional Affairs, Sherrie Nist, University of Georgia and Michael Martin, Eastern Michigan University
> Public Information, Frederick J. Fedorko, East Stroudsburg University and Jeanne Schumm, University of Miami (FL)
> Awards, Lonnie D. McIntyre, University of Tennessee
> Media, Maria Valeri-Gold, Georgia State University
> Historian, James E. Walker, Clarion University
> Photographer, Frederick J. Fedorko, East Stroudsburg
> Research, D. Ray Reutzel, Brigham Young University
> Elections, June B. Ewing, Georgia Southwestern College

Resolutions and Rules, Terry McEdchern, Nipissing University College
Publications, J. Estill Alexander, University of Tennessee
Legislative and Social Issues, Barbara Fox, North Carolina State University

Division Chairpersons
Teacher Education, Robert J. Rickelman, University of North Carolina at Charlotte
College Reading, Michele Simpson, University of Georgia
Clinical, Rose Ann Khoury, West Chester University
Adult Learning, Linda Thistlethwaite, Western Illinois University

Reading Research and Instruction
William E. Blanton, Co-Editor, Appalachian State University
Karen D. Wood, Co-Editor, University of North Carolina at Charlotte

The Reading News
Susan Argyle, Co-Editor, Deborah Wells (Co-Editor) Slippery Rock

University Monographs
Alan D. Frager, Editor, Miami University, Ohio

Yearbook
Nancy D. Padak, Co-Editor, Kent State University
Timothy V. Rasinski, Co-Editor, Kent State University
John Logan, Co-Editor, Community Consolidated School District 21, IL

1992-1993
President, Victoria J. Risko, Vanderbilt University
President-Elect, Patricia Koskinen, University of Maryland
Past-President, Norman A. Stahl, Northern Illinois University
Executive Secretary, Linda Thistlethwaite, Western Illinois University
Treasurer, E. Sutton Flynt, Pittsburg State University

Board of Directors
William A. Henk, Penn State University-Harrisburg
Marino C. Alvarez, Tennessee State University
Judy Richardson, Virginia Commonwealth University
Alan D. Frager, Miami University (Ohio)
Timothy V. Rasinski, Kent State University
Karen M. Bromley, SUNY-Binghamton
June B. Ewing, Georgia Southwestern College
Lonnie D. McIntyre, University of Tennessee

Committees and Commissions
Conference, Marion L. Patterson, Morgan State University
Program, Patricia S. Koskinen, University of Maryland
Membership, Donna Mealey, Louisiana State University and Bonnie Higginson, Murray State University
Professional Affairs, Sherrie Nist, University of Geotgia and Michael Martin, Eastern Michigan University
Public Information, Federick J. Fedorko, East Stroudsburg and Jeanne Schumm, University of Miami (FL)
Awards, Norman A. Stahl, Northern Illinois University

Media, Maria Valeri-Gold, Georgia State University
Historian, Albert J. Mazurkiewicz, Kean College of New Jersey and Janet Miller, Northern Kentucky University
Photographer, Federick Fedorko, East Stroudsburg University
Research, Naomi Feldman, Baldwin-Wallace College and Jon Shapiro, The University of British Columbia
Elections, Lonnie D. McIntyre, University of Tennessee
Resolutions and Rules, Joan Elliott and Gary L. Shaffer, James Madison University
Publications, J. Estill Alexander, University of Tennessee
Legislative and Social Issues, Barbara Fox, North Carolina State University

Division Chairpersons
Teacher Education Division, Robert J. Rickelman, University of North Carolina at Charlotte
College Reading Division, Cathie Kellogg Anderson, Mercyhurst College
Clinical Division, Rose Ann Khoury, West Chester University
Adult Learning Division, Gerald Parker, Appalachian State University

Reading Research and Instruction
Robert B. Cooter, Jr., Editor, Texas Christian University

The Reading News
Ellen Jampole, Co-Editor, Deborah Wells, Co-Editor, Slippery Rock University

CRA Monographs
Martha Collins, Co-Editor and Barbara Moss, Co-Editor, University of Akron

CRA Yearbook
Nancy D. Padak, Co-Editor, Kent State University,
Timothy J. Rasinski, Co-Editor, Kent State University
John Logan, Co-Editor, Community Consolidated School District 21, IL

1993-1994
President, Patricia S. Koskinen, University of Maryland
President-Elect, Betty S. Heathington, University of Tennessee
Past-President, Victoria J. Risko, Vanderbilt University
Executive Secretary, Linda Thistlethwaite, Western Illinois University
Treasurer, E. Sutton Flynt, Pittsburg State University

Board of Directors
James King, University of South Florida
Barbara Walker, Eastern Montana College
Judy Richardson, Virginia Commonwealth University
Alan D. Frager, Miami University (Ohio)
Timothy V. Rasinski, Kent State University
Karen M. Bromley, SUNY-Binghamton
Lonnie D. McIntyre, University of Tennessee
Norman A. Stahl, Northern Illinois University
Jane B. Matanzo

Committees and Commissions
Conference, Maria Valeri-Gold, Georgia State University
Program, Betty S. Heathington, University of Tennessee

Membership, Donna Mealey Pierce, Louisiana State University, and Bonnie Higginson, Murray State University

Professional Affairs, Sherrie Nist, University of Georgia, and Michael Martin, Eastern Michigan University

Public Information, Frederick J. Fedorko, East Stroudsburg University and Jeanne Schumm, University of Miami (FL)

Awards, Victoria J. Risko, Vanderbilt University

Media, Barbara Martin Palmer, Mount Saint Mary's College and Marion Patterson, Morgan State University

Historian, Albert J. Mazurkiewicz, Kean College of New Jersey and Janet Miller, Northern Kentucky University

Photographer, Frederick J. Fedorko, East Stroudsburg

Research, Naomi Feldman and Jon Shapiro, The University of British Columbia

Elections, Norman A. Stahl, Northern Illinois University

Resolutions and Rules, Joan Elliott and Gary L Shaffer, James Madison University

Publications, William A. Henk, Penn State University-Harrisburg

Legislative and Social Issues, Barbara Fox, North Carolina State University

Division Chairpersons

Teacher Education, Mary M. Brittain, Virginia Commonwealth University

College Reading, Cathie Kellogg Anderson, Mercyhurst College

Clinical, Katherine Wiesendanger, Alfred University

Adult Learning, Nancy Boraks, Virginia Commonwealth University

Reading, Research and Instruction

Robert B. Cooter, Jr., Editor, Texas Christian University

The Reading News

Ellen Jampole, Co-Editor and Deborah Wells, Co-Editor, Slippery Rock University

CRA Monographs

Martha D. Collins, Co-Editor

Barbara Moss, Co-Editor, University of Akron

CRA Yearbook

Elizabeth G. Sturtevant, Co-Editor, Marymount University

Wayne M. Linek, Co-Editor, East Texas State University

1994-1995

President, Betty S. Heathington, University of Tennessee
President-Elect, Judy Richardson, Virginia Commonwealth University
Past-President, Patricia S. Koskinen, University of Maryland
Executive Secretary, Linda Thistlethwaite, Western Illinois University
Treasurer, E. Sutton Flynt, Pittsburg State University

Board of Directors

James King, University of South Florida

Barbara Walker, Eastern Montana College

Judy Richardson, Virginia Commonwealth University

Michele Simpson, University of Georgia

Timothy V. Rasinski, Kent State University

Karen M. Bromley, SUNY-Binghamton

Victoria J. Risko, Peabody College of Vanderbilt

Jack Cassidy, Millersville State University
Norman A. Stahl, Northern Illinois University
D. Ray Reuztel, Brigham Young University
Barbara Walker, Eastern Montana College

Committees and Commissions

Conference, Maria Valeri-Gold, Georgia State University
Program, Judy S. Richardson, Virginia Commonwealth University
Membership, Robin Erwin, Jr., Niagara University and Gail Gayeski, Wilkes University
Professional Affairs, Gwendolyn Turner, University of Missouri, St. Louis
Public Information, Jane B. Matanzo, Florida Atlantic University
Awards, Patricia Koskinen, University of Maryland
Media, Barbara Palmer, Mount St. Mary's College and Marion Patterson, Morgan State University
Historian, Albert J. Mazurkiewicz, Kean College of New Jersey and Janet Miller, Northern Kentucky University
Photographer, Frederick J. Fedorko, East Stroudsburg University
Research, Naomi Feldman and Jon Shapiro, The University of British Columbia
Elections, Victoria J. Risko, Vanderbilt University
Resolutions and Rules, Joan Elliott and Gary L. Shaffer, James Madison University
Publications, William A. Henk, Penn State University-Harrisburg
Legislative and Social Issues, Barbara Fox, North Carolina State University

Division Chairpersons

Teacher Education, Mary M. Brittain, Virginia Commonwealth University
College Reading, Jeannie Shay Schumm, University of Miami
Clinical, Katherine Wiesendanger, Alfred University
Adult Learning, Nancy Boraks, Virginia Commonwealth University

Reading Research and Instruction

Robert B. Cooter, Jr., Editor, Texas Christian University

The Reading News

Ellen Jampole, Co-Editor and Deborah Wells, Co-Editor, Slippery Rock University

CRA Monographs

Martha D. Collins, Co-Editor, and Barbara Moss, Co-Editor, University of Akron

CRA Yearbook

Elizabeth G. Sturtevant, Co-Editor, Marymount University
Wayne M. Linek, Co-Editor, East Texas State University

1995-1996

President, Judy Richardson, Virginia Commonwealth University
President-Elect, Marino C. Alvarez, Tennessee State University
Past-President, Betty S. Heathington, University of Tennessee
Executive Secretary, Linda Thistlethwaite, Western Illinois University
Treasurer, Gary L. Shaffer, James Madison University

Board of Directors
> James King, University of South Florida
> Barbara Walker, Eastern Montana College
> Nancy D. Padak, Kent State University
> Robert B. Cooter, Jr., Austin Peay State University
> Jon Shapiro, The University of British Colombia
> Jack Cassidy, Millersville University
> D. Ray Reutzel, Brigham Young University
> Victoria J. Risko, Vanderbilt University
> Patricia S. Koskinen, University of Maryland

Committees and Commissions
> Conference, Maria Valeri-Gold, Georgia State University
> Program, Marino C. Alvarez, Tennessee State University
> Membership, Robin Erwin, Jr., Niagara University, and Susan Davis Lenski, Illinois State University
> Professional Affairs, Gwendolyn Turner, University of Missouri, St. Louis
> Public Information, Jane B. Matanzo, Florida Atlantic University
> Awards, Patricia S. Koskinen, University of Maryland
> Media, Barbara Martin Palmer, Mount Saint Mary's College, and Marion Patterson, Morgan State University
> Historians, J. Estill Alexander, University of Tennessee and Susan Strode, Jefferson City, MO
> Photographer, Frederick J. Fedorko, East Stroudsburg University
> Research, Evangeline Newton, John Carol University and Steven Rinehart, West Virginia University
> Elections, Patricia S. Koskinen, University of Maryland
> Resolutions and Rules, Patricia Linder, Texas A&M-Commerce
> Publications, William A. Henk, Penn State University-Harrisburg
> Legislative and Social Issues, Sherry Kragler, Ball State University

Division Chairpersons
> Teacher Education, Arthur E. Smith, SUNY-Brockport
> College Reading, Jeanne Shay Schumm, University of Miami
> Clinical, Diane Allen, University of North Texas
> Adult Learning, Nancy Boraks, Virginia Commonwealth University

Reading, Research and Instruction
> Robert B. Cooter, Jr., Editor, Austin Peay State University

The Reading News
> Ellen Jampole, Co-Editor and Deborah Wells, Co-Editor, Slippery Rock University

CRA Monographs
> Barbara Martin Palmer, Editor, Mount St. Mary's College

CRA Yearbook
> Elizabeth G. Sturtevant, Co-Editor, George Mason University
> Wayne M. Linek, Co-Editor, Texas A&M University-Commerce

1996-1997

President, Marino C. Alvarez, Tennessee State University
President-Elect & Programs Chair, Timothy V. Rasinski, Kent State University
Past President & Awards Chair, Judy Richardson, Virginia Commonwealth University
Second Past President, Betty S. Heathington, University of Tennessee
Executive Secretary, Ora Sterling King, Coppin State College
Treasurer, Gary L. Shaffer, University of Wisconsin-Platteville

Board of Directors
Gwendolyn Turner, University of Missouri, St. Louis
Nancy D. Padak, Kent State University
Jon Shapiro, The University of British Columbia
Jack Cassidy, Millersville University
D. Ray Reutzel, Brigham Young University
Victoria J. Risko, Vanderbilt University
Patricia S. Koskinen, University of Maryland
Robert J. Rickleman, University of North Carolina, Charlotte
Alan Frager, Miami University, Ohio
Patricia S. Koshinen, University of Maryland

Committees and Commissions
Conferences, Maria Valeri-Gold, Georgia State University
Membership, Robin Erwin, Jr., Niagara State University and Susan Davis Lenski, Illinois State University
Professional Affairs, Gwendolyn Turner, University of Missouri-St. Louis
Public Information, Jane B. Matanzo, Florida Atlantic University
Media, Nancy Bertrand, Middle Tennessee State University and John Bertrand, Tennessee State University
Historians, J. Estill Alexander, University of Tennessee and Susan Strode, Jefferson City, MO
Photographer Frederick J. Fedorco, East Stroudsburg University
Research, Evangeline Newton, University of Akron and Steven Rinehart, West Virginia University
Elections, Betty S. Heathington, University of Tennessee
Resolutions and Rules, Patricia Linder, Texas A&M University-Commerce
Publications, Michael McKenna, Georgia Southern University
Legislative and Social Issues, Sherry Kragler, Ball State University
Ad Hoc Technology, Carolyn Andrews-Beck, Miami University
Program, Timothy V. Rasinski, Kent State University
Legislative and Social Issues, Sherry Kragler, Ball State University

Division Chairpersons
Teacher Education, Arthur E. Smith, SUNY-Brockport
College Reading, Cathy Leist, University of Louisville
Clinical, Diane Allen, University of North Texas
Adult Learning, Laurie Elish-Piper, Northern Illinois University

Reading Research and Instruction
D. Ray Reutzel, Editor, Brigham Young University

The Reading News
Ellen Jampole, Editor, SUNY-Cortland

CRA Monographs
>Barbara Martin Palmer, Editor, Mount St. Mary's College

CRA Yearbook
>Wayne M. Linek, Co-Editor, Texas A&M University-Commerce
>Elizabeth G. Sturtevant, Co-Editor, George Mason University

1997-1998

President, Timothy V. Rasinski, Kent State University
President-Elect, Nancy D. Padak, Kent State University
Past President, Marino C. Alvarez, Tennessee State University
Executive Secretary, Ora Sterling King, Coppin State College
Treasurer, Gary L. Shaffer. University of Wisconsin-Platteville

Board of Directors
>Donna Alvermann, University of Georgia
>Jon Shapiro, The University of British Columbia
>Wayne M. Linek, Texas A&M University-Commerce
>Robert J. Rickelman, University of North Carolina at Charlotte
>Patricia Skoskinen, University of Maryland
>Gwendolyn Turner, University of Missouri-St. Louis
>Alan D. Frager, Miami University, Ohio
>Betty S. Heathington, University of Tennessee
>Judy Richardson, Virginia Commonwealth University

Committees and Commission Chairpersons
>Conference, MariaValeri-Gold, Georgia State University
>Program, Nancy D. Padak, Kent State University
>Membership, Robin Erwin, Jr., Niagara State University and Susan Davis Lenski, Illinois State University
>Professional Affairs, Gwendolyn Turner, University of Missouri-St. Louis
>Public Information, Jane B. Matanzo, Florida Atlantic University
>Awards, Marino C. Alvarez, Tennessee State University
>Media, Nancy Bertrand, Middle Tennessee State University and John Bertrand, Tennessee State University
>Historian, J. Estill Alexander, University of Tennessee and Susan Strode, Jefferson City, MO
>Photographer, Frederick J. Fedorko, East Stroudsburg University
>Research, Evangeline Newton, University of Akron and Steven Rinehart, West Virginia University
>Elections, Judy Richardson, Virginia Commonwealth University
>Resolutions and Rules, Patricia Linder, Texas A&M University-Commerce
>Publications, Michael McKenna, Georgia Southern University
>Legislative and Social Issues, Sherry Kragler, Ball State University
>Technology, Marino C. Alvarez, Tennessee State University

Division Chairpersons
>Teacher Education, Joan Elliott, James Madison University
>College Reading, Cathy Leist, University of Louisville
>Clinical, Madlyn L. Hanes, University of South Carolina, Clinical Division
>Adult Learning, Laurie Elish-Piper, Northern Illinois University

Reading Research and Instruction
>D. Ray Reutzel, Editor, Brigham Young University

The Reading News
Ellen Jampole, Editor, SUNY-Cortland

CRA Monograph
Barbara Martin Palmer, Editor, Mount St. Mary's College

CRA Yearbook
Elizabeth G. Sturtevant, Co-Editor, George Mason University
Wayne M. Linek, Co-Editor, Texas A&M University-Commerce
JoAnn Dugan, Co-Editor, Clarion University of Pennsylvania
Patricia Linder,Co-Editor, Texas A&M University-Commerce

1998-1999

President, Nancy D. Padak, Kent State University
President-Elect, Jack Cassidy, Texas A&M University-Corpus Christi
Past President, Timothy V. Rasinski, Kent State University
Executive Secretary, Ora Sterling King, Coppin State College
Treasurer/Business Manager, Gary L. Shaffer, State University of West Georgia

Board of Directors
Donna Alvermann, University of Georgia
Elizabeth G. Sturtevant, George Mason University
Wayne M. Linek, Texas A&M University-Commerce
Robert Rickelman, University of North Carolina-Charlotte
Gwendolyn Turner, University of Missouri-St. Louis
Alan Frager, Miami University, Ohio
Barbara J. Walker, Oklahoma State University
Maria Valeri-Gold, Georgia State University
Marino C. Alvarez, Tennessee State University
Judy Richardson, Virginia Commonwealth University

Division Chairpersons
Teacher Education, Joan Elliot, Indiana University of Pennsylvania
College Reading, Phyllis Kremen, Middlesex Community College
Clinical, Madlyn L. Hanes, Penn State University-Great Valley
Adult Learning, Sarah Nixon-Ponder, Southwest Missouri State University

Committees and Commissions
Conference Coordinator, Maria Valeri-Gold, Georgia State University
Program, Jack Cassidy, Texas A&M University-Corpus Christi
Membership, Peggy Daisey, Eastern Michigan University; Cindy Gillespie, Bowl-
ing Green State University
Professional Affairs, Michael Martin, University of Southern Mississippi
Public Information, Jane Brady Matanzo, Florida Atlantic University
Awards, Timothy V. Rasinski, Kent State University
Media, Nancy Bertrand, Middle Tennessee State University; John Bertrand, Ten-
nessee State University
Historian, J. Estill Alexander, University of Tennessee
Photographer, Frederick J. Fedorko, East Stroudsburg University
Research, Evangeline Newton, University of Akron; Jacqueline Peck, The Cleve-
land State University
Elections, Marino C. Alvarez, Tennessee State University
Resolutions and Rules, William Dee Nichols, University of North Carolina-
Charlotte; John Helfeldt, University of Arkansas

Publications, Michael McKenna, Georgia Southern University
Legislative and Social Issues, Betty Goerss, Indiana University-East Richmond

Reading Research and Instruction
Sam Miller, University of North Carolina-Greensboro
Robert Rickelman, University of North Carolina-Charlotte
Ernest Dishner, Penn State University-Harrisburg
William Henk, Penn State University-Harrisburg

The Reading News
Ellen Jampole, State University of New York-Cortland

CRA Monographs
Barbara Martin Palmer, Mount St. Mary's College

CRA Yearbook
JoAnn R. Dugan, Clarion University of Pennsylvania
Elizabeth Sturtevant, George Mason University
Wayne M. Linek, Texas A&M University-Commerce
Patricia E. Linder, Texas A&M University-Commerce

1999-2000

President, Jack Cassidy, Texas A&M University, Corpus Christi
President-Elect, Maria Valeri-Gold, Georgia State University
Past President, Nancy D. Padak, Kent State University
Executive Secretary, Linda L. Thistlethwaite, Western Illinois University
Treasurer/Business Manager, John E. Bertrand, Tennessee State University

Board of Directors
Donna Alvermann, University of Georgia
Wayne M. Linek, Texas A&M University-Commerce
Elizabeth G. Sturtevant, George Mason University
Maria Valeri-Gold, Georgia State University
Karen Bromley, State University of New York-Binghamton
Michael McKenna, Georgia Southern University
Jon Shapiro, University of British Columbia
Marino C. Alvarez, Tennessee State University
Timothy V. Rasinski, Kent State University

Division Chairpersons
Teacher Education, Bonnie Higginson, Murray State University
College Reading, Maryann Errico, Georgia Perimeter College
Clinical, H. Jon Jones, Western Illinois University
Adult Learning, Sarah Nixon-Ponder, Southwest Missouri State University

Committee and Commissions
Conference Coordinator, Katharine D. Wiesendanger, Alfred University
Program, Maria Valeri-Gold, Georgia State University
Elections, Timothy V. Rasinski, Kent State University
Awards, Nancy D. Padak, Kent State University
Research, Evangeline V. Newton, University of Akron; Jacqueline Peck, The Cleveland
State University
Publications, Michael McKenna, Georgia Southern University
Membership, Peggy Daisey, Eastern Michigan University; Cindy Gillespie, Bowling
Green State University
Professional Affairs, Michael A. Martin, University of Southern Mississippi

Public Information, Jane Brady Matanzo, Florida Atlantic University; Marie F. Holbein, Florida Atlantic University

Media, Nancy Bertrand, Middle Tennessee State University; John Bertrand, Tennessee State University

Historian, J. Estill Alexander, University of Tennessee

Photographer, Frederick J. Fedorko, East Stroudsburg University

Resolutions and Rules, William Dee Nichols, University of North Carolina-Charlotte; John Helfeldt, University of Arkansas

Legislative and Social Issues, Betty Goerss, Indiana University-East Richmond; Carolyn Ann Walker, Ball State University

Reading Research and Instruction,

Sam Miller, University of North Carolina-Greensboro
Robert Rickelman, University of North Carolina-Charlotte
Ernest Dishner, Penn State University-Harrisburg
William Henk, Penn State University-Harrisburg

The Reading News

Ellen Jampole, State University of New York-Cortland

CRA Yearbook

Patricia E. Linder, Texas A&M University-Commerce
Wayne M. Linek, Texas A&M University-Commerce
Elizabeth G. Sturtevant, George Mason University
JoAnn R. Dugan, Clarion University of Pennsylvania

2000-2001

President, Maria Valeri-Gold, Georgia State University
President-Elect, Jane Brady Matanzo, Florida Atlantic University
Past President, Jack Cassidy, Texas A&M University, Corpus Christi
Executive Secretary, Linda L. Thistlethwaite, Western Illinois University
Treasurer/Business Manager, John E. Bertrand, Tennessee State University

Board of Directors

Elizabeth G. Sturtevant, George Mason University
Maria Valeri-Gold, Georgia State University
Karen Bromley, State University of New York-Binghamton
Michael McKenna, Georgia Southern University
Laurie Elish-Piper, Northern Illinois University
Joan Elliot, Indiana University of Pennsylvania
John Helfeldt, Texas A&M University
Timothy V. Rasinski, Kent State University
Nancy D. Padak, Kent State University

Division Chairpersons

Teacher Education, Bonnie Higginson, Murray State University
College Reading, Linda Saumell, University of Miami
Clinical, H. Jon Jones, Western Illinois University
Adult Learning, Bryan Bardine, Kent State University

Committee and Commissions

Conference Coordinator, Katherine D. Wiesendanger, Alfred University
Program, Jane Brady Matanzo, Florida Atlantic University
Membership, Angela Ferree, Western Illinois University

Professional Affairs, Richard Harlan, Piedmont College

Public Information, Marie F. Holbein, State University of West Georgia; Donna Harkins, State University of West Georgia

Awards, Jack Cassidy, Texas A&M University, Corpus Christi

Media, Nancy Bertrand, Middle Tennessee State University; John Bertrand, Tennessee State University

Historians, Gary Shaffer, Middle Tennessee State University, the late J. Estill Alexander, Emeritus University of Tennessee

Photographer, Frederick J. Fedorko, East Stroudsburg University

Research, Evangeline Newton, University of Akron; Jacqueline Peck, Kent State University

Elections, Nancy D. Padak, Kent State University

Resolutions and Rules, William Dee Nichols, Virginia Polytechnic Institute and State University; John Helfeldt, Texas A&M University

Publications, Michael McKenna, Georgia Southern University

Legislative and Social Issues, Betty Goerss, Indiana University-East Richmond; Carolyn Ann Walker, Ball State University

Technology, Marino C. Alvarez, Tennessee State University

Reading Research and Instruction

Sam Miller, University of North Carolina-Greensboro

Robert Rickelman, University of North Carolina-Charlotte

Ernest Dishner, Penn State University-Harrisburg

William Henk, Penn State University-Harrisburg

The Reading News

Ellen Jampole, State University of New York-Cortland

CRA Yearbook

Wayne M. Linek, Texas A&M University-Commerce

Elizabeth G. Sturtevant, George Mason University

JoAnn R. Dugan, Clarion University of Pennsylvania

Patricia E. Linder, Texas A&M University-Commerce

2001-2002

President, Jane Brady Matanzo, Florida Atlantic University

President-Elect, Robert J. Rickelman, University of North Carolina-Charlotte

Past President, Maria Valeri-Gold, Georgia State University

Executive Secretary, Linda Thistlethwaite, Western Illinois University

Treasurer/Business Manager, John E. Bertrand, Middle Tennessee State University

Board of Directors

Karen Bromley, Binghamton University, SUNY

Michael McKenna, Georgia Southern University

Laurie Elish-Piper, Northern Illinois University

Joan Elliott, Indiana University of Pennsylvania

Caryn King, Grand Valley State University

Lillian Putnam, Kean College (Emerita)

Ellen Jampole, State University of New York-Cortland

Nancy D. Padak, Kent State University

Jack Cassidy, Texas A&M University-Corpus Christi

Division Chairpersons

Teacher Education, Mona Matthews, Georgia State University

College Reading, Linda Saumell, University of Miami
Clinical, Connie Briggs, Emporia State University
Adult Learning, Bryan Bardine, University of Dayton

Committee and Commissions
Conference Coordinator, Barbara J. Reinken, Grand Valley State University
Program, Robert J. Rickelman, University of North Carolina-Charlotte
Reading Room, Karen Bromley, Binghamton University-SUNY; Linda Rogers, East Stroudsburg University
Exhibits, Naomi Feldman, Balwin-Wallace College; Lisa Henderson, Balwin-Wallace College
Elections, Jack Cassidy, Texas A&M University-Corpus Christi
Awards, Maria Valeri-Gold, Georgia State University
Research, Wayne M. Linek, Texas A&M University-Commerce; Evangeline Newton, University of Akron; Jacqueline Peck, Kent State University
Publications, Michael McKenna, Georgia Southern University
Membership, Angela Ferree, Western Illinois University
Public Information, Marie F. Holbein, State University of West Georgia; Donna Harkins, State University of West Georgia
Media, Nancy Bertrand, Middle Tennessee State University; Nancy Anderson, University of South Florida
Historian, Gary Shaffer, Middle Tennessee State University
Photographer, Frederick J. Fedorko, East Stroudsburg University
Professional Affairs, Richard Harlan, Piedmont College
Resolutions and Rules, William Dee Nichols, Virginia Tech; John Helfeldt, Texas A&M University
Legislative and Social Issues, Barbara Fox, North Carolina State University
Technology, Marino C. Alvarez, Tennessee State University

Reading Research and Instruction
Sam Miller, University of North Carolina-Greensboro
Robert Rickelman, University of North Carolina-Charlotte
Ernest Dishner, Penn State University-Harrisburg
William Henk, Penn State University-Harrisburg

The Reading News
Ellen Jampole, State University of New York-Cortland

Literacy Cases Online
Barbara J. Walker, Oklahoma State University
Sandra Goetze, Oklahoma State University

CRA Yearbook
Patricia E. Linder, Texas A&M University-Commerce
Mary Beth Sampson, Texas A&M University-Commerce
JoAnn R. Dugan, Clarion University of Pennsylvania
Barrie Brancato, Clarion University of Pennsylvania

2002-2003
President, Robert J. Rickelman, University of North Carolina-Charlotte
President-Elect, Wayne M. Linek, Texas A&M University-Commerce
Vice President, Jon Shapiro, University of British Columbia
Past President, Jane Brady Matanzo, Florida Atlantic University
Executive Secretary, Joan Elliot, Indiana University of Pennsylvania
Treasurer/Business Manager, John A. Smith, Utah State University

Board of Directors
   D. Ray Reutzel, Utah State University
   Gary Shaffer, Middle Tennessee State University
   Laurie Elish-Piper, Northern Illinois University
   Joanne Kilgour Dowdy, Kent State University
   Caryn King, Grand Valley State University
   Maria Valeri-Gold, Georgia State University
   Jacqueline Peck, Kent State University
   Frederick J. Fedorko, East Stroudsburg University (Emeritus)
   Lillian Putnam, Kean College (Emerita)

Division Chairpersons
   Teacher Education, Mona Matthews, Georgia State University
   College Reading, Linda Saumell, University of Miami
   Clinical, Connie Briggs, Emporia State University
   Adult Learning, Patricia E. Linder, Texas A&M University-Commerce

Committee and Commissions
      Conference Coordinator, Barbara J. Reinken, Grand Valley State University
      Program, Wayne M. Linek, Texas A&M University-Commerce
      Exhibits, Naomi Feldman, Balwin-Wallace College; Lisa Henderson, Balwin-Wallace
         College
      Elections, Maria Valeri-Gold, Georgia State University
      Awards, Jane Brady Matanzo, Florida Atlantic University
      Research, Julie K. Kidd, George Mason University; Charlene E. Fleener, Old Do-
         minion University
      Publications, Timothy G. Morrison, Brigham Young University
      Membership, Angela Ferree, Western Illinois University; Linda Thistlethwaite,
         Western Illinois University
      Public Information, Marie F. Holbein, State University of West Georgia; Donna
         Harkins, State University of West Georgia
      Media, Patricia Douville, University of North Carolina-Charlotte
      Historian, Gary L. Shaffer, Middle Tennessee State University
      Photographer, Frederick J. Fedorko, East Stroudsburg University (Emeritus)
      Resolutions and Rules, William Dee Nichols, Virginia Tech; John Helfeldt, Texas
         A&M University
      Legislative and Social Issues, Barbara J. Fox, North Carolina State University
      Technology, Marino C. Alvarez, Tennessee State University

Reading Research and Instruction
   Dianne D. Allen, University of North Texas
   Alexandra G. Leavell, University of North Texas
   Janelle B. Mathis, University of North Texas
   Kathleen A. J. Mohr, University of North Texas

The Reading News
   Ellen Jampole, State University of New York-Cortland

Literacy Cases Online
   Barbara J. Walker, Oklahoma State University
   Sandra Goetze, Oklahoma State University

CRA Yearbook
   Mary Beth Sampson, Texas A& M University-Commerce
   Patricia E. Linder, Texas A&M University-Commerce
   JoAnn R. Dugan, Ohio University
   Barrie Brancato, Clarion University of Pennsylvania

2003-2004

President, Wayne M. Linek, Texas A&M University-Commerce
President-Elect, Jon Shapiro, University of British Columbia
Vice President, Karen M. Bromley, Binghamton University, SUNY
Past President, Robert J. Rickelman, University of North Carolina-Charlotte
Executive Secretary, Joan Elliot, Indiana University of Pennsylvania (Emerita)
Treasurer/Business Manager, John A. Smith, Utah State University

Board of Directors
   D. Ray Reutzel, Utah State University
   Bonnie Higginson, Murray State University
   Caryn King, Grand Valley State University
   Jacqueline Peck, Kent State University
   Frederick J. Fedorko, East Stroudsburg University (Emeritus)
   Elizabeth G. Sturtevant, George Mason University
   Jane Brady Matanzo, Florida Atlantic University
   Lillian Putnam, Kean College (Emerita)

Division Chairpersons
   Teacher Education, Mary Beth Sampson, Texas A&M University-Commerce
   College Reading, Donna Marie Colonna, Sandhills Community College
   Clinical, Jeanne Cobb, Eastern New Mexico University
   Adult Learning, Patricia E. Linder, Texas A&M University-Commerce

Committee and Commissions
      Conference Coordinator, Barbara Reinken, Grand Valley State University
      Program, Jon Shapiro, University of British Columbia
      Reading Room, Linda K. Rogers, East Stroudsburg University; Allison Swan Dagen, West Virginia University
      Exhibits, Naomi Feldman, Balwin Wallace College; Lisa Henderson, Balwin Wallace College
      Elections, Jane Brady Matanzo, Florida Atlantic University
      Awards, Robert J. Rickelman, University of North Carolina-Charlotte
      Research, Julie K. Kidd, George Mason University; Charlene E. Fleener, Old Dominion University
      Publications, Timothy G. Morrison, Brigham Young University
      Membership, Angela Ferree, Western Illinois University; Doris Walker-Dalhouse, Minnesota State University-Moorhead
      Public Information, Marie F. Holbein, State University of West Georgia; Parker Fawson, Utah State University; Donna Harkins, State University of West Georgia
      Media, Patricia Douville, University of North Carolina at Charlotte
      Historian, Gary L. Shaffer, Middle Tennessee State University
      Photographer, Frederick J. Fedorko, East Stroudsburg University (Emeritus)
      Resolutions and Rules, William Dee Nichols, Virginia Tech University; John Helfeldt, Texas A&M University
      Legislative and Social Issues, Barbara J. Fox, North Carolina State University
      Professional Affairs, Maryann Mraz, University of North Carolina-Charlotte; Jill Mizell Reddish, State University of West Georgia
      Technology, Marino C. Alvarez, Tennessee State University

Reading Research and Instruction
   Dianne D. Allen, University of North Texas
   Alexandra G. Leavell, University of North Texas

Janelle B. Mathis, University of North Texas
Kathleen A. J. Mohr, University of North Texas

The Reading News
Ellen Jampole, State University of New York-Cortland

Literacy Cases Online
Barbara J. Walker, Oklahoma State University
Sandra Goetze, Oklahoma State University

CRA Yearbook
Mary Beth Sampson, Texas A&M University-Commerce
Patricia E. Linder, Texas A&M University-Commerce
JoAnn R. Dugan, Ohio University
Barrie Brancato, Clarion University

2004-2005

President, Jon Shapiro, University of British Columbia
President-Elect, Karen Bromley, Binghamton University, SUNY
Vice President, Ellen Jampole, State University of New York-Cortland
Past President, Wayne M. Linek, Texas A&M University-Commerce
Executive Secretary, Joan Elliot, Indiana University of Pennsylvania (Emerita)
Treasurer/Business Manager, John A. Smith, Utah State University

Board of Directors
Jacqueline Peck, Kent State University
Frederick J. Fedorko, East Stroudsburg University (Emeritus)
Bonnie Higginson, Murray State University
Michael Martin, Eastern Kentucky University
Connie Briggs, Emporia State University
Mary Roe, Washington State University
William Dee Nichols, Virginia Tech University
Robert J. Rickelman, University of North Carolina-Charlotte

Division Chairpersons
Teacher Education, Mary Beth Sampson, Texas A&M University-Commerce
College Reading, Donna Marie Colonna, Sandhills Community College
Clinical, Jeanne Cobb, Eastern New Mexico University
Adult Learning, Gary Padak, Kent State University

Committee and Commissions
Conference Coordinator, Barbara J. Reinken, Grand Valley State University
Program, Karen Bromley, Binghamton University-SUNY
Reading Room, Linda Rogers, East Stroudsburg University; Allison Swan Dagen, West Virginia University
Exhibits, Linda Hurst, Texas A&M University-Commerce; Elaine Marker, Rowan University
Elections, Robert J. Rickelman, University of North Carolina-Charlotte
Awards, Wayne M. Linek, Texas A&M University-Commerce
Research, Julie Kidd, George Mason University; Charlene E. Fleener, Old Dominion University; Kristy Dunlap, George Mason University
Publications, Timothy G. Morrison, Brigham Young University
Membership, Angela Ferree, Western Illinois University; Doris Walker-Dalhouse, Minnesota State University-Moorhead

Public Information, Marie F. Holbein, State University of West Georgia; Parker Fawson, Utah State University; Donna Harkins, State University of West Georgia, Sylvia Read (Webmaster), Utah State University

Scholarship, Patricia Douville, University of North Carolina-Charlotte

Historian, Dixie Massey, Pacific Lutheran University

Photographer, Frederick J. Fedorko, East Stroudsburg University (Emeritus)

Resolutions and Rules, Diana Quatroche, Indiana State University; H. Jon Jones, Western Illinois University

Legislative and Social Issues, Barbara J. Fox, North Carolina State University

Professional Affairs, Maryann Mraz, University of North Carolina-Charlotte; Jill Mizell Reddish, State University of West Georgia

Reading Research and Instruction
Kathleen A. J. Mohr, University of North Texas
Janelle B. Mathis, University of North Texas
Dianne Allen, University of North Texas

The Reading News
Julie Kidd, George Mason University

Literacy Cases Online
Barbara J. Walker, Oklahoma State University

CRA Yearbook
Patricia E. Linder, Texas A&M University-Commerce
JoAnn R. Dugan, Ohio University
Mary Beth Sampson, Texas A&M University-Commerce
Barrie Brancato, Clarion University

2005-2006

President, Karen Bromley, Binghamton University, SUNY
President-Elect, Ellen Jampole, State University of New York-Cortland
Vice President, D. Ray Reutzel, Utah State University
Past President, Jon Shapiro, University of British Columbia
Executive Secretary, Kathleen A. J. Mohr, University of North Texas
Treasurer/Business Manager, John A. Smith, Utah State University

Board of Directors
Bonnie Higginson, Murray State University
Michael Martin, Eastern Kentucky University
Laurie Elish-Piper, Northern Illinois University
Connie Briggs, Emporia State University
Mary Roe, Washington State University
JoAnn R. Dugan, Ohio University
Gary Padak, Kent State University
Wayne M. Linek, Texas A&M University-Commerce

Division Chairperson
Teacher Education, Francine Falk-Ross, Northern Illinois University
College Reading, Donna Marie Colonna, Sandhills Community College
Clinical, J. Helen Perkins, University of Memphis
Adult Learning, Christine McKeon, Walsh University

Committee and Commissions
 Conference Coordinator, Barbara J. Reinken, Grand Valley State University
 Program, Ellen Jampole, State University of New York-Cortland
 Reading Room, Allison Swan Dagen, West Virginia University; Pamela F. Summers, State University of New York-Cortland
 Exhibits, Linda Hurst, Texas A&M University-Commerce; Elaine Marker, Rowan University
 Elections, Wayne M. Linek, Texas A&M University-Commerce
 Awards, Jon Shapiro, University of British Columbia
 Research, Kristy Dunlap, George Mason University; Ruth Oswald, University of Akron
 Publications, Timothy G. Morrison, Brigham Young University
 Membership, Doris Walker-Dalhouse, Minnesota State University-Moorhead; Mary DeKonty Applegate, Holy Family University
 Public Information, Marie F. Holbein, State University of West Georgia; Parker C. Fawson, Utah State University; Donna M. Harkins, State University of West Georgia; Sylvia Read (Webmaster), Utah State University
 Scholarship, Patricia Douville, University of North Carolina-Charlotte
 Historian, Dixie D. Massey, University of Puget Sound
 Photographer, Frederick J. Fedorko, East Stroudsburg University (Emeritus)
 Resolutions and Rules, Diana Quatroche, Indiana State University; H. Jon Jones, Western Illinois University
 Legislative and Social Issues, Barbara J. Fox, North Carolina State University
 Professional Affairs, Maryann Mraz, University of North Carolina-Charlotte; Jill Mizell Reddish, State University of West Georgia

Reading Research and Instruction
 Sherry Kragler, University of South Florida-Lakeland
 Carolyn Ann Walker, Ball State University

The Reading News
 Julie K. Kidd, George Mason University

Literacy Cases Online
 Barbara J. Walker, Oklahoma State University

CRA Yearbook
 Patricia E. Linder, Texas A&M University-Commerce
 Mary Beth Sampson, Texas A&M University-Commerce
 Francine Falk-Ross, Northern Illinois University
 Martha Foote, Texas A&M-Commerc
 Susan Szabo, Texas A&M University-Commerce

2006-2007

President, Ellen Jampole, State University of New York-Cortland
President-Elect, D. Ray Reutzel, Utah State University
Vice President, Mona Matthews, Georgia State University
Past President, Karen Bromley, Binghamton University, SUNY
Executive Secretary, Kathleen A. J. Mohr, University of North Texas
Treasurer/Business Manager, John A. Smith, Utah State University

Board of Directors
 Connie Briggs, Emporia State University
 Mary F. Roe, Washington State University
 JoAnn R. Dugan, Ohio University

Gary Padak, Kent State University
Rona Flippo, University of Massachusetts-Boston
Patricia E. Linder, Texas A&M University-Commerce
Jon Shapiro, University of British Columbia
Jacqueline Peck, Kent State University

Division Chairpersons

Teacher Education, Francine C. Falk-Ross, Northern Illinois University
College Reading, Bettina P. Murray, John Jay College of Criminal Justice
Clinical, J. Helen Perkins, University of Memphis
Adult Learning, Christine A. McKeon, Walsh University

Committee and Commissions

Conference Coordinator, Barbara Reinken, Grand Valley State University
Program, D. Ray Reutzel, Utah State University
Reading Room, Tami Craft Al-Hazza, Old Dominion University; Pamela Summers, State University of New York-Cortland
Exhibits, Barbara J. Reinken, Grand Valley State University
Elections, Jon Shapiro, University of British Columbia
Awards, Karen Bromley, Binghamton University, SUNY
Research, Kristy Dunlap, George Mason University; Ruth A. Oswald, University of Akron
Publications, Timothy G. Morrison, Brigham Young University
Membership, Doris Walker-Dalhouse, Minnesota State University-Moorhead; Mary DeKonty Applegate, St. Joseph's University
Public Information, Marie F. Holbein, University of West Georgia; Parker Fawson, Utah State University; Donna M. Harkins, University of West Georgia; Sylvia Read (Webmaster), Utah State University
Scholarship, Patricia Douville, University of North Carolina-Charlotte
Historian, Dixie Massey, University of Puget Sound
Photographer, Rob Erwin, Niagara University
Resolutions and Rules, Diana Quatroche, Indiana State University; H. Jon Jones, Western Illinois University
Legislative and Social Issues, Barbara J. Fox, North Carolina State University
Professional Affairs, Jill Mizell Reddish, University of West Georgia

Reading Research and Instruction

Sherry Kragler, University of South Florida-Lakeland
Carolyn Ann Walker, Ball State University

The Reading News

Julie K. Kidd, George Mason University

CRA Yearbook

Mary Beth Sampson, Texas A&M University-Commerce
Francine C. Falk-Ross, Northern Illinois University
Martha M. Foote, Texas A&M University-Commerce
Susan Szabo, Texas A&M University-Commerce

2007-2008

President, D. Ray Reutzel, Utah State University
President-Elect, Mona W. Matthews, Georgia State University
Vice President, Laurie Elish-Piper, Northern Illinois University

Past President, Ellen Jampole, State University of New York-Cortland
Executive Secretary, Kathleen A. J. Mohr, University of North Texas
Treasurer/Business Manager, John A. Smith, University of Texas-Arlington

Board of Directors
   Mary F. Roe, Washington State University
   JoAnn R. Dugan, Ohio University
   Gary Padak, Kent State University
   Rona Flippo, University of Massachusetts-Boston
   Patricia E. Linder, Texas A&M-Commerce
   Jon Shapiro, University of British Columbia
   Julie Kidd, George Mason University
   Mary Beth Sampson, Texas A&M University-Commerce
   Karen Bromley, Binghamton University, SUNY

Division Chairpersons
   Teacher Education, Angela Ferree, Western Illinois University
   College Reading, Bettina Murray, John Jay College of Criminal Justice
   Clinical, Virginia Modla, LaSalle University
   Adult Learning, Dianna Baycich, Kent State University

Committee Chairpersons
   Conference Coordinator, Barbara J. Reinken, Grand Valley State University
   Program, Mona W. Matthews, Georgia State University
   Reading Room, Tami Craft Al-Hazza, Old Dominion University; Pamela Summers,
      State University of New York-Cortland
   Elections, Karen Bromley, Binghamton University, SUNY
   Awards, Ellen Jampole, State University of New York-Cortland
   Research, Kristy Dunlap, George Mason University; Ruth A. Oswald, University
      of Akron
   Publications, Timothy Morrison, Brigham Young University
   Membership, Doris Walker-Dalhouse, Minnesota State University-Moorhead; Mary
      DeKonty Applegate, St. Joseph's University
   Public Information, Marie F. Holbein, University of West Georgia; Parker Fawson,
      Utah State University; Donna Harkins, University of West Georgia; Sylvia Read
      (Webmaster), Utah State University
   Historian, Dixie D. Massey, University of Puget Sound
   Photographer, Robin Erwin, Niagara University
   Resolutions and Rules, H. Jon Jones, Western Illinois University
   Legislative and Social Issues, JoAnn R. Dugan, Ohio University
   Professional Affairs, Jill Mizell Drake, University of West Georgia; John Ponder,
      University of West Georgia

Literacy Research and Instruction
   Parker C. Fawson, Utah State University
   Sylvia Read, Utah State University
   Brad Wilcox, Brigham Young University

The Reading News
   Larkin Page, Texas A&M University-Commerce

CRA Yearbook
   Mary Beth Sampson, Texas A&M University-Commerce
   Francine C. Falk-Ross, Northern Illinois University
   Martha M. Foote, Texas A&M University-Commerce
   Susan Szabo, Texas A&M University-Commerce